Contents

Hegel
by H. B. Acton*

GEORG WILHELM FRIEDRICH HEGEL (1770–1831), German idealist philosopher, was born at Stuttgart and entered the theological seminary at the
University of Tübingen in 1788. Among his fellow students were Schelling
and the poet Friedrich Hölderlin. After graduating he became, in 1793, a
resident tutor in the home of an aristocratic family at Bern, and in 1796 he
took a similar post in Frankfurt. In 1800 he went to Jena, where Schelling
had succeeded Fichte as professor of philosophy and was developing an
idealist philosophy of nature and metaphysics. Having been accepted as a
teacher at Jena on the strength of his dissertation, *De Orbitis Planetarum*
(1801), Hegel collaborated with Schelling in editing the philosophical
journal *Kritisches Journal der Philosophie* and published his first book, *Differ-
enz des Fichte'schen und Schelling'schen Systems der Philosophie* (1801). Nota-
ble articles by Hegel in the *Kritisches Journal* were "Glauben und Wissen"
(1802) and "Über die wissenschaftlichen Behandlungsarten des Natur-
rechts" (1802–1803). At Jena, Hegel wrote his first major work, *Phäno-
menologie des Geistes* (*Phenomenology of Mind*). Completed about the time of
Napoleon's victory over the Prussians at Jena in 1806, it was not published
until 1807, after Hegel had left Jena to become editor of a daily paper at
Bamberg in Bavaria.

In 1808, Hegel was appointed headmaster of a school in Nuremberg, a
post he held until 1816. While at Nuremberg, Hegel published his *Wissenschaft der Logik (Science of Logic)* — Vol. I, *Die objective Logik* (2 vols.,
1812–1813), and Vol. II, *Die subjective Logik oder Lehre vom Begriff* (1816).

Note: As I argue in my Introduction, Hegel's writings are difficult for a variety of reasons
and consequently an explanatory introduction to them may approach them in several different
ways. Arguably more than one such approach is required if the student is to be enabled to read
Hegel with understanding. I have therefore reprinted the late H. B. Acton's masterly survey
of Hegel's life and thought, in the hope it may lighten the reader's task. - M. J. Inwood, Ed.

*"Hegel" by H. B. Acton. Reprinted with permission of Macmillan Publishing Company
from *Encyclopedia of Philosophy*, Paul A. Edwards, Editor in Chief. Volume III, pages 435–
451. Copyright © 1967 by Macmillan, Inc.

From 1816 to 1818, Hegel was professor of philosophy at Heidelberg. There he published *Encyklopädie der philosophischen Wissenschaften im Grundrisse (Encyclopedia of the Philosophical Sciences in Outline)* in 1817. In 1818, Hegel was appointed professor at the University of Berlin, where he became famous and influential. *Naturrecht und Staatswissenschaft im Grundrisse (Philosophy of Right)* appeared there in 1821; a second edition, edited by E. Gans as *Grundlinien der Philosophie des Rechts*, was published in Berlin in 1833. In 1827 a second, much enlarged edition of the *Encyclopedia* appeared.

Hegel died during a cholera epidemic in 1831. After his death a group of his friends compiled an edition of his works in 18 volumes (Berlin, 1832–1840). Several of Hegel's works were published for the first time in this edition: *Vorlesungen über die Aesthetik* ("Lectures on Aesthetics," translated as *The Philosophy of Fine Art*); *Vorlesungen über die Philosophie der Geschichte (Lectures on the Philosophy of History, 1837)*; *Vorlesungen über die Philosophie der Religion (Lectures on the Philosophy of Religion);* and *Vorlesungen über die Geschichte der Philosophie (Lectures on the History of Philosophy, 2 vols.).* This edition also contains notes taken by students of Hegel's comments on the *Encyclopedia* and on *Philosophy of Right*, which he was in the habit of using as textbooks.

In his biography, *Georg Wilhelm Friedrich Hegels Leben* (1844), Karl Rosenkranz referred to and quoted from the manuscripts of works written by Hegel prior to the publication of the *Phenomenology of Mind*. Not all the manuscripts known to Rosenkranz have survived, but toward the end of the nineteenth century Wilhelm Dilthey made a study of those that have and published an account and discussion of them in the *Proceedings of the Berlin Academy* in 1905. This has since received the title *Die Jugendgeschichte Hegels* and is reprinted in the fourth volume of Dilthey's collected works. Dilthey's pupil and editor, Herman Nohl, then published, under the title *Hegels theologische Jugendschriften*, the text of a great part of what Hegel had written while he was in Bern and Frankfurt. The chief of the writings unpublished during Hegel's lifetime are the essay "Das Leben Jesu" (Life of Jesus," 1795), *Die Positivität der christlichen Religion (The Positivity of the Christian Religion*, 1796), and *Der Geist des Christentums und sein Schicksal (Spirit of Christianity and Its Destiny*, 1799). In 1915, Hans Ehrenberg and Herbert Link published, under the title *Hegels erstes System*, an early version, written at Jena but never published by Hegel, of what later became the system sketched in the *Encyclopedia*. Since then Georg Lasson (*Hegels Jenenser Logik*, 1928) and Johannes Hoffmeister (*Hegels Jenenser Realphilosophie*, 2 vols., 1932) have published still other writings that Hegel had left unpublished. Thus, much more is now known about Hegel's writings and philosophical development than was generally known in the nineteenth century.

MAIN THEMES OF HEGEL'S PHILOSOPHY

Mind

In the Preface to the *Phenomenology*, Hegel wrote that only mind (*Geist*) is real, and he constantly reiterated this view. (I have translated Hegel's *Geist* as "mind," in agreement with Wallace's view that "to average English ears the word Spiritual would carry us over the medium line into the proper land of religiosity.") Thus, he must be regarded as a philosophical idealist. He wrote rather slightingly of Berkeley, however, whose works he does not seem to have studied closely, and is sometimes described as an objective idealist in order to absolve him from suspicion of the subjective idealism that has often been attributed to Berkeley. Hegel's idealism presupposed the work of Kant and was influenced by Fichte and Schelling, but his early unpublished writings show that he had preoccupations of his own, independent of his famous German predecessors.

When Hegel said that only mind is real, he did not mean that material things do not exist and that only minds do. Mind was not, in Hegel's view, a plurality of immaterial substances but a system of individuals actively developing their potentialities by embodying them in increasingly complex forms. A fundamental feature of mind, according to Hegel, is freedom, and nothing that is partial or finite can be wholly free. The mind that is the only reality is therefore infinite. Furthermore, no one is free unless he is conscious of what he is doing, and infinite mind is therefore self-conscious mind. Artists and statesmen, merchants and saints, all busy themselves with their more or less partial tasks without necessarily concerning themselves with what it is that they are doing. According to Hegel, it is the function of the philosopher to make men conscious of what art and politics, commerce and religion, are, so that mind can exert itself to its utmost range and thus become absolute. Like Pythagoras, Plotinus, and Spinoza, Hegel was a philosopher who held that philosophy is an activity which purifies and frees the mind.

Dialectic

Hegel is, of course, famous for his dialectical method, but it is enormously difficult to explain this in a brief compass. It should first be noted that Hegel set out his systematic writings in dialectical triads comprising a thesis, antithesis, and synthesis. Thus, he divided his *Encyclopedia*, in which he expounded his system as a whole, into three fundamental division sections—"Logic," "Philosophy of Nature," and "Philosophy of Mind." In the first he expounded the categories as developing forms of thought; in the second, he said "the Idea" is considered in its "otherness" (*Anderssein*) or externality; and in the third, mind is considered as existing "for itself," as conscious of itself and of the institutions it has given rise to. Within these main divisions there are further triadic subdivisions, although a very large number of subdivisions are not of this nature. It is therefore clear that Hegel himself regarded his whole work as a dialectical construction, with thought and nature as opposites united in mind and society, in the artistic and religious products of man, and, ultimately, in the activity of philosophical self-consciousness.

Hegel's system, then, has a dialectical structure, but what is his dialectical method? Hegel, like Spinoza, held that error resides in incompleteness and abstraction, but, unlike Spinoza, he held that the incompleteness and abstraction can be recognized by the contradictions they generate. It is the business of the philosopher, he held, to bring out the contradictions latent in partial or abstract views and to emphasize and elaborate them in such a way that less partial and less abstract views can be constructed that nevertheless retain in themselves what there was of truth in the original views. The same method is to be brought to bear on the less partial and less abstract views in their turn and to be pressed as thoroughly as it can be. This method of pressing and accentuating contradictions is not to be used merely to discard error but also to preserve truth. Because of the happy circumstance that in German *aufheben* means both "to cancel" and "to preserve" — its literal meaning is "to lift up" — Hegel was able to express this aspect of his view with brevity and acuity. The concept or view that is *aufgehoben* is transcended without being wholly discarded. Hegel's *Phenomenology of Mind* was an account of how various human attitudes — reliance on sense experience, the belief in substance, otherworldliness, strenuous moralism, and so on — all have some point and are yet contradictory, leading to the conclusion that "truth is a bacchanalian revel where not a member is sober," as Hegel put it in the Preface. His *Logic* gave an account of how the categories are related in this way. In his *Lectures on the History of Philosophy* he sought to show that the major philosophical outlooks from that of the Ionians on are, on the one hand, positive contributions that we could not do without and, on the other hand, contradictions that we have to overcome.

History

Another feature of Hegel's philosophy is its concern with history. Much as Hegel admired Plato's philosophy, he held that it was impossible to be a Platonist in the nineteenth century, when the philosophical context differed so greatly from that of Plato's day. In his *Lectures on the Philosophy of History*, Hegel argued that the history of man in the concrete was as much a progression as the history of his thought. This he deduced from the thesis that mind is of its very nature free. Thus, each historical epoch, according to Hegel, embodied some aspect of or stage in the development of man's free mind, and it would be absurd for an individual to go counter to his time except insofar as he was preparing the way for future epochs. Hegel borrowed this "progressivism," as it may be called, from the philosophers of the Enlightenment. It has greatly influenced Marxism.

Christianity

Hegel thought his system provided a defense of Christianity, and both supporters and opponents of his system have taken this view of it. Those known as right Hegelians considered Hegel's apologetic successful, whereas the left Hegelians argued that his Christianity had been only superficial and his Christian terminology a disguise for something very different. In his system Hegel placed philosophy above religion in the dialectical scale, and this may give some support for the interpretations of the left. Yet there is ambiguity in Hegel's view on this, as on other important matters. On one hand, he held that only infinite mind is real; on the other hand, he held that infinite mind cannot be distinct from or beyond the finite and partial. He thought that these views were not incompatible, but it has been argued that the second is a denial of the first and, hence, a denial of any form of theism.

This article will briefly describe Hegel's early works that were posthumously published in *Hegels theologische Jugendschriften*. It will continue with an account of the *Phenomenology of Mind*, Hegel's first important book, and conclude with a brief discussion of the Hegelian system based chiefly on the *Encyclopedia*.

EARLY UNPUBLISHED WRITINGS

"Life of Jesus"

Even before he wrote his "Life of Jesus," Hegel had written some comments on Christianity in which he criticized it for its belief in the efficacy of prayer and had contrasted it, to its detriment, with the this-worldly, social religion of the Greeks. Jesus, he held, was obscurantist and narrow-minded in comparison with Socrates. In the "Life of Jesus" it almost seems as if Hegel had decided to rewrite the Gospels in the form of a Kantian manifesto. He began by claiming that God is pure reason. He described Jesus as the son of Joseph and Mary. The only miracles Hegel mentioned he interpreted naturalistically, bringing the work to an end with the death and burial of Jesus. The central theme is the conflict between the virtuous Jesus acting dutifully for the sake of the moral law and the Jewish priesthood calling for the meticulous observance of a set of irrational rules said to be commanded by God. Jesus is depicted as saying to the Pharisees, "When you regard your ecclesiastical statutes and positive commands as the supreme law given to mankind, you fail to understand the dignity of man and the power he has of creating out of himself the idea of the divinity and knowledge of his will." This improbable allocution is typical of the way in which this work denudes the Gospel narrative of what is individual and poetical.

"The Positivity of the Christian Religion"

The theme of *The Positivity of the Christian Religion* — the place in the Christian religion of the rational, on the one hand, and of the merely factual and historical, on the other — was already raised in the "Life of Jesus." Developing the implications of the then current distinctions between natural law and positive law and between natural religion and positive religion, Hegel argued that the positive element rested on authority and was not wholly based on the dignity of man. In Christianity, according to Hegel, the main positive element was provided by Judaism, a highly authoritarian religion. But Jesus himself brought elements of positivity into the rational morality that it was his prime aim to teach; he could not have obtained a hearing from the Jews of his day if he had not claimed God's authority for his teachings. "Jesus therefore demands attention for his teachings, not because they are adapted to the moral needs of our spirit, but because they are God's will" (*Early Theological Writings*, p. 76). In claiming to be the Messiah, Jesus was using the language his listeners would understand. His followers, from a natural interest in the details of his life, developed these positive elements into Christianity. They appealed to miracles as proofs of Jesus' divinity and virtue, and instead of revering him for his teaching about virtue, they revered his teaching about virtue because of the miracles he was supposed to have performed.

Hegel asked how it happened that the pagan religion of the Greeks and Romans was overcome by Christianity. His answer was that at the periods of their greatness the Greeks and Romans were free peoples each individual of which regarded his own good as inseparable from the good of his community. When they lost their freedom, they lost the motives that bound them to their fellows; government and authority were now imposed from without, weighing down upon isolated individuals who came to regard their lives as individual possessions to be preserved irrespective of the social whole that alone gave them meaning.

> Thus the despotism of the Roman emperors had chased the human spirit from the earth and spread a misery which compelled men to seek and expect happiness in heaven, robbed of freedom, their spirit, their eternal and absolute element, was forced to take flight to the deity. [The doctrine of] God's objectivity is a counterpart to the corruption and slavery of man. [*Ibid.*, pp. 162–163]

"The Spirit of Christianity"

In *The Spirit of Christianity* Hegel continued and sharpened his attack on Judaism, which he regarded as a religion of domination. He now criticized

Kantian ethics as well, however, finding in it elements of the same positivity he had criticized in the Jewish religion and had seen as a contamination in the teachings of Jesus. Kant had contrasted his rational religion with the religion of the Siberian shamans on the ground that these primitive men, as well as some civilized prelates and puritans, irrationally worshiped alien forces that they regarded as exerting domination over men. But according to Hegel, the difference between the believers in these positive creeds and the follower of the religion approved by Kant is "not that the former make themselves slaves, while the latter is free, but that the former have their lord outside themselves, while the latter carries his lord in himself, yet at the same time is his own slave" (*ibid.*, p. 211). Hegel here first used the word "morality" (*Moralität*) as a pejorative description of the Kantian morality, which he now considered to be a submission of man's inclinations, including his impulses and his feelings of love, to a universal reason held to be free from and above all passion. He held that virtue demands more than this and that in the Sermon on the Mount Jesus made higher demands. "The Sermon does not teach reverance for the laws; on the contrary, it exhibits that which fulfils the law but annuls it as law and so is something higher than obedience to law and makes law superfluous" (*ibid.*, p. 212). Thus, duty takes a lower place than love. " . . . Jesus makes a general demand on his hearers to surrender their rights, to lift themselves above the whole sphere of justice or injustice by love, for in love there vanish not only rights but also the feeling of inequality and the hatred of enemies which this feeling's imperative demand for equality implies" (*ibid.*, p. 218). Hegel here saw in the ethics of the Sermon on the Mount and in the conduct of Jesus something of the "beautiful soul" described by Goethe in *Wilhelm Meister*. Jesus retained his dignity by refusing to defend himself or to uphold his rights.

Hegel went on to discuss with subtlety the possible consequences for the individual and for other men of resistance to evil, on the one hand, and of withdrawal from conflict, on the other. In this part of the work the beginnings of dialectical method as it was used a few years later in *Phenomenology of Mind* may already be discerned.

"PHENOMENOLOGY OF MIND"

The *Phenomenology* is the most obscure and the most interesting of Hegel's works. On the title page it is described as a "System of Science, Part I. The Phenomenology of Mind," but this arrangement of Hegel's system was not continued in the *Encyclopedia*, where the section headed "Phenomenology of Mind" is contained in the third part and deals with only some of the topics of the original *Phenomenology*. Hegel put the *Phenomenology* together rather hastily and was uncertain what to call it. Different copies of the first edition have slightly differing titles, and what

ke a new title, "Science of the Experience of Consciousness," is
ter the Preface and before the Introduction. Insofar as there is a
heme, it consists of an account of the various stages of human
consciousness from mere sense awareness to absolute knowledge, but there
are many digressions into topics of current interest, such as Goethe's
description of the "beautiful soul," the Reign of Terror, and F. J. Gall's
phrenology. The difference between the dialectical progression of the
Phenomenology and of the *Encyclopedia* was cited soon after Hegel's death as
evidence of the inadequacy of the dialectical method (C. F. Bachmann,
*Über Hegels System und die Nothwendigkeit einer nochmaligen Umgestaltung der
Philosophie*, 1833). In the twentieth century Marxists have preferred the
Phenomenology to Hegel's other writings because Marx himself admired it
and because of its account of how man develops by transforming the natural
world through his labor. Existentialists have preferred it to the later system
because of its account of man as maker of himself; no doubt they are also
impressed by Hegel's references to death and the fear of death.

The *Phenomenology* begins with a dialectical discussion of sense perception in which it is argued that knowledge of physical things presupposes the
view that the physical world consists of forces interacting according to laws.
Hegel maintained that knowledge of such a world is really a type of
self-knowledge, since in penetrating to the forces behind phenomena we
become aware of what we ourselves have devised and put there. "Behind
the so-called curtain which is to hide the internal constitution of things,
there is nothing to be seen unless *we ourselves* go behind." The physical
world of scientific theory presupposes self-conscious beings. When he
analyzed self-consciousness, Hegel argued that it presupposed a plurality
of living and desiring beings each of whom seeks to subdue the world to his
own wishes, to make it part of himself.

Master and Slave

No individual will rest satisfied with a conquest that fails to secure the
conscious acknowledgment of other men. Hence, there is a struggle for
both power and recognition. In this struggle some will take greater risks
than their competitors; those who risk the least will become the slaves or
bondsmen of those who face death by risking their lives. In order to
preserve his life, the slave submits to the master, who regards the slave as
nothing but a means to his own designs. The slave is forced to work,
whereas the master can enjoy leisure in the knowledge that the slave is
reshaping the natural world to provide the products of his labor for the
master to consume. Thus, the master's leisure protects him from experience of the negativity of nature, whereas the slave, in struggling with
nature's recalcitrance, learns its secrets and puts mind into it. The master,
in consuming, destroys; the slave, in working, creates. But the master's

consumption depends upon the slave's work and is thus impermanent, whereas the slave's labor passes into things that have a permanent existence. Hegel argued, too, that the slave's work in transforming the natural world is a consequence of his fear of the master, who can kill him. Death is overcome by the works of civilization. The man who risks his life and becomes the first master breaks the bonds of nature and starts the process that will incorporate mind into it.

It is not surprising that this section in the *Phenomenology* has greatly interested Marxists. Both Georg Lukács, in *Der junge Hegel*, and Herbert Marcuse, in *Reason and Revolution* (1955), contrived to discuss it without mentioning Hegel's emphasis on the fear of death. In *Introduction à la lecture de Hegel*, Alexandre Kojève brought out the importance of the fear of death and showed, too, that Hegel was here concerned with the transition from nature to history, from mere life to thought, from animality to freedom.

The Unhappy Consciousness

The next dialectical transition is from mind that is attempting to master nature to mind that seeks freedom and independence in itself, that says, "It is in thinking that I am free because I am not in another but remain completely with myself alone," an attitude exemplified in stoicism. But stoicism passes over into skepticism, for the stoic finds freedom in himself as a rational, thinking being, whereas the skeptic, pushing freedom still further, uses thought to dissipate its own categories. This, according to Hegel, was the state of mind that prevailed when the Roman Empire was dissolving. Christianity was an attempt on the part of men in intellectual despair to find stability in an eternal and infinite God.

Hegel called this frame of mind the unhappy consciousness. The individual is divided within himself, conscious of his own isolation, attributing all that is good to the activity of God. What Hegel said here was elaborated from a passage in *The Postivity of the Christian Religion* describing how the eternal and absolute in man had been "forced to take flight to the Deity." The unhappy consciousness was regarded by Hegel as a characteristic of both Judaism and Christianity and as the condition of all men at all times who believe in a transcendent God before whom they are as nothing. It is a stage on the way to higher forms of self-mastery.

It will be noted that in this part of the *Phenomenology* Hegel passed from epistemology through a sort of speculative sociology to an account of historical stages in human consciousness. According to Rosenkranz, Hegel, in his last years, used to refer to the *Phenomenology* as his philosophical "voyage of discovery," and it does seem that the course of the argument, although arresting, was not altogether foreseen. Royce was right when he said that in this book Hegel described "in serial order, some varieties of experience which . . . are at once characteristic of the general evolution of the higher intellectual life, and are examples of the transition from common sense naiveté to philosophical reflection and to the threshold of an idealistic system" (*Lectures on Modern Idealism*, J. Loewenberg, ed., New Haven, 1919, p. 139).

Reason As "Objectivity"

After discussing certain scientific theories of his time under the heading "Reason as Observer," Hegel went on to consider some of the ways in which reason becomes practical. He depicted the man who, like Faust, tries to make the passing moment stay. When this attempt fails, as inevitably it must, ideals are sought in a spirit of sentimental disillusionment, but such romantic crusades are never really serious. In reaction to this frivolity there develops a taste for the hard intellectual pursuits of disinterested scholarship, the concern for "objectivity," for facts, for "the thing itself." But these allegedly disinterested researchers actually go into a sort of intellectual jungle (*das geistige Thierreich*) where, deceiving one another and themselves, they tear one another to pieces in the service of truth. It soon emerges that it is not the facts that matter but a certain proprietorship that scholars working in their special fields claim over the facts.

The Dialectic of Morality

In the next part of the *Phenomenology*, entitled "Mind," Hegel considered how the mind of man is embodied in his rules and institutions. This part constitutes both an account of the main types of moral attitude and a philosophy of history. These two lines of thought come together insofar as Hegel regarded the historical development from the Greek and Roman civilizations through early and medieval Christianity to Protestantism and the French Revolution as an unfolding of the main aspects and stages of freedom and, hence, as a dialectical actualization of what was merely latent and implicit in the morality of the ancient world. This unfolding is dialectical because it proceeds by oscillations and because it is made possible by conflict, in the ancient world by the conflict between the gods of the family and the laws of the city and in the modern world by the conflict between the claims of the individual and the demands of society.

In this part Hegel gave indications of the doctrine of alienation that attracted Marx in the 1840s. In building his civilization, man creates institutions and rules that are simultaneously his own products and alien constraints upon him. He may not even understand them, so that they appear strange to him. It was Hegel's view, of course, that without these institutions and rules and without the restrictions upon willfulness that they impose, mind could not reach its higher levels.

Religion and Absolute Knowledge

In the last two parts of the *Phenomenology*, Hegel presented the dialectic of religion and the passage to absolute knowledge. In the earlier developments of mind the individual has to find his place in the natural world and in society, but in religion he gains consciousness of the Absolute Being. This is first approached in the primitive religions of nature, in which men worship trees, streams, or animals. Next come those forms of religion in which the Absolute Being is approached through such works of art as temples and statues. This type of religion reached a high level in ancient Greece, but when God was represented in human form, he came to be regarded as merely human and hence was lost sight of in the tragic heroes of Greek drama. As the religious element was discarded from tragedy, it gave way to comedy, in which the contingencies of human life were paraded and criticized, and God was completely ignored in favor of human self-knowledge. "The individual self is the negative force through and in which the gods . . . disappear."

This skeptical and sophisticated humanism is succeeded by Christianity, in which God is revealed to man in Christ. Here the human and the divine are no longer sundered, and God is seen to be present in the world. But it is easy to overemphasize the historical features of Christianity and, as Hegel put it, to neglect the spiritual revelation in the attempt to uncover the often commonplace ideas of the early Christians and to gain knowledge of the mere externality and particularity of Jesus. Thus, no religious experience, not even that of Christianity, can bring absolute knowledge. The historical element in Christianity, although necessary in order to avoid regarding the Absolute Being as apart from the world, is nevertheless inseparable from perception and imagination. The events of the Gospels are, so to speak, pictured or represented. Religion therefore leads on but is subordinate tu the supreme form of knowledge, the philosophical, in which human history is "conceived history, the recollection of the Absolute Mind and its grave-yard, the actuality, truth and certainty of its throne, without which it would be for ever alone and devoid of life." In these last words of the *Phenomenology*, Hegel made it clear that the course of history, philosophically conceived, was in his view the incarnation of the Absolute Mind. Apart from the history of man God would be alone and lifeless (*das leblose Einsame*). It would seem, indeed, that without the historical development of man and his freedom there would be no God.

THE HEGELIAN SYSTEM

It has already been mentioned that before writing the *Phenomenology*, Hegel had written but had left unpublished some attempts at a complete system of philosophy and that the *Phenomenology* was described on its title page as the first part of a system of science. It turned out that the *Science of Logic* (1812–1816) became the first part of Hegel's final system. A shortened and revised version of the *Science of Logic* appeared in 1817 as the first part of the *Encyclopedia*, a book intended for use at his lectures. A second, very much elaborated edition of the *Encyclopedia* appeared in 1827, and a third in 1830. This last edition was reprinted in the edition of Hegel's collected works published soon after his death, with inserted "additions" taken from the notebooks of students who had attended Hegel's lectures. These additions, which are most frequent in the first and second parts of the *Encyclopedia*, help greatly in the understanding Hegel's argument but do not have quite the authority of the main text. Such additions are less frequent at the end, since the editors considered that the *Philosophy of Right*, first published in 1821, and some of the sets of lectures, provide commentary of this sort.

The "Encyclopedia"

The *Encyclopedia* starts with a discussion of "Logic" — a revision of *Science of Logic* — and proceeds to the sections "Philosophy of Nature" and "Philosophy of Mind." The transition from the "Logic" to the "Philosophy of Nature" is not easy to understand. There are statements which say that the idea decides to allow nature to go forth freely from itself (Sec. 244), that "Nature has come to pass as the Idea in the form of otherness" (Sec. 247), and that nature is "the unresolved contradiction" (Sec. 248). The last main heading in the "Philosophy of Nature" is "The Animal Organism." Toward the end of this section there is an account of the individual animal as having "an original sickness" and "an innate germ of death" (Sec. 375), which leads to the assertion that with the subjectivity of living organisms the "outside-itself-ness" (*Aussersichsein*) of nature is transcended by the "interiority" (*Insichsein*) of actuality (Sec. 376). Hegel later claimed (Sec. 381) that mind presupposes nature but is "the truth [of nature] and its absolute ground [*deren absolut Erstes*]." He also stated that the essence of mind is freedom (Sec. 382). A fundamental comment on the dominating triadic division must be made before going further into the details of the system. The revised "Science of Logic" that appeared in the *Encyclopedia* was concerned with the categories of thought, proceeding from the most inadequate and abstract to the most concrete and adequate, from being to the Absolute Idea. The inadequacies of the abstract categories show themselves through the contradictions they give rise to. Being is more abstract than becoming; becoming, more abstract than being-for-self; these early categories, more abstract than the latter categories of life, and so on. But Hegel was always concerned with the categories of thought and their relations to one another. When he wrote that the idea decided to allow nature to go forth freely from itself, was he saying that thought is the Divine Being that created nature? The religious overtones that accompany

Hegel's major transitions cannot be ignored, but those who wish to interpret him naturalistically—an interpretation his early writings and the *Phenomenology* may well justify—can take the view that the decision and the free going forth are meant to indicate that nature is not deducible from the categories of thought, that there is a contingency about it that no system of logic and no elaboration of concepts can eliminate. In *Subjekt–Objekt* (Berlin, 1951) Ernst Bloch suggested that the free decision of the Absolute Idea is reminiscent of the arbitrary act of an absolute monarch, and he quoted a passage from Schelling's *Philosophie und Religion* (Tübingen, 1804) which held that "the descent of finite things from the Absolute" is a "primal accident [*Urzufall*]." In the third part of the *Encyclopedia*, Hegel described mind as it develops in the natural world, mind as it transforms the natural world in creating the works of civilization, and mind fully aware of itself in the complete self-consciousness of philosophical thought. The "Logic" culminates in the Absolute Idea, the most adequate category but still a category. In the "Philosophy of Nature," where there is no Absolute, the culminating point consists of mortal individuals belonging to persisting animal species. The "Philosophy of Mind" culminates in Absolute Mind, the consciousness man gains of himself through understanding his own history in a civilization that he has imposed upon the contingencies of nature.

"Logic"

Like the Hegelian system as a whole, each of its three main sections—"Logic," "Philosophy of Nature," and "Philosophy of Mind"—is again divided into three. The "Logic" is divided into the "Doctrine of Being," the "Doctrine of Essence," and the "Doctrine of the Concept [*Begriff*]." The difficulties in presenting a comprehensible summary of Hegel's views are at their greatest in relation to the "Logic," and all that will be attempted is an indication of a few of Hegel's most characteristic views.

"Doctrine of Being"

In the "Doctrine of Being" Hegel was concerned with the most abstract categories. Being itself, the most abstract of all, amounts to the same as nothing. Like Russell in his theory of descriptions, Hegel held that nothing can be said to be unless some characteristic is attributed to it; hence, in Hegel's terminology being leads on to determinate being, which involves the notion of quality. On the ground that a quality is something distinct from other qualities, Hegel argued that quality implies the category of a unit (*das Eins*) and that this in turn leads on to quantity. This part of the "Logic" was completed by transitions to degree and measure.

Hegel's object in the "Doctrine of Being" was to show that these categories are not independent of one another but develop from one to the other in an ascending order of adequacy. We know more about something when we know the proportions of its parts than when we know only how many parts it has, that it is, or that it is something or other. An important element in this part of the "Logic" is Hegel's criticism of infinite numerical series as the false infinite and his contrast between the false and the true infinite, which is not an incompletable progression of similar items but a completed, complex whole of supplementary parts. The true infinite is not to be reached by attempting the impossible task of moving from one finite to the next but must comprise the finite.

"Doctrine of Essence"

The "Doctrine of Essence" is concerned with such distinctions as that between a thing's nature and its appearances, forces and their manifestations, form and matter. Hegel exploited the difficulties ("contradictions") that arise when these oppositions are so accentuated that we are left with featureless essences, on the one hand, and unattached appearances, on the other. Typical of his treatment of these topics is his claim that "the explanation of an appearance in terms of a force is an empty tautology" (Sec. 136) and his assertion that as a man's outward actions are, so his inner aims and intentions must be (Sec. 140).

"Doctrine of the Concept"

A prominent feature in the "Doctrine of the Concept" is Hegel's critical treatment and reorganization of the traditional formal logic. Thus, he classified judgments in terms of his own division of "Logic" into being, essence, and concept. The classification progresses from the mere factual attribution of a quality, through disjunctive and necessary judgments in which the predicate belongs essentially to the subject, to judgments of value which assert that a thing is good or bad just because it is that individual thing. Judgments gain in adequacy as they advance from mere factual attribution to attribution for reasons contained in the subject. Hence, the more developed forms of judgment are indistinguishable from inferences. In his account of the syllogism Hegel placed inferences in which the terms are only contingently connected at the bottom of a scale leading up to the disjunctive syllogism, in which a genus is exhaustively specified.

Although Hegel retained the terms and distinctions of the traditional formal logic, the use he made of them was highly original. Instead of setting out the types of judgment and the figures and moods of the syllogism as equally valid forms, he regarded judgment as implicit inference and inference as ordered in a scale of ascending rationality. This conception of logic influenced such later writers as Christoff Sigwart and R. H. Lotze and was developed in both F. H. Bradley's *Principles of Logic* (London, 1883) and Bernard Bosanquet's *Logic: The Morphology of Knowledge* (2 vols., Oxford, 1888).

The argument of Hegel's "Logic" can be very briefly summarized. The least that can be said about anything is that it is. More is said about it when it is qualified, numbered, or measured; still more is said about it when it is explained in terms of essences, grounds, or causes. Most is said about it when it is placed in the context of life, purpose, will, and value.

"Philosophy of Nature"

At the end of the eighteenth and the beginning of the nineteenth century there was a great deal of philosophizing about nature. Electricity was held to have cosmic significance, and Schelling made much of the opposition between positive and negative poles. Poets as dissimilar as Blake and Goethe rejected what they regarded as the unduly quantitative physics of Newton. Spinoza was revived, and among German poets and philosophers much was said about the ἐν καὶ πᾶν, the one and the all. It is not surprising, therefore, that Hegel's dissertation of 1801, *De Orbitis Planetarum*, was critical of Newton and sought to provide an a priori justification of Kepler's laws. At the end of the dissertation Hegel mentioned some numerological accounts of the distances and number of the planets and expressed the opinion that if Plato was right in the *Timaeus*, there could be no planet between Mars and Jupiter. Hegel did not then know that Ceres, an asteroid between these two planets, had been discovered at the beginning of the year. However, even after he had heard of this discovery and of the discovery of several other asteroids soon after, he continued to hope that philosophical reasons could be given for the positions of the heavenly bodies. In an addition to Section 270 of the *Encyclopedia*, Hegel tried to show that these asteroids filled a gap that would otherwise have been unreasonable. The addition ends with the words: "Specialists do not think about such matters. But a time will come when in this science there will be a demand for concepts of the Reason."

It should be mentioned here that Hegel accepted and developed Kant's distinction between the reason and the understanding. According to Hegel, the understanding, although a necessary stage of thought, is less philosophical than the reason. To think in terms of the understanding, as is done in mathematics, the natural sciences, and traditional metaphysics, is to think in terms of fixed and uncriticized categories, to think undialectically or in prephilosophical terms. The reason moves dialectically toward completeness in terms of fluid categories that constantly amend themselves. Thus, when Hegel wanted astronomers to pay attention to "concepts of Reason," he wanted astronomy to take its place within a system of philosophy. This place must be a subordinate one, for Hegel wrote in the Introduction to the "Philosophy of Nature" (Sec. 248): "Even if arbitrary will, the contingency of mind, leads on to wickedness, this is nevertheless something infinitely higher than the regular movements of the planets or than the innocence of the plants: for what goes wrong in that way is nevertheless mind." Here Hegel was emphasizing the gulf between mind and nature, even though he held that the understanding does not give a complete knowledge of nature.

Mechanics

The three main divisions of the "Philosophy of Nature" are concerned with mechanics, physics, and organic nature. The astronomical theories expounded in the first part have already been touched upon. This part also contains a brief discussion of space and time. Following Kant, Hegel regarded them both as "forms of sensibility," or, more strikingly, as "the non-sensible sensible." Although he regarded arithmetic and geometry as sciences of the understanding, he considered the possibility of a philosophical mathematics at the level of measure or proportion (*Mass*).

Physics

The second part of the "Philosophy of Nature" moves through various triads from light, the elements, sound, heat, to electricity and chemical combination. Hegel commented upon the philosophical significance of each form of matter. The comment on heat is characteristic:

> Heat is the re-establishment of matter in its formlessness, its fluidity, the triumph of its abstract homogeneity over its specific determinations. . . . Formally, that is in relation to spatial determinations in general, heat therefore appears expansive, as cancelling the limitations which the specification of the indifferent occupation of space is. [Sec. 303]

That is, when heat spreads out from a heated thing, that thing is not confined to one place, as it would be if it were not heated. Or as Hegel put it in the next section, heat is the "real negation of what is specific and exclusive in body."

Organic Nature

In the last main triad of the "Philosophy of Nature," Hegel passed from geological nature through vegetable nature to the animal organism. The most interesting part of this triad is the last, in which Hegel discussed animal species and their relationships. He seems to have thought that violent death is, in the animal world, "the natural fate of the individual" and that because of the contingency of nature animal life is "uncertain, anxious, and unhappy" (Sec. 369). But other members of the same species are not only hostile to the individual; they are also, like him, continuations of the species, and, hence, the individual feels a need to unite himself to the species (*Gattung*) and to continue it by copulation (*Begattung*) — the play on words is, of course, deliberate. Thus, Hegel seems to have held that animal sexual union is not merely a contingent affair. On the other hand, since the new individuals produced in this way only repeat the features of their parents and other ancestors, their constant reproduction is an instance of the false infinite, nor of the true infinite in which completeness and perfection are achieved.

"Philosophy of Mind"

The major triad in the "Philosophy of Mind" consists of "Subjective Mind," "Objective Mind," and "Absolute Mind."

"Subjective Mind"

Under the heading "Subjective Mind" and the subheading "Anthropology," Hegel dealt with the soul as a natural entity in the physical world: the soul as a sensitive, feeling being, and the soul as a being that can express itself and act upon the world through its body. The upright body, the hand "as the absolute tool" (Sec. 411), the mouth, and the power of weeping and laughing all enable man to express in nature — to externalize — his thoughts and feelings. Furthermore, the world has effects upon man's body that are internalized by him — Hegel here made a play on the word *Erinnerung*, which means "recollection" but, if taken in the literal sense of its German etymology, can be taken to mean "internalization." When the organism reacts to immediate stimuli in the light of its own experience, mind has evolved beyond the mere animal level and has reached the stage of consciousness.

Hegel discussed the next moment of subjective mind under the heading of the "Phenomenology of Mind," going through the main phases distinguished in the earlier chapters of his book with that title — namely, sense experience, perception, understanding, desire, the self-consciousness that recognizes others (containing the discussion of master and slave), reason.

The third triad of subjective mind, which is headed "Psychology," contains descriptions of such intellectual functions as intention, representation, recollection, imagination, memory, and thought and descriptions of the practical drives, impulses, and seekings after satisfaction.

This part ends with a brief section headed "Free Mind." Here it is asserted that the unity of theoretical and practical mind is free will. Hegel meant that human freedom is possible only on the dual basis of thought and impulse and consists of the rationalizing and systematizing of the impulses and passions. "This will to freedom," he said, "is no longer an impulse that demands satisfaction, but the character — the mind's consciousness grown into something non-impulsive" (Sec. 482).

"Objective Mind"

At the very end of his discussion of subjective mind Hegel wrote that the freedom which is the culmination of subjective mind is only a concept, "a principle of mind and heart destined to develop into the objective phase, into legal, moral, religious and scientific actuality" (Sec. 482). The rest of the system is therefore concerned with the ways in which the human will, in which thought and impulse ("mind and heart") are combined in freedom, becomes effective (this is the idea behind the word "actuality," which translates *Wirklichkeit*) in the public world, the world in which men act and in which their thoughts and deeds give rise to rules, institutions, and organizations. These rules, institutions, and organizations are independent of each man and thus may be regarded as kinds of objects, though not as physical objects. Men build up in the natural world a world other than the natural world by working on nature and transforming it and by creating systems of property, economic organizations, class differentiations, and the like. The triad that makes up objective mind comprises law (*Recht*), subjective morality (as Wallace translated *Moralität*), and social morality (as Wallace translated *Sittlichkeit*; Knox translated it as "ethical life"). The first part covers legal rights and duties as exemplified in property, contract, and punishment. The second is concerned largely with the morality of intention and conscience — the term *Moralität* was used by Hegel somewhat pejoratively to mean a sort of ethics (of which Kant was, in his view, the chief exponent) in which the agent is unduly governed by the subjective and internal aspects of decision and action.

The third part is itself a triad. The first stage of social morality is the family, "the natural or immediate phase" of objective mind (*Philosophy of Right*, Sec. 152). When members of the family have matured, they detach themselves from it and enter the world of independent men who compete in an economic arena free from tribal allegiances. This phase of social life Hegel called "civil society." It is the world of intelligent, responsible individuals in their business relationships, free from irrational tribal loyalties, allowing their connections with one another to be formed by the coincidence of wants in a market of wide extent. Indeed, it is the aspect of human society that the classical economists, whom Hegel admired, had analyzed and justified. But civil society cannot exist as a mere market, for markets need to be policed, whereas trades and industries themselves find common concerns that unite the individuals in corporations of various kinds.

There is thus a double necessity for the state — as the upholder of fair dealing and as the ultimate curb on the selfishness of corporations within civil society. In the *Encyclopedia*, Hegel wrote of "the unification of the family principle with that of Civil Society" and described it as a unification of the love that is essential to the family with the conscious universality that is the mark of civil society (Sec. 535). In the *Philosophy of Right* (Sec. 257) the state was described as "the actuality [*Wirklichkeit*] of the ethical Idea" — that is, as its effective embodiment. In the same section of the *Philosophy of Right*, Hegel wrote that "the mind of a nation (Athene for instance) is the divine, knowing and willing itself," and in an addition to Section 258 is the famous phrase "The march of God in the world, that is what the State is." But this section has been misunderstood. In the sentence before that in which he had written that the state is divine, Hegel had said, with the family in mind, "The *Penates* are inward gods, gods of the underworld," so that it is not only to the state that he attributed divinity. Furthermore, in the same addition as that in which he claimed that the state is "the march of God in the world," he said that the state "stands on earth and so in the sphere of caprice, chance and error, and bad behaviour may disfigure it in many respects." Hegel's main concern was, as he stated, to analyze the state at its best. Although, like Aristotle, he regarded the state as the highest social achievement of man, he also held, again like Aristotle, that within the state there should be guarantees against arbitrariness and despotism. He did not take a favorable view of "popular suffrage" on the grounds that "in large states it leads inevitably to electoral indifference" and that "election falls into the power of a few, of a caucus" (*Philosophy of Right*, Sec. 311). He strongly believed that all important interests should be represented and thought that there should be a constitutional monarchy with considerable powers advised by an upper and a lower house.

This brings us to the most controversial part of Hegel's account of objective mind, his philosophy of history. Whatever else is involved in his view that the state is man's highest social achievement, it undoubtedly implies that there is no superior body or group by which its claims may be assessed. States are necessarily independent beings. Their relations are regulated to some degree by custom, and there is an international law that regulates dealings between subjects of different states and requires adherence to treaties, as if they were a sort of contract. When the vital interests of states clash, however, there is no alternative except war. War between states, Hegel had said in his "Die Verfassung Deutschlands" (Constitution of Germany," 1802, first published in Georg Lasson, ed., *Schriften zur Politik und Rechtsphilosophie*, 2d ed., Leipzig, 1923), does not decide which of the rights of the conflicting states is the true right—for both are—"but which right has to give way to the other." Hegel believed that war performs the function of keeping before the minds of men the realities of death and destruction. He held that states are individuals and that all individuals persist in their existence by ensuring that other individuals recognize them as they recognize the others. The very concept of a state therefore requires that there be a plurality of them, and this makes war a part of the system of states even though war is not their natural condition but an interruption of the normal state of peace. Hegel argued that since war is a relation between states and not a relation of individual men to one another, the rights and interests of noncombatants should be maintained to the utmost. For the same reason he was in favor of professional armies and against conscription or any form of levy en masse.

Each nation is limited by geographical and other accidental features and hence can build up only a particular culture and can have only a particular, not a universal, history. Thus, nations, when they reach the level of statehood, make their contribution to the whole in the part they play in world history (*Encyclopedia*, Sec. 548). World history is not wholly an affair of chance or contingency: as the work of mind it could not be. Therefore, the history of the world has a rational structure; any historical writing that ignored this "would be only an imbecile mental divagation, not as good as a fairy-tale" (Sec. 549). This rational structure, according to Hegel, is the development of freedom.

"Absolute Mind"

The triad which completes the Hegelian system is composed of art, revealed religion, and philosophy. It will be remembered that at the end of the *Phenomenology* Hegel proceeded from the religion of nature to the religion of art and then to the philosophical knowledge of the history of the world. In the *Encyclopedia* art is given what seems to be a more independent status, but the details of the argument hardly bear out the general scheme, since the transitional sections describe a transition from objective mind to religion, as in the *Phenomenology*. Thus, in the concluding sections of the *Encyclopedia* art is regarded as an inadequate form of religion, religion as a more adequate form of art, philosophy as religion freed from picture thinking and wholly rationalized, and all three as manifestations of Absolute Mind. Art is the embodiment of Absolute Mind in material things fashioned by the artist, who, in a sense, is thus "the master of the God" (*Encyclopedia*, Sec. 560). In classical art the embodiment takes place without any antithesis between the embodiment and the mind that is embodied. In the art of the sublime, which preceded classical art, the Absolute Mind is regarded as something that defies embodiment and remains forever beyond and behind the sensible forms that succeed only in symbolizing it. The defect of artistic representation is that the sensible symbols may be taken to refer to another world beyond, which is as limited as this world is falsely taken to be. Thus, men worship idols or even bones, "which point to the unspiritual objectivity of that other world" (*ibid.*, Sec. 562).

God is therefore not something grander and more powerful than the natural world yet fundamentally like it, nor is he something beyond the world that must remain forever inaccessible to man. God is manifested in the world, and this is the truth that revealed religion has expressed most adequately in the Christian doctrine of the Incarnation. Without this doctrine God would still be regarded as beyond the world and, thus, as incomplete and finite. Even with this doctrine he is conceived of through the medium of particular historical events that introduce an element of contingency and irrelevance into our conception of him. In philosophy the artist's external vision and the mystic's internal vision are united in a mode of thought in which there is no further conflict. The philosopher who achieves ultimate self-knowledge is freed from the conflicts that inevitably disturb the inferior levels of knowledge. By philosophizing to the end, he has made himself free (*ibid.*, Sec. 576).

THE DIALECTICAL METHOD

Contradiction

It is now necessary to give more detailed attention to Hegel's dialectical method. There are interpreters of Hegel who say that Hegel denied the principle of contradiction in that he held that contradictories can both exist and that contradictory propositions can therefore both be true. Others deny this interpretation, maintaining, instead that, according to Hegel, since contradiction is a mark of inadequacy and falsehood, contradictions are to be found in the lower categories but are absent from or resolved in the Absolute Idea. This view is summed up in Michael Oakeshott's reference to "the element of self-contradiction inherent in all abstraction" (*Experience and Its Modes*, Cambridge, 1933, p. 328). Those who take the first view can quote some convincing passages from Hegel's *Science of Logic*. For example, there he wrote that "all things are in themselves contradictory," that "movement is existing contradiction itself," and that "only insofar as something has contradiction in itself does it move, have impulse or activity."

If Hegel had rejected the principle of contradiction in the sense that that principle is understood by formal logicians, his case would indeed be serious, for it follows from the rejection of this principle that any proposition can be true and false and that there is thus no means of distinguishing truth from falsehood. It is important, therefore, to see whether Hegel did reject the principle of contradiction in this sense and whether its rejection is part of his dialectical method. That these questions are not easy to answer becomes apparent if we consult some of the commentators on the passages I have just quoted. J. M. E. McTaggart, in his *Commentary on Hegel's Logic*, was dissatisfied with the whole section and claimed that in it Hegel had allowed himself to be too much influenced by Schelling's view on polarity and opposition. "The whole point of the dialectic," McTaggart protested, "is that the perception of a contradiction is a reason for abandoning the category which we find contradictory." Indeed, he found this part of the *Logic* so unsatisfactory that he proposed to amend the sequence of categories by leaving out contradiction altogether.

McTaggart said nothing, however, about Hegel's statement that there are existing contradictions. G. R. G. Mure, in his *A Study of Hegel's Logic*, did not evade this difficulty. Examining Hegel's text more closely than McTaggart had done, he pointed out that on the ground that "the contradictory cannot be imagined or thought" Hegel rejected the common-sense view that things cannot be self-contradictory but that thought can be. Mure called attention, too, to Hegel's statement that self-contradiction is not a mere disease of thought but something which it must pass through on its way to truth. Furthermore, according to Hegel, it is finite things that are self-contradictory, and they are contradictory not in relation to one another but by virtue of their relation to what is infinite; Hegel "is not suggesting that Big Ben can now read both 9 P.M. and not 9 P.M." (p.105). Although this is an improvement on McTaggart, it left out of account Hegel's statement that for something to move, it must be both here and not here at the same time. What Hegel said about movement is not altogether unlike Mure's example of Big Ben. So the difficulty remains.

In the "Logic" sections of the *Encyclopedia* which was written later than the *Science of Logic* contradiction is not a separate category at all. Perhaps the reason for this difference is that Hegel had second thoughts and gave up the idea of contradiction in the nature of things. But although contradiction is no longer a category in the *Encyclopedia*, Hegel still sometimes wrote as if there were contradictions in the nature of things. For example, he stated that although such concepts as "square circle," "many-sided circle," and "straight curve" are self-contradictory, geometers nevertheless regard circles as polygons composed of very short sides and "the center and circumference of a circle as opposite and contradictory to one another" (*Encyclopedia*, Sec. 119). Hegel also suggested that polarity in physics goes against the ordinary logic—but he used the word "opposition" (*Entgegensetzung*) rather than "contradiction" (*Widerspruch*).

In *Geschichte der neueren Philosophie* (Heidelberg, 1901, Vol. VIII, Part 2) Kuno Fischer tried to overcome the difficulty by distinguishing between two sorts of contradiction, "necessary contradiction" and "impossible contradiction." The example of a square circle illustrates the notion of an impossible contradiction, a *contradictio in adjecto*, for it is impossible for the same thing to be both circular and square. When a circle is regarded as a many-sided polygon, however, the contradiction is not *in adjecto* but *in subjecto*, for the circle is then being regarded as in the process of being formed or generated from these many sides. This, Fischer held, is the contradiction involved in all becoming (the first concrete category of the "Logic," the synthesis of being and nothing). Fischer's suggestion is therefore that there is not a vicious or stultifying contradiction involved in becoming or in movement, contradictory though they must in some sense be. But although this may be a correct exposition of Hegel's view, it is hardly a defense of it, since it merely repeats without explaining his claim that there are contradictions in the objective world.

By drawing this distinction, Fischer has nevertheless raised the question of whether Hegel intended the word "contradiction" to be used in the way it is used in formal logic. The answer is clear enough. Hegel did not regard formal logic as a philosophical science, and he therefore rejected any idea that its categories should dominate philosophical thought. Thus, the fact that the word "contradiction" is used in a certain way by formal logicians was not for him a reason for confining himself to that meaning. When Hegel was advocating the dialectical method, he had in mind a method in which oppositions, conflicts, tensions, and refutations were courted than avoided or evaded. Hegel was a student of the classical, laissez-faire economists who held that wealth would be maximized by the free play of competition. In this view if traders and producers ceased to compete with one another, the whole level of economic life would be lowered. General prosperity could be reached only at the expense of labor and anxiety. So it is, Hegel believed, with the categories of our thought, the systems of philosophers, and the forms of life and society. There is no tranquillity to be had by withdrawal and isolation. Our categories compete with one another, and out of their competition emerges something better than either of them could have accomplished alone. But it is not possible for the superior category to go into retirement, for without the spur of competition it would fall into decay. Furthermore, just as competition requires the competitors to continue in business — for if one destroys the others, there is monopoly and stagnation — so the competing categories cannot be swallowed up and lost in the Absolute Idea but must all play their part in maintaining its life and stability. There is nothing fanciful in this comparison. Indeed, it gains support from Hegel's "System der Sittlichkeit" of 1802 ("System of Morality"; in *Schriften zur Politik und Rechtsphilosophie*, Georg Lasson, ed., 2d ed., Leipzig, 1923), in which it is quite clear that Hegel's systematic thinking was influenced by his understanding of economic theory. For example, in this essay he developed the triad need – labor – enjoyment and described labor as "the destruction of the object . . . but in such a way that another is put in its place." Here Hegel compared labor with knowledge and undoubtedly had in mind (in accord with his tendency to take German words in the sense of their roots) the element of negation (*nicht*) in the word for destruction (*Vernichtung*). The destruction of the natural object is the creation of an artificial one.

Negation

Negation, indeed, is the vital notion in Hegel's account of the dialectic. In the Preface to the *Phenomenology* Hegel wrote, "The life of God and divine knowledge may, if we wish, be described as love disporting with itself; but this idea is degraded into mere edification and insipidity if it lacks the seriousness, the pain, the patience and the labour of the negative." "Seriousness," "pain," "patience," and "labor" would be strange words to use of the negative symbol of formal logic. Expressed in theological-economic terms Hegel's view is that God cannot be a mere consumer, for there is no consumption without labor, and labor has to face a recalcitrant nature that has to be understood and humored. Thus, there is no God apart from nature. In moral terms there is no good without evil, and in logical terms there is no truth without error. These, according to Hegel, are central truths of dialectics.

But surely, it will be said, this conflicts with such obvious facts as that there are some who consume without working, that in mathematics there are sequences of necessarily true propositions with no admixture of falsity, and that some things — for example, conscientious action — are good without qualification. As to the first point, Hegel argued in the *Phenomenology* that the master who consumes what his slave produces for him destroys what he consumes, whereas the slave shapes the external world in such a way that mind is embodied in it. Hence, the slave is on the road to freedom, whereas the master, who does not work, destroys without creating. As to mathematics, Hegel was inclined to hold it in contempt. There is no space here to consider the strange things he said about it, and it need only be remarked that he held that philosophical truth is utterly different from mathematical truth in that false philosophical views are taken up into true philosophy whereas false mathematics is not taken up into true mathematics. As to the alleged unmixed goodness of conscientious action (the Kantian "good will"), Hegel held that the morality of conscience contained in itself the seeds of willfulness and arbitrariness, for the most atrocious deeds can be defended on the ground that the man who committed them genuinely thought them right. Obedience to one's own conscience, Hegel thought, is an advance over obedience to the commands of an external lord but is nevertheless an unstable basis for morality.

Several ways in which the negative element is important in Hegel's method have been discussed. There is the conceptual competition without which thought must decay. Then, there is the polar character of certain fundamental notions which makes the one unthinkable without its opposite. At the prephilosophical level Hegel gave above and below, right and left, father and son, as examples. At the philosophical level his examples, were good and bad, master and slave, thought and nature. But not only do these opposites require each other; they also pass into each other. Good will can pass over into atrocity; philosophical truth is the result of errors that supplement each other; the master satisfies his desires but becomes dependent upon the labor of the slave in order to do so; and the slave, by work, controls his desires and develops a rational will. The life of thought in conceptual conflict, the mutual dependence of polar opposites, and the instability or oscillations of philosophical and moral attitudes are different sorts of dialectic which Hegel emphasized on different occasions. If they have anything in common, it is the activity of negation.

There are two other aspects of the dialectic to discuss, the role of reason and understanding and the role of skepticism.

Reason and Understanding

First, Hegel, following Kant, contrasted the reason, the source of dialectical thinking, with the understanding, the predialectical mode of thought.

The understanding, as Hegel saw it, is the type of thinking that prevails in common sense, in the natural sciences, and in mathematics and those types of philosophy that are argued in quasi-scientific or quasi-mathematical ways. Fixed categories are uncritically adhered to, demonstrations are produced (only to be demolished), analyses are made, and distinctions are drawn. Analyzing and distinguishing are necessary foundations of philosophical activity but only to prepare the way for the more sinuous and subtle method of the dialectic. Once an analysis has been made, the elements of it are seen to conflict and collide as well as to cohere. First, the understanding isolates, then comes the Reason's negative moment of criticism or conflict, and after that its speculative moment of synthesis. It should be mentioned that distinctions somewhat similar to the distinction between the understanding and the reason had already been made by Plato when he distinguished between the highest knowledge and knowledge in the various sciences, by Spinoza in his second and third kinds of knowledge, by Pascal with his *esprit de géométrie* and *esprit de finesse*, by Hume with his reason and imagination, and by Burke when he contrasted the abstract rationalism of the Enlightenment with the organic, evolutionary view of society that he preferred. These distinctions are not all quite like that drawn by Hegel, but in his theory there is something corresponding to each of them.

Skepticism

Second, Hegel thought that skepticism was an important forerunner and essential ingredient of the dialectical method. In a review of a book by G. E Schulze that appeared in 1802, Hegel wrote appreciatively of the skepticism of Sextus Empiricus and of the skeptical features in the philosophy of Parmenides, of whom he wrote, "This skepticism, which in its pure *explicit* form comes forward in Parmenides, is to be found *implicit* in every genuinely philosophical system, for it is the free aspect [*die freie Seite*] of every philosophy" ("Verhältnis des Skeptizismus zur Philosophie," in *Kritisches Journal der Philosophie*, Vol. 2, (1802), 1–74, quoted from *Sämtliche Werke*, Georg Lasson, ed., Vol. 1, pp. 174–175). In the same essay Hegel wrote that when Spinoza held that God is the immanent but not the transcendent cause of the world, he was equating the cause with the effect, even though the very notion of an effect implies that it is distinct from the cause. Hegel agreed with Spinoza's equation but concluded that it shows that the reason can accept the principle of contradiction only as a formal principle. In "genuine" philosophy cause and effect are seen as both distinct and identical.

Hegel illustrated his comment that skepticism is "the free aspect" of philosophy in the following way. Dogmatists, he said, regard individual men as objects in the power of rules, laws, and customs. The more the dogmatists study man, the more they show him in subjection to these forces. When, however, the skeptics attack dogmatism, "they raise the freedom of Reason above this necessity of nature." An example of this is the way in which Europeans came to question their own concepts of law and morals when they were brought face to face with cultures very different from their own. When such skeptics as Montaigne mockingly insisted on these differences, men became more conscious of their own institutions and recognized the possibility of changing them. In theoretically breaking down men's traditional views and institutions, the skeptic frees men from the unconscious power of these views and institutions. Hegel repeated his general assessment of skepticism in the *Encyclopedia* (Sec. 81, addition 2) and in his *Lectures on the History of Philosophy.* In these lectures Hegel said that skepticism is "the demonstration that all that is determinate and finite is unstable." Hegel went on to say that "positive philosophy," by which he meant philosophy that is not content to remain in total skepticism, "has the negative to Scepticism in itself; thus it does not oppose, nor is it outside of it, for Scepticism is a moment in it" (Haldane and Simpson, 1955, Vol. II, p. 330).

FREEDOM

From what has just been said, it is clear that Hegel's account of dialectic and of reason is closely linked with his view of freedom. The exercise of thought in its most developed forms involves the negation of what had seemed firm and certain and the opening up of new possibilities. That mind is freedom applies both to the understanding and the reason, since both are spontaneous activities that interpret and arrange. But because the understanding is confined to a fixed system of categories, it is less free than the reason that criticizes, stretches, and transforms the categories of the understanding.

Freedom is, of course, logically connected with will, and according to Hegel, will is as essential to mind as intellect is. Reference has already been made to Section 482 of the *Encyclopedia,* in which Hegel asserted that the unity of theoretical and practical mind is free will. In the preceding sections he had argued that thought presupposes mind as practical, since classifying and explaining are activities through which the world is, so to speak, appropriated by the mind. In the sections of the *Encyclopedia* in which he expounded the categories of cognition and of will, Hegel endeavored to show that mere cognition is at a lower stage than will and that will is thus the actuality of what is only potential in knowledge. He also argued that the freedom and necessity that are opposed to each other are abstractions and that what is concrete must combine both. The very nature of necessity, he continued, presupposes a will on which it is a constraint.

At the logical-metaphysical level, therefore, Hegel held a view which implied that freedom is essential to mind, both the presupposition and outcome of intelligence, and in its concrete form inseparable from constraint and necessity. This view of the matter pervaded his account of freedom in the social and political sphere. Freedom is not something merely opposed to constraint, on the contrary, it presupposes and requires restraint. This is true of concrete freedom. However, abstract or negative freedom, when it is more than a moment in actual or positive freedom, is a purely destructive force. Hegel considered that this negative freedom played a large part in the French Revolution. The old corporations and institutions were destroyed in such a frenzy of annihilation that it took several years for new institutions to be created and recognized as authoritative. Furthermore, when the conflicting interests in society are overcome, individuals come to be treated as equal, undifferentiated, replaceable, and expendable units. The events of the Reign of Terror thus led Hegel to hold that purely negative freedom was associated with force and death. The logical connections are not altogether clear, but it may well be that the links between egalitarianism, antinomianism, violence, and contempt for human life are not wholly accidental.

Freedom, according to Hegel, is something that has to be achieved, and it therefore would be impossible in the absence of opposition and negation. Hence, although negative freedom in its abstract form is a "fury of destruction," it is a necessary element in concrete freedom. Free will is not the liberty of indifference but the rational organization of the feelings and impulses.

Rationality is not a power that could reside in an isolated individual, however. To be rational, the individual must draw upon the resources of an organized and differentiated society and must be "formed" and educated to do this. His will is then in harmony with the ends of the various social groups by which he has been influenced and, in civilized societies, with the more complex ends of the state. In conforming to these pressures and in obeying the laws of the state, the individual is achieving his own rational ends and in so doing is free.

Hegel, like Rousseau, also held that an individual might be free even when he was being coerced, for although he might dislike the force applied against him, this dislike would be an expression of his particular whims, not of his rational insight, as can be seen when he approves of the imposition of a like force upon other people in like circumstances. Insofar as the criminal who is being punished would wish others to be punished who committed a like crime against him, he wills his own punishment.

Freedom in History

Hegel considered that the history of the human race is a development from less to greater freedom and from less adequate forms of freedom to freedom in its perfection. Thus, his philosophy of history can be understood only in terms of his conception of freedom. In the Oriental world there was no freedom for the subjects and only an arbitrary, irrational freedom for the despot who ruled over them. In the classical world of Greece and Rome there was a more adequate conception of freedom, and more men achieved freedom than in the Oriental despotisms. In the Greek city-state the citizens often regarded themselves as finding their fulfillment in the achievements of their city, apart from which they conceived of no life for themselves. Indeed, they might accept personal defeat and misfortune and submit to what they called destiny and still regard themselves as free in so doing. Of course, there were slaves who had no part in this activity and had no freedom.

Christianity offered the prospect of freedom to all men, a freedom, furthermore, that transcended the given social order. In what Hegel called the Germanic world — that is, the Christian civilization that grew out of Protestantism — this latest form of freedom was being realized in the manifold institutions of Europe and America and in the states in which these institutions flourished and by which they were regulated and protected. In Christianity the individual is regarded as of infinite value, as a candidate for eternal salvation, and although the emphasis on subjective freedom can lead, as it did in the French Revolution, to contempt for social institutions, it comprises the form and aspect of freedom that gives its special quality to modern civilization, with its romantic art, romantic love, and support for the rights of conscience (*Philosophy of Right*, Sec. 124).

It is apparent from the foregoing that Hegel rejected the liberal view that man is free to the extent that he is guaranteed a sphere within which he can do what he wishes without interference from others who are guaranteed a like position. Such freedom he stigmatized as negative, abstract, or merely willful. Men enjoy concrete freedom when the various orders and groups of civilized life are maintained in and by the state. In this passage of the *Lectures on the Philosophy of History* (Hoffmeister, Vol. XVIIIA, p.111) Hegel also emphasized that in submitting their private wills to the laws of the state and to the rules of its subordinate but free institutions, men were submitting their passions to the control of reason. Thus, the argument comes full circle. The theoretical reason is inseparable from will and from freedom; necessity and negative freedom are only abstractions; in concrete freedom the negative, destructive element is held in check and rendered fruitful by being realized in institutions; the individual enjoys concrete freedom when he is educated to live in a civilized state and to be guided by the reason that permeates it.

There is no space here to criticize this view in any detail, for in a way it is a cross section of the whole Hegelian metaphysic. It should be noted, however, that when a critic maintains that real freedom is what Hegel called negative or abstract freedom and when he goes on to maintain that "concrete freedom" is not freedom but indoctrinated submission, then he is criticizing Hegel's terminology rather than the substance of his view. To say that freedom consists of a willing acceptance of the tasks imposed by a civilized state is certainly to extend and perhaps to distort the ordinary senses of the term and to capture a word from the liberal vocabulary for use in a far from liberal scheme of concepts. It was Hegel's view, however, that the thoughts that the liberal phraseology expressed necessarily move in the directions he described and that societies themselves, the embodiments of men's thoughts and aims, move in these directions, too.

AESTHETIC THEORY

We have already seen that Hegel discussed the nature of art and of beauty toward the end of both the *Phenomenology* and the *Encyclopedia*. Art, according to Hegel, is one of the manifestations of Absolute Mind, of which religion and philosophy are the other two. Thus, although art presupposes the civilized life of the state, it also transcends it. In his lengthy *Vorlesungen über die Aesthetik* ("Lectures on Aesthetics") Hegel developed his theories of art and beauty in great detail. The lectures possess great power and attraction, and so much of their value resides in the details that a summary treatment is bound to be difficult.

Three Styles of Art

Hegel's account of beauty is a modification of Schiller's view, in his *Letters on the Aesthetic Education of Mankind* (1795), that beauty is the mediation between the sensible and the rational. According to Hegel, beauty is the rational rendered sensible, the sensible appearance being the form in which the rational content is made manifest. This sensible embodiment of the rational, he held, can take place in three principal ways, symbolic art, classical art, and romantic art.

Symbolic Art

In the first and least adequate form, symbolic art, the sensible shape merely symbolizes the rational content without penetrating and transforming it. A lion may symbolize courage; a bird, the soul; or a temple, the presence of a god who nevertheless remains a mystery. Thus, in symbolic art the sensible object refers away from itself to a rationality that is enigmatically and mysteriously beyond it. In thus referring away from the sensible symbol to something vast and merely adumbrated, symbolic art sometimes achieves the sublime.

Classical Art

In classical art, the second form of sensible embodiment, the sensible expression is adequate to the idea that it gives expression to and does not point vaguely beyond itself. This is typified in sculptures of the human body so formed that the divine ideal is realized in the stone, not merely hinted at. A temple makes us think of the god but is not the god. In a statue of Apollo the god is visible and tangible in the stone. Hegel pointed out that works of classical art have independence and completeness, so that when they have been created, it seems that there is nothing more left to do done. "Nothing more beautiful," he wrote, "can be or become."

Romantic Art

Christianity, however, with its emphasis on the infinite value of the individual and upon subjective freedom, made classical art seem somewhat unsatisfactory. More is required than works of art in which reason, as Hegel put it, "stands in quiet and blessedness in bodily form." When the self and its inner life are regarded as of infinite value, the forms of art must move on from balance and harmony to the storm and turmoil of the subjective. According to Hegel, it is in romantic art that this progress to subjectivity and self-consciousness is achieved. Romantic art turns its back on the quiet and balanced beauty of the classical and "weaves the inner life of beauty into the contingency of the external form, and allows full scope to the emphatic features of the unbeautiful." In romantic art, as in symbolic art, there is much that is bizarre and even grotesque, but romantic art is on a higher level than symbolic art because the mind expressed in it is more complex and sophisticated. And in romantic art the mind has achieved a greater measure of freedom than in classical art because romantic art is less involved in and hampered by the sensible embodiment.

Products of Art

Hegel's view of the three main types of beauty is closely linked with his view of the main types of artistic product. Hegel divided the arts into architecture, sculpture, painting, music, and poetry. Works in any of these mediums may be produced in the symbolic, classical, or romantic styles, but, according to Hegel, architecture is particularly appropriate to symbolic art, sculpture to classical art, and painting, music, and poetry to romantic art.

Architecture

Architecture, Hegel held, is the basic art, the art that men first practice, for its material is mindless and its forms depend upon the weight and physical properties of this mindless medium. The architecture of early men, by bringing them together to worship the gods in temples, served to bring unity into their societies. Hegel imagined the men who built the first temples as they cleared the ground on which to build them, and he described this as "clearing the undergrowth of finitude."

Sculpture

In architecture a house is provided for the god, and the god is prepared for and expected. He is not, however, embodied or manifested in the stones of a mere building. In classical sculpture the god is embodied in the stone in such a way that all the parts of the statue combine in expressing and proclaiming him. Hence, it is not a mindless symbol of the mind beyond but a unified expression of it. Hegel contrasted the stiff regularity of Egyptian sculpture with the harmonious independence of the Greek, the acme of classical art. In Christian sculpture this Greek ideal does not predominate, and even when, as with Michelangelo, it is fully understood and mastered, it is associated with "the kind of inspiration that is found in romantic art."

Painting, Music, and Poetry

The three romantic arts of painting, music, and poetry differ from the arts of sculpture and architecture, according to Hegel, by being more "ideal." One thing he seems to have meant was that the productions of these arts are not three-dimensional like the productions of architecture and sculpture. Painting, of course, is two-dimensional, and Hegel thought it is more ideal than sculpture because it is further removed from the solid substance of material things. He appears to have argued that the painter transforms to an extent that the sculptor has no need to do. In reducing the three dimensions to two, space is somehow rendered more "inward" and "subjective," and the first step has been taken on the road to poetry.

The next step toward subjectivity is taken by music, which abandons all the dimensions of space as well as the senses of sight and touch. Hearing, according to Hegel, is a "more subjective" sense than sight because it is less practical and more contemplative.

In poetry the sensible elements of music, the notes or tones, are replaced by words that stand for thoughts. "The art of poetry," Hegel wrote, "is the universal art of mind that has become free and is no longer dependent upon external sensible material for its realization." Within poetry as a whole he distinguished epic, lyric, and dramatic poetry. Hegel's account of dramatic poetry is particularly interesting. "In tragedy," he wrote, "individuals destroy themselves through the onesidedness of their upright will and character, or they are forced to resign themselves and identify themselves with a course of action to which they are fundamentally opposed." In comedy, on the other hand, there is no such reconciliation, the characters pursue courses of action that have only subjective significance. Indeed, in comedy, according to Hegel, the subjectivity characteristic of romantic art is taken to such an extreme that all unity is dissolved; with it goes beauty, too. In comedy there is merely a series of subjective interests playing against one another, as opposed to the aim of all art, which is the revelation of the eternal and divine in sensible form.

Natural Beauty

The discussion has thus far been confined to the beauty of works of art (*das Kunstschöne*). It is with this that by far the greater part of the "Lectures on Aesthetics" is concerned. In the second chapter, however, Hegel did say something about natural beauty (*das Naturschöne*). He discussed the notions of regularity, symmetry, harmony, and conformity to law and also the beauty claimed for plants, animals, and human beings. He concluded his discussion of the subject with some comments on how natural beauty falls short of artistic beauty. Plants and animals, he granted, are more beautiful than inanimate natural objects, but what we see of them is their outward coverings, not the soul that works within, for that is concealed by the visible feathers, hair, scales, fur, and the like that cover them. Hegel referred to natural beauty as the "prose of the world." Although Hegel did not altogether deny the beauty of nature, it is clear that he ranked it very low. Indeed, the structure of his system made this inevitable, for it is the self-conscious achievements of man that form its culmination.

It would seem that the triadic divisions of the "Lectures on Aesthetics" constrained and even corrupted Hegel's argument. An example of this occurs in his account of dramatic poetry, into which he introduced a species called "drama," the function of which was to add one species to tragedy and comedy and thus make three species of dramatic poetry.

Hegel also tended to confuse conceptual and historical relationships. For example, the distinction between symbolic, classical, and romantic art was intended to be made on conceptual grounds, but, on the other hand, Hegel had in mind historical progression. Here, as elsewhere, Hegel confused historical types, such as romanticism, with conceptual types, such as tragedy, which have no necessary temporal sequence. Perhaps the most interesting case of this is Hegel's suggestion that art comes to an end with the highest flights of romanticism. We have already seen that Hegel brought his account of dramatic poetry to an end with comedy, the most subjective of all art forms. At the very end of the "Lectures on Aesthetics" he said that "in this culmination comedy is leading straight to the dissolution of art in general." It is unlikely that Hegel believed that art was coming to an end, any more than he believed that with the Prussian state, history was coming to an end. Yet in each case he argued in such a way as to suggest that the culmination of a conceptual sequence must also be the conclusion of a historical progress. Insofar as he held that history was the movement of the Divine in the world, it was natural to make this identification, extravagant as it is. Bosanquet, who denied that Hegel believed that art was on the point of final dissolution, held that he did foresee that it was about to suffer an eclipse in the new form of society. "But we must claim extraordinary insight for him, who, still under the spell of Schiller and Goethe, described the present exhaustion of the art-impulse and the conditions hostile to it in language approaching that of Ruskin and William Morris" (*A History of Aesthetic*, 4th ed., London, 1917, p. 361).

PHILOSOPHY OF RELIGION

A few commentators have regarded Hegel's philosophy as atheistic, but most have considered it to be either theistic or pantheistic. Certainly religious expressions abound in his writings, even in the *Logic*. It has been shown how closely he associated art with religion and how he applied religious epithets to the state. It was also pointed out that the *Phenomenology* might with some justification be interpreted in atheistic terms. It would be obviously overstraining the evidence, however, to interpret Hegel's mature system in this way, for in the system religion is a form of Absolute Mind, along with art and philosophy, which is the supreme expression of the Absolute Mind. According to Hegel, religion represents or pictures the Absolute, whereas philosophy conceives or thinks it. The same truth, that is, expressed in quasi-imaginative form in one and in conceptual form in the other.

Christianity

Since the concept is supreme and ultimate, philosophy surpasses religion to this extent, but in doing this, it finally and fully justifies Christianity, which is the absolute religion. The doctrine that elevates Christianity above all other religions is the doctrine of the Incarnation, which, according to Hegel, is the religious expression of the philosophical truth that the Infinite Being is not distinct from what is finite but is necessarily manifested in it. Hegel also interpreted the doctrine of the Trinity in philosophical terms. In the "Science of Logic" God is revealed as he is before the creation of the world; in the "Philosophy of Nature," in his material embodiment, and in the "Philosophy of Mind," as reconciling the finite and the Infinite. In this way the Father, the Son, and the Holy Spirit are explained in terms of the main themes of the Hegelian system. Again, Hegel interpreted the doctrine that God is love to mean that although the Infinite Being cannot exist without negation and opposition, the negation and opposition are finally reconciled. Finally, it should be mentioned that Hegel gave a series of lectures on the traditional proofs for the existence of God. He admitted the force of Kant's criticisms of these proofs but claimed to have reformulated the arguments so as to meet the criticisms. In particular, he held that the Ontological Argument, which Kant had regarded as vital but unsound, was valid when properly understood.

Undoubtedly, Hegel's later writings are much closer to orthodox Christianity than his earlier ones. The early "Life of Jesus" had nothing to say about the Resurrection, whereas in the *Lectures on the Philosophy of Religion* this doctrine was stated and defended. Hegel here wrote of "the death of death," of "the triumph over the negative," of mind as "the negative of this negative which thus contains the negative in itself," and of "the division of the divine idea and its reunion" that is "the whole of history." Although Hegel said that God appeared in the flesh at a particular time and in a particular individual, his account of the matter seems to be extremely general. In the Christian doctrine of the Incarnation, God became man in Jesus Christ at a particular time and place, whereas Hegel's God is incorporated in the finite world. It would seem that a highly specific historical view is replaced by a highly general metaphysical one. Hegel himself did not take this view of his own work, nor did a younger contemporary of his, Karl Friedrich Göschel, in his *Aphorismen über Nichtwissen und absolutes Wissen im Verhälnisse zur christlichen Glaubenserkenntnis* (Berlin, 1829). In the *Encyclopedia* (Sec. 564) Hegel recommended this book, which is generally regarded as giving a theistic account of the Absolute. Just before referring to Göschel's book, Hegel had written, "God is only God in so far as he knows himself; his self-knowledge is moreover his consciousness of himself in man and man's knowledge *of* God, a knowledge that extends itself into the self-knowledge of man *in* God."

What cannot be doubted is that Hegel's philosophy of religion contained elements that could easily be developed in ways that go counter to orthodox Christianity. Thus, when D. F. Strauss argued, in his *Life of Jesus* (1835), that the Gospel story was a set of myths, he was consciously working out what he thought was the consequence of Hegel's view that in religion the truth about God is understood in representative or pictorial terms. Again, Ludwig Feuerbach, in his *The Essence of Christianity* (1841), endeavored to interpret the Christian doctrines in human and psychological terms as the imaginary fulfillment of wishes that cannot be satisfied here on earth. We have already referred to the passage in Hegel's *The Positivity of the Christian Religion*, in which he said that in the days of imperial Rome men who had been robbed of their freedom in this world sought for it in a heaven beyond. Feuerbach, who, of course, had not seen this work, could have read something similar in the *Phenomenology*. It is a very short step from Hegel's view that the infinite is manifested in the finite to the view that it is a projection of it. Perhaps the truth of the matter is that the Christian religion, according to Hegel, is adequate in its own sphere and that the philosophy of religion is required to counteract false religious views and false views about religion but is not a substitute for it. This is the interpretation given by Lasson in the Introduction to Hegel's philosophy of religion printed at the end of his edition of Hegel's *Lectures on the Philosophy of Religion*.

Introduction

Do you know when one can say "I"? When a man struggles all by himself and all by himself makes or breaks something, then he may say "I". But when many people join together in the struggle and accomplish something, then they should say "We." In the life that we live it is "We" and not "I." [General Makryannis][1]

Hegel is one of the greatest and yet one of the most difficult of all philosophers. There are several reasons for his difficulty. First, there is the sheer magnitude of the problems that he is attempting to solve. It is a matter of controversy whether he is, like Schelling, attempting to explain why there is anything at all rather than nothing, why God created the world, or, more ambitiously, why the world takes precisely the form it does and not some other form. But at any rate Hegel operates against a background in which it seems reasonable to ask such questions and in which one's unwillingness to ask them or inability to answer them requires explanation. Again, philosophy must, in Hegel's view, be both systematic and more or less all-embracing: The whole of human experience, both theoretical and practical—nature, psychology, morality, politics, history, art, religion, and above all philosophy itself—must be accounted for in a single, rationally interrelated system. Naturally enough Hegel often draws connections that seem to us obscure between topics that seem to us, if not unconnected, yet more remotely related than Hegel supposes. Moreover, Hegel is attempting to philosophize without any assumptions or presuppositions; any concept we use, any claim we make, in fact any question we ask (for even questions involve presuppositions) must be justified within philosophy itself. The questions that Hegel is attempting to answer, then, and the self-imposed constraints on his manner both of asking and of answering them account in good part for the difficulty of his texts.

A second reason for Hegel's difficulty is that whereas most earlier German philosophers—Kant, for example—are often content to use words of Latin origin or even Latin words to express their meaning and see no great significance in the German language as such, Hegel is a peculiarly German philosopher: He attaches immense importance to the structure and etymology of the German language and makes it his aim to "teach philosophy to speak German".[2] The English reader's difficulties in following what Hegel says about, for example, essence, judgment, or condition are often eased by the realization that for Hegel the notion of essence (*Wesen*) is closely connected with the past tense of the verb "to be" (*gewesen*): that judgment (*Urteil*) is seen as an "original" or "primitive division" (*Ur-teil*); and that the German words for "conditioned" and "to condition" (*bedingt, bedingen*) are associated, in Hegel's mind, with the notion of a "thing" (*Ding*) and carry the additional connotation of reification or of making something into a thing. Hegel is not of course the only or the first philosopher to make such claims: Schelling, Hegel's friend and collaborator, maintained six years before Hegel's first publications that German is an "original language" and that its structure and vocabulary are especially revealing. It would thus be a mistake to regard the "I" or self as a thing, since this would imply that it is conditioned or determined by other things.[3] Again, German has a variety of words roughly equivalent to "existence": *Sein* ("being"), *Dasein* (literally "being there"), *Existenz*, and *Wirklichkeit* ("actuality"). Kant is prepared to use these words interchangeably, but this, Schelling argues, is a mistake; in particular we should not say that an unconditioned entity like God or the self exists in the same way or sense that a stone or a tree exists.[4] At about the same time, another friend of Hegel's student days, the poet Hölderlin, argued that "judgment is the original division between subject and object" and that the "most fitting example of this concept" is the self-awareness expressed by "I am I," the state, that is, in which I become an object to myself and thus, as it were, bifurcate into a subject and an object.[5] Hegel takes up this procedure and, especially in his works on logic, applies it more rigorously and systematically than do Schelling or Hölderlin, but even when he does not explicitly advert to such intricacies of the German language, they generally lie in the background and account for much of the difficulty of his writings.

Finally, the philosophical and cultural context in which Hegel wrote is rich and intricate, although relatively unfamiliar to Hegel's English readers. For a time Hegel was, for example, under the spell of the younger but more precocious Schelling, and even in his later writings Hegel was often influenced by, or alternatively reacting against, Schelling. In fact Hegel saw the history of philosophy after Kant as passing from Fichte via Schelling to Hegel (with a detour through a lesser figure rated highly by Hegel—F. H. Jacobi).[6] But these were not the only philosophers operating in Germany at the time. The period in which Hegel lived was a golden age of German philosophy and of German culture in general. Many other considerable talents—K. L. Reinhold, G. E. Schulze, S. Maimon, J. S. Beck, for example—were inspired by the work of Kant to develop or criticize it; others, like J. G. Herder, made significant advances in the philosophy of history and that of language; the romantics—Novalis, the

Schlegels, and Friedrich Schleiermacher — reacted against the Enlightenment in several spheres: religion, politics, history, literature, and so forth. All of these movements left their mark on Hegel and it is impossible to understand his writings fully without some appreciation of them. However a full mastery of any one of these thinkers would require a lifetime; the writings of many of them — Schelling, for example — are hardly less difficult than those of Hegel, and in fact few of Hegel's English-speaking readers have more than a passing acquaintance even with Schelling, let alone the other writers whose influence on Hegel was, though less intense than Schelling's, nevertheless significant. This then is a further reason for the apparent obscurity of Hegel's thought — our relative unfamiliarity with its background.

These considerations suggest at least three ways in which an introduction to Hegel might alleviate the difficulties of his writings for the Anglo-American reader. First it might supply a general survey of his writings and of the problems they attempt to solve. Second, it might consider some of the thinkers who influenced Hegel, and attempt to trace the route by which he developed his own thought from theirs. Third, it might provide a glossary of some of the terms Hegel uses and an account of the use he makes of them. In this volume Hegel's thought is approached in each of these three ways. First, H. B. Acton supplies a masterly survey of Hegel's thought and writings. In this Introduction, I attempt to reconstruct the route taken by German philosophy between Kant and Hegel. Finally, I provide a brief glossary of some of Hegel's key terms.

I.
THE BACKGROUND TO HEGEL: SOME PROBLEMS

It may seem obvious that in order to understand and assess the thought of Hegel or of any other philosopher, we need some acquaintance with the writers who influenced him. Only in this way can we see what concepts and questions he inherited from others and what, by contrast, is original to him. This approach to Hegel faces considerable difficulties, however. For first, Hegel possesses vast learning in the history of philosophy and he explicitly attempts to incorporate the whole of past philosophy into his own thought. Arguably his thought owes more to the ancient Greeks (and perhaps to the Bible) than it does to his contemporaries. For the historical approach to Hegel's thought there is therefore no obvious point of departure. Second, even if we agree to adopt some starting point — Kant, for example — and ask how philosophy moved from Kant to Hegel, we are confronted by a host of significant philosophers who, although they would not figure largely, if at all, in a modern history of philosophy, nevertheless played a part in this transition. This in itself is enough to make any answer to the question either chaotic (if it attempts to take in everything) or arbitrary (if it does not), even if we determinedly exclude from our account those earlier thinkers, such as the Greeks and Spinoza, whose revival in this period also played a significant role. Hegel himself sees the history of German idealism as a fairly self-contained narrative centering on Kant, Fichte, Schelling, and Hegel himself, and this verdict has been more or less accepted by subsequent historians of the period. But Hegel is not necessarily the final authority on his own position in history or even perhaps on the significant influences on his own thought. Third, even if we can settle on a manageable list of participants in the story, it would be a mistake to represent them as related to one another like runners in a relay race, in which each philosopher would cease to function as soon as he has passed the baton on to his successor. For one thing, a philosopher does not simply proceed from where his predecessor left off: He attempts to make a fresh start and to produce his own assessment of past philosophers. Hegel, for example, does not simply accept Schelling's account of Kant and confine himself to criticizing and developing Schelling; he criticizes Kant independently, as well as philosophers of the remoter past. For another, a philosopher does not retire from the field as soon as his successor enters it. Fichte, for example, made significant criticisms of Schelling's philosophy, some of them similar to criticisms later made by Hegel. Schelling in turn did not retire gracefully in favour of Hegel; he continued to produce important work and, after Hegel's death, criticized him in some detail, as well as claiming to have originated the method employed by Hegel. This implies that the course of the narrative cannot be settled uncontroversially. Schelling in particular did not accept Hegel's view that German idealism proceeded from Kant to Hegel by way of Schelling, arguing instead that it proceeded to (the later) Schelling by way of Hegel (and the earlier Schelling). Thus the scope, characters, and direction of our narrative are all problematic. Nevertheless, given these caveats, there is some justification for asking the question "How do we get from Kant to Hegel?" and for restricting our answer to manageable proportions. For first of all a thinker is likely to be more deeply influenced, at least initially, by the conversation, lectures, and writings of his contemporaries than by thinkers of the past. It is after all in such contemporary influences that we must look for answers to such questions as "Why did Hegel think it important to read past philosophers at all?" "Why did he read some rather than others, Spinoza, say, and Böhme rather than Hume?" and "Why did he understand them in this way rather than that?" Second, it is not unreasonable to present the story of German idealism as Hegel himself saw it, at least in respect of its central characters. The claims of Kant, Fichte, and Schelling to a place in the story are undisputable in a way that other claims are not. Finally, in telling the story in one way we need not deny the possibility of other versions of the same story. In fact we can indicate within the story itself how Schelling, for example, might have seen matters differently. How, then, do we get from Kant to Hegel?

II.
STARTING WITH KANT

In his first major work, the *Critique of Pure Reason* of 1781, Kant starts from the problem "How can we have knowledge of an external world?" and in particular "How can we have knowledge that is synthetic (i.e., that does not consist in the elucidation of concepts) and yet is also a priori (i.e., that can be acquired independently of our sense-experience) — knowledge, for example, of arithmetic and geometry and of such truths as that every event has a cause?" His answer is that our experience is largely, though not wholly, the product of our own minds. It is we who contribute to our experience the "forms of sensibility" — space and time — and such "categories" as those of causality and substance. "Things in themselves" are not causally ordered in space and time; that is simply how we, in virtue of our own sensory and conceptual equipment, must view them. However, they are not, in Kant's view, dispensable; it is things in themselves that supply the sensory material, the material of "intuition", that we unify into a coherent, objective experience. It is not, however, only external objects that are constituted in this way. We ourselves, insofar as we have bodies and even sensations and emotions (the objects of "inner" as opposed to "outer" sense) are constituted by ourselves — ourselves, that is, not as embodied creatures with a diverse inner life, but as "transcendental apperception" or the "transcendental ego". This transcendental ego is the "I think" that must "accompany all our representations."[7] It cannot be known to us in any substantial sense, any more than things in themselves can be known to us; they are known only as "phenomena," as they appear to us — that is, through the spectacles of our own sensibility (space and time) and understanding (categories). The world of "noumena," while we can coherently if emptily think about it, cannot be known to us. This implies that certain questions, though we inevitably ask them, cannot be reliably answered — such questions as "Does God exist?" "Is the world finite or infinite in space and in time?" "Is the will free?" and "Is the soul immortal?" We could answer such questions as these only if we had knowledge of things in themselves, which, Kant has argued, we do not and cannot possess. Kant strengthens his case by arguing that in the case of some of these questions, equally valid arguments can be devised for incompatible answers to them ("antinomies"). We can argue with equal validity, for example, both that the world has a beginning in time and that it does not. Since both answers cannot be right and since, if the question were an appropriate one for us to ask with respect to things in themselves, one of them would have to be right, we must confess that our theoretical reason cannot give us access to things in themselves. Such metaphysical claims can at most have a "regulative" use, guiding our enquiries into empirical phenomena but not extending or supplementing them. The belief that, for example, the world has no beginning has a use in enjoining us to pursue our enquiries as far as we can, and the belief in God encourages us to bring system and order into the results of our enquiries, a system and order that go beyond what is required by our "constitutive" (as opposed to "regulative") principles — the categories.

The apparent effect of Kant's *Critique of Pure Reason* was to curb our metaphysical pretensions and to restrict us to empirical enquiry. When Kant turns to moral philosophy, however, especially in the *Critique of Practical Reason* of 1788, he is not content to leave matters there. Theoretical reason presents us with a view of the world as wholly causally ordered and determined, and we ourselves are involved in this causal network insofar as we are embodied creatures with sensations and desires. However, we are not wholly and inextricably embedded in the causal network, since it is, after all, only a phenomenon and one that is in good part produced by us. We cannot be wholly subject to laws that we ourselves impose. The core self, the transcendental ego, may well be free for all that theoretical reason tells us. Kant believes that if we are to be genuinely morally responsible, then we must be free — our decisions, that is, must be determined by ourselves and not by the causal processes in which we are involved. That we are free, however, is a requirement of morality, of our practical reason, and not of theoretical reason. If we are to do justice to our freedom — to our innermost selves — then we must not, in Kant's view, be guided by our desires and inclinations, for these belong to the causal network of the phenomenal world. We must, as it were, break loose from the phenomenal world by following reason, by imposing on ourselves "categorical imperatives," certified by reason alone and not by our desires or by our long-term happiness. Freedom is not, however, the only "postulate" of practical reason. The existence of God and the immortality of the soul, doctrines that theoretical reason was unable to establish, are required by our practical reason. God is needed in order to guarantee that moral worth, the "good will," though not motivated by the desire for happiness, is nevertheless rewarded with happiness in proportion to its worth. Immortality is needed to ensure that we can continue to strive toward perfection and that our moral efforts are not cut short by death. Humanity is advancing toward the condition of purely rational beings, a condition in which decisions will be guided solely by reason. This is not a condition to which we shall ever attain in fact, but it is one to which our practical reason requires us to believe that we shall get ever closer. Kant held a similar view of human history. We must, he argues, conceive it is progressing toward a community of free, enlightened republics, living together in "perpetual peace."[8]

In his third *Critique*, the *Critique of Judgment* of 1790, Kant attempted to build a bridge between the theoretical reason of the first *Critique* and the practical reason of the second. The contemplation of objects of beauty, he argues, stands midway between the theoretical understanding of the world and the practical desire to change it. On the one hand, aesthetic contemplation involves a specific type of delight or pleasure, but on the other, this delight is *disinterested* in a way in which practical reason is not. In the second part of the *Critique of Judgment* Kant turns to teleology in nature, which he regards as importantly related to aesthetics. By *teleology* he means not the fact that natural organisms serve purposes external to themselves —as grass, for example, serves the purpose of feeding cows—but that natural organisms form integrated wholes the nature and workings of which cannot be accounted for by the mechanical principles considered in the *Critique of Pure Reason*. A living organism is in this respect analogous to a work of art, though Kant does not believe that our need to regard an organism *as if* it were intrinsically purposive entitles us to infer that it is actually the product of a purposive cosmic designer.

This, then, in brief outline, is the thought of Kant, the thought from which the German idealists began, but with which they could not remain satisfied.

III.
IDEALIST CRITICISMS OF KANT: FICHTE, SCHELLING, AND HEGEL

Before we turn to Fichte we should note some of the difficulties experienced by the idealists in general when they considered Kant's system. First they felt that, despite Kant's stress on the importance of system, his own thought was insufficiently systematic in several respects. Why are there, in the first *Critique*, just two faculties—sensibility and the understanding (or just three, if we include the imagination)? Why are there just two forms of sensibility—space and time? Why do we have just the categories that we do have? Kant derives the categories from the "forms of judgment"—causality, for example, is associated with the hypothetical judgment-form —but he does not explain why the forms of judgment are as they are.[9] In each of these cases Kant simply accepts something empirically when a proper system should derive and explain it. Even Kant's system as a whole, consisting of all three *Critiques*, is inadequately knit together. Schelling complained in 1803 that "Kant posits as many different reasons as he wrote Critiques. There is a well known epigram in which an observer listening to several art-critics discussing various tastes cries out 'But where is the taste of all your tastes?' Similarly Kant might be asked 'Where is the reason of all your reasons?'" (Werke, I/V, vii).[10] A major concern of the German idealists, then, is *system*. Every concept, every area of human experience—knowledge, morality, art, and so forth—must have its place in a single, integrated system. Nothing can be simply accepted either from experience or from traditional belief.

Another feature of Kant's thought to which the idealists in general objected was its retention of unknowable things in themselves. The reasons for their objection are complex and various, but one reason is connected with their concern for system. If in order to explain experience we need to postulate things in themselves as well as the human subject, our account of experience is less than fully systematic, since it requires two independent principles and not simply one. Kant himself had suggested that we and things in themselves might derive from a "common root," but in accordance with his principles he made no attempt to establish that this was in fact the case and the suggestion could play no part in the "architectonic" of his system. But the idealists also felt that the thought of a thing in itself was essentially empty or incoherent. According to Fichte it was a "non-thought," while Schelling held that "it is a true wooden iron; for insofar as it is a thing, it is not in itself, and if it is in itself it is not a thing" (I/X 84; cf. 81).[11] Both Fichte and Schelling raised the objection that since in Kant's view categories are applicable only within the realm of appearances, things in themselves cannot consistently be said to cause or ground our "representations" of objects (Fichte, I, 482; Schelling, I/II, 21).[12] Hegel argued that things "are said to be in themselves insofar as we abstract from all being for another, i.e. in general insofar as they are thought of without any determination, as nothing" (WL. I 108).[13] Jacobi summed up their feelings when he wrote that without the presupposition of the thing in itself he could not enter into Kant's system, while with that presupposition he could not remain in it (*Werke*, II, 304).

The idealists were not deterred from their attempt to eliminate unknowable things in themselves by the *antinomies*. While they on the whole accepted the validity of Kant's arguments, they rejected his conclusion that our concepts are inapplicable to things in themselves or to the "absolute." Schelling and Hegel argued that it is only the rigid, "finite" concepts of the *understanding* that are inapplicable to the absolute. If for example the concepts of infinity and of finitude are seen as incompatible with each other, then the absolute can be neither finite nor infinite. But if these concepts are seen from the point of view of *reason* then the absolute can, and in fact must, be both finite and infinite. If our concepts are reconstructed by reason, then there is no longer any cause to suppose that the absolute must elude them. Both Schelling and Hegel were concerned to break down sharp boundaries between concepts, and they were inspired in this in part by Kant's antinomies.

One problem for an idealism of the Kantian sort is the existence of *other* people. In the *Critique of Pure Reason* Kant conceals this problem by regularly speaking of "we" rather than of "I." Insofar as other people are physical bodies, it should be *I* who construct or constitute them. But since others are not simply bodies but also, like myself, transcendental egos, they cannot be wholly my products; they too must play a part in constructing the (or *a*) world for themselves. How do their constructions mesh in with one another? And what guarantee have I that there are any other people similar in status to myself? Could there in fact be more than one transcendental ego, given Kant's prohibition on applying concepts, including numerical concepts, beyond the range of experience? The idealists, as we shall see, made a variety of attempts to answer these questions, and their abandonment of idealism in Kant's sense seems to have been in part the result of these attempts. [See especially Fichte's *Vocation of Man* (II, 167ff.) esp. Book III; his *Lectures on the Vocation of the Scholar* (VI, 289ff.), esp. Lecture II; and Schelling's *System of Transcendental Idealism* (I/III, 329ff., esp. 540ff.)].[14]

Kant's moral doctrines were received in different ways by the different idealists. They were all (with the occasional exception of Schelling) inclined to agree with Kant that men are of equal rationality, that this rationality constitutes the core of the person, and that morality consists in the cultivation and expression of this rationality. (These beliefs were later challenged by Schopenhauer and more radically by Nietzsche.) They tended, however, to interpret rationality in different ways. Hegel in particular, as we shall see, considered rationality to be more social and less purely formal than Kant regarded it. Kant's belief in the "primacy of practical reason," the doctrine that metaphysical doctrines that cannot be proved by theoretical reason receive support from practical reason, made its strongest impact on Fichte, who argued that my belief in an objective world and in particular in rational beings independent of myself depends on "the necessary faith in our own freedom and power, in our own real activity, and in the definite laws of human action" (II, 263). In a similar vein, Schelling too held that it is my "consciousness of freedom" that requires me to believe in the existence of other rational beings and hence in an objective world: "an isolated rational being would be unable to attain not only to the consciousness of freedom, but also to the consciousness of the objective world as such" (I/III, 556f.; cf. I/II, 52). For it is only other rational beings that can make moral demands on me — if I were alone in the world I would have no reason to do anything else than satisfy my own desires — and it is only because there are other rational beings equal in status to myself that I am compelled to regard the world as more than simply the product of my own mind. Schelling, however, unlike Fichte, did not regard the practical as the pinnacle of his system. What is primary for Schelling — at least after about 1800 — is the "absolute identity" of the objective, or unconscious, and the subjective, or conscious, and this is best represented by the purposive organism in nature and by the work of art in human affairs. Practical considerations also play a part in Hegel's view of the world. His account of the emergence of self-consciousness in interaction with another self-conscious being, though strikingly original, echoes several themes in Fichte and Schelling. Nevertheless, practice is not the culmination of Hegel's system; that is rather philosophy itself. Moreover, Hegel does not accept Kant's view that the doctrines of God, freedom, and immortality rest on a moral faith. They have, on his account, a securer foundation in conceptual thought itself. Similarly, Hegel differs from Fichte and Schelling in that he rejected Kant's doctrine that the destiny of humanity, whether in this world or the next, consists in an "infinite progress" toward an ideal that can never be fully realized (e.g., Fichte's second *Lecture on the Vocation of Scholar*, Schelling, I/III, 560f.). Hegel criticizes this doctrine at more than one level. In his *Philosophy of Right*, for example, he argues that philosophy is a reflective, retrospective enterprise that can have no truck with unrealized ideals, and in his *Logic*, he rejects the concept of "bad infinity" involved in the doctrine of infinite progress (e.g., E, 94).

In fact several of Hegel's differences from Kant and Fichte depend on his reflections on the concept of *infinity*. Kant often came close to Hegel's concept of infinity in his thoughts on the unity of a philosophical system — and also of a living organism — but by and large he (and Fichte) adhered to what Hegel regarded as *bad* infinity. Hegel sees two defects in the customary conception of infinity. The first is that the infinite is represented as sharply distinct from the finite; the infinite deity, for example, is conceived as distinct from the finite world that he creates. Second, the infinite is represented as running on *forever* and never being *complete*; space, time, and number are generally thought of as infinite in this way. Each of these features, Hegel argues, implies that the infinite is really only finite, in the first case because the infinite is *bounded* by something else — the finite — and is not unbounded, as the infinite should be; and in the second case because the infinite itself is never complete and surveyable, but only a *finite* segment of it. The *true* infinite, as Hegel conceives it, remedies both these defects: It is not distinct from and bounded by the finite, and it does not run on forever. It is, like a circle rather than a straight line, complete and self-contained; it is, we might say, *finite but unbounded*. This notion of infinity pervades Hegel's thought: the "absolute," as we have seen, cannot be exclusively infinite but must also be in some sense finite, or — in theological terms — God cannot be sharply distinct from his finite creatures; the destiny of man cannot consist in an infinite process of gradual improvement; the true philosophical system must not, as Fichte supposed, sharply contrast with other philosophical doctrines, but must in some sense embrace — or *sublimate* — them; and, as we shall see, it must take the form of a *circle* and not proceed in a rectilinear fashion from assumed premises.

The idealists were, like Kant himself, interested in history, and none more so than Hegel, for whom history was integral to philosophy. Idealism here confronts a difficulty that is admirably expressed by Schelling: "how in general a history is conceivable, since if everything which is is posited for everyone only through his consciousness, the whole of past history too can only be posited for everyone through his consciousness" (I/III, 590). Schelling replies to this by distinguishing between the transcendental ego, which "posits" history (along with everything else), and the "determinate individuality," which is determined by and therefore cannot posit past history: "Past history thus belongs of course merely to appearance, just as the individuality of consciousness itself does; it is thus neither more nor less real for everyone than his own individuality is" (ibid.). As we shall see, however, this reply is not adequate for Hegel's purpose, since Hegel believes that it is not only our "determinate individuality" that changes over time, but also the concepts or categories with which, in Kant's view, we in part constitute the world, including its history. It is hard to see how it can be maintained without circularity that what constitutes history is itself subject to historical change. This problem too plays a part in Hegel's rejection of *Kantian* idealism.

There is, finally, a more general problem that is related to the problem of *system* with which we began — the problem of the philosopher's own thought or discourse and of its relationship to what it is about. This problem arises in a variety of forms. First, the idealists felt that Kant himself had paid insufficient attention to his own thought. Hegel in particular argued that in presenting the categories Kant had ignored his own thought *about* the categories and that had he not done so, he would have had to devise a far more elaborate and integrated system of categories, a system that would do justice to our thought about categories as well as to our thought about the world. Hegel's *Logic* is an attempt to develop such a system, and it owes much of its difficulty to the fact that he is trying not only to think but to think about his own thinking. But Hegel was not the only idealist to face this problem. Schelling too believed that philosophy, or rather *Wissenschaftslehre*, the science of knowledge, is peculiarly self-reflexive in that whereas other sciences can simply presuppose that they are to be of a certain form, the science of knowledge is concerned with its own form. Schelling's resolution of this "circle" is that the philosopher must find a "principle" in which form and content reciprocally determine one another; in Schelling's view only the principle "I = I" can fulfill this requirement. Secondly, Kant and the idealists claim that the philosopher is aware of certain things of which the ordinary person (and the philosopher in his nonphilosophical moments) is unaware. In particular, while the philosopher is an idealist, holding that the "external world" and indeed the "empirical self" are, at least in part, our own products, the ordinary person (or ordinary "consciousness") is a realist, believing that the external world exists independently of himself. The idealists acknowledge this feature of consciousness, including their own nonphilosophical consciousness, which explains why they regard themselves as "empirical realists" as well as "transcendental idealists." In consequence they need to distinguish between what we as philosophers are aware of and what the consciousness we are examining is aware of. This distinction is most famously present in Hegel's *Phenomenology of Mind*, but it also plays an important and similar role in Fichte's and Schelling's science of knowledge (Fichte, I, 453ff.; Schelling, I/III, 388f., etc.). Since the philosopher is obliged to account not only for ordinary consciousness, but also for philosophical consciousness itself, one of the aims of the science of knowledge is to show how the philosopher's consciousness develops out of ordinary consciousness. As Schelling puts it: "our enquiry will . . . have to go on until what is posited for us in the self *qua* object is also posited for us in the self *qua* subject, that is, until for us the consciousness of our object coincides with our own consciousness, and thus until the self has for us arrived at the point from which we started" (I/III, 389). A similar aim underlies Hegel's *Phenomenology*. If this aim is to be fulfilled, philosophy must again be more systematic than Kant supposed. Third, the idealists have a special problem concerning their own thought or discourse insofar as they are attempting to give a complete account of reality as a whole, for reality must of course include their own thought *about* reality. This is especially clear in the case of Schelling, who believed at one stage of his career that knowledge or consciousness, on the one hand, and being or nature, on the other, are both manifestations of a neutral "absolute" or "identity." This absolute is all that really exists. What, then, is the relationship between the absolute and the philosopher's own knowledge of it? Evidently they cannot be distinct, since in that case the absolute would not be all that exists. Sometimes Schelling argues, as we have seen, that the philosopher's knowledge simply develops out of ordinary knowledge or consciousness. But at other times he takes the view that our knowledge of the absolute must be identical with it and must therefore be, like the absolute itself, simple and immediate (e.g., Bw. 136).[15] Fichte's objection to this anticipates Hegel's: "You went straight to the absolute with your thinking, without considering your thinking and the fact that it could well be only this that surreptitiously *formed* the absolute for you through its own immanent laws" (Bw. 143). Hegel did not believe that our knowledge of the absolute can be simple and immediate, but, for reasons similar to Schelling's, he is reluctant to distinguish sharply between the absolute and our knowledge of it. The idealists, then, were concerned with a cluster of problems about the status of their own thought, problems that seemed closely connected with the requirement of *system* in philosophy.

These, then, are some of the problems that the idealists found in Kant, problems that helped to shape their response both to Kant and to each other. I turn now to a fuller account of the idealists themselves.

IV.
THE PERFECTION OF KANTIAN IDEALISM: FICHTE

Fichte believed that the aim of philosophy was to "furnish the ground of all experience," that is, of "the system of presentations which are accompanied by the feeling of necessity, and of this feeling of necessity itself" (I,423). There are, he argued, only two ways in which this can be done: dogmatism (or realism), which attempts to explain experience on the basis of *things*, and idealism, which explains experience on the basis of the intelligence or the self. It might be objected that these are not the only two possible ways of explaining our experience and that we might alternatively (and more plausibly) explain it, as Kant tried to do, in terms both of things and of intelligence. Fichte's reply however is this: *Either* the things that figure in this proposed alternative are things as we experience them, things *for us*, and in that case they are already a part of our experience and cannot be referred to to explain it. For, Fichte argues, "the ground is always external to the grounded" (I, 456). *Or* the things in question are things in *themselves*, conceived quite independently of ourselves, in which case, Fichte argues, they cannot interact causally with ourselves and cannot therefore ground our experience jointly with ourselves. Idealism and dogmatism are then the only coherent alternatives.

The idealism in question bears little resemblance to the idealism of Berkeley or to that of J.S.Mill and twentieth-century phenomenalists. Roughly speaking, these idealisms attempt to reduce our experience to "ideas," but they do not explain, or even attempt to explain, why we have these ideas rather than others or why we have any ideas at all. They do not, that is, furnish the "ground" of our experience. (Berkeley, it is true, tried to explain our ideas in terms of *God's* ideas, but for this reason Fichte regards him as a dogmatist rather than an idealist: I, 438.) For Fichte, by contrast, idealism derives the whole of our experience from a single principle, the I or ego itself, and thus furnishes a ground of experience. Similarly dogmatism, if it is to provide a proper ground of experience, cannot consist simply in the claim that our diverse experience is grounded in a diversity of things or objects. It must attempt to derive the multiplicity of objects from a single principle. For this reason Fichte, and at one stage Schelling, regarded Spinoza as the paradigmatic dogmatist. In his *Ethics* Spinoza had argued that the world is a single self-causing substance (or "God"). This substance has an infinity of attributes but only two of them are known to us—extension and thought. Finite entities such as ourselves are "modifications" of the attributes of substance. A human being, for example, is a modification of the attributes of extension (his body) and of thought (his mind or intellect). Spinoza held that finite entities and their states follow from the nature of substance somewhat as the conclusion of a deductive

argument follows from its premises, but that we are unable to reconstruct
the argument since it involves an infinite number of steps. Spinoza thus
attempts to ground our experience in a single principle and is in this
respect close to idealism. But since his substance is manifestly something
other than myself and my ideas, his system is dogmatist rather than idealist.

If both idealism and dogmatism can each provide a systematic answer to
the question "What is the ground of experience?" what reason could there
be for preferring one of these systems to the other? Fichte often suggests
that one's choice of a system depends on the type of person one is, but
since this refers primarily to the intellectual and moral deficiencies of
dogmatists, it does not imply that Fichte has no respectable reason for his
preference of idealism over dogmatism. The reasons that he, and at one
stage Schelling, opted for idealism are various. First, there are epistemolog-
ical reasons. Schelling expresses this most clearly: "The chain of our
knowledge goes from one conditioned item to another; now either the
whole must have no support, or one must be able to believe that it goes on
to infinity in this way, or there must be some one final point on which the
whole depends. But this final point must for that very reason be directly
opposed in respect of the principle of its being to everything that still falls
within the sphere of the conditioned, i.e. not only unconditioned but
absolutely unconditionable" (I/I, 163f.). Schelling would of course have to
say more than he has to exclude the possibility that there is more than one
unconditioned point on which our knowledge depends, but he has said
enough to suggest that one motive for the adoption of idealism is that the
existence of the self or I is certain and ineliminable in a way that the
existence of a *thing* cannot be. I cannot, Schelling argues, disentangle
things from my view of them. A dogmatist is thus like someone attempting
to stand on his own shoulders in order to look beyond himself (I/I, 296).
Fichte argues in a similar vein: the existence of the thing in itself to which
the dogmatist appeals is a hypothesis that can be accepted if and only if it
explains, and is required in order to explain, our experience. The I, by
contrast, is immediately manifest in our consciousness. But, more than this,
insofar as the I provides a rival, equally satisfactory account of our experience, it undermines the only reason that the dogmatist has for believing in
the thing in itself (I, 428). Second, there are metaphysical or ontological
reasons. Dogmatism, Fichte argues, cannot explain what it purports to
explain, namely the self and its ideas or (re)presentations. There is no
conceivable explanatory route from unconscious things to conscious ideas:
"Intellect and thing are thus exact opposites: they inhabit two worlds
between which there is no bridge" (I, 436;cf.Schelling, I/II, 17ff.). Still
less can the dogmatist explain the emergence of the I itself. And yet, as
Schelling argues, we cannot think away the self (I/I, 320). The tendency of
dogmatism, in fact, is to explain away the self, regarding it as epipheno-
menal to objects, and Fichte often thinks of idealism as requiring a special

act of self-concentration, of withdrawal into oneself, an act that dogmatists are unable to perform since, in keeping with their doctrine, they are not proper selves. Third, there are moral reasons for preferring idealism. Both Fichte and Schelling held that if dogmatism is true, then fatalism or determinism is true and there is no free will (Fichte, I, 509; Schelling, I/I, 339f.). Only idealism can guarantee that we are free and morally responsible for what we do. At times they gave more weight to this consideration than to any other. Schelling, for example, sometimes regards idealism and dogmatism less as theoretical doctrines than as moral programs, and he argues that dogmatism is not refutable theoretically, but only practically — that is, if "one realises in oneself an absolutely opposed system. But it is irrefutable for him who is able to realise it practically, for him who can bear the thought of working at his own annihilation, of doing away with all free causality in himself, and of being the modification of an object in whose infinity he will find, sooner or later, his own (moral) extinction" (I/I, 339; cf.Fichte's *Vocation of Man*). Fichte often suggests that dogmatism appeals to those who are not properly free and he shows less respect for it than Schelling does. These, then, are the main reasons for Fichte's and Schelling's preference for idealism.

The I or self from which idealism begins is of course quite remote from the person of everyday experience, and if it were not so it could not function as the ground of that experience. This is why Fichte and Schelling suggest that idealism presupposes a special act of self-concentration (esp. Schelling, I/I, 395ff.). The I in question is not an embodied person, nor does it have any object other than itself. For a subject that is relative to an object is itself a part of experience rather than its ground. There can be, as Schelling makes plain, only one such I: "Since the I is conditioned only by itself and is determinable only in intellectual intuition, it must be identical with itself (not at all determinable by number)" (I/I, 182). This I, then, a near descendent of Kant's transcendental ego, is the principle from which idealism begins.

Where does it go from there? Fichte describes his procedure as follows: "[Idealism] shows that what it first set up as fundamental principle and directly demonstrated in consciousness, is impossible unless something else occurs along with it, and that this something else is impossible unless a third something also takes place, and so on until the conditions of what was first exhibited are completely exhausted, and this latter is, with respect to its possibility, fully intelligible" (I, 446). Thus we begin with the pure I, which has no object apart from itself and whose being consists solely in its self-awareness or "intellectual intuition" of itself. (Fichte associated it with the formula "A = A" or, more specifically, "I = I," in part because he believed, in common with Schelling and Hegel but in opposition to Kant, that idealist philosophy *grounds* formal logic rather than presupposes it.) But the I could have no intuition of itself unless there were something other than itself, a "not-self," which restricts or limits the self. (A is not equal to not-A.) Thus the self "posits" or "counter-posits" a not-self. (The verb *setzen* means to seat, set, place, put up, assert, posit, etc.). The third step is to see the self and the not-self as reciprocally limiting or determining each other. Thus the self posits the not-self as limited by the self and itself as limited by the not-self (A = B). And so the derivation proceeds until all the conditions of self-consciousness, of the original I, have been established. In the course of the derivation, Kant's categories emerge as consequences of more fundamental laws of the operation of the intellect. Causality, for example, is involved in the reciprocal determination of the self and the not-self (I, 136, 441). It is because Kant started with the categories and did not derive them from these more fundamental laws that he seemed to require the thing in itself to account for the content of experience and did not see that "form and matter are not separate items; the totality of form is the matter" (I, 443).

It is important to remember that Fichte is not simply attempting to deduce or infer the structure and content of experience from the I. He is also attempting to explain or ground it. The I itself is an active, striving entity, which, as it were, produces or generates its own conditions. It is, as Schelling puts it, the "principium essendi" as well as the "principium cognoscendi" (I/I, 237 n.). Thus when Fichte and Schelling say that the I is "unconditioned" they mean not only that it is *epistemically* unconditioned, that we can be certain of its existence without inferring it from anything else, but also that it is *ontologically* unconditioned, that it does not depend on anything else for its existence. The I then produces the world of our experience and the philosopher retraces the path by which it does so: the self is "a living and active thing which engenders insights from and through itself, and which the philosopher merely contemplates" (I, 454). What motivates this constructive activity of the self is above all morality. It constructs the world as a field in which it can realize its moral ideals: "The concept of action, which becomes possible only through this intellectual intuition of the self-active self, is the only concept which unites the two worlds that exist for us, the sensible and the intelligible. That which stands opposed to my action . . . is the sensible world; that which is to come about through my action is the intelligible world" (I, 467). In order to act morally, however, the self must first have a body — a portion of the external world, that is, which it regards as belonging to itself, and second it must acknowledge the existence of other rational beings on a par with itself. Fichte thinks of one's own individuality as closely bound up with one's recognition of *others*: "the consciousness of individuality is necessarily accompanied by another consciousness, that of a *Thou*" (I, 476). These two features then are derived in the course of the *Wissenschaftslehre* (e.g., I, 188f., 495; cf. *Vocation of Scholar*. Lecture II). Since men necessarily live together in a society and since they are not as yet perfectly rational or perfectly moral beings, they require a *state* to ensure that they do not infringe each other's freedom and to guarantee to each person a realm in which he can exercise his freedom. The state is required, however, only in virtue of our present imperfection and is not an essential feature of the human condition. We are progressing toward a condition in which pure reason will replace the state and in which men will live together in perfect harmony and uniformity. This is a condition that we cannot actually reach without ceasing to be men and becoming gods, but we can and ought to approach this goal ever closer to infinity (*Vocation of Scholar*, II). Fichte, like Schelling and Hegel after him, argues that in a sense his system returns to its beginning: the self strives to return to the pure I with which the *Wissenschaftslehre* began. But the correspondence is not, he concedes, exact: while the pure I lacks individuality "because selfhood there has not yet been particularized into individuality," in the self to which we gradually approximate—the "Idea" of the self—"individuality has vanished through cultivation according to general laws" (I,516). Schelling is regularly less cautious in this matter and speaks as if the goal of the "absolute I" is the restoration of itself out of the "finite I"—"the absolute I demands that the finite I should become equal to it, that is, that it should destroy in itself all multiplicity and all mutability"—but he agrees with Fichte that this is possible only through the "idea of moral progress, of progress in infinity" (I/I, 198ff.).

This, then, is Fichte's system at the height of his fame. As I have indicated, Fichte's development did not stop at this point and his thought underwent a variety of changes and refinements. Its broad outlines remained unchanged, however, and I now leave Fichte and turn to Schelling.

V.
IDEALISM, NATURE, AND THE ABSOLUTE: SCHELLING

Schelling, though more mercurial and less persistent than Fichte, was perhaps a more brilliant thinker. While Fichte labored at what was essentially a single system, attempting to perfect it and explain it to the public, Schelling produced in rapid succession the beginnings of what appear to be several systems—idealism, philosophy of nature, the philosophy of identity—and each of these in several different versions. In his first philosophical writings he appeared as a follower of Fichte, with whom he had corresponded since 1794, when Schelling was 19. From an early date, however, differences appeared between the two philosophers. In a letter to Hegel of February 4, 1795, Schelling wrote: "I have meanwhile become a Spinozist! . . . For Spinoza, the world (the object as opposed to the subject) was—*everything*; for me this is true of the *ego*. The real difference between the Critical [Kantian] and the dogmatic philosophy seems to me to lie in the fact that the former starts from the absolute ego (not yet conditioned by any object), while the latter starts from the absolute object or non-ego. The latter, pushed to its ultimate consequences, leads to Spinoza's system, the former to Kant's. Philosophy has got to start from the *unconditional*. The only question is what is unconditional, the ego or the non-ego. . . . For me the highest principle of all philosophy is the pure, absolute ego, i.e. the ego insofar as it is mere ego, not yet conditioned by objects but posited through *freedom*. The alpha and omega of all philosophy is freedom. . . . [16] Even at this stage Schelling shows more sympathy for Spinoza and puts less emphasis on the intellectual defects of dogmatism than Fichte did. In *Of the I as Principle of Philosophy* (1795) Schelling argues that Spinoza's consistent dogmatism turns against his will into a sort of idealism: "he elevated the not-I to the I, and demeaned the I to a not-I. For him, the world is no longer world, the absolute object no longer object. No sense perception, no concept reaches his one substance whose infinitude is present only to intellectual intuition" (I/I, 171). In his *Philosophical Letters on Dogmatism and Criticism* (1795) he argued that Spinoza's intellectual intuition of substance was essentially an intuition of the absolute ego but was misinterpreted by Spinoza in an objective way. Spinoza is a covert idealist: "He could not think of himself as *lost* in that state; he thought of his personality as expanded into it" (I/I, 321f.). In this work Schelling places great weight on the practical consequences of adopting a philosophical system. But idealism and dogmatism, he argues, amount to the same thing if we think of them as having achieved their goal: "Realism, conceived in its perfection, . . . becomes idealism. For perfect realism comes to pass only where the objects cease to be objects, that is, appearances opposed to the subject — in short, only where the representation is identical with the represented objects, hence where subject and object are absolutely identical" (I/I, 330) — which is just what would happen, in Schelling's view, if perfect idealism came to pass. But since neither idealism nor realism can come to pass in their full perfection, it remains a possibility that they differ in their practical consequences. Schelling argues that dogmatism in fact encourages passivity and the attempt to "annihilate all free causality in me", whereas idealism enjoins us to exert our freedom against the objective world (I/I, 334). While Fichte sharply distinguishes dogmatism from idealism, Schelling tends to argue that dogmatism, if it is consistently developed, turns into idealism. (This tendency later became a marked feature of Hegel's treatment of other philosophers.)

At least two factors seem to have led Schelling away from Fichte's idealism. First, since the I from which idealism begins is manifestly not the I of everyday experience, doubt arose as to whether it could properly be regarded as an I at all and therefore whether an idealism based on such an I was in fact distinct from dogmatism. This doubt has already emerged in Schelling's 1795 writings, but it is most clearly expressed by Hölderlin in a letter to Hegel of January 26, 1795: "At first I suspected him [Fichte] very much of dogmatism. . . . His absolute ego (= Spinoza's substance) contains all reality; it is everything, and outside it there is nothing. Thus there is no object for this absolute ego, for otherwise it would not contain all of reality; but a consciousness without object is not thinkable, and when I myself am this object, then I am necessarily limited as such, even if it should only be in time, and thus not absolute. Thus no consciousness is thinkable in the absolute ego; as the absolute ego, I have no consciousness, and insofar as I have no consciousness, I am (for myself) nothing; thus the absolute ego is (for me) nothing."[17]

A second factor in Schelling's abandonment of Fichtean idealism was his interest in nature and his attempt to develop a philosophy of nature — that is, to derive or construct the main features of nature from rational principles. Fichte himself was not much interested in nature except insofar as it provides the necessary conditions for human conduct. In a letter to Fichte of October 3, 1801, Schelling remarks: "For you it [nature] has absolutely no speculative significance, only teleological significance. But can you really be of the opinion that, e.g., light only exists so that rational beings can, when they speak to each other, also see each other, and air so that when they see one another, they can speak to each other?" (Bw. 140). But while this may be an objection to Fichte's *moral* idealism, it is not an objection to idealism as such, and neither Schelling nor Fichte initially saw any incompatibility between idealism and Schelling's early ventures in the philosophy of nature. The philosophy of nature does of course proceed in the opposite direction from the science of knowledge. It begins not with the self-conscious ego of the *Wissenschaftslehre* but with the simplest of natural phenomena — matter occupying space, for example — and tries to "construct" the progressively higher "potencies" or "powers" of nature — magnetism, the organism, and so on — until eventually we arrive at the human mind itself. Thus the mind is seen in some sense as a product of nature rather than, as in the *Wissenschaftslehre*, its producer. There are, however, at least two ways in which this project might be interpreted so as to remain compatible with idealism. First, Schelling had already argued in his *Of the I* that the argument of the science of knowledge can be taken in reverse order: "If it [the I] is determined at the same time as the dominant element throughout the whole system of my knowledge, then a *regress* too must be possible, i.e., I must be able to *ascend* even from the lowest conditioned proposition to the unconditioned, as conversely I can *descend* from the unconditioned proposition to the lowest in the series of conditioned propositions" (I/I, 169). For example, I can not only descend from the absolute I to the I that is correlative to an object, I can also ascend from the latter to the former. The arguments will differ in that the descent from the absolute to the relative I corresponds to and mirrors the fact that the absolute I produces the relative I, whereas the relative I does not produce the absolute I and the *ascent* does not therefore mirror an ontological process. Is the philosophy of nature simply the "ascent" corresponding to the "descent" of the science of knowledge? It cannot plausibly be regarded in this way. First, Schelling's philosophy of nature is not simply the mirror image of his *Wissenschaftslehre*, dealing with the same topics in reverse order; the two types of work cover significantly different ground. Second, there is a sense in which the human mind is a product of nature, dependent on more primitive natural phenomena for its emergence and functioning, and an idealist must take account of this. Thus the attempt of the philosophy of nature to accommodate it cannot be seen as simply a process of reasoning that corresponds to no real process in nature. A second interpretation, then, of the philosophy of nature that would leave it compatible with idealism is this: the philosophy of nature simply unearths and systematizes those features of nature that *Wissenschaftslehre* will subsequently have to derive from the absolute I. On this account the philosophy of nature approaches the matter from the other end, as it were, and there is clearly no inconsistency in this. Facts about nature need to be discovered and presented in a suitable form before they can be derived from the I. Further, the idealist need not balk at the claim that nature *produces* the human mind, as long as this is not taken to imply that it produces the *absolute I* in the same way that the absolute I produces nature. As we have already seen, if idealism is to be plausible it must do justice to the apparent dependence of the mind on nature. If the philosophy of nature is interpreted in this way, then it is subordinate to the *Wissenschaftslehre* and will ultimately be dispensable when *Wissenschaftslehre* is fully developed; it will become just a part of a complete *Wissenschaftslehre* that derives nature from the absolute I and the human mind from nature.

Schelling, however, resisted this interpretation of the philosophy of nature and argued that the two branches of philosophy were coordinate; neither could be dispensed with in favor of the other. Fichte failed to understand how this could be so. In his letters to Schelling he obliquely condemned Schelling's procedure as circular: "Now conversely the I cannot in turn be explained by that which elsewhere is entirely explained *by the I*" (Bw. 114); and: "It would not occur to me to remind you of the palpable circle in the derivation of a nature from the intelligence and of the intelligence in turn from nature" (Bw. 125). How can Schelling avoid this charge? He seems to have done so in two successive steps. The first step is to argue that the absolute I does not, as Fichte supposed, operate only on one level. It is at work both in nature, objectively, and in mind or history, subjectively. The philosophy of nature records its operations in nature, while "transcendental philosophy" traces its development in history. It is one and the same I at work in both spheres, only in different powers or potencies. The I in nature is at a lower potency than the I of *Wissenschaftslehre*. This doctrine, though quite different from Fichte's, still retains some claim to the title of "idealism," in virtue of the dual role played by the I. But Schelling's next step removes this claim. He ceases to speak of the I as operating at these two levels and speaks instead of the "absolute" or of the "absolute identity," for the reason that the "I" in nature is too remote from what we ordinarily take the I to be to count as an I. The absolute is the "point of indifference" between the objective and the subjective, between nature and mind, and it manifests itself in both. Schelling made a number of attempts to explain how and why it does so, how and why the "infinite" manifests itself in a plurality of finite entities. He never wholly abandoned his claim to be in some sense an idealist. Nature is not, on his view, exclusively objective. It is both subjective and objective, with a quantitative preponderance of objectivity over subjectivity, and mind is correspondingly the preponderance of subjectivity over objectivity. The "identity" of nature and mind receives additional confirmation from the fact that up to a certain point (the point, on Schelling's account, where theoretical philosophy gives way to practical philosophy), nature and mind follow parallel paths and the same stages or "potencies" occur in both (I/III, 331f.; I/IV, 418). He remained resolutely opposed to the mechanistic view of nature and conceived it as organic and mindlike in its structure and development. But his theory, he acknowledges, is rather a combination of idealism and realism than idealism alone: "This indifference of form and essence contains the only possible and necessary point of unification of idealism and realism" (I/IV, 370; cf. I/IV, 108ff.). Schelling again appeals to Spinoza: "Since A is the cognitive principle, but B . . . is infinite extension or in itself unlimited, we have here exactly the two attributes of Spinoza's absolute substance, thought and extension." (I/IV, 136). Spinoza is no longer seen as a dogmatist or a realist, but as a precursor of ideal-realism. In 1802 Schelling began to postulate a realm of Platonic ideas lying between the absolute and the phenomenal world (I/IV, 223f; 405). In this Schelling (like Schopenhauer, who proposed a similar doctrine some years later) seems to have been motivated primarily by his interest in aesthetics.

As we have seen, Fichte's idealism undergoes another modification in Schelling's hands. The predominantly moral tendency of Fichte's thought becomes in Schelling an aesthetic tendency. The work of art, not the moral action, is the pinnacle of Schelling's transcendental idealism. It is the work of art that represents in the subjective sphere the "identity of the unconscious activity which has produced nature and the conscious activity which expresses itself in willing" (I/III, 349). The work of art thus concludes the system by bringing it back, as it were, to its starting point: "The ultimate ground of all harmony between subjective and objective could be exhibited in its original identity only through intellectual intuition; and it is precisely this ground which, by means of the work of art, has been brought forth entirely from the subjective, and rendered wholly objective, in such a way that we have gradually led our object, the I itself up to the point where we

ourselves stood when we began to philosophise" (I/III, 628f.). "The objective world," Schelling believes, "is just the original, as yet unconscious
poetry of the spirit; the universal organon of philosophy—and the keystone of its entire vault is *the philosophy of art*" (I/III, 349).

In his ethical doctrines, however, Schelling does not differ greatly from
Fichte. There is a similar belief, submerged but not eradicated by the role
assigned to art, in an "infinite progress" toward the "idea" (I/III, 560f.), in
the eventual attainment of "perpetual peace," and in the ultimate dispen-
sability of the state. In contrast to Fichte and Hegel, however, Schelling
was essentially an apolitical thinker. Insofar as he has a distinctive view of
the state, it is again an *aesthetic* view: "The state ought to appear as a work
of art" (I/V, 312). In a way reminiscent of Hegel he criticized Fichte for
regarding the state solely as a means to the safeguarding of rights and for
ignoring "all positive arrangements for the energy, the rhythmic movement
and the beauty of public life" (I/V, 316). The state should not be seen as a
means to some specific end such as happiness or the maximization of
freedom, but as an organic unity that is as much its own end as nature is.
Schelling did not, however, work out these ideas in any detail.

As we have indicated, the development of Schelling's thought did not
stop at this point. However, Schelling's subsequent thought had little
influence on Hegel. It is now appropriate, therefore, to consider Schelling's
relationship to Hegel.

VI.
HEGEL AND SCHELLING: RESEMBLANCES

Before we ask how Hegel's thought differed from Schelling's, we should
first consider some of the respects in which they are similar. Many of the
ideas that are now regarded as characteristically Hegelian appeared earlier
in the writings of Schelling. The two thinkers share a general conception of
what philosophy is. Schelling, like Hegel, aims at "absolute knowledge"
and believes that philosophy should constitute a single system that depends
on no prior assumptions. Before we embark on philosophy, for example, we
do not even know what philosophy is or what requirements it is to meet:
"The idea of philosophy is simply the result of philosophy itself, which as
an infinite science is also the science of itself" (I/II, 11; cf. I/III, 359). The
system is knit together by an interconnecting dialectic that depends on the
fact that the divisions erected by the "understanding" are not stable, but
give rise to "contradictions" that can be allayed only when the system is
complete (I/IV, 402). Schelling believed, as Hegel did, that philosophy
arises from a condition of "separation." When men were in harmony with
nature, they had no need of philosophy, no need to ask, for example, how a
world outside themselves was possible. But because the human spirit is
essentially free, they broke loose from this natural condition and entered

into a state of separation from or contradiction with the external world, and "with that separation reflection first begins; from now on he separates . . . the object from the intuition, the concept from the image, finally . . . himself from himself" (I/II, 13). It is the task of philosophy freely to reunite these separated fragments and thus to restore us to our original state, albeit on a higher level. Schelling, like Hegel, consistently attempts to unite concepts that are customarily regarded as distinct: thought and intuition, infinity and finitude, thought and being, universality and particularity, the ideal and the real, freedom and necessity (I/III, 395).[18] Since no rigid dichotomy is philosophically tenable, Schelling cannot even sharply contrast his own philosophy to other philosophies, and for this reason among others, he — like Hegel but unlike Fichte — argued that there was only one philosophy and that past "philosophies" were "pictures, distorted in various directions, of the uniquely true system" (I/IV, 401). To speak of "my philosophy" is, in Schelling's view, as absurd as speaking of "my geometry" (I/IV, 352).

After Hegel's death, Schelling claimed that the method later made famous by Hegel had been originated by himself (I/X, 96, 108). The method Schelling has in mind was already prefigured in his *Explanatory Essays on the Idealism of the Science of Knowledge* (1796/97), in which he proposed a "history of self-consciousness," which would trace the various actions or states by which the "spirit . . . gradually attains to the intuition of itself, to pure self-consciousness" (I/I, 382). The mind, Schelling argues, "can be conceived only *in its action* . . . ; thus it is only in *becoming* or rather it is itself nothing but an eternal becoming" (I/I, 367). These suggestions (which are entirely in the spirit of Hegel) receive more substance in the *System of Transcendental Idealism* (1800), where Schelling claims to have found a method that will guarantee that no phase or "epoch" in this history has been omitted. The history presents a "progressive series of intuitions through which the I rises up to consciousness in the highest potency" (I/III, 331). The basic idea of the method is this: At any given stage the I or spirit is conscious of itself as an object of a certain sort. It is, that is, "limited" in a certain way. But to be conscious of itself as limited, the I must already have transcended that limit in a way that "we philosophers," but not as yet the I itself, can see. At the next stage, the I becomes conscious of what it must be if it is to be conscious of the object of the first stage; the subject of the first stage becomes the object of the next stage. But this in turn implies a limit that the I must again transcend, and so the process continues until "what for us is posited in the I as object is also posited for us in the I as subject, until, that is, for us the consciousness of our object coincides with our own consciousness, thus until the I itself has for us reached the point from which we set out" (I/III, 389). Schelling argues, for example, that the I senses or feels and is to that extent limited. But to be aware that it senses, the I must transcend this limit, "for even the judgment that the impression stems from an object presupposes an activity which does not cling to the impression but is directed at something *beyond* the impression" (I/III, 413). When the I becomes aware in turn of this transcending activity, it sees it as the thing in itself, the thing that produces its sensations: "The ideal activity which has transcended the limit and has now become the object has thus now disappeared from consciousness and been transformed into the thing in itself" (I/III, 421). Schelling thus sees the thing in itself as a product of the mind itself in its drive to become fully self-conscious. Arguments of this type abound in Schelling's writings (cf., e.g., I/II, 16f., 53f.), as well as in those of Hegel. Hegel argues, in the Introduction to his *Phenomenology of Mind*, that it is by such successive elevations in its self-awareness that "consciousness" advances to "absolute knowledge," and the history of self-consciousness that Hegel provides is similar in its essential design to Schelling's conception.

Apart from these central doctrines several other features of Hegel's thought were anticipated by Schelling. Like Hegel, Schelling believed that the mind is objectified in nature: "The principle and element of philosophy is absolute ideality, but this would be eternally unknowable, concealed within itself, if it did not transform itself, as subjectivity, into objectivity, and the finite nature which appears is the symbol of this transformation" (I/V, 324). Like Hegel, he believes that the mind reconciles itself to nature by "idealizing" it: "the mind can emerge from that struggle with nature reconciled to it only if nature transfigures itself for it into complete indifference with itself and into the ideal" (I/V, 326). Nevertheless, Schelling dissents as much as Hegel from idealism in Kant's and Fichte's sense. He rejects Kant's doctrine that objects are put together by us from materials supplied by "sensibility," preferring the view (already implicit in Kant's third *Critique*) that living organisms are self-constituting purposive unities independently of us: "Or if it lies in your power whether or not to transfer the idea of purposiveness to things outside yourselves, how does it come about that you transfer this idea only to *certain* things and not to *all* . . . ?" (I/II, 44). Schelling, like Hegel, stresses that I must acknowledge or "recognize" rational beings equal in status to myself and in turn be recognized by them: "this relationship is fully reciprocal and no rational being can prove itself to be such except through the recognition of others as such" (I/III, 550; cf. I/II, 52f.). The *state* in which such beings are organized should not be, for Schelling any more than Hegel, a merely external arrangement designed to regulate their relationships to one another, but an organic unity comparable to a work of art.

Finally, Schelling's thoughts on history contain the germ of Hegel's. In 1798 Schelling had argued that there can be no philosophy of history, since history is produced by our free activity and cannot therefore be determined a priori (I/I, 466ff.), but he soon came to believe that history is not a succession of accidents but "comes from an eternal unity and has its roots in the absolute as much as nature or any other object of knowledge" (I/V, 291). To the objection that actions are performed *freely* by individuals, Schelling replies that there may be no more to an individual than the actions he performs and that "if the action was necessary, then so too was the individual" (I/V, 291). In the *System of Transcendental Idealism*, he attempts to reconcile the apparent freedom of historical agents with his belief that "history as a whole is a progressive, gradually self-disclosing revelation of the absolute" (I/III, 603), by comparing history to a drama the author of which is "one spirit who speaks in everyone and . . . the author, whose mere fragments . . . the individual players are, has so harmonised in advance the objective outcome of the whole with the free play of all individuals that in the end something rational is actually bound to emerge." The author, however, does not exist independently of his drama: "If he *is* not, independently of us, but reveals and discloses himself only successively through the play of our very freedom, so that without this freedom he himself would not *be*, then we are co-authors of the whole and have ourselves invented the particular roles which we play" (I/III, 602). This *Geist* of Schelling's is a near relative of Hegel's *Geist*.

Schelling anticipated, then, several ideas that have come to be associated with Hegel. Our final question then is "How does Hegel differ from Schelling?"

VII.
HEGEL: THE CULMINATION OF GERMAN IDEALISM

Hegel's most obvious divergence from Schelling is his rejection of the various "absolutes" that Schelling successively espoused. As we have seen, Schelling's absolute, like Fichte's, performs two distinct roles. First, it is the *principium cognoscendi*, the principle of cognition from which our knowledge begins. Second, it is the *principium essendi*, the absolute ground or essence that manifests itself in phenomenal reality. In this role the absolute is often conceived as the "point of indifference" between the realms of nature and mind. Hegel by contrast does not believe that there is an absolute ground or beginning either of knowledge or of reality. Thus he rejects the absolute in each of these roles.

First, the free act of "intellectual intuition" to which Schelling (and Fichte) ascribe our acquaintance with the absolute (Schelling, I/I, 318; I/IV, 391ff.), cannot be, Hegel argues, even in the works of Fichte and Schelling themselves, the first step in the cognitive process. We require some preparatory argument to enable us both to perform the act and to see the point of doing so. Such argument cannot be dismissed as irrelevant to the system itself: It is an essential part of it. Thus, for example, Hegel declines to begin his logic with the I, since "this pure I is *not* an immediate given, nor is it the familiar, the usual I of our consciousness" (WL I, 76). It is not, then, an appropriate starting point but rather requires an introduction of its own.

Second, although Hegel does not wholly reject the notion of intellectual intuition, he argues that Fichte and Schelling were mistaken in regarding it as simple, immediate, and free of concepts and argument (WLII, 286). Such intuition cannot be detached from the arguments that lead up to it and from those that proceed from it, as if it were entirely unaffected by them. Schelling in particular tended to make such claims as that the absolute is "in itself an absolute unity of the finite and the infinite" (I/IV, 346), distinguishing this type of infinity, as Hegel did, from the bogus infinity of an endless series (I/IV, 382ff.). But this, Hegel argues, cannot be discerned by immediate intuition. It requires an examination of the concepts of infinity and finitude and an attempt to show that the finite "contains a contradiction in itself and makes itself into the infinite" (VGP, III, 435). The absolute and our claims about it cannot be simply intuited, but must be argued for.

Third, however, Hegel denies that there is a single, simple absolute of the type postulated by Fichte and Schelling. He has a variety of reasons for this. He argues, for example, that an essence or ground can be no more (and no less) than its manifestations (E, 112ff.), implicitly denying Fichte's claim that the ground of our experience must lie outside our experience (while somehow remaining demonstrable within it). In Hegel's view, the ground of our experience is to be found not outside it, but in the systematic structure that it displays. This line of thought is supported by his belief that the absolute is a subject or spirit, which, in his view as well as Schelling's, simply is what it *becomes* (*Phen.*,Preface, 6). Again, Hegel argues that the absolute is not something additional to the concepts that we apply to it (ibid., 17) or the arguments by which we arrive at it (ibid., 13). Our knowledge of the absolute cannot lie outside the absolute, and Hegel takes this to imply that the absolute is, as it were, a "logical construction" out of our arguments for it. Finally, Hegel argues that Schelling's absolute plays no useful role in his system. He cannot explain how or why the absolute differentiates itself into the realms of nature and mind, but simply assures us that "in the absolute everything is one" (ibid., 4). It might be objected that Hegel here overlooks Schelling's attempts to derive the "finite" from the "infinite" (e.g., I/IV, 412ff.), as well as his idea of a history of self-consciousness. But rather than revive these issues, I shall now consider some of Hegel's own works in more detail.

In his *Phenomenology of Mind* Hegel provides a "ladder" from the simplest form of human experience—"sense certainty"—up to absolute knowledge (Preface, 7). Absolute knowledge is not knowledge of the absolute in Schelling's sense—the *Phenomenology* ends, as it began, with criticism of the "empty abyss of the absolute" (*Phen.* 587)—but philosophical knowledge, especially the phenomenologist's own knowledge.

Hegel's *Phenomenology*, like Schelling's *System of Transcendental Idealism*, purports to end by deriving from ordinary consciousness the philosophical knowledge with which "we" began. But Hegel's conception differs from Schelling's in a crucial respect. Idealism and the philosophy of nature are, in Schelling's view, coordinate sciences determined in the following way: "All knowledge," Schelling says, "rests on the agreement of an objective element with a subjective element," of "nature" with "intelligence" (I/III, 339). These two "poles" of knowledge form the basis for our two sciences. Transcendental idealism sets out from the subjective and asks "how an objective element is annexed to it, which agrees with it" (I/III, 342). Conversely, philosophy of nature sets out from the objective and asks "how a subjective element is annexed to it, which agrees with it" (I/III, 340). Several questions can be raised here. Why does Schelling assume that the object of knowledge is "nature," when so much of our knowledge is of other people and of artifacts? If his aim is simply to explain how there can be "agreement" between the subjective and the objective, why are *both* sciences required? How does the philosophy of nature, in this interpretation, differ from "dogmatism," which Schelling still describes as the attempt to "bring forth a knowledge from a being assumed as independent" (I/III, 358)? But the objection that weighed most heavily with Hegel is that the distinction between the subject and its object arises *within* our consciousness, and that it is inconsistent with the spirit of idealism and with sound philosophical procedure to assume at the outset an object that is wholly distinct from and coordinate with the conscious subject (*Phen.*, Intro.).[19] Phenomenology, then, is not, for Hegel, coordinate with philosophy of nature, but preparatory to it. It is only when we have ascended to absolute knowledge by way of an examination of the subject and the object *together* that we can turn to nature itself. In this respect Hegel is more consistently idealist, in fact more Fichtean, than Schelling.

Before he turns to nature, however, Hegel provides a logic that has no parallel in Schelling, but bears on Schelling's enterprise in several respects. First, Schelling is, Hegel argues, relatively unreflective about the concepts and procedures that he employs. He does not examine, as Hegel does in his *Logic*, such concepts as those of a ground, of a subject and an object, of truth, and of the absolute itself (e.g., *Phen.*, Preface, 9). But concepts such as these, Hegel believes, require investigation before we can deploy them with any confidence. Second, it is logic, Hegel argues, that supplies conceptual support for Schelling's occasional intuitive glimpses of the interconnections between such concepts as those of finitude and infinity, of their coincidence "in the absolute." In fact, logic, Hegel believes, can solve a problem raised by Kant's first *Critique*—namely, how can we bring unity and system into the categories of the understanding? Schelling, like Hegel, expresses his conviction of such unity by saying that there is at bottom only *one* category (Schelling, I/III, 514; Hegel, *Phen.*, 181), but he does not attempt to substantiate this claim, as Hegel does, by displaying all of Kant's categories (and many more) as a single interlocking system of concepts. Third, these concepts are not, as we have seen, concepts to be applied to an absolute of Schelling's type (e.g., E, 85). They rather *are* the absolute. Nor are they concepts *possessed* and deployed by a Kantian or Fichtean ego. They rather constitute the ego; they form the rational core of the human mind (E, 20). (The ego has, as it were, become identical with its spectacles.) Finally, these concepts are not separate from the realms of nature and society, but are embedded in them. They constitute the rational core not only of the mind, but of the objective world (E, 24).

Logic, Hegel believed, enabled him to overcome the defects of Fichte and Schelling while retaining their virtues. Since in his view the world is informed and structured by an overarching system of concepts that also forms the core of the mind, Hegel returns in a sense from Schelling's dualistic parallelism to the unitary idealism of Fichte. Since, however, this conceptual system (or "the concept," E, 159) is no longer Fichte's empty "I = I," he need not regard the objective world simply as a sounding board for the moral endeavors of human beings, but can, like Schelling, grant it a relatively independent status. The "concept," however, does more work than Schelling's absolute. For embedded as it is in the realms of nature and "mind," it provides Hegel with a systematic framework for exploring these realms.

As we have seen, Hegel purports to embrace within his system every area of human experience — barring the contingent details (E, 16) — not only nature, but psychology, politics (or "right"), history, art, and religion. Each of these areas, and indeed the system as a whole, is, in Hegel's view, governed and structured by the concept. I shall focus on Hegel's account of "objective mind" (or "spirit") — the mind that is "an I that is a We, and a We that is an I" (*Phen.*, B, IV). Hegel, like Fichte and Schelling, has a strong inclination to speak as if there were at bottom only one self or mind. This supposition perhaps seems less fanciful if we view the ego as simply the concept: There is, in Hegel's view, only one such conceptual system. But Hegel's reasons for speaking in this way are not confined to logic. What he primarily has in mind when he speaks of *one Geist* are those interpersonal norms and institutions that shape, and are shaped by, our conduct and our relations with each other. Objective mind is Hegel's solution (or one of his solutions) to the problem of *other* people, which, as we have seen, arose from Kant's first *Critique*. Objective mind is, like a language, a unitary system that allows for and embraces the diversity of individual participants in it. Hegel's inclination to regard it as a single *mind* is strengthened by his belief that it embodies the conceptual system of the *Logic*. For Hegel's account of objective mind, in his *Encyclopaedia* and more especially in the *Philosophy of Right*, is explicitly structured according to the "concept," and this enables him to provide a more detailed and systematic account of moral and political life than Schelling ever did.

Hegel's account differs from Fichte's and Schelling's, however, in substance as well as in form. In contrast to Fichte, Hegel regards "right" neither as a merely external arrangement for governing men's relationships to each other nor as ultimately dispensable in favour of morality. Kantian *Moralität*, he argues, is defective; in particular, its prescriptions remain unsatisfactorily indeterminate unless they are supplemented by *Sittlichkeit*, those values embodied in the institutions of our society. These values find their highest expression, Hegel argues, in the state itself, which, far from being an external and alien imposition on the individual, confers on him a freedom that he could not procure from his own resources and thus makes him a proper individual. Since the state, together with other "ethical" (*sittlich*) institutions, embodies the concepts that form the core of the human mind, a person is more truly free if he submits to them than if he follows his own nonrational drives and inclinations or the empty dictates of Kantian morality. Unlike Schelling however, Hegel is little inclined to suppose that the modern (as opposed to the ancient Greek) state either can or should be a work of art. The modern state inevitably allows considerable free play to the nonrational desires of individuals and these find expression primarily in "civil society," the realm of economic behavior that Hegel distinguished sharply from the state itself, Hegel pays far more attention to the actual condition of his own and other societies than Schelling did, and for this reason, among others, his work has had more influence on students of and participants in political life.

Objective mind, unlike (in Hegel's view) nature, has a significant history, and Hegel provides lectures on history, not only "world history," but also the history of art, religion, and above all philosophy itself. Some of the central ideas of Hegel's historiography—that, for example, of a single spirit whose gradual revelation supplies a rational plan to the story without thereby depriving individual agents of their freedom or residual contingency—are, as we have seen, to be found in Schelling. But Schelling's own attempts at history are sketchy and lack empirical foundation in contrast. Once again it seems to be Hegel's logic that enables him to integrate a wealth of empirical material into a single system. Unlike Kant, Hegel does not assume that all men at all times (or places) think in the same way. They have, or at least deploy, different categories[20] at different times, but since the categories that they deploy develop in roughly the order in which they appear in the conceptual system of the *Logic*, Hegel's account of their activities and products can be patterned on that system. The fact that any given historical period (except Hegel's own) reveals only a fragment of this system implies, as we have seen, that the *Geist* that reveals itself in the course of history is no single finite human mind and is considerably remote from its origins in the Kantian-Fichtean ego. Nevertheless, Hegel insists that history develops in a mindlike way by the successive elevations of human self-awareness that we have already seen in Schelling.

A distinctive feature of Hegel's mature thought, in contrast to Fichte and Schelling, is his resolute opposition to utopianism, indeed, his impatience with any claim that things *ought* to be other than they are. This strand in his thought has a variety of sources: his doubts about Kantian *Moralität*; his logical reflections on the "bad infinity" of "infinite progress"; his conviction that philosophy is a reflective, retrospective discipline that cannot predict or prescribe the future; and his belief that the sharp dichotomy between what is and what ought to be is no more tenable than any other such dichotomy. Above all, unlike Fichte and Schelling, Hegel will countenance, in contrast to the actual world, no ideal world or "*beyond*" that might provide a foothold for criticizing the actual world. Hegel thus abandons the high political hopes of the other idealists (and of his own youth) —including the expectation of a perpetual peace—and attempts to see "the rose in the cross of the present" (PR, Preface)—that is, the rational structure inherent in the actual world. Similarly he avoids on principle any attempt to predict the course of future history, and he hovers uneasily between the claim that history has already reached its fulfilment in the complete self-consciousness of humanity and the admission that there is more history to come—perhaps in America (VPG, 114)—even if we cannot foresee what it will be like. Hegel's belief that he can discern rationality, the "concept," in the actual world of the present means that he is a more thoroughly this-worldly thinker than the other idealists.

Hegel's system culminates, however, not in objective mind, but in "absolute mind," the interpersonal structures of art, religion, and philosophy that develop historically, and yet express the concept in different, increasingly adequate forms—art in the form of intuition, religion in that of "conception" (*Vorstellung*), and philosophy in the form of thought. Hegel's most striking divergence from Schelling here is his dissent from Schelling's claim that philosophy culminates in art. It is, Hegel argues, a result of Schelling's reluctance to give conceptual thought its due that he takes the work of art to be the "highest and unique way in which the idea presents itself to the spirit" (VGPIII, 454). But firstly "the highest mode of the idea is its own element; thinking, the conceptualised idea, is higher than the work of art" (*loc.cit.*). And second, art has now lost such power as it once had to express the latest development of conceptual thought. "Where and how," Hegel asks, "could there be a work of art which would correspond to the spirit, to the idea of spirit?" (VGPIII, 449). Even Schelling, who shared Hegel's view that the Christian trinity is the most fitting symbol for the "unity of the finite with the infinite in and with the eternal" (Schelling, I/IV, 390), agreed with Hegel that the trinity is not well expressed in art (Schelling, I/V, 431f.). It is, in Hegel's view, philosophy, not art, that supplies the best insight into the nature of things, and he concludes his system with philosophy itself. Thus his system returns to its beginning in a stricter sense than Schelling's. In Hegel's thought the circle finally displaces the straight line with its "unconditioned beginning," as the dominant model for a philosophical system.

As we have seen, however, many though not all of the ideas characteristically associated with Hegel are to be found in the works of Fichte and more especially Schelling. It does not follow of course that none of these ideas was originated by Hegel. Schelling may have derived them from him in conversation. But if we consider only their published writings, our verdict on Hegel's contribution to German idealism should perhaps be this. Hegel's originality lies less in the production of wholly novel ideas or the proposal of a wholly novel program than in the persistence and thoroughness with which he attempts to fulfil Schelling's program, to weld isolated insights into a single system, to pay due regard both to empirical detail and to reflection on his own philosophical procedures, and to prune away the romantic and utopian extravagances of his friend. Paradoxically, Hegel appears as a model of sobriety when seen against the background of his immediate predecessors. With Hegel, we might say, German idealism has at last come down to earth.

NOTES

1. Quoted from Makryannis's *Memoirs* by G. Seferis in his *On the Greek Style*, trans. R. Warner and T. D. Frangopoulos (Athens, 1982), pp. 28f.
2. From a letter to J. H. Voss in May, 1805, translated by W. Kaufmann in his *Hegel: Reinterpretation, Texts and Commentary*, pp. 313f.
3. *Of the I as Principle of Philosophy* (1795) (I/I, 166). References to Schelling are to the volumes and pages of the Collected Works posthumously edited by his son, K. F. A. Schelling (1856–1861). The pages of this edition are indicated in most subsequent editions and translations. In addition, I have used the following translations of works by Schelling:
   a. *The Unconditional in Human Knowledge: Four Early Essays (1794–1796)*, trans. A. Marti (New Jersey, 1980). This contains (1) *On the Possibility of a Form of all Philosophy;* (2) *Of the I as Principle of Philosophy;* (3) *Philosophical Letters on Dogmatism and Criticism;* and (4) *New Deduction of Natural Right*.
   b. *System of Transcendental Idealism (1800)*, trans. P. Heath (Virginia, 1978).
   c. *Bruno or On the Natural and The Divine Principle of Things (1802)*, trans. M. Vater (Albany, 1984).
   d. *On University Studies* (1803), trans. E. S. Morgan (Athens, Ohio, 1966).
4. *Of the I* (I/I, 209).
5. *Urteil und Sein (Judgment and Being)* (probably early 1795), trans. A. Marti, *op. cit.*, pp. 261f.
6. Jacobi later attacked Schelling in *Of Divine Things and their Revelation* (1811) (*Werke*, III, 247ff.). Schelling—who, like Fichte, was a far more acrimonious polemicist than Hegel—replied in his *Memorial to F. H. Jacobi's "Of Divine Things, etc."* (1812) (VIII, 19ff.). Nevertheless, one probable reason for

Hegel's considering Jacobi at such length is that he saw an affinity between Jacobi's doctrine of "immediate knowledge" (see, e.g., *Encyclopaedia*, 50 and 61ff.) and Schelling's "intellectual intuition." Hegel seems to have tried to avoid overt, public criticism of Schelling, and, conversely, Schelling reserved his main attack on Hegel until after Hegel's death (in his Berlin lectures of 1841/2).

7. E.g., *Critique of Pure Reason*, B131f; A347ff., B405ff. ("A" indicates the pages of the first edition, 1781; "B" those of the second edition, 1787.)

8. For these doctrines, see especially Kant's *Idea for a Universal History from a Cosmopolitan Point of View* (1784) and his *Perpetual Peace* (1795).

9. *Critique of Pure Reason*, A70ff., B95ff.

10. The passage continues: "Fichte expressly declared his intention to be to give a common scientific principle to theoretical and practical reason. But with him the strict point of indifference of the two [reasons] lies ultimately not in knowledge but in faith, and the opposition of the two sides is removed by the subordination and sacrifice of one [the theoretical] to the other."

11. This quotation comes from a later period—the superb Munich lectures of 1827—but it represents his earlier views as well.

12. References to Fichte are to the volumes and pages of the *Collected Works* posthumously edited by his son, I. H. Fichte, in 1845/6. The pages of this edition are indicated in most subsequent editions and translations. In addition I have used the following translations of works by Fichte:
    a. *Science of Knowledge (Wissenschaftslehre) with the First and Second Introductions*, trans. P. Heath and J. Lachs (New York, 1970) (I, 83–328 and 417–518).
    b. *The Vocation of Man*, trans. W. Smith, revised and introduced by R. M. Chisholm (New York, 1956) (II, 165–319).

13. References to Hegel are, for the most part, to pages of the edition of E. Moldenhauer and K. M. Michel (Frankfurt am Main, 1971). I use the following abbreviations:
    a. WLI and WLII refer to the two Moldenhauer/Michel volumes (5 and 6 in their edition) of the *Science of Logic (Wissenschaft der Logik)*.
    b. VGP refers to the three volumes of lectures on the history of philosophy (18–20).
    c. VPG refers to the volume of lectures on the philosophy of history(12).
    d. *Phen.* refers to the *Phenomenology of Mind*. In the case of the Preface to this work, I refer to the paragraph numbers indicated in the translation in this volume, but other references, unless specified otherwise, are to the pages of the Moldenhauer/Michel edition (3).
    e. E refers to the *Encyclopaedia*, and all references to this work are to Hegel's own numbered paragraphs.

14. I have discussed this, as well as some of the other problems raised by Kantian idealism, in relation to *Schopenhauer's* version of it, in *The Bulletin of the Hegel Society of Great Britain*, no. 11 (Spring/Summer 1985), pp. 40ff.

15. This reference is to the pages of Fichte's and Schelling's *Briefwechsel* ("Correspondence"), edited and introduced by W. Schulz (Frankfurt am Main, 1968).

16. The letter is translated by W. Kaufmann, *op. cit.*, pp. 302f.

17. The letter is translated by W. Kaufmann, *op. cit.*, pp. 301f.

18. Schelling speaks of "the ambiguity of all determinations of reflection and concepts, which reveal themselves in their isolation as empty understanding precisely by the fact that what appears from one side to be something real or to be finite, can be shown from the other side to be something ideal or to be

infinite . . . , and everything which the understanding fixes lacks stability" (I/IV, 402). But he did not develop this thought with the persistence of Hegel. His postulation of a realm of static ideas, an "archetypal life of things [that] has neither ever begun nor will ever end", in contrast to their earthly copies that "arise and pass away again under the compulsion of circumstances" (I/IV, 224), is essentially alien to Hegel's dialectic, which attempts to portray the dynamic interrelatedness of such concepts.

19. Schelling seems to anticipate Hegel's objection when he writes, later in the same book: "The question how our concepts agree with objects thus has no transcendental sense, insofar as the question presupposes an original difference between them. The object and its concept, and conversely concept and object, are one and the same beyond consciousness and the separation of them first arises together with the emergence of consciousness" (I/III, 506).

20. Although Hegel often uses the word *Kategorie*, he does so primarily in contexts where he has Kant in mind. His own favored term is "determination" (or "thought-determination"), *Bestimmung*—a word with a variety of meanings, including "destination," "destiny," "vocation" (as in Fichte's *Vocation of Man*), "definition," "provision," and "regulation." The verb from which it derives, *bestimmen*, has a similar range of meanings: "determine," "characterize," "fix," "decide," "define," etc. Other words in the same group are *bestimmt* ["definite(ly)," "determinate(ly)," etc.] and *Bestimmtheit* ("determinacy," "definiteness," etc.). Hegel's use of these words is connected with his idea that the understanding fixes or determines sharp boundaries that are then "sublimated" by reason.

Glossary

I list here some of the important terms used by Hegel. The translations often use a variety of English words for the same German word. *Begriff*, for example, is translated as "concept" and as "notion"; *Vorstellung* as "idea", "conception," or "representation." I have extensively revised most of the older translations included in this volume, but I have not imposed a uniform translation of all of Hegel's key terms. Such a procedure might, in any case, be taken to carry the unhegelian implication that some one English rendering is correct and the others incorrect. I have, as an alternative, often indicated the occurrence of a word, or of one of a group of cognate words, in Hegel's text by a superscript numeral in the translation. For example, "notion[9]" means that the word translated by "notion" is *Begriff* or a close relative such as *begreifen*. I have done this only when the occurrence of a word is significant and not otherwise obvious from the context.

1. **absolut; das Absolute:** absolute; the absolute

2. **allgemein; Allgemeinheit:** universal, general; universality, generality (contrasting with 10 and 17)

3. **anerkennen:** to recognize, acknowledge

4. **Anschauung; anschauen:** intuition; to intuit, to look at

5. **an sich; das Ansichsein:** in itself, implicit(ly), potential(ly), taken by itself, superficially; being-in-itself, etc.

6. **für sich; das Fürsichsein:** for itself, explicit(ly), actual(ly), by itself, in itself; being-for-itself, etc.

7. **an und für sich, etc.:** in and for itself, absolute(ly), etc.

8. **aufheben; Aufhebung:** to pick up, cancel, annul, subl(im)ate, merge, supersede, etc.; cancellation, etc. (These words have three senses (a) "cancel," (b) "preserve," and (c) "elevate." Hegel intends to convey all three senses whenever he uses them. Our expression "kick upstairs" conveys a similar idea.)

9. **begreifen; Begriff:** to include, comprehend, conceptualize, etc.; concept, notion.

10. **besonder; Besonderheit:** particular; particularity [Contrasting with 2 and 17. This is distinct from individuality. It is connected with the ideas of (a) a determinate, e.g., "red," as opposed to a determinable or universal, e.g., "colored"; (b) a "particular" judgment, viz a judgment of the form "Some Fs are G."]

11. bewusst; Bewusstsein: conscious, aware; consciousness, etc.

12. Dasein: determinate being, existence, being

13. denken; Denken; Gedanke: to think; thinking, thought; thought, idea

14. nachdenken; Nachdenken: to after-think, meta-think, reflect, think over; after-thinking, etc.

15. eigen; Eigenschaft: own, proper; property (of a thing)

16. Eigentum: (owned) property

17. einzeln; Einzelheit: individual, singular; individuality, singularity (contrasting with 2 and 10)

18. erfahren; Erfahrung: to learn, come to know, hear, experience; experience

19. erkennen; Erkenntnis: to know, (re)cognize; knowledge, (re)cognition

20. erscheinen; Erscheinung: to appear; appearance, phenomenon

21. Ethik: ethic(s)

22. Existenz: existence

23. frei; Freiheit: free; freedom, liberty

24. fühlen, Gefühl: to feel; feeling

25. Geist; geistig; Geistigkeit: mind, spirit; intellectual, spiritual, mental; spirituality, etc.

26. Gesetz: law, statute

27. Gestalt; Gestaltung: form, figure, shape; shaping, shape, formation, structure

28. gewiss; Gewissheit: sure, certain; certainty

29. Gewissen: conscience

30. Grund: soil, bottom, ground, reason (cf. *zugrunde gehen; zugrunde richten* go to ruin, perish; ruin, destroy, wreck)

31. ich; Ich; das Ich: I; I, ego; the ego, the I, the self

32. Idee: idea, ideal, Idea

33. meinen, Meinung: to think, believe, opine, mean; opinion, meaning

34. Moment: moment, stage, element, aspect (rarely "instant")

35. Moral; moralisch; Moralität: morality, morals; moral; morality (contrasting with 44)

36. recht; Recht: right, correct, etc.; right, justice, law

37. reflektieren; Reflexion: to reflect; reflection (with the same ambiguity as the English words)

38. Sache: thing, matter, concern, subject-matter

39. scheinen; Schein: to shine, appear, seem, show; shine, appearance, show, illusion, semblance (Hegel often exploits the resemblance to *Sein*, "being." The words carry a suggestion of illusoriness that is generally absent from 20.)

40. schliessen; Schluss: to shut, close, finish, conclude, infer, etc.; end, close, closure, conclusion, inference, syllogism [cf. *zusammenschliessen* to close, join, connect (together)] [Hegel insists that in, e.g., the syllogism "All men are mortal; all Greeks are men; so all Greeks are mortal," the middle term ("men") joins or connects the two extremes ("Greeks" and "mortal").]

41. sein; Sein; seiend: to be, exist; being, existence; being, existent

42. selbstbewusst; Selbstbewusstsein: self-conscious, self-assertive, self-confident; self-consciousness, etc.

43. Sinn; sinnlich; Sinnlichkeit: sense; sensual, sensory, sensible, material, physical; sensuality, etc.

44. Sitte; sittlich; Sittlichkeit: custom, usage; ethical, moral; ethical life, social ethics, morality, etc.

45. sollen, das Sollen: shall, to be to, be said to, be supposed to, should, ought; the ought

46. Teleologie: teleology

47. unmittelbar; Unmittelbarkeit: immediate, direct; immediacy, directness

48. Ursache: cause (Ur-, "original," + *Sache*).

49. urteilen; Urteil: to judge; judgment

50. vermitteln; Vermittlung: to mediate; mediation

51. Vernunft; vernünftig: reason; rational

52. verstehen; Verstand; verständig; verständlich: understand; understanding, intellect; intelligent, etc.; intelligible, etc.

53. vorstellen; Vorstellung: to put forward, introduce, (re)present, imagine; (re)presentation, idea, notion, conception, (general) image, imagination, etc.

54. wahr; das Wahre; Wahrheit: true; the true, the truth; truth

55. wahrnehmen; Wahrnehmung: to perceive; perception (*wahr+nehmen*, "to take, accept")

56. Wesen; wesentlich: being, entity, essence; essential

57. Wille(n); wollen: will, volition; to want, wish, will, etc.

58. Willkür; willkürlich: arbitrariness, arbitrary will, choice, self-will, willfulness; arbitrary, willful (For Hegel, the word implies choosing or doing as one likes, with, in contrast to 57, no rational constraint on the manner or object of one's choice.)

59. wirken; Wirkung; wirklich; Wirklichkeit: work, cause, operate; effect, action, result; real, actual; reality, actuality

60. wissen; Wissen; Wissenschaft: to know; knowledge; science, philosophy

61. Zweck; zweckmässig; Zweckmässigkeit: purpose, end, design, aim; purposive, final, expedient, suitable; purposiveness, teleology, finality, expediency, suitability

I. The Positivity of the Christian Religion*

1. "IS JUDAEA, THEN, THE TEUTONS' FATHERLAND?"

Every nation has its own imagery, its gods, angels, devils, or saints who live on in the nation's traditions, whose stories and deeds the nurse tells to her charges and so wins them over by impressing their imagination. In this way these tales are given permanence. In addition to these creatures of the imagination, there also live in the memory of most nations, especially free nations, the ancient heroes of their country's history, i.e., the founders or liberators of their states scarcely less than the men of valor in the days before the nation was united into a state under civil laws. These heroes do not live solely in their nation's imagination; their history, the recollection of their deeds, is linked with public festivals, national games, with many of the state's domestic institutions or foreign affairs, with well-known houses and districts, with public memorials and temples. Every nation which has its own religion and polity, or which has made wholly its own any part of the religion and culture it has acquired from other peoples, has had its own national imagery of this kind; consider, for example, the Egyptians, the Jews, the Greeks, the Romans. The ancient Germans too, the Gauls, the Scandinavians, had their Valhalla (the home of their gods) as well as their heroes who lived in their songs, whose deeds inspired them in battle or filled their souls with great resolves on festal occasions; and they had their sacred groves where these deities drew nearer to them.

Christianity has emptied Valhalla, felled the sacred groves, extirpated the national imagery as a shameful superstition, as a devilish poison, and given us instead the imagery of a nation whose climate, laws, culture, and interests are strange to us and whose history has no connection whatever

*"The Positivity of the Christian Religion," reprinted from *Early Theological Writings* by G. W. F. Hegel. Translated by T. M. Knox, with an Introduction and Fragments translated by Richard Kroner. University of Pennsylvania Press: Philadelphia, 1971. Reprinted by permission of the University of Pennsylvania Press. This selection is a fragment that was not incorporated in the main body of the work. It was composed in 1795 or 1796.

with our own. A David or a Solomon lives in our popular imagination, but our country's own heroes slumber in learned history books, and, for the scholars who write them, Alexander or Caesar is as interesting as the story of Charlemagne or Frederick Barbarossa. Except perhaps for Luther in the eyes of Protestants, what heroes could we have had, we who were never a nation? Who could be our Theseus, who founded a state and was its legislator? Where are our Harmodius and Aristogiton to whom we could sing scolia as the liberators of our land? The wars which have engulfed millions of Germans were wars waged by princes out of ambition or for their own independence; the people were only tools, and even if they fought with rage and exasperation, they still could only ask at the end: "Why?" or "What have we gained?" The Reformation, and the bloody vindication of the right to make reforms in religion, is one of the few events in which a part of the nation took an interest, an interest which did not evaporate, like the interest in the Crusades, as the imagination cooled, but which was animated by a sense of an abiding right, the right in matters of religious opinion to follow one's own self-wrought or self-acquired conviction. But apart from the usual annual readings of the Augsburg Confession in some Protestant churches (readings usually wearisome to every hearer) and apart from the dull sermon which follows these, what is the festival which celebrates the memory of this event? It looks as if the authorities in church and state were content that the memory of how our forefathers had a sense of this right, how thousands could stake their lives to vindicate it, should slumber in our hearts and not be retained in any living fashion.

Anyone who did not know the history of the city, the culture, and the laws of Athens could almost have learned them from the festivals if he had lived a year within its gates.

Thus we are without any religious imagery which is home-grown or linked with our history, and we are without any political imagery whatever; all that we have is the remains of an imagery of our own, lurking amid the common people under the name of superstition. As a belief in ghosts it retains the memory of a hill where knights once did their mischief or a house where monks and nuns walked or where a supposedly faithless trustee or neighbor has still failed to find rest in the grave. As a product of fancy, drawing nothing from history, it befools weak or evil men with the possibility of witchcraft. These are sad and indigent remains of an attempted independence and an attempted possession, and the general attitude to them is that it is the duty of all enlightened people to extirpate them altogether. As a result of this temper in the upper classes, quite apart from the coarseness and intractability of the available material, it has become totally impossible to ennoble these remnants of mythology and thereby refine the imagination and sensibility of the common people. The delightful *jeux d'esprit* of Hölty, Bürger, and Musäus in this department are altogether lost on the masses because they are too backward in the rest of their culture to be capable of enjoying them. Similarly, the imagery of our more educated classes has an entirely different orbit from that of the common people, and the latter do not understand in the least the characters and scenes of those authors and artists who cater for the former. On the other hand, the Athenian citizen whose poverty deprived him of the chance to vote in the public assembly, or who even had to sell himself as a slave, still knew as well as Pericles and Alcibiades who Agamemnon and Oedipus were when Sophocles or Euripides brought them on the stage as noble types of beautiful and sublime manhood or when Phidias or Apelles exhibited them as pure models of physical beauty.

Shakespeare delineated his characters so truly that, quite apart from the fact that many of them are familiar historical figures, they have been deeply impressed on the English people and have formed for them a group of imaginative pictures that are wholly their own. The result is that the people can understand and freely enjoy the Shakespeare gallery, i.e., that part of the Academy exhibitions in which the greatest masters compete.

In the sphere of imaginative ideas which would be common to both the educated and the vulgar among us, i.e., the story of our religion, there are certain obstacles to that poetic adaptation which might be a means of refining our people. Apart from anything else, there is the disadvantage, so far as the vulgar are concerned, that they cling too rigidly to the material in question as to a matter of faith; while so far as the educated are concerned, the trouble is that, however fine the poet's treatment of the subject, the very names bring with them the idea of something Gothic or Old Frankish and, because of the compulsion by which they have been proclaimed to our reason from our youth onward, they carry a sense of uneasiness running counter to that enjoyment of beauty which arises from the free play of our mental powers. Even if in some heads the imagination has made itself free and has come to aspire solely to the beautiful and good, still if we look closely at its ideals or its susceptibility to these we can see that they have been cut up for it out of the catechism.

As the taste for ancient literature spread, and with it the taste for fine art, the more educated part of our people adopted the Greek mythology into their imagination. Their susceptibility to it proves that its ideas were more self-subsistent, more independent of the intellect, which otherwise could not have refrained from disturbing their free enjoyment. Others, trying to give the Germans an imagery of their own once more, an imagery that was home-grown, cried: "Is Achaea, then, the Teutons' fatherland?" But this imagery is not that of Germans today. The project of restoring to a nation an imagery once lost was always doomed to failure; and on the whole it was bound to be even less fortunate than Julian's attempt to inculcate the mythology of his forefathers into his contemporaries in its old strength and universality. The outcome of that attempt was to all appearance far more promising because at the date much of the old mythology was still left in men's hearts and because the Emperor had plenty of means at his command for giving it pre-eminence. The old German imagery has nothing in our day to connect or adapt itself to; it stands as cut off from the whole circle of our ideas, opinions, and beliefs, and is as strange to us as the imagery of Ossian or of India. And what the poet cried to his people in relation to Greek mythology could be said both to him and his nation with just as much right in relation to the Jewish; they could be asked: Is Judaea, then, the Teutons' fatherland?

In proportion as the imagination loves freedom, it requires that the religious imagery of a people shall be permanent, i.e., shall be less linked with specific dates than with certain familiar places. For the vulgar, familiarity with the place is generally one proof more, or the most certain proof, that the story told of it is true. This is why the mythology of the Greeks was a living reality in their hearts, and why the Catholics have such a strong faith in their saints and miracle workers. To the Catholics, the miracles worked in their own country are much more real and important than far greater ones worked elsewhere or even than those worked by Christ himself. Nearly every country has its patron saint who worked special miracles and receives exceptional honor there. Moreover, every nation believes, on the strength of the special notice devoted to it by its protecting deity, that it is pre-eminently distinguished and honored, and this precedence over other nations increases its dependence on him, as is the case with the Jews. This is how an imaginative picture of this kind becomes domiciled in a nation's heart.

What in our Holy Scriptures is properly history, like the greater part of the Old Testament, and is not something, like the New Testament, which it is strictly our duty to believe, is precisely what may become a content of the popular imagination; but it is so alien to our customs, to our polity, to the culture attained by our mental and physical powers that we can hardly make contact with it at any point except at the occasional references to universal human nature which it contains. For anyone who begins to be enlightened, i.e., to demand universality for the laws of his intellect and his experience, and this means for people whose numbers are continually increasing, it is in the main unpalatable, and it is useful for only two types of reader: the first consists of those who with saintly simplicity take the whole thing for gospel in the sense of being convinced that the recorded events would have been open to everyone's experience; the second never stumbles on this question about truth or falsehood for the intellect, but thinks only on the subjective aspect of this material, on its truth for the imagination. (See Herder's works, for example.)*

---

*The different ways of reading the old sagas, whether with the intellect or the imagination, may be seen, for example, in the story of Moses. It is told of him that he saw God on Sinai. (*a*) The ordinary Christian reader takes this as a case of sense-perception and one which accords with the rules governing all our sense-perceptions. (*b*) The enlightened and intellectualistic Recha [in Lessing's *Nathan der Weise*, III, 2 (1653)] says: "Wherever Moses stood, it was before his God." She grants the objective existence of God but denies that he can be apprehended by man's sense-perception. She holds that God was present to him at all times

The Greeks had their religious sagas almost exclusively for the purpose of having gods to whom they could devote their gratitude, build altars, and offer sacrifices. Our sacred history, on the other hand, is supposed to have many uses; we are supposed to learn and derive from it all sorts of moral truths. But a sound moral judgment which approaches it on purpose to learn from it is often compelled first to read the morality into most of the stories before it can find morality in them; and in many instances it encounters difficulty in squaring them with its principles. The chief utility of these stories to a pious man, and the chief effect of them he can detect in himself, is edification, i.e., the awakening of obscure feelings of saintliness (because he is now occupied with ideas about God). The confusedness of these feelings gives up any claim to a gain in moral insight, though generally it brings with it an intensification of the so-called holy passions such as a misconceived holy zeal for God's glory, a pious pride and conceit, and a lethargical submission to God.

2. HOW CHRISTIANITY CONQUERED PAGANISM

One of the pleasantest feelings enjoyed by Christians arises from comparing their good fortune and knowledge with the misfortune and darkness of the heathen, and one of the commonplaces the spiritual shepherds are most fond of using to lead their sheep to the pastures of self-satisfaction and proud humility is to put this good fortune vividly before their eyes, a process in which the blind heathen generally come off very badly. Special commiseration is given to them on the score of their *comfortless* religion, since it does not promise forgiveness of sins and, in particular, leaves them without faith in a Providence governing their destinies to wise and beneficent ends. But we can soon be aware that our sympathy is superfluous, since in the Greeks we do not encounter the needs which our practical

---

even if he was not thinking of him, and she denies in particular that God was *visibly* present to him. (*c*) A third possibility is to maintain that at that place and moment where Moses believed he had felt the presence of God, the Deity was truly present to him in the same sense in which any and every feeling has truth for us. But there is no intention here of dogmatizing about the *object* of the feeling, since in the judgment "I feel so-and-so" no question arises about objective reality; all that is implied is that at any place or moment where a man does not think of God, God is not present.

The first of these three judgments upholds the perceptivity of God as an object; the second denies his perceptivity but upholds his existence; the third upholds the perceptivity of God but not of God as an object. The first ascribes sensation and understanding to Moses, the second imagination alone, the third the activity of both imagination and reason. Objectivity alone speaks to the maker of the second judgment, and it is judged as an object according to the laws of his understanding and experience. The maker of the third judgment is heedless of the object; the spirit of Moses speaks directly to his spirit; it is revealed to him, and he understands it.

The first judgment asserts subjective and objective truth; the second, objective truth accompanied by subjective error; the third, subjective truth accompanied, if the expression be allowed, by objective error.

reason has today when we have learned how to saddle it with plenty of them.

The supplanting of paganism by Christianity is one of those remarkable revolutions whose causes the thoughtful historian must labor to discover. Great revolutions which strike the eye at a glance must have been preceded by a still and secret revolution in the spirit of the age, a revolution not visible to every eye, especially imperceptible to contemporaries, and as hard to discern as to describe in words. It is lack of acquaintance with this spiritual revolution which makes the resulting changes astonishing. The supersession of a native and immemorial religion by a foreign one is a revolution which occurs in the spiritual realm itself, and it is thus of a kind whose causes must be found all the more directly in the spirit of the times.

How could a religion have been supplanted after it had been established in states for centuries and intimately connected with their constitutions? What can have caused the cessation of a belief in gods to whom cities and empires ascribed their origin, to whom the people made daily offerings, whose blessings were invoked on every enterprise, under whose banners alone the armies had conquered, who had been thanked for victories, who received joyful songs and earnest prayers, whose temples and altars, wealth and statues, were the pride of the people and the glory of the arts, and whose worship and festivals were but occasions for universal joy? How could the faith in the gods have been reft from the web of human life with which it had been interwoven by a thousand threads? A habit of body can be opposed by other physical capacities operating together with the will; the habitual exercise of one psychical capacity (fixity of will excepted) can be opposed by other psychical capacities. But how strong must the counterweight have been to overcome the power of a psychical habit which was not isolated, as our religion frequently is today, but was intertwined in every direction with all men's capacities and most intimately interwoven even with the most spontaneously active of them?

"Acquaintance with Christianity had the negative effect of drawing people's attention to the poverty and comfortlessness of their religion, of giving their minds an insight into the foolish and ridiculous elements in their fabulous mythology and making them dissatisfied with it. The positive effect was their adoption of Christianity, the religion which was so well adapted to all the needs of the human mind and heart, which answered so satisfactorily all the questions of human reason, and which into the bargain had its divine origin authenticated by miracles." This is the usual answer to the questions in the last paragraph. The expressions used by those who give this answer: "intellectual enlightenment," "fresh insight," etc., are so familiar to us that we think great things of them and suppose that they have explained everything. We make so light of this intellectual operation and look on its effects as so natural simply because it is so very easy for us to make any child understand how silly is the belief that up in heaven a troop of gods, like those the heathen believed in, walk about, eat, drink, indulge in horseplay, and do other things that any decent person would be ashamed to do on earth.

But anyone who has made the simple observation that the heathen too had intellects, and that in everything great, beautiful, noble, and free they are so far our superiors that we can hardly make them our examples, but must rather look up to them as a different species at whose achievements we can only marvel; anyone who knows that religion, particularly an imaginative religion, cannot be torn from the heart, especially from the whole life and heart of a people, by cold syllogisms constructed in the study; anyone who knows that in the expansion of Christianity use was made of anything and everything rather than reason and intellect; anyone who, before explaining the vogue of Christianity by miracles, knows to raise the prior question: What must have been the character of the age which made possible the occurrence of miracles at that time, especially those miracles which history records?; anyone who knows all this will find unsatisfactory the usual answers to the question about the supersession of paganism.

Free Rome subjected to her sway a number of states which had lost their freedom, some (those in Asia) earlier, others (those further west) later; a few which had remained free she destroyed altogether, because they refused to bow to the yoke. All that was left to the conqueror of the world was the honor of being the last to lose her freedom. Greek and Roman religion was a religion for free peoples only, and, with the loss of freedom, its significance and strength, its fitness to men's needs, were also bound to perish. What can divisions of artillery do if they have no ammunition left? They must seek other weapons. What is the use of a net to a fisherman if the stream has run dry?

As free men the Greeks and Romans obeyed laws laid down by themselves, obeyed men whom they had themselves appointed to office, waged wars on which they had themselves decided, gave their property, exhausted their passions, and sacrificed their lives by thousands for an end which was their own. They neither learned nor taught [a moral system] but evinced by their actions the moral maxims which they could call their very own. In public as in private and domestic life, every individual was a free man, one who lived by his own laws. The idea[32]* of his country or of his state was the invisible and higher reality for which he strove, which impelled him to effort; it was the final end of *his* world or in his eyes the final end of *the* world, an end which he found manifested in the realities of his daily life or which he himself co-operated in manifesting and maintaining. Confronted by this idea, his own individuality vanished; it was only this idea's maintenance, life, and persistence that he asked for, and these were things which he himself could make realities. It could never or hardly ever have struck

*Superscript numbers throughout the text refer to items in the Glossary.

him to ask or beg for persistence or eternal life for his own individuality. Only in moments of inactivity or lethargy could he feel the growing strength of a purely self-regarding wish. Cato turned to Plato's *Phaedo* only when his world, his republic, hitherto the highest order of things in his eyes, had been destroyed; at that point only did he take flight to a higher order still.

The Greek and Roman gods held sway in the realm of nature and over everything which could bring grief or happiness to men. Strong passions were their work, just as it was they who bestowed great gifts of wisdom, eloquence, and counsel. They were asked to advise whether an undertaking would turn out well or ill; they were implored for their blessings and thanked for gifts of every kind. If a man clashed with these lords of nature and their power, he could set over against them his freedom and his own self. His will was free and obeyed its own laws; he knew no divine commands, or, if he called the moral law a divine command, the command was nowhere given in words but ruled him invisibly (*Antigone*). This implied that he recognized everyone's right to have a will of his own, be it good or bad. Good men acknowledged in their own case the duty of being good, yet at the same time they respected other people's freedom not to be so; thus they did not set up and impose on others any moral system, whether one that was divine or one manufactured or abstracted [from experience] by themselves.

Fortunate campaigns, increase of wealth, and acquaintance with luxury and more and more of life's comforts created in Athens and Rome an aristocracy of wealth and military glory. The aristocrats then acquired a dominion and an influence over the masses and corrupted them by their deeds and still more by the use they made of their riches. The masses then readily and willingly ceded power and preponderance in the state to the aristocrats, conscious as they were that they had given them their power and could take it away again at the first fit of bad temper. But gradually the masses ceased to deserve a reproof so often brought against them on the score of their ingratitude to their leaders; when they could choose between [subjection] and this wrong [of ingratitude], they ceased to prefer the latter and [were now ready] to curse in an individual those virtues which had saved their country from ruin. Soon the preponderance freely granted to the rulers was upheld by force, and the fact that this could happen already presupposes the loss of that type of feeling and consciousness which, under the name of "virtue," Montesquieu makes the principle of a republican regime and which is readiness to sacrifice one's life for an ideal,[32] an ideal realized for republicans in their country.

The picture of the state as a product of his own energies disappeared from the citizen's soul. The care and oversight of the whole rested on the soul of one man or a few. Each individual had his own allotted place, a place more or less restricted and different from his neighbor's. The administration of the state machine was intrusted to a small number of citizens, and these served only as single cogs deriving their worth solely from their connection with others. Each man's allotted part in the congeries which formed the whole was so inconsiderable in relation to the whole that the individual did not need to realize this relation or to keep it in view. Usefulness to the state was the great end which the state set before its subjects, and the end they set before themselves in their political life was gain, self-maintenance, and perhaps vanity. All activity and every purpose now had a bearing on something individual; activity was no longer for the sake of a whole or an ideal. Either everyone worked for himself or else he was compelled to work for some other individual. Freedom to obey self-given laws, to follow self-chosen leaders in peacetime and self-chosen generals in war, to carry out plans in whose formulation one had had one's share—all this vanished. All political freedom vanished also; the citizen's right gave him only a right to the security of that property which now filled his entire world. Death, the phenomenon which demolished the whole structure of his purposes and the activity of his entire life, must have become something terrifying, since nothing survived him. But the republican's whole soul was in the republic; the republic survived him, and there hovered before his mind the thought of its immortality.

But since all his aims and all his activities were directed on something individual, since he no longer found as their object any universal ideal for which he might live or die, he also found no refuge in his gods. They too were individual and incomplete beings and could not satisfy the demands of a universal ideal. Greeks and Romans were satisfied with gods so poorly equipped, with gods possessed of human weaknesses, only because they had the eternal and the self-subsistent within their own hearts. They could tolerate the mockery of their gods on the stage because to mock them could never be to mock holiness. A slave in Plautus dared to say: *si summus Jupiter hoc facit, ego homuncio idem non facerem?*—an inference that his audience must have found singular and droll because they were quite unfamiliar with the principle of finding in the god what man's duty was; a Christian, on the other hand, would have been bound to find the slave's reasoning correct. In this situation, faith in something stable or absolute was impossible; obedience to another's will and another's legislation was habitual. Without a country of his own, the citizen lived in a polity with which no joy could be associated, and all he felt was its pressure. He had a worship to whose celebration and festivals he could no longer bring a cheerful heart, because cheerfulness had flown away out of his life. A slave, besides being often more than a match for his lord in natural capacity and education, could no longer descry in him the freedom and independence in which his superiority might otherwise have consisted. In this situation men were offered a religion which either was already adapted to the needs of the age (since it had arisen in a people characterized by a similar degeneracy and a similar

though differently colored emptiness and deficiency) or else was one out of
which men could form what their needs demanded and what they could
then adhere to.

Reason could never give up finding practical principles, the absolute and
self-subsistent reality, somewhere or other; but these were no longer to be
met with in man's will. They now showed themselves in the deity proffered
by the Christian religion, a deity beyond the reach of our powers and our
will but not of our supplications and prayers. Thus the realization of a
moral ideal could now no longer be willed but only wished for, since what
we wish for we cannot achieve of ourselves but expect to acquire without
our cooperation. The first disseminators of the Christian religion hoped for
a revolution to be brought about by these means, i.e., to be accomplished
by a Divine Being while men looked on passively. When this hope finally
evaporated, men were content to await this universal revolution at the end
of the world. Once the realization of an ideal was placed beyond the
boundaries of human powers, and once men felt themselves incapable of
achieving much more, it did not matter how boundlessly enlarged the
object of their hopes became; this made that object capable of incorporat-
ing everything with which an enthusiastic oriental imagination could adorn
it, and what was thus incorporated was not a fantasy but something expected to be actual.

Similarly, so long as the Jewish state found spirit and strength enough in
itself for the maintenance of its independence, the Jews seldom, or, as
many hold, never, had recourse to the expectation of a Messiah. Not until
they were subjugated by foreign nations, not until they had a sense of their
impotence and weakness, do we find them burrowing in their sacred books
for a consolation of that kind. Then when they were offered a Messiah who
did not fulfil their political expectations, they thought it worth toiling to
insure that their state should still remain a state;* they very soon discarded
their ineffective messianic hopes and took up arms. After doing everything
the most enthusiastic courage could achieve, they endured the most appall-
ing of human calamities and were buried with their polity under the ruins
of their city. In history and the judgment of nations they would stand
alongside the Carthaginians and Saguntines, and above the Greeks and
Romans, whose cities outlived their polities, if the sense of what a nation
may do for its independence were not too foreign to us, and if we had not
the impertinence to order a nation not to manage its affairs in its own way
but to follow our opinions and live and die for them, though we do not lift a
finger to uphold them ourselves. The scattered remnant of the Jews have
not abandoned the idea of the Jewish state, but they have reverted not to
the banners of their own courage but only to the standards of an ineffective
messianic hope.

---

*A nation to which this is a matter of indifference will soon cease to be a nation.

The adherents of paganism also sensed this lack of ideals for conduct; Lucian and Longinus sensed that there should be such ideals in human affairs, and their sad experience in this matter was poured out in bitter lamentations. Others again, like Porphyry and Iamblichus, attempted to equip their gods with the wealth which human beings no longer possessed and then to conjure some of it back in the form of a gift. Apart from some earlier attempts, it has been reserved in the main for our epoch to vindicate at least in theory the human ownership of the treasures formerly squandered on heaven; but what age will have the strength to validate this right in practice and make itself its possessor?

Men thus corrupt, men who must have despised themselves from the moral point of view, even though in other respects they prided themselves on being God's favorites, were bound to create the doctrine of the corruption of human nature and adopt it gladly. For one thing, it corresponded with experience; for another, it satisfied their pride by exculpating them and giving them in the very sense of calamity a reason for pride; it brought disgrace into honor, since it sanctified and perpetuated every incapacity by turning into a sin any possible belief in human potentialities. The scope of the dominion exercised by the pagan gods, who hitherto had haunted nature only, was extended, like that of the Christian God, over the free world of mind. The right of legislation was ceded to God exclusively, but, not content with this, men looked to him for every good impulse, every better purpose and decision. These were regarded as his work, not in the sense in which the Stoics ascribed every good thing to the deity because they thought of their souls as sparks of the divine or as generated by God, but as the work of a being outside us in whom we have no part, a being foreign to us with whom we have nothing in common. Again, even our ability to submit passively to God's operation was supposed to be weakened by the unceasing machinations and cunning of an evil spirit who made constant inroads into the other's domain in the realms of both nature and mind. While the Manichaeans seemed to allow the evil principle an undivided dominion in the realm of nature, orthodox theology took this doctrine as a dishonor to God's majesty and vindicated God's mastery of most of nature, though at the same time it compensated the evil principle for this loss by allowing it some power in the realm of freedom.

With an upright heart and a well-meaning zeal the helpless human race fled to the altar where it found and worshiped what was self-subsistent and moral.[35] But as Christianity penetrated into the upper and more corrupt classes, as great differences arose within its own organization between the distinguished and the inferior, as despotism poisoned more and more of the sources of life and reality, the age revealed its hopeless triviality in the turn taken by its conceptions of God's divinity and its disputes about these. And it displayed its indigence all the more nakedly by surrounding it with a nimbus of sanctity and lauding it to the skies as the supreme honor of mankind.

The ideal of perfection was the sole abiding-place left to the holy, but morality now disappeared from this ideal, or at any rate it was cast into oblivion. The sight of morality, the true divinity, would have reflected a warming ray into men's hearts, but instead of this the mirror now revealed nothing save the picture of its own age, the picture of nature fashioned to a purpose bestowed on it at discretion by human pride and passion; I say "nature" because every interest of knowledge and faith was now concentrated on the metaphysical or transcendental side of the idea of God. We see humanity less occupied with dynamical categories, which theoretical reason is capable of stretching to cover the infinite, than with applying to its infinite object numerical categories, reflective categories like difference, etc., and mere ideas drawn from sense-perception, such as origin, creation, and engendering, and with deriving the characteristics of that object from events in its nature. These definitions and subtleties, unlike those in other sciences, were not confined to the theologians' study; their public was the whole of Christendom. All classes, all ages, both sexes, took an equal share in them, and differences of opinion about them roused the most deadly hatred, the bloodiest persecutions, and often a complete disruption of all moral ties and the most sacred relationships. Such a perversion of nature could only entail a most frightful revenge.

The purpose which the Christians ascribed to this Infinite Being was poles apart from the world's *moral* goal and purpose; it was whittled down not simply to the propagation of Christianity but to ends adopted by a single sect or by individuals, particularly priests, and suggested by the individual's passions, by vainglory, pride, ambition, envy, hatred, and the like. At this early date, however, there was still no question of that keystone of our eudaemonism, its picturesque and comforting theory of Providence. The situation of the Christians was for the most part too unhappy for them to expect much happiness on earth, and the general conception of a church lay too deep in their souls for any individual to expect or demand much for himself. And yet their demands were all the stronger as soon as they linked their interest with the church's. They despised the mundane joys and earthly blessings they had to forgo and found ample compensation in heaven. The idea of the church took the place of a motherland and a free polity, and the difference between these two was that, in the idea of the church, freedom could have no place, and, while the state was complete on earth, the church was most intimately connected with heaven. Heaven stood so close to the cycle of Christian feelings that the renunciation of all joys and goods could seem no sacrifice at all, and only to those spectators of martyrdom who did not know this sense of heaven's nearness was it bound to appear extraordinary.

Thus the despotism of the Roman emperors had chased the human spirit from the earth and spread a misery which compelled men to seek and expect happiness in heaven; robbed of freedom, their spirit, their eternal and absolute element, was forced to take flight to the deity. God's objectivity is a counterpart to the corruption and slavery of man, and it is strictly only a revelation, only a manifestation of the spirit of the age. This spirit was revealed by its conception of God as objective when men began to know such a surprising amount about God, when so many secrets about his nature, comprised in so many formulas, were no longer secrets whispered from ear to ear but were proclaimed on the housetops and known to children by heart. The spirit of the age was revealed in its objective conception of God when he was no longer regarded as like ourselves, though infinitely greater, but was put into another world in whose confines we had no part, to which we contributed nothing by our activity, but into which, at best, we could beg or conjure our way. It was revealed again when man himself became a non-ego and his God another non-ego. Its clearest revelation was in the mass of miracles which it engendered and which took the place of the individual's reason when decisions were made and convictions adopted. But its most dreadful revelation was when on this God's behalf men fought, murdered, defamed, burned at the stake, stole, lied, and betrayed. In a period like this, God must have ceased altogether to be something subjective and have entirely become an object, and the perversion of the maxims of morality is then easily and logically justified in theory.

Christians know through God's self-revelation that he is the supreme Lord, Lord of heaven and the whole earth, of nature, both organic and inorganic, Lord too of the world of mind and spirit. To refuse this king the veneration which he has himself ordained is inevitably an ingratitude and a crime. This is the system of all the churches; differences about who is to judge and punish this crime are only secondary. One church administers this judicial office itself. The other condemns in accordance with the system but does not lift a finger to execute judgment on earth. It is assured that God himself will execute it, and the zeal to help him by warnings, by various petty bribes, or by an oppression that only stops short of death, seems to be gradually cooling off; sympathy, or a sense of impotence, is taking the place of hatred, and this is preferable even if its basis be a pride self-persuaded that it possesses the truth. A free man could share neither the zeal nor the sympathy; as a free man, living among others equally free, he would grant no one a right to try to change and improve him or to interfere with his moral principles, nor would he presume to dispute the right of others to be what they are and what they wish, whether good or bad. Piety and sin are two concepts which in our sense of the words the Greeks lacked; for us the former is a disposition which acts from respect for God as lawgiver, and the latter is an action in contravention of a divine command. Ἅγιον and ἀνάγιον, *pietas* and *impietas*, express holy human feelings together with the dispositions and actions which correspond or are at variance with these. They were also called divine commands by the ancients, but the commands were not regarded as positive or authoritarian. If anyone had been able to hit upon the question, "How would you prove the divine origin of a command or a prohibition"? he could not have called on any historical fact for his answer, but only on the feelings of his own heart and the agreement of all good men.

3. HOW A DISINCLINATION FOR MILITARY SERVICE HELPED THE SUCCESS OF CHRISTIANITY

With the total extinction of political freedom, all interest in the state has disappeared, because we take an interest in a thing only if we can be active on its behalf. In such a position, when the purpose of life is whittled down to gaining one's daily bread plus a greater or lesser degree of comfort and luxury, and when interest in the state becomes a wholly self-seeking one because it is confined to the hope that its persistence will guard the achievement of our aims or else achieve them for us, then among the traits discernible in the spirit of the time there is necessarily present a disinclination for military service, because this service is the opposite of the universal wish for quiet and uniform enjoyment. It brings with it hardships and even death, the loss of the chance to enjoy anything. A man whose indolence or debauchery or ennui has left him only soldiering as a last resort if he is to earn his living and gratify his passions, will be nothing but a coward in face of the enemy. Among the Romans we find large numbers of men who, in a situation of oppression and political inactivity, escaped military service by flight, bribery, or self-mutilation. A nation in this mood must have welcomed a religion which branded the dominant spirit of the age, i.e., moral impotence and the dishonor of being trampled underfoot, with the name of "passive obedience" and then made it an honor and the supreme virtue. This operation gave men a pleasant surprise because it transformed the contempt felt by others and their own sense of disgrace into a glory and a pride. They must have welcomed a religion which preached that to shed human blood was a sin. For this reason we now see St. Ambrose or St. Antony with their numerous flock not hastening to man the walls in defense of their city against an approaching horde of barbarians but kneeling in the churches and on the streets and imploring God to avert their terrifying misfortune. And indeed how could they have willed to die in battle? The preservation of the city could only have been important to them as a means to the preservation of their property and its enjoyment. Therefore, to have exposed themselves to the danger of death would have been to do something ridiculous, since the means, death, would have forthwith annulled the end, property and enjoyment. The sense that in defending one's property one was dying to uphold not so much this property itself as the right to it (for to die in defense of a right is to uphold it) was foreign to an oppressed nation which was a satisfied to hold its property only by grace.

4. MIRACLES

There is a close connection between the need for an objective and given religion and the possibility of a belief in miracles. An event whose condition is supposed to have been its condition only on one single occasion, or a reported observation which cannot possibly be lifted into the sphere of our experience, is absolutely unthinkable by the *understanding*, and decisions in matters of experience are made in a court where the understanding is the sole judge. It cannot refrain from thinking of the event's conditions as exhaustive, even if the report of it makes no reference to data of that sort, and it thus must abstain from thinking of special and unique conditions. If proof be offered that a condition which it now envisages did not in fact condition the event in question, then it looks for others; if the improbability of every condition which ingenuity can excogitate is shown, it does not give up its claim that even if this or that condition were absent, there still must have been conditions completely determinant of the event. If it now be supposed that its fruitless quest for such conditions may be satisfied by the explanation that there is a higher Being who caused the event, then the understanding is dumb and speechless because this explanation was advanced by someone who had turned his back on it and had not addressed it.

But the *imagination* is readily satisfied on these lines, and to proffer this explanation is to cast one's self onto its field. The understanding makes no objection to this and almost laughs at it, but it has no interest in depriving imagination of its playthings, since nothing further is asked of it in connection with them. It even lowers itself to relinquish or lend its general concept of causality for use by the imagination, but it is not the understanding which operates if that concept is applied in this way. The reporter of the miracle, however, is not content with the understanding's negative attitude here; he now clamors and yells about godlessness, blasphemy, and knavery. The unbeliever remains unmoved; he sees no connection between upholding the rights of his understanding, on the one hand, and immorality and irreligion, on the other.

Now, however, the scene changes. Defenders of miracles turn to *reason* and hold up to it the great moral ends served by these miracles, the improvement and beatification of the human race. They turn to the sense of reason's impotence and kindle the flames of imagination. Reason, now helpless, can offer no resistance to these terrors and this predominance [of imagination], and in its dread it adopts the laws given to it and silences the understanding's protest. It is with this mood that the belief in miracles stands or falls. To raise questions against miracles on the understanding's ground is always futile; the outcome has always shown that nothing is achieved along those lines. Decisions in favor of miracles or against them have always depended on the interests of reason.

II. The "Oldest System-Programme" of German Idealism*

. . . *an ethic.*[21] Since the whole of metaphysics henceforth falls into *morality*[35] — Kant with his two practical postulates only gave an *example* of it and did not *exhaust* it at all — this ethics will be nothing less than a complete system of all Ideas or, which is the same thing, of all practical postulates. The first Idea is naturally the conception *of myself* as an absolutely free entity. Together with the free, self-conscious entity, a whole *world* emerges — from nothing — the only true and conceivable *creation out of nothing*. Here I shall descend to the fields of physics; the question is this: How must a world be constituted for a moral being? I would like to give wings once more to our physics, which proceeds so slowly and laboriously with its experiments. So if philosophy provides the Ideas and experience the data, we can at last get the physics on a grand scale that I expect from later generations. It does not seem as if the physics of the present can satisfy a spirit that is creative, as ours is or ought to be. I turn from nature to the *work of man*. Starting out from the Idea of mankind I will show that there is no Idea of the *state*, because the state is something *mechanical*, any more than there is an Idea of a *machine*. Only what is an object of *freedom* is called an *Idea*. Thus we must get beyond the state too! For every state inevitably treats free men as mechanical clockwork; and it should not do that; so it should *cease*. You can see for yourselves that here all the Ideas of eternal peace, etc. are simply Ideas *subordinate* to a higher Idea. At the same time I will here lay down the principles for a *history of mankind*, and strip to the skin that whole wretched work of man — state, constitution, government, legislation. Finally come the Ideas of a moral world, divinity, immortality — overthrow of all superstition, persecution of the priesthood, which in recent times simulates reason, by means of reason itself. Absolute freedom of all spirits who bear the intellectual world within themselves, and may seek neither God nor immortality *outside themselves*. Last, the Idea that unites them all, the Idea of *beauty*, taking this word in a higher,

*Translated by M. J. Inwood. This fragment, discovered in Hegel's handwriting, is variously attributed to Hegel, Hölderlin, and Schelling, who held similar views at the time of its composition in 1796 or 1797.

Platonic sense. I am now convinced that the highest act of reason, the act in which reason embraces all the Ideas, is an aesthetic act, and that *truth and goodness* become kindred *only in beauty* — the philosopher must possess just as much aesthetic power as the poet. Men without aesthetic sense are our philosophers of the letter. The philosophy of the spirit is an aesthetic philosophy. One cannot be spirited in anything, one cannot even argue about history spiritedly — without aesthetic sense. Here it should become apparent what is lacking in men who understand no Ideas, — and who confess frankly enough that everything is obscure to them as soon as it goes beyond tables and records.

Poetry thereby acquires a higher dignity; it becomes again at the end what it was at the beginning — the *teacher of mankind*; for there is no longer any philosophy, any history — the poetic art alone will survive all the other sciences and arts.

At the same time we hear it said again and again that the masses must have a *sensuous religion*. Not only the masses, the philosopher needs it too. Monotheism of reason and the heart, polytheism of the imagination and art, that is what we need!

First of all I shall here speak of an Idea that as far as I know, has not yet occurred to any man — we must have a new mythology, but this mythology must stand in the service of Ideas, it must become a mythology of *reason*.

Until we make the Ideas aesthetic — i.e., mythological — they are of no interest to the *people* and, conversely, until mythology is rational, the philosopher is inevitably ashamed of it. So at last the enlightened and the unenlightened must join hands, mythology must become philosophical and the people rational, and philosophy must become mythological in order to make philosophers sensuous. Then eternal unity reigns among us. Never the contemptuous glance, never the blind trembling of the people before its sages and priests. Then there awaits us for the first time the *equal* development of *all* powers, those of the person taken singly as well as those of all individuals. No power will be suppressed any more, then universal freedom and equality of spirits reigns! A higher spirit sent from heaven must found this new religion among us; it will be the last and greatest work of mankind.

III. Difference between the Systems of Fichte and Schelling*

PREFACE

In those few public utterances in which a feeling for the difference between Fichte's and Schelling's systems of philosophy can be recognized, the aim seems to be more to hide their distinctness or to get round it than to gain a clear awareness of it. Neither the systems as they lie before the public for direct inspection, nor among other things, Schelling's answer to Eschenmayer's idealistic objections against the philosophy of nature have brought the distinctness of the two systems out into open discussion. On the contrary, *Reinhold*, for example, is so far from an inkling of it that he takes the complete identity of both systems for granted. So his view of Schelling's system is distorted in this way too [as well as in other ways]. The occasion for the following treatise is this confusion of Reinhold's, rather than his revolution of bringing philosophy back to logic—a revolution that he has not merely threatened us with, but has proclaimed as already accomplished.

The Kantian philosophy needed to have its spirit distinguished from its letter, and to have its purely speculative principle lifted out of the remainder that belonged to, or could be used for, the arguments of reflection. In the principle of the deduction of the categories Kant's philosophy is authentic idealism; and it is this principle that Fichte extracted in a purer, stricter form and called the spirit of Kantian philosophy. The things in themselves—which are nothing but an objective expression of the empty form of opposition—had been hypostasized anew by Kant, and posited as absolute objectivity like the things of the dogmatic philosophers. On the one hand, he made the categories into static, dead pigeonholes of the intellect; and on the other hand he made them into the supreme principles capable of nullifying the language that expresses the Absolute itself—e.g., "substance" in Spinoza. Thus he allowed argumentation to go on replacing philosophy, as before, only more pretentiously than ever under the name of

*Reprinted from *The Difference between Fichte's and Schelling's System of Philosophy* by G. W. F. Hegel, translated by H. S. Harris and W. Cerf, by permission of the State University of New York Press. Translation © 1977 State University of New York.

critical philosophy. But all this springs at best from the form of the Kantian deduction of the categories, not from its principle or spirit. Indeed, if we had no part of Kant's philosophy but the deduction, the transformation of his philosophy [from speculation into reflection] would be almost incomprehensible. The principle of speculation is the identity of subject and object, and this principle is most definitely articulated in the deduction of the forms of the intellect.[52] It was Reason[51] itself that baptized this theory of the intellect.

However, Kant turns this identity itself, which is Reason, into an object of philosophical reflection, and thus this identity vanishes from its home ground. Whereas intellect had previously been handled by Reason, it is now, by contrast, Reason that is handled by the intellect. This makes clear what a subordinate stage the identity of subject and object was grasped at. The identity of subject and object is limited to twelve acts of pure thought —or rather to nine only, for modality really determines nothing objectively; the nonidentity of subject and object essentially pertains to it. Outside what is objectively determined by the categories there remained an enormous empirical realm of sensibility and perception, an absolute *a posteriori* realm. For this realm the only a priori principle discovered is a merely subjective maxim of the faculty of reflecting judgment. That is to say, nonidentity is raised to an absolute principle. Nothing else was to be expected, once the identity, i.e., the rational, had been removed from the Idea, which is the product of Reason, and the Idea had been posited in absolute opposition to being. Reason as a practical faculty had been presented as it must be conceived by finite thought, i.e., by the intellect: not as absolute identity, but in infinite opposition, as a faculty of the pure unity [typical] of the intellect. Hence there arises this contrast: there are no absolute objective determinations for the intellect [i.e., in critical philosophy], but they are present for Reason [i.e., in speculative philosophy].

The principle of Fichte's system is the pure thinking that thinks itself, the identity of subject and object, in the form Ego = Ego. If one holds solely and directly to this principle and to the transcendental principle at the basis of Kant's deduction of the categories, one has the authentic principle of speculation boldly expressed. However, as soon as [Fichte's] speculation steps outside of the concept that it establishes of itself and evolves into a system, it abandons itself and its principle and does not come back to it again. It surrenders Reason to the intellect and passes over into the chain of finite [acts and objects] of consciousness from which it never reconstructs itself again as identity and true infinity. Transcendental intuition, the very principle [of speculation], thereby assumes the awkward posture of something that is in opposition to the manifold deduced from it. The Absolute of the system shows itself as apprehended only in the form in which it appears to philosophical reflection. This determinacy which is given to the Absolute by reflection is not removed—so finitude and opposition are not removed. The principle, the Subject-Object, turns out to be a subjective Subject-Object. What is deduced from it thereby gets the form of a conditioning of pure consciousness, of the Ego = Ego; and pure consciousness itself takes on the form of something conditioned by an objective infinity, namely the temporal progression *ad infinitum*. Transcendental intuition loses itself in this infinite progression and the Ego fails to constitute itself as absolute self-intuition. Hence, Ego = Ego is transformed into the principle 'Ego *ought* to be equal to Ego.' Reason is placed in absolute opposition, i.e., it is degraded to the level of intellect, and it is this degraded Reason that becomes the principle of the shapes that the Absolute must give itself, and of the Sciences of these shapes.

These are the two sides of Fichte's system. On the one hand it has established the pure concept of Reason and of speculation and so made philosophy possible. On the other hand, it has equated Reason with pure consciousness and raised Reason as apprehended in a finite shape to the status of principle. That these two sides should be distinguished must be shown to be an inner necessity of the problem[38] itself, even though the external occasion for making the distinctions is a need of the time and is now provided by a bit of contemporary flotsam in time's stream, namely Reinhold's *Contributions* to a Survey of the State of Philosophy at the Beginning of the New Century. In these *Contributions* the aspect of authentic speculation and hence of philosophy in Fichte's system is overlooked; and so is the aspect of Schelling's system that distinguishes it from Fichte's — the distinction being that in the philosophy of nature Schelling sets the objective Subject-Object beside the subjective Subject-Object and presents both as united in something higher than the subject.

As to the need of the times, Fichte's philosophy has caused so much of a stir and has made an epoch to the extent that even those who declare themselves against it and strain themselves to get speculative systems of their own on the road, still cling to its principle, though in a more turbid and impure way, and are incapable of resisting it. The most obvious symptoms of an epoch-making system are the misunderstandings and the awkward conduct of its adversaries. However, when one can say of a system that fortune has smiled on it, it is because some widespread philosophical need, itself unable to give birth to philosophy — for otherwise it would have achieved fulfilment through the creation of a system — turns to it with an instinct-like propensity. The acceptance of the system seems to be passive but this is only because what it articulates is already present in the time's inner core and everyone will soon be proclaiming it in his sphere of science or life.

In this sense one cannot say of Fichte's system that fortune has smiled on it. While this is partly due to the unphilosophical tendencies of the age, there is something else that should also be taken into account. The greater the influence that intellect and utility succeed in acquiring, and the wider the currency of limited aims, the more powerful will the urge of the better spirit be, particularly in the more openminded world of youth. A phenomenon such as the *Speeches on Religion* may not immediately concern the speculative need. Yet they and their reception — and even more so the dignity that is beginning to be accorded, more or less clearly or obscurely, to poetry and art in general in all their true scope — indicate the need for a philosophy that will recompense nature for the mishandling that it suffered in Kant and Fichte's systems, and set Reason itself in harmony with nature, not by having Reason renounce itself or become an insipid imitator of nature, but by Reason recasting itself into nature out of its own inner strength.

This essay begins with general reflections about the need, presupposition, basic principles, etc. of philosophy. It is a fault in them that they are general reflections, but they are occasioned by the fact that presupposition, principles, and such like forms still adorn the entrance to philosophy with their cobwebs. So, up to a point it is still necessary to deal with them until the day comes when from beginning to end it is philosophy itself whose voice will be heard. Some of the more interesting of these topics will be more extensively treated elsewhere.

Jena, July 1801.

VARIOUS FORMS OCCURRING IN
CONTEMPORARY PHILOSOPHY

Historical View of Philosophical Systems

An age which has so many philosophical systems lying behind it in its past must apparently arrive at the same indifference which life acquires after it has tried all forms. The urge toward totality continues to express itself, but only as an urge toward completeness of information. Individuality becomes fossilized and no longer ventures out into life. Through the variety of what he has, the individual tries to procure the illusion of being what he is not. He refuses the living participation demanded by science, transforming it into mere information, keeping it at a distance and in purely objective shape. Deaf to all demands that he should raise himself to universality, he maintains himself imperturbably in his self-willed particularity. If indifference of this sort escalates into curiosity, it may believe nothing to be more vital than giving a name to a newly developed philosophy, expressing dominion over it by finding a name for it, just as Adam showed his dominance over the animals by giving names to them. In this way philosophy is transposed to the plane of information. Information is concerned with alien objects. In the philosophical knowledge that is only erudition, the inward totality does not bestir itself, and neutrality retains its perfect freedom [from commitment].

No philosophical system can escape the possibility of this sort of reception; every philosophical system can be treated historically. As every living form belongs at the same time to the realm of appearance, so too does philosophy. As appearance, philosophy surrenders to the power capable of transforming it into dead opinion and into something that belonged to the past from the very beginning. The living spirit that dwells in a philosophy demands to be born of a kindred spirit if it is to unveil itself. It brushes past the historical concern which is moved by some interest, to [collect] information about opinions. For this concern it is an alien phenomenon and does not reveal its own inwardness. It matters little to the spirit that it is forced to augment the extant collection of mummies and the general heap of contingent oddities; for the spirit itself slipped away between the fingers of the curious collector of information. The collector stands firm in his neutral attitude towards truth; he preserves his independence whether he accepts opinions, rejects them, or abstains from decision. He can give philosophical systems only one relation to himself: they are opinions — and such incidental things as opinions can do him no harm. He has not learned that there is truth to be had.

The history of philosophy [seems to] acquire a more useful aspect, however, when the impulse to enlarge science takes hold of it, for according to Reinhold, the history of philosophy should serve as a means "to penetrate more profoundly than ever into the spirit of philosophy, and to develop the idiosyncratic views of one's predecessors about the grounding of the reality of human cognition further in new views of one's own." Only if this sort of information concerning previous attempts to solve the problem of philosophy were available could the attempt actually succeed in the end — if mankind is fated to succeed in it at all.

As can be seen, the project of such an investigation presupposes an image of philosophy as a kind of handicraft, something that can be improved by newly invented turns of skill. Each new invention presupposes acquaintance with the turns already in use and with the purposes they serve; but after all the improvements made so far, the principal task remains. Reinhold evidently seems to think of this task as the finding of a universally valid and ultimate turn of skill such that the work completes itself automatically for anyone who can get acquainted with it. If the aim were such an invention, and if science were a lifeless product of alien ingenuity, science would indeed have the perfectibility of which mechanical arts are capable. The preceding philosophical systems would at all times be nothing but practice studies for the big brains. But if the Absolute, like Reason which is its appearance, is eternally one and the same — as indeed it is — then every Reason that is directed toward itself and comes to recognize itself, produces a true philosophy and solves for itself the problem which, like its solution, is at all times the same. In philosophy, Reason comes to know itself and deals only with itself so that its whole work and activity are grounded in itself, and with respect to the inner essence of philosophy there are neither predecessors nor successors.

Nor is it any more correct to speak of *personal views* entertained in philosophy than of its steady improvement. How could the rational be a personal idiosyncrasy? Whatever is thus peculiar in a philosophy must *ipso facto* belong to the form of the system and not to the essence of the philosophy. If something idiosyncratic actually constituted the essence of a philosophy, it would not be a philosophy, though even where the system itself declared its essence to be something idiosyncratic it could nevertheless have sprung from authentic speculation which suffered shipwreck when it tried to express itself in the form of science. One who is caught up in his own idiosyncrasy can see in others only their idiosyncrasies. If one allows personal views to have a place in essential philosophy, and if Reinhold regards what he has recently turned to as a philosophy peculiar to himself, then it is indeed possible generally to regard all preceding ways of presenting and solving the problem of philosophy as merely personal idiosyncrasies and mental exercises. But the exercises are still supposed to prepare the way for the attempt that finally succeeds — for though we see that the shores of those philosophical Islands of the Blest that we yearn for are only littered with the hulks of wrecked ships, and there is no vessel safe at anchor in their bays, yet we must not let go of the teleological perspective.

Fichte dared to assert that Spinoza could not possibly have believed in his philosophy, that he could not possibly have had a full inner living conviction; and he said of the ancients that it is even doubtful that they had a clear conception of the task of philosophy. This, too, must be explained in terms of the idiosyncratic form in which his philosophy expressed itself.

In Fichte, the peculiar form of his own system, the vigor that characterizes it as a whole produces utterances of this sort. The peculiarity of Reinhold's philosophy, on the other hand, consists in its founding and grounding concern with different philosophical views, making a great to-do about the historical investigation of their idiosyncrasies. His love of, and faith in, truth have risen to an elevation so pure and so sickening that in order to found and ground the step into the temple properly, Reinhold has built a spacious vestibule in which philosophy keeps itself so busy with analysis, with methodology and with storytelling, that it saves itself from taking the step altogether; and in the end, as a consolation for his incapacity to do philosophy, Reinhold persuades himself that the bold steps others have taken had been nothing but preparatory exercises or mental confusions.

The essence of philosophy, on the contrary, is a bottomless abyss for personal idiosyncrasy. In order to reach philosophy it is necessary to throw oneself into it *à corps perdu* — meaning by 'body' here, the sum of one's idiosyncrasies. For Reason, finding consciousness caught in particularities, only becomes philosophical speculation by raising itself to itself, putting its trust only in itself and the Absolute which at that moment becomes its object. In this process Reason stakes nothing but finitudes of consciousness. In order to overcome these finitudes and construct the Absolute in consciousness, Reason lifts itself into speculation, and in the groundlessness of the limitations and personal peculiarities it grasps its own grounding within itself. Speculation is the activity of the one universal Reason directed upon itself. Reason, therefore, does not view the philosophical systems of different epochs and different heads merely as different modes [of doing philosophy] and purely idiosyncratic views. Once it has liberated its own view from contingencies and limitations, Reason necessarily finds itself throughout all the particular forms—or else a mere manifold of the concepts and opinions of the intellect; and such a manifold is no philosophy. The true peculiarity of a philosophy lies in the interesting individuality which is the organic shape that Reason has built for itself out of the material of a particular age. The particular speculative Reason [of a later time] finds in it spirit of its spirit, flesh of its flesh, it intuits itself in it as one and the same and yet as another living being. Every philosophy is complete in itself, and like an authentic work of art, carries the totality within itself. Just as the works of Apelles or Sophocles would not have appeared to Raphael and Shakespeare—had they known them—as mere preparatory studies, but as a kindred force of the spirit, so Reason cannot regard its former shapes as merely useful preludes to itself. Virgil, to be sure, regarded Homer to be such a prelude to himself and his refined era, and for this reason Virgil's work remains a mere postlude.

The Need of Philosophy

If we look more closely at the particular form worn by a philosophy we see that it arises, on the one hand, from the living originality of the spirit whose work and spontaneity have reestablished and shaped the harmony that has been rent; and on the other hand, from the particular form of the dichotomy from which the system emerges. Dichotomy is the source of *the need of philosophy*; and as the culture of the era, it is the unfree and given aspect of the whole configuration. In [any] culture, the appearance of the Absolute has become isolated from the Absolute and fixated into independence. But at the same time the appearance cannot disown its origin, and must aim to constitute the manifold of its limitations into one whole. The intellect, as the capacity to set limits, erects a building and places it between man and the Absolute, linking everything that man thinks worthy and holy to this building, fortifying it through all the powers of nature and talent and expanding it *ad infinitum*. The entire totality of limitations is to be found in it, but not the Absolute itself. [The Absolute is] lost in the parts, where it drives the intellect in its ceaseless development of manifoldness. But in its striving to enlarge itself into the Absolute, the intellect only reproduces itself *ad infinitum* and so mocks itself. Reason reaches the Absolute only in stepping out of this manifold of parts. The more stable and splendid the edifice of the intellect is, the more restless becomes the striving of the life that is caught up in it as a part to get out of it, and raise itself to freedom. When life as Reason steps away into the distance, the totality of limitations is at the same time nullified, and connected with the Absolute in this nullification, and hence conceived and posited as mere appearance. The split between the Absolute and the totality of limitations vanishes.

The intellect copies Reason's absolute positing and through the form [of absolute positing] it gives itself the semblance of Reason even though the posits are in themselves opposites, and hence finite. The semblance grows that much stronger when intellect transforms and fixes Reason's negating activity [as distinct from its positing activity] into a product. The infinite, insofar as it gets opposed to the finite, is a thing of this kind, i.e., it is something rational as posited by the intellect. Taken by itself, as something rational, it merely expresses the negating of the finite. By fixing it, the intellect sets it up in absolute opposition to the finite; and reflection which had risen to the plane of Reason when it suspended the finite, now lowers itself again to being intellect because it has fixed Reason's activity into [an activity of] opposition. Moreover, reflection still pretends to be rational even in its relapse.

The cultures of various times have established opposites of this kind, which were supposed to be products of Reason and absolutes, in various ways, and the intellect has labored over them as such. Antitheses such as spirit and matter, soul and body, faith and intellect, freedom and necessity, etc. used to be important; and in more limited spheres they appeared in a variety of other guises. The whole weight of human interests hung upon them. With the progress of culture they have passed over into such forms as the antithesis of Reason and sensibility, intelligence and nature and, with respect to the universal concept, of absolute subjectivity and absolute objectivity.

The sole interest of Reason is to suspend such rigid antitheses. But this does not mean that Reason is altogether opposed to opposition and limitation. For the necessary dichotomy is one factor in life. Life eternally forms itself by setting up oppositions, and totality at the highest pitch of living energy is only possible through its own re-establishment out of the deepest fission. What Reason opposes, rather, is just the absolute fixity which the intellect gives to the dichotomy; and it does so all the more if the absolute opposites themselves originated in Reason.

When the might of union vanishes from the life of men and the antitheses lose their living connection and reciprocity and gain independence, the need of philosophy arises. From this point of view the need is contingent. But with respect to the given dichotomy the need is the necessary attempt to suspend the rigidified opposition between subjectivity and objectivity; to comprehend the achieved existence of the intellectual and real world as a becoming. Its being as a product must be comprehended as a producing. In the infinite activity of becoming and producing, Reason has united what was sundered and it has reduced the absolute dichotomy to a relative one, one that is conditioned by the original identity. When, where and in what forms such self-reproductions of reason occur as philosophies is contingent. This contingency must be comprehended on the basis of the Absolute positing itself as an objective totality. The contingency is temporal insofar as the objectivity of the Absolute is intuited as a going forth in time. But insofar as it makes its appearance as spatial compresence, the dichotomy is a matter of regional climate. In the form of fixed reflection, as a world of thinking and thought essence in antithesis to a world of actuality, this dichotomy falls into the Northwest.

As culture grows and spreads, and the development of those outward expressions of life into which dichotomy can entwine itself becomes more manifold, the power of dichotomy becomes greater, its regional sanctity is more firmly established and the strivings of life to give birth once more to its harmony become more meaningless, more alien to the cultural whole. Such few attempts as there have been on behalf of the cultural whole against more recent culture, like the more significant beautiful embodiments of far away or long ago, have only been able to arouse that modicum of attention which remains possible when the more profound, serious connection of living art [to culture as a living whole] can no longer be understood. The entire system of relations constituting life has become detached from art, and thus the concept of art's all-embracing coherence has been lost, and transformed into the concept either of superstition or of entertainment. The highest aesthetic perfection, as it evolves in a determinate religion in which man lifts himself above all dichotomy and sees both the freedom of the subject and the necessity of the object vanish in the kingdom of grace, could only be energized up to a certain stage of culture, and within general or mob barbarism. As it progressed, civilization has split away from it [i.e., this aesthetic religious perfection], and juxtaposed it to itself or vice-versa. Because the intellect has grown sure of itself, both [intellect and the aesthetic religious perfection] have come to enjoy a measure of mutual peace by separating into realms that are completely set apart from one another. What happens in one has no significance in the other.

However, the intellect can also be directly attacked by Reason in its own realm. These attempts to nullify the dichotomy, and hence the absoluteness of intellect, through reflection itself are easier to understand. Dichotomy felt itself attacked, and so turned with hate and fury against Reason, until the realm of the intellect rose to such power that it could regard itself as secure from Reason. — But just as we often say of virtue that the greatest witness for its reality is the semblance that hypocrisy borrows from it, so intellect cannot keep Reason off. It seeks to protect itself against the feeling of its inner emptiness, and from the secret fear that plagues anything limited, by whitewashing its particularities with a semblance of Reason. The contempt for Reason shows itself most strongly, not in Reason's being freely scorned and abused, but by the boasting of the limited that it has mastered philosophy and lives in amity with it. Philosophy must refuse friendship with these false attempts that boast insincerely of having nullified the particularities, but which issue from limitation, and use philosophy as a means to save and secure these limitations.

In the struggle of the intellect with Reason the intellect has strength only to the degree that Reason forsakes itself. Its success in the struggle therefore depends upon Reason itself, and upon the authenticity of the need for the reconstitution of totality, the need from which Reason emerges.

The need of philosophy can be called the *presupposition* of philosophy if philosophy, which begins with itself, has to be furnished with some sort of vestibule; and there has been much talk nowadays about an absolute presupposition. What is called the presupposition of philosophy is nothing else but the need that has come to utterance. Once uttered, the need is posited for reflection, so that [because of the very nature of reflection] there must be two presuppositions.

One is the Absolute itself. It is the goal that is being sought; but it is already present, or how otherwise could it be sought? Reason produces it, merely by freeing consciousness from its limitations. This suspension of the limitations is conditioned by the presupposed unlimitedness.

The other presupposition may be taken to be that consciousness has stepped out of the totality, that is, it may be taken to be the split into being and not-being, concept and being, finitude and infinity. From the standpoint of the dichotomy, the absolute synthesis is a beyond, it is the undetermined and the shapeless as opposed to the determinacies of the dichotomy. The Absolute is the night, and the light is younger than it; and the distinction between them, like the emergence of the light out of the night, is an absolute difference — the nothing is the first out of which all being, all the manifoldness of the finite has emerged. But the task of philosophy consists in uniting these presuppositions: to posit being in non-being, as becoming; to posit dichotomy in the Absolute, as its appearance; to posit the finite in the infinite, as life.

Still, it is clumsy to express the need of philosophy as a presupposition of philosophy, for the need acquires in this way a reflective form. This reflective form appears as contradictory propositions, which we shall discuss below. One may require of propositions that they be justified. But the justification of these propositions as presuppositions is still not supposed to be philosophy itself, so that the founding and grounding gets going before, and outside of, philosophy.

Reflection as Instrument of Philosophizing

The form that the need of philosophy would assume, if it were to be expressed as a presupposition, allows for a transition from the need of philosophy to the *instrument of philosophizing*, to *reflection* as Reason. The task of philosophy is to construct the Absolute for consciousness. But since the productive activity of reflection is, like its products, mere limitation, this task involves a contradiction. The Absolute is to be posited in reflection. But then it is not posited, but cancelled; for in having been posited it was limited [by its opposite]. Philosophical reflection is the mediation of this contradiction. What must be shown above all is how far reflection is capable of grasping the Absolute, and how far in its speculative activity it carries with it the necessity and possibility of being synthesized with absolute intuition. To what extent can reflection be as complete for itself, subjectively, as its product must be, which is constructed in consciousness as the Absolute that is both conscious and non-conscious at the same time?

Reflection in isolation is the positing of opposites, and this would be a suspension of the Absolute, reflection being the faculty of being and limitation. But reflection as Reason has connection with the Absolute, and it is Reason only because of this connection. In this respect, reflection nullifies itself and all being and everything limited, because it connects them with the Absolute. But at the same time the limited gains standing precisely on account of its connection with the Absolute.

Reason presents itself as the force of the negative Absolute, and hence as a negating that is absolute; and at the same time, it presents itself as the force that posits the opposed objective and subjective totality. Reason raises the intellect above itself, driving it toward a whole of the intellect's own kind. Reason seduces the intellect into producing an objective totality. Every being, because it is posited, is an opposite, it is conditioned and conditioning. The intellect completes these its limitations by positing the opposite limitations as conditions. These need to be completed in the same way, so the intellect's task expands *ad infinitum*. In all this, reflection appears to be merely intellect, but this guidance toward the totality of necessity is the contribution and secret efficacy of Reason. Reason makes the intellect boundless, and in this infinite wealth the intellect and its objective world meet their downfall. For every being that the intellect produces is something determinate, and the determinate has an indeterminate before it and after it. The manifoldness of being lies between two nights, without support. It rests on nothing—for the indeterminate is nothing to the intellect—and it ends in nothing. The determinate and the indeterminate, finitude and the infinite that is to be given up for lost, are not united. The intellect stubbornly allows them to subsist side by side in their opposition. And stubbornly it holds fast to being as against not-being; yet being and not-being are equally necessary to it. The intellect essentially aims at thoroughgoing determination. But what is determinate for it is at once bounded by an indeterminate. Thus its positings and determinings never accomplish the task; in the very positing and determining that have occurred there lies a non-positing and something indeterminate, and hence the task of positing and determining recurs perpetually.

If the intellect fixes these opposites, the finite and the infinite, so that both are supposed to subsist together as opposed to each other, then it destroys itself. For the opposition of finite and infinite means that to posit the one is to cancel the other. When Reason recognizes this, it has suspended the intellect itself. Its positing then appears to Reason to be non-positing, its products to be negations. If Reason is placed in opposition to the objective infinite, this nullification of the intellect or Reason's pure positing without oppositing is subjective infinity: the realm of freedom as opposed to the objective world. But in this form, the realm of freedom is itself something opposite and conditioned. In order to suspend opposition absolutely, Reason must also nullify the independence of this realm. It nullifies both of the opposed realms by uniting them; for they only are in virtue of their not being united. Within the union, however, they subsist together; for what is opposite and therefore limited is, in this union, connected with the Absolute. But it does not have standing on its own account, but only insofar as it is posited in the Absolute, that is, as identity. The limited is either necessary or free, according to whether it belongs to one or the other of the mutually opposed and therefore relative totalities. Insofar as the limited belongs to the synthesis of both totalities, its limitation ceases: it is free and necessary at the same time, conscious and nonconscious. This conscious identity of the finite and infinite, the union of both worlds, the sensuous and the intelligible, the necessary and the free, in consciousness, is *knowledge*. Reflection, the faculty of the finite, and the infinite opposed to it are synthesized in Reason whose infinity embraces the finite within it.

So far as reflection makes itself its own object, its supreme law, given to it by Reason and moving it to become Reason, is to nullify itself. Like everything else, reflection has standing only in the Absolute; but as reflection it stands in opposition to it. In order to gain standing, therefore, reflection must give itself the law of self-destruction. The immanent law, the law through which reflection by its own power would constitute itself as absolute, would be the law of contradiction: namely that, being posited, reflection shall be and remain posited. Reflection would thus fix its products as absolutely opposed to the Absolute. It would have as its eternal law to remain intellect and not to become Reason and to hold fast to its own work, which, as limited, is opposed to the Absolute and as opposed to the Absolute, is nothing.

When placed in an opposition, Reason operates as intellect and its infinity becomes subjective. Similarly, the form which expresses the activity of reflecting as an activity of thinking, is capable of this very same ambiguity and misuse. Thinking is the absolute activity of Reason itself and there simply cannot be anything opposite to it. But if it is not so posited, if it is taken to be nothing but reflection of a purer kind, that is, a reflection in which one merely abstracts from the opposition, then thinking of this abstracting kind cannot advance beyond the intellect, not even to a Logic supposed capable of comprehending Reason within itself, still less to philosophy. Reinhold sets up identity as "the essence or inward character of thinking as such": "the infinite repeatability of one and the same as one and the same, in and through one and the same." One might be tempted by this semblance of identity into regarding this thinking as Reason. But because this thinking has its antithesis (a) in an application of thinking and (b) in absolute materiality, it is clear that this is not the absolute identity, the identity of subject and object which suspends both in their opposition and grasps them within itself, but a *pure* identity, that is, an identity originating through abstraction and conditioned by opposition, the abstract intellectual concept of unity, one of a pair of fixed opposites.

Reinhold sees the fault of all past philosophy in "the habit, so deeply rooted and widespread among contemporary philosophers, of regarding thinking both in general and in its application as something merely subjective." If Reinhold were truly serious about the identity and non-subjectivity of this thinking, he could not make any distinction between thinking and its application. If thinking is true identity, and not something subjective, where could this application that is so distinct from it come from, let alone the stuff that is postulated for the sake of the application? To the analytic method an activity must appear to be synthetic precisely because it is to be analysed. The elements that originate in the analysis are unity and a manifold opposed to it. What analysis presents as unity is called subjective; and thinking is characterized as a unity of this sort opposed to the manifold, that is, it is an abstract identity. In this way thinking has become something purely limited, and its activity is an application [of the identity] to some independently extant material, an application which conforms to a law and is directed by a rule, but which cannot pierce through to knowledge.

Only so far as reflection has connection with the Absolute is it Reason and its deed a knowing. Through this connection with the Absolute, however, reflection's work passes away; only the connection persists, and it is the sole reality of the cognition. There is therefore no truth in isolated reflection, in pure thinking, save the truth of its nullification. But because in philosophizing the Absolute gets produced by reflection for consciousness, it becomes thereby an objective totality, a whole of knowledge, an organization of cognitions. Within this organization, every part is at the same time the whole; for its standing is its connection with the Absolute. As a part that has other parts outside of it, it is something limited, and is only through the others. Isolated in its limitation the part is defective; meaning and significance it has solely through its coherence with the whole. Hence, single concepts by themselves and singular cognitions[19] must not be called knowledge.[60] There can be plenty of singular empirical known items. As known from experience they exhibit their justification in experience, that is, in the identity of concept and being, of subject and object. Precisely for this reason, they are not scientific knowledge: they find their justification only in a limited, relative identity. They do not justify themselves as necessary parts of a totality of cognitions organized in consciousness, nor has speculation recognized the absolute identity in them, i.e., their connection with the Absolute.

Relation of Speculation to Common Sense

What the so-called common sense takes to be the rational, consists similarly of single items drawn out of the Absolute into consciousness. They are points of light that rise out of the night of totality and aid men to get through life in an intelligent way. They serve as correct standpoints from which one takes off and to which one returns.

In fact, however, men only have this confidence in the truth of these points of light because they have a feeling of the Absolute attending these points; and it is this feeling alone that gives them their significance. As soon as one takes these truths of common sense by themselves and isolates them as cognitions of the intellect, they look odd and turn into half-truths. Reflection can confound common sense. When common sense permits itself to reflect, the proposition it states for the benefit of reflection claims to be by itself knowledge and valid cognition. Thus sound sense has given up its strength, the strength of supporting its pronouncements and counteracting unsteady reflection solely by the obscure totality which is present as feeling. Although common sense expresses itself for reflection, its dicta do not contain the consciousness of their connection with the absolute totality. The totality remains inward and unexpressed.

For this reason, speculation understands sound intellect well enough, but the sound intellect cannot understand what speculation is doing. Speculation acknowledges as the reality of cognition only the being of cognition in the totality. For speculation everything determinate has reality and truth only in the cognition of its connection with the Absolute. So it recognizes the Absolute in what lies at the basis of the pronouncements of sound sense too. But since, for speculation, cognition has reality only within the Absolute, what is cognized and known in the reflective mode of expression and therefore has a determinate form, becomes nothing in the presence of speculation. The relative identities of common sense which pretend to absoluteness in the limited form in which they appear, become contingencies for philosophical reflection. Common sense cannot grasp how what has immediate certainty for it, can at the same time be nothing to philosophy. For in its immediate truths it only feels their connection with the Absolute, and it does not separate this feeling from their appearance, wherein they are limitations, and yet they are supposed as such to have standing and absolute being. But in the face of speculation they vanish.

Common sense cannot understand speculation; and what is more, it must come to hate speculation when it has experience of it; and, unless it is in the state of perfect indifference that security confers, it is bound to detest and persecute it. For common sense, the essential and the contingent in its utterances are identical and this identity is absolute; and, just as it cannot separate the limits of appearance from the Absolute, so what it does separate in its consciousness, becomes absolutely opposed, and what it cognizes as limited it cannot in consciousness unite with the unlimited. Limited and unlimited are, to be sure, identical for common sense, but this identity is and remains something internal, a feeling, something unknown and unexpressed. Whenever it calls the limited to mind, and the limited is raised into consciousness, the unlimited is for consciousness absolutely opposed to the limited.

In this relation or connection of the limited with the Absolute there is consciousness of their opposition only; there is no consciousness at all of their identity. This relation is called *faith*. Faith does not express the synthesis inherent in feeling or intuition. It is, rather, a relation of reflection to the Absolute, and one in which reflection is certainly Reason. But though it nullifies itself as something that sunders and is sundered, and also nullifies its product too — an individual consciousness — it still preserves the form of sundering. The immediate certitude of faith, which has been much talked of as the ultimate and highest consciousness, is nothing but the identity itself, Reason, which, however does not recognize itself, and is accompanied by the consciousness of opposition. Speculation, however, lifts the identity of which sound sense is not conscious into consciousness. In other words, speculation constructs conscious identity out of what, in the consciousness of the ordinary intellect, are necessarily opposites; and this synthesis of what is sundered in faith is an abomination to faith. In its consciousness the holy and the divine only have standing as objects. So the healthy intellect sees only destruction of the divine in the suspended opposition, in the identity brought into consciousness.

In particular, ordinary common sense is bound to see nothing but nullification in those philosophical systems that satisfy the demand for conscious identity by suspending dichotomy in such a way that one of the opposites is raised to be the absolute and the other nullified. This is particularly offensive if the culture of the time has already fixed one of the opposites otherwise. Speculation, as philosophy, has here indeed suspended the opposition, but speculation, as system, has elevated something which in its ordinary familiar form is limited, to absolute status. The only aspect here relevant is the speculative, and this is simply not present for ordinary common sense. Viewed from this speculative aspect, the limited is something totally different from what it appears to ordinary common sense; having been elevated into being the Absolute, it is no longer the limited thing that it was. The matter of the materialist is no longer inert matter which has life as its opposite and its formative agent; the Ego of the idealist is no longer an empirical consciousness which, as limited, must posit an infinite outside itself. The question that philosophy has to raise is whether the system has truly purified all finitude out of the finite appearance that it has advanced to absolute status; or whether speculation, even at its furthest distance from ordinary common sense with its typical fixation of opposites, has not still succumbed to the fate of its time, the fate of positing absolutely one form of the Absolute, that is, something that is essentially an opposite. But even where speculation has actually succeeded in freeing from all forms of appearance the finite which it has made infinite, ordinary common sense primarily takes offense over the name though it may take no other notice of the business of speculation. Speculation does indeed elevate finite things — matter, the Ego — to the infinite and thus nullifies them: matter and Ego so far as they are meant to embrace totality, are no longer matter and Ego. Yet the final act or philosophical reflection is still lacking: that is to say, the consciousness of the nullification of these finite things. And even though the Absolute within the system has still preserved a determinate form, in spite of the fact that this nullification has actually been accomplished, still the genuinely speculative tendency is unmistakable anyway. But ordinary common sense understands nothing about it, and does not even see the philosophic principle of suspending the dichotomy. It only sees the systematic principle by which one of the opposites is raised to the Absolute and the other nullified. So it has an advantage over the system with respect to the dichotomy. For there is an absolute opposition present in both of them. But in ordinary common sense there is *completeness* of opposition [whereas the system makes one of the opposites explicitly absolute]; and hence common sense is enraged on two counts.

Nevertheless, apart from its philosophical side, there accrues to a philosophical system of this kind, encumbered as it is with the defect of raising to the Absolute something that is still in some respect an opposite, another advantage and a further merit, which are not only incomprehensible but must be abhorrent to the ordinary intellect. The advantage is that by raising something finite to an infinite principle, the system has struck down with one stroke the whole mass of finitudes that adhere to the opposite principle. And the merit with regard to culture consists in having made the dichotomy that much more rigid and hence strengthened the urge toward unification in totality in the same measure.

Common sense is stubborn; it stubbornly believes itself secure in the force of its inertia, believes the non-conscious secure in its primordial gravity and opposition to consciousness; believes matter secure against the difference that light brings into it just in order to reconstruct the difference into a new synthesis at a higher level. In northern climates this stubborness perhaps requires a longer period of time to be so far conquered that the atomic matter itself has become more diversified, and inertia has first been set in motion on its own ground by a greater variety of their combination and dissolution and next by the multitude of fixed atoms thus generated. Thus the human intellect becomes more and more confused in its own proper doings and knowings, to the point where it makes itself capable of enduring the suspension of this confusion and the opposition itself.

The only aspect of speculation visible to common sense is its nullifying activity; and even this nullification is not visible in its entire scope. If common sense could grasp this scope, it would not believe speculation to be its enemy. For in its highest synthesis of the conscious and the non-conscious, speculation also demands the nullification of consciousness itself. Reason thus drowns itself and its knowledge and its reflection of the absolute identity, in its own abyss: and in this night of mere reflection and of the calculating intellect, in this night which is the noonday of life, common sense and speculation can meet one another.

Principle of a Philosophy in the Form of an Absolute Basic Proposition

Philosophy, as a totality of knowledge produced by reflection, becomes a system, that is, an organic whole of concepts, whose highest law is not the intellect, but Reason. The intellect has to exhibit correctly the opposites of what it has posited, as well as its bounds, ground and condition. Reason, on the other hand, unites these contradictories, posits both together and suspends them both. One might demand that the system as an organization of propositions should present the Absolute which lies at the basis of reflection in the fashion of reflection, that is, as the highest, or absolutely fundamental proposition. But such a demand at once entails its own nullity. For a proposition, as something posited by reflection, is something limited and conditioned on its own account. It requires another proposition as its foundation, and so on *ad infinitum*. Suppose that the Absolute is expressed in a fundamental proposition, validated by and for thinking, a proposition whose form and matter are the same. Then either mere sameness is posited, and the inequality of form and matter is excluded, so that the fundamental proposition is conditioned by this inequality. In this case the fundamental proposition is not absolute but defective; it expresses only a concept of the intellect, an abstraction. Or else the fundamental proposition also contains both form and matter as inequality, so that it is analytic and synthetic simultaneously. In that case the fundamental proposition is an antinomy, and therefore not a proposition. As a proposition it is subject to the law of the intellect, the law that it must not contradict itself, that it cannot suspend itself, that it be something posited. As an antinomy, however, it does suspend itself.

It is a delusion that something merely posited for reflection must necessarily stand at the summit of a system as the highest or absolute and basic proposition; or that the essence of any system is expressible as a proposition that has absolute validity for thinking. This delusion makes the business of judging a system easy. For of any thought expressed by a proposition it can be shown very easily that it is conditioned by an opposite and therefore is not absolute: and one proves for this opposite that it must be posited, hence that the thought expressed by the fundamental proposition is a nullity. The delusion accounts itself all the more justified if the system itself expresses the Absolute which is its principle, in the form of a proposition or definition which is basically an antinomy, and for this reason suspends itself as something posited for mere reflection. For example, Spinoza's concept of substance, defined as both cause and effect, concept and being, ceases to be a concept because the opposites are united in a contradiction.

No philosophical beginning could look worse than to begin with a definition as Spinoza does. This offers the starkest contrast to 'founding and grounding,' or the 'deduction of the principles of knowledge,' or the laborious reduction of all philosophy to the 'highest facts of consciousness,' etc. But when Reason has purified itself of the subjectivity of reflection, then Spinoza's artlessness which makes philosophy begin with philosophy itself, and Reason come forward at once with an antinomy, can be properly appreciated too.

If the principle of philosophy is to be stated in formal propositions for reflection, the only thing that is present, at the outset, as the object of this task is knowledge, i.e., in general terms the synthesis of the subjective and objective, or absolute thinking. But reflection cannot express the absolute synthesis in one proposition, if this proposition has to be valid as a proper proposition for the intellect. Reflection must separate what is one in the absolute Identity; it must express synthesis and antithesis separately, in two propositions, one containing the identity, the other dichotomy.

In A = A, as principle of identity, it is connectedness that is reflected on, and in this connecting, this being one, the equality, is contained in this pure identity; reflection abstracts from all inequality. A = A, the expression of absolute thought or Reason, has only one meaning for the formal reflection that expresses itself in the propositions of the intellect. This is the meaning of pure unity as conceived by the intellect, or in other words a unity in abstraction from opposition.

Reason, however, does not find itself expressed in this onesidedness of abstract unity. It postulates also the positing of what in the pure equality had been abstracted from, the positing of the opposite, of inequality. One A is subject, the other object; and the expression of their difference is A ≠ A, or A = B. This proposition directly contradicts the first. It abstracts from pure identity and posits the non-identity, the pure form of non-thinking, just as the first proposition is the form of pure thinking, which is not the same thing as absolute thinking, or Reason. Only because non-thinking too, is thought, only because A ≠ A is posited through thinking, can it be posited at all. In A ≠ A, or A = B there also is the identity, the connection, the " = " of the first proposition, but it is here only subjective, that is, only insofar as non-thinking is posited by thinking. But if non-thinking is posited for thinking this is entirely incidental to the non-thinking, it is a mere form for the second proposition. One must abstract from this form in order to have its matter pure.

This second proposition is as unconditioned as the first and *qua* unconditioned it is condition of the first, as the first is condition of the second. The first is conditioned by the second in that it is what it is through abstraction from the inequality that the second proposition contains; the second conditioned by the first, in that it is in need of a connection in order to be a proposition.

The second proposition has also been stated in the subordinate form of the principle of sufficient reason. Or rather, it was first brought down to this extremely subordinate meaning when it was turned into the principle of causality. A has a ground means: to A pertains an existence that is not an existence of A: A is a being posited that is not the being posited of A. Hence, A ≠ A, A = B. If one abstracts from A's being something posited, as one must in order to have the second proposition in its purity, it expresses A's not being posited. To posit A as something posited and also as something not posited is already the synthesis of the first and second proposition.

Both propositions are principles of contradiction, but in an inverse sense. The first, the principle of identity, states that contradiction is = 0. The second proposition, insofar as one relates it to the first, states that contradiction is as necessary as non-contradiction. Taken separately[6] both propositions are posits on the same level. [But] if the second one is so stated that the first proposition is connected with it at the same time, then it is the highest possible expression of Reason by the intellect. This connection of the two propositions expresses the antinomy; and as an antinomy, as an expression of the absolute identity, it makes no difference whether we posit A = A or A = B as long as each of them, A = B and A = A, is taken as connection of both propositions. A = A contains the difference of A as subject and A as object together with their identity, just as A = B contains the identity of A and B together with their difference.

The intellect has not grown into Reason if it does not recognize the antinomy in the principle of sufficient reason which is a connection of both propositions. In that case the second proposition is not, *formaliter*, a new one for it: for the mere intellect A = B does not say more than the first proposition and consequently it conceives A's being posited as B only as a repetition of A. That is to say, the intellect just holds fast to the identity and abstracts from the fact that when A is repeated as B or as posited in B, something else, a non-A, is posited and posited as A, hence, A is posited as non-A. If one reflects only on the formal aspect of speculation and holds fast to the synthesis of knowledge [only] in analytic form, then antinomy, that is, the contradiction that cancels itself, is the highest formal expression of knowledge and truth.

Once antinomy is acknowledged as the explicit formula of truth, Reason has brought the formal essence of reflection under its control. The formal essence still has the upper hand, however, if thought, [conceived merely] in its character of abstract unity, i.e., exclusively in the form of the first proposition as opposed to the second, is posited as the first truth of philosophy, and a system of the reality of cognition is supposed to be erected by analysis of the application of thinking. In that case, the entire course of this purely analytic business will be as follows:

Thought, as infinite repeatability of A as A, is an abstraction, the first proposition expressed as activity. But now the second proposition is lacking, the non-thought. There must necessarily be a transition to it as the condition of the first; it, too, i.e., the matter, must be posited. Then the opposites will be complete; the transition from the first to the second is a certain kind of reciprocal connection between them, which is a very inadequate synthesis called an application of thought. But even this weak synthesis goes counter to the presupposition that thought is a positing of A as A *ad infinitum*. For in the *application*, A is at the same time posited as non-A; and thought, in its absolute standing as infinite repetition of A as A, is suspended.

What is opposite to thought is, through its connection with thought, determined as something thought = A. But such a thought, such a positing = A is conditioned by an abstraction and is hence something opposite. Hence, that which is thought, besides the fact that it has been thought = A, has still other determinations = B, entirely independent of being merely determined [as something thought] by pure thought. These other determinations are brute data for thought. Hence for thought as the principle of the analytic way of philosophizing, there must be an absolute stuff. We shall discuss this further below. With this absolute opposition as foundation the formal programme, in which the famous discovery that philosophy must be reduced to logic consists, is allowed no immanent synthesis save that provided by the identity of the intellect, i.e., the repetition of A *ad infinitum*. But even for this repetition the identity needs some B, C, etc. in which the repeated A can be posited. In order for A to be repeatable, B, C, D, etc. have to be a manifold, in which each is opposed to the other. Each of them has particular determinations not posited by A. That is to say, there exists an absolutely manifold stuff. Its B, C, D, etc. must *fit in* with A, as best it can. This fitting in without rhyme or reason takes the place of an original identity. The basic fault can be presented as follows. There is no reflection, in respect to form, on the antinomy of the A = A and A = B. This whole analytic approach lacks the basic consciousness that the purely formal appearance of the Absolute is contradiction. Such consciousness can only come into being where speculation takes its point of departure in Reason and in the $A = A$ as absolute identity of subject and object.

Transcendental Intuition

When speculation is viewed from the standpoint of mere reflection, the absolute identity appears in syntheses of opposites, i.e., in antinomies. The relative identities into which absolute identity differentiates itself are limited to be sure; they belong to the intellect and are not antinomic. At the same time, however, since they are identities, they are not pure concepts of the intellect. And they must be identities because nothing can stand as posited in a philosophy unless it is connected with the Absolute. But on the side of its connection with the Absolute, everything limited is a (relative) identity and hence something that is antinomic for reflection. —And this is the negative side of knowing, the formal aspect which, ruled by Reason, destroys itself. Besides this negative side knowing has a positive side, namely intuition. Pure knowing, which would be knowing without intuition, is the nullification of the opposites in contradiction. Intuition without this synthesis of opposites, [on the other hand,] is empirical, given, nonconscious. Transcendental knowledge unites both reflection and intuition. It is at once concept and being. Because intuition becomes transcendental, the identity of the subjective and objective, which are separated in empirical intuition, enters consciousness. Knowledge, insofar as it becomes transcendental, posits not merely the concept and its condition—or the antinomy of both, the subjective—but at the same time the objective, that is, being.

In philosophical knowledge, what is intuited is an activity of both intelligence and nature, of consciousness and the unconscious together. It belongs to both worlds at once, the ideal and the real. It belongs to the ideal world because it is posited in the intelligence and, hence, in freedom. It belongs to the real world because it gets its place in the objective totality, it is deduced as a link in the chain of necessity. If we take up the standpoint of reflection or freedom, the ideal is the first, and essence and being are only schematized intelligence. If we take up the standpoint of necessity or being, thought is only a schema of absolute being. In transcendental knowledge both being and intelligence are united. Likewise, transcendental knowledge and transcendental intuition are one and the same. The variation of expression merely indicates the prevalence of the ideal or real factor.

It is of the profoundest significance that it has been affirmed with so much seriousness that one cannot philosophize without transcendental intuition. For what would this be, philosophizing without intuition? One would disperse oneself endlessly in absolute finitudes. Whether these finitudes are subjective concepts or objective things and even though one may pass from one to the other, philosophizing without intuition moves along an endless chain of finitudes, and the transition from being to concept or from concept to being is an unjustified leap. Philosophizing of this sort is called formal. For thing as well as concept is, each taken by itself, just a form of the Absolute. Formal philosophizing presupposes destruction of the transcendental intuition, an absolute opposition of being and concept. If it talks of the unconditioned, it converts even that into something formal, say the form of an Idea that is opposed to Being for instance. The better the method, the more glaring the results. To speculation, [on the contrary,] the finitudes are radii of the infinite focus which irradiates them at the same time that it is formed by them. In the radii the focus is posited and in the focus the radii. In the transcendental intuition all opposition is suspended, all distinction between the universe as constructed by and for the intelligence, and the universe as an organization intuited as objective and appearing independent, is nullified. Speculation produces the consciousness of this identity, and because ideality and reality are one in it, it is intuition.

Postulates of Reason

As a work of reflection the synthesis of the two opposites posited by reflection required its completion; as antinomy that suspends itself, it needs its standing in intuition. Speculative knowledge has to be conceived as identity of reflection and intuition. So if one posits only the share of reflection, which, as rational, is antinomic, but stands in a necessary connection with intuition, one can in that case say of intuition that it is postulated by reflection. Postulating Ideas is out of the question; for Ideas are the products of Reason or rather, they are the rational, posited as a product by the intellect. The rational must be deduced in its determinate content, that is, it must be deduced starting from the contradiction of determinate opposites, the rational being their synthesis. The only thing that can be postulated is the intuition that fills and sustains this antinomic aspect. This sort of 'Idea' that used to get postulated, is the 'infinite progress,' which is a mixture of empirical and rational elements: the intuition of time is empirical, while the suspension of all time, its expansion to infinity is rational. But in the empirical progress, time is not purely infinitized, for in this progress time is supposed to have standing as something finite, as limited moments. It is an empirical infinitude. The true antinomy which posits both the limited and unlimited, not just side by side but together as identical, must *ipso facto* suspend the opposition. The antinomy postulates the determinate intuition of time, and this determinate intuition must be both the limited moment of the present and the unlimitedness of the moment's being self-externalized. That is to say, it must be eternity. —

It is equally impossible to postulate intuition as something that is opposed to the Idea or rather, to the necessary antinomy. The intuition that is opposed to the Idea is a limited existent, precisely because it excludes the

Idea. Intuition is indeed postulated by Reason, but not as something limited; it is postulated in order to complement the onesidedness of the work of reflection in such a way that the intuitive complement does not remain opposed to reflection but is one with it. In general one can see that this whole manner of postulating has its sole ground in the fact that the onesidedness of reflection is accepted as a starting point. This onesidedness requires, as the complement of its deficiency, the postulation of the opposite that is excluded from it. But this point of view places the essence of Reason in distorted perspective, for it here appears as something that is not self-sufficient but needy. When Reason recognizes itself as absolute, however, philosophy begins where reflection and its style of thinking ends, that is, it begins with the identity of Idea and Being. Philosophy does not have to postulate one of the opposites for in positing absoluteness it immediately posits both Idea and Being, and the absoluteness of Reason is nothing else but the identity of both.

Relation of Philosophizing to a Philosophical System

The need of philosophy can satisfy itself by simply penetrating to the principle of nullifying all fixed opposition and connecting the limited to the Absolute. This satisfaction found in the principle of absolute identity is characteristic of philosophy as such. [For a philosophizing that did no more than this] the known, as to its content, would be something contingent; the dichotomies, from whose nullification the known emerged, would have been given and would have vanished, but they would not themselves be reconstructed syntheses. The content of such philosophizing would have no internal coherence and would not constitute an objective totality of knowledge. But the philosophizing would not necessarily be abstract reasoning simply on account of the incoherence of its content. Abstract reasoning only disperses the posited into ever greater manifoldness; thrown into this stream the intellect drifts without an anchor, yet the whole extension of its manifold is supposed to stand fast unanchored. For true philosophizing on the other hand, even though it may be incoherent, the posited and its opposites disappear because it does not simply put them in context with other finite things, but connects them with the Absolute and so suspends them.

Since the finite things are a manifold, the connection of the finite to the Absolute is a manifold. Hence, philosophizing must aim to posit this manifold as internally connected, and there necessarily arises the need to produce a totality of knowing, a system of science. As a result, the manifold of these connections finally frees itself from contingency: they get their places in the context of the objective totality of knowledge and their objective completeness is accomplished. The philosophizing that does not construct itself into a system is a constant flight from limitations—it is Reason's struggle for freedom rather than the pure self-cognition of Reason that has become secure in itself and clear about itself. Free Reason and its action are one, and Reason's activity is a pure self-exposition.

In this self-production of Reason the Absolute shapes itself into an objective totality, which is a whole in itself held fast and complete, having no ground outside itself, but founded by itself in its beginning, middle and end. A whole of this sort appears as an organization of propositions and intuitions. Every synthesis of Reason is united in speculation with the intuition corresponding to it; as identity of the conscious and non-conscious it is for itself in the Absolute and infinite. But at the same time, the synthesis is finite and limited, insofar as it is posited within the objective totality and has other syntheses outside itself. The identity that is least dichotomous—at the objective pole, matter, at the subjective pole, feeling (self-consciousness)—is at the same time an infinitely opposed identity, a thoroughly relative identity. Reason, the faculty of totality (*qua* objective totality), complements this relative identity with its opposite, producing through their synthesis a new identity which is in turn a defective one in the face of Reason, and which completes itself anew in the same way. The method of the system should be called neither synthetic nor analytic. It shows itself at its purest, when it appears as a development of Reason itself. Reason does not recall its appearance, which emanates from it as a duplicate, back into itself—for then, it would only nullify it. Rather, Reason constructs itself in its emanation as an identity that is conditioned by this very duplicate; it opposes this relative identity to itself once more, and in this way the system advances until the objective totality is completed. Reason then unites this objective totality with the opposite subjective totality to form the infinite world-intuition, whose expansion has at the same time contracted into the richest and simplest identity.

It can happen that an authentic speculation does not express itself completely in its system, or that the philosophy of the system and the system itself do not coincide. A system may express the tendency to nullify all oppositions in the most definite way, and yet not pierce through to the most perfect identity on its own account. So in judging philosophical systems it is particularly important to distinguish the philosophy from the system. If the fundamental need has not achieved perfect embodiment in the system, if it has elevated to the Absolute something that is conditioned and that exists only as an opposite, then as a system it becomes dogmatism. Yet true speculation can be found in the most divergent philosophies, in philosophies that decry one another as sheer dogmatism or as mental aberration. The history of philosophy only has value and interest if it holds fast to this viewpoint. For otherwise, it will not give us the history of the one, eternal Reason, presenting itself in infinitely manifold forms; instead it will give us nothing but a tale of the accidental vicissitudes of the human spirit and of senseless opinions, which the teller imputes to Reason, though they should be laid only to his own charge, because he does not recognize what is rational in them, and so turns them inside out.

An authentic speculation, even when it does not succeed in constructing itself completely into a system, necessarily begins from the absolute identity. The dichotomy of the absolute identity into subjective and objective is a production by [or of] the Absolute. The basic principle then, is completely transcendental, and from its standpoint there is no absolute opposition of the subjective and objective. But as a result the appearance of the Absolute is an opposition. The Absolute is not in its appearance, they are themselves opposites. The appearance is not identity. This opposition cannot be suspended transcendentally, that is to say, it cannot be suspended in such a fashion that there is no opposition in principle.[5] For then appearance would just be nullified, whereas it is supposed to have being just like [the Absolute does]. It is as if one were to claim that the Absolute, in its appearance, had stepped out of itself. So, the Absolute must posit itself in the appearance itself, i.e., it must not nullify appearance but must construct it into identity.

The causal relation between the Absolute and its appearance is a false identity; for absolute opposition is at the basis of this relation. In the causal relation both opposites have standing, but they are distinct in rank. The union is forcible. The one subjugates the other. The one rules, the other is subservient. The unity is forced, and forced into a mere relative identity. The identity which *ought* to be absolute, *is* incomplete. Contrary to its philosophy, the system has turned into a dogmatism, it has either turned into realism positing objectivity absolutely, or into idealism positing subjectivity absolutely. Yet both realism and idealism emerged from authentic speculation, though this is more doubtful with respect to realism than to idealism.

Pure dogmatism, if it is a dogmatism of philosophy, remains within the opposition even as a tendency. The basic governing principle in it is the relation of causality in its more complete form as reciprocal interaction: the intelligible realm has effects upon the sensible realm or the sensible upon the intelligible. In consistent realism and idealism the relation of causality plays only a subordinate role, even though it appears to govern — for in realism the subject is posited as produced by the object, and in idealism the object as produced by the subject. But the causal relation is essentially suspended, for the producing is an absolute producing, the product an absolute product; that is to say, the product has no standing apart from the producing; it is not posited as something self-sustaining, as something that has standing prior to and independent of the producing, as is the case with the pure causality relation, the formal principle of dogmatism. In dogmatism, the product is something posited by A and also, at the same time, not posited by A, so A is absolutely only subject, and A = A expresses merely an identity of the intellect. Even though philosophy in its transcendental business makes use of the causal relation yet B, which appears to be opposed to the subject, is in its oppositeness a mere possibility and it remains absolutely a possibility, i.e., it is only an accident. Thus the true relation of speculation, the substantiality relation [i.e., the relation of substance and accident] is the transcendental principle, though it appears under the guise of the causal relation. Or again, we might express this formally thus: genuine dogmatism acknowledges both principles A = A and A = B, but they remain in their antinomy side by side, unsynthesized. Dogmatism does not recognize that there is an antinomy in this and hence does not recognize the necessity of suspending the subsistence of the opposites. The transition from one to the other by way of the causality relation is the only synthesis possible to dogmatism, and this is an incomplete synthesis.

Notwithstanding this sharp difference between transcendental philosophy and dogmatism, the former is apt to pass over into the latter, when it constructs itself into a system. This is the case if transcendental philosophy while [rightly] refusing to allow any real causal relation on the ground that nothing exists but the absolute identity in which all difference and standing of opposites is suspended, yet introduces the causality relation, insofar as appearance is also supposed to have a standing so that the Absolute must have a relation to appearance other than that of nullification. Thus appearance is turned into something subservient, and likewise transcendental intuition is posited as something merely subjective and not objective, which is to say that the identity is not posited in the appearance. A = A and A = B remain both unconditioned whereas only A = A *ought* to be absolutely valid; that is, their identity is not set forth in their true synthesis which is no mere ought.

Thus in Fichte's system Ego = Ego in the Absolute. The totality sought by Reason leads to the second proposition which posits a non-Ego. Not only is this antinomy of the positing of both complete, but also their synthesis is postulated. But in this synthesis the opposition remains. It is not the case that both, Ego as well as non-Ego, are to be nullified, but one proposition is to survive, is to be higher in rank than the other. The speculation at the basis of the system demands the suspension of the opposites, but the system itself does not suspend them. The absolute synthesis which the system achieves is not Ego = Ego, but Ego *ought* to be equal to Ego. The Absolute is constructed for the transcendental viewpoint but not for the viewpoint of appearance. Both still contradict each other. The identity was not also placed in the appearance, or [in other words] the identity did not also pass completely into objectivity. Therefore transcendentality is itself something opposite, the subjective. One may also say that the appearance was not completely nullified.

In the following presentation of Fichte's system an attempt will be made to show that pure consciousness, the identity of subject and object, established as absolute in the system, is a *subjective* identity of subject and object. The presentation will proceed by showing that the Ego, the principle of the system, is a subjective Subject-Object. This will be shown directly, as well as by inspecting [not only] the deduction of nature, [but also] and particularly, the relations of identity in the special sciences of morality and natural law and the relation of the whole system to the aesthetic sphere.

It will be clear from what has been said that we are concerned in this presentation with Fichte's philosophy as a system and not as authentic philosophizing. As philosophy it is the most thorough and profound speculation, all the more remarkable because at the time when it appeared even the Kantian philosophy had proved unable to awaken Reason to the lost concept of genuine speculation.

IV.   Phenomenology of Spirit: Preface*

1.   OF SCIENTIFIC KNOWLEDGE

In the preface of a book it is customary to explain the author's aim, the reasons why he wrote the book, and what he takes to be its relationship to other treatments, earlier or contemporary, of the same subject. In the case of a philosophical work, however, such an explanation seems not only superfluous but, owing to the nature of the subject matter,[38] altogether improper and unsuited to the end in view. For what contents and tone would be appropriate for a preface to a philosophical work? Perhaps a historical statement concerning the tendency and point of view, the general contents and results of the work, an attempt to connect sundry claims and assertions about the truth? Philosophical truth cannot be presented in this manner.

Philosophy deals essentially with the general in which the particular is subsumed. Therefore it *seems*, more than in the case of other sciences, as if the aim or the final results gave expression to the subject matter itself, even as if they did entire justice to its very essence, while the way in which things are worked out in detail may seem to be unessential. Yet people do not suppose that the general idea of, say, the nature of anatomy—perhaps as the knowledge of the parts of the body, considered *qua* their lifeless existence—automatically furnishes us with the subject matter itself. Everybody realizes that, if we want possession of the contents of this science, we must also exert ourselves to master the particulars, the detail.

Moreover, such an aggregate of information really has no right to the name of science; and any discussion of its aim and other such generalities is usually no different from the manner in which the content—i.e., the nerves, the muscles, etc.—is discussed, too: in both cases, the manner is equally historical and void of Concepts. In the case of philosophy, however, such an introductory discussion would be an oddity; for it would employ

*Excerpt from *Hegel: Reinterpretation, Texts, and Commentary,* translated by Walter Kaufmann. Copyright © 1965 by Walter Kaufmann. Reprinted by permission of Weidenfeld & Nicolson Ltd., and Doubleday, a division of Bantam, Doubleday, Dell Publishing Group, Inc.

this same manner while demonstrating that this manner is incapable of grasping the truth.

The very attempt to determine the relationship of a philosophical work to other efforts concerning the same subject, introduces an alien and irrelevant interest which obscures precisely that which matters for the recognition of the truth. Opinion considers the opposition of what is true and false quite rigid, and, confronted with a philosophical system, it expects agreement or contradiction. And in an explanation of such a system, opinion still expects to find one or the other. It does not comprehend the difference of the philosophical systems in terms of the progressive development of the truth, but sees only the contradiction in this difference. The bud disappears as the blossom bursts forth, and one could say that the former is refuted by the latter. In the same way, the fruit declares the blossom to be a false existence of the plant, and the fruit supplants the blossom as the truth of the plant. These forms do not only differ, they also displace each other because they are incompatible. Their fluid nature, however, makes them, at the same time, elements of an organic unity in which they not only do not conflict, but in which one is as necessary as the other, and it is only this equal necessity that constitutes the life of the whole.

The opposition to a philosophical system, however, usually does not understand itself in this way. And the consciousness that is confronted with this opposition usually does not know how to liberate it, or how to keep it free, from its one-sidedness. Nor does it know how to penetrate this appearance of contention and mutual opposition in order to recognize elements which are necessary to each other.

The demand for such explanations or confessions and the satisfaction of this demand are easily mistaken for a concern with what is essential. Where could one hope for a better expression of the core of a philosophical work than in its aims and results? And how could these be determined better than by noting their difference from that which the age generally produces in the same sphere? But when this procedure is taken for more than the beginning of knowledge, when it is mistaken for knowledge itself, then we must indeed count it among the devices for bypassing the real subject matter, while combining the semblance of seriousness and exertion with a dispensation from both.

For the subject matter is not exhausted by any aim, but only by the way in which things are worked out in detail; nor is the result the actual whole, but only the result together with its becoming. The aim, taken by itself, is a lifeless generality; the tendency is a mere drift which still lacks actuality; and the naked result is the corpse which has left the tendency behind.

In the same way, the difference is really the limit of the subject matter: it indicates where the subject matter ceases, or it is what the subject matter is not. Such exertions concerning the aim, the results, the differences that may exist in this respect, or the critical judgments of aim and results, are therefore easier work than they may seem to be. For instead of dealing with the subject matter, such talk is always outside it; instead of abiding in the subject matter and forgetting itself in it, such knowledge always reaches out for something else and really remains preoccupied with itself instead of sticking to, and devoting itself to, the subject matter.

To judge that which has contents and workmanship is the easiest thing; to grasp it is more difficult; and what is most difficult it to combine both by producing an account of it.

How should education begin, and how the process of working oneself up out of the immediacy of the substance of life? The beginning will always have to be made by acquiring some cognizance of general principles and points of view and by working oneself up, first of all, to the idea[13] of the subject matter. No less, one must learn to support or refute it with reasons, to comprehend a concrete and copious fullness in terms of exact determinations, and to be able to offer accurate information and serious judgments. Then, however, this beginning of education will have to give way to the seriousness of life in its fullness which leads us into the experience of the subject matter itself. And when, in addition to all this, the seriousness of the Concept descends into the depth of the subject matter, then such knowledge and judgment will always retain a proper place in discussion.

2. THE ELEMENT OF TRUTH IS THE CONCEPT, AND ITS TRUE FORM THE SCIENTIFIC SYSTEM

The true form in which truth exists can only be the scientific system of it. To contribute to this end, that philosophy might come closer to the form of science—the goal being that it might be able to relinquish the name of love of knowledge and be actual knowledge—that is what I have resolved to try. The *inner* necessity according to which knowledge is science is grounded in the nature of knowledge, and the only satisfactory explanation of this is to be found in the presentation of philosophy itself. The *external* necessity, however, can also be understood more generally, apart from the accidents of the author's person or his individual motivation; and so understood, it coincides with the inner necessity; only the form is different in accordance with the manner in which time exhibits the existence of its stages. To demonstrate that the time has come for the elevation of philosophy to a science—this would be the only true justification of the attempts which have this aim. For this would show the necessity of this aim even while accomplishing it.

Truth can attain its true form only by becoming scientific, or, in other words, I claim that truth finds the element of its existence only in the

Concept. I know that this view seems to contradict a notion[53] and its consequences that are as presumptuous as they are as widely accepted in our time. Therefore some discussion of this contradiction seems hardly superfluous, although at this point it can only take the form of a mere assertion —just like the view against which it is aimed.

Others say that truth exists only in that, or rather as that, which is called now intuition,[4] now immediate knowledge of the absolute, religion, or being—not *at* the center of divine love but the being itself of this very center. It follows that what is then demanded for the presentation of philosophy is the opposite of the form of the Concept. The absolute is supposed to be not comprehended[9] but felt and intuited; it is not its Concept that is meant to prevail and be proclaimed but its feeling and intuition.

3.   PRESENT POSITION OF THE SPIRIT

The appearance of such a demand should be considered in its more general context, and one should see what stage the self-conscious spirit occupies at present. Clearly, it has passed beyond the substantial life that it formerly led in the element of thought—beyond this immediacy of its faith, beyond the satisfaction and security of that certainty which consciousness possessed about its reconciliation with the essence and its general, internal as well as external, presence. The spirit has not only passed beyond all this into the other extreme of its insubstantial reflection in itself; it has also passed beyond that. Not only has it lost its essential life; it is also conscious of this loss and of the finitude that is its contents. The spirit is turning away from the husks and, confessing that it is in trouble and cursing, it now demands from philosophy not so much self-knowledge as that philosophy should help the spirit to establish such substantiality and the solidity of being. Philosophy is asked to answer this need not by unlocking the locks of substance and raising it to the level of self-consciousness, nor by returning the chaotic consciousness to the order of thought and the simplicity of the Concept, but rather by confounding the distinctions of thought, by suppressing the discriminating Concept, and by establishing the *feeling* of the essence, granting not so much insight as edification.

The beautiful, the holy, the eternal, religion, and love are the bait that is required to arouse the desire to bite. Not the Concept but ecstasy, not the coldly progressing necessity of the subject matter but fermenting enthusiasm is held to be the best attitude and guide to the spread-out riches of the substance.

In line with such demands one exerts oneself almost zealously and angrily to tear men out of their absorption in the sensuous, the vulgar, the particular, and to raise their sights to the stars—as if, utterly forgetful of the divine, they were at the point of satisfying themselves with dust and water, like worms. Formerly they had a heaven, furnished with abundant riches of thoughts and images. The significance of all that is used to lie in the thread of light that tied it to the heavens; and following this thread, the eye, instead of abiding in the present, rose above that to the divine essence, to, if one may say so, a presence beyond. The eye of the spirit had to be directed forcibly to the things of this earth and kept there. Indeed, it took a long time to work that clarity which only the supernatural possessed into the must and confusion in which the sense of this world lay imprisoned; it took a long time to make attention to the present as such—what was called, in one word, experience—interesting and valid.

Now the opposite need meets the eye: sense[43] seems to be so firmly rooted in what is wordly that it takes an equal force to raise it higher. The spirit appears so poor that, like a wanderer in the desert who languishes for a simple drink of water, it seems to crave for its refreshment merely the bare feeling of the divine in general. By that which suffices the spirit one can measure the extent of its loss.

This modest contentment in accepting, or stinginess in giving, is, however, improper for science. Whoever seeks mere edification, whoever desires to shroud the worldly multiplicity of his existence and of thought in a fog to attain the indeterminate enjoyment of this indeterminate divinity, may look out for himself where he can find this; he will easily find the means to impress himself with his enthusiasm and thus to puff himself up. Philosophy, however, must beware of wishing to be edifying.

Least of all should such modest contentment which renounces science make claims that such ecstasy and dimness are something higher than science. Such prophetic talk supposes that it abides right in the center and in the depths, views the determinate (*the horos*) contemptuously, and deliberately keeps its distance from the Concept and from necessity, associating them with reflection[37] that makes its home in the finite. But even as there is an empty breadth, there is also an empty depth; even as there is an extension of the substance that pours itself out into finite multiplicity without the strength to hold it together, there is also an intensity void of content—pure force without any spread—which is identical with superficiality. The strength of the spirit is only as great as its expression; its depth is only as deep as it dares to spread and lose itself in its explication.

Moreover, when this substantial knowledge without Concept pretends to have drowned the personality of the self in the essence and to philosophize in a true and holy manner, it really hides the truth from itself: for instead of devoting itself to the god, it is undone because it spurns measure and determination, and now the accidental contents, now personal arbitrariness will lord it. —As they abandon themselves to the untamed ferment of the substance, they suppose that by shrouding self-consciousness and yielding up the understanding they become His beloved to whom God gives wisdom in sleep; what they thus conceive and give birth to in sleep indeed are, naturally, dreams.

It is surely not difficult to see that our time is a time of birth and transition to a new period. The spirit has broken with what was hitherto the world of its existence and imagination[53] and is about to submerge all this in the past; it is at work giving itself a new form. To be sure, the spirit is never at rest but always engaged in ever progressing motion. But just as in the case of a child the first breath it draws after long silent nourishment terminates the gradualness of the merely quantitative progression — a qualitative leap — and now the child is born, so, too, the spirit that educates itself matures slowly and quietly toward the new form, dissolving one particle of the edifice of its previous world after the other, while its tottering is suggested only by some symptoms here and there: frivolity as well as the boredom that open up in the establishment and the indeterminate apprehension of something unknown are harbingers of a forthcoming change. This gradual crumbling which did not alter the physiognomy of the whole is interrupted by the break of day that, like lightning, all at once reveals the edifice of the new world.

Yet what is new here does not have perfect actuality any more than the newborn child; and it is essential not to overlook this. The first emergence is only its immediacy or its Concept. Even as a building is not finished when its foundation has been laid, the attained Concept of the whole is not the whole itself. When we wish to see an oak — the strength of its trunk, the spread of its branches, and the mass of its foliage — we are not satisfied when in its place we are shown an acorn. Thus science, the crown of a world of the spirit, is not complete in its beginning. The beginning of the new spirit is the product of a far-reaching revolution in ever so many forms of culture and education; it is the prize for an immensely tangled path and an equally immense amount of exertion and toil. It is the whole which has returned into itself from succession as well as extension, the resultant simple Concept of it. But the actuality of this simple whole consists in this, that these forms which have become mere moments now develop anew and give themselves form, but in their new element, in the sense that has emerged.

4. THE PRINCIPLE IS NOT THE COMPLETION; AGAINST FORMALISM

While on the one hand the first appearance of the new world is only the whole shrouded in simplicity or its general basis, the wealth of its previous existence is, on the other hand, still present to consciousness in memory. In the newly appearing form it misses the spread and the particularization of the contents; but even more it misses the cultivation of the form whereby the distinctions are determined with certainty and ordered according to their firm relationships. Without this elaboration science lacks universal intelligibility[52] and has the appearance of being an esoteric possession of a few individuals. An esoteric possession: for it is present only in its Concept —only its inside is there. Of a few individuals: for its inarticulate appearance makes its existence merely individual. Only what is completely determinate is at the same time exoteric, comprehensible, and capable of being learned and of thus becoming the property of all. The intelligible[52] form of science is the way to science which is offered to all and made equal for all; and to reach rational knowledge by means of the understanding[52] is the just demand of consciousness as it approaches science. For the understanding is thinking, the pure ego; and the sensible[52] is the already familiar and that which science and the unscientific consciousness have in common — that whereby the latter can immediately enter science.

The science which is still close to its beginnings and thus has achieved neither completeness of detail nor perfection of form is open to reproach for this reason. But if such censure is aimed at the very essence of science it is as unjust as it would be to refuse to recognize the demand for such elaboration. This opposition seems to be the most important knot on which scientific education is working today, wearying itself without as yet properly understanding the situation. One side insists on the wealth of its material and its intelligibility; the other side spurns at least the latter and insists on immediate rationality and divinity. Even though the first party has been reduced to silence, whether by the power of truth alone or also by the impetuosity of the other party, and though they feel overwhelmed in respect to the fundamentals of the case, they still have not been satisfied regarding their demands: their demands are just but have not been fulfilled. Their silence is only half due to victory — half to the boredom and indifference which are usually the consequences of constantly excited expectations when the promises made are never fulfilled.

Regarding the contents, the others certainly sometimes make it easy enough for themselves to have great spread. They drag a lot of material into their field, namely material that is already familiar and well ordered. And when they deal preferably with the queer and curious, they only seem that much more to have firm possession of the rest which knowledge has long taken care of in its way, as if their mastery of the unruly came in addition to all this. Thus they subject everything to the absolute idea which then appears to be recognized in everything and to have developed into a comprehensive science. But when this comprehensiveness is considered more closely, it becomes manifest that it was not attained insofar as one and the same principle differentiated itself into different forms, but it is rather the formless repetition of one and the same principle which is merely applied externally to different material and thus receives a dull semblance of differentiation. The idea, true enough by itself, remains in fact just where it was in the beginning as long as the development consists merely in such repetition of the same formula. When the knowing subject applies the one unmoved form to whatever is presented, and the material is externally dipped into this resting element, this is not, any more than arbitrary notions about the contents, the fulfillment of that which is in fact required — to wit, the wealth that wells forth out of itself and the self-differentiation of the forms. Rather it is a drab monochromatic formalism that gets to the differentiation of the material solely because this is long prepared and familiar.

Yet he proclaims this monotony and abstract generality as the absolute; he assures us that any dissatisfaction with this is mere incapacity to master the absolute point of view and to abide there. Formerly, the mere possibility that one could also imagine[53] something in another way was sufficient to refute a notion,[53] and this same bare possibility, the general thought, also had the full positive value of actual knowledge. Now here we find that all value is also ascribed to the general idea in this form of non-actuality, while the dissolution of the distinct and determinate — or rather the resolve, which is neither developed further nor self-justifying, to thrust the distinct and determinate into the abyss of emptiness — is presented as the speculative mode of study.

To study anything as it is in the absolute here means merely that one says of it: to be sure, it has just been spoken of as something, but in the absolute, the $A = A$, there is nothing of the sort, for in the absolute everything is one. To pit this one piece of information, that in the absolute all is one, against all the distinctions of knowledge, both attained knowledge and the search and demand for knowledge — or to pass off one's absolute as the night in which, as one says, all cows are black — that is the naïveté of the emptiness of knowledge.

Recent philosophy accuses and derogates formalism, and yet formalism has regenerated itself in its very midst. But though the inadequacy of formalism is familiar and felt, it will not disappear from science until the knowledge of absolute actuality has gained perfect clarity about its nature.

Since the general notion, if it precedes an attempt to execute it, makes it easier to understand the latter, it may be helpful to offer some suggestions at this point. At the same time, this occasion may be used to eliminate a few forms whose customary acceptance constitutes an obstacle for philosophical knowledge.

5. THE ABSOLUTE IS SUBJECT —

According to my view, which must justify itself by the presentation of the system, everything depends on this, that we comprehend and express the true not as substance but just as much as subject. At the same time it should be noted that substantiality involves the generality or immediacy both of knowledge itself and of that which is being or immediacy *for* knowledge.

Comprehending God as the one substance outraged the age in which this definition was proclaimed. On the one hand, this was due to the instinctive recognition that self-consciousness was only drowned in it and not preserved; on the other hand, however, the opposite view which clings to thinking as thinking is generality as such and the same simplicity or undifferentiated, unmoved substantiality. And when, thirdly, thinking unites with itself the being of the substance and comprehends immediacy or intuition as thinking, it still remains decisive whether this intellectual intuition does not fall back into inert simplicity and present actuality in a non-actual manner.

6.   — AND WHAT THIS IS

The living substance is, further, that being which is in truth subject or — to say the same thing in other words — which is in truth actual only insofar as it is the movement of positing itself, or the mediation between a self and its development into something different. As subject, it is pure, simple negativity and thus the bifurcation of the simple, that which produces its own double and opposition, a process that again negates this indifferent diversity and its opposite: only this sameness which reconstitutes itself, or the reflection into itself in being different — not an original unity as such, or an immediate unity as such — is the true. The true is its own becoming, the circle that presupposes its end as its aim and thus has it for its beginning — that which is actual only through its execution and end.

Thus the life of God and divine knowledge may indeed be spoken of as love's playing with itself; yet this idea descends to the level of edification and even insipidity when seriousness, pain, and the patience and work of the negative have no place in it. In itself[5] this life is indeed unstained sameness and unity with itself which is not serious about otherness, estrangement, and the overcoming of this estrangement. But this in-itself is abstract generality in which the nature of this life to be *for itself*,[6] and thus also the self-movement of the form, are ignored.

When the form is said to be the same as the essence, it is plainly a misunderstanding to suppose that knowledge can be satisfied with the in-itself or the essence while sparing itself concern with the form — as if the absolute principle or the absolute intuition made the explication of the former or the development of the latter dispensable. Precisely because the form is no less essential to the existence than the essence itself, the essence is to be comprehended and spoken of not merely as essence, i.e., as immediate substance or as the pure self-contemplation of the divine, but just as much as form — and in the whole wealth of the developed form. Only in that way is it comprehended and spoken of in its actuality.

The true is the whole. But the whole is only the essence perfecting itself through its development. Of the absolute it should be said that it is essentially result, that it is only in the end what it is in truth; and precisely in this consists its nature: to be actual, subject, or that which becomes itself.

Though it may seem contradictory that the absolute is to be comprehended essentially as result, it requires only a little reflection to clear up
this semblance of contradiction. The beginning, the principle, or the absolute, as it is spoken of at first and immediately is merely the general. Just as
when I say, "all animals," this phrase is not acceptable as a zoology, it is
obvious that such words as the divine, absolute, eternal, etc., do not express
what they contain. And only such words do indeed express the intuition as
something immediate. Whatever is more than such a word, even the
transition to a mere proposition, contains a becoming something other
which must then be taken back, and is thus a mediation. This, however, is
precisely what some people abhor, as if absolute knowledge has been
abandoned as soon as one makes more of mediation than to say that it is
nothing absolute and that it has no place in the absolute.

This abhorrence, however, is really rooted in ignorance of the nature of
both mediation and absolute knowledge. For mediation is nothing else than
self-identity that moves itself; or it is reflection into itself, the moment of
the ego which is for itself, pure negativity or, reduced to its pure abstraction, simple becoming. The ego or becoming in general — this mediation is
on account of its simplicity precisely growing immediacy and the immediate itself.

It is therefore a misapprehension about reason when reflection is excluded from the true instead of being comprehended as a positive moment
of the absolute. It is reflection that makes the true a result while also
sublimating[8] this opposition to its becoming; for this becoming is also quite
simple and therefore not different from the form of the true which manifests itself in the result as something simple: rather it is precisely this
return into simplicity.

While the embryo is surely in itself human, it still is not human for itself:
human for itself is only the educated reason which has made itself that
which it is in itself. Only this is its actuality. But this result is itself simple
immediacy; for it is self-conscious freedom which rests in itself and has not
laid opposition aside to let it lie there, but is reconciled to it.

What has been said here can also be expressed by saying that reason is
purposive activity. The elevation of what is supposed to be nature above
thinking, which is also misunderstood, and especially the banishment of
external purposiveness, have brought the form of purpose in general into
disrepute. Yet even as Aristotle, too, defines nature as purposive activity,
purpose is the immediate, that which is at rest, the unmoved mover; thus it
is subject. Its power to move, taken abstractly, is being-for-itself or pure
negativity. The result is the same as the beginning only because the
beginning is purpose. In other words, the actual is the same as its Concept
only because the immediate, being purpose, contains the self or pure
actuality in itself. The executed purpose or the actual as existent is movement and unfolded becoming; but precisely this unrest is the self. And it is

like the immediacy and simplicity of the beginning because it is the result, that which has returned into itself—and that which has returned into itself is the self, and the self is the identity and simplicity that relates itself to itself.

The need to represent the absolute as subject has employed the propositions: God is what is eternal, or the moral world order, or love, and so forth. In such propositions the true is only posited straightway as the subject, but it is not represented as the movement of that which reflects itself into itself. In a proposition of this kind one begins with the word God. This by itself is a senseless sound, a mere name; only the predicate says what he is and fills the name with content and meaning; the empty beginning becomes actual knowledge only in this end. For this reason, it is not clear why they do not speak merely of the eternal, of the moral world order, and so forth—or as the ancients did, of pure Concepts, such as being, the One, and so forth—in sum, only of that which supplies the meaning, without adding the senseless sound as well. But this word signifies that what is posited is not a being or essence or mere generality, but rather something reflected into itself—a subject. Yet at the same time this is only anticipated. The subject is accepted as a fixed point to which the predicates are affixed as to their support—by a movement which belongs to those who know of the subject and which is not supposed to belong to the fixed point—though only this [recognition] could represent the content as a subject. In the way in which the movement is here constituted, it could not belong to the point; but after this point has been presupposed it really cannot be constituted differently and is bound to be merely external. This anticipation that the absolute is subject is therefore not only not the actuality of this Concept but even makes this actuality impossible; for it posits a point at rest, while the actuality is self-movement.

Among several implications of what has here been said, one may be singled out for special emphasis: it is only as science or system that knowledge is actual[59] and can be expounded. Further, any so-called basic proposition or principle of philosophy, if true, is also false simply insofar as it is merely a basic proposition or principle.

It is therefore easy to refute it. The refutation consists in demonstrating its deficiency; and it is deficient because it is merely general or a principle —the mere beginning. If the refutation is thorough, it is taken and developed out of the principle itself—and not effected externally by opposite assurances and notions. Thus it would really be the development of this principle and the completion of its deficiency, if only the refutation would not misunderstand itself by paying attention solely to its negative activity without also becoming conscious of its progress and results on their positive side.

The positive explication of the beginning is at the same time also, conversely, a negative treatment of it insofar as it is directed against the one-sided form of the beginning which is only immediate or purpose. Therefore it can also be taken for a refutation of that which constitutes the basis of the system; but it would be more correct to look upon it as a demonstration that the basis or the principle of the system is in fact only its beginning.

That the true is actual only as system, or that the substance is essentially subject, is expressed in the conception which speaks of the absolute as spirit. This is the most sublime Concept, and it belongs to the modern age and its religion. The spiritual alone is the actual; it is [i] the essence or being-in-itself; [ii] that which relates itself and is determinate, that which is other and for itself; and [iii] that which in this determinateness and being outside itself remains in itself—or, in other words, it is in and for itself.

This being-in-and-for-itself, however, it is first for us or in itself: it is the spiritual substance. Then it must also become this for itself and attain the knowledge of the spiritual and of itself as the spirit; i.e., it must become an object for itself, but just as immediately an object which is sublimated, reflected into itself. It is for itself only for us, insofar as its spiritual content is generated by it itself. But insofar as it is for itself also for itself, this self-generation, the pure Concept is for it at the same time the objective element in which it has its existence; and in this way it is in its existence for itself an object reflected into itself.

The spirit that, so developed, knows itself as spirit is science. Science is the actuality of the spirit and the realm that the spirit builds for itself in its own element.

7. THE ELEMENT OF KNOWLEDGE

Pure self-recognition in absolute otherness, this ether as such, is the ground and basis of science or knowledge in general. The beginning of philosophy presupposes or demands that consciousness dwell in this element. But this element itself receives its perfection and transparence only through the movement of its becoming. It is pure spirituality as the general that has the manner of simple immediacy; this simple, as it has existence as such, is the basis that is thinking and only in the spirit. Because this element, this immediacy of the spirit, is the very substance of the spirit, it is the transfigured essence and the reflection which itself is simple and immediacy as such for itself—being that is reflection into itself. Science on her part demands of self-consciousness that it should have elevated itself into this ether to be able to live—and to live—with her and in her. Conversely, the individual has the right to demand that science should at least furnish him with the ladder to this standpoint—and show him this standpoint within himself. His right is based on his absolute independence which he possesses in every form of his knowledge; for in all of them, whether they are recognized by science or not and regardless of their contents, the individual is the absolute form, i.e., he is the immediate certainty of himself and, if this expression should be preferred, he is therefore unconditioned being. It is the standpoint of consciousness to know of objective things in opposition to itself, and to know of itself in opposition to them. Science considers this standpoint as the other—and precisely that through which consciousness knows itself to be at home with itself is for science the loss of the spirit. Conversely, the element of science is for consciousness a distant beyond in which consciousness no longer has possession of itself. Each of these two appears to the other as the perversion of truth. That the natural consciousness immediately entrusts itself to science is an attempt it makes, attracted by it knows not what, to walk for once also on its head. The compulsion to adopt this unaccustomed position and to move in it amounts to the presumption that the natural consciousness should do itself violence in a manner as unexpected as it must seem unnecessary.

Whatever science may be in itself, in relation to immediate self-consciousness it presents itself as something topsy-turvy. Or: because immediate self-consciousness has the principle of its actuality in its certainty of itself, science bears the form of unactuality for this immediate self-consciousness which seems to itself to stand outside science. Science must therefore join this element to herself, or rather she must show that and how it belongs to her. As long as she lacks such actuality, she is merely the content as the in-itself, the purpose which is still only something inward— not yet spirit, only spiritual substance. This in-itself has to express itself and become for itself; in other words, it has to posit self-consciousness as one with itself.

8. THE ASCENT INTO THIS IS THE PHENOMENOLOGY OF THE SPIRIT

This becoming of science in general or of knowledge is what this phenomenology of the spirit represents. Knowledge in its initial form, or immediate spirit, is that which lacks spirit, the consciousness of the senses. To become true knowledge, or to generate the element of science which is her pure Concept itself, it has to work its way through a long journey.

This becoming, as it will appear in its content and the forms that will show themselves in it, will not be anything like what one would at first associate with an introduction to science for the unscientific consciousness. It will also be quite different from a foundation of science. Above all, it will differ from that enthusiasm which, as shot from a pistol, begins immediately with absolute knowledge, having done with other standpoints simply by declaring that it will not deign to take notice of them.

The task of leading the individual from his uneducated standpoint to knowledge had to be taken in its general sense, and the general individual, the self-conscious spirit, had to be considered in its education.

As for the relation of the two: in the general individual every moment shows itself as it gains concrete form and its own shape. The particular individual is the incomplete spirit, a concrete form in whose whole existence one determination predominates, while the others are present only in blurred features. In the spirit who stands on a higher level than another, the lower concrete existence has been reduced to an insignificant moment; what formerly was the matter itself has become a mere trace; its form is shrouded and become a simple shade.

Through this past the individual whose substance is the spirit that stands on a higher level passes in the same manner in which the student of a higher science goes once more through the preparatory knowledge that he has long mastered, to present the contents to his mind: he recalls these memories without being interested in them for their own sake or wishing to abide in them. The individual must also pass through the contents of the educational stages of the general spirit, but as forms that have long been outgrown by the spirit, as stages of a way that has been prepared and evened for him. Thus we see that as far as information is concerned, what in former ages occupied the mature spirits of men has been reduced to information, exercises, and even games suitable for boyhood; and in the boy's pedagogical progress we recognize the history of the education of the world as if it had been traced in a silhouette. This past existence is property that has already been acquired by the general spirit which constitutes the substance of the individual and, by thus appearing to him externally, his inorganic nature.

In this respect, education, considered from the point of view of the individual, consists in his acquiring what is thus given to him; he must digest his inorganic nature and take possession of it for himself. But from the point of view of the general spirit as the substance this means nothing else than that this should acquire self-consciousness and produce its becoming and reflection in itself.

Science represents this educational movement both in its detail and necessity and also as that which has already been reduced to a moment and property of the spirit. The aim is the spirit's insight into what constitutes knowledge. Impatience demands the impossible, namely the attainment of the aim without the means. First, the length of this way must be endured, for every moment is necessary. Secondly, one must take time over every one, for each is itself an individual and entire form and is considered absolutely insofar as one considers its determinateness as something whole and concrete, or the whole in the individuality of this determination.

Because the substance of the individual, because the world spirit has had the patience to pass through these forms in the long expanse of time, taking upon itself the tremendous labor of world history in which it imparted as much of its content to every form as that form was capable of holding, and because it could not attain consciousness about itself with less labor, therefore the individual cannot in the nature of the case comprehend his own substance with less than this; and yet he has less trouble because this is already accomplished in itself: the content is by now the actuality reduced to a possibility, vanquished immediacy, and the forms have been reduced to abbreviations and to the simple determinations of thought. Having already been thought, the content is the possession of the substance. No longer must existence be transformed into the in-itself; only the in-itself—which is neither raw any more, nor immersed in existence, but rather something recalled—needs to be transmitted into the form of the for-itself. How this is to be done must now be described in some detail.

9. THE TRANSMUTATION OF THE NOTION[53] AND THE FAMILIAR INTO THOUGHT—

What is no longer necessary at the point at which we are here taking up this movement is the sublimation of existence. But what remains and still requires a higher transformation is the notion of and familiarity with the forms. Existence, taken back into the substance, has merely been transposed immediately by this first negation into the element of the self. This possession which the self has acquired thus still has the same character of uncomprehended immediacy and unmoved difference as does existence itself: all this is retained in the notion.

At the same time it is thus something familiar, something that the existing spirit has mastered so that its activity and interest no longer abide in it. The activity that masters existence is itself only the movement of the particular spirit which does not comprehend itself; but knowledge is directed against the notion that arises in this way, against this familiarity; knowledge is the activity of the general self and the interest of thinking.

What is familiar is not known simply because it is familiar. It is the most common self-deception and deception of others to presuppose something as familiar when it comes to knowledge, and to accept this; but with all its talking back and forth such knowledge, without knowing what is happening to it, never gets anywhere. The subject and object, etc., God, nature, the understanding, the sensibility, etc., are presupposed as familiar and valid foundations without having been scrutinized, and they are accepted as fixed points of both departure and return. They remain unmoved as one moves back and forth between them—and thus only on their surfaces. Thus apprehension and examination, too, consist merely in seeing whether everybody finds what has been said of them in his notion, too, whether it seems and is familiar to him that way or not.

The analysis of a notion, as it used to be performed, was nothing else than the sublimation of the form of its familiarity. Dissecting a notion into its original elements means going back to its moments which at least do not have the form of the notion encountered as a datum, constituting rather the immediate property of the self. To be sure, this analysis only reaches thoughts which are themselves familiar, fixed, and static determinations. But what is thus differentiated and unactual is itself an essential moment; for it is only because the concrete differentiates itself and makes itself what is unactual, that it is that which moves itself. The activity of differentiating is the strength and work of the understanding, which is the most astonishing and the greatest, or rather the absolute, power.

The circle that rests closed in itself and, being substance, holds its moments, is the immediate and therefore not perplexing relation. But that the accidental as such, separated from its circumference, that the bounded which is actual only in its connection with others, should gain an existence of its own and separate freedom, this is the tremendous power of the negative; this is the energy of thought, of the pure ego. Death, if we care to call this unactuality by this name, is what is most terrible, and to hold on to what is dead requires the greatest strength. That beauty which lacks strength hates the understanding because it asks this of her and she cannot do it. But not the life that shrinks from death and keeps itself undefiled by devastation, but the life that endures, and preserves itself through, death is the life of the spirit. Spirit gains its truth only by finding itself in absolute dismemberment. This power it is not as the positive that looks away from the negative — as when we say of something, this is nothing or false, and then, finished with it, turn away from it to something else: the spirit is this power only by looking the negative in the face and abiding with it. This abiding is the magic force which converts the negative into being.

It is the same which above was called the subject which, by giving determinateness existence in its element, sublimates abstract immediacy — i.e., immediacy which barely *is* — and thus is true substance: that being or that immediacy which does not leave mediation outside itself but which is mediation itself.

10. — AND THIS INTO THE CONCEPT

That notions become the property of pure self-consciousness, this elevation to generality is only one side and not yet the completed education. — Study in antiquity differed from that current in modern times: it was nothing less than the thorough education of the natural consciousness. Testing itself against every separate part of its existence, and philosophizing about everything it encountered, it made itself into a generality that was active through and through. In modern times, on the other hand, the individual finds the abstract form ready-made: the exertion of grasping it and appropriating it is rather more the unmediated production of the inward and the cut-off generation of the general than the emergence of the general out of the concrete and the multiplicity of existence. The work cut out for us now, therefore, is less to purify the individual from the manner of immediacy and the senses while making it into a thinking and thought substance, than to attempt the opposite: to sublimate fixed, determinate thoughts and thus to actualize the general and infuse it with spirit. But it is far more difficult to make fixed thoughts fluid than sense existence. The reason for this has been mentioned above: the substance and the element of existence of these determinations is the ego, the power of the negative, or pure actuality; but the element of the sense determinations is merely powerless, abstract immediacy, or being as such. Thoughts become fluid when pure thinking, this inner immediacy, recognizes itself as a moment, or when pure self-certainty abstracts from itself—not by leaving itself out or setting itself aside, but by abandoning the fixity of its self-positing— both the fixity of the pure concreteness which characterizes the ego even in its opposition to differentiated content and the fixity of differentiations which, posited in the element of pure thinking, share in the unconditionality of the ego. Through this movement the pure thoughts become Concepts and come to be what they are in truth: self-movements, circles, that which is their substance, spiritual entities.

This movement of the pure entities constitutes the nature of what is scientific. As far as the coherence of the contents is concerned, it means the necessity and elaboration of the contents into an organic whole. The way in which the Concept of knowledge is reached thus also becomes a necessary and complete becoming. Hence this preparation ceases to be a fortuitous bit of philosophizing that takes off from these or those objects, relationships, and thoughts of the imperfect consciousness, depending on fortuitous circumstances, nor does it seek to establish what is true by reasoning back and forth, inferring and drawing consequences from determinate thoughts. Rather this way will encompass, by virtue of the movement of the Concept, the complete worldliness of consciousness in its necessity.

Such a presentation constitutes the first part of science because the existence of the spirit is at first nothing else than the immediate or the beginning, but the beginning is not yet its return into itself. The element of immediate existence is therefore that which distinguishes this part of science from the others. —The indication of this difference leads us into a discussion of a few fixed thoughts which usually crop up in this connection.

The immediate existence of the spirit, i.e., consciousness, contains the two moments of knowledge and the objectivity which is negative to knowledge. It is in this element [of consciousness] that the spirit develops itself and explicates its moments which are therefore characterized by this opposition and, without exception, appear as forms of consciousness. The science of this way is the science of the experience made by consciousness: the substance is studied insofar as it and its movement are objects of consciousness. Consciousness knows and comprehends nothing but what lies within its experience; for what is within that is only the spriritual substance — specifically, as the object of its self. The spirit, however, becomes an object, for the spirit is this movement of becoming something other for itself, i.e., an object for its self, and then to sublimate this otherhood. And experience is the name we give to just this movement in which the immediate, the unexperienced, i.e., the abstract, whether of sensible being or of a bare, simple thought, becomes estranged and then returns to itself from estrangement, and is only then presented in its actuality and truth and becomes the property of consciousness.

The non-identity we find in consciousness between the ego and the substance that is its object, is their difference, the negative in general. It can be considered as the defect of both, but is really their soul or that which moves them. Therefore some of the ancients comprehended the void as that which moves, seeing well that that which moves is the negative, but not yet that it is the self.

When the negative thus appears at first as the non-identity of the ego and its object, it is just as much the non-identity of the substance with itself. What seems to happen outside it, as an activity directed against it, is its own doing; and thus the substance shows that it is essentially subject. When it has shown this completely, the spirit has made its existence equal to its essence; it becomes an object for itself as it is, and the abstract element of immediacy and of the separation of knowledge and truth is overcome. Being is mediated absolutely; it is substantial content which is just as immediately property of the ego, self-like, or Concept. With this the phenomenology of the spirit is concluded. What the spirit prepares for itself in this phenomenology is the element of knowledge. In this element the moments of the spirit spread themselves out in the form of simplicity which knows its object as itself. They no longer fall apart into the opposition of being and knowledge but abide in the simplicity of knowledge; they are now the true in the form of the true, and their difference is only the difference of content. Their movement which in this element organizes itself into a whole is Logic or speculative philosophy.

11. IN WHAT WAY THE PHENOMENOLOGY OF THE SPIRIT IS NEGATIVE OR CONTAINS WHAT IS FALSE

The system of the experience of the spirit deals only with the appearance of the spirit. Hence the progression from this system to the science of the true that also has the form of the true seems to be merely negative. Therefore one might wish to be spared the negative as something false, and one might ask to be led to truth without delay: Why bother with the false?

This demand, mentioned previously, that one should begin straightway with science, one has to answer here by considering quite generally the nature of the negative as something false. The conceptions people have about this are pre-eminent obstacles on the way to truth. This also provides an occasion for speaking of mathematical knowledge which unphilosophical knowledge considers the ideal that philosophy should strive to reach, though so far it has striven in vain.

True and false are among the determinate thoughts which are considered immobile separate essences, as if one stood here and the other there, without community, fixed and isolated. Against this view one must insist that truth is not a minted coin which can be given and pocketed readymade. Nor does something false exist any more than something evil exists. To be sure, the evil and the false are not as bad as the devil, for in the devil they are even made into a particular subject; as the false and evil they are merely something general but still have opposed individual essences.

The false (for only this has a place in our discussion) would be the other, the negative of the substance which, as the content of knowledge, is the true. But the substance is itself essentially the negative, partly as the differentiation and determination of the content, partly as simple discrimination, i.e., as self and knowledge in general. One can know something falsely. That something is known falsely means that knowledge is not identical with its substance. Yet precisely this non-identity is differentiation which is an essential moment. Out of this differentiation their identity comes, and this resulting identity is the truth. But it is not truth as if non-identity had been thrown away, like dross from pure metal — nor even as the tool is excluded from the finished vessel; rather non-identity is, as the negative, as the self, still immediately present in the true as such. Yet it does not follow that the false may be called a moment of the true, let alone a part of it. That in everything false there is something true — in this dictum both are treated like oil and water which are unmixable and united only externally. Precisely on account of the meaning associated with the moment of complete otherhood, such expressions must no longer be used where such otherhood is sublimated. Talk of the unity of subject and object, of the finite and the infinite, of being and thinking, etc., is misleading because object and subject, etc., signify that which they are outside their unity, and in the unity they are not meant in the sense suggested by such an expression. Just so, the false is no longer something false as a moment of truth.

Dogmatism as a style of thought in knowledge and in the study of philosophy is nothing else than the opinion that the true consists in a proposition that is a fixed result or that is known immediately. To such questions as, when Caesar was born, or how many feet there were in a stadium, etc., a neat answer should be given, just as it is surely true that the square of the hypotenuse equals the sum of the squares of the other two sides of a right-angled triangle. But the nature of such so-called truths is different from the nature of philosophical truths.

12.   HISTORICAL AND MATHEMATICAL TRUTH

Regarding historical truths — to mention these briefly — insofar as their purely historical aspect is considered, it will be readily granted that they concern particular existence and the accidental and arbitrary side, the features that are not necessary.

But even such bare truths as those adduced here as examples do not lack the movement of self-consciousness. To know one of them one must compare much, consult books, or inquire in some manner; and even where one might appeal to immediate intuition, such knowledge is held to have true value only when it is backed up by reasons, although it may be alleged that only the bare result matters.

As for mathematical truths, it is even more obvious that one would not consider a man a geometer if he knew Euclid's theorems by *heart*, but without their proofs — without, as one might say by way of juxtaposition, also knowing them by *mind*. In the same way, if a man by measuring many right-angled triangles acquired the knowledge that their sides have the well-known relation to each other, such knowledge would be considered unsatisfactory. Yet even in mathematical knowledge, the importance of the demonstration still does not have the significance and characteristic that it is a moment of the result itself; in the result the demonstration is over and has disappeared. As a result, to be sure, the theorem is something whose truth is apprehended. But this additional circumstance does not concern its content but only its relation to the subject; the movement of the mathematical demonstration does not belong to that which is the object but is an activity that remains external to the matter. Thus the nature of the right-angled triangle does not take itself apart after the manner of the construction that is required for the demonstration of the proposition that expresses the relations; the whole production of the result is a way and means of knowledge.

In philosophical knowledge, too, the becoming of the existence as existence is different from the becoming of the essence or inner nature of the matter. But in the first place philosophical knowledge contains both, while mathematical knowledge represents only the becoming of the existence, i.e., the emergence of the nature of the matter in knowledge. Secondly, philosophical knowledge also unites these two separate movements. The internal genesis or becoming of the substance is undivided transition into the external or into existence, into being for another; and, conversely, the becoming of existence is a retreat into essence. In this way the movement is the double process and becoming of the whole: each posits the other simultaneously, and therefore each also has both as two aspects of itself. Together they constitute the whole by dissolving themselves and making themselves into its moments.

In mathematical knowledge, insight is an event that is external to the matter; it follows that the true matter is changed by it. The means, construction and demonstration, contain true propositions; but at the same time it must be said that the content is false. In the above example, the triangle is dismembered and its parts are allotted to other figures which the construction brings into being alongside it. Only in the end one reconstitutes the triangle which really matters, but which during the procedure was lost from view and appeared only in pieces which belonged to other wholes. — Here, then, we also see the negativity of the content enter, which would just as much have to be called a falseness of the content as is the disappearance in the movement of the Concept of the thought that had been considered fixed.

The real defectiveness of mathematical knowledge, however, concerns both the knowledge itself and its content. — Regarding the knowledge, the first point is that the necessity of the construction is not apprehended. This does not issue from the Concept of the theorem; rather it is commanded, and one must blindly obey the command to draw precisely these lines instead of an indefinite number of others, not because one knows anything but merely in the good faith that this will turn out to be expedient for the conduct of the demonstration. Afterwards this expediency does indeed become manifest, but it is an external expediency because it manifests itself only after the demonstration.

Just so, the demonstration follows a path that begins somewhere — one does not yet know in what relation to the result that is to be attained. As it proceeds, these determinations and relations are taken up while others are ignored, although one does not by any means see immediately according to what necessity. An external purpose rules this movement.

The evident certainty of this defective knowledge, of which mathematics is proud and of which it also boasts as against philosophy, rests solely on the poverty of its purpose and the defectiveness of its material and is therefore of a kind that philosophy must spurn. — Its purpose or Concept is magnitude. This is precisely the relation that is not essential and is void of Concept. The movement of knowledge therefore proceeds on the surface, does not touch the matter itself, not the essence or the Concept, and is therefore not comprehension.

The material about which mathematics offers such a pleasing treasure of truths is space and the unit. Space is the existence into which the Concept writes its distinctions as into an empty, dead element in which they are equally immobile and lifeless. The actual is not something spatial the way it is considered in mathematics; with such unactuality as is exemplified by the things of mathematics neither concrete sense intuition nor philosophy concerns itself. In such an unactual element there are only unactual truths, i.e., fixed, dead propositions: one can stop with any one of them; the following one starts anew for itself, and the first one does not move itself on to the next, nor does a necessary connection come about in this way through the nature of the matter. — Also, on account of this principle and element — and in this consists the formalism of the evident certainty of mathematics — knowledge proceeds along the line of equality. For what is dead and does not move itself does not attain the differentiation of its essence or the essential opposition and inequality; and therefore it also does not attain the transition from the opposed into the opposed, nor the qualitative, immanent movement, nor self-movement. For mathematics considers only magnitude which is the unessential difference. Mathematics abstracts from the fact that it is the Concept that bifurcates space into its dimensions and determines the relations of and in these. It does not consider, e.g., the relation of the line to the plain; and when it compares the diameter of the circle with the circumference it comes up against incommensurability, i.e., a relation of the Concept, something infinite that escapes mathematical determination.

Immanent or so-called pure mathematics also does not juxtapose time as time with space, as the second material for its consideration. Applied mathematics, to be sure, does treat of it as well as of movement and other actual things. But it takes the synthetic propositions, i.e., those about their relations which are determined by their Concept, from experience, and it merely applies its formulas to these assumptions. The so-called demonstrations of such propositions as those about the equilibrium of the lever, or the relation of space and time in the movement of a fall, etc., are often given and accepted as demonstrations; but this only demonstrates how great a need knowledge has of demonstrations: where it lacks anything more, it respects even the empty semblance of a demonstration and thus gains some satisfaction. A critique of these demonstrations would be as remarkable as it would be instructive and might both cleanse mathematics of this false finery and show the limitations of mathematics and thus also the necessity of another kind of knowledge.

As for time, of which one should think that, juxtaposed with space, it would constitute the material of the other part of pure mathematics, it is the existing[12] Concept itself. The principle of magnitude, that difference void of Concept, and the principle of equality, that abstract and lifeless unity, are incapable of concerning themselves with this pure unrest of life and this absolute differentiation. This negativity, therefore, becomes the second material for this knowledge only in paralyzed form, namely as the unit; and this knowledge, being external to its content, reduces that which moves itself to mere material in which it then has an indifferent, external, lifeless content.

13. THE NATURE OF PHILOSOPHICAL TRUTH AND ITS METHOD

Philosophy, on the other hand, considers not the inessential determination but the determination insofar as it is essential. Not the abstract or unactual is its element and contents but the actual, that which posits itself and lives in itself, existence in its Concept. It is the process that generates and runs through its moments, and this whole movement constitutes the positive and its truth. This truth, then, includes the negative as well — that which might be called the false if it could be considered as something from which one should abstract. The evanescent must, however, be considered essential — not in the determination of something fixed that is to be severed from the true and left lying outside it, one does not know where; nor does the true rest on the other side, dead and positive. The appearance is the coming to be and passing away that itself does not come to be or pass away; it is in itself and constitutes the actuality and the movement of the life of the truth. The true is thus the bacchanalian whirl in which no member is not drunken; and because each, as soon as it detaches itself, dissolves immediately — the whirl is just as much transparent and simple repose. In the court of justice of this movement, to be sure, the individual forms of the spirit endure no more than determinate thoughts do, yet they are just as much positive and necessary moments as they are negative and evanescent. — In the whole of the movement, considering it as repose, that which distinguishes itself in it and gives particular existence is preserved as something that remembers, and its existence is knowledge of itself even as this knowledge is just as immediately existence.

It might seem necessary to devote a lengthy preamble to the method of this movement or of science. But the Concept of this method is implicit in what has been said, and its real exposition belongs to the Logic, or rather constitutes the Logic. For the method is nothing else than the edifice of the whole, constructed in its pure essence. But the entire system of prevalent notions of philosophical method belongs to an extinct form of education.

If this should sound boastful or revolutionary, though I know that my tone is altogether different, it should be noted that the scientific finery furnished by mathematics — such as explanations, divisions, axioms, rows of theorems, their demonstrations, principles, and deductions and inferences from them — is at least according to current opinion quite outmoded. Even if the unfitness of these procedures is not yet clearly understood, one makes little or no use of them; and if one does not disapprove of them, at least they are not loved. And we must have the prejudice in favor of what is excellent that it will get itself used and loved.

But it is not difficult to see that positing a proposition, adducing reasons for it, and in the same way refuting the opposite by giving reasons, cannot be the form in which truth appears. Truth is its own self-movement, while this is the method of knowledge that remains external to its material. It is peculiar to, and must be left to, mathematics which, as we have noted, has for its principle the relation of magnitude — a relation void of Concept — and for its material dead space and the equally dead unit. In a somewhat freer style, i.e., mixed more with the arbitrary and the accidental, this method may retain its place in ordinary life, in conversation, or in historical instruction which is aimed at curiosity more than at knowledge — and therefore perhaps also in a preface. In ordinary life, consciousness has for its contents information, experience, sense concretions, also thoughts, principles — altogether, what is considered as a datum or as a being or essence in fixed repose. Now consciousness follows this thread, now it interrupts the connection by freely and arbitrarily disposing of such contents, and altogether consciousness here treats and determines its contents from the outside. Things are led back to some certainty, even if that is only the feeling of the moment; and conviction is satisfied when it has reached a familiar point of rest.

While the necessity of the Concept banishes the looser gait of conversational arguments as well as the stiffer gait of scientific pomp, it has been pointed out above that their place must not be taken by the unmethod of intimation and enthusiasm and the arbitrariness of prophetic speech which despises not only this scientific pomp but scientific procedures quite generally.

14. AGAINST SCHEMATIZING FORMALISM

Now that Kant, by instinct, has rediscovered triplicity, albeit still dead and still uncomprehended, and it has subsequently been raised to its absolute importance, and with it the true form in its true content has been presented and the Concept of science has emerged, it is equally obvious that we must not consider scientific that use of this form which reduces it to a lifeless schema, really to a phantom, and scientific organization to a table.

In a general way this formalism has already been discussed above, but we now want to describe its manner in a little more detail. This formalism supposes it has comprehended and expressed the nature and life of a form when it merely ascribes to it as a predicate some determination of the schema; e.g., subjectivity or objectivity, or magnetism, electricity, etc., contraction or expansion, east or west, *et al*. This sort of thing can be multiplied *ad infinitum* because in this manner every determination or form can be used again as a form or moment of the schema when it comes to another, and each can gratefully perform the same service for another. But in this circle of reciprocity one never learns what the matter itself is — neither what the one nor what the other is. In this process one sometimes uses sense determinations from common intuition—but then these are supposed to mean something different from what they say—and sometimes one uses the pure determinations of thoughts, meaningful in themselves, such as subject, object, substance, cause, the general, etc.—but just as uncritically and without examination as in ordinary life and as strengths and weaknesses, expansion and contraction. This metaphysics, then, is as unscientific as these sense conceptions.

Instead of the inner life and the self-movement of its existence, such a simple determinateness is taken from intuition, which here means the knowledge of the senses, and expressed according to a superficial analogy, and then this external and empty application of a formula is called construction.—Such formalism is like any other. How dull would a mind have to be that could not learn in a quarter of an hour the theory that there are asthenic, sthenic, and indirectly asthenic diseases, and equally many attempts at cures! And since such instruction was until quite recently considered sufficient, anybody but a dullard could in such a short span of time be transformed from a *routinier* into a theoretical physician. The formalism of such philosophy of nature teaches, say, that the understanding is electricity, or that animals are nitrogen or equal the south or north, etc., or represent it—whether all this is expressed as nakedly as here or brewed up with a little more terminology. Confronted with such power that brings together what had seemed far apart, and with the violence that the calmly restful things of sense suffer from such connections while they thus receive the semblance of a Concept, though they are spared the main thing, namely to express the Concept itself or the significance of the notion of the senses—confronted with all this, inexperience may well be plunged into admiration and amazement, and it may even venerate in all this the signs of profound genius. Inexperience may also be delighted by the good cheer of such determinations, since they substitute something that can be intuited for the abstract Concept and thus make things more pleasing, and inexperience may even congratulate itself on its intimation of an affinity of souls with such glorious activity.

The trick of such wisdom is learned as quickly as it is easy to master it; its repetition, once it is known, becomes as insufferable as the repetition of a sleight of hand one sees through. The instrument of this monotonous formalism is no more difficult to handle than a painter's palette on which there are only two colors, say, red and green, one if an historical piece is wanted, the other for landscapes.

It would be difficult to decide what is greater—the smugness with which everything in the heavens, on earth, and beneath the earth is coated with such a broth of paint, or the conceit that is based on the supposed excellence of this panacea: each supports the other. The product of this method of labeling everything in heaven and earth, all natural and spiritual forms, with a few determinations of the general schema, and thus pigeonholing everything, is nothing less than a sun-clear report on the organism of the universe — namely a tabulation that is like a skeleton with little pieces of paper stuck all over it, or like the rows of closed, labeled jars in a spicer's stall. While it is as explicit as both of these, it is like them in other ways too: here, flesh and blood are removed from the bones; there, the also not living matter is concealed in jars; and in the report, the living essence of the matter is left out.

This manner has been further perfected into monochromatic absolute painting: ashamed of the distinctions of the schema, one drowns them in the emptiness of the absolute because they belong to reflection, and the new product is then pure identity, formless white. But this has been noted above. That monotony of the schema and its lifeless determinations and this absolute identity, and the transition from one to the other — all are equally dead understanding and equally external knowledge.

The excellent, however, not only cannot escape the fate of being thus deprived of life and spirit, of being flayed and then seeing its skin wrapped around lifeless knowledge and its vanity. Rather we can recognize even in this fate the power of the excellent over the hearts, even if not over minds; also the development toward the generality and determinateness of the form which constitutes its perfection and which alone makes it possible that this generality can be used in the service of superficiality.

Science may organize itself only through the life of the Concept; the determinateness which some would take externally from the schema to affix it to existence is in science the self-moving soul of the abundant content. The movement of beings is, first, to become something other and thus to become their own immanent content; secondly, they take back into themselves this unfolding or this existence of theirs, i.e., they make themselves into a mere moment and simplify themselves into determinateness. In the first movement negativity consists in the differentiation and positing of existence; in the return into oneself it is the becoming of determinate simplicity. In this way, the content does not receive its determinateness from another, like a label; instead it determines itself and assigns itself its place as a moment of the whole. The tabular understanding keeps to itself the necessity and the Concept of the contents — that which constitutes the concreteness, the actuality, and the living movement of the matter that it arranges — or rather, the tabular understanding does not keep this to itself, it does not know this; for if it had this insight it would surely show it. It does not even know the need for it; otherwise it would stop schematizing, or at least know that this process produces no more than a table of contents: it gives only the table of contents; the content itself, however, it does not furnish.

Suppose even that the determinateness is, like magnetism, e.g., concrete in itself and actual: even then it is reduced to something dead, as it is merely predicated of some other existence instead of being known as the immanent life of this existence, or as that which has its native and characteristic self-generation and presentation in this existence. The formal understanding leaves it to others to add this main point.

Instead of entering into the immanent content of the matter, it always looks over the whole and stands above the individual existence of which it speaks, i.e., it simply overlooks it. Scientific knowledge, however, demands precisely that we surrender to the life of the object or—and this is the same—that we confront and express its inner necessity. Thus immersed in its object, scientific knowledge forgets that survey which is merely the reflection of knowledge out of the content into itself. But absorbed in the matter and following the movement of that, it returns to itself—but not until the abundance of the content, simplified into determinateness, returns into itself, reduces itself to one side of existence, and develops into its higher truth. Thus the simple whole that surveys itself emerges from the riches in which its reflection had seemed lost.

Because, as we put it above, the substance is in itself subject, all content is its own reflection in itself. The subsistence or substance of an existence is self-identity; for its non-identity with itself would be its dissolution. But self-identity is pure abstraction; but this is thinking. When I say quality, I say simple determinateness. By its quality an existence is different from another, or is existence; it is for itself, or it subsists through this simplicity with itself. But through this it is essentially thought.—In this the fact is comprehended that being is thinking; and this includes the insight that eludes the usual talk, void of Concept, of the identity of thinking and being.

Inasmuch as the subsistence of existence is self-identity or pure abstraction, it is its own abstraction from itself, or it is itself its non-identity with itself and its dissolution—its own inwardness and return into itself—its becoming. Insofar as this is the nature of beings, and beings have this nature for knowledge, knowledge is not an activity that handles its content as something strange—not reflection into itself, away from the content. Science is not that idealism that replaced the dogmatism of assertions with a dogmatism of assurances or a dogmatism of self-certainty. Rather, when knowledge sees the content return into its own inwardness, the activity of knowledge is both absorbed in the content, being its immanent self, and at the same time this knowledge has returned into itself, for it is pure self-identity in otherhood. Thus it is the cunning that seems to abstain from activity while it looks on as determinateness and its concrete life suppose that they are pursuing their self-preservation and particular interests though in fact they are the converse, an activity that dissolves itself and makes itself a moment of the whole.

Above, we indicated the significance of the understanding with reference to the self-consciousness of substance; from what has now been said one can see its significance with reference to the determination of substance as having being. Existence is quality, self-identical determinateness or determinate simplicity, determinate thought; this is the understanding of existence. Thus it is *nous*, as Anaxagoras was the first to recognize. Those who came after him comprehended the nature of existence more determinately as *eidos* or *idea*, i.e., determinate generality, species. The expression "species" may seem too common and inferior for the Ideas, for the beautiful, holy, and eternal which are now in fashion. But in fact the Idea expresses no more, nor less, than the species. Yet in our day an expression that designates a Concept precisely is often spurned in favor of another term which, if only because it belongs to a foreign language, shrouds the Concept in a fog and thus sounds more edifying.

Precisely when existence is determined as species it is simple thought; the *nous*, the simplicity, is the substance. On account of its simplicity or self-identity it appears firm and enduring. But this self-identity is also negativity; therefore this firm existence passes over into its dissolution. The determinateness at first seems merely due to the fact that it is related to something else, and the movement seems imposed on it by an alien power; but what is contained in this simplicity of thinking is precisely that this determinateness is qualified by its own otherhood and is thus self-movement. For it is the thought that moves and differentiates itself, its own inwardness, the pure Concept. Thus reasonableness is a becoming, and as such becoming it is rationality.

In this nature of beings, to be their Concept in their being, consists logical necessity. This alone is the rational and the rhythm of the organic whole; it is just as much the knowledge of the content as the content is Concept and essence — or it alone is what is speculative.

The concrete form, moving itself, makes itself into simple determinateness. Thus it raises itself to become logical form and attain its essential nature. Its concrete existence is nothing but this movement and is immediately logical existence. Therefore it is unnecessary to impose formalism externally on the concrete content: the content is in itself the transition into formalism which, however, ceases to be this external formalism because the form is the native development of the concrete content itself.

This nature of the scientific method — to be partly not separate from the content, and partly to determine its rhythm by itself — receives, as already mentioned, its proper exposition in speculative philosophy.

What has here been said, to be sure, expresses the Concept, but cannot count for more than an anticipatory assurance. Its truth does not lie in this partly narrative exposition; therefore it also cannot be refuted by the opposed assurance that things are not so but otherwise, or by recalling and recounting conventional conceptions as if they were established and familiar truths, or by assurances of something newly dished up from the shrine of inward divine intuition.

A reception of this sort is usually the first reaction of knowledge to something unfamiliar: one wants to save one's freedom and one's own insight and authority from the alien one — for that which is now first encountered appears in this form. Also, one wants to remove the appearance, and the sort of shame that is supposed to lie in this, that something has been learned. Similarly, when the unfamiliar is accepted with applause, the reaction is motivated the same way and consists in what in another sphere would take the form of ultra-revolutionary speech and action.

15. THE DEMANDS OF THE STUDY OF PHILOSOPHY

What therefore matters in the study of science is taking upon oneself the exertion of the Concept. What is wanted is attention to the Concept as such, to the simple determinations, e.g., of being in itself, being for itself, self-identity, etc.; for these are such pure self-movements which one might call souls if their Concept did not designate something higher. To those accustomed to progress from notion to notion, being interrupted by the Concept seems just as bothersome as it does to formalistic thinking that argues back and forth in unactual thoughts. The former custom should be called material thinking — an accidental consciousness that is merely absorbed in the material and therefore finds it hard to lift the self at the same time clear out of the material to be with itself. The other type, argumentative thinking, is, on the contrary, the freedom from the content and the vanity that looks down on it. This vanity is expected to exert itself, to give up this freedom and to immerse it in the content, instead of merely being the arbitrary moving principle of the content: the content should be made to move itself by virtue of its own nature, i.e., through the self as its own self, and then to contemplate this movement. One should not intrude into the immanent rhythm of the Concepts either arbitrarily or with wisdom gained elsewhere: such restraint is itself an essential moment of attention to the Concept.

16. ARGUMENTATIVE THINKING IN ITS NEGATIVE ATTITUDE —

One should note the two ways in which the argumentative manner is opposed to the thinking that comprehends. — First, such reasoning adopts a negative attitude against its content and knows how to refute and destroy it. That things are otherwise — this insight is merely negative; it is a finality that does not proceed beyond to a new content. Rather, to gain a content again one has to find something somewhere else. This is the reflection into the empty ego, the vanity of its knowledge.

This vanity, however, does not only express that this content is vain but also that this insight itself is vain; for this insight is the negative that does not see what is positive in itself. By never making its own negativity its content, such reflection is never in the matter but always beyond it; therefore it imagines that with its claim of emptiness it is always more advanced than a contentful insight. On the other hand, as shown above, in the thinking that comprehends the negative belongs to the content itself and is the positive both as the immanent movement and determination of the content and as the whole of this. Seen as a result, it is the determinate negative that comes out of this movement, and thus just as much a positive content.

But considering that such thinking has a content, whether it be of notions or of thoughts or of a mixture of both, it has another side that makes comprehension difficult for it. The strange nature of this second side is closely connected with the above-mentioned essence of the idea[32] — or rather expresses it as it appears as the movement which is thinking apprehension.

17.   —IN ITS POSITIVE ATTITUDE; ITS SUBJECT

In its negative behavior, just discussed, argumentative thinking is itself the self into which the content returns; in its positive knowledge, on the other hand, the self is a represented[53] subject to which the content is related as an accident and predicate. This subject constitutes the basis to which the content is tied and on which the movement runs back and forth.

It is different with the thinking that comprehends. The Concept is the object's own self which presents itself as its becoming; thus it is not a subject at rest that carries its attributes unmoved, but it is the Concept that moves itself and takes its determinations back into itself. In this movement the resting subject itself perishes: it enters into the differences and the content and constitutes the determinateness, i.e., the differentiated content and its movement, instead of abiding outside it. The firm ground that argumentative reasoning found in the resting subject thus quakes, and only this movement itself becomes the object. The subject that fills its content ceases to go beyond that and cannot have any other predicates or attributes. The dispersion of the content, conversely, is bound under the self, and the content is not something general that, free from the subject, could be assigned to several others. The content is thus in fact no longer the predicate of the subject; rather it is the substance and the essence and Concept of that which is discussed. It is of the nature of representational[53] thinking to follow the attributes or predicates and to go beyond them, quite rightly, too, because they are mere predicates and attributes; but because that which in a proposition has the form of a predicate is really the substance itself, representational thinking is stopped in its advance. To represent it that way: it suffers a counterthrust. Beginning with the subject, as if this remained the basis, it finds, because the predicate is really the substance, that the subject has moved into the predicate and has thus been sublimated. Thus that which seemed to be predicate has become the whole and independent mass, and thinking can no longer stray freely but is brought to a stop by this gravity.

Usually, the subject is first made the basis as the objective, fixed self, and the necessary movement to the multiplicity of the determinations or predicates proceeds from there. Here, however, this subject is replaced by the knowing ego itself which connects the predicates and becomes the subject that holds them. The first subject enters into the determinations and is their soul; thus the second subject, which knows, still finds in the predicate that with which it had wished to be done so it could return into itself; and instead of being in a position to function as the active element in the movement of the predicate—arguing back and forth whether this or that predicate would be suitable—the second subject is still preoccupied with the self of the content and has to stay with that instead of being by itself.

What has here been said can be expressed more formally: the nature of the judgment or proposition which involves the distinction between subject and predicate, is destroyed by the speculative proposition; and the identical proposition into which the former turns contains the counterthrust against this relation.—This conflict between the form of a proposition and the unity of the Concept that destroys it resembles the conflict between meter and accent in rhythm. Rhythm results from the floating center and unification of both. Thus, in the philosophical proposition, too, the identity of subject and predicate is not meant to destroy the difference between both that is expressed by the form of the proposition; rather their unity is meant to emerge as a harmony. The form of the proposition is the appearance of the determinate sense, or the accent that distinguishes its fulfillment; but that the predicate expresses the substance, and the subject itself falls into the general, that is the unity in which this accent fades away.

Examples may help to explain this. In the proposition "God is being," the predicate is "being." It has substantial meaning in which the subject dissolves. Being here is not meant to be a mere predicate but rather the essence, and God apparently ceases to be the firm subject, in spite of his position in the sentence.—Thinking here does not progress in the transition from the subject to the predicate: the subject gets lost, and thinking feels inhibited and, missing the subject, is thrown back to the thought of the subject. Or, because the predicate is expressed as itself a subject, as being, as the essence which exhausts the nature of the subject, thinking finds the subject immediately in the predicate; and now, instead of attaining in the predicate the free position to argue, it is still absorbed in the content—or at least the demand is present that it ought to be so absorbed.

It is similar when one says: the actual is the general. The actual as a subject vanishes in the predicate. The general is not meant to have merely the meaning of the predicate, as if the proposition were merely meant to say that the actual is general. Rather, the general is supposed to express the essence of the actual. — Thus thinking loses the firm objective ground it had in the subject whenever the predicate throws it back to the subject, so that in the predicate it returns not to itself but to the subject of the content.

This unaccustomed inhibition is the main source of the complaints about the unintelligibility of philosophical writings — at least from those who do not lack other educational prerequisites for understanding them. In what has here been said we find the reason for the specific reproach, which is often heard, that many passages have to be read several times before one can understand them. This is considered improper, and it is supposed that this reproach, if well founded, is final and unanswerable. — From the above it should be clear what this amounts to. The philosophical proposition, being a proposition, gives rise to the opinion that the relation of subject and predicate and the procedure of knowledge are as usual. But the philosophical content destroys this procedure and this opinion; one learns that what one supposed[33] was not what one was supposed to suppose; and this correction of one's opinion requires knowledge to return to the sentence and to reinterpret it.

One difficulty should be avoided: mixing up the speculative style with the argumentative style so that what is said of the subject sometimes has the meaning of its Concept, at other times only the meaning of its predicate or attribute. — One style interferes with the other, and only a philosophical exposition that strictly precluded the usual relation of the parts of a sentence would attain the goal of being really vivid.

Yet non-speculative thinking also has its valid rights that are ignored in the style of the speculative proposition. That the form of the proposition is sublimated should not merely happen immediately, through the mere content of the proposition. Rather, this opposite movement must be expressed; it must not be a mere internal inhibition, but the return of the Concept into itself must be represented expressly. This movement which takes the place of that which proof was once supposed to accomplish is the dialectical movement of the proposition itself. This alone is the actually speculative, and only the expression of this is speculative exposition. As a proposition the speculative is merely internal inhibition and the failure of the essence to return into itself. Therefore we often find that philosophical expositions refer us to this internal intuition and thus spare themselves the presentation of the dialectical movement of the proposition, which we demanded.

The proposition should express what the true is, but essentially this is subject; as such it is merely the dialectical movement, this way that generates itself, leads itself on, and returns into itself. — In non-speculative knowledge proof constitutes this side of expressed inwardness. But since dialectic has been separated from proof, the Concept of philosophical proof has been lost.

Here it may be recalled that the dialectical movement also has propositions for its parts or elements; the difficulty shown here therefore appears to recur always and to be a feature of the matter itself. —This is similar to the situation in ordinary proof where the reasons used require reasons in turn, and so forth ad infinitum. Yet this form of finding reasons and conditions is a feature of those proofs which differ from dialectical movement; it belongs to external knowledge. But the element of the dialectical movement is the pure Concept; thus it has a content that is through and through subject in itself. Thus no content occurs that functions as an underlying subject and receives its meaning as a predicate; the proposition is immediately a merely empty form.

Apart from the self that is intuited or represented by the senses, it is above all the name as name that designates the pure subject, the empty unit void of Concept. For this reason it may be expedient, e.g., to avoid the name "God" because this word is not immediately also a Concept but rather the proper name, the fixed repose of the underlying subject, while, e.g., being or the One, the particular, the subject, etc., also immediately suggest Concepts.

Although speculative truths are formulated about this subject, their content lacks the immanent Concept because it is present only as a subject at rest, and owing to this such truths easily acquire the form of mere edification. —The habit of construing the speculative predicate on the model of a proposition and not as Concept and essence constitutes an obstacle that can be increased or diminished by the manner of the philosophic exposition. In keeping with our insight into the nature of the speculative, the presentation should retain the dialectical form and include nothing except insofar as it is Concept and comprehended.

There is another obstacle that is as serious as the argumentative manner. The study of philosophy is obstructed no less by a conceit that does not deign to argue: one supposes that one is in possession of established truths which do not require discussion but can be assumed as the basis of what follows: one feels free to pronounce them and to judge and condemn by appealing to them. At this point it is particularly necessary that philosophy should again be made a serious pursuit. Of all sciences, arts, skills, and crafts one is convinced that mastery requires a multiple effort of learning and exercise. But when it comes to philosophy, quite another prejudice is prevalent today: although one grants that having eyes and fingers is not enough to enable everyone who is given leather and tools to make shoes, it is held that everybody can immediately philosophize and judge philosophy merely because he possesses the measure in his natural reason — as if one did not equally possess the measure for a shoe in one's foot.

It seems that the mastery of philosophy is found precisely in the lack of knowledge and study, as if philosophy ceased where these begin. Philosophy is often considered a merely formal knowledge, void of content, and the insight is sadly lacking that whatever content of knowledge or science is truth does not deserve this name unless it has been produced by philosophy. Let the other sciences try to get somewhere by arguing without philosophy as much as they please: without it, they cannot contain life, spirit, or truth.

18. NATURAL PHILOSOPHIZING AS HEALTHY COMMON SENSE AND AS GENIUS

When it comes to real philosophy, the long path of education and the movement, as rich as it is profound, through which the spirit reaches knowledge are now considered dispensable, and the immediate revelation of the divine and a healthy common sense that has never troubled or educated itself with other knowledge or with philosophy proper are held to be just as good and as perfect a substitute as some claim chicory is for coffee. It is not pleasant to remark that ignorance, indeed even crudeness that lacks form as much as taste and is incapable of concentrating thought on an abstract sentence, not to speak of the connection of several, assures us now that it is the freedom and tolerance of thought, now that it is nothing less than genius. As is well known, such genius, now the rage in philosophy, once raged no less in poetry; but when the products of such genius had any meaning at all, they were not poetry but trivial prose or, when they were more, mad oratory. Thus a supposedly natural philosophizing that considers itself too good for Concepts and thinks that this lack makes it an intuitive or visionary and poetical thinking, in fact brings to market arbitrary combinations of an imagination that has merely been disorganized by thought — fabrications that are neither flesh nor fish, neither poetry nor philosophy.

Flowing along in the calmer bed of healthy common sense, natural philosophizing entertains us with a rhetoric of trivial truths. Reproached with the insignificance of all this, it assures us that meaning and fulfillment reside in its heart and must reside in other hearts, too — and one supposes that such references to the innocence of the heart, the purity of conscience, *et al.*, represent final matters which brook no objection or further demands. But the task was not to leave the best deep inside but to bring it to light out of these depths. To produce final truths of that sort was trouble one might easily have spared oneself, for it has long been easy to find them in the catechism, in popular proverbs, etc.

It is not difficult to show how indeterminate and vague, or how misleading, such truths are, or even to show to consciousness how it also contains diametrically opposite truths. As consciousness tries to extricate itself from this confusion it is likely to fall into new confusions and may finally expostulate that as a matter of fact things are thus and thus while those supposed truths are sophistries. "Sophistries" is a slogan that common sense likes to use against educated reason, even as ignorance of philosophy likes to apply the expression "idle dreams" to philosophy.

Those who invoke feeling as their internal oracle are finished with anyone who does not agree: they have to own that they have nothing further to say to anyone who does not find and feel the same in his heart—in other words, they trample under foot the roots of humanity. For it is the nature of humanity to struggle for agreement with others, and humanity exists only in the accomplished community of consciousness. The anti-human, the animalic consists in remaining at the level of feeling and being able to communicate only through feelings.

If someone asked for a royal road to science, no road could be more comfortable than this: to rely on healthy common sense and, in order to progress with the times and with philosophy, to read reviews of philosophic essays, at most the prefaces and first paragraphs; for the latter offer the general principles, which are all-important, and the former, in addition to a historical notice, also some judgment which, being a judgment, goes beyond what is judged. This vulgar road can be taken in one's dressing gown; but the elevated feeling of the eternal, the holy, and the infinite struts about in a high priest's robes—on a road that itself is immediate being at the core, the genius of profound and original ideas and lofty flashes of inspiration. Yet even as such profundity still does not reveal the fount of essence, so, too, such rockets are not yet the empyrean. True thoughts and scientific insight are to be won only through the work of the Concept. This alone can produce the generality of knowledge which is neither the common vagueness and paltriness of common sense, but educated and complete knowledge, nor the uncommon generality of the disposition of reason that has corrupted itself through laziness and the conceit of genius, but truth that has developed into its native form—and is thus capable of being owned by all self-conscious reason.

19. CONCLUSION: THE AUTHOR'S RELATION TO THE PUBLIC

I find the distinctive mark of science in the self-movement of the Concept but have to admit that the above-mentioned, as well as several other peripheral, features of the notions of our time about the nature and form of truth are different and indeed quite opposed to my view. It would therefore seem that an attempt to present the System of Science from this point of view is not likely to meet with a favorable reception. But there are other considerations. Occasionally, e.g., the excellence of Plato's philosophy was supposed to be due to his scientifically worthless myths; but there have also been times, which are even called times of wild enthusiasm, when Aristotle's philosophy was esteemed for its speculative profundity and Plato's *Parmenides*, probably the greatest work of art of ancient dialectic, was considered the true disclosure and the positive expression of the divine life, and in spite of the frequent turbidity of the products of ecstasy, this misunderstood ecstasy was in fact supposed to be nothing less than the pure Concept. Furthermore, what has excellence in the philosophy of our time finds its own value in being scientific; and although others understand this differently, it is only through this scientific posture that it actually gains credit. Therefore I can also hope that this attempt to vindicate science for the Concept and to present it in this, its proper, element may win acceptance through the inner truth of the matter.

We must have the conviction that it is of the nature of truth to prevail when its time has come, and that truth appears only when its time has come — and therefore never appears too early, nor ever finds that the public is not ready for it. And the individual needs public acceptance to prove the truth of what is as yet his solitary concern; he needs to see how the conviction that is as yet particular becomes general. But at this point the public must often be distinguished from those who act as if they were its representatives and spokesmen. In some respects the public behaves differently from these people, even in the opposite way. When a philosophical essay is not found appealing, the public may good-naturedly ascribe the fault to itself, but the others, sure of their competence, ascribe the sole fault to the author. In the public the effect is quieter than the activity of these dead men when they bury their dead.

The general level of insight now is more educated, curiosity is wide awake, and judgments are made more quickly than formerly; so the feet of them which shall carry thee out are already at the door. But from this we must often distinguish the slower effect which corrects the attention that was extorted by imposing assurances as well as disdainful reproaches: some writers find an audience only after a time, while others after a time have none any more.

In our time general participation in the life of the spirit has been greatly strengthened, and every particular, as is fitting, counts for that much less. Moreover, this vast public clings to and demands its full extent and the wealth of its education; so the share of the total work of the spirit that can be assigned to the activity of any individual has to be small. Hence the individual—and this is in any case in keeping with the nature of science —should forget himself that much more. To be sure, he should become and do what he can; but less should be demanded of him, even as he must expect less of himself and demand less for himself.

V. The Phenomenology of Spirit or Science of the Experience of Consciousness: Introduction*

It is a natural idea that before getting down to business in philosophy, that is, to really knowing what truly is, it is necessary first to be clear about knowing, this being regarded as the instrument with which we gain possession of the Absolute, or as the means through which we catch sight of it. The concern seems well founded that on the one hand there may be various kinds of knowledge, and among them one handier than another for reaching this goal, and so by choosing the wrong one — and on the other that, since knowing is a faculty of particular kind and scope, without a rather particular determination of its nature and limits — clouds of error instead of the heaven of truth will be seized. This concern cannot, indeed, but turn into the conviction that the whole undertaking, through knowing to secure for consciousness that which is 'in itself' is in its very conception absurd, and that between knowing and the Absolute there falls a line which utterly divides them. For, if knowing is the instrument for gaining possession of the absolute nature of things, then it is immediately obvious that using an instrument on a thing does not in fact leave it as it is by itself, but rather effects a fashioning and alteration of it. Or, if knowing is not an instrument we use, but as it were a passive medium through which the light of truth comes down to us, then here too we obtain this, the truth, not as it is in itself, but as it is in and through this medium. In both cases we use a means which without meaning to produces the very reverse of what is intended with it; or what is really absurd is that we make use of a means at all. It seems admittedly that this drawback could be overcome through a knowledge of the kind of effect the *instrument* has, for that would enable us at the final stage to subtract from the idea we receive by means of it of the Absolute that part which is due to the instrument, and so to obtain the truth in its purity. However, this remedy would in the event simply take us back to where we were previously. When we subtract from a thing that has been modified in some way whatever the instrument has done to it, then as

*Newly translated by J. L. H. Thomas.

far as we are concerned the thing—here the Absolute—is once again exactly what it was before this now wasted effort. If the instrument is supposed merely to draw the Absolute somewhat closer to us without changing it in any way—as a bait draws a bird, say—then, were it not in and for itself already with us and willing to be so, the Absolute would surely scorn the subterfuge: for a subterfuge is just what knowing would be in this case, in pretending with all its efforts to be up to something quite other than simply establishing a relation that is immediate and so effortless. Or, if the examination of knowledge, which we picture to ourselves as a *medium*, yields us its index of refraction, still nothing whatsoever is gained by subtracting the refraction from the result; for it is not the way the ray is refracted, but the ray itself, by which truth comes into contact with us, that is knowledge, and were the latter subtracted we should have been shown merely its direction or point of origin.

However, if the concern that we may fall into error is the source of a mistrust in the Science which without any such misgivings gets down to work and actually knows, it is difficult to see why, conversely, a mistrust should not be placed in this mistrust, and one not be concerned that this fear of erring is itself the very error. And, in fact, this fear does presuppose something, indeed the truth of a great deal, and it is upon this that its misgivings and inferences are based, although it is precisely the truth of these presuppositions that has first to be examined. What it presupposes is, first, certain *models* of *knowing* as an *instrument* or *medium*; further, a *distinction between ourselves and this knowing*; but above all this, that *the Absolute* lies *on the one side* and *knowing on the other*, by itself, divided from the Absolute, and yet something real, or in these terms, that knowing, lying outside the Absolute and so of course outside the truth as well, is nevertheless truthful, an assumption, the upshot of which is that what calls itself a fear of error reveals itself rather to be a fear of truth.

This conclusion follows from the Absolute's alone being true, or the truth's alone being absolute. It can be declined by drawing a distinction to the effect that a knowing which does not know the Absolute, as Science intends, can still be true too; and that any knowing, though it may be incapable of grasping the Absolute, can still be capable of some other truth. But sooner or later we see that such prevarication comes down to an obscure distinction between what is true absolutely and some other kind of truth, and that 'the Absolute', 'knowledge', and so on, are words supposing a significance which it is our first task to establish.

Instead of worrying oneself, first, with such unhelpful models and slo-gans, as of knowledge being an instrument for gaining possession of the Absolute or a medium through which we catch sight of the truth, and so on—terms to which in the end all these models of a knowing divided from the Absolute, and of an Absolute divided from knowing, come down; then, with excuses, which on the basis of these terms make out the incapacity of

Science, so as at one and the same time to free oneself from the effort of Science and to give oneself the air of serious and zealous effort; and, finally, with answers to all these difficulties, they could be rejected out of hand as fortuitous and arbitrary models, and the associated use of words like 'the Absolute', 'knowledge', as well as 'objective', 'subjective', and countless others, the meaning of which is supposed to be generally known, simply be regarded as a fraud. For the claim, on the one hand that their meaning is generally known, on the other that one has the concept of them oneself, seems designed rather only to avoid the main task, namely that of providing this concept. On the contrary, and with more justification, one could spare oneself the effort of paying any attention at all to such models and slogans, with which Science itself is intended to be kept at bay, for they are nothing but an empty show of knowledge, a show which vanishes the moment Science itself comes on the scene. But Science, in coming on, is itself putting in an appearance; its debut is not yet Science itself carried out and set out in its truth. It is a matter of indifference in all this whether òne thinks of *Science* as the appearance, because it comes on *along with other things*, or calls that other, truthless knowledge the way it appears. Either way, Science must free itself of this semblance; and this it can do only by facing up to it. For Science cannot simply repudiate a knowing that is not truthful as a vulgar perspective of things, and claim that it itself is a quite different kind of knowledge, to which that other kind of knowing means nothing whatsoever; nor can Science appeal to the inkling of something better within the latter. With that first *claim* Science would be declaring its *might* to be its right; but truthless knowledge can equally appeal to the fact that *it is*, and *claim* that Science means nothing to it either; and *one* bare claim is worth just as much as another. Still less can Science appeal to the inkling of better things which is supposed to be present in the knowledge that is not truthful, and to be within the latter the signpost to Science; because, for one thing, Science would again be appealing no less to 'how it is'; and, for another, appealing to itself in the form in which it is present in truthless knowledge — that is, to a lowly form in which it itself exists, and so to its appearance rather than to how it is in and for itself. It is for this reason that the presentation of knowing as it appears is here to be undertaken.

Now because this presentation has only knowing as it appears for its object, it itself seems not to be the free Science, moving in its characteristic shape, but can from the latter standpoint be taken as the path of natural consciousness pressing on towards true knowledge; or as the way of the soul passing through the sequence of its transformations, stages set it in advance by its own nature, so that it may purify itself to Spirit and, through the complete experience of itself, come to a knowledge of what it is in itself.

Natural consciousness will prove itself to be solely a conception of knowing, or a knowing that is not real. But as natural consciousness takes itself from the first to be real knowledge rather, this path has for it a negative value, and it regards as its personal loss what is rather the realization of the conception, for on this path it loses its truth. It can accordingly be seen as the way of *doubt*, or more correctly as the way of redoubtable despair; for on it there does not take place what is commonly understood by doubting, a shaking of some supposed truth or other, conveniently followed by the disappearance of the doubt and a return to the earlier truth, so that in the end the matter stands as before. Rather, this path is the conscious insight into the untruth of knowing as it appears, a knowing which takes to be most real what is in truth only the unrealized conception. This self-consummating scepticism is consequently not what an earnest zeal for Truth and Science doubtless fancies it has expressly prepared and equipped itself with either: namely, the *maxim*, never to submit oneself upon authority to the ideas of others, but to examine everything for oneself and to follow solely one's own conviction; or, even better, always to do it yourself and to regard only what one has done oneself as true. The series of transformations through which consciousness passes on this path is rather the full record of consciousness's own *education* to Science. The maxim mentioned above pictured education as over and done with and now past in the simplified manner of a maxim; contrary to this untruth, however, the present path is the actual doing of it. To follow one's own conviction is, true enough, to do more than submit to authority; but the change from assent through authority into assent through personal conviction does not necessarily mean that the content of what is assented to has changed and truth come to take the place of error. To stay put in a tissue of opinion and prejudice on the authority of others, and to do so from personal conviction are distinguished solely by the vanity attaching to the latter. That scepticism which directs itself upon the whole compass of consciousness as it appears is, by contrast, what first puts Spirit in a position to assess what truth is, by provoking a despair in so-called natural models, ideas, and opinions—it does not matter whether these are called one's own or others'—with which the consciousness that gets down to testing *without further ado* is still preoccupied and encumbered, and as a result incapable, when it comes to it, of doing what it wants.

The *completeness* of the forms of the consciousness that is not real will follow of itself from the necessity of the progression and interconnexion. To make this intelligible, the general observation can be made in advance that the presentation of truthless consciousness in its untruth is not a merely *negative* movement. It is such a one-sided view that natural consciousness has of it throughout; and a knowing which makes of this one-sidedness its very essence is one of the forms of unfinished consciousness, which will come up in the course of this journey and there present itself. This is, to wit, the scepticism which only ever sees in the result *pure nothing*, abstracting from the fact that this 'nothing' is specified as the nothing *of that from which it results*. But 'nothing,' taken as the nothing of what it comes from, just is in the event the true result; it is consequently itself *determinate* and has a *content*. The scepticism which ends up with the abstraction of 'nothing' or the void cannot go on from there, but must wait and see what next may be offered it for it to cast into the same bottomless abyss. When, on the other hand, the result is grasped as it truly is, as *determinate* negation, then, by that very token, a new form has arisen, and in the negation the transition been made, whereby the advance through the entire sequence of forms follows of itself.

Knowing, however, has its *destination* laid down just as necessarily as the sequence of stages: it lies where knowing no longer finds it necessary to go out beyond itself, where it finds itself and the concept matches the object and the object the concept. The advance to this destination is hence inexorable as well, and at no earlier stage is satisfaction to be found. Whatever is confined to a natural existence cannot of its own accord go out beyond its present form of life, but is driven out beyond it by something else; and to be so torn out is for it very death. But consciousness is of itself its own *concept*, so by that very token a going beyond limitations and, since these limitations are part of it, beyond itself; as well as the particular thing, consciousness is also set a 'beyond', albeit only, in spatial terms, *beside* what is limited. Consequently, consciousness suffers the violence of having its narrow satisfaction spoiled at its own hands. On sensing this violence, fear may well draw back before the truth and seek to preserve for itself what threatens to be lost. However, this fear can find no rest — unless, that is, it wants to remain in thoughtless indolence; but thought spoils thoughtlessness, and its restlessness disturbs indolence — or unless it entrenches itself as a sensibility which claims to find everything *good of its kind*; but this claim likewise suffers violence from reason, which finds something no good precisely to the extent that it is of a kind. Or the fear of the truth may hide itself from itself, as well as from others, behind the illusion that it is precisely its burning zeal for truth that makes it so difficult, nay impossible, for it to find any truth other than the sole one of the conceit of always being even cleverer than any ideas one has got from oneself or others; this conceit, which knows how to defeat every truth to its own satisfaction and thereafter return into itself to gloat over this capacity it has to understand, that is, to pull apart any idea you please and in lieu of any content find merely the same old 'I', is a gratification which must be left to its own devices, for it shuns what is universal and seeks only to be its own company.

In keeping with these preliminary remarks in general terms about the manner and necessity of the progression, it may be helpful to say something too about *the way it is carried out*. It would seem that this account, pictured as *the way Science stands* to knowing *as it appears*, and as an *investigation* and *assessment of the reality of knowing*, cannot be implemented without some presupposition or other, which is laid down as a *criterion*. For assessment consists in the application of an accepted criterion, and upon the resulting correspondence or lack of correspondence between what is being assessed and the criterion rests the decision whether the former is correct or incorrect; and whatever criterion is used, and so Science too, were it the criterion, is thereby taken as the *essence* or '*in itself*'. But here, where Science first comes on, neither Science itself nor anything else has legitimated itself as the essence or 'in itself'; and without something of the kind it would seem that no assessment can take place.

The nature of this objection and how it is dealt with will emerge more sharply, if we first recall the abstract determinations of knowing and of truth as they are found in consciousness. Consciousness, namely, *distinguishes* something from itself, to which it at the same time *relates* itself; or, as this is put, there is something *for consciousness*; and the specific facet of this *relating*, or of something's *being for a consciousness*, is *knowledge*. From this being for something else we distinguish now '*being in itself*': that which is related to knowing is no less distinguished from the latter and laid down as also *being* apart from this relation; and this facet of 'in itself' is called *truth*. How it really is with these determinations does not concern us here any further, for inasmuch as knowledge as it appears is our object, so too its determinations are first taken as they immediately present themselves; and it is very much as they have been set out that they present themselves.

If now we examine the truth of knowing, then it seems we are investigating what it, knowing, is *in itself*. But in this investigation knowing is *our* object, it is *for us*; and the 'in itself' purportedly obtained in respect of it would thus be rather its being *for us*; what we should declare to be its essence would not be its truth, but only our knowledge of the essence. The essence or criterion would lie in us, and that which is supposedly being compared with it, and concerning which a decision is to be taken as a result of this comparison, would not be obliged to recognize it.

But the nature of the object which we are investigating spares us this division, or this semblance of division and presupposition. Consciousness provides its criterion in its own person, and the investigation will consequently be a comparison of consciousness with itself; for the distinction which has just been made falls within it. There is in consciousness one thing *for another* thing, or consciousness as such has about itself the determinateness of the moment of knowing; at the same time this other thing is to consciousness not only *for consciousness*, but also apart from this relation or *in itself*—the moment of truth. In what consciousness declares within itself to be the '*in itself*' or the truth we have then the criterion, which consciousness itself sets up, for measuring its knowledge against it. If we call *knowing* the *concept*, the essence or *truth* on the other hand that which is, or the *object*, then the assessment consists in seeing whether the concept matches the object. But if we call *the essence* or 'in itself' *of the object* the *concept*, and conversely understand by the *object* the latter qua *object*, namely as it is *for something else*, then the assessment consists in our seeing whether the object matches its concept. It will be seen that both amount to one and the same; the essential thing, however, is to bear the following in mind throughout the whole investigation, that both these moments, *concept* and *object*, '*being-for-another*' and '*being-in-itself*', themselves lie within the knowing which we are investigating, and that consequently we shall not find it necessary to provide criteria of our own, and to apply *our* ideas and thoughts in the course of the investigation; and, by leaving these on one side, we shall succeed in viewing the matter as it is *in* and *for itself*.

But it is not only in this respect—namely, that concept and object, criterion and that which is to be assessed, are present in consciousness itself—that anything we do will be superfluous; we are also spared the effort of comparing the two and actually *assessing* them, so that, as consciousness assesses itself, all that remains for us in the latter respect too is simply to look on. For consciousness is on the one hand consciousness of the object, on the other consciousness of itself: consciousness of what to it is the truth, and consciousness of its knowing of the latter. As both are *for consciousness*, it itself is their comparison; it will be a matter *for consciousness* itself whether its knowledge of the object matches the latter or not. Admittedly, the object seems to be for consciousness only as consciousness knows it; consciousness seems unable, as it were, to get round at the object, *not* as it is *for consciousness*, but as it is *in itself*, and so too unable to assess its knowledge against it. But it is precisely in the fact that consciousness knows of an object at all that the distinction is already present to the effect that *consciousness* has one thing as the '*in itself*', and another moment as the knowledge, or the being of the object *for* consciousness. It is upon the making of this distinction, which is actually to hand, that the assessment rests. If in this comparison the two do not match, then it seems that consciousness must change its knowledge to make it adequate to the object; but, in the event, through the change in the knowing the very object of consciousness too is changed: for the knowledge in question was essentially a knowledge of the object; along with the knowledge, the object too becomes another, for it was essentially part and parcel of this knowledge. Hence consciousness comes to see that what it took previously as the '*in itself*' is not in itself, or that it was *in itself* only *for consciousness*. Consequently, as consciousness finds with its object that its knowledge does not match the latter, the object itself does not hold out either; that is, the criterion used in the assessment changes when that of which it is intended to be the criterion does not pass the test; and the assessment is not only an assessment of knowledge, but of the criterion used as well.

This *dialectical* movement, which consciousness exercises upon itself, as much upon its knowledge as upon its object, *insofar as its new, true object arises out of it*, is really what is meant by *experience*. In this connexion there is one moment of the process just mentioned to be examined more closely, and this will shed a new light on the scientific aspect of the following account. Consciousness knows *something*, this object is the essence or '*in itself*'; but the object is also the '*in itself*' for consciousness; thus it is that the ambivalence of this 'truth' comes in. We see that consciousness now has two objects, one being the first '*in itself*', the other *the 'being-for-conscious-ness' of this 'in itself'*. The latter seems at first to be merely the reflexion of consciousness into itself, a representing, not of an object, but only of consciousness's knowing of that first object. But, as shown above, consciousness thereby has its first object changed; the latter ceases to be the 'in itself', and becomes to consciousness an object that is only *for consciousness* the '*in itself*'; and so then the latter, *the being-for-consciousness of this 'in itself'*, is what is true, and that means that this is the *essence*, or the *object* of consciousness. This new object contains the nullity of the first; it is what experience has made of it.

In this account of the course of experience there is a moment, or factor, which does not seem to agree with what is commonly understood by experience. The transition, namely, from the first object and the knowing of it to the second object, *with which*, as one says, the experience has been had, was expressed by saying that the knowing of the first object, or the being-*for*-consciousness of the first 'in itself', is itself supposed to become the second object. By contrast, it seems in other cases that we learn by experience of the untruth of our first conception *with another* object which we happen to find lying around somewhere, so that all in all it is only the mere *taking in* of what is in and for itself that falls to us. On the above view, however, the new object reveals itself to have arisen through a *turning-about of consciousness* itself. This way of viewing the matter is our addition, and it is by virtue of it that the sequence of the experiences of consciousness is raised to a scientific movement, although this view is not for the consciousness which we are observing. This is in actual fact, however, just the same feature as that already discussed above in connexion with the relation of this presentation to scepticism, namely that each result arising from a knowing that is not truthful should not be left to dwindle into an empty 'nothing,' but must needs be understood as the nothing *of that of which* it is *the result*, a result which contains whatever truth the previous knowledge had in it. This presents itself here in such a way that, as consciousness has what first appeared as the object sink to a knowing of it, and the 'in itself' become a '*being-for-consciousness*' *of the 'in itself'*, the latter is the new object, whereupon also a new form of consciousness emerges which has as essence something different from that of the previous form. This feature it is which leads the whole sequence of the forms of consciousness on in their necessity. It is simply and solely this necessity, or the *arising* of the new object to present itself to consciousness without the latter's knowing what is happening to it, that for us, as it were, goes on behind consciousness's back.

Thus there enters its movement a moment of '*being-in-itself*' or '*being-for-us*,' which does not present itself to the consciousness which is caught up in the experience itself; the *content*, however, of what we see arise is *for it*, and we grasp only its formal aspect, or just the way it arises; *for consciousness* what has thus arisen is only as object, *for us* it is at the same time movement and becoming.

By virtue of this necessity this path to Science is already itself *Science* and, having the content it has, Science of the *Experience of Consciousness*.

The experience which consciousness has concerning itself can, given the concept of experience, comprehend in itself nothing less than the whole system of consciousness, or the whole realm of the truth of Spirit, so that the moments of this truth present themselves with the specific characteristic of not being abstract moments and nothing more, but of being as they are for consciousness, or as the latter itself emerges in its relation to them, whereby the moments of the whole are *forms of consciousness*. In pressing on to its true form of existence, consciousness will reach a point at which it will lay aside its semblance of being burdened with something alien that is only for it, or as an other, that is, where appearance becomes equal to essence, the presentation of consciousness consequently coinciding at this very point with the true Science of Spirit; and finally, by itself grasping this its essence, consciousness will betoken the nature of Absolute Knowing itself.

VI.   Phenomenology of Spirit: Consciousness*

THE SENSUOUS CERTITUDE, OR THE THIS AND THE MEANING.

The knowing which is, at first or immediately, our object, can be no other than that which is itself immediate knowing—a knowing of the immediate or that which is. We have, likewise, to conduct ourselves toward it, in an immediate manner, i.e. *apprehending* it, and taking care to change nothing that is presented in it,—in short, we must simply *apprehend* and hold back all tendency to *comprehend*.

The concrete content of the sensuous certitude appears immediately as the *richest* knowing, even as a knowing of infinite wealth, for which no limit is to be found, whether we go out into space and time in which it expands itself, or whether, selecting a specimen out of this fullness we go through analysis into the same. Besides this, it appears as the most true; for it has omitted nothing from the object, but has the same before it in its entire completeness. This certitude, however, turns out in point of fact to be the most abstract and poorest truth. It says, of what it knows, only this: It is; and its truth contains merely the *being* of the subject-matter; the consciousness for its part, in this certitude, is merely as pure *Ego*; or the Ego is therein merely as a pure This and the object, likewise, as a pure This. I—This one—am certain of this subject-matter, not for the reason that I, as consciousness, have unfolded myself in this, and my thought has been active; nor for the reason that the subject-matter of which I am certain, is, in a variety of respects, rich in relations to itself or a state of manifold relation to other things; neither of these circumstances has anything to do with the truth of sensuous certitude. Neither the Ego nor the subject-matter contains a manifold mediation; the Ego has not the signification of a manifold representing or thinking, nor has the subject-matter the signification of manifold properties. The subject-matter *is*; and *it is merely because it is.* "It is,"—this is the essential point for sensuous knowing, this pure

*Translated by W. T. Harris in the *Journal of Speculative Philosophy*, II (1868), with revision by M. J. Inwood.

being, or this simple immediateness, constitutes its truth. Moreover, the certitude as relation, is immediate, pure relation; consciousness is the Ego, and nothing more, a pure This; the individual knows purely this, or the individual.

But to the pure being which constitutes the essence of this certitude, and which it asserts as truth, much else is attached, if we examine closely. A given, real, sensuous certitude, is not merely this pure immediateness, but an *example* of the same. Among countless distinctions which occur on every hand in this, we find everywhere the main distinction, viz: that in it the two already named This's at once separate from the pure being—one This as Ego, the other This as object. If we reflect upon this distinction, it becomes obvious that neither the one nor the other is merely immediate in the sensuous certitude, but both are at the same time mediate; the Ego possesses its certitude through another, namely, the subject-matter, and the latter is likewise in the certitude through another, namely, the Ego.

This distinction of essence and example, of immediateness and mediation, is not one that is made merely by us, but we find it in the sensuous certitude itself, and we must proceed to take it up in the form which it has there, and not in the [reflective] mode which we have just now been using. One "This" is posited in the certitude as the simple, immediately existent, or as the essence, *the Object*; the other "This," however, is posited as the unessential and mediated which is therein not in itself but through another —the ego, a knowing which knows the object only because the object *is*, and which may or may not be. The object, however, is the true and the essence; it *is*, indifferent whether it is known or not; it remains even if it is not known; but the knowing is not if the object is not.

The object, therefore, is to be considered in order to ascertain whether it, in point of fact, is, in the sensuous certitude, such an essence as that for which it is given out by the certitude; whether this, which is defined to be essence, proves to be so in reality. For this purpose we have not to reflect and think, concerning it, inquiring what it is in truth, but only to consider it as found in the sensuous certitude.

It, therefore, is itself to be interrogated: What is the This? If we take it in the two-fold form of its being, as the Now and the Here, its dialectic will obtain as intelligible a form as the subject possesses. To the question: What is the Now? We answer, for example: The Now is night. In order to test the truth of this sensuous certitude, a simple experiment is sufficient. We write this truth down; a truth can lose nothing by being written down, for that is the way to preserve it. If we look now, this noon, at this truth that was written down, we shall have to say that it is become stale.

The Now which is night is preserved, i.e. it is treated as that which it professes to be—as an existent; but it proves itself to be a non-existent, rather. Although the Now preserves itself, yet it is as a somewhat which is not night; the same thing happens to the day which it is now, namely, the

Now proves itself to be not the day, but a negative somewhat in general. This Now which preserves itself, therefore, is not an immediate, but a mediate somewhat; for it is determined as an abiding and self-preserving somewhat, through this, that while others, namely, the day and night are not, nevertheless, *it* is just as simply a Now as before, and in this simplicity it is indifferent to whatever else plays around it; as little as day and night are its being, just as much is it also both day and night; it is not affected, at all, through this—its other being. Such a simple, which is through negation neither This nor That—a Not-this, and likewise indifferent whether it *is* This or that—we call a Universal; the Universal, therefore, is in point of fact the True of sensuous certitude.

We also *express* the sensuous fact as a universal; what we say is: "This," i.e. the universal This; or: "It is," i.e. Being in general. Of course, we do not, on this occasion, *represent* to ourselves the universal This, or Being in general, but we *express* the universal; in other words, we do not *speak* what we *mean* in this sensuous certitude. But language is, we see, the more true; in it we refute immediately our meaning,—and since the Universal is the True of sensuous certitude and language expresses only *this* True, it is entirely impossible that we should ever be able to express a sensuous being which we *mean*.

The same will be the case with the other form of the This, with the Here. The Here is, e.g. the tree. I turn around and this truth has vanished and has converted itself into its opposite: the Here is not a tree but rather a house. The Here itself vanishes not, but it abides in the vanishing of the house, the tree, &c., and is indifferent whether it is house or tree. The This (somewhat) therefore shows itself again to be a mediated simplicity, or Universality.

For this sensuous certitude, therefore, while it shows the Universal to be the truth of its object, pure Being remains as its essence, not as an immediate, however, but as a somewhat to which negation and mediation are essential; hence, not what we *mean* by Being, but *Being with the determination that it is the abstraction or the pure Universal;* and our *meaning* for which the true of the sensuous certitude is not the Universal is left alone, standing opposite to this empty or indifferent Now and Here.

If we compare the relation in which the knowing and the object stood to each other when they first entered upon the scene, with the relation in which they stand now in this result, we shall discover that it has become inverted. The object which was taken for the Essential, is now the Unessential of sensuous certitude; for the Universal into which it has been changed, is no longer such a somewhat as it was supposed to be essentially by itself, but it is now in the contrary somewhat, namely, in the Knowing, which previously was taken for the Unessential. Its truth is in the object as *mine*, or in the *meaning*—it is, because *I* know it. The sensuous certitude is therefore driven out of the object; but through that, it is not yet cancelled, but only driven back into the Ego; it remains to be seen what experience teaches us with reference to this its reality.

The force of its truth lies, therefore, in the Ego — in the immediateness of my *seeing, hearing,* &c.; the vanishing of the particular Now and Here, which we mean, is prevented through the fact that the Ego holds them fast. The Now is day, because the Ego sees it; the Here is a tree, for the same reason. But the sensuous certitude experiences, in this relation, the same dialectic as in the former case. I, *this* Ego, see the tree and assert the tree to be the Here; but another Ego sees the house and asserts that the Here is not a tree but a house. Both truths have the same evidence, namely, the immediateness of seeing, and the certainty and testimony of each concerning its knowing; but the one vanishes in the other.

That which does not vanish is the Ego as universal, whose seeing is neither a seeing of the tree nor of this house, but a simple seeing which is mediated through the negation of this house, &c., and is simple and indifferent in respect to that which still plays around it — i.e. the house and the tree. The Ego is merely universal, as Now, Here, or This, in general; although I *mean* a particular Ego, yet just as little as I can say what I mean by Now and Here, just so little can I say what I mean by Ego. When I say this Here, Now, or a particular, I say all This's, all Here's, all Now's, all particulars; likewise when I say Ego, *this particular* Ego, I say in general all Ego's; for each is what I say — Ego, this particular Ego. If the demand is made upon science, as a test by which it must prove its adequacy, that it deduce a so-called *this thing* or a *this man* — or to construct it a priori, if one wishes to express it so — it is surely not more than fair that the demand express *which* "this thing," or *which* "this Ego" it means; but to say this is impossible.

The sensuous certitude discovers, therefore, that its essence is neither in the object nor in the Ego, and that the immediateness is neither an immediateness of the one nor of the other; for to either that which I *mean* is rather an Unessential, and the object and Ego are Universals in which that particular Now and Here and Ego which I *mean* do not remain or be. Through this we are forced to posit the whole of the sensuous certitude as its essence, and no longer to do this of a mere moment thereof — as we did in the two instances already considered, wherein, first, the object opposed to the Ego was taken for the reality, and second, the Ego itself for such. It is therefore only the entire sensuous certitude which holds fast to it as immediateness, and thereby excludes all opposition which was present in the former cases.

With this pure immediateness, the other-being of the Here, as a tree, which passes over into a Here, which is not a tree; the other-being of the Now, as day, which passes over into a Now, that is Night, or another Ego to whom something else is object, has therefore nothing to do. Its truth preserves itself as a relation which remains equal to itself, and which causes no distinction between the Ego and the object, of essentiality and unessentiality, and into which, therefore, no distinction in general can possibly penetrate. I, this Ego, assert, therefore, the Here as a tree, and do not turn around so that the Here would become a not-tree; neither do I take any notice of the fact that another Ego sees the Here as a not-tree, or that I myself, at some other time, took the Here as a not-tree, the now as not-day — but I am pure intuition; I, for myself, insist that the Now is day, or in like manner that the Here is a tree, and moreover I do not compare the Here and Now themselves with each other, but I cling to one immediate relation: the Now is day.

Since this certitude refuses to notice when we call its attention to a Now which is night, or to an Ego for which it is night, we must go to it and permit it to show to us the Now which it asserts. We must allow it to be shown to us, for the truth of this immediate relation is the truth of this Ego which limits itself to a Now or a Here. If we were to hear of this truth subsequently, or to stand at a distance from it, it would have no significance at all; for we should then cancel the immediateness which is essential to it. We are bound, therefore, to enter into the same moment of time, or of space, and let it be shown to us, i.e. we must let ourselves be transformed into the same Ego which is subject of the certitude in question. Let us, then, see what is the nature of this Immediate which is shown to us.

The Now is shown; *this* Now. Now; while it is being shown, it has already ceased to be; the Now which is, is another from the one shown, and we see that the Now is precisely this; to be no more, while it is. The Now which is shown to us is a Been; and this is its truth; it has not the truth of Being. This, then, is surely true, that it *has been.* But what has been, is, in point of fact, no essence; it is not, and Being was the very thing in question.

Hence we see in this exhibition merely a movement and the following course thereof: (1) I exhibit the Now; it is asserted as the true; but I show it as a Been or as a cancelled, I cancel the first truth and (2) now I assert as the second truth that it *has been,* that it is cancelled. (3) But that which has been is not; I cancel the Been (or cancelled Being,) the second truth, and thus negate the negation of the Now, and return to the first assertion: the Now is. The Now and the exhibition of the Now possess, therefore, this nature, that neither the Now nor the showing of the Now is an immediate Simple, but an activity which consists of different moments; the This is posited, but instead of it another is posited rather, or the This is cancelled; and this other being or the cancelling of the first is itself again cancelled and thus there is a return to the first. But this first, reflected into itself, is not quite the same that it was in the beginning, namely, an immediate; but it is precisely a somewhat which is reflected into itself, or a Simple which remains in the other being what it is; a Now which is absolutely many Nows; and this is the true Now; the Now as simple day, which has many Nows within it, hours; such a Now, an hour, is likewise many minutes, and this Now also many Nows and so on. The showing is, therefore, the activity which expresses what the Now in truth is, namely, a result, or a manifold of Nows taken together; and the showing is the experiencing that the Now is universal.

The exhibited Here, which I hold fast, is likewise a this Here, which, in fact, is not *this* Here, but a Before and Behind, an Above and Below, a Right and Left. The Above is itself likewise this manifold other-being, an Above and Below, &c. The Here which was to be shown vanishes in other Heres, but the latter vanish no less; the "Shown," the Retained and Remaining is a negative This, which is only so while the Here is taken for what it offers itself, but therein cancels itself; it is a simple complex of many Heres. The Here which is *meant* would be the point; but it does not exist, but while it is shown as being, the process of such "showing" shows itself to be not an immediate knowing but a movement proceeding from the "meant" Here through many Heres into the universal Here, which, just as the day is a simple multiplicity of Nows, is a simple multiplicity of Heres.

It is obvious that the dialectic of the sensuous certitude is nothing else than the simple history of its activity or its experience, and the sensuous certitude itself is nothing else than merely this history. The natural consciousness, therefore, for this reason also always goes forward to this result, and makes this experience concerning it; but it likewise always forgets it again, and begins the movement from the beginning. It is therefore surprising that in the face of this experience we hear it asserted as a matter of universal experience (and even as a philosophical conclusion or a result of skepticism) that the reality or Being of external things as This's or sensuous particulars has absolute truth for the consciousness. Such an assertion does not know at the same time what it says; it knows not that it says the opposite of what it meant to say. The truth of the sensuous This's is asserted to be universal experience for the consciousness; but the converse rather is universal experience; every consciousness cancels such a truth as e.g.: "the Here is a tree," or "the Now is noon," of itself, and expresses the converse: "The Here is not a tree but a house," or whatever else takes its place is again cancelled in the same manner; and in all sensuous certitude it only experiences in truth what we have seen, namely, the This as a universal, the converse of that which the mentioned assertion assures us to be the universal experience.

On the occasion of this appeal to universal experience it may be permitted to anticipate the practical result. In this respect it may be said to those who assert the truth and certitude of the reality of sensuous objects that they ought to be sent back to the lowest school of Wisdom, viz.: into the ancient Eleusinian Mysteries of Ceres and Bacchus in order to learn the secret of the eating of the bread and the drinking of the wine; for he who is initiated into these mysteries does not arrive merely at a *doubt* of the Being of sensuous things, but to despair of the same, and partly accomplishes in them their nugatoriness and partly sees it accomplished. Even the animals are not shut out from this wisdom, but rather show that they are deeply initiated; for they do not stand before the sensuous things as in themselves existent ones, but they despair of this reality and in the full certitude of their nugatoriness, they "help themselves" to them and eat them up; and all nature celebrates, like them, these open mysteries, which demonstrate what the truth of sensuous things is.

But those who make such assertions, say, as above remarked, immediately the converse of what they mean; a phenomenon which is perhaps the best calculated to arouse reflection concerning the nature of sensuous certitude. They speak of the extant being of *external* objects, which, more closely, may be determined as *real* ones, as absolutely particular, wholly personal, individual things, each one of which has no longer its absolute equivalent; that this extant Being has absolute certitude and truth. They mean *this* piece of paper upon which I write (or rather have written); but they do not say what they mean. If they really wanted to say this piece of paper which they mean, (and they do,) this is impossible, since the sensuous This which is meant, is unapproachable by language; for that belongs to consciousness—the in itself Universal. During the actual attempt to express it, it would rot; those who had commenced its description could not complete it but would have to leave it to others who would finally themselves acknowledge that they were engaged in describing what no longer existed. Hence although they mean *this* piece of paper which is entirely a different one from that above, yet they speak of "actual things," "external or sensuous objects," "absolute individual essence," &c, i.e. they say of them only the Universal; for this reason that which is called the unspeakable is nothing else than the untrue, the unreasonable, that which is merely "meant."—If nothing more is said of something than that it is an actual thing, an external object, then one has said only the most general thing of it, and with this has been expressed rather its likeness with everything, than its difference. If I say *a particular thing*, I say it rather as a universal, for each is a particular thing; and moreover, a *This thing* is anything which one pleases. More closely designated as *this piece of paper*,—so is every piece of paper *a this piece of paper*, and I have still merely said the general. But if I will not allow language which possesses the divine nature, immediately to invert the meaning and thus not permit it to put in a word, but hasten to its assistance by *exhibiting* this piece of paper, then I learn by experience what the truth of sensuous certitude is in fact; I point it out as a Here which is a Here of other Here's; or in itself a simple complex of many Here's, i.e. a Universal, and thus I apprehend it as it in truth is, and instead of *knowing* an Immediate, I PERCEIVE it.

VII. Phenomenology of Spirit: Self-Consciousness*

IV

The Truth of the Certainty of Oneself

In the previous ways of certainty, or of being sure, the truth is to consciousness something other than consciousness itself. The concept of this truth vanishes, however, in the experience of it: how the object was immediately *in itself*—the mere being of sense certainty, the concrete thing of perception, the force of understanding—thus, on the contrary, the object does not show itself in truth to be; instead this '*in-itself*' reveals itself as a way in which the object is merely for another; the concept of the object does away with itself when confronted with the actual object, or the first immediate idea does away with itself in the experience, and the certainty has been lost in the truth. Now, however, something has arisen which did not come about in those earilier relationships, namely a certainty which is equal to its truth; for the certainty has itself as its object, consciousness has itself as the truth. There is indeed an otherness here, too; consciousness does distinguish, but distinguishes something which is for it at the same time something not distinct. If we mean by *concept* the movement of knowing, and by *object* the knowledge as a unity at rest, or as 'I', then we see that, not only for us, but for knowing itself, the object matches the concept. Or, put the other way, the *concept* meaning what the object is *in itself*; and the object meaning what it is as *object* or *for* another, then it is evident that the 'being-in-itself' and the 'being-for-another' are one and the same: for the '*in-itself*' is consciousness; but the latter is equally that *for which* another thing (the '*in itself*') is; and it is for consciousness that the 'it-itself' of the object and the being of the object for another are the same: 'I' is the content of the relation and the relating itself; it is itself as distinct from another, and at the same time reaches over round this other, which for 'I' is equally only 'I' itself.

With self-consciousness, then, we have now entered the native realm of truth. We have next to see how the form of self-consciousness first presents

*Newly translated by J. L. H. Thomas.

168

itself. If we look at this new form of knowing, the knowledge of oneself, in relation to what has gone before, the knowledge of another, then the latter, the other, has indeed vanished; but at the same time its moments have no less preserved themselves, and the loss consists in their being present here as they are in themselves. The *being* of opinion, the *individuality* and the *universality* opposed to this of perception, as well as the *empty 'inner'* of understanding are no longer as entities, but as moments of self-consciousness, that is, as abstractions or differences, which *for* consciousness are themselves also null, or not differences at all, but sheerly vanishing entities. It seems then that only the principal moment itself has been lost, namely the *simple independent subsistence* for consciousness. But, in actual fact, self-consciousness is the reflexion out of the being of the world of sense and perception, and essentially the return out of *otherness*. It is as self-consciousness movement, but in distinguishing from itself *only itself as* itself self-consciousness has the distinction as an otherness *immediately done away with*; the distinction *is* not, and *it*, self-consciousness, is merely the motionless tautology of 'I am I'; as long as the distinction, or difference, does not to self-consciousness also have the form of *being*, it is not self-consciousness. Consequently, for self-consciousness the otherness is *as an existence*, or as a *moment* that has been *differentiated*; but there is for it also the unity of itself with this difference as a *second distinct* moment. With that first moment self-consciousness is as *consciousness*, and for it the whole extent of the world of sense is preserved, though at the same time only as related to the second moment, the unity of self-consciousness with itself; the world of sense is consequently for self-consciousness an existence, but one which is only *appearance*, or a difference that *in itself* has no being. This opposition between its appearance and its truth has, however, only the truth, namely the unity of self-consciousness with itself, for its essence; this unity must prove essential to self-consciousness, that is, self-consciousness is *desire* in the abstract. Consciousness now has as self-consciousness a double object: one, the immediate object, the object of sense-certainty and perception, which however *for self-consciousness* is marked with the *character of something negative*; the other, namely *itself*, which is the true being, or essence, and at first now present only in opposition to the first object. Self-consciousness presents itself here as the movement in which this opposition is done away with and self-consciousness has the equality of itself with itself come about.

The object, which for self-consciousness is what is negative, has for its part, however, as much gone back into itself, *for us* or *in itself*, as consciousness has for its part. Through this reflexion into itself the object has become *life*. That which self-consciousness distinguishes from itself *as existing* not merely has in it, inasmuch as it is established as existing, the way of sense-certainty and perception; in addition it is being reflected into itself, and the object of immediate desire is a *living being*. For the '*in itself*', or the *general* result of the relationship of understanding to the interior of things, is the distinguishing of what is not to be distinguished, or the unity of what has been distinguished. But this unity is, as we saw, no less its repulsion from itself, and this concept thus *divides* itself into the opposition of self-consciousness and life: the former, the unity *for which* the boundless unity of the differences exists; while the latter, life, just *is* this self-same unity, so that the unity is not in addition *for itself*. Hence, just as consciousness is independent, so equally independent is, *in itself*, its object. The self-consciousness which is unqualifiedly *for itself*, and immediately marks its objects with the character of negativity, or is to begin with *desire*, will instead therefore learn by experience of the independence of its object.

The characterization of life, as it follows from the concept or general result with which we enter this sphere, is adequate to pick it out, without it being possible on that basis to develop its nature any further; the circuit of the latter is completed with the following moments. The *essence* is boundlessness, or infinitude, qua the *having-been-done-away-with* of all differences, the pure motion about an axis, the being at rest of itself as absolutely restless infinitude: *self-dependence* itself, in which the differences of the movement are dissolved; the simple essence of time that in its equality-with-itself has the solid figure of space. But the *differences* are no less present in this *simple universal* medium as *differences*, for this general fluidity has its negative nature only through being a *doing-away-with of these differences*; the fluidity, however, cannot do away with the differences unless the latter have some subsistence. It is precisely this fluidity, as self-equal independence, that is the *subsistence*, or the substance of the differences, in which consequently they are as distinct members and parts *existing-for-themselves*. *Being* no longer has the sense of the *abstraction of being*, nor the members' pure essentiality that of the *abstraction of universality*; rather, their being is precisely that simple fluid substance of pure movement within itself. The *distinction* of these members *among themselves*, however, qua distinction, consists all in all in no other *determination* than the determination of the moments of infinitude, or of the pure movement itself.

The independent members are *for themselves*; but this *being-for-themselves* is no less *immediately* their reflexion into the unity than this unity is the division into the independent forms. The unity is divided because it is an absolutely negative or boundless unity; and because *it*, the unity, is the subsistence, or *permanence*, so too the difference has independence only *in it*. This independence of the form appears as *something determinate, for another*, since the form is something divided; and the *doing-away-with* of the division is to that extent effected by another. But the doing-away-with goes on just as much in the form itself; for it is precisely that fluidity which is the substance of the independent forms; this substance, however, is boundless, or infinite; the form is therefore in its permanence itself the dividing, or the doing-away-with of its being-for-itself.

If we distinguish the moments contained here more carefully, then we see that we have as the *first* moment the *permanence of the independent forms*, or the suppression of what the differentiating is in itself, namely, not to be in itself and to have no permanence. The *second* moment, by contrast, is the *subjection* of that permanence to the infinitude of the difference. In the first moment there is the permanent form; as *existing-for-itself*, or within its specificity infinite substance, it comes on in opposition to the *universal* substance, denies this fluidity and its continuity with it, and asserts itself not be dissolved in this universal element, but rather to be maintaining itself through the separation from this inorganic nature it has, and through the consumption of the same. Life in the universal fluid medium, a *quiet* laying-apart of the forms, precisely thereby becomes a movement of the latter, or life as *process*. The simple universal fluidity is the '*in itself*', and the difference of the forms the *other*. But this very fluidity becomes through this difference *the other*; for the fluidity is now *for the difference*, which is in and for itself and hence the infinite movement by which that quiet medium is consumed, life as *living beings*. — But this *reversal* is consequently in turn the *being-reversed against itself*: what is consumed is the essence; the individuality, which maintains itself at the expense of the universal and gives itself the feeling of its unity with itself, precisely thereby does away with *its opposition to the other, through which it is for itself*; the *unity* with itself, which it gives itself, is precisely the *fluidity* of the differences, or the *general dissolution*. But, conversely, the doing away with the individual permanence is equally the generation of that permanence. For since the *essence* of the individual form is the universal life, and since what is for itself is in itself simple substance, so the essence, in setting the *other* into itself, does away with this simplicity or essence it has — that is, it divides it, and this dividing of the undifferentiated fluidity is precisely the establishing of individuality. The simple substance of life is thus the division of this very substance into forms, and simultaneously the dissolution of these existing differences; and the dissolution of the division is no less a dividing or an articulating. Thus there coincide the two facets of the whole movement which were distinguished, namely the form-giving, quietly laid out in the general medium of independence, and the process of life; the second is just as much a form-giving as it is a doing-away-with of the form; and the first, the form-giving, is just as much a doing-away as it is an articulation. The fluid element is itself only the *abstraction* of the essence, and it is *actual* only as form; and its articulating of itself is in turn a dividing of what is articulated, or a dissolving of it. This entire cycle is what constitutes life; not what was stated first, the immediate continuity and homogeneity of its essence; nor the enduring form and the discrete element existing for itself; nor the pure process of these; nor even the simple putting together of these moments; but rather the whole, unfolding itself, and dissolving what is unfolded, and in this movement simply preserving itself as a whole.

Inasmuch as the first immediate unity is the starting-point, from which, through the moments of form-giving and of process, a return is made to the unity of these moments, and so back to the first simple substance, this *reflected unity* is hence another unity than the first. In contrast to the first unity, stated to be an *immediate* unity or an *existence*, this second unity is the *universal* unity, which has all these moments as done-away within itself. This is the *simple species*, which in the movement of life itself does not *exist for itself as* this *simple thing*; rather, in this *result* life refers to something other than it, life, is, namely to consciousness, for which it is as this unity, or as species.

This other life, however, for which the *species* is as such, and which for itself is species, self-consciousness, is to itself at first only as this simple entity, and has itself as *pure 'I'* for its object; in its experience, which we have now to follow, it will have this abstract object enrich itself and acquire the development that we have seen in the case of life.

The simple 'I' is this species or the simple universal, for which the differences are not such, only through being the *negative essence* of the independent moments that have been given form; and self-consciousness is consequently only certain of itself through doing away with this other, which presents itself to self-consciousness as self-sufficient life: self-consciousness is *desire*. In the certainty of the nullity of this other, self-consciousness establishes *for itself* this nullity as its truth, destroys the independent object, and thereby gives itself the certainty of itself, as *true* certainty, as a certainty which self-consciousness itself has had come about in *the manner of an object*.

In the course of this satisfaction, however, self-consciousness learns by experience of the independence of its object. The desire and the certainty of oneself attained in the satisfaction of desire is conditional upon the object, for the certainty exists only through the doing-away-with of this other; for there to be this doing-away, this other must exist. Self-consciousness is unable, therefore, by means of its negative bearing to do away with the object; instead, it thereby generates the object again, as likewise the desire. It is in the event something other than self-consciousness that is the essence of desire; and through this experience self-consciousness itself has come to realise this truth. At the same time, however, self-consciousness is no less absolutely for itself, and it is this only through doing away with the object, and it must get its satisfaction, for self-consciousness is the truth. For the sake of the object's independence, therefore, self-consciousness can only attain satisfaction through the object's itself carrying out the negation upon itself; and the object must carry out this negation of itself upon itself, for it is *in itself* what is negative, and must be for the other what it is. Through being the negation upon itself, and at the same time in that negation being independent, the object is consciousness. In life, which is the object of desire, the *negation* is either *in another*, namely in the desire, or as a *determination* opposed to another indifferent form, or as its *inorganic, universal nature*. This universal independent nature, however, in which the negation is an absolute negation, is the species as such, or as *self-consciousness*. *Self-consciousness attains its satisfaction only in another self-consciousness*.

In these three moments the concept of self-consciousness is now, and only now, complete: (a) pure, undifferentiated 'I' is its first immediate object. But (b) this immediacy is itself absolute mediation, it is only as the doing-away-with of the independent object, or it is desire. The satisfaction of desire is, to be sure, the reflexion of self-consciousness into itself, or the certainty become truth. But (c) the truth of desire is rather the reflexion twice over, or the duplication of self-consciousness. The object for consciousness is one which within itself establishes its otherness, or the difference, as a difference that is null, and is thereby independent. The distinct, merely *living* form certainly also does away with its independence in the process of life itself, but it ceases, along with its difference, to be what it is; the object of self-consciousness, however, is equally independent in this negativity of itself; and thereby it is for itself species, universal fluidity in the distinctiveness of its separation: the object is living self-consciousness.

There is a *self-consciousness for a self-consciousness*. Only now through this is it in fact; for only now in this does there come to be for it the unity of itself in its otherness; 'I', which is the object of its concept, is in the event not an *object*; the object of desire, however, is just *independent*, for it is the universal indestructible substance, the fluid self-equal essence. Inasmuch as a self-consciousness is the object, the object is as much 'I' as object. — With this is already present for us the concept *of Spirit*. What lies ahead for consciousness is the experience of what Spirit is, this absolute substance, which, in the complete freedom and independence of its antithesis, that is, of distinct self-consciousnesses existing for themselves, is the unity of these: 'I' that is 'we', and 'we' that is 'I'. Consciousness has only now in self-consciousness, as the concept of Spirit, its turning-point, at which, from the coloured glitter of the sensible hither-side, and from the empty night of the supersensible beyond, it steps into the spiritual daylight of the here-and-now.

A.

Independence and Dependence of Self-Consciousness: Relations of Master and Servant

Self-consciousness is *in* and *for itself* in and through being in and for itself for another self-consciousness; that is, it is only as something acknowledged, or recognized. The concept of this unity of self-consciousness in its duplication, of the infinitude realising itself in self-consciousness, is a many-sided and many-sensed complex, so that the moments of this complex must both be held carefully apart, and at the same time taken and understood in this differentiation as not distinct, or always also in their opposed sense. The double-sensedness of what is distinguished lies in the essence of self-consciousness, of being infinite, or boundless, that is, immediately the contrary of the determination in which it is established. The laying-apart of the concept of this spiritual unity in its duplication presents to us the movement of *acknowledging*.

There is for self-consciousness another self-consciousness; it has come *outside itself*. This has a twofold significance: *first*, self-consciousness has lost itself, for it finds itself as *another* being; *second*, it has thereby done away with the other, for it does not see the other either as the essential being, but *it itself* in the *other*.

Self-consciousness must do away with this *otherness it* has; this is the doing away with of the first double-sense, and hence itself a second double-sense: *first*, it must set out to do away with *the other* independent being in order thereby to become certain of *itself* as the essential being; *second*, in so doing it sets out to do away with *itself*, for this other being is itself.

This double-sensed doing away with its double-sensed otherness is equally a double-sensed return *into itself*; for, *first*, through doing away it gets itself back, for it becomes once more equal to itself through doing away with *its* otherness; *second*, however, it no less gives back the other self-consciousness to the latter again, for it had itself in the other, it does away with this being *it* has in the other, thus letting the other go free again.

This movement of self-consciousness in its relation to another self-consciousness has been presented in this way now, as *the doing of the one*; but this doing of the one has itself the two-fold significance of being as much *its doing* as *the doing of the other*; for the other is no less independent, shut up within itself, and there is nothing in it that is not owing to itself. The first self-consciousness does not have the object before it as the latter to begin with is merely for desire, but an independent object existing for itself, over which therefore it has of itself no power, unless the object does with itself what self-consciousness does with it. The movement is thus in all respects the double movement of both self-consciousnesses. Each sees the *other one* do the same as it does; each does itself what it demands of the other, and so does what it does only inasmuch as the other does the same; a one-sided doing would be unavailing, because what it is intended should occur can come about only through both.

The doing is therefore double-sensed not only inasmuch as it is a doing as much *to itself* as *to the other*, but also inasmuch as it is undividedly as much the *doing of the one* as *of the other*.

In this movement we see the process repeat itself which presented itself as the play of forces, but in consciousness. What in the earlier process was for us, is here for the extremes themselves. The centre is self-consciousness, which puts itself apart into the extremes; and each extreme is this exchanging of its determination and absolute going over into the opposed extreme. But though, as consciousness, it does indeed come *out of itself*, yet it is in its being-out-of-itself at the same time held back within itself, is *for itself*, and its 'outside-itself' is *for it*. It is for consciousness that it immediately *is* and *is not* another consciousness; and, equally, that this other is only for itself in doing away with itself as something being for itself, and only in the being-for-itself of the other is for itself. Each is to the other the centre through which each brings into relation and connects itself with itself, and each is to itself and to the other an immediate entity existing for itself, which at the same time is thus for itself only through this relating, or mediation. They *acknowledge* one another as *mutually acknowledging one other*.

This pure concept of acknowledgement, the duplication of self-consciousness in its unity, will now be studied in the way in which its process appears for self-consciousness. This process will first present the facet of the *inequality* of the two, or the coming out of the centre into the extremes, which, being extremes, are opposed to one another, the one acknowledged only, the other acknowledging only.

Self-consciousness is to begin with simple being-for-itself, equal-with-itself through the exclusion of everything *other from itself*; its essence and absolute object is to it '*I*'; and it is in this *immediacy*, or in this *being* of its being-for-itself, an *individual*. Whatever else there is for it, is as an inessential object, one marked with the character of the negative. But the other is also a self-consciousness: an individual comes on opposite an individual. Thus *immediately* coming on, they are for each other in the way of common objects: *independent* forms, consciousnesses immersed in the *existence* of *life* — for it is as life that the existent object has here determined itself — which have not yet carried out *for each other* the movement of absolute abstraction, of expunging all immediate existence and of being merely the purely negative existence of consciousness equal-with-itself, or which have not yet presented themselves to each other as pure *being-for-self*, that is, as *self*-consciousness. Each is indeed certain of itself, but not of the other, and consequently each's own certainty of itself has as yet no truth; for its truth could only be that its own being-for-itself had presented itself to it as an independent object or, what amounts to the same thing, that the object had presented itself as this pure certainty of itself. This, however, on the concept of acknowledgement is not possible, save that as the other does for the one, so the one does for the other, each with itself through its own activity, and again through the activity of the other, carrying out this pure abstraction of being-for-itself.

The *presentation* of oneself as the pure abstraction of self-consciousness, however, consists in showing oneself to be the pure negation of one's objective way of being, that is, in showing oneself not to be attached to a particular *concrete existence*, nor to the universal individuality of concrete existence in general, nor even to life. This presentation is a *double* doing: doing of the other, and doing through oneself. Inasmuch as it is the doing *of the other*, each then is set upon the death of the other. But in this there is present also the second doing, *the doing through oneself*; for the former contains within itself the staking of one's own life. The relation of the two self-consciousnesses is hence determined in such a way that through the combat for life and death they *prove* themselves and each other. — They must enter this combat, for they must raise the certainty of themselves, *of being for themselves*, to truth in the other and in themselves. And it is solely through the staking of life that freedom arises, that it is confirmed to self-consciousness that it is not *being*, not the *immediate* way in which it comes on, not its being immersed in the expanse of life which is its essence — but that there is nothing present in it which is not for it a vanishing moment, that it is just pure *being-for-itself*. The individual that has not risked life can indeed be acknowledged as a *person*; but it has not attained the truth of this state of acknowledgement as that of an independent self-consciousness. Likewise, each must as much aim at the death of the other as it stakes its own life; for the other means no more to it than it itself does; the individual's essence presents itself to it as another, it is outside itself, it must do away with its being-outside-itself; the other is a consciousness engaged and existing in manifold ways; it must view its otherness as pure being-for-self, or as absolute negation.

This proving through death does away, however, with the truth that was to result from it, just as much as it thereby also does away with the certainty of oneself altogether; for just as life was the *natural* position of consciousness, independence without absolute negativity, so death is the *natural* negation of consciousness, negation without independence, which therefore remains without the required sense of acknowledgement. Through death the certainty has indeed arisen that both risked their life and despised it in themselves and in the other; though not for those who underwent this combat. They do away with their consciousness set in this alien essentiality that is natural concrete existence, or they do away with themselves, and are done away with as the *extremes* which would be for themselves. There thereby vanishes, however, from the play of exchange the essential moment of setting oneself apart into extremes of opposed determinations; and the centre collapses into a dead unity, which is set apart into dead, merely existent, not opposed, extremes; and the two do not mutually give back and receive back themselves from each other through consciousness, but let each other free merely indifferently, as things. Their deed is abstract negation, not the negation of consciousness, which *does away* in such a manner that it *puts by* and *preserves* what is done away, and consequently survives its being-done-away.

In this experience self-consciousness comes to realise that life is as essential to it as pure self-consciousness is. In immediate self-consciousness the simple 'I' is the absolute object, which however, for us or in itself, is absolute mediation and has existent independence as an essential moment. The dissolution of that simple unity is the result of the first experience; through it there is established a pure self-consciousness, and a consciousness which is not purely for itself, but is for another consciousness, that is, is as *existent*, or is consciousness in the form of *thinghood*. Both moments are essential; — but as they are to begin with unequal and opposed, and their reflexion into unity is not yet a reality, they are as two opposed forms of consciousness: one, the independent consciousness, to which being-for-self is the essence; the other, the dependent consciousness, to which life or being for another is the essence: the former is the *master*, the latter the *servant*.

The master is the consciousness existing *for itself*, though no longer merely the concept of the latter, but a consciousness existing for itself which is in mediate relation with itself through *another* consciousness, namely through one to whose essence it pertains to be synthesised with independent *being* or thinghood in general. The master relates himself to both these moments, to a *thing* as such, the object of desire, and to the consciousness to whom thinghood is what is essential; and since he (a), qua concept of self-consciousness, is immediate relation of *being-for-himself*, but (b) now is also as mediation, or as a being-for-self which is for itself only through another, so he relates himself (a) immediately to both and (b) mediately to each through the other. The master relates himself *to the servant mediately through independent being*; for it is precisely to this that the servant is kept; it is his chain, from which in the combat he could not abstract, and consequently showed himself to be dependent, to have his independence in thinghood. The master, however, is the power over the being in question, for he showed in the combat that it meant merely something negative to him; since he is the power over this being, while this being is the power over the other, the master thus has in this conjunction the other under himself. Likewise the master relates himself *mediately through the servant to the thing*; the servant relates himself, qua self-consciousness as such, to the thing negatively also, and does away with it; but the thing is at the same time independent for him, and hence he cannot through his negating dispose of it so far as to destroy it, or he *works* it merely. The master on the other hand *gains* through this mediation the *immediate* relation as the pure negation of the thing, or the *enjoyment*; where desire did not succeed, he succeeds, namely in disposing of the thing and in satisfying himself in the enjoyment of it. Desire did not succeed in this on account of the independence of the thing; the master, however, who has interposed the servant between the thing and himself, thereby connects himself only with the non-independence of the thing, and enjoys it in its purity; the facet of independence, on the other hand, he leaves to the servant, who works it.

In these two moments the master has his acknowledgement, or recognition, by another consciousness granted him; for the other consciousness establishes itself in these moments as something inessential, first, in the working of the thing, second, in the dependence upon a particular existence; in both it cannot achieve mastery over being and attain absolute negation. There is therefore present here the following moment of recognition, that the other consciousness does away with itself as being-for-itself, and so itself does what the other does to it. Likewise the other moment is present, that this doing of the second consciousness is the first's own doing; for what the servant does is really the doing of the master; to the latter, solely being-for-himself is the essence; he is the pure negative power to which the thing is nothing, and hence the pure essential doing in this situation; while the servant is not a pure doing, but an inessential one. But for true recognition there is lacking the moment that what the master does to the other he also does to himself, and what the servant does to himself he also does to the other. Thus there has arisen a one-sided and unequal recognizing.

The inessential consciousness is here for the master the object which constitutes the *truth* of the certainty of oneself. But it is evident that this object does not match its concept, and that there where the master has fulfilled himself, he has instead had something quite other than an independent consciousness come to be. It is not such a consciousness that is for him, but a dependent one rather; he is consequently not certain of *being-for-himself* as the truth, and his truth is rather the inessential consciousness, and the inessential doing of the latter.

The *truth* of independent consciousness is accordingly the servile or *subject consciousness*. The latter admittedly appears at first *outside* itself, and not as the truth of self-consciousness. But just as masterhood or dominion, showed that its essence is the converse of what it itself would be, so too, as we shall see, subjection will in its fulfillment turn rather into the contrary of what it is immediately; it will, qua consciousness *driven back* into itself, go into itself and turn about to true independence.

We have seen only what subjection is in the context of dominion. But the former is self-consciousness, and accordingly we shall now see what it is in and for itself. First of all, for subjection the master is the essence; hence the *independent consciousness existing for itself* is to subjection *the truth*, which however *for subjection* is not yet *in subjection*. But it has this truth of pure negativity and of *being-for-itself in the event in itself*, for subjection has *experienced* this essence within itself. This consciousness was, namely, not afraid for this or that, or for this instant or that, but for its whole being; for it has felt the fear of death, the absolute lord, or master. In this fear it has been internally broken up, it has been thoroughly shaken in itself, and everything fixed has trembled within it. This pure universal movement, the absolute becoming fluid of all that is permanent, is however the simple essence of self-consciousness, absolute negativity, *pure being-for-itself,* which is consequently *in* this consciousness. This moment of pure being-for-itself is also *for it,* for in the master it has it as its *object.* It is further not merely this universal dissolution *in general,* but in serving it *actually* brings it about; in serving it does away in all *particular* moments with its dependency on natural existence, and works that existence off.

But the feeling of absolute power, in general and in the particulars of service, is only the dissolution *in itself,* and although "the fear of the Lord is the beginning of wisdom," consciousness in this fear is *for its self,* not *being-for-itself.* Through work, however, it comes to itself. In the moment which corresponds to desire in the consciousness of the master, the facet of the inessential relation to the thing seemed to have fallen to the consciousness that serves, inasmuch as in this relation the thing retains its independence. Desire has reserved to itself the pure negating of the object and thereby the unmixed feeling-of-self. This satisfaction is on that account, however, itself just a vanishing, for it lacks the facet of the *object,* or *permanency.* Work by contrast is *contained* desire, *arrested* vanishing, or work *improves.* The negative relation to the object turns into the *form* of the object and into something *enduring,* precisely because to the worker the object has independence. This *negative* centre, or the *activity* that forms, or fashions, is at the same time *the particularity,* or the pure being-for-self of consciousness, which now in work steps out of consciousness into the element of permanency; the consciousness that works therefore attains as a consequence a view of independent being *as itself.*

The fashioning has not only this positive significance, however, that in it the consciousness that serves has itself as pure *being-for-itself* become something *existent;* but also a negative significance as against its first moment, the fear. For, in the improving of the thing, the consciousness which serves has its own negativity, its being-for-itself, become object only by doing away with the opposed existent *form.* But this objective, *negative* thing is precisely the alien being before which it trembled. Now, however, it destroys this alien negative thing, sets *itself* as something negative into the element of permanency, and thereby comes to be *for itself,* something *existing-for-itself.* In the master it has being-for-self as *an other,* or as merely *for it;* in the fear being-for-self is *in the consciousness itself that serves;* in the improving being-for-self comes to be for the consciousness that serves as *its own,* and the latter becomes conscious that it itself is in and for itself. Through being *set outside,* the form does not become to the consciousness that serves something other than the consciousness itself; for it is precisely the form that is its pure being-for-itself, which thereby to consciousness becomes the truth. Through this refinding of itself by itself, then, the consciousness that serves becomes a mind or *sense of its own*, and in the very work in which it seemed to be only *another's sense*. — For this reflexion both moments, that of fear and service in general, as well as that of improving, are necessary, and at the same time both in a general way. Without the discipline of service and obedience, fear remains at the formal stage, and does not spread itself upon the known reality of concrete existence. Without the improving, fear remains inward and silent, and consciousness does not become for itself. If consciousness fashions, or forms, without the initial absolute fear, it is merely a vain sense of self; for its form or negativity is not negativity *in itself*, and its fashioning cannot therefore give it the consciousness of itself as the essence. If it has not endured absolute fear, but only some anxiety, then it has the negative essence remain something external, its substance has not been infected through and through by the negative essence. Inasmuch as not all aspects of its natural consciousness have become insecure, it still *in itself* belongs to some particular existence; its self-sense is *self-will*, a freedom which as yet remains within subjection. No more than it can have the pure form become essence, no more is the form, regarded as something spread over individual things, a universal cultivating, an absolute concept, but is instead a dexterity which has power over merely some things, not over universal power and the whole objective realm of being.

VIII. Encyclopaedia: Introduction and Logic*

INTRODUCTION

1. Philosophy lacks an advantage enjoyed by the other sciences. It cannot like them presuppose its objects on the immediate admissions of conception, nor can it assume that its method of cognition, either for beginning or continuing, is already accepted. The objects of philosophy, it is true, are to begin with the same as those of religion. In both the object is truth, in that supreme sense in which God and God alone is truth. Both then go on to consider the finite realm of nature and the human mind, with their relation to each other and to their truth in God. Thus philosophy may—indeed must—presume some acquaintance with its objects, and an interest in them besides, if only for the reason that in point of time consciousness forms *conceptions*[53] of objects before it forms *concepts*[9] of them, and that it is only through conception,[53] and by recourse to it, that the thinking mind rises to know and comprehend *thinkingly*.

But in the thinking study of things, it soon becomes clear that it involves the requirement of showing the *necessity* of its content, of demonstrating the being of its objects, as well as their determinations. Our original acquaintance with them thus appears inadequate. We can assume nothing, and assert nothing dogmatically; nor can we accept the assertions and assumptions of others. Yet we must make a beginning; and a beginning, as immediate, involves, or rather is, an assumption. Thus it is difficult to *begin* at all.

2. This *thinking study of objects* may serve in general as a definition of philosophy. But the definition is too wide. If it is correct to say that thought makes the difference between man and animals, then everything human is human for the sole and simple reason that it is due to the operation of thought. Philosophy, on the other hand, is a peculiar mode of thinking, a mode in which thinking becomes knowledge, and conceptual knowledge. Thus however great the identity and essential unity of the two modes of

---

*From the third (1830) edition of *The Encyclopaedia of the Philosophical Sciences in Outline*. Translated by William Wallace, with revisions by M. J. Inwood.

thought, the philosophical mode will be *different* from the thinking that is active in all that is human and gives humanity its distinctive character. This difference relates to the fact that the strictly human and thought-induced contents of consciousness do not originally appear in the form of a thought, but as feeling, intuition, conception — all of which forms must be distinguished from the form of thought proper.

According to an old prejudice, which has become a commonplace, it is thought that marks man off from animals. Yet trivial as this old belief may seem, it must, strangely enough, be recalled to mind in view of a prejudice of the present day. This prejudice sets feeling and thought so far apart as to make them opposites, and supposes them to be so antagonistic that feeling, particularly religious feeling, is contaminated, perverted and even annihilated by thought, and religion and religiosity do not essentially grow out of and rest on thinking. But those who make this separation forget that only man has the capacity for religion, and animals no more have religion than law and morality.

Those who insist on this separation of religion from thinking usually have in mind the sort of thinking that may be called "meta-thinking,"[14] reflective thinking that considers thoughts as thoughts and brings them into consciousness. Failure to see and observe this definite distinction that philosophy draws in respect of thinking is the source of the crudest ideas and reproaches against philosophy. Man, just because it is his essence to think, is the only being that possesses law, religion, and ethics. In these spheres, therefore, thinking, in the guise of feeling, faith, or conception, has not been inactive; its activity and productions are present and contained in them. But it is one thing to have such feelings and conceptions determined and permeated by thought, and another to have thoughts about them. The thoughts to which meta-thinking on those modes of consciousness gives rise are what comprise reflection, argumentation, and the like, as well as philosophy itself.

Neglect of this distinction has led to another frequent misunderstanding. Such meta-thinking has often been held to be the condition, or even the only way, of attaining a conception and certainty of the eternal and true. The (now somewhat antiquated) metaphysical proofs of God's existence, for example, have been treated as if knowledge of them and a conviction of their validity were the sole and essential means of producing a belief and conviction that there is a God. This claim would find its parallel, if we said that eating was impossible before we had acquired a knowledge of the chemical, botanical, and zoological characters of our food; and that we must delay digestion until we have completed the study of anatomy and physiology. Were it so, these sciences in their field, like philosophy in its, would gain greatly in utility; in fact, their utility would rise to absolute and universal indispensableness. Or rather, instead of being indispensable, they would not exist at all.

3. The *content*, of whatever kind, that fills our consciousness, constitutes the *determinacy* of our feelings, intuitions, images, and ideas; of our aims and duties; and of our thoughts and concepts. Thus feeling, intuition, image, etc. are the *forms* assumed by these contents. The contents remain the same whether they are felt, intuited, represented or willed, and whether they are merely felt, or felt with an admixture of thoughts, or merely and simply thought. In any one of these forms, or in the mixture of several, the content is consciousness' *object*. But when they are thus objects of consciousness, the *determinacies of these forms* ally themselves with the content, so that each form seems to give rise to a particular object. Thus, what is at bottom the same may look like a different content.

The determinacies of feeling, intuition, desire, and will, so far as we are *aware* of them, are in general called "ideas" or "conceptions";[53] and, roughly speaking, philosophy puts thoughts, categories, or, more precisely, concepts, in the place of ideas. Ideas in general may be regarded as metaphors of thoughts and concepts. But to have these ideas does not imply that we appreciate their meaning for thinking, i.e., their thoughts and concepts. Conversely, it is one thing to have thoughts and concepts, and another to know what ideas, intuitions, and feelings correspond to them.

This explains in part what people call the "unintelligibility" of philosophy. The difficulty lies partly in an incapacity — which in itself is just want of habit — for abstract thinking, an inability to grasp pure thoughts and move about in them. In our ordinary consciousness the thoughts are clothed in and combined with familiar sensuous and spiritual material; and in meta-thinking, reflection, and argumentation we introduce a blend of thoughts into feelings, ideas, and intuitions. (Thus in propositions where the content is wholly sensuous — e.g., "This leaf is green" — such categories as being and individuality are introduced.) But to make thoughts pure and simple our object is a different matter.

But there is also another reason for the complaint that philosophy is unintelligible: an impatience to have before one as an idea that which is in consciousness as a thought or concept. When people are asked to apprehend some concept, they often complain that they do not know what they are supposed to *think*. In a concept there is nothing more to be thought than the concept itself. What the phrase reveals is a hankering after an idea with which we are already familiar. Consciousness, denied its familiar ideas, feels the ground where it once stood firm and at home taken from it, and, when transported into the pure region of concepts, cannot tell where in the world it is. Thus authors, preachers, and orators are found most intelligible when they speak of things that their readers or hearers already know by rote, which are familiar to them and are understood as a matter of course.

4. In connection with our ordinary consciousness, philosophy will first have to prove and even to awaken the need for its peculiar mode of knowledge. But in connection with the objects of religion, with truth in

general, it will have to show that it is capable of knowing them from its own resources; and if a difference from religious conceptions comes to light, it will have to *justify* the points in which it diverges.

5.   To give a preliminary explanation of this distinction and of the connected insight that the real content of our consciousness is retained, and even put in its proper light for the first time, when translated into the form of the thought and the concept, it may be well to recall another old prejudice: that to learn the truth of any object or event, even of feelings, intuitions, opinions, and ideas, we must first think it over.[14] Now in any case to think things over is at least to transform feelings, ideas, etc. into thoughts.

Nature has given everyone an ability to think. But thought is all that philosophy claims as the form proper to her business: and thus neglect of the distinction stated in §3 leads to a new delusion, the reverse of the complaint about the unintelligibility of philosophy. This science must often submit to the slight of hearing even people who have never taken any trouble with it talk as if they thoroughly understood all about it. With no preparation beyond an ordinary education they do not hesitate, especially under the influence of religious feelings, to philosophize and to criticize philosophy. Everybody allows that to know any other science you must have first studied it, and that you can express a judgement on it only in virtue of such knowledge. Everybody allows that to make a shoe you must have learned and practised the craft of the shoemaker, though every man has a model in his own foot, and possesses in his hands the natural endowments for the operations required. For philosophy alone, it is supposed, such study, care, and application are not requisite. This comfortable view has recently received corroboration through the theory of immediate or intuitive knowledge.

6.   So much for the form of philosophical knowledge. It is no less desirable, on the other hand, that philosophy should understand that its content is no other than *actuality*, that content which, originally produced and producing itself within the precincts of the living mind, has become the *world*, the inward and outward world, of consciousness. At first we become aware of these contents in what we call experience. Even a judicious consideration of the world, of the wide range of inward and outward existence, enables us to distinguish mere appearance, transient and meaningless, from what in itself really deserves the name of actuality. As it is only in form that philosophy is distinguished from other modes of attaining an awareness of this same content, it must necessarily be in harmony with actuality and experience. In fact, this harmony may be viewed as at least an extrinsic test of the truth of a philosophy. Similarly it may be held the highest and final aim of philosophic science to bring about, by knowledge of this harmony, a reconciliation of the self-conscious reason with the reason that is in the world, with actuality.

In the preface to my *Philosophy of Right*, are found the propositions:

What is rational is actual;
and,
What is actual is rational.

These simple statements have given rise to expressions of surprise and hostility, even in quarters where it would be reckoned an insult to presume absence of philosophy, and still more of religion. Religion at least need not be brought in evidence; its doctrines of the divine government of the world affirm these propositions too decidedly. For their philosophic sense, we must presuppose cultivation enough to know, not only that God is actual, that He is the supreme actuality, that He alone is truly actual; but also, as regards the formal side, that existence is in part appearance, and only in part actuality. In common life, any brain wave, error, evil, and everything of the nature of evil, as well as every degenerate and transitory existence whatever, gets indiscriminately called an actuality. But even our ordinary feelings forbid a contingent existence getting the emphatic name of an actual; for the contingent is an existence that has no greater value than that of something possible, which may as well not be as be. As for the term 'actuality,' these critics would have done well to consider the sense in which I employ it. In a detailed Logic I have treated among other things of actuality, and accurately distinguished it not only from the contingent, which, after all, has existence, but more precisely from determinate being, existence, and other determinations.

The actuality of the rational is opposed by the notion that Ideas and ideals are nothing but chimeras, and philosophy a mere system of such figments. It is also opposed by the contrary notion that Ideas and ideals are too excellent to have actuality, too impotent to procure it for themselves. This divorce between idea and reality is especially dear to the understanding that regards its dreamlike abstractions as something true and real, and prides itself on the 'ought,' which it takes especial pleasure in prescribing even in the field of politics. As if the world had waited on it to learn how it ought to be, and was not! For, if it were as it ought to be, what would come of the precocious wisdom of that 'ought'? When understanding turns this 'ought' against trivial external and transitory objects, against social regulations or conditions, which very likely possess a great relative importance for a certain time and special circles, it may often be right, and in such a case may find much that fails to satisfy general requirements; for who is not acute enough to see a great deal in his own surroundings which is really far from being as it ought to be? But such acuteness is mistaken to imagine that, in these objects and their 'ought,' it is dealing with questions of philosophical interest. The sole concern of philosophy is the Idea: and the Idea is not so impotent that it merely ought to be without actually being. The object of philosophy is an actuality of which those objects, social regulations, and conditions, are only the superficial surface.

7. Thus meta-thinking in general contains the principle (which also

means the beginning) of philosophy, and when it arose again in its independence in modern times, after the epoch of the Lutheran Reformation, it
did not, as in the philosophical beginnings among the Greeks, stand merely
aloof and abstract, but at once turned its energies also on the apparently
illimitable material of the phenomenal world. In this way the name 'philosophy' came to be applied to all those branches of knowledge that are
engaged in ascertaining the fixed measure and universal in the ocean of
empirical individualities, as well as the necessity, the laws, in the apparent
disorder of the endless masses of the contingent; and which thus derive
their content from their own intuition and perception of the external and
internal world, from the very presence of nature and of the mind and heart
of man.

The principle of experience involves the infinitely important condition
that, to accept and believe any fact the person must be present; or, more
exactly, that he must find the fact unified and combined with the certainty
of his own self. He must himself be present, whether only with his external
senses, or else with his profounder mind, his essential self-consciousness.
This principle is the same as that which has in the present day been termed
faith, immediate knowledge, the revelation in the outward world, and,
above all, in our own heart. Those sciences, which thus got the name of
philosophy, we call *empirical* sciences, since they take their departure from
experience. Still the essential results that they aim at and provide, are laws,
general propositions, a theory—the thoughts of what is found existing.
Thus Newtonian physics was called Natural Philosophy. Hugo Grotius,
again, by putting together and comparing the behavior of nations toward
each other in history, set up, with the help of the ordinary general reasoning, general principles, a theory that may be termed the Philosophy of
International Law. In England this is still the usual signification of the term
philosophy. Newton continues to be celebrated as the greatest of philosophers: and the name goes down as far as the price-lists of instrument
makers. All instruments, such as the thermometer and barometer, that do
not come under the special head of magnetic or electric apparatus are
styled philosophical instruments. Surely thought, and not a mere combination of wood, iron, etc. ought to be called the instrument of philosophy!
The recent science of Political Economy in particular is also called
philosophy—what we are wont to call 'rational' political economy, or,
perhaps, the political economy of *intelligence*.

8. In its own field this knowledge may at first give satisfaction; but in
two ways it falls short. In the first place there is another realm of objects
that it does not embrace—freedom, spirit, and God. They are excluded,
not because it can be said that they have nothing to do with experience; for
though they are certainly not experiences of the senses, it is quite a
tautological proposition to say that whatever is in consciousness is experienced. The reason for their exclusion is that in their *content* these objects
evidently show themselves as infinite.

There is an old dictum often wrongly attributed to Aristotle, and supposed to express the general tenor of his philosophy. *'Nihil est in intellectu quod non fuerit in sensu'*: there is nothing in thought that has not been in sense, in experience. If speculative philosophy refused to admit this maxim, it can have done so only by a misunderstanding. It will, however, conversely, also assert: *'Nihil est in sensu quod non fuerit in intellectu.'* And this in two senses: in the general sense that *nous* or spirit (the more profound counterpart of *nous*) is the cause of the world; and in the specific sense (§2) that the feeling of right, ethics and religion is a feeling (and thus an experience) of such content as can only spring from and rest on thought.

9. In the second place in point of *form* the subjective reason requires further satisfaction; this form is, in general, necessity (§1). The method of empirical science exhibits two defects. The first is that the universal contained in it—the genus, etc.—is, on its own account, indeterminate, and therefore not on its own account connected with the particular. Each is external and accidental to the other; and it is the same with the particulars that are brought into union: each is external and accidental to the others. The second defect is that the beginnings are in every case data and postulates, neither accounted for nor deduced. In both these points the form of necessity fails to get its due. Hence meta-thinking, whenever it sets itself to remedy these defects, becomes speculative thinking, strictly philosophical thinking. As a species of meta-thinking, therefore, that, though it has much in common with the first variety, is nevertheless different from it, it thus possesses, in addition to the common forms, some forms of its own, of which the concept is the universal one.

The relation of speculative science to the other sciences is just this. It does not neglect the empirical content of the sciences, but recognizes and adopts it; it recognizes and applies to its own content the universal of these sciences, their laws and classifications: but besides all this, into the categories of science it introduces and applies other categories. The difference thus relates only to this change of categories. Speculative logic contains all previous logic and metaphysics: it preserves the same forms of thought, laws, and objects,—while at the same time remodeling and expanding them with further categories.

From concept in the speculative sense we should distinguish what is ordinarily called a concept. The claim that no concept can comprehend the infinite, a claim that has been repeated over and over again till it has grown axiomatic, is based on this ordinary, one-sided sense of 'concept.'

10. The thinking involved in philosophical knowledge itself calls for explanation. We must understand in what way it possesses necessity, and its claim to be able to apprehend absolute objects (God, spirit, freedom) must be substantiated. Such an insight, however, is itself a philosophical cognition and thus falls within philosophy itself. A preliminary attempt to make matters plain would only be unphilosophical, and consist of a tissue of assumptions, assertions, and inferential pros and cons, of dogmatism

without cogency, against which there would be an equal right of counter-dogmatism.

A main line of argument in the Critical Philosophy bids us pause before proceeding to inquire into God or the essence of things, and first of all examine the faculty of cognition and see whether it is equal to the task. We ought, says Kant, to become acquainted with the instrument, before we undertake the work for which it is to be employed; for if the instrument be insufficient, all our trouble will be in vain. The plausibility of this thought has won general assent and admiration; the result of which has been to withdraw cognition from an interest in its objects and absorption in them, and to direct it back to itself, to the question of form. Unless we wish to be deceived by words, it is easy to see through this. In the case of other instruments, we can examine and assess them in other ways than by setting about the special work for which they are destined. But the examination of knowledge can only be carried out by *knowing*. To examine this so-called instrument is the same thing as to know it. But to seek to know before we know is as absurd as the wise resolution of the scholastic, not to venture into the water until he had learned to swim.

Reinhold saw the confusion in this style of beginning, and tried to get out of the difficulty by starting with a hypothetical and problematical stage of philosophizing, and by continuing in it, somehow, until we find ourselves, further on, at the primary truth. His method, when closely looked into, will be seen to amount to a common procedure. It starts from a substratum of experiential fact, or from a provisional assumption that has been brought into a definition; and then proceeds to analyze this starting point. We can detect in Reinhold's argument a perception of the truth, that the usual course that proceeds by assumptions and anticipations is a hypothetical and problematical procedure. But perceiving this does not alter the character of this method; it only makes clear its imperfections.

11. The need for philosophy may be specified thus. The mind, when it feels or intuits, finds its object in something sensuous; when it imagines, in an image; when it wills, in an aim. But in contrast to, or it may be only in distinction from, these forms of its existence and of its objects, the mind has also to gratify its highest and most inward life, *thought*. Thus the mind renders thought its object. In the deepest meaning of the phrase, it comes *to itself*; for thought is its principle, its unadulterated self. But while thus occupied, thought entangles itself in contradictions, loses itself in the hard-and-fast nonidentity of thoughts, and so, instead of reaching itself, is caught in its opposite. This result of the thinking of the mere understanding is resisted by the higher need, which is grounded in the perseverance of thought, which continues true to itself, even in this conscious loss of its consonance with itself, 'that it may overcome' and work out in thinking itself the solution of its own contradictions.

To see that thought in its very nature is dialectical, and that, as understanding, it must fall into contradictions, the negative of itself, forms one of the main lessons of logic. When thought despairs of achieving, by its own means, the solution of the contradiction that it has brought upon itself, it turns back to those solutions with which the mind has learned to console itself in some of its other modes and forms. Unfortunately, however, the retreat of thought has led it, as Plato noticed even in his time, to an unnecessary 'misology'; and it then takes up against itself that hostile attitude of which an example is seen in the doctrine that immediate knowledge, as it is called, is the exclusive form in which we are conscious of the truth.

12.   The rise of philosophy is due to this need. Its point of departure is experience; our immediate and our inferential consciousness. Awakened by this stimulus, thought's essential procedure is to raise itself above natural consciousness, above the senses and inferences, into its own unadulterated element, and to assume, accordingly, at first a stand-aloof, negative attitude toward that beginning. Its first satisfaction it finds in itself, in the Idea of the universal essence of these phenomena: this Idea (the absolute, God) may be more or less abstract. Conversely, the experiential sciences contain a stimulus to overcome the form in which their varied contents are presented, and to elevate these contents to necessity. For these contents have the form of a vast conglomerate, one thing side by side with another, as if they were merely given and immediate, — as in general contingent. This stimulus drags thought out of that universality and its merely *implicit* guarantee of satisfaction, and impels it on to a development out of itself. This development involves, on the one hand, merely receiving the content and the determinations that it presents; but, on the other, it also gives the content a new form: it lets it emerge freely, in the sense of original thinking and in accordance only with the necessity of the subject-matter itself.

On the relation between 'immediacy' and 'mediation' in consciousness we shall speak later, expressly and with more detail. Here it may suffice that, though the two moments present themselves as distinct, still neither of them can be absent, nor can one exist apart from the other. Thus the knowledge of God, as of every supersensible reality, is essentially an elevation above sensations or intuitions: it consequently involves a negative attitude to the initial data, and to that extent mediation. For to mediate is to begin and to go on to a second thing; so that the existence of this second thing depends on our having reached it from something other than it. In spite of this, the knowledge of God is no less independent of the empirical phase: in fact, its independence is essentially secured through this negation and elevation. If we attach an unfair prominence to mediation, and represent it as conditionedness, it may be said — not that it would amount to much — that philosophy is the child of experience, of the *a posteriori*. (In fact, thinking is the negation of what we have immediately before us.) With as much truth, however, we may be said to owe eating to the means of nourishment, for we cannot eat without them. If we take this view, eating is certainly represented as ungrateful: it devours that to which it owes itself. Thinking, in this sense, is equally ungrateful.

But there is also an *a priori* aspect of thought, where by a mediation, not made by anything external but by a reflection into self, we have that immediacy that is universality, the self-containment of thought that is so much at home with itself that it feels an innate indifference to particularization, and thus to development of itself. It is thus also with religion, which, whether it be rude or elaborate, whether it be developed to scientific consciousness or confined to the simple faith of the heart, possesses the same intensive nature of contentment and felicity. But if thought gets no further than the universality of Ideas, as was perforce the case in the first philosophies (e.g., Eleatic being, or Heraclitus' becoming), it is open to the charge of formalism. Even in a developed philosophy, we may find a mastery merely of abstract propositions or determinations such as, 'In the absolute all is one,' and 'Subject and object are identical,' which are only repeated when it comes to particulars. In respect of this first period of thought, the period of mere generality, we may safely say that experience is the real author of *growth* and *advance* in philosophy. For, first, the empirical sciences do not stop short at the mere perception of the individual features of a phenomenon. By the aid of thought, they have met philosophy with materials prepared for it, in the form of general uniformities, laws, and classifications of phenomena. Thus the content of the particular is made ready to be received into philosophy. This, second, implies a compulsion on thought itself to proceed to these concrete determinations. The reception of these contents, now that thought has removed their immediacy and made them cease to be mere data, forms at the same time a development of thought out of itself. Philosophy, then, owes its development to the empirical sciences. In return it gives their contents the most essential form: the *freedom* (the *a priori*) of thinking. The contents are now warranted necessary, and no longer depend on the evidence of facts merely, that they were so found and so experienced. The fact as experienced thus becomes an illustration and a copy of the original and completely self-supporting activity of thought.

13.   In the peculiar form of external history the origin and development of philosophy is presented as the history of the science. The stages in the evolution of the Idea there seem to follow each other by accident, and to present merely a number of different and unconnected principles, which the several philosophies develop. But for thousands of years the same architect has directed the work: the one living mind whose nature is to think, to bring to consciousness what it is, and, with this thus set as object before it, to be at the same time raised above it, and so to reach a higher stage of its own being. The different systems that the history of philosophy presents are, first, only one philosophy at different degrees of maturity;

second, the particular principle, which is the groundwork of each system, is but a branch of one and the same whole. The last philosophy in time is the result of all the systems that preceded it, and must include their principles; and so, if indeed it is philosophy, will be the fullest, most comprehensive, and most adequate philosophy.

The spectacle of so many and so various philosophies suggests the necessity of defining strictly the universal and the particular. When the universal is taken formally and *coordinated* with the particular, it sinks into a particular itself. Even common sense in everyday matters is above the absurdity of setting a universal *beside* the particulars. Would anyone who wished for fruit reject cherries, pears, and grapes, on the ground that they were cherries, pears, or grapes, and not fruit? But when philosophy is in question, the excuse of many is that philosophies are so different, and none of them is *the* philosophy, each is only *a* philosophy. Such a plea is assumed to justify contempt for philosophy. And yet cherries too are fruit. Often, too, a system, of which the principle is the universal, is put on a level with another of which the principle is a particular, and with theories that deny the existence of philosophy altogether. Such systems are said to be only different views of philosophy. With equal justice, light and darkness might be styled different kinds of light.

14. The same development of thought that is exhibited in the history of philosophy is presented in philosophy itself, only *purely in the element of thinking* and freed of that historical externality. The free and genuine thought is internally concrete, and is thus an Idea; and in its whole universality, it is *the* Idea or *the absolute*. The science of it is essentially a *system*. For the truth is concrete; it unfolds within itself, and gathers and holds itself together in unity; that is, it is a totality; and the freedom of the whole, as well as the necessity of its distinct moments, are possible only when these are discriminated and defined.

Unless it is a system, philosophy is not in the least scientific. Unsystematic philosophising can only express personal pecularities of mind, and is contingent in its contents. Apart from the whole of which it is a moment, a content lacks justification, and is a baseless assumption, or personal conviction. Yet many philosophical treatises confine themselves to such an exposition of opinions and sentiments.

The term '*system*' is often misunderstood. It does not denote a philosophy, the principle of which is narrow and distinguished from others. On the contrary, a genuine philosophy makes it a principle to include every particular principle.

15. Each of the parts of philosophy is a philosophical whole, a circle rounded and complete in itself. In each of these parts, however, the philosophical Idea is found in a particular specificality or medium. The individual circle, because it is internally a totality, bursts through the limits imposed by its special medium, and gives rise to a wider circle. The whole thus resembles a circle of circles. The Idea appears in each single circle, but the whole Idea is constituted by the system of these peculiar media and each is a necessary moment.

16.   In the form of an encyclopaedia, science has no room for a detailed exposition of particulars, and must be limited to setting forth the beginnings of the special sciences and their basic concepts.

How much of the particular parts is requisite to constitute a particular science is indeterminate; but the part, if it is to be something true, must be not an isolated moment merely, but itself a totality. The entire field of philosophy therefore really forms a single science; but it may also be viewed as a whole composed of several particular sciences. The encyclopaedia of philosophy must not be confounded with ordinary encyclopaedias. An ordinary encyclopaedia does not pretend to be more than an aggregation of sciences, regulated by no principle, and merely as experience offers them. Sometimes it even includes what merely bear the name of sciences, but are merely collections of information. In an aggregate like this, the sciences owe their place in it to extrinsic reasons and their unity is therefore extrinsic: an *arrangement*. For the same reason, especially as the materials also depend on no principle, the arrangement is at best an experiment, and will always exhibit awkwardnesses. An encyclopaedia of philosophy excludes three kinds of partial science: (I) Mere aggregates of information. Philology *prima facie* belongs to this class. (II) The quasi-sciences, founded on arbitrary will alone, such as heraldry. Sciences of this class are positive from beginning to end. (III) In other sciences, also styled positive, but which have a rational basis and beginning, philosophy claims that constituent as its own. The positive features remain the property of the sciences themselves.

The positive element in sciences is of different sorts. (I) Their beginning, though implicitly rational, yields to contingency, when they have to bring the universal into contact with empirical individuality and actuality. In this region of chance and change, the concept cannot be brought to bear, only *grounds*. Thus *e.g.* jurisprudence, or the system of direct and indirect taxation, require certain precise and definitive decisions that lie beyond the absolute determinacy of the concept. A latitude for settlement is accordingly left, which may be determined in one way on one principle, in another way on another, and admits of no definitive certainty. Similarly the Idea of nature, when individualized, is dissipated into contingencies. Natural history, geography, and medicine stumble on determinations of existence, on kinds and distinctions, which are not determined by reason, but by hazard and external chance. Even history belongs here. The Idea is its essence; but its appearance lies in contingency and in the field of self-will. (II) These sciences are positive also in failing to recognize the finite nature of their determinations and to show how they and their whole sphere pass into a higher. They assume them to possess an authority beyond appeal.

Here finitude lies in the form, as in the previous instance it lay in the matter. (III) Related to this is the ground of cognition: partly inference, partly feeling, faith, and the authority of others, in general the authority of inward and outward intuition. Under this head falls also the philosophy that proposes to build on anthropology, facts of consciousness, inner or outward experience. It may happen, however, that only the form of scientific exposition is empirical; while intuitive sagacity arranges what are mere phenomena, according to the inner sequence of the concept. In such a case the contrasts between the varied phenomena brought together serve to eliminate the external, contingent circumstances of the conditions, and the universal thus comes into view. A judicious experimental physics in this way will present the rational science of nature, — as history will present the science of human affairs and actions — in an external picture, which mirrors the concept.

17. It may seem as if philosophy, in order to begin, had, like the rest of the sciences, to start with a subjective presupposition, viz to make a particular object, thinking, the object of thinking, just as space, number, etc. are objects elsewhere. However, it is by a free act of thought that it occupies the point of view in which it is for its own self, and thus gives itself an object of its own production. Moreover the point of view, which thus appears as *immediate*, must within science be converted to a result, — the ultimate result in which philosophy returns into itself and reaches the point with which it began. In this manner philosophy exhibits the appearance of a circle which closes with itself, and has no beginning in the same way as the other sciences. It has a beginning only in relation to a person who proposes to study it, and not in relation to the science as science. In other words, the concept of science — the first concept, which, since it is the first, implies a separation between the thought that is our object, and the subject philosophizing that is, as it were, external — must be grasped by science itself. This is even the one single aim, action, and goal of philosophy — to arrive at the concept of its concept, and thus secure its return and its satisfaction.

18. As only the whole of science can exhibit the Idea, it is impossible to give a preliminary general conception of a philosophy. Nor can the division of philosophy be intelligible, except in connection with the Idea. A preliminary division, like the conception from which it comes, can only be an anticipation. But the Idea turns out to be the thinking that is completely identical with itself and this also in its activity of setting itself over against itself, so as to be for itself, and of being in full possession of itself in this other. Thus philosophy falls into three parts:

I. Logic, the science of the Idea in and for itself.

II. The Philosophy of Nature: the science of the Idea in its otherness.

III. The Philosophy of Mind, of the Idea come back to itself out of that otherness.

As observed in §15, the differences between the particular philosophical sciences are only determinations of the Idea that alone is exhibited in these different media. In nature nothing else would be discerned, except the Idea: but the Idea has the form of alienation. In mind, again, the Idea is for itself, and is becoming absolute. Every such determination in which the Idea appears, is at the same time a fleeting stage; hence each subdivision has not only to know its contents as an object that has being, but also how these contents pass into their higher circle. To represent it as a division, therefore, leads to misconception; for it coordinates the several parts or sciences one beside another, as if they had no development, but were, like species, radically distinct.

FIRST PART: SCIENCE OF LOGIC
PRELIMINARY CONCEPT

19. Logic is the science of the pure Idea, that is, the Idea in the abstract medium of thought.

This definition, and the others that occur in this introductory concept, derive from and are subsequent to a survey of the whole. This applies to all prefatory concepts whatever about philosophy.

Logic might be defined as the science of thought, and of its laws and determinations. But thought, as thought, constitutes only the medium, or universal determinacy, that renders the Idea logical. If the Idea is thought, thought must not be taken as formal, but as the self-developing totality of its laws and peculiar determinations. These laws are given by thought to itself, and not something it finds in itself and already has.

From different points of view, logic is both the hardest and the easiest science. Logic is hard, because it deals not with intuitions, nor, like geometry, with representations of the senses, but with pure abstractions; and it demands a force and facility of withdrawing into pure thought, of keeping hold of it, and of moving in such an element. Logic is easy, because its content is nothing but our own thought and its familiar determinations; and these are the acme of simplicity, the a b c of everything else. They are also what we are best acquainted with: being and nothing; quality and magnitude: being-for-self and being-in-itself; one, many, and so on. But such an acquaintance only adds to the difficulties of the study; for while, on the one hand, we readily think it not worth bothering any longer with things so familiar, on the other hand, the problem is to become acquainted with them in a new way, quite opposite to that in which we are already.

The utility of logic concerns its bearings on the student, and the training it gives for other purposes. This logical training consists in exercise in thinking (for this science is the thinking of thinking); and storing his head with thoughts. But the logical, being the absolute form of truth, and, even more, the pure truth itself, is far more than merely useful. Yet if what is noblest, most free, and independent is also most useful, logic can be so conceived. Its utility must then be estimated otherwise than as merely formal exercise in thinking.

20. If we take our *prima facie* idea of thought, we find first (a) that, in its usual subjective meaning, thought is one out of many activities or faculties of the mind, coordinate with such others as sensation, intuition, imagination, desire, volition. The product of this activity, the form or determinacy of the thought, is the *universal*, or, in general, the abstract. Thought, as an *activity*, is thus the *active* universal, and, since the deed, its product, is just the universal, it is the *self*-actuating universal. Thought conceived as a *subject* is a thinker, and the subject existing as a thinker is simply expressed as 'I.'

The definitions in this and the following sections are not offered as assertions or opinions of mine on thinking. But in these preliminary remarks deduction or proof would be impossible and they may be taken as *facts*. In other words, everyone, when he has and considers thoughts, will discover empirically in his consciousness that they possess the character of universality as well as other determinations to be enumerated. Of course his powers of attention and abstraction need previous training, to observe the facts of his consciousness and his conceptions.

This introductory exposition has already alluded to the distinction between the sensuous, conception, and thought. As the distinction is crucial for understanding the nature and kinds of knowledge, it will help to explain matters if we here call attention to it. To explain the sensuous, the readiest method is to refer to its external source—the sense-organs or senses. But to name the organ does not help to explain what is apprehended by it. The distinction between the sensuous and thought lies in this: the essential feature of the sensible is individuality, and as the individual (at its most abstract, the atom) is also in a context, the sensuous is mutual externality, whose more definite, abstract forms are juxtaposition and succession. *Conception* has such sensuous stuff as content, but characterized as in *me* and *mine*; and second, as universal, simple, and related-to-self. Nor is sense the only source of conception. There are conceptions of a content emanating from self-conscious thought, such as those of law, ethics, religion, and even of thought itself, and it requires effort to detect the difference between such conceptions and thoughts of the same content. For here a thought is the content, and there is the form of universality, without which no content could be in me, or be a conception at all. Yet here also the peculiarity of conception is, in general, to be sought in the individualisation of its contents. Law and legal provisions do not of course exist in sensible space, mutually external. Nor as regards time, though they appear perhaps in succession, are their contents themselves conceived as

affected by time, as transient and changeable in it. But these determinations, though implicitly spiritual, stand *isolated* on the broad ground of
conception, its inward, abstract generality. Thus isolated, each is simple:
right, duty, God. Conception now either rests satisfied with declaring that
right is right, God is God; or in a higher culture, it enunciates determinations; as, for instance, God is the creator of the world, omniscient, almighty,
etc. Here too several isolated, simple determinations are strung together;
but in spite of the link supplied by their subject, they remain mutually
external. In this, conception coincides with understanding; the only distinction being that the latter introduces relations of universal and particular, of cause and effect, etc., and in this way supplies necessary connections
to the isolated ideas of conception, which leaves them side by side in its
indeterminate space, connected only by a bare 'also.'

The difference between conception and thought is of special importance,
because philosophy can be said to do nothing but transform conceptions
into thoughts, — though it goes on to transform the mere thought into the
concept.

The sensuous has been characterized by determinations of individuality
and mutual externality. We can add that these determinations are themselves thoughts and universals. It will be shown in the Logic that thought
and the universal is just this: it lets nothing escape it, but outflanking its
other, is that other and itself. Language is the work of thought; hence all
that is said in language must be universal. What I only *mean* is *mine*: it
belongs to me, — this particular individual. But language expresses nothing
but universality; and so I cannot say what I merely *mean*. And the
unutterable, — feeling, sensation — far from being the highest truth, is the
most unimportant and untrue. If I say 'The individual,' 'This individual,'
'here,' 'now,' all these are universal terms. Everything and anything is an
individual, a 'this,' and, if it be sensible, here and now. Similarly when I
say, 'I,' I *mean* myself to the exclusion of all others: but what I *say*, 'I,' is just
everyone: I, which excludes all others from itself. In an awkward expression
Kant said that I *accompany* all my conceptions, — sensations, too, desires,
actions, etc. I is in essence and act the universal, and community is also a
form, though an external form, of universality. All other men have it in
common with me to be I; just as it is common to all my sensations and
conceptions to be mine. But I, in the abstract, as such, is pure self-relation,
in which we abstract from conception and feeling, from every state and
every peculiarity of nature, talent, and experience. To this extent, I is the
existence of wholly *abstract* universality, of the abstractly free. Hence the I
is thought as a subject, and since I am at the same time in all my sensations,
conceptions, and states, the thought is everywhere present, and is a category that runs through all these determinations.

21.   (b) If thinking is taken as active in relation to objects, as meta-
thinking about something, then the universal or product of its activity

contains the value of the thing, the essential, inward, and true core of it.

In §5 the old belief was quoted that the reality in object, circumstance, or event, the intrinsic worth or essence, the thing on which everything depends, is not an immediate datum of consciousness, or coincident with the first appearance and impression of the object; that, on the contrary, meta-thinking is required to discover the real constitution of the object, and that by meta-thinking it will be ascertained.

22. (c) By meta-thinking something is altered in the way in which the content first occurs in sensation, intuition, or conception. Thus an alteration must be interposed before the true nature of the object can come to consciousness.

23. (d) The real nature of the object comes to light in meta-thinking; but this thinking is my activity. Thus the real nature is a *product of my* mind, in its character of thinking subject, of me in my simple universality, as the simply self-collected I, or of my freedom.

'Think for yourself' is a phrase often used as if it had some significance. In fact no one can think for another, any more than he can eat or drink for him; the expression is a pleonasm. To think is *ipso facto* to be free, for thought as the activity of the universal is an abstract relating of self to self, which, being self-contained and, as regards subjectivity, utterly featureless, finds it content only in the subject-matter and its determinations. If therefore humility or modesty consists in ascribing to subjectivity no particularity of act or quality, it is easy to solve the question concerning the humility or pride of philosophy. For in content thought is only true insofar as it sinks itself in the subject-matter, and in form is no particular state or act of the subject, but rather that attitude of consciousness where the abstract I, freed from all the particularity of its ordinary states or qualities, restricts itself to the universal in which it is identical with all individuals. Thus philosophy may be acquitted of pride. When Aristotle urges us to be worthy of that attitude, consciousness becomes worthy by letting go all particular opinions and prejudices, and submitting to the subject-matter.

24. These determinations entitle us to call thoughts 'objective thoughts,' which also include the forms primarily discussed in the common logic, which are usually treated as forms of *conscious* thought only. *Logic therefore coincides with metaphysics, the science of things grasped in thoughts,* — thoughts accredited able to express the essentialities of things.

The relation of such forms as concept, judgment, and syllogism to others, such as causality, is a matter for the science itself. But this much is evident beforehand. If thought tries to form a concept of things, this concept (and thus its most immediate forms, the judgment and syllogism) cannot consist of determinations and relations that are alien and irrelevant to the things. Meta-thinking, we said, leads to the universal of things: which universal is itself one of the conceptual moments. To say that reason, understanding is in the world, is equivalent to the phrase 'objective thought.' The phrase however has the inconvenience that 'thought' is too often confined to the mind or consciousness, while 'objective' is applied primarily only to the nonmental.

25. The term 'objective thoughts' indicates the *truth*—the truth that is to be the absolute *object* of philosophy, and not merely its goal. But the expression reveals an opposition, to characterize and evaluate which is the main interest of contemporary philosophy and which forms the nub of the question of truth and of our knowledge of it. If the thought-forms are burdened with a fixed antithesis, *i.e.*, if they are only of a finite character, they are unsuitable for the truth that is absolutely in and for itself, and truth can find no place in thought. Thought that produces only finite categories and proceeds by their means, is, in the strict sense, understanding. The finitude of these categories lies in two points. First, they are only subjective, and have a permanent antithesis in the objective. Second, they are of restricted content, and so persist in antithesis to one another and still more to the absolute. To explain the position and import here attributed to logic, the attitudes in which thought is supposed to stand to objectivity will next be examined by way of further introduction.

In my *Phenomenology of Spirit*, which on that account was at its publication described as the first part of the System of Science, the method adopted was to begin with the first and simplest appearance of mind, immediate consciousness, and to develop its dialectic up to the philosophical point of view, the necessity of that view being proved by the process. But, for this, it was impossible to restrict myself to the mere form of consciousness. For the stage of philosophical knowledge is the richest in material and organization, and therefore, as it emerged as a result, it presupposed the concrete formations of consciousness, such as morality, ethics, art and religion. The development of consciousness, which at first appears limited to form merely, thus at the same time includes the development of the content of the objects of the special branches of philosophy. But the process must, so to speak, go on behind consciousness's back, since the content is related to consciousness as the in-itself. The exposition thus becomes more intricate, and much that belongs to the concrete branches already appears in the introduction. The survey that follows has even more the inconvenience of being only historical and inferential in its method. But it tries especially to show how the questions we face, in our conception, on the nature of knowledge, faith and the like,—questions that we regard as wholly concrete—are really reducible to *simple* categories, which first get cleared up in logic.

FIRST ATTITUDE OF THOUGHT TO OBJECTIVITY

26. The first attitude is the naive procedure that has no awareness of the opposition of thinking in and against itself. It involves the *belief* that the truth is *known* by meta-thinking, and objects brought before consciousness as they really are. In this belief, thinking heads straight for objects, transforms the content of sensations and intuitions into a content of thought, and is satisfied with this as the truth. All philosophy in its beginnings, all sciences, and even the daily activities of consciousness, live in this belief.

27. This thinking is not aware of its antithesis; thus there is nothing to prevent it from possessing a genuinely philosophical and speculative content, though it is just as possible that it may never get beyond finite categories, or the still unresolved opposition. In this introduction the main question is to observe this attitude of thought in its extreme form, and thus first to examine its second form. The clearest instance of it, and one lying nearest to ourselves, is the old, pre-Kantian metaphysics. It is, however, only for the history of philosophy that this metaphysic belongs to the past: the thing is always to be found, as the view that the mere understanding takes of the objects of reason. It is here that the real and immediate good lies of a closer examination of its main content and its *modus operandi.*

28. This science took the determinations of thought to be the fundamental determinations of things. It assumed that to think what is, is to know in itself; to that extent it occupied higher ground than the critical philosophy that succeeded it. But (1) *these determinations were cut off from their connection*; each was believed valid by itself and a possible predicate of the truth. It was a general assumption of this metaphysic that a knowledge of the absolute was gained by assigning predicates to it. It investigated neither the peculiar content and value of the determinations of the understanding, nor even this way of determining the absolute by assigning predicates to it.

Examples of such predicates are: 'existence,' in the proposition, 'God has existence;' 'finitude' or 'infinity,' as in the question, 'Is the world finite or infinite?'; 'simple' and 'complex,' in the proposition, 'The soul is simple' or again, 'The thing is a unity, a whole,' etc. Nobody asked whether such predicates had any intrinsic and independent truth, or if the judgmental form could be a form of truth.

29. Predicates of this kind, taken individually, have a restricted content, and evidently fall short of the fullness of conception (of God, nature, spirit, etc.), which they in no way exhaust. Besides, though their being predicates of one subject supplies them with connection, their contents keep them apart; and so each is brought in from outside in relation to the others.

The first of these defects the Orientals sought to remedy, when, for example, they defined God by attributing to Him many names; but still the number of names was supposed to be infinite.

30. (2) Their objects were no doubt totalities that intrinsically belong to reason, to the thinking of the internally concrete universal. But these totalities—God, the soul, the world—were taken by the metaphysician as subjects made and ready, to form the basis for an application of the

categories of the understanding. They were adopted from conception. Accordingly, conception was the only criterion for whether or not the predicates were suitable and sufficient.

31. The conceptions of God, the soul, the world, may be supposed to afford thought a firm footing. But besides having a particular, subjective character clinging to them, and thus leaving room for great variety of interpretation, they themselves first require a firm definition by thought. This may be seen in any proposition where the predicate, or in philosophy the category, needs to indicate *what* the subject, or the conception we start with, is.

In such a sentence as 'God is eternal,' we begin with the conception of God, not knowing as yet what he is; to tell us that is the business of the predicate. In logic, accordingly, where the content is determined in the form of thought only, it is not merely superfluous to make these categories predicates of propositions in which God, or, still vaguer, the absolute, is the subject, but it would also have the disadvantage of suggesting another criterion than the nature of thought. Besides, the form of the proposition, or, more precisely, judgment, is not suited to express the concrete—and the true is concrete—or the speculative. The judgment is by its form one-sided and, to that extent, false.

32. (3) *This metaphysics turned into dogmatism.* By the nature of finite determinations, it had to assume that of two opposite assertions, such as the above propositions, one must be true and the other false.

33. The *first* part of this metaphysic in its systematic form is ontology, the doctrine of the abstract determinations of the essence. The multitude of these determinations and their finite validity lack a principle. They have in consequence to be enumerated empirically and contingently, and their detailed content can be founded only on conceptions, on assertions that words are used in a particular sense, and even perhaps on etymology. If experience pronounces the list to be complete, and if linguistic usage, by its agreement, shows the analysis to be correct, the metaphysician is satisfied; and the truth and necessity of such determinations is never investigated in its own right.

To ask if being, existence, finitude, simplicity, complexity, etc. are intrinsically and independently true concepts must surpise those who believe that questions of truth concern only propositions (whether a concept is or is not with truth to be attributed, as the phrase is, to a subject), and that untruth lies in the contradiction between the subject of the idea, and the concept to be predicated of it. Now as the concept is concrete, it and every determinacy in general is essentially a self-contained unity of distinct determinations. If truth, then, were nothing more than absence of contradiction, it would be first necessary in the case of every concept to examine whether it, taken individually, contains such an intrinsic contradiction.

34. The *second* branch was rational psychology or pneumatology. It dealt with the metaphysical nature of the soul—that is, of the mind regarded as a thing. It expected to find immortality in a sphere dominated by composition, time, qualitative change, and quantitative increase or decrease.

35. The *third* branch, cosmology, considered the world, its contingency, necessity, eternity, limitation in time and space; the formal laws of its changes; the freedom of man and the origin of evil.

Here it applied supposedly absolute contrasts: contingency and necessity; external and internal necessity; efficient and final cause, or causality in general and design; essence or substance and appearance; form and matter; freedom and necessity; happiness and pain; good and evil.

36. The *fourth* branch, natural or rational theology, considered the concept of God, or God as a possibility, the proofs of his existence, and his properties.

(a) When understanding thus considers God, its main purpose is to find what predicates correspond or do not to our *conception* of God. In so doing it assumes the contrast between reality and negation as absolute; hence, in the end, nothing is left for the concept as understanding takes it, but the empty abstraction of indeterminate essence, of pure reality or positivity, the lifeless product of modern enlightenment.

(b) The *demonstration* employed in finite cognition in general leads to an inversion of the true order. For it requires the statement of some objective ground for God's being, which thus presents itself as *mediated* by something else. This mode of proof, guided as it is by the understanding's notion of identity, is embarrassed by the difficulty of passing from the finite to the infinite. Either the finitude of the existing world, which remains positive, clings to God, and God has to be defined as the immediate substance of that world (pantheism); or He remains an object set over against the subject, and in this way, finite (dualism).

(c) The attributes of God, which ought to be various and determinate, actually disappeared in the abstract concept of pure reality, of indeterminate essence. Yet in our conception the finite world continues still to be a true being, with God as its antithesis; and thus arises the further conception of different relations of God to the world. These, formulated as properties, must, on the one hand, as relations to finite states, themselves be finite (e.g., just, gracious, mighty, wise, etc.); on the other hand they should be infinite. On this level of thought the contradiction admits of only the nebulous solution of quantitative exaltation of the properties, forcing them into indeterminateness, into the *sensus eminentior*. But this expedient really destroyed the property and left a mere name. . . .

THE CONCEPT AND SUBDIVISION OF LOGIC

79. In form the logical has three aspects: (α) the abstract or that of understanding; (β) the dialectical, or that of negative reason; (γ) the speculative, or that of positive reason.

These three aspects do not make three *parts* of logic, but are moments in every logical entity, that is, of every concept and truth whatever. They may all be put under the first stage, that of understanding, and so kept isolated from each other; but this would not give their truth. The statement of the division and determinations of logic is here only historical and anticipatory.

80. (α) Thought, as *understanding*, sticks to the fixed determinacy and its distinctiveness from others; every such limited abstract it treats as having a substance and being of its own.

81. (β) In the dialectical moment these finite determinations supersede *themselves*, and pass into their opposites.

(1) When the dialectical is taken by the understanding separately and independently, especially as shown in scientific concepts, it constitutes skepticism; this contains mere negation as the result of the dialectical.

(2) It is customary to view dialectic as an external art, which willfully introduces confusion and a mere semblance of contradictions into determinate concepts, so that the semblance is a nullity, while the true reality is the determinations of understanding. Often, indeed, dialectic is nothing more than a subjective seesaw of arguments *pro* and *con*, where the absence of substance is disguised by the subtlety that produces the arguments. But in its proper character, dialectic is the very nature and essence of the determinations of understanding, of things and of the finite as a whole. In the first instance, reflection is that movement beyond the isolated determinacy that connects it, and brings it into relation, while in other respects leaving it its isolated validity. But dialectic is the immanent movement beyond, in which the one-sidedness and limitation of the determinations of understanding is seen in its true light, as their negation. To be finite is just to sublimate itself. Thus the dialectical constitutes the life and soul of scientific progress, the principle that alone gives immanent connection and necessity to the content of science; and in it lies the true, as opposed to the external, elevation above the finite.

82. (γ) The speculative or positively rational apprehends the unity of determinations in their opposition, the affirmative that is involved in their disintegration and in their transition.

(1) The result of dialectic is positive, because it has a definite content, or because its result is not empty, abstract nothing, but the negation of certain determinations that are contained in the result, for the very reason that it is a result and not an immediate nothing. (2) Thus this rational, though it be a thought and abstract, is still a concrete, being not a plain formal unity, but a unity of distinct determinations. Bare abstractions or formal thoughts are therefore no business of philosophy, only concrete thoughts. (3) The logic of mere understanding is involved in speculative

logic, and can at will be elicited from it, by simply omitting the dialectical and rational. Then it becomes what the common logic is, a descriptive collection of sundry thought-determinations, which, finite though they are, are taken to be something infinite.

83. Logic is subdivided into three parts:

I. The Doctrine of Being:
II. The Doctrine of Essence:
III. The Doctrine of the Concept and Idea.

That is, into the doctrine of the thought:

I. In its immediacy: the concept in itself;
II. In its reflection and mediation: being-for-self and show of the concept;
III. In its return into itself, and its developed abiding by itself: the concept in and for itself.

FIRST SUBDIVISION OF LOGIC:
THE DOCTRINE OF BEING

84. Being is the concept implicit only: its determinations are beings; when they are distinguished they are each of them an other; and the form of the dialectical, *i.e.*, their further determination, is a passing over into another. This further determination is at once a forth-putting, and in that way an unfolding, of the implicit concept; and at the same time the withdrawing of being inwards, its sinking deeper into itself. The explication of the concept in the sphere of being does two things: it brings out the totality of being, and it abolishes the immediacy of being, or the form of being as such.

85. Being itself and the determinations of it that follow, as well as those of logic in general, may be viewed as definitions of the absolute, as metaphysical definitions of God; but strictly only the first and third in every sphere—the first, simple determination, and the third, the return from differentiation to simple self-relation. For a metaphysical definition of God is the expression of His nature in thoughts as such: and logic embraces all thoughts so long as they continue in the form of thought. The second determination, where the sphere is in its differentiation, is, on the other hand, a definition of the finite. The objection to the form of definition is that it implies in the mind's eye a substrate of conception. Thus even the absolute (though it purports to express God in the sense and form of thought) in relation to its predicate (the real and determinate expression in thought) is as yet only a putative thought, an indeterminate substrate. The thought, which is here the only matter of importance, is contained only in the predicate; hence the propositional form, like the said subject, is a mere superfluity (cf. §31, and below, on the judgment).

A. Quality

a. Being

86. Pure being makes the beginning: because it is both a pure thought, and immediacy, simple and indeterminate; and the first beginning cannot be anything mediated or further determined.

All doubts about, and admonitions against, beginning science with abstract empty being, disappear, if we only perceive what a beginning naturally implies. It is possible to define being as 'I = I,' as absolute indifference or identity, and so on. Where we need to begin either with what is absolutely certain, *i.e.*, the certainty of oneself, or with a definition or intuition of the absolute truth, these and other forms of the kind may be viewed as if they must be the first. But each of these forms contains mediation, and hence cannot be the real first; mediation is an advance from a first on to a second, and an emergence from distinct items. If I = I, or even intellectual intuition, is really taken only as the first, they are in this pure immediacy just being; conversely, pure being, if abstract no longer, but involving mediation, is pure thinking or intuition.

If we enunciate being as a predicate of the absolute, we get the first definition of it: 'the absolute is being.' This is (in the thought) the absolutely initial definition, the most abstract and poor. It is the definition of the Eleatics, but at the same time is also the familiar definition of God as the sum of all realities. We are to set aside that limitation that is in every reality, so that God shall be only the real in all reality, the superlatively real. Since reality implies a reflection, we get a more immediate statement of this when Jacobi says that the God of Spinoza is the *principium* of being in all existence.

87. But this pure being, as it is pure abstraction, is therefore the absolutely negative: which taken similarly immediately, is nothing.

(1) From this follows the second definition of the absolute: The absolute is nothing. In fact this definition is implied in saying that the thing-in-itself is the indeterminate, utterly without form and so without content, or that God *is* only the supreme essence and nothing more; for this is declaring Him to be the same negativity. The nothing that Buddhists make the principle as well as the final aim and goal, of everything, is the same abstraction.

(2) If the opposition is stated in this immediacy as being and nothing, the shock of its nullity is too great not to stimulate the attempt to fix being and secure it against transition. In this regard, meta-thinking inevitably hits on the plan of finding a fixed determination for being, to distinguish it from nothing. Thus being is taken as what persists in all change, as infinitely determinable matter, or even, unreflectingly, as some individual existence, any chance sensuous or mental entity. But all such further and more concrete determinations make being more than the pure being which it is

here immediately in the beginning. Only in and because of this indeterminacy is it nothing — something inexpressible; its distinction from nothing is a mere *meaning*.

All that is wanted is to realize that these beginnings are nothing but these empty abstractions, one as empty as the other. The urge to find a fixed meaning in being or in both is the very necessity that leads to the onward movement of being and nothing, and gives them a true or concrete meaning. This advance is the logical exposition and the movement exhibited later. The meta-thinking that finds profounder determinations for them is the logical thinking through which such determinations emerge, not, however, in a contingent, but a necessary way. Every meaning, therefore, which they afterwards acquire, is only a more precise determination and truer definition of the absolute. Here emptily abstract being and nothing are replaced by a concrete in which both are elements. The supreme form of nothing in itself would be freedom: but freedom is negativity when it sinks self-absorbed to supreme intensity, and is itself an affirmation, an *absolute* affirmation.

88. Nothing as thus immediate and equal to itself, is also conversely the same as being is. The truth of being and of nothing is accordingly the unity of the two: this unity is becoming.

(1) The proposition 'Being and nothing are the same' seems so paradoxical to conception or understanding that it is perhaps taken for a joke. And indeed it is one of the hardest things thought expects of itself; for being and nothing are the antithesis in all its immediacy, that is, without the one being invested with a determination that would involve its connection with the other. They involve, however, as this paragraph points out, this determination — the determination that is just the same in both. So far the deduction of their unity is completely analytical: Indeed the whole progress of philosophizing in general, if it be methodical — that is, necessary — merely renders explicit what is implicit in a concept. It is as correct, however, to say that being and nothing are altogether different, as to assert their unity. The one is *not* what the other is. But since the distinction has not yet become determinate (being and nothing are still the immediate), it is, in the way that they have it, something unutterable, which we merely mean.

(2) No great expenditure of wit is needed to make fun of the proposition that being and nothing are the same, or rather to adduce absurdities that, it is falsely asserted, are consequences and applications of that proposition: e.g., that it makes no difference whether my home, my property, the air I breathe, this city, the sun, law, mind, God, are or not. In some of these cases, they introduce private aims, the utility a thing has for me, and ask, whether it be the same to me if the thing is or is not. In fact the teaching of philosophy is precisely to free man from the endless crowd of finite aims and intentions, by making him so indifferent to them that their being or

non-being is all the same to him. But in general, reference to a content at once establishes a connection with other existences and other purposes that are assumed valid: It is now made to depend on such assumptions whether the being or not-being of a determinate content is all the same or not. A substantial distinction is in these cases substituted for the empty distinction of being and nothing. In other cases, it is implicitly essential purposes, absolute existences, and Ideas that are placed in the mere category of being or not-being. But there is more to be said of these concrete objects than that they merely are or are not. Barren abstractions, like being and nothing — the initial categories that, for that reason, are the scantiest to be found — are utterly inadequate to the nature of these objects. Genuine content is far above these abstractions and their opposition. In general when a concrete is substituted for being and not-being, thoughtlessness makes its usual mistake of speaking about, and having in conception, something other than what is in question: and here the question is abstract being and nothing.

(3) It may be said that nobody can comprehend the unity of being and nothing. But the concept of it is stated in the sections preceding, and that is all there is to it. What they really mean by 'comprehension' is more than the strict concept: They want a richer and more complex consciousness, a conception that presents the concept as a concrete case, more familiar to the ordinary operations of thought. Insofar as incomprehensibility means only want of habituation in holding onto abstract thoughts, free from all sensuous admixture, and grasping speculative propositions, the reply is just that philosophical knowledge certainly differs in kind from the knowledge usual in common life, as well as from that dominant in the other sciences. But if non-comprehension merely means that we cannot form a conception of the unity of being and nothing, this is far from true; everyone has countless conceptions of this unity. To say that we have no such conception can only mean that in none of these conceptions do we recognize the concept in question, and we are not aware that they exemplify it. The readiest example is becoming. Everyone has a conception of becoming, and will even allow that it is *one* idea; he will further allow that, when analyzed, it involves the determination of being, and also the very other of being, nothing; and that these two determinations lie undivided in the one idea: so that becoming is the unity of being and nothing. Another obvious example is a beginning. In its beginning, the thing is not yet, but it is more than merely nothing, for its being is already in the beginning. Beginning is itself a case of becoming; only it involves a reference to the further advance. If we were to adapt logic to the more usual method of the sciences, we might start with the representation of a beginning as abstractly thought, or with beginning as such, and analyze this representation; and perhaps people would more readily admit, as a result of this analysis, that being and nothing present themselves as undivided in unity.

(4) It remains to note that such phrases as 'Being and nothing are the same,' or 'The unity of being and nothing'—like all other such unities, that of subject and object, and others—give rise to reasonable objection. They misrepresent the case, by giving an exclusive prominence to the unity, and leaving the difference that undoubtedly lies in it (because it is being and nothing, for example, the unity of which is posited) with no express mention or notice. It accordingly seems as if the diversity is unduly abstracted from and neglected. In fact no speculative determination can be correctly expressed by any such propositional form, for the unity has to be conceived *in* the diversity, which is all the while present and explicit. Becoming is the true expression for the result of being and nothing; it is the unity of the two; but not only is it the unity, it is also inherent unrest—the unity that is no mere connection-with-self and therefore motionless, but, through the diversity of being and nothing that is in it, at war with itself. Determinate being, on the other hand, is this unity, or becoming in this form of unity: hence determinate being is one-sided and finite. The opposition seems to have vanished; it is only implied in the unity, it is not explicitly put in it.

(5) The proposition of becoming, that being is the passage into nothing, and nothing the passage into being, is countered by the proposition of pantheism, of the eternity of matter: 'From nothing comes nothing,' and 'Something only comes out of something.' The ancients made the simple reflection that the proposition 'From nothing comes nothing, from something something,' really abolishes becoming: for what it comes from and what it becomes are one and the same: it is just the proposition of the abstract identity of the understanding. It cannot but seem strange, therefore, to hear the propositions 'Out of nothing comes nothing: Out of something only comes something,' calmly taught in these days, with no awareness that they are the basis of pantheism, or that the ancients have exhausted all that is to be said about them.

b. Determinate Being

89.   In becoming, the being that is one with nothing, and the nothing that is one with being are only vanishing factors; by its inherent contradiction becoming collapses into itself, into the unity in which the two are absorbed. Its result is accordingly determinate being.

In this first example we must call to mind, once for all, what was stated in §82: the only way to secure development and advance in knowledge is to hold results fast in their truth. In anything whatever we can and must point to contradiction or opposite determinations; the abstraction made by understanding is a forcible insistence on one determinacy, and an effort to obscure and remove all consciousness of the other determinacy involved. Whenever such contradiction, then, is discovered in any object or notion, the usual inference is, *Hence* this object is *nothing*. Thus Zeno, who first showed the contradiction in motion, concluded that there is no motion: and the ancients, who recognized origin and decease, the two species of becoming, as untrue categories, made use of the expression that the one or absolute neither arises nor perishes. Such dialectic looks only at the negative aspect of its result, and fails to notice, what is at the same time really present, the determinate result, here a pure nothing, but a nothing that includes being, and, in like manner, a being that includes nothing. Hence being determinate is (1) the unity of being and nothing, in which the immediacy of these determinations, and their contradiction vanishes in their connection, a unity in which they are now only moments. (2) Since the result is the sublimated contradiction, it is in the form of simple unity with itself; it also is being, but being with negation or determinateness; it is becoming expressly put in the form of one of its elements, being.

90.   (α) Determinate being is being with a determinacy—which simply *is*; this immediate determinacy is quality. As reflected into itself in this its determinacy, determinate being is something, a determinate entity. The categories that develop in determinate being need be mentioned only briefly.

91.   Quality, as determinateness that *is*, as contrasted with the negation involved in it but distinguished from it, is reality. Negation is no longer abstract nothing, but, as a determinate being and something, is only a form in it—it is as otherness. Since this otherness, though a determination of quality itself, is in the first instance distinct from it, quality is being-for-another—an expanse of determinate being, of something. The being as such of quality, contrasted with this connection with an other, is being-in-self.

92.   (β) Being, if kept distinct from determinateness, being-in-itself, would be only the empty abstraction of being. In determinate being, the determinateness is one with being; yet at the same time, when explicitly made a negation, it is a limit, a barrier. Hence otherness is not something indifferent outside it, but a moment proper to it. Something is by its quality, first finite, second, alterable; so that finitude and variability pertain to its being.

93.   Something becomes an other; this other is itself a something, so it likewise becomes an other, and so *ad infinitum*.

94.   This infinity is bad or negative infinity: it is only negation of the finite; but the finite rises again the same as ever, and is never sublimated. Or this infinity only expresses the '*ought*' of the sublimation of finitude. The progression to infinity never gets further than a statement of the contradiction involved in the finite, that it is something as well as its other. It sets up with endless iteration the alternation between these determinations, each of which calls up the other.

95.   (γ) What we now in fact have is that something comes to be an other, and the other in general comes to be an other. In relation to another,

something is itself already an other against it; since what is passed into is quite the same as what passes over (both have one and the same determination, to be an other), so something in its passage into other only joins with itself. To be thus self-related in the passage, and in the other, is genuine infinity. Or, seen negatively: what is altered is the other, it becomes the other of the other. Thus being, but as negation of the negation, is restored again: it is now being-for-self.

Dualism, in putting an insuperable opposition between finite and infinite, fails to make the simple observation that the infinite is thereby only one of two, and is reduced to a particular, to which the finite is the other particular. Such an infinite, which is only a particular, is alongside the finite, in which it thus has its limit, barrier: it is not what it ought to be, not the infinite, but is only finite. In such a relation, where the finite is on this side and the infinite on that, the one here and the other there, an equal dignity of permanence and independence is ascribed to finite and to infinite. The being of the finite is made an absolute being, and in this dualism it stands firm on its own. Touched, so to speak, by the infinite, it would be annihilated. But it is supposed not to be able to be touched by the infinite. There must be an abyss, an impassable gulf between the two, with the infinite abiding on that side and the finite on this. Those who assert that the finite firmly persists over against the infinite are not, as they imagine, far above metaphysic: they are still on the level of the most ordinary metaphysic of understanding. For the same thing occurs here as the infinite progression expresses. At one time it is admitted that the finite has no independent actuality, no absolute being, is not in and for itself, but is only a transient. But the very next moment this is forgotten; the finite, merely over against the infinite, wholly separated from it, and rescued from annihilation, is conceived as persistent in its independence. While thought thus imagines itself elevated to the infinite, it meets with the opposite: it comes to an infinite that is only a finite, and the finite, which it had left behind, is still retained and made an absolute.

After this examination (with which we could usefully compare Plato's *Philebus*) of the nullity of the distinction made by understanding between the finite and the infinite, we are again liable to hit on the expression that the infinite and the finite are therefore one, and that genuine infinity, the truth, must be defined and expressed as unity of the finite and infinite. This is to some extent correct; but is just as perverse and false as the unity of being and nothing already noticed. Besides it may fairly be charged with reducing the infinite to finitude, with a *finite* infinite. For in the expression the finite seems left in place, it is not expressly expressed as sublimated. Or, if we reflect that the finite, when united with the infinite, certainly cannot remain what it was out of such unity, and will at least suffer some change in its determination (as an alkali combined with an acid loses some of its properties), the same will happen to the infinite, which, as the negative, will on its part also get blunted on the other. This in fact happens to the abstract, one-sided infinite of understanding. The genuine infinite, however, does not merely behave like the one-sided acid; it preserves itself. The negation of negation is not a neutralization: The infinite is the affirmative, and only the finite is sublimated.

In being-for-self enters the category of ideality. Determinate being, in the first instance apprehended only in its being or affirmation, has reality (§91); thus even finitude in the first instance is in the determination of reality. But the truth of the finite is rather its ideality. Similarly, the infinite of understanding, which is coordinated with the finite, itself only one of two finites, is untrue, ideal. This ideality of the finite is the chief maxim of philosophy; and for that reason every genuine philosophy is idealism. But everything depends on not taking for the infinite what, in its very determination, is at once made a particular and finite. For this reason we have paid more attention to this distinction. The fundamental concept of philosophy, the genuine infinite, depends on it. The distinction is cleared up by these simple, and for that reason seemingly insignificant, but incontrovertible reflections.

c. *Being-for-self*

96.   (α) Being-for-self, as connection with itself, is immediacy, and as connection of the negative with itself, is *a* being-for-self, the one, which, being without distinction in itself, thus excludes the other from itself.

97.   (β) The connection of the negative with itself is a negative connection, and so a distinguishing of the one from itself, the repulsion of the one; that is, a positing of many ones. The being-for-self is also immediate, and hence these many are *beings*; and the repulsion of the ones that *are* becomes to that extent their repulsion against each other as entities at hand or reciprocal exclusion.

98.   (γ) But each one of the many is what the other is: each is one, or even one of the many; they are consequently one and the same. Or, considered in itself, repulsion, as negative behavior of many ones to one another, is just as essentially their connection with each other; and as what the one connects with in its repelling are ones, in them it connects itself with itself. The repulsion therefore is just as essentially attraction; and the exclusive one, or being-for-self, sublimates itself. The qualitative determinacy that in the one has attained to its determinedness in and for itself, has thus passed into the determinacy as sublimated, into being as quantity.

The philosophy of atomism is this standpoint where the absolute is as being-for-self, as one, and many ones. And the repulsion that appears in the concept of the one is taken as their fundamental force. But instead of attraction, it is chance — that is, mere absence of thought — that is supposed to bring them together. Since the one is fixed as one, it is certainly impossible to regard its congression with others as anything but external.

The void, which is assumed as the complementary principle to the atoms, is repulsion itself, represented as the nothing that *is*, between the atoms. Modern atomism—and physics still retains this principle—has given up the atoms insofar as it keeps to molecules or small particles. Thus it has come closer to sensuous conception, but has abandoned the determination of thought. Besides, when an attractive is placed by the side of a repulsive force, the opposition is certainly made complete; and much stress has been laid on the discovery of this natural force, as it is called. But the connection between the two, which constitutes what is true and concrete in them, would have to be rescued from the obscurity and confusion in which they were left even in Kant's *Metaphysical Principles of Natural Science*. In modern times the atomic theory is even more important in politics than in physics. According to it, the will of individuals as such is the principle of the state: The attracting force consists of the particularity of needs and inclinations; and the universal, the state itself, is the external relation of a compact. . . .

SECOND SUBDIVISION OF LOGIC:
THE DOCTRINE OF ESSENCE

112. The essence is the concept as posited concept, the determinations in the essence are relative only, and not yet simply reflected into self; thus the concept is not yet for itself. The essence, as being that mediates itself with itself through the negativity of itself, is connection with self only to the same extent as it is a connection with another. But the other is not immediately a being, but is posited and mediated. Being has not vanished: for first, the essence as a simple connection-with-self is being; but second, being, in respect of the one-sided determination by which it is immediate, is reduced to a mere negative, a *show* or seeming. The essence is accordingly being as *showing* in itself.

The absolute is the essence. This is the same definition as the one that the absolute is being, insofar as being is similarly a simple connection with self. It is at the same time higher, since the essence is being that has gone into itself: that is, its simple connection-to-self is this connection as a negation of the negative, as a mediation of it in itself with itself. But when the absolute is defined as essence, the negativity is often taken only in the sense of an abstraction from all determinate predicates. This negative action, abstraction, thus falls outside the essence—which is then presented as a result apart from its premises, the *caput mortuum* of abstraction. But as this negativity is not external to being, but its own dialectic, the truth of being, the essence, is as being gone into itself or being in itself. That reflection, its showing in itself, constitutes its difference from immediate being, and it is the peculiar determination of the essence itself.

113.   The connection-with-self in the essence is the form of identity, of reflection-into-self; this here takes the place of the immediacy of being. They are both the same abstractions of connection-with-self.

The senses, with their lack of thought, take everything limited and finite as a being. This leads to the obstinacy of the understanding, which views the finite as something self-identical, not inherently self-contradictory.

114.   This identity, as descended from being, appears in the first place only possessed of the determinations of being, and connected to being as to something external. This external being, taken in separation from the essence, is the inessential. But essence is being-within-self, it is essential, only to the extent that it contains in itself its negative, connection with another, mediation. Consequently it has the inessential within itself as its, essence's, own show. But to show or seem, or to mediate, involves distinguishing; and since what is distinguished (as distinct from the identity out of which it arises and in which it is not or lies as a show) receives the form of identity, it is still in the mode of being or of immediacy connecting itself to itself. The sphere of essence thus becomes a still imperfect combination of immediacy and mediation. In it everything is so posited that it connects itself to itself, and yet so that we at the same time go beyond it — as a being of reflection, a being in which another shows and which shows in another. Thus it is also the sphere in which contradiction, still only implicit in the sphere of being, is *posited*.

As the one concept is the substance of everything, there appear in the development of essence the same determinations as in the development of being, but in a reflected form. Instead of being and nothing we have now the forms of the positive and the negative; the former at first as identity corresponding to oppositionless being, the latter developed (showing in itself) as difference. So also we have becoming as the ground of determinate being; and determinate being, reflected on the ground, is existence, and so on.

Essence, the hardest part of logic, includes the categories of metaphysics and of the sciences in general. These are products of reflective understanding, which both assumes the differences to be independent and also posits their relativity. It combines the two thoughts, side by side or one after the other, by an '*also*,' without bringing them together or uniting them in the concept.

A.   Essence as Ground of Existence

a.   *The Pure Determinations of Reflection*

α.   IDENTITY

115.   Essence shows in itself or is pure reflection, and so is only connection with itself, not as immediate but as reflected — identity with self.

This identity is formal identity or identity of the understanding, if it is held fast in abstraction from difference. Or rather abstraction is the positing of this formal identity, the change of something inherently concrete into this form of simplicity. This may be done in two ways: We may omit a part of the manifold found in the concrete (by so-called analysis) and select only one part; or neglecting their diversity, we may concentrate the manifold determinacies into one.

If we combine identity with the absolute as the subject of a proposition, we get: "The absolute is the self-identical." However true this proposition may be, it leaves unclear whether it is meant in its truth; therefore it is at least imperfect in expression. For it is undecided whether what is meant is the abstract identity of understanding — i.e., in contrast to the other determinations of essence — or identity as inherently concrete. The latter, as we shall see, is first the ground and in higher truth the concept. Even the word "absolute" often means no more than "abstract." Thus "absolute" space and "absolute" time just mean "abstract" space and "abstract" time.

When the determinations of essence are taken as essential determinations, they become predicates of a presupposed subject, which, because they are essential, is *everything*. The propositions thus arising have been expressed as the universal laws of thought. The proposition of identity runs: "Everything is identical with itself, $A = A$"; and, negatively, "A cannot at the same time be A and not A." Far from being a true law of thought, this proposition is just the law of the abstract understanding. The form of the proposition is already self-contradictory: for a proposition also promises a distinction between subject and predicate, while this one does not fulfill what its form requires. But it is expressly sublimated by the following so-called laws of thought, which make laws out of the contrary of this law. It is asserted that the proposition of identity, though it cannot be proved, regulates everyone's consciousness and that experience shows it to be accepted as soon as it is heard. To this alleged experience of the school we can oppose the universal experience that no consciousness thinks or has conceptions or speaks in accordance with this law, and that no existence of any kind conforms to it. The speech conforming to this supposed law of truth ("A planet is a planet"; "Magnetism is magnetism"; "Mind is a mind") is rightly viewed as silly. That is certainly a general experience. The logic that seriously propounds such laws has long since lost the school, in which they alone are valid, its credit with common sense as well as with reason.

β. DIFFERENCE

116. Essence is pure identity and show in itself, only as it is the negativity that connects self with self, and is thus a thrusting of itself away from itself. It therefore contains essentially the determinations of difference.

Other-being is here no longer qualitative, the determinacy or limit. It is in the essence, which connects self with self, and is thus the negation that is at the same time a connection, *difference, positedness, mediatedness*.

117.   Difference is (1) immediate difference, diversity. In diversity each of the different items is for itself what it is and indifferent to its connection with the other. This connection is therefore external to it. Owing to the indifference of the diverse items to their difference, it falls outside them into a third factor, the act of comparison. This external difference, as an identity of the items connected, is likeness; as non-identity of them it is unlikeness.

The understanding lets these determinations fall so far apart that although comparison has one and the same substratum, in which likeness and unlikeness are supposed to be diverse sides and aspects, still likeness for itself is only the former, identity, and unlikeness for itself is difference.

Diversity, like identity, has been transformed into a proposition: "Everything is diverse" or "No two things are completely alike." Here *everything* is assigned a predicate that is the opposite of the identity attributed to it in the first proposition and thus a law contradicting the first. As diversity is for outer comparison only, something is supposed to be for itself only identical to itself, so that the second proposition is supposed not to contradict the first. But then too, diversity does not belong to the something or everything; it constitutes no essential determination of this subject; on this showing the second proposition cannot be stated at all. But if the something itself is, as the proposition says, diverse, it must be in virtue of its own determinacy; but in this case what is meant is *determinate* difference, not diversity as such. This is the sense of Leibniz's proposition too.

118.   Likeness is an identity only of those items that are not the same, not identical to each other, and unlikeness is a connection of unlike items. Thus the two do not fall into diverse sides or aspects that are indifferent to each other. The one is a showing into the other. Thus diversity is a difference of reflection, or difference in its own self, *determinate* difference.

119.   Difference in itself is the essential difference, the positive and negative. The positive is identical connection with self in such a way as not to be the negative, and the negative is the different for itself so as not to be the positive. Thus each is for itself insofar as it is not the other. Each shows in the other and is only insofar as that other is. The difference of essence is therefore opposition, according to which the different is not faced by an other in general but by *its* other. That is, each has its own determinacy only in its connection with the other, is only reflected into itself as it is reflected into the other. Each is thus the other of its other.

Difference in itself gives the proposition "Everything is essentially distinct" or, as it may be expressed, "Of two opposite predicates, the one only belongs to the something and there is no third possibility." This proposition of opposition expressly contradicts the proposition of identity: by the one, something is supposed to be only a connection with self; by the other, it is supposed to be an opposite, a connection with its other. The thoughtlessness of abstraction is to juxtapose two such contradictory propositions, as laws, without even comparing them. The proposition of the excluded middle is the proposition of the determinate understanding, which falls into contradiction in attempting to avoid it. A is to be either +A or −A. This already implies a third A that is neither + nor −. If +W means 6 miles to the west and −W 6 miles to the east, and if + and − cancel each other, the 6 miles of way or space remain what they were with and without the contrast. Even the mere *plus* and *minus* of number or abstract direction have, if we like, zero as their third; but it cannot be denied that understanding's empty contrast between *plus* and *minus* has a place in such abstractions as number, direction, etc.

In the doctrine of contradictory concepts, the one concept is, e.g., 'blue' and the other 'not-blue.' (In this doctrine even the conception of a color is called a concept.) This other then is not an affirmative, such as 'yellow,' but is merely to be kept as the abstract negative. That the negative in itself is just as much positive is implied in the determination that what is opposite to another is *its* other. The vacuity of the opposition between so-called contradictory concepts is fully exhibited in the, so to say, grandiose expression of a general law: that every thing has the one and not the other of all predicates that are so opposed. Thus mind is either white or not-white, yellow or not-yellow, etc. *ad infinitum.*

It was forgotten that identity and opposition are themselves opposed, and the proposition of opposition was taken for that of identity in the form of the proposition of contradiction. A concept that has neither or both of two contradictory marks, such as a square circle, is held to be logically false. Now though a polygonal circle and a rectilineal arc also conflict with this proposition, geometers never hesitate to treat the circle as a polygon with rectilineal sides. But such a thing as a circle (its mere determinacy) is still no concept. In the concept of a circle, center and circumference are equally essential; both marks belong to it; and yet center and circumference are mutually opposed and contradictory.

The conception of polarity, so dominant in physics, contains the more correct determination of opposition. But when physics has to deal with thoughts, it adheres to ordinary logic; thus it may well be shocked if it develops the conception of polarity and sees the thoughts implied in it.

120. The positive is that diverse item that is supposed to be for itself and at the same time not indifferent to its connection with its other. The negative is supposed to be no less independent, the negative connection with self, for itself, but at the same time, as negative, simply to have this connection with itself, its positive, only in the other. Both are thus the posited contradiction; both are in themselves the same. Both are so for themselves too, since each is the sublimation of the other and of itself.

Thus they fall to the ground—or immediately the essential difference, as difference in and for itself, is the difference of it from itself and thus implies the identical; so that to the whole of difference in and for itself there belongs itself as well as identity. As a difference that connects self to self it is likewise enunciated to be the self-identical. And the opposite is in general that which contains the one and its other, itself and its opposite. The being within itself of the essence so determined is the ground.

γ. THE GROUND

121. The ground is the unity of identity and difference, the truth of what difference and identity have turned out to be—the reflection-into-self that is equally a reflection-into-other and vice versa. It is essence posited as a totality.

The proposition of the ground runs: "Everything has its sufficient ground;" that is, the true essentiality of something is not the determination of something as self-identical or diverse or merely positive or merely negative, but that it has its being in an other that, as its self-identical, is its essence. Essence is equally not abstract reflection into self, but into an other. The ground is the essence within itself; the essence is essentially a ground; and it is a ground only when it is a ground of something, of an other.

122. At first essence is showing and mediation in itself. But as a totality of mediation, its unity with itself is posited as the self-sublimation of difference and thus of mediation. This is thus the restoration of immediacy or being, but being insofar as it is mediated by the sublimation of mediation: existence.

The ground still has no content determined in and for itself; nor is it a purpose; hence it is not active or productive. An existence only *proceeds from* the ground. The determinate ground is therefore somewhat formal: any determinacy (if it is posited as connected to its own self, as an affirmation) in relation to the immediate existence cohering with it. If it is a ground at all, it is a good ground: for "good" means abstractly just an affirmative; and any determinacy is good that can in any way be enunciated as admittedly affirmative. Thus a ground can be found and adduced for everything: and a good ground (e.g., a motivating ground for action) may have effect or may not, may have a consequence or may not. It becomes a motive and effects something, e.g., by its reception into a will that first makes it active and a cause.

b. Existence

123. Existence is the immediate unity of reflection-into-self and reflection-into-other. Thus existence is the indeterminate mass of existents as reflected-into-themselves, which at the same time are equally a showing into another, are relative, and form a world of reciprocal dependence and of infinite interconnection between grounds and grounded. The grounds are themselves existences; and the existences are grounds in as many directions as they are grounded.

124. The reflection-into-other of the existent is, however, inseparable from reflection-into-self; the ground is their unity, from which existence has issued. The existent thus contains, in its own self, relativity and its manifold interconnection with other existents, and it is reflected into itself as ground. The existent is thus a thing.

The thing-in-itself, famous in Kant's philosophy, shows itself here in its genesis. It is the abstract reflection-into-self, which is retained, to the exclusion of reflection-into-other and of the distinct determinations in general, as their empty groundwork.

c. The Thing

125. The thing is that totality where the development of the determinations of the ground and of existence is posited as one. By one of its moments, reflection-into-other, it has in it the differences in virtue of which it is a determinate and concrete thing. (α) These determinations are diverse from each other; they have their reflection-into-self not in themselves but in the thing. They are properties of the thing, and their connection with the thing is that of *having*.

As a connection *having* replaces being. True *something* has qualities in it too, but this transference of *having* to what *is* is inexact, since the determinacy as quality is directly one with the something and the something ceases to be when it loses its quality. But the thing is reflection-into-self as the identity that is different even from the difference, its determinations. In many languages "have" is used to indicate past time — and with reason: for the past is sublimated being, and the mind is its reflection-into-self; in the mind alone it continues to subsist, but the mind distinguishes from itself this sublimated being in it.

126. (β) Even in the ground, however, the reflection-into-other is directly, in itself, reflection-into-self. Hence the properties are also self-identical, independent and freed of their attachment to the thing. Still, as they are the determinacies of the thing distinguished from each other (as reflected-into-self), they are not themselves things, if things be concrete, but only existences reflected into themselves as abstract determinacies, *matters*.

Nor are matters, e.g., magnetic and electrical matters, called "things." They are qualities proper, one with their being, the determinacy that has reached immediacy, but a reflected being, existence.

127. This matter is the abstract or indeterminate reflection-into-other, or reflection-into-self at the same time as determinate; it is therefore thinghood as a determinate being, the subsistence of the thing. In this way the thing finds in the matters its reflection-into-self (the reverse of §125); it subsists not in its own self but in the matters and is only their superficial interconnection, an external combination of them.

128.   (γ) Matter, as the immediate unity of existence with itself, is also indifferent to determinacy. Hence the diverse matters coalesce into the one matter, existence in the reflective determination of identity. In contrast to this one matter these distinct determinacies and their external connection, which they have to each other in the thing, are the form—the reflective determination of difference, but a difference that exists and is a totality.

This one indeterminate matter is also the same as the thing-in-itself, only the latter is quite abstract within itself, while the former, in itself, is also for an other and first of all for the form.

129.   Thus the thing divides into matter and form. Each of these is the totality of thinghood and independent for itself. But matter, which is supposed to be the positive, indeterminate existence, contains, as existence, reflection-into-other just as much as being-within-self. As a unity of these determinations it is itself the totality of form. But form, as a totality of determinations, *ipso facto* involves reflection-into-self; or, as form that connects itself to itself, it has what is supposed to constitute the determination of matter. Both are in themselves the same. This posited unity of them is in general the connection of matter and form, which are also distinguished.

130.   The thing, as this totality, is a contradiction. By its negative unity it is the form in which matter is determined and reduced to properties (§125). At the same time it consists of matters that in the reflection of the thing into-self are as much independent as they are at the same time negated. Thus the thing is the essential existence in such a way as to be an existence that sublimates itself within itself, appearance.

In physics porosity represents the posited negation and the posited independence of matters. Each of the many matters (coloring matter, smelling matter, and, according to some, even sound matter, then too caloric, electric matter, etc.) is also negated; and in this negation of them, in their pores, are the many other independent matters that, being similarly porous, let the others in turn exist in themselves. Pores are not empirical; they are figments of the understanding, which uses them to represent the moment of negation in independent matters. The further development of the contradictions is concealed by the nebulous confusion in which all matters are independent and all are no less negated in each other. If the faculties or activities of the mind are similarly hypostatized their living unity also turns into a confusion of interaction.

These pores (not the pores of wood or of the skin but those in so-called matters, like coloring matter, caloric, or metals and crystals) cannot be verified by observation. So too matter itself; the form separated from matter; above all the thing and its consistence from matters, or that the thing itself subsists and only *has* properties—all are products of the reflective understanding that, while it observes and professes to retail what it observes, rather creates a metaphysic, bristling with contradictions that remain hidden from it.

B. Appearance

131. Essence must appear. In the essence there is a showing that sublimates itself to immediacy. That immediacy, as reflection-into-self, is matter or subsistence; it is also form, reflection-into-other, a subsistence that sublimates itself. Showing is the determination by which the essence is not being but essence; and this show, when developed, is appearance. The essence is accordingly not beyond or behind appearance. Existence is appearance by the very fact that the essence is what exists.

a. The World of Appearance

132. The apparent exists in such a way that its subsistence is immediately sublimated and is made only one moment in the form itself. The form embraces in it the matter or subsistence as one of its determinations. Thus the apparent has its ground in this matter as its essence, its reflection-into-self in contrast to its immediacy, but only in another determinacy of the form. This ground is no less apparent than the appearance itself, and appearance thus passes into an infinite mediation of subsistence by form, and thus equally by non-subsistence. This infinite mediation is at the same time a unity of connection with self; and existence is developed into a totality and world of appearance, of reflected finitude.

b. Content and Form

133. The self-externality of appearance is a totality and is wholly contained in its connection with self. Thus the connection of appearance with self is fully determined, it has the form in itself, and, since it is in this identity, has it as essential subsistence. So the form is *content* and, in its developed determinacy, the *law* of appearance. Into the form as not reflected into-self falls the negative of appearance, the dependent and changeable: that is the indifferent, external form.

The essential point in the opposition of form and content is that content is not formless but has form in its own self just as much as the form is external to it. There is a duplication of form. At one time it is reflected into itself and identical with the content. At another it is not reflected into self and is the external existence, indifferent to the content. We have here in itself the absolute relation of content and form: change of one into the other, so that content is nothing but the change of form into content and form nothing but the change of content into form. This change is one of the most important determinations. But it is first posited only in the absolute relation.

134. But immediate existence is a determinacy of the subsistence itself as well as of the form: the form is thus external to the determinacy of the content, but equally this externality that the content has by the moment of its subsistence is essential to it. When thus posited appearance is the *relation*, in which one and the same item, the content as the developed form, is *both* the externality and opposition of independent existences *and* their identical connection. In this connection alone the items distinguished are what they are.

c. Relation

135. (α) The immediate relation is that of whole and parts. The content is the whole and consists of parts; these parts are the form and the reverse of the content. The parts are diverse from each other and independent. But they are parts only in their connection with each other or insofar as, taken together, they constitute the whole. But this *together* is the reverse and negation of the part.

136. (β) The one-and-same of this relation, the connection with self present in it, is thus immediately a negative connection with itself, and indeed as the mediation by which one and the same is *both* indifferent to the difference *and* the negative connection with itself that repels itself (as reflection-into-self) to difference and posits itself (as reflection-into-other) as existing. Conversely it leads back this reflection-into-other to a connection with self and to indifference — force and its manifestation.

The relation of whole and parts is the immediate, and therefore thoughtless, relation and change of identity-with-self to diversity. We pass from whole to parts and from parts to whole; in one we forget its opposition to the other, while each for itself, at one time the whole, at another the parts, is taken as an independent existence. Or since the parts are supposed to subsist in the whole and the whole to consist of the parts, each is at different times taken to be the subsistent, while the other is the inessential. In its superficial form the mechanical relation consists in the parts' being independent of each other and of the whole.

This relation may be adopted for the infinite progression in the divisibility of matter, and then it is the thoughtless alternation between its two sides. A thing is at one time taken as a whole; then we go on to determine the parts; this determining is forgotten and what was a part is regarded as a whole; then the determining of the part reemerges, and so on forever. But taken as the negative that it is, this infinity is the negative connection with itself of the relation, force, the self-identical whole, as being-within-itself; and then again as sublimating this being-in-self and manifesting itself; conversely it is the manifestation that vanishes and returns into force.

Despite this infinity, force is also finite: for the content, the one and the same of the force and its manifestation, is this identity at first only in itself; the two sides of the relation are not yet, each for itself, the concrete identity of it, not yet the totality. For each other they are thus diverse and the relation is a finite one. Force consequently requires solicitation from without; it works blindly; and owing to this deficiency of form, the content is also limited and contingent. It is not yet genuinely identical to the form, is not yet as concept and purpose—which is what is determined in and for itself. This difference is most essential but not easy to grasp; it must first be more closely determined in the purpose-concept itself. If it is overlooked it leads to the error of viewing God as force, a confusion that especially mars Herder's *God*.

It is often said that the nature of force itself is unknown and that only its manifestation is known. But first, the whole content-determination of force is the same as that of the manifestation; the explanation of an appearance by a force is thus an empty tautology. Thus what is supposed to remain unknown is really nothing but the empty form of reflection-into-self, by which alone force is distinguished from manifestation—a form that is equally well known. This form does not make the slightest addition to the content and the law, which are supposed to be known from appearance alone. It is also always affirmed that this is not supposed to tell us anything about the force; thus it is hard to see why the form of force has been introduced into the sciences. Second, the nature of force is undoubtedly known: it still lacks the necessity interconnecting its content in itself and there is no necessity in the content insofar as it is for itself limited and thus has its determinacy by means of an other outside it.

137. Force is the whole that is in its own self the negative connection with self; and as such it repels itself from itself and manifests itself. But since this reflection-into-other (the distinction of parts) is equally a reflection-into-self, this manifestation is the mediation by which force that returns into itself is as a force. Its manifestation itself sublimates the diversity of the two sides that is found in this relation, and posits the identity that in itself constitutes the content. Thus the truth of force and manifestation is that relation in which the two sides are distinguished only as outer and inner.

138. (γ) The inner is the ground when it is as the mere form of the one side of the appearance and the relation, the empty form of reflection-into-self. Over against it stands the outer. It is existence, as the form of the other side of the relation, with the empty determination of reflection-into-other. Their identity is fulfilled identity, the content, that unity of reflection-into-self and reflection-into-other posited in the movement of force. Both are the same one totality and this unity makes them the content.

139. First, then, the outer is the same content as the inner. What is internal is also present externally, and vice versa. The appearance shows nothing that is not in the essence and there is nothing in the essence that is not manifested.

140. Second, inner and outer, as determinations of form, are reciprocally opposed, and that thoroughly. The one is the abstraction of self-identity, the other that of manifoldness or reality. But as moments of the one form they are essentially identical: so that whatever is at first posited only in the one abstraction is also immediately *only* in the other. Thus what is only internal is thereby also only external, and what is only external is also only internal.

It is the usual error of reflection to take the essence to be the merely inner. If it is so taken, this view of it too is a wholly external one and that essence is the empty external abstraction.

> *"Into the inner of nature,"* says a poet *(Goethe):*
> *No created spirit enters,*
> *Lucky enough, if it knows the outer shell.*

He should rather have said that it is when the essence of nature is determined as the *inner* that the spirit only knows its outer shell. In being in general or even in mere sense-perception the concept is at first only the inner, and so it is external to being, a subjective and truthless being and thinking. In nature as well as mind so far as the concept, purpose or law are only inner dispositions, pure possibilities, they are only an external inorganic nature, the science of a third party, an alien imposition, etc. As a person is externally — i.e., in his actions (not of course in his mere bodily externality) — so he is internally; and if he is virtuous, moral, etc. only internally — i.e., only in intentions, sentiments — and his outer is not identical thereto, the one is as hollow and empty as the other.

141. The empty abstractions by which the one identical content is still supposed to be in the relation sublimate each other in the immediate transition, the one in the other. The content itself is nothing but their identity (§138); they are the show of essence, posited as show. By the manifestation of force the inner is posited into existence; this positing is mediation by empty abstractions. In its own self it vanishes into the immediacy in which the inner and outer are in and for themselves identical, and the distinction between them is determined only as positedness. This identity is actuality.

C. Actuality

142. Actuality is the unity, which has become immediate, of essence and existence or of inner and outer. The manifestation of the actual is the actual itself; so that in this manifestation it remains just as essential, and is essential only insofar as it is in immediate and external existence.

Earlier we met being and existence as forms of the immediate. Being is in general unreflected immediacy and transition into other. Existence is immediate unity of being and reflection, hence appearance; it comes from the ground and falls to the ground. The actual is this unity's positedness, the relation become self-identical. Hence the actual is exempted from transition and its externality is its energy. In that energy it is reflected into itself; its determinate being is only the manifestation of itself, not of another.

143. Such a concrete as actuality contains those determinations and the distinction between them, and is thus also the development of them, so that they are at the same time in it as show, as merely posited (§141). (1) As identity in general, actuality first appears as *possibility* — the reflection-into-self that, as against the concrete unity of the actual, is posited as the abstract and inessential essentiality. Possibility is what is essential to actuality, but in such a way that it is at the same time *only* possibility.

It was the determination of possibility that Kant was able to regard, along with actuality and necessity, as modalities, "since these determinations do not in the least increase the concept as object but only express its relation to the faculty of knowledge." In fact, possibility is the empty abstraction of reflection-into-self, what was earlier called the inner, only now determined as the external inner that is sublimated and only posited. So of course it is also posited as a mere modality, as an insufficient abstraction or, taken more concretely, as belonging to subjective thought only. By contrast, actuality and necessity are anything but a mere kind and mode for another; in fact the very reverse. They are posited as a concrete completed in itself and as not merely posited. As possibility is, at first, the mere form of self-identity (in contrast to the concrete as actual), its rule is only that something not be self-contradictory. Thus everything is possible, for abstraction can give any content this form of identity. But everything is equally impossible. In every content, since it is a concrete, the determinacy may be seen as an opposition and so as a contradiction. Thus nothing is more empty than to speak of such possibility and impossibility. In philosophy in particular we should never speak of showing that something is possible or that there is still something else possible and that, as it is also expressed, something is thinkable. The historian is no less directly advised not to use this category that has been explained to be for itself untrue. But the subtlety of empty understanding finds its chief pleasure in a hollow devising of possibilities and a good many of them.

144. (2) But the actual, as distinguished from possibility (which is reflection-into-self), is itself only the external concrete, the inessential immediate. Or, immediately, insofar as the actual is primarily (§142) the simple, itself immediate unity of inner and outer, it is an inessential outer, and thus at the same time (§140) it is merely inner, the abstraction of reflection-into-self. Hence it is itself determined as merely possible. With this value of a mere possibility, the actual is a contingency; and conversely, possibility is mere chance itself.

145. Possibility and contingency are the moments of actuality, inner and outer, posited as mere forms that constitute the externality of the actual. They have their reflection-into-self in the intrinsically determined actual, the content, as the essential ground of their determination. The finitude of the contingent and the possible thus lies, more precisely, in the distinction between the form-determination and the content; and thus it depends on the content alone whether something is contingent and possible.

146. More precisely, that externality of actuality involves this: contingency, which is actuality in its immediacy, is self-identical, essentially only as positedness, but positedness is equally sublimated, an externality with determinate being. Consequently it is a presupposition whose immediate determinate being is at the same time a possibility and has the determination of being sublimated, of being the possibility of an other—the condition.

147. (3) When this externality of actuality is so developed, it is a circle of the determinations of possibility and immediate actuality, the mediation of one by the other, in general *real possibility*. As such a circle, it is also the totality, thus the content, the matter[38] determined in and for itself. Equally, by the distinction between the determinations in this unity, it is the concrete totality of the form for itself, the immediate self-translation of inner into outer and of outer into inner. This movement of the form is activity, actuation of the matter,[38] as the real ground that sublimates itself to actuality; and it is the actuation of the contingent actuality, of the conditions, viz their reflection-into-self and their self-sublimation to another actuality, the actuality of the matter. If all conditions are at hand the matter must become actual, and the matter is itself one of the conditions, for at first, being only inner, it is itself only presupposed. Developed actuality, as the alternation of inner and outer falling into one, the alternation of their opposite motions that are unified in a single motion, is *necessity*.

Necessity has been rightly defined as the unity of possibility and actuality. But so expressed this definition is superficial and thus unintelligible. The concept of necessity is very difficult just because it is the concept itself, but with its moments still as actualities, though they are at the same time to be seen as forms only, as internally fragmented and transient. So in the next two sections we must give a more detailed account of the moments constituting necessity.

148. Of the three moments—the condition, the matter,[38] and the activity:

a. The condition is (α) what is presupposed [pre-posited]: as only *posited* it is only relative to the matter; but as *prior*, it is for itself, a contingent, external circumstance that exists without respect to the matter. But while thus contingent, this presupposition is in respect of the matter, which is the totality, a complete circle of conditions. (β) The conditions are passive, are used as material for the matter, and thus enter into its content. They also conform to this content and within themselves already contain its whole determination.

b. The matter is also (α) a presupposition: only as posited is it an inner and a possibility, and, as prior, an independent content for itself. (β) By using up the conditions it acquires its external existence, the realization of its determinations of content, which reciprocally correspond to the conditions, so that equally it presents itself as matter out of these and emerges from them.

c. The activity similarly has (α) an independent existence for itself (a man, a character) and at the same time has its possibility only in the conditions and the matter. (β) It is the movement that translates the conditions into the matter and the latter into the former as the side of existence, or rather that educes the matter from the conditions in which it is in itself present, and gives it existence by sublimating the existence of the conditions.

Insofar as these three moments stand to each other in the shape of independent existences, this process takes the form of an outer necessity. This necessity has a limited content as its matter. For the matter is the whole process in simple determinacy. But since in its form this whole is self-external, it is thereby self-external even in its own self and in its content, and this externality in the matter is a limit of its content.

149. Necessity, then, is the one self-identical but contentful essence, which shows into itself, so that its distinctions take the form of independent actualities. This self-identical is at the same time, as absolute form, the activity of sublimating into mediatedness and of mediating into immediacy. Whatever is necessary is through another, which is divided into the mediating ground (the matter and the activity) and an immediate actuality, a contingency, which is at the same time a condition. The necessary, as through another, is not in and for itself; it is merely posited. But this mediation is just as immediately the sublimation of itself. The ground and contingent condition are translated into immediacy, by which that positedness is sublimated to actuality and the matter has closed with itself. In this return to itself the necessary simply *is*, as unconditioned actuality. The necessary is so, mediated by a circle of circumstances: it is so because the circumstances are so, and at the same time it is so unmediated: it is so because it is.

a. Relation of Substantiality

150. The necessary is within itself absolute relation, i.e., the process developed (in the preceding sections), in which the relation sublimates itself to absolute identity.

In its immediate form it is the relation of substantiality and accidentality. The absolute self-identity of this relation is substance as such, which, as necessity, is the negativity of this form of internality and thus posits itself as actuality, but it is also the negativity of this external. By this negativity, the actual, as immediate, is only an accident, which owing to its mere possibility passes into another actuality; this transition is substantial identity as the activity of form (§§148,149).

151. Substance is thus the totality of accidents, revealing itself in them as their absolute negativity, i.e., as absolute power and at the same time as the wealth of all content. But this content is nothing but that very manifestation, since the determinacy reflected in itself to the content is only a moment of the form and it passes on in the power of substance.

Substantiality is the absolute activity of form and the power of necessity; all content is but a moment, which belongs only to this process — the absolute change of form and content into each other.

152.   By the moment where substance, as absolute power, is the power that connects itself to itself and thus determines itself to accidentality, and the externality thus posited is distinguished from it, it is relation proper just as in the first form of necessity it is substance: the relation of causality.

b. Relation of Causality

153.   The substance is cause, insofar as it reflects into self as against its passage into accidentality and so is the original matter, but equally sublimates this reflection-into-self or its mere possibility, posits itself as the negative of itself and thus produces an effect, an actuality that is thus only a posited actuality, but by the process that effects it at the same time necessary.

As the original matter, the cause has the determination of absolute independence and a subsistence that endures against the effect; but in the necessity whose identity is constituted by that originality itself it has only passed into the effect. So far as we can again speak of a determinate content, there is no content in the effect that is not in the cause. That identity is the absolute content itself: but it is equally also the form-determination; the originality of the cause is sublimated in the effect, in which the cause makes itself a positedness. But the cause has not thereby vanished and left the effect alone as the actual. For this positedness is equally immediately sublimated and is rather the reflection of the cause into itself, its originality; it is in the effect that the cause is first actual and a cause. Thus the cause is, in and for itself, *causa sui*. Jacobi stuck to the one-sided conception of mediation (*Letters on Spinoza*. 2nd. ed., p. 416) and regarded the *causa sui* (the *effectus sui* is the same), this absolute truth of the cause, merely as a formalism. He also stated that God must be determined not as ground but essentially as cause. If Jacobi had reflected more thoroughly on the nature of cause he would have seen that this does not achieve what he intended. This identity with regard to content is present even in the finite cause and its conception: rain (the cause) and wetness (the effect) are one and the same existing water. With regard to form the cause (rain) falls away in the effect (wet); but therewith the determination of effect also falls away, for without the cause it is nothing and only the indifferent wet remains. In the ordinary sense of the causal relation the cause is finite insofar as its content is finite (as in the finite substance) and insofar as cause and effect are represented as two diverse, independent existences — which they are, however, only if we abstract from the causal relation. In finitude we never get beyond the *distinction* of form-determinations in their connection; hence the cause in turn is also determined as posited or as an effect. This again has another cause, and thus arises a progress to infinity from effects to causes. There is a descending progress too: The effect by its identity with the cause is itself determined as a cause and at the same time as *another* cause, which again has other effects, and so on to infinity.

154. The effect is diverse from the cause; the effect as such is positedness. But the positedness is likewise reflection-into-self and immediacy, and the action of the cause, its positing, is at the same time *presupposing*, insofar as the effect is kept diverse from the cause. Hence there is another substance present on which the effect takes place. As immediate this substance is not negativity connecting self to self and *active*, but *passive*. But as substance it is also active, sublimates the presupposed immediacy and the effect posited in it, and *reacts*, i.e., it sublimates the activity of the first substance. But the latter too is the sublimation of its immediacy or of the effect posited in it, and thus sublimates the activity of the other substance and reacts. Thus causality has passed into the new relation of reciprocity.

In reciprocity, though causality is not yet posited in its true determination, the rectilinear movement from causes to effects and from effects to causes is curved round and back into itself, and thus the progress to infinity of causes and effects is, as a progress, sublimated in a genuine way. This bending round of the infinite progression into a self-contained relation is here as always the simple reflection that in that thoughtless repetition there is only one and the same, viz one cause and another, and their connection with each other. The development of this connection, the reciprocal action, is itself, however, the alternation of distinguishing, not the causes, but the moments, in each of which for itself, again by the identity that the cause is a cause in the effect and vice versa, by this inseparability, the other moment is also posited.

c. Reciprocity

155. The determinations kept distinct in reciprocity are (α) in themselves the same: the one side is a cause, original, active, passive, etc. just as the other is. Similarly, the presupposing of another side and the action on it, the immediate originality and the positedness by the alternation, are one and the same. The cause assumed to be first is owing to its immediacy passive, positedness and an effect. The distinction of the causes spoken of as two is thus empty and, in itself, there is only one cause, sublimating itself as substance in its effect and in this action as a cause first making itself independent.

156. But this unity is also (β) for itself, since this whole interchange is the cause's own positing, and this positing is its being. The nullity of the distinctions is not only in itself or a reflection of ours (§155). Reciprocity itself is this: each of the posited determinations is also sublimated and inverted into its opposite, and thus the nullity of the moments is posited. An effect is posited in the originality, i.e., the originality is sublimated; the action of a cause becomes reaction, etc.

157. (γ) This pure interchange with its own self is thus necessity disclosed or posited. The bond of necessity as such is identity, as still inner and hidden, since it is the identity of what pass for actualities, though their independence is supposed to be just necessity. The circulation of substance through causality and reciprocity thus only posits that independence is the infinite negative connection with self: it is negative in general, for in it the distinguishing and mediating become an originality of actualities independent against each other; it is infinite connection with self, since their independence lies only in their identity.

158. This truth of necessity is thus freedom, and the truth of substance is the concept. The concept is that independence which is a repulsion of itself from itself into distinct, independent items and which in this repulsion is self-identical; it is a movement of interchange only with itself and it remains self-contained.

159. Thus the concept is the truth of being and essence, inasmuch as the showing of the reflection in its own self is at the same time an independent immediacy, and this being of a diverse actuality is immediately only a showing in itself.

The concept has proved to be the truth of being and essence, which revert to it as their ground. Conversely it has developed out of being as its ground. The former aspect of the advance may be regarded as a deepening of being in itself, the inner of which has thus been disclosed by this advance; the latter aspect as emergence of the more from the less perfect. When such development is viewed in the latter aspect only, this has been made an objection to philosophy. The more determinate content that these superficial thoughts of *more imperfect* and *more perfect* have here is the distinction of being as immediate unity with itself from the concept as free mediation with itself. Since being has shown that it is a moment of the concept, the concept has thus proved to be the truth of being. As this its reflection-into-self and as sublimation of mediation, the concept is the presupposing of the immediate — a presupposing that is identical to the return-to-self, and this identity constitutes freedom and the concept. Thus if the moment is called the imperfect then the concept, the perfect, is of course a development from the imperfect, since it is essentially this sublimation of its presupposition. At the same time it is the concept alone that, when it posits itself, makes the presupposition — as has emerged in causality in general and especially in reciprocity.

Thus in connection with being and essence, the concept is defined as the essence that has reverted to the simple immediacy of being, the showing of essence thereby having actuality and its actuality being at the same time a free showing in itself. In this way the concept has being as its simple connection with itself or as the immediacy of its unity in its own self. Being is so poor a determination that it is the least that can be exhibited in the concept.

The passage from necessity to freedom or from actuality into the concept is the hardest, since the independent actuality is supposed to be thought as having its substantiality only in the passage and in the identity with the *other* independent actuality. The concept too is the hardest, for it is this very identity. But the actual substance as such, the cause, which in its being-for-self will let nothing penetrate into itself, is *ipso facto* subject to necessity and the fate of passing into positedness, and it is rather this subjection that is the hardest. The *thinking* of necessity by contrast is rather the dissolution of that hardness; for it is to join together in the other with one's own self — the liberation that is not the flight of abstraction but this: the actual has itself not as other, but its own being and positing, in the other actuality with which it is bound up by the power of necessity. As existing for itself this liberation is called *I*; as developed to its totality it is *free mind*; as sensation it is *love*; as enjoyment it is *bliss*. The great intuition of substance in Spinoza is only *in itself* liberation from finite being-for-self; but the concept is *for itself* the power of necessity and *actual* freedom.

IX.   Science of Logic: From Objectivity to Absolute Idea*

OBJECTIVITY

In the First Book of the *Objective Logic* abstract *being* was exhibited as passing over into determinate being, but no less retiring into *essence*. In the Second Book we see how essence determines itself as *ground*, enters thereby into *existence*[22] and realizes itself as *substance*, but again retires into the *concept*. Of the concept, now, we have shown, to begin with, that it determines itself to *objectivity*. It is self-evident that this latter transition is identical in character with what has elsewhere appeared in *Metaphysics* as the *inference* from the *concept*, that is to say, from the *concept of God*, to *His existence*,[12] or as the so-called *ontological proof* of the *existence of God*. — It is no less familiar that Descartes' sublimest thought, that God is that *whose concept contains within itself its being*, was later degraded into the faulty form of the formal syllogism, that is, into the form of the proof just mentioned, and finally fell a victim to the Critique of Reason, and to the thought that *existence cannot be extracted from the concept*. Some points connected with this proof have been already elucidated. In the First Part, where *being* has vanished in its immediate opposite, *not-being*, and *becoming* has shown itself as the truth of the two, attention was drawn to what is a common confusion. One takes a particular determinate being and fixes, not on its *being*, but on its *particular content*, then, comparing *this particular content*, e.g. a hundred dollars, with another *particular content*, e.g. the context of my perception, or my finances, one finds that it makes a difference whether the former content is attached to the latter or not; and then one imagines that this is a case of the difference between being and not being, or even of the difference between being and concept. Further in the same Part, and in Part II, we elucidated a term that occurs in the ontological proof, *the sum-total of all realities*. — But the essential matter of that proof, *the connexion of concept and existence*, is the concern of our examination, just closed, of the *concept* and of the whole course through which the concept determines itself to *objectivity*. The concept, in virtue of being absolutely self-identical negativity, is the

*Translated from the *Wissenschaft der Logik* (1812–1816), by H. S. Macran, with revisions by M. J. Inwood.

self-determinant; it has been observed that, even in resolving itself in singularity into the *judgement*—it is positing itself as *real*, as *being*, this as yet abstract reality finds its completion in *objectivity*.

Now it might seem as though the transition of concept into objectivity was not the same thing as the transition from the concept of God to His existence. It should be observed, however, on the one hand, that the determinate *content*, God, makes no difference in the logical process, and the ontological proof is merely an application of this logical process to that particular content. On the other hand, it is essential to bear in mind the remark above, that the subject only obtains determinateness and content in its predicate, and that, until it has a predicate, whatever it may be for feeling, intuition, and representation, for rational cognition it is nothing but a *name*: it is in the predicate that determinateness first appears, and with it begins *realization* in general.—The predicates, however, must be taken as themselves still included within the concept, consequently as something subjective, that does not carry one as far as determinate being; to that extent we must admit, on the one hand, that the *realization* of the concept in the judgement is not yet complete. On the other hand, however, the mere determination of an object by predicates, without that determination being at the same time the realization and objectifying of the concept, remains something subjective in the sense that it is not even the genuine cognition and *determination of the concept* of the object—subjective in the sense of abstract reflexion, and unconceptualized representation.[53] God as the living God, and still more as the absolute Spirit, is only cognized in His *operation*. Mankind was early admonished to cognize Him in His *works*, for thence alone can proceed the *determinations*, which are called His *properties*, just as also His *being* is contained in them. Thus the conceptual cognition of His *working*, i.e. of Himself, grasps the *concept* of God in His *being*, and His being in His concept. *Being* taken by itself, or, for that matter, determinate being, is such a poor and limited determination that surely the difficulty of finding it in the concept can only have arisen from the fact that it has not been considered what *being* or determinate being itself really is.—*Being* is the wholly *abstract immediate relation to self*, and is therefore nothing else than an abstract moment of the concept, namely abstract universality. This universality at the same time supplies the feature that one demands in being, that of standing *outside* the concept; for, though it is a moment of the concept, it is no less the concept's difference or abstract judgement, where the concept opposes itself to itself. The concept, even in its formal character, immediately contains *being* in a *truer* and *richer* form when it appears as self-referred negativity or *singularity*.

But the difficulty of finding *being* in the concept in general, and equally in the concept of God, certainly becomes insuperable when *being* is taken to be something that is to occur *in the context of outer experience*, or *in the form of sensuous perception*, like *the hundred dollars in my finances*, a thing grasped with the hand and not with the mind, a thing visible essentially to the outer, not to the inner, eye; when the names of being, reality, and truth are given to what belongs to things as sensuous, temporal and perishable. — When a philosophy in its view of being fails to rise above sense, it follows that in its view of the concept also it never quits mere abstract thought; this latter stands opposed to being.

The mental habit that takes the concept merely for a one-sided thing, such as abstract thought is, will boggle at accepting even the above proposal, namely, to regard the transition from the *concept of God* to His *being* as an *application* of the above presented logical course of the objectification of the concept. Yet, if it is granted, as it commonly is, that the logical element, in virtue of being the formal element, constitutes the form for the cognition of every determinate content, the above relationship at least would have to be admitted, unless this very opposition between concept and objectivity, with its untrue concept and its equally untrue reality, is accepted outright as ultimate and final. — But in the exposition *of the pure concept*, it has been further indicated that this is the absolute divine concept itself, so that in truth this would not be a case of the relationship of *application*, and the logical process in question would be the immediate presentation of the self-determination of God to being. But on this point it is to be remarked that, where the concept is to be presented as the concept of God, it must be comprehended in the form in which it appears when taken up into the *idea*. The pure concept traverses the finite forms of the judgement and syllogism, because it is not yet posited as in its own absolute nature one with objectivity, but is only in process of becoming it. Similarly, this objectivity is not yet the divine existence, not yet the reality manifesting itself in the idea. Yet objectivity is just so much richer and higher than the *being* or determinate being of the ontological proof as the pure concept is richer and higher than the old metaphysical void of the *sum total* of all *reality*. — I reserve, however, for another occasion the closer examination of the manifold misunderstanding that has been brought by logical formalism into the ontological and other so-called proofs of God's existence, as also the closer examination of the Kantian criticism of them. I hope then, by re-establishing their true significance, to restore the fundamental thoughts of these proofs to their proper status and dignity.

We have already encountered, as before remarked, several forms of immediacy; but in different phases of determination. In the sphere of being immediacy is being itself and determinate being; in the sphere of essence it is existence, and then actuality and substantiality; in the sphere of the concept, besides immediacy as abstract universality, we have now objectivity. When the exactitude of philosophical and conceptual distinctions is not at stake, these expressions may doubtless be used as synonymous; but the categories just mentioned have proceeded from the necessity of the concept. — *Being* is in general the *first* immediacy, and determinate being is the same along with the first determinateness. *Existence*, with the *thing*, is the immediacy that proceeds from the *ground* — from the self-merging[8] mediation of the simple reflexion of essence. Again, *actuality* and *substantiality* is the immediacy that has proceeded from the merged[8] opposition between the still unessential existence as appearance and its essentiality. *Objectivity*, finally, is the immediacy to which the concept determines itself by the merging of its abstraction and mediation. — Philosophy is justified in selecting from the language of common life, which is made for the world of representations, such expressions as *seem to approximate* to the determinations of the concept. It cannot be a question of *demonstrating* for a word selected from the speech of common life that even in common life it is connected with the same concept for which philosophy employs it: for common life possesses no concepts, but only representations,[53] and philosophy itself consists in cognizing the concept of what, but for philosophy, is a mere representation. It must suffice, therefore, if the representative faculty in the use of its expressions that are employed for philosophical terms has some dim vision of their distinctive signification; just as in the case of the expressions before us it may be the case that one recognizes in them shades of representation more nearly related to the corresponding concepts. — One will, perhaps, find it harder to grant that something can *be* without *existing*; but at least one will not use as interchangeable terms the expression *being* for the copula of the judgement and the expression *existence*. One will not say 'this article *exists* dear, suitable, &c.', — 'gold *exists* a metal, or metallic', instead of 'this article *is* dear, suitable, &c.', 'gold *is* a metal'.* And surely, it is usual to distinguish between *being* and *appearance, phenomenon* and *actuality*, as well as to distinguish mere *being* from *actuality*, and still more all these expressions from *objectivity*. — Even should they, however, be employed synonymously, philosophy will in any case be free to utilize such empty superfluity of language to denote its distinctions.

In our treatment of the apodeictic judgement, in which, as the consummation of the judgement, the subject loses its determinate character as against the predicate, mention was made of the consequent ambiguity of the term *subjectivity*, which is used sometimes for the concept and sometimes for the externality and contingency that is opposed to the concept. A similar ambiguity attaches to the term objectivity, which signifies sometimes what stands *opposed* to the self-dependent *concept*, but at other times *absolute* being.[7] The object in the former sense is opposed to the I = I which is enunciated as the absolute truth in subjective idealism, and in that

*In a French report, where the officer in command is stating that he was waiting for the wind, which generally rose near the island towards morning, in order to steer to shore, the expression occurs — 'le vent ayant été longtemps sans exister'; here the distinction has arisen merely from the common idiom, e.g. 'il a été longtemps sans m'écrire'.

case it is the manifold world in its immediate determinate being, with which the ego or the concept only enters into an eternal struggle, in order by the negation of this *intrinsically nonentical* antithesis to give the primary consciousness of itself *the actual truth* of its identity with self. — In a vaguer sense it denotes, similarly, an object in general for any interest or activity of the subject.

In the opposite sense, however, objectivity signifies *absolute existence* that knows neither limitation nor opposition. Rational principles, perfect works of art, and so forth, are called *objective* in so far as they are free and above all contingency. Although rational principles, theoretical or moral, only belong to the subjective side or to consciousness, yet the absolute element[7] in consciousness is called objective. The cognition of truth is placed in cognizing the object as object, free from the admixture of subjective reflexion, and right action in the following of objective laws that have no subjective origin and exclude all self-will and all treatment that might reverse their necessity.

At the present standpoint of our exposition, objectivity signifies, to begin with, the *absolute being of the concept*, or the concept that has superseded the *mediation* posited in its self-determination and merged it in *immediate* relation to self. Consequently this immediacy is itself immediately and wholly pervaded by the concept, just as the concept's totality is immediately identical with its being. But, since, once more, the concept has also to restore the free being-for-self of its subjectivity, there arises a relationship between the latter as *end*[61] and objectivity. In this relationship the immediacy of objectivity becomes the negative element in contrast to the end, an element to be determined by the activity of the end, and consequently takes on the other significance of being the absolute nullity, as opposed to the concept.

First, then, objectivity appears in its immediacy, where its moments, in virtue of the totality of all the moments, subsist in self-dependent indifference as *objects outside one another*, and in their relationship possess the *subjective unity* of the concept only as *internal* or as *external*. This is *mechanism*.

But *secondly*, through this unity exhibiting itself as the *immanent* law of the objects themselves, their relationship becomes their *peculiar* specific difference founded on their law; it becomes a relation in which their determinate self-dependence is merged. This is *chemism*.

Thirdly, this essential unity of the objects is thereby posited as distinct from their self-dependence; it is the subjective concept, but posited as in its own absolute nature related to objectivity, as *end*. This is *teleology*.

As the end is the concept that is posited as relating in itself to objectivity and merging by its own act its defect of being subjective, the finality that is at first *external* passes through the realization of the end into *internal* finality and the *idea*. . . .

Teleology[46]

Where we discern *finality*,[61] we assume an intellect as its author; thus for the end we demand the concept's own free existence. *Teleology* is especially opposed to mechanism, in which the determinateness posited in the object, being an external determinateness, is essentially one in which no *self-determination* manifests itself. The opposition between *causae efficientes* and *causae finales*, between merely *efficient* and *final* causes, relates to this distinction; which also, taken in more concrete form, is at the bottom of the question whether the absolute essence of the world is to be conceived as blind natural mechanism or as an understanding determining itself in accordance with ends. The antinomy between *fatalism* and *determinism* on the one hand and *freedom* on the other is likewise concerned with the opposition between mechanism and teleology; for the free is the concept in its existence.

Earlier metaphysics has adopted the same procedure with these concepts as with its other ones; it has, for one thing, presupposed a certain world-representation, and takes pains to show that one of the two concepts fitted it while the opposite one was faulty because failing to *explain* it; and again, while thus engaged, it has not examined the concept of the mechanical cause and of the end, to see which possesses truth *by its own absolute nature*.[7] When this question is settled on its own merits, the objective world may present us with mechanical and final causes, but their existence is not the standard of *truth*, but on the contrary truth is the criterion that decides which of these existences is the true one. As the subjective understanding exhibits errors of its own, so the objective world also exhibits aspects and stages of truth that taken in themselves are as yet one-sided and incomplete, and are merely phenomenal relationships. If mechanism and finality stand in opposition to one another, they cannot for that very reason be taken as *equally valid* concepts, each of them correct on its own account and possessing as much validity as the other, the only question being where each may be applied. This equal validity of the two concepts relies merely on the fact that they *are*, that is to say, that we *have* them both. But since they are opposed, the necessary first question is, which of the two is the true one; and the higher real question is *whether their truth does not lie in a third thing, or whether one of them is the truth of the other.* — But we have found the *final relation* to be the truth of *mechanism.* — What we have presented as *chemism* is included with *mechanism* to the extent that the end is the concept in free existence, and therefore is opposed in general to the bondage of the concept and its submersion in externality; both of them therefore, mechanism and chemism, are included under natural necessity; for in mechanism the concept has no real existence in the object, since the object as mechanical does not contain self-determination, while in chemism the concept either has a tense one-sided existence, or, in emerging as the unity that expands the neutral object into the extremes, is external to itself as merging this separation.

The more the teleological principle was associated with the concept of an *extramundane* intellect and so countenanced by piety, the further it seemed to depart from the true investigation of nature, which insists on cognizing nature's properties, not as extraneous, but as *immanent determinatenesses*, and accepts such cognition alone as a comprehension. As the end is the concept itself in its existence, it may seem strange that the cognition of objects from their concept appears rather as an unjustified excursion into a *heterogeneous* element, while mechanism, for which the determinateness of an object is a determinateness posited in it externally and by another object, passes for a *more immanent* view of things than teleology. Undoubtedly mechanism, at least the ordinary unfree mechanism, as well as chemism, must be regarded as an immanent principle to this extent that the *external* determinant is itself again *just such another object*, externally determined, and indifferent to such determination, — or in chemism the other object is one likewise chemically determined — and that in general an essential moment of the totality always lies in something outside. These principles, therefore, remain within the same natural form of finitude; yet, though they do not ask to transcend the finite, and in their explanation of phenomena only lead to finite causes which themselves demand a further progress, at the same time they enlarge themselves to a formal totality, not only in the concept of force, cause, and such reflective terms which purport to denote an *originality*, but also through the abstract *universality* of a *sum total of forces*, a *whole* of reciprocal causes. Mechanism shows itself to be a striving after totality in the very fact that it seeks to grasp nature *by itself* as a *whole* that needs nothing else for *its* concept — a totality that is not found in the end and the extramundane intellect connected with it.

Finality, then, shows itself in the first instance as a *higher being* in general; as an intellect that *externally* determines the multiplicity of objects *by an absolute unity*, so that the indifferent determinatenesses of the objects become *essential by means of this relation*. In mechanism they become so by the *mere form of necessity*, their *content* being indifferent; for from this standpoint they remain externalities, and it is only the understanding as such that finds satisfaction in cognizing its own connexion, abstract identity. In teleology, on the contrary, the content becomes important; for teleology presupposes a concept, something *absolutely determined* and therewith self-determining, and so has made a distinction between the *relation* of the opposed members and their reciprocal determination on the one hand, which is the *form*, and on the other hand *introflected unity*, *something determined absolutely*, which is therefore *a content*. When, however, this content is otherwise a *finite* and insignificant one, it contradicts its own purport, for the end is from the nature of its form a totality *infinite within itself* — especially when the activity that works in accordance with ends is regarded as *absolute* will and intellect. The reason that teleology has brought upon itself so much the reproach of fatuity, is that the ends that it presented are more important or more insignificant as the case may be; and it could not be but that this final relation of objects should often seem trifling, since it appears so external and therefore contingent. Mechanism, on the contrary, leaves to the determinatenesses of objects in respect of import their status of contingencies to which the object is indifferent, and which do not purport to have any higher value in themselves or for the subjective understanding. This principle, therefore, in its connexion of external necessity gives the consciousness of infinite freedom as compared with teleology, which sets up for something absolute the most paltry and even contemptible of its contents, in which more universal thought can only find itself infinitely straitened, and even disgusted.

The formal disadvantage under which this teleology in the first instance labours is that it gets no further than *external finality*. The concept being thus posited as a formality, the content for such teleology is also a thing given externally to the concept in the multiplicity of the objective world — in those very determinatenesses which also constitute the content of mechanism, though appearing there as something external and contingent. On account of this community of content it is the *form of finality* that by itself alone constitutes the essential element of the teleological. In this respect, without as yet looking to the difference of external and internal finality, the final relation has in general proved itself by its own absolute nature to be the *truth of mechanism*. Teleology possesses in general the higher principle, the concept in its existence, which is by its own very nature the infinite and absolute; a principle of freedom, a principle that in the perfect assurance of its self-determination is absolutely emancipated from the *external determination* of mechanism.

One of *Kant's* great services to philosophy consists in the distinction which he has drawn between relative or *external* finality and *internal* finality; in the latter he has opened up the concept of *life*, the *idea*, and in so doing has effected *positively* for philosophy what the *Critique of Reason* did but imperfectly, crookedly, and *negatively*; namely, to raise it above the reflective categories and relative world of metaphysics. — It has been remarked that the opposition of teleology and mechanism is in the first instance the more general opposition of *freedom* and *necessity*. Kant has exhibited the opposition in this form among the *antinomies* of reason, namely, as the *third conflict of the transcendental ideas*. — His exposition, which was referred to at an earlier stage, I cite quite briefly, as the essential gist of it is so simple as to require no diffuse statement, and the way and manner of the Kantian antinomies has been explained with more detail elsewhere.

The *thesis* of the antinomy runs: 'Causality according to natural laws is not the sole causality, from which the phenomena of the world can be all derived without exception. For their explanation a causality through freedom must be assumed as well.'

The *antithesis* is: 'There is no freedom, but everything in the world happens solely according to natural laws.'

As in the case of the other antinomies, the proof sets to work in the apagogic manner, and the opposite of each thesis is assumed; secondly and conversely, in order to show the contradictory nature of this assumption, its opposite, which is accordingly the proposition to be proved, is assumed and presupposed as valid. The whole detour of the argument might therefore have been spared; the proof consists of nothing but the assertorical affirmation of the two opposed propositions.

Thus to prove the *thesis* we have first to assume that there is *no other causality* than that by *natural laws*, i.e., by the necessity of mechanism in general, including chemism. This proposition we find to be self-contradictory, because we take natural law to consist just in this that nothing takes place *without a cause sufficiently determined a priori*, which cause consequently contains an absolute spontaneity within itself; in other words, the assumption opposed to the thesis is a contradiction because it contradicts the thesis.

To prove the *antithesis* we *assume* that there exists a *freedom*, as a particular species of causality, that absolutely initiates a state of things, and with it also a series of the effects of that state. But, now, a beginning such as this *presupposes* a state that has *no causal connexion* whatever with its predecessor, and therefore contradicts *the law of causality*, which alone makes unity of experience, and experience in general, possible; in other words, the assumption of freedom, which is opposed to the antithesis, cannot be made because it contradicts the antithesis.

What is essentially the same antinomy recurs in the *Critique* of the *teleological judgement* as the opposition between the position that *every production of material things takes place under merely mechanical laws*, and the position that *certain cases of such production are not possible under those laws*. Kant's solution of this antinomy is the same as the general solution of the others; namely, that reason can prove neither the one proposition nor the other, because we *cannot have a priori any determining principle* of the possibility of things according to merely empirical natural laws; that further, therefore, both must be regarded not *as objective propositions* but as *subjective maxims*; that *on the one hand I* am in every case to *reflect* on all natural events according to the principle of mere natural mechanism, but that this does not prevent me, *when occasion calls for it*, from *investigating* certain natural forms in accordance with *another maxim*, namely, on the principle of final causes; as though, now, these *two maxims*, which moreover are supposed to be necessary only for the *human reason*, did not stand in the same opposition as the *propositions*. As was remarked before, this whole standpoint ignores the one and only question to which the philosophic interest demands an answer, namely, which of the two principles is in its own essential nature true; from this point of view it makes no difference whether the principles are to be regarded as *objective*, that is, in this case, externally existing determinations of nature, or as mere *maxims* of a *subjective* cognition. Rather, that is a subjective, i.e. contingent, cognition which *on the occasion's demand* applies this or that maxim as it finds them suitable for given objects, without any further question as to the *truth* of these determinations, be they determinations of objects or of cognition.

Unsatisfactory as is, therefore, Kant's discussion of the teleological principle in respect of its essential point of view, nevertheless the position that Kant gives to the principle is worthy of note. In ascribing it to a *reflecting judgement*, he makes it a connecting *link* between *the universal of reason* and *the singular of intuition*; further, he distinguishes that *reflecting* judgement from the *determining* judgement, the latter merely *subsuming* the particular under the universal. A universal of this kind, which merely *subsumes*, is an *abstraction* that only becomes *concrete* in something *else*, in the particular. The end, on the contrary, is the *concrete universal*, which possesses within itself the moment of particularity and externality, and therefore is active and the impulse to self-repulsion. The concept as end is, certainly, an *objective judgement* with one term as subject, namely the concrete concept as self-determined, while the other term is not merely a predicate, but external objectivity. But the final relation is not for that reason a *reflecting* judgement that only regards external objects under a certain unity given *as it were* by an intellect *for the behoof of our cognitive faculty*; on the contrary, it is the absolute truth, that judges *objectively* and determines external objectivity unconditionally. Thus the final relation is more than *judgement*; it is the *syllogism* of the self-dependent free concept that closes into unity with itself through objectivity.

The end we have found to be the *third* to mechanism and chemism; it is their truth. Since it still stands within the sphere of objectivity, or the immediacy of the total concept, it is still affected by externality as such, and is confronted by an external world to which it relates. It follows from this aspect that mechanical causality, with which in general chemism is also to be included, still appears in the case of this *external finality*, but as *subordinate* to it and in its own essential nature merged. As regards the more precise relation, the mechanical object as immediate totality is indifferent to its determination, and on the other hand equally indifferent to being a determinant. This external determination has now developed into self-determination, and accordingly the concept, which in the object was merely *internal*, or what is the same thing, merely *external* concept, is now *posited*; the *end* is in the first instance this concept itself that is external to the mechanical. Similarly, the end is for chemism the self-determinant which reduces the external determination by which it is conditioned to the unity of the concept. — This gives us the nature of the subordination of the two previous forms of the objective process; the other, which in them lies in the infinite progress, is the concept posited in the first instance as external to them, which is the end; the concept is not only their substance, but also externality is the essential moment that constitutes their determinateness. Thus mechanical or chemical technique, through its character of being outwardly determined, offers itself spontaneously to the final relation, which we have now to examine more closely. . . .

THE IDEA[32]

   The idea is the *adequate concept*, the objective *truth*, or the *truth as such*. When anything whatever possesses truth, it possesses it through its idea; or, we may say, *a thing possesses truth only in so far as it is idea.* —The term *idea* is often employed in another way in philosophy, as in common life, for *concept*, nay even for a mere *representation*;[53] 'I have no *idea* yet of this law-suit, building, neighbourhood' means nothing more than the *representation*. Kant has re-established the claim of reason's concept to the expression *idea*. — Now, according to Kant, the concept of reason is the concept of the *unconditioned*, but a concept *transcendent* in regard to phenomena, that is, one of which *no adequate use* can be made *in experience*. The concepts of reason, on this view, serve to the comprehension[9] of perceptions, the concepts of the understanding to the *understanding* of them. —But, as a matter of fact, if the latter are actually *concepts*, then *they are concepts*—they enable one to comprehend, and an *understanding* of perceptions through concepts of the understanding will be a comprehension. But if understanding is only a determining of perceptions by such categories, for example, as whole and parts, force, cause, and the like, it signifies only a determining by reflection. In the same way one may mean by *understanding* only the definite *representation* of a completely determined sensuous content; thus, when a traveller is shown the way, that he must turn to the left at the end of the wood, and he replies 'I *understand*', *understanding* means no more than the grasping of a thing in representation and memory. —*Concept of reason*, too, is a rather awkward expression; for the concept in general is something rational, and in so far as reason is distinguished from the understanding and the concept as such, it is the totality of concept and objectivity. —In this sense the idea is the *rational*; it is the unconditioned, because that alone has conditions which relates essentially to an objectivity that is not determined by it itself, but still confronts it in the form of indifference and externality. In this way the external end still had conditions.

   Reserving then the expression *idea* for the objective or real concept, and distinguishing it from the concept itself and still more from the mere representation, we must further and still more strongly reject that estimate according to which the idea is denied actuality, and it is said of true thoughts that *they are only ideas*. If *thoughts* are merely something *subjective* and contingent, they certainly possess no further worth; yet in this respect they are not inferior to temporal and contingent *actualities*, for these likewise have no further status than that of contingencies and phenomena. But if, on the contrary, the idea is taken to lack the status of truth because it is *transcendent* in respect to phenomena, because no conformable object can be given it in the world of sense, it is a strange misunderstanding that thus denies objective validity to the idea because it lacks the element that constitutes the phenomenal side or *untrue being* of the objective world. In regard to practical ideals Kant recognizes that 'nothing can be found more pernicious and more unworthy of a philosopher than the *vulgar* appeal to an *experience* presumably conflicting with the idea. This very experience would not exist at all, if, for example, political institutions had been established at the proper time in conformity with ideas, and if *crude concepts*, crude for the very reason *that they were drawn from experience*, had not supplanted the ideas, and made all good intention of no effect.' Kant sees the idea as a necessity, as the aim, which as the *archetype* it must be our endeavour to set up for a maximum, and to which we must endeavour to bring ever more closely the condition of the actual world.

Having, however, arrived at the result that the idea is the unity of concept and objectivity, the truth, we must not regard it merely as an *aim* to which we have to approximate, while it remains itself always a kind of *world beyond*; rather must we recognize that everything actual only *is* in so far as it contains and expresses the idea. It is not merely that the object, the objective and subjective world, *ought to be congruous* with the idea, but those worlds are themselves the congruence of concept and reality; the reality that does not correspond to the concept is mere *phenomenon*, the subjective, contingent, arbitrary element that is not the truth. When it is said that no object is to be found in experience completely congruous with the *idea*, one is opposing the idea as a subjective standard to the actual. But what an actual thing is really to *be*, if its concept is not in it, and its objectivity is not in any way conformable to the concept, it is impossible to say; for it would be nothing. No doubt, the mechanical and chemical object, as also the unspiritual subject, and the spirit conscious only of the finite and not of its essence, do not, in their various natures, possess their concept existent *in its own free form*. But they can only be true things at all in so far as they are the union of their concept and reality, of their soul and their body. Wholes such as the state and the church, when the unity of their concept and their reality is dissolved, cease to exist; the man, the living being, is dead when soul and body part in him; dead nature, the mechanical and chemical world — that is, taking the dead world to mean the inorganic world, otherwise it would have no positive significance whatever — dead nature, then, if it is divided into its concept and its reality, is nothing but the subjective abstraction of a thought form and a formless matter. The spirit that was not idea, not the unity of the concept with itself — the concept that had the concept itself for its reality—would be dead spiritless spirit, a material object.

The idea being the unity of concept and reality, *being* has attained the significance of *truth*; now, therefore, nothing *is* but what is idea. Finite things are finite because they do not possess the reality of their concept completely in themselves, but require other things for it—or, conversely, because they are presupposed as objects, and consequently possess the concept as an external determination. The highest point they attain on the side of this finitude is external finality. That actual things are not congruous with the idea is the side of their *finitude* and *untruth*; from this side they are *objects*, each in its different sphere, and determined in the relationships of objectivity mechanically, chemically, or by an external end. That the idea has not completely moulded its reality, and has imperfectly subdued it to the concept, is made possible by the fact that the idea itself possesses a *limited content*, that it is no less essentially the difference, that it is essentially the unity, of concept and reality; for the object is only their immediate, or merely *intrinsic*[5] unity. But if an object, for example, the state, were *not at all* conformable to its idea, that is, if it were on the contrary not the idea of the state at all, if its reality, which is the self-conscious individuals, wholly failed to correspond to the concept, then its soul and its body would have parted; the former would escape into the abstract regions of thought, the latter would have broken up into the single individualities. But, because the concept of the state so essentially constitutes the nature of these individualities, it appears in them as a motive so powerful that they are constrained to translate it into reality, be it only in the form of external finality, or to put up with it as it is; otherwise they would of necessity perish. The worst state, whose reality least corresponds to the concept, so long as it still exists, is still idea; the individuals still obey a dominating concept.

But the idea not merely signifies in general *veritable being*, the unity of *concept* and *reality*, but more definitely the unity of *subjective concept* and *objectivity*. That is, the concept as such is itself already the identity of itself and *reality*: for the indefinite expression *reality* means in general nothing but *determinate being*, and this the concept possesses in its particularity and singularity. Similarly, too, *objectivity* is the total *concept* that has converged out of its determinateness into self-*identity*. In subjectivity, on the one hand, the determinateness or distinction of the concept is a semblance that is immediately merged and falls back into being-for-self or negative unity; it is an *inhering* predicate. In objectivity, on the other hand, the determinateness is posited as an immediate totality, as an external whole. Now the idea has exhibited itself as the concept liberated once more into its subjectivity from the immediacy in which it is immersed in the object; as the concept that distinguishes itself from its objectivity while, nevertheless, this objectivity is determined by it, and has its substantiality only in the concept. This identity has, therefore, rightly been defined as the *subject-ob-*

ject; in the sense that it is *at one and the same time* the formal or subjective concept and the object as such. But this requires to be conceived more precisely. The concept, having veritably attained its reality, is the absolute judgement whose *subject*, as self-related negative unity, distinguishes itself from its objectivity, of which it is the absolute being,[7] while at the same time it essentially relates to it by its own nature—being therefore its own end, and impulse;—but, for this very reason, the subject does not possess objectivity immediately, in which case it would be merely the totality of the object as such lost in objectivity; on the contrary, objectivity is here the realization of the end, an objectivity *posited* by the activity of the end, an objectivity that as *positedness* possesses its subsistence and its form only as permeated by its subject. As objectivity, it has in it the moment of the *externality* of the concept, and is therefore in general the side of finiteness, change, and the phenomenal, a side, however, that has its demise in falling back into the negative unity of the concept; the negativity whereby its indifferent mutual externality proves itself inessential and posited is the concept itself. Hence the idea, in spite of this objectivity, is absolutely *simple* and *immaterial*, for the externality is only there as determined by the concept and adopted into its negative unity; so far as it subsists as indifferent externality, it is not only the prey of mechanism in general, but appears merely as the perishable and untrue. — Although, therefore, the idea has its reality in a material, this material is not an abstract *being* that subsists in its own right confronting the concept; on the contrary, it appears merely as a *becoming* through the negativity of indifferent being, as a simple determinateness of the concept.

This gives the following more precise definitions of the idea. — It is *first* the simple truth, the identity of concept and objectivity as *a universal* in which the opposition and subsistence of the particular is dissolved in its self-identical negativity, and appears as equality with self. *Secondly*, it is the *relation* of the self-existent[6] subjectivity of the simple concept and its objectivity as *distinct* therefrom; the former is essentially the *impulse* to merge this separation, and the latter is the indifferent positivity, the subsistence that is by its own very nature a nullity. Regarded as this relation, the idea is the *process* of sundering itself into individuality and its inorganic nature, and of again reducing this inorganic nature under the sway of the subject, and returning to the original simple universality. The self-*identity* of the idea is one with the *process*; thought which liberates actuality from the semblance of aimless alteration and clarifies it into the *idea* must not represent this truth of actuality as a dead repose, as a mere *picture*, inert, without impulse and movement, as a genus or number, or an abstract thought; by virtue of the freedom which the concept attains in the idea, the idea possesses within itself the *most obstinate opposition* also; its repose consists in the sureness and certainty with which it eternally creates and eternally overcomes that opposition, and in it comes into contact with itself.

In the first instance, however, the idea, once again, is as yet only *immediate*, or only in its *concept*; the objective reality is indeed conformable to the concept, but not yet liberated into the concept, and the concept has no existence *of its own as concept*. In this state the concept is indeed *soul*, but the soul exists in the way of an *immediacy*; that is, its determinateness does not appear as its own self, it has not grasped itself as soul, it does not possess its objective reality within itself; the concept appears as a soul that is not yet *psychical*.

In this *first* phase the idea is *life*: the concept that, distinct from its objectivity and simple within itself, pervades its objectivity, and, having itself for end, possesses its means in objectivity, and posits objectivity as its means, yet is immanent in this means, and is therein the realized self-identical end. By reason of its immediacy this idea has *singularity* for the form of its existence. But the introflection of its absolute process is the merging of this immediate singularity; thereby the concept, which, as universality, is its *inwardness*, converts the externality into universality or posits its objectivity as self-equality.

In this *second* phase the idea is the idea of the *true* and the *good*, as *cognition* and *volition*. In the first instance it is finite cognition and finite volition, in which the true and good are still distinct, and both as yet appear only as *aims*. The concept has, to begin with, liberated *itself* into itself, and as yet given itself only an *abstract objectivity* for reality. But the process of this finite cognition and action converts the initially abstract universality into a totality, whereby it becomes *complete objectivity*. — Or, to look at it from the other aspect, the finite, that is, the subjective spirit, *makes* for itself the *presupposition* of an objective world, just as life *has* such a presupposition; but its activity consists in merging this presupposition, and converting it into a thing posited. In this way its reality is for it the objective world, or, conversely, the objective world is the ideality in which it cognizes itself.

Thirdly, the spirit cognizes the idea as its *absolute truth*, as the truth that is in and for itself; the infinite idea, in which cognition and action have cancelled their difference, and which is the *absolute knowledge of itself*. . . .

The Absolute Idea

The absolute idea, by the manner of its coming to be, is the identity of the theoretical and the practical idea. Each of these taken by itself is still one-sided, and only involves the idea itself as a *world beyond* desiderated, and an aim unattained. Thus each is a *synthesis of endeavour*, and has *not*, as much as has, the idea in it; and passes from one thought to the other, but, instead of bringing the two together, remains in their contradiction. The absolute idea is the rational concept that in its reality only comes into contact with itself. As such, by virtue of this immediacy of its objective identity, it is on the one hand the return to *life*; but it has no less merged this form of its immediacy, and contains within itself the highest opposition. The concept is not merely *soul*, but free subjective concept that exists for itself and therefore possesses *personality*—the practical, absolutely determined, objective concept, which, as person, is impenetrable atomic subjectivity—but which none the less is not exclusive singularity, but for itself *universality* and *cognition*, and in its opposite has *its own* objectivity for object. Everything else is error, obscurity, opinion, endeavour, caprice, and transience; the absolute idea alone is *being*, everlasting *life, self-knowing truth*, and is *all truth*.

It is the sole object and content of philosophy. As it contains *all determinateness* within itself, and its essence is to return to itself through its self-determination or particularization, it takes various shapes, and it is the business of philosophy to cognize it in these. Nature and spirit are in general different modes of presenting *its determinate being*, art and religion its different modes of apprehending itself and giving itself an adequate determinate being. Philosophy has the same content and the same aim as art and religion; but it is the highest mode of apprehending the absolute idea, for its mode is the supreme mode, namely the concept. Hence it includes within itself those formations of real and ideal finiteness as well as of infinity and holiness, and comprehends them and itself. The deduction and cognition of these particular modes is then the further business of the particular philosophical sciences. The *logic* of the absolute idea may also be called a *mode* of it; but whereas 'mode' signifies a *particular* species, a *determinateness* of form, logic on the contrary is the universal mode in which all particular modes are merged and enveloped. The logical idea is the idea itself in its pure essence, the idea enclosed in simple identity within its concept before it has entered the stage of *showing itself* in a determinate form. Hence logic exhibits the self-movement of the absolute idea only as the original *word*, which, though an *utterance*, is yet an utterance that in being has immediately vanished again as an outer thing; the idea is therefore only in this self-determination *of apprehending itself*, it is in *pure thought*, in which difference is not yet otherness, but is and remains completely translucent to itself.—The logical idea, consequently, has for its content itself as *infinite form*.—*Form* constitutes the opposite to *content* insofar as the content is the formal determination so withdrawn into itself and merged in identity that this concrete identity stands opposed to the identity developed as form. Content figures as an other and a *datum* as against the form; for form as such stands altogether in *relation*, and its determinateness is at the same time posited as semblance.—More precisely, the absolute idea has for its content merely this, that the formal determination is its own completed totality, the pure concept. Now the *determinateness* of the idea and the whole career of this determinateness has constituted the object of logical science, and from this career the absolute idea itself has issued *in its being-for-self*, for itself, however, it has shown its nature to be this, that determinateness does not figure as a *content*, but altogether as *form*, and that the idea accordingly is the altogether *universal idea*. Therefore what remains for consideration here is not a content as such, but the universal character of its form—that is, the *method*.

Method may initially appear as the mere *mode and manner* of cognition, and as a matter of fact it has the nature of such. But mode and manner, as method, is not merely an *absolutely determined* modality of *being*, it is a modality of cognition, and as such is posited as determined by the *concept*, and as form, where form is the soul of all objectivity, and all otherwise determined content has its truth in the form alone. If the content of method again is regarded as given and of a peculiar nature of its own, then method, like logic in general when so characterized, is a merely *external* form. Against this, however, not only can we appeal to the fundamental concept of logic, but its whole career, in which all versions of a given content and of objects have occurred, has proved their transition and untruth; and, so far from the possibility of a given object being the foundation, with the absolute form standing to it merely as external and contingent determination, the absolute form has proved itself the absolute foundation and ultimate truth. From this career has emerged the method, as *the concept that knows itself, that has itself*, as the absolute, both subjective and objective, *for its object*; consequently, as the pure correspondence of the concept and its reality, as an existence that is the concept itself.

Thus what is to be considered here as method is only the movement of the *concept* itself, the nature of which movement has been already cognized; but *in the first place* there is now the additional *significance* that the *concept* is *everything*, and its movement *universal absolute activity*, a movement that determines and realizes itself. Therefore the method is to be recognized as the unlimitedly universal, internal and external, mode; and as the absolutely infinite force, to which no object, presenting itself as an external thing, remote from reason and independent of it, can offer resistance, or be of a nature particular as against it, or escape its penetration. It is therefore *soul* and *substance*, and anything whatever is only comprehended and known in its truth where it is *completely subjugated to the method*; it is the proper method of every subject-matter, for its activity is the concept. This is also the truer meaning of its *universality*; in the light of the universality of reflection it is merely regarded as the method for *everything*; but, in the light of the universality of the idea, it is at once the mode and manner of cognition, of the *subjectively* self-knowing concept, and at the same time the *objective* mode and manner, or rather the *substantiality*, of *things*—that is, of concepts, in so far as they appear at first to *representation* and *reflection* as *others*. It is therefore the highest *force*, or rather the *sole* and absolute *force* of reason; and not only this, but also its supreme and sole *impulse* to find and cognize *itself by means of itself in everything*.—This brings us *secondly* to the *distinction between the method and the concept as such,* to the method's *particularity.* The concept, regarded in itself, appeared in its immediacy; the *reflection,* or *the concept that regards* the concept, fell within *our* knowledge. The method is that knowledge itself, for which the concept is not merely an object, but knowledge's own subjective act, as the *instrument* and means of the cognizing activity, distinguished from that activity but as that activity's own essentiality. In the cognition of quest likewise the method holds the position of an *instrument,* of a means standing on the subjective side by which this side relates itself to the object. In this syllogism the subject is one extreme, and the object the other, and the former by means of its method forms a conclusion[40] with the latter, but in doing so does not in itself form a *conclusion with itself.* The extremes remain diverse because subject, method, and object are not posited as the *one identical concept;* hence the syllogism is still the formal syllogism; the premiss in which the subject posits the form on its side as its method is an *immediate* determination, and therefore contains the determinations of form, as we have seen, of definition, division, and so forth as facts *found in the subject.* In veritable cognition, on the contrary, the method is not merely a mass of certain determinations, but the absolute determinedness of the concept, which concept is the middle term only because it has no less the significance of the objective; consequently in the conclusion the objective does not merely attain an external determinateness by means of the method, but is posited in its identity with the subjective concept.

1. Thus what constitute the method are the determinations of the concept itself and their relations, which we have now to examine in their significance as determinations of the method. — In doing so we must *first* begin with the *beginning.* Of this beginning we have already spoken at the beginning of the *Logic* itself, as also above in dealing with subjective cognition, and we have shown that, if it is not made arbitrarily and with a categorical unconsciousness, it may seem indeed to raise numerous difficulties but nevertheless is of the most simple nature. Because it is the beginning, its content is an *immediate,* yet such an immediate as possesses the significance and form *of abstract universality.* Be it otherwise a content of *being,* or of *essence,* or of *concept,* as an *immediacy* it is a thing *assumed, found, assertorical.* But, *first of all,* it is not an immediate of *sensible intuition* or *representation* but an immediate of *thinking,* which thinking on account of its immediacy may also be called a supersensible *inner intuition.* The immediate of sensible intuition is a *manifold* and *singular.* But cognition is conceptual thinking, and therefore its beginning also lies *only in the element of thinking;* it is a *simple* and *universal.* — We have dealt with this form already in reference to definition. In the beginning of finite cognition universality is similarly recognized as an essential determination, but it is taken only as a determination of thought and concept in opposition to being. As a matter of fact, this *first* universality is an *immediate* one, and for

that reason has no less the significance of *being*, for being is just this abstract relation to self. Being requires no further deduction, as though it attached to the abstract of definition only because it is taken from sensible intuition or elsewhere, and only in so far as it is produced for us to see. This demonstration and deduction is a matter of *mediation*, which is more than a mere beginning, and is a mediation of a kind that does not belong to thinking comprehension but is the elevation of representation, of empirical and ratiocinative consciousness, to the standpoint of thought. According to the current contrast between thought or concept and being it is regarded as a weighty truth that to the former taken by itself no being belongs as yet, and that the latter has a ground of its own, independent of thought. The simple determination of *being*, however, is so poor in itself, that for that reason, if for no other, there is no need to make a fuss about it; the universal is immediately itself this immediate, since, as an abstract, it is also merely the abstract relation to self, which is being. As a fact, the demand that being should be produced for us to see has a further inner meaning involving more than this abstract determination; what is meant by this is in general the demand for the *realization of the concept*, which realization does not reside in the mere *beginning*, but is rather the aim and task of the whole further evolution of cognition. Further, in so far as the *content* of the beginning is supposed to be justified and to receive the credentials of its truth or correctness through the evidence of internal or external perception, it is no longer the *form* of universality as such that is meant by it, but its *determinateness*, of which we shall have need to speak presently. The confirmation of the *determinate content* with which the beginning is made seems to lie *behind* it; but in fact confirmation is to be regarded as an advance, that is, if it belongs to conceptual cognition.

Hence the beginning has for the method no other determinateness than that of being the simple and universal; this is itself the *determinateness* by reason of which it is deficient. Universality is the pure simple concept, and the method as the consciousness of the concept knows that universality is only a moment and that in it the concept has not reached its absolute determination. But with this consciousness that would carry the beginning further only for the sake of the method, the method would be a formality posited in external reflection. Since, however, the method is the objective immanent form, the immediacy of the beginning must be *intrinsically* defective, and endowed with the *impulse* to carry itself further. But the universal in the absolute method has the value not of a mere abstraction, but of the objective universal, that is, the universal that is *in itself* the *concrete totality*, though that totality is not yet *posited* or *for itself*. Even the abstract universal as such, considered in its concept, that is, in its truth, is not merely the *simple*, but, in being *abstract*, is already *posited* as burdened with a *negation*. For this reason, too, *there is* nothing, whether in *actuality* or in *thought*, that is as simple and as abstract as one commonly imagines. A simple thing of this kind is a mere *opinion* that has its ground solely in the unconsciousness of what is really present. Just now the beginning was determined as the immediate; the *immediacy of the universal* is the same thing that is here expressed as being-in-itself without being-for-itself. — Hence it may, no doubt, be said that all beginning must be made with the *absolute*, just as all advance is only the presentation of it, in so far as what is in itself is the concept. But because the absolute exists at first only in itself, it is equally *not* the absolute, nor the posited concept, and also not the idea; for these terms involve just this, that being-in-itself is only an abstract one-sided moment. Hence the advance is not a kind of *superfluity*; it would be so if the beginning were in truth already the absolute; the advance consists rather in the universal determining itself, and being for itself the universal, i.e. is no less individual and subject. Only in its consummation is it the absolute.

One may be reminded that the beginning, which *in itself* is concrete totality, may as beginning also be *free* and its immediacy have the determination of an *external* determinate being; the *germ of the living being* and the *subjective end* in general have proved themselves such beginnings, and hence both are themselves *impulses*. The non-spiritual and inanimate, on the contrary, are the concrete concept only as *real possibility*; the *cause* is the highest stage in which the concrete concept has an immediate determinate being as beginning in the sphere of necessity; but it is not yet a subject maintaining itself as such even in its actual realization. The *sun*, for example, and in general all inanimate things are determinate existences in which the real possibility remains an *inner* totality, and the moments of the totality are not *posited* in subjective form in them and, in so far as they realize themselves, attain an existence by means of *other* corporeal individuals.

2. The concrete totality which makes the beginning contains, as such, within itself the beginning of progress and evolution. As a concrete it is *differentiated within itself*, but on account of its initial *immediacy* the first distinguished items are, to begin with, a *diversity*. The immediate, however, as self-related universality, as subject, is also the *unity* of these diverse items. — This reflection is the first step of the advance — the emergence of *difference, judgement, determination* in general. The essential point is that the absolute method finds and cognizes the *determination* of the universal in the universal itself. The procedure of the finite cognition of understanding in its process of determination consists in adopting again no less externally from the concrete what it has laid aside in its process of creating the universal by abstraction. The absolute method, on the contrary, does not behave like external reflection, but takes the determinate from its own very object, since it is itself that object's immanent principle and soul. This is the meaning of *Plato's* demand that cognition should *consider things in and for themselves*; that is, partly, that it should consider them in their universal-

ity, but, partly, that it should not stray away from them and grasp at circumstances, instances and comparisons, but keep them alone before it, and bring to consciousness what is immanent in them.—The method of absolute cognition is to this extent *analytical*. That it *finds* the further determination of its initial universal simply and solely in that universal, is the absolute objectivity of the concept, of which objectivity the method is the certainty.—But the method is no less *synthetical*, inasmuch as its object, immediately determined as a *simple universal*, by virtue of the determinateness which it possesses in its very immediacy and universality, exhibits itself as an *other*. This relation of the diverse, which the object of the method thus is within itself, is nevertheless no longer what is meant by synthesis in finite cognition; by the mere fact of the object's no less analytical determination in general—that the relation is relation within the *concept*—it is completely distinguished from the latter synthesis.

This no less synthetical than analytical moment of *judgement*, by which the initial universal of itself determines itself as the *other of itself*, is to be termed the *dialectical* moment. *Dialectic* is one of those ancient sciences that have been most misunderstood in the metaphysics of the moderns, as well as by popular philosophy in general, both old and new. Diogenes Laertius says of *Plato* that, as Thales was the founder of natural philosophy, and Socrates of moral philosophy, so Plato was the founder of the third science pertaining to philosophy, *dialectic*—a service which the ancients reckoned his highest, but which often remains entirely unnoticed by those who have him most in their mouths. Dialectic has often been regarded as an *art*, as though it rested on a subjective *talent* and did not belong to the objectivity of the concept. The shape it takes and the results it reaches in the philosophy of Kant have been pointed out in the particular examples of that theory. The recognition once more of dialectic as necessary to reason must be regarded as a stride of infinite importance, although the result to be drawn from it must be the very opposite of that arrived at by Kant.

Besides the fact that dialectic is commonly regarded as something contingent, it usually takes the following more precise form. It is shown in reference to some object or other, for example, the world, motion, the point, or the like, that some or other determination belongs to it, for example (taking the objects in the order named) finiteness in space or time, presence in *this* place, absolute negation of space; but, further, that with equal necessity the opposite determination belongs to it also, for example, infinity in space and time, non-presence in this place, relation to space and so spatiality. The older Eleatic school has directed its dialectic pre-eminently against motion, Plato frequently against the representations and concepts of his time, especially those of the Sophists, but also against the pure categories and the determinations of reflection; the later cultivated scepticism has extended it not only to the immediate so-called facts of consciousness and maxims of common life, but also to all the concepts of science. Now the consequence drawn from dialectic of this kind is in general the *contradiction* and *nullity* of the assertions propounded. But this consequence can be drawn in either of two senses — either in the objective sense that the *object* which contradicts itself in such a manner merges itself and is null and void; — this was, for example, the conclusion of the Eleatics, according to which *truth* was denied, for example, to the world, motion, the point; — or again, in the subjective sense that *the cognition is defective*. One meaning of the latter conclusion is that the illusion is merely the artificial imposition of this dialectic. This is the usual view of so-called common sense, which takes its stand on *sensible* evidence, and *familiar representations* and *expressions*. Sometimes common sense takes this dialectic easily, as when Diogenes the cynic exposes the dialectic of motion by walking up and down without a word; but often it rises in indignation against it, seeing in it, may be, a mere folly, or, when ethically important objects are concerned, an outrage that tries to unsettle the essential bed-rock of things and teaches how to supply vice with grounds. This view comes out in the Socratic dialectic against the Sophists, and this indignation, turned in the opposite direction, cost the same Socrates his life. As to the vulgar refutation that confronts thinking, as did Diogenes, with *sensuous consciousness* and believes that in the latter it has got the truth, we must leave that to itself; in so far, however, as dialectic abrogates ethical determinations, we must have confidence in reason that it will know how to restore these determinations, but restore them in their truth and in the consciousness of their right, though also of their limitations. — Again from the other alternative standpoint the result of subjective nullity does not affect dialectic itself, but rather the cognition against which it is directed, and in the view of scepticism and likewise of the Kantian philosophy, *cognition in general*.

The fundamental prejudice on this question is the notion that dialectic has *only a negative result*, a point which will presently be more precisely defined. But first of all in respect of the above cited *form*, in which dialectic is usually presented, it is to be observed that in that form the dialectic and its result affect the *object* under consideration or else the subjective *cognition*, and declare one or the other null and void, while on the other hand the determinations exhibited in the object as in a *third* thing remain unnoticed, and are presupposed as valid in themselves. It is an infinite merit of the Kantian philosophy to have drawn attention to this uncritical procedure, and thereby to have given the impetus to the restoration of logic and dialectic in the sense of the examination of the *determinations of thought in their own absolute nature*. The object, if taken apart from thinking and the concept, is a representation or even a name; it is in the determinations of thought and concept that it *is* what it *is*. Hence in reality these determinations are the one thing that matters; they are the true object and content of reason, and anything else that one understands by object and content in distinction from them has its validity solely through and in them. It must not, therefore, be assumed that through the fault of some object or of cognition these determinations, owing to their condition and external connexion, show themselves dialectical. On that assumption the object or the cognition is represented as a subject into which the *determinations* are introduced in the form of predicates, properties, self-dependent universals, with the result that these determinations, in themselves correct and constant, are, by extraneous and contingent connexion in and by a third thing, brought into dialectical relationships and contradiction. This kind of external and static subject of representation and understanding and these abstract determinations are so far from deserving to pass for *ultimate* fundamental certainties, that they are rather to be regarded as an immediacy, and a presupposed and initial immediacy that, as before shown, must in its own very nature submit to dialectic, because it is to be taken as *in itself* concept. Thus all the oppositions that are assumed as constant, as, for example, finite and infinite, singular and universal, are not in contradiction through, say, an external connexion; on the contrary, as the consideration of their character has shown, they are in their own essential nature transition; the synthesis and the subject in which they appear is the product of their concept's own reflection. If unconceptual consideration stops short at their external relationship, isolates them, and leaves them as static presuppositions, it is the concept on the other hand that views them in themselves, moves them as their soul, and brings out their dialectic.

Now this is the very standpoint indicated above, from which an initial universal *regarded in its own essential nature* proves to be the other of its self. Conceived quite generally, this determination may be taken to signify that the initially *immediate* is now posited as *mediated*, as *related* to an other, or that the universal is posited as a particular. The *second* term that has thus arisen is consequently the *negative* of the first, and if in anticipation we take into account the subsequent progress, the *first negative*. From this negative aspect the immediate has been *lost* in its other, but that other is essentially not the *empty negative*, the *nothing* that is taken as the common result of dialectic; rather, it is the *other of the first*, the *negative* of the *immediate*, and therefore it is determined as the *mediated*—that is, it *contains* in general within itself the *determination of the first*. Thus the first is essentially *preserved* and *retained* even in its other. —To maintain the positive in *its* negative, the content of the presupposition in the result, is the most important point in rational cognition; it is at once a matter merely of the simplest reflection to convince oneself of the absolute truth and necessity of this requirement, and as far as *examples* to prove it are concerned, the whole of logic consists of such.

Accordingly, what we have now before us is the *mediated*, and if, to begin with, we take this in the same immediacy as we did the first term, it is also a *simple* determination; for as the first is lost in it, we have only the second before us. Now since also the first term is *contained* in the second and the latter is the truth of the former, this unity may be expressed as a proposition in which the immediate is put as subject, and the mediated as its predicate; for example, *the finite is infinite, one is many, the singular is the universal.* The inadequate form, however, of such propositions and judgements is immediately obvious. In discussing the *judgement* it has been shown that its form in general, and most of all the immediate form of the *positive* judgement, is incapable of accommodating speculation and truth. The direct supplement to it, the *negative* judgement, would at least have to be added as well. In the judgement the first term as subject has the semblance of a self-dependent subsistence, whereas it is merged in its predicate as in its other; this negation is indeed contained in the content of the above propositions, but their positive form contradicts the content; consequently they fail to posit what is contained in them — which would be precisely the purpose of employing a proposition.

The second term, the *negative* or *mediated*, is further at the same time the *mediating* term. Initially it may be regarded as a simple determination, but in its truth it is a *relation* or *relationship*; for it is the negative *of the positive*, and includes the positive in itself. Hence it is an other, not in the sense of the other of something to which it is indifferent, in which case it would not be an other, nor a relation or relationship; rather it is the *intrinsically other*, the *other of an other*; therefore it includes *its* own other in itself, and is consequently, *as contradiction*, the *posited dialectic of itself.* — Since the first or immediate term is the concept in itself, it is therefore only *in itself*, the negative, and thus with it the dialectical moment consists in the *difference* which it *in itself* contains being posited in it. The second term, on the contrary, is itself the *determinate, difference* or relationship; hence with it the dialectical moment consists in positing the *unity* that is contained in it. — If, then, the negative, the determinate, relationship, judgement, and all the terms which come under this second moment of the method do not at once appear on their own account as contradiction and as dialectical, the fault lies solely with the thinking that does not bring its thoughts together. For the material, the *opposed* terms in *one relation*, is already *posited* and at hand for thought. Formal thinking, however, makes identity its law and allows the contradictory content before it to fall away into the sphere of representation, into space and time, where the contradictories are held *asunder* in juxtaposition and succession and so come before consciousness lacking the reciprocal contact. Formal thinking lays down the definite principle on this point that contradiction is unthinkable; but, as a matter of fact, the thinking of contradiction is the essential moment of the concept. Formal thinking does in fact think contradiction, only it immediately looks away from it, and in the above pronouncement passes over into mere abstract negation.

Now the negativity just considered constitutes the *turning-point* of the movement of the concept. It is the *simple point of negative self-relation*, the innermost source of all activity, of all animate and spiritual self-movement, the dialectical soul that everything true possesses and by which alone it is true; for on this subjectivity alone rests the merging of the opposition between concept and reality, and the unity that is truth. — The *second* negative, the negative of the negative, at which we have arrived, is this merging of contradiction, but just as little as the contradiction is it *an act of an external reflection*, but rather the *innermost, most objective factor* of life and spirit, which results in a *subject, person, free being.* — The *self-relation of the negative* is to be regarded as the *second premiss* of the whole syllogism. If the terms *analytical* and *synthetical* are employed in their opposition, the *first* premiss may be regarded as the *analytical* moment, for in it the immediate stands in *immediate* relationship to its other, and hence *passes over*, or rather has passed over, into it: — although this relation, as already remarked, is also synthetical, since that into which it passes is its other. The second premiss here under consideration may be determined as the *synthetical* premiss, since it is the relation of the *distinct as such* to *its distinct.* — As the first premiss is the moment of *universality* and *communication*, so the second is characterized by *singularity*, which initially stands to its other in a relation of exclusion, independence, and diversity. The negative appears as the *mediator*, since it includes both itself and the immediate whose negation it is. So far as these two terms are taken in the light of any relationship whatever as externally related, the negative is only the *formal* mediator; but as absolute negativity, the negative moment of absolute mediation is the unity which is subjectivity and soul.

In this turning-point of the method the course of cognition at the same time returns upon itself. This negativity as self-merging contradiction is the *restoration* of the *first immediacy*, of simple universality; for the other of the other, the negative of the negative, is immediately the *positive, identical, universal.* If we choose to *count*, this *second* immediate is the *third* term in the course of thought as a whole to the first immediate and the mediated. It is also, however, the third to the first or formal negativity, and to the absolute negativity or the second negative; now as the first negative is already the second term, what is reckoned as the *third* may also be reckoned as the *fourth*, and instead of a *triplicity*, the abstract form may be taken as a *quadruplicity*; in the latter case the negative or *distinction* is counted as a duality. — The third or fourth is in general the unity of the first and second moments, of the immediate and the mediated. — That it is this *unity*, as also that the whole form of the method is a *triplicity*, is, no doubt, merely the superficial external aspect of the mode of cognition; yet to have demonstrated even merely this, and that too in determinate application — for it is common knowledge that the abstract numerical form itself has been put forward at quite an early period, but without concept and therefore without result, — must be regarded as another infinite merit of the Kantian philosophy. The *syllogism*, which is also threefold, has always been recognized as the universal form of reason; but, for one thing, it passed generally for a wholly external form that did not determine the nature of the content, and, for another, as it proceeds in the formal sense merely in the understanding's determination of *identity*, it lacks the essential *dialectical* moment of *negativity*; yet this moment makes itself apparent in the triplicity of terms, since the third is the unity of the first two, and the latter, as they are diverse, can only be in unity *as merged*. — Formalism has, it is true, taken possession also of triplicity and fastened on to its empty *schema*; the shallow ineptitude and barrenness of the modern philosophic *construction* so-called, that consists in nothing but appending this schema everywhere without concept and immanent determination and using it for an external arrangement, has made this form a nuisance and a by-word. Yet the banality of this employment of it cannot take from its inner worth, and we must always prize highly the first discovery of even the mere uncomprehended shape of the rational.

Now, more precisely, the *third* term is the immediate, but the immediate *due to the merging of mediation*, the simple due to the *merging of difference*, the positive due to the merging of the negative, the concept that has realized itself through otherness, and through merging of this reality has rejoined itself and restored its absolute reality, its *simple* self-relation. This *result* is therefore the *truth*. It is *equally* immediacy *and* mediation; but such forms of judgement as 'the third is immediacy and mediation' or 'it is the unity of them' are not capable of grasping it; for it is not a quiescent third, but, just because it is this unity, is self-mediating movement and activity. As the beginning was the *universal*, so the result is the *singular*, the *concrete*, the *subject*; what the former was *in itself*, the latter is no less *for itself*; the universal is *posited* in the subject. The two first moments of the triplicity are the *abstract* untrue moments that for that very reason are dialectical, and by this their negativity convert themselves into the subject. The concept itself is, *for us* in the first instance, *alike* the universal in its being-in-itself, *and* the negative in its being-for-itself, *and* the third in which being-in-itself and being-for-itself are united, the *universal* that runs through all the moments of the syllogism; but the third term is the conclusion in which the concept through its negativity is mediated with itself and thereby posited for-itself as the *universal* and the *identity of its moments*.

Now this result, as the introverted and self-*identical* whole, has given itself again the form of *immediacy*. Thus it is now itself of the same kind as the *initial* term had determined itself to be. As simple self-relation it is a universal, and in this universality the *negativity* that constituted its dialectic and mediation has collapsed again into *simple determinateness*, which can again be a beginning. It may seem at first that this cognition of the result must be an analysis of it, and hence must again dissect these determinations and the process by which the result arose and which has been observed. But if the treatment of the object is actually carried out in this analytical manner, it belongs to the stage of the idea above considered, the cognition of inquiry, which merely states of its object what *is*, apart from the necessity of its concrete identity and the concept of it. But though the method of truth, which comprehends the object, is, as we have seen, itself analytical, since it abides simply within the concept, yet it is none the less synthetical, for by the concept the object is determined dialectically and as an other. On the new foundation constituted by the result as the fresh object the method remains the same as with the foregoing. The difference is solely one of the relationship of the foundation as such; it is, no doubt, a foundation in this case also, yet its immediacy is only a *form* since it was result as well; hence its determinateness as content is no longer a mere assumption, but something *deduced* and *proved*.

It is here first that the *content* of cognition as such enters into the circle of consideration, since, as deduced, it now has a place in the method. By means of this moment the method enlarges itself into a *system*. At first the method had to have a beginning wholly indeterminate in respect of content; to this extent the method appears as the merely formal soul, for and by which the beginning was determined simply and solely in regard to its *form*, namely as the immediate and universal. By the movement presented the object has obtained for itself a *determinateness* that is a *content*, since the negativity that has collapsed into simplicity is the merged form, and as simple determinateness confronts its development, and, in the first instance, its very opposition to universality.

Now, as this determinateness is the proximate truth of the undetermined beginning, it condemns that beginning as an imperfect thing, as well as the method itself, which in starting from that beginning was merely formal. This may be expressed as the now determinate demand that the beginning, since it is itself a determinate in contrast with the determinateness of the result, shall be taken not as an immediate but as something mediated and deduced. This may appear as the demand for infinite *retrogression* in proof and deduction; just as from the new beginning that has been obtained the progress of the method again brings forth another result, so that the process moves forwards also in an infinite *progression*.

It has been shown more than once that the infinite progress in general belongs to unconceptual reflection; the absolute method, which has the concept for its soul and content, cannot lead to that. At the first blush such beginnings as *being, essence, universality*, may seem to be of such a kind as to possess the complete universality and absence of content required for a purely formal beginning, as it is supposed to be, and therefore, as absolutely first beginnings, to require and admit no further retrogression. As they are pure self-relations, immediate and indeterminate, they certainly do not possess in them the difference which in any other kind of beginning is directly posited between the universality of its form and its content. But the indeterminateness which the above logical beginnings have for their sole content is the very thing that constitutes their determinateness; that is, their determinateness consists in their negativity as merged mediation; the particularity of this latter gives even their indeterminateness a particularity, whereby *being, essence,* and *universality* are distinguished from one another. The determinateness then which attaches to them severally is their *immediate determinateness* respectively, just as much as the determinateness of any content whatever, and requires therefore a deduction; for the method it is a matter of indifference whether the determinateness be taken as determinateness of *form* or of *content*. In fact, the fact that a content has been determined by the first of its results is not the beginning for the method of a new mode; the method remains as it was, neither more or less formal than before. For as it is the absolute form, the concept that knows itself and everything as concept, there is no content to confront it and determine it as one-sided external form. Hence, while the absence of content in the beginnings does not make them absolute beginnings, neither is it content as such that could lead the method into an infinite progression or retrogression. From one aspect, the *determinateness* which the method creates for itself in its result is the moment whereby the method is self-mediation and converts *the immediate beginning into a mediated*. But, conversely, it is through the determinateness that this mediation of the method runs its course; it returns *through a content*, as through an apparent *other* of itself, to its beginning in such wise that not only does it restore that beginning, this time as a *determinate* beginning, but the result is no less merged determinateness and so the restoration of the first indeterminateness in which it began. This is the achievement of the method as *a system of totality*. We have still to consider it in this character.

We have seen that the determinateness which was a result is itself, in virtue of the form of simplicity into which it has collapsed, a new beginning; as this beginning is distinguished from its predecessor precisely by that determinateness, cognition sweeps on from content to content. The first characterization of this advance springs from the fact that it begins from simple determinatenesses and the succeeding ones are ever getting *richer and more concrete*. For the result contains its beginning, and its course has enriched it with a new determinateness. The *universal* constitutes the foundation; hence the advance is not to be taken as a *flux* from *other* to *other*. In the absolute method the concept *maintains* itself in its otherness, the universal in its particularization, in judgement and reality; at every stage of its further determination it lifts with it the whole mass of its preceding content, and, far from losing anything or leaving anything behind in its dialectical advance, it carries along with it all its winnings, and is ever enriching and adding new layers to itself.

This *enlargement* may be regarded as the moment of content and in general as the first premiss; the universal is *communicated* to the wealth of the content and immediately maintained in it. But the relationship has also its second, negative or dialectical, aspect. The enrichment proceeds in the *necessity* of the concept, it is maintained by the concept, and each determination is a reflection into self. Each new stage of *expansion*, in other words, of *further determination*, is also a *concentration*, and the *greater extension* is no less a higher *intensity*. Hence the richest term is the most concrete and *most subjective*, and that which retreats into the simplest depth is the most potent and overarching. The apex and summit is the *pure personality*, which, solely through the absolute dialectic which is its nature, no less holds and *embraces everything within itself* than it makes itself the supremely free — the simplicity which is the primary immediacy and universality.

Thus it is that each step of the *advance* in further determination, while moving further from the undetermined beginning, *is bringing us back nearer* to it again, and that, consequently, what may appear at first as diverse, the *retrogression to the grounds* of the beginning and the *progression to the wider determination* of it, coincide and are the same. The method, which thus winds itself into a circle, cannot, however, in a temporal development anticipate that the beginning as such is already a deduction; for the beginning in its immediacy it is sufficient that it is simple universality. In being that, it has its conditions complete; and there is no need to fear a mere *provisional* and *hypothetical* acceptance of it. Whatever considerations might be brought against it — say, from the limits of human knowledge, from the necessity of examining critically the instrument of cognition before we attack the subject-matter — are themselves *presuppositions*, which, as *concrete determinations*, involve the necessity for their mediation and grounding. So far, therefore, from having a formal advantage over the *beginning* with the subject-matter against which they protest, they themselves require a deduction on account of their more concrete content, and so we may look on them as merely vain pretensions to prior consideration. They have a false content, for they make what we have come to know as finite and false into an irrefragable and absolute, namely, a *limited* cognition, determined as *form* and *instrument in contrast* to its *content*; this untrue cognition itself is the retrogressive form or process of seeking grounds. The method, too, knows that the beginning is incomplete, because it is a beginning; but at the same time it knows that this incomplete in general is a necessity, since truth is nothing but self-recovery through the negativity of immediacy. The impatience that insists on *merely* getting beyond the *determinate* — whether called beginning, object, finite, or in whatever other form it be taken — and finding itself immediately in the absolute, has nothing before it as cognition but the empty negative, the abstract infinity; — in other words, a *presumed*[33] absolute, that is presumed because it is not *posited* or *apprehended*; apprehended it can only be through the *mediation* of cognition, of which mediation the universal and immediate is a moment, while the truth itself lies only in the extended course of the process and in the conclusion. To meet the subjective needs of unfamiliarity and the impatience that goes with it, a survey *of the whole* may, indeed, be given *in anticipation* — by a division for reflection, which, in the mode of finite cognition, enters the particular under the universal as a thing *already there* and to be expected in the process of knowledge. Yet this gives no more than a picture for our *representative* faculty; for the true transition from the universal to the particular and to the whole determined in its own essential nature, in which whole that first universal itself according to its true determination is now a moment, is alien to this method of division, and is only the mediation of science itself.

By virtue of the nature of the method exhibited, science presents itself as a *circle* returning upon itself, whose mediation carries round its conclusion into its beginning, the simple ground. Moreover this circle is a *circle of circles*; for each individual link, as animated by the method, is introflection that in returning into the beginning is at the same time the beginning of a new link. Fragments of this chain are the individual sciences, of which each has a *before* and *after*—or, to speak more exactly, only *has* the *before*, and in its conclusion[40] *indicates* its *after*.

Thus then logic, too, in the absolute idea has returned to that simple unity which is its beginning; the pure immediacy of being, in which at first all determination appears as extinguished or dropped by abstraction, is the idea that has arrived through mediation, that is, the merging of mediation, at its corresponding equality with itself. The method is the pure concept that stands in relationship to itself alone; it is therefore the *simple self-relation* that is *being*. But it is now also being *fulfilled*, the *self-comprehending concept*, being as the *concrete* and absolutely intensive totality.—Of this idea it only remains to remark in conclusion, *first*, that in it *logical science* has apprehended its own concept. In the case of *being*, the beginning of its *content*, its concept appears as a knowledge lying outside the content in subjective reflection. But in the idea of absolute cognition the concept has become the idea's own content. The idea is itself the pure concept, that has itself for its object, and which, in running itself as object through the totality of its determinations, develops itself into the totality of its reality, into the system of science, and concludes by apprehending this comprehension of itself, merging thereby its standing as content and object, and cognizing the concept of science.—*Secondly*, this idea is still logical; it is enclosed in pure thought, the science only of the divine *concept*. The systematic development of it is, no doubt, itself a realization, but confined within the same sphere. Since the pure idea of cognition is so far enclosed in subjectivity, it is the *impulse* to merge this subjectivity, and pure truth as the last result becomes also the *beginning of another sphere and science*. It only remains here to indicate this transition.

The idea, namely, posits itself as the absolute *unity* of the pure concept and its reality, and therewith contracts into the immediacy of *being*, as *the totality* in this form the idea is *nature*.—This determination, however, is not a *result of becoming* or a *transition*, as when, above, the subjective

concept in its totality becomes *objectivity* and the *subjective end becomes life.*
On the contrary, the pure idea, in which the determinateness or reality of
the concept has itself been raised into concept, is absolute *liberation*, for
which there is no longer any immediate determination that is not at the
same time *posited* and the concept. In this freedom therefore there is no
room for transition; the simple being to which the idea determines itself
remains completely transparent to it, and is the concept that in its determination abides with itself. Accordingly instead of transition we have here to
say that the idea *freely releases* itself in its absolute self-certainty and inner
peace. In virtue of this freedom the *form of its determinateness* is just as
completely free — the *externality of space and time* that is absolutely for itself
without subjectivity. In so far as this latter appears in the abstract immediacy of being and is apprehended by consciousness, it is as mere objectivity
and external life; but in the idea it remains in its own essential nature the
totality of the concept, and science in the relationship of divine cognition to
nature. This primary resolution of the pure idea to determine itself as
external idea, nevertheless, only posits thereby for itself the mediation
from which the concept soars as a free real existence that has withdrawn
into itself out of externality, that completes of itself its liberation in the
science of spirit, and that finds the highest concept of itself in logical science
as the pure concept that comprehends itself.

X. Philosophy of Nature: Introduction*

§245. In man's *practical* approach to Nature, the latter is, for him, something immediate and external; and he himself is an external and therefore sensuous individual, although in relation to natural objects, he correctly regards himself as *end*. A consideration of Nature according to this relationship yields the standpoint of *finite* teleology (§205). In this, we find the correct presupposition that Nature does not itself contain the absolute, final end (§§207–11). But if this way of considering the matter starts from particular, *finite* ends, on the one hand it makes them into presuppositions whose contingent content may in itself be even insignificant and trivial. On the other hand, the end-relationship demands for itself a deeper mode of treatment than that appropriate to external and finite relationships, namely, the mode of treatment of the Notion,[9] which in its own general nature is immanent and therefore is immanent in Nature as such.

§246. What is now called *physics* was formerly called *natural philosophy*, and it is also a *theoretical*, and indeed a *thinking* consideration of Nature; but, on the one hand, it does not start from determinations which are external to Nature, like those ends already mentioned; and secondly, it is directed to a knowledge of the *universal* aspect of Nature, a universal which is also *determined* within itself—directed to a knowledge of forces, laws and genera, whose content must not be a simple aggregate, but arranged in orders and classes, must present itself as an organism. As the Philosophy of Nature is a *comprehending* treatment, it has as its object the same *universal*, but *explicitly*, and it considers this universal in its *own immanent necessity* in accordance with the self-determination of the Notion.

Remark. The relation of philosophy to the empirical sciences was discussed in the general introduction [to the *Encyclopaedia*]. Not only must philosophy be in agreement with our empirical knowledge of Nature, but the *origin* and *formation* of the Philosophy of Nature presupposes and is

---

*Pages 4–42 (omitting *Zusätze*) from Hegel's *Philosophy of Nature* translated by A. V. Miller (1970). Reprinted by permission of Oxford University Press.

Translated from the third (1830) edition of the *Encyclopaedia of the Philosophical Sciences in Outline*, Part II.

261

conditioned by empirical physics. However, the course of a science's origin and the preliminaries of its construction are one thing, while the science itself is another. In the latter, the former can no longer appear as the foundation of the science; here, the foundation must be the necessity of the Notion.

It has already been mentioned that, in the progress of philosophical knowledge, we must not only give an account of the object *as determined by its Notion*, but we must also name the *empirical* appearance corresponding to it, and we must show that the appearance does, in fact, correspond to its Notion. However, this is not an appeal to experience in regard to the necessity of the content. Even less admissible is an appeal to what is called *intuition*,[4] which is usually nothing but a fanciful and sometimes fantastic exercise of the imagination on the lines of *analogies*, which may be more or less significant, and which impress determinations and schemata on objects only *externally* (§231 *Remark*).

B. The Notion of Nature

§247. Nature has presented itself as the Idea in the form of *otherness*. Since therefore the Idea is the negative of itself, or is *external to itself*, Nature is not merely external in relation to this Idea (and to its subjective existence Spirit); the truth is rather that *externality* constitutes the specific character in which Nature, as Nature, exists.

§248. In this externality, the determinations of the Notion have the show of an *indifferent subsistence* and *isolation* in regard to each other, and the Notion, therefore, is present only as something inward. Consequently, Nature exhibits no freedom in its existence, but only *necessity* and *contingency*.

Remark. For this reason, Nature in the determinate existence which makes it Nature, is not to be deified; nor are sun, moon, animals, plants, etc., to be regarded and cited as more excellent, as works of God, than human actions and events. *In itself*, in the Idea, Nature is divine: but as it *is*, the being of Nature does not accord with its Notion; rather is Nature the *unresolved contradiction*. Its characteristic is *positedness*, the negative, in the same way that the ancients grasped matter in general as the *non-ens*. Thus Nature has also been spoken of as the *self-degradation of the Idea*, in that the Idea, in this form of externality, is in a disparity with its own self. It is only to the external and immediate stage of consciousness, that is, to *sensuous* consciousness, that Nature appears as the First, the immediate, as mere being. But because, even in this element of externality, Nature is a representation of the *Idea*, one may, and indeed ought, to admire in it the wisdom of God. Vanini said that a stalk of straw suffices to demonstrate God's being: but every mental image, the slightest fancy of mind, the play of its most capricious whims, every word, affords a superior ground for a knowledge of God's being than any single object of Nature. In Nature, not only is the play of forms a prey to boundless and unchecked contingency, but each separate entity is without the Notion of itself. The highest level to which Nature attains is life; but this, as only a natural mode of the Idea, is at the mercy of the unreason of externality, and the living creature is throughout its whole life entangled with other alien existences, whereas in every expression of Spirit there is contained the moment of free, universal self-relation. It is equally an error to regard the products of mind as inferior to natural objects, and to regard the latter as superior to *human works of art*, on the ground that these must take their material from outside, and that they are not alive. As if the spiritual form did not contain a higher kind of life, and were not more worthy of the Spirit, than the natural form, and as though form generally were not superior to matter, and throughout the ethical sphere even what can be called matter did not belong to Spirit alone: as if in Nature the higher form, the living creature, did not also receive its matter from outside. It is put forward as a further superiority of Nature that throughout all the contingency of its manifold existence it remains obedient to eternal laws. But surely this is also true of the realm of self-consciousness, a fact which finds recognition in the belief that human affairs are governed by Providence; or are the laws of this Providence in the field of human affairs supposed to be only contingent and irrational? But if the contingency of Spirit, the free will[58] does *evil*, this is still infinitely superior to the regular motions of the celestial bodies, or to the innocence of plant life; for what thus errs is still Spirit.

§249. Nature is to be regarded as a *system of stages*, one arising necessarily from the other and being the proximate truth of the stage from which it results: but it is not generated *naturally* out of the other but only in the inner Idea which constitutes the ground of Nature. *Metamorphosis* pertains only to the Notion as such, since only *its* alteration is development. But in Nature, the Notion is partly only something inward, partly existent only as a living individual: *existent* metamorphosis, therefore, is limited to this individual alone.

Remark. It has been an inept conception of ancient and also recent Philosophy of Nature to regard the progression and transition of one natural form and sphere into a higher as an outwardly-actual production which, however, to be made *clearer*, is relegated to the *obscurity* of the past. It is precisely externality which is characteristic of Nature, that is, differences are allowed to fall apart and to appear as indifferent to each other: the dialectical Notion which leads forward the *stages*, is the inner side of them. A thinking consideration must reject such nebulous, at bottom, sensuous ideas, as in particular the so-called *origination*, for example, of plants and animals from water, and then the *origination* of the more highly developed animal organisms from the lower, and so on.

§250. The *contradiction* of the Idea, arising from the fact that, as

Nature, it is external to itself, is more precisely this: that on the one hand there is the *necessity* of its forms which is generated by the Notion, and their rational determination in the organic totality; while on the other hand, there is their indifferent *contingency* and indeterminable irregularity. In the sphere of Nature contingency and determination from without has its right, and this contingency is at its greatest in the realm of concrete individual forms, which however, as products of Nature, are concrete only in an *immediate* manner. The *immediately* concrete thing is a group of properties, external to one another and more or less indifferently related to each other; and for that very reason, the simple subjectivity which exists for itself is also indifferent and abandons them to contingent and external determination. This is the *impotence* of Nature, that it preserves the determinations of the Notion only *abstractly*, and leaves their detailed specification to external determination.

Remark. The infinite wealth and variety of forms and, what is most irrational, the contingency which enters into the external arrangement of natural things, have been extolled as the sublime freedom of Nature, even as the divinity *of* Nature, or at least the divinity present *in* it. This confusion of contingency, caprice, and disorder, with freedom and rationality is characteristic of sensuous and unphilosophical thinking. This impotence of Nature sets limits to philosophy and it is quite improper to expect the Notion to comprehend — or as it is said, construe or deduce — these contingent products of Nature. It is even imagined that the more trivial and isolated the object, the easier is the task of deducing it.* Undoubtedly, traces of determination by the Notion are to be found even in the most particularized object, although these traces do not exhaust its nature. Traces of this influence of the Notion and of this inner coherence of natural objects will often surprise the investigator, but especially will they seem startling, or rather incredible, to those who are accustomed to see only contingency in natural, as in human, history. One must, however, be careful to avoid taking such trace of the Notion for the total determination of the object, for that is the route to the analogies previously mentioned.

In the impotence of Nature to adhere strictly to the Notion in its realization, lies the difficulty and, in many cases, the impossibility of finding fixed distinctions for classes and orders from an empirical consideration of Nature. Nature everywhere blurs the essential limits of species and genera by intermediate and defective forms, which continually furnish counter examples to every fixed distinction; this even occurs within a specific genus, that of man, for example, where monstrous births, on the

---

*It was in this — and other respects too — quite naïve sense that Herr Krug once challenged the Philosophy of Nature to perform the feat of deducing *only* his pen. One could perhaps give him hope that *his* pen would have the glory of being deduced, if ever philosophy should advance so far and have such a clear insight into every great theme in heaven and on earth, past and present, that there was nothing more important to comprehend.

one hand, must be considered as belonging to the genus, while on the other hand, they lack certain essential determinations characteristic of the genus. In order to be able to consider such forms as defective, imperfect and deformed, one must presuppose a fixed, invariable type. This type, however, cannot be furnished by experience, for it is experience which also presents these so-called monstrosities, deformities, intermediate products, etc. The fixed type rather presupposes the self-subsistence and dignity of the determination stemming from the Notion.

§251. Nature is, in itself, a living Whole. The movement through its stages is more precisely this: that the Idea *posits* itself as that which it is *in itself*; or what is the same thing, that it returns *into itself* out of its immediacy and externality which is *death*, in order to be, first a *living creature*, but further, to sublate this determinateness also in which it is only Life, and to give itself an existence as Spirit, which is the truth and the final goal of Nature and the genuine actuality of the Idea.

C. Division

§252. The Idea as Nature is:

I. in the determination of asunderness or mutual outsideness, of infinite separatedness, the unity of form being outside it; this unity, as *ideal*, is only *in itself* and is consequently a unity which is only *sought*. This is *matter* and its ideal system — Mechanics;

II. in the determination of *particularity*, so that reality is posited with an immanent determinateness of form and with an existent difference in it. This is a relationship of Reflection whose being-within-self is natural *individuality* — Physics;

III. in the determination of *subjectivity*, in which the real differences of form are also brought back to the *ideal* unity which has found itself and is for itself — Organics.

SECTION ONE — MECHANICS

§253. Mechanics treats of:

A. self-externality in its complete abstraction — Space and Time;

B. self-externality as individualized and its relation in that state of abstraction, i.e. *Matter* and *Motion* — Finite Mechanics;

C. Matter in the freedom of its intrinsic Notion, in its *free motion* — *Absolute* Mechanics.

A. Space and Time

1. Space

§254. The first or immediate determination of Nature is *Space*: the abstract *universality of Nature's self-externality*, self-externality's mediation-less indifference. It is a wholly ideal *side-by-sideness* because it is self-externality; and it is absolutely *continuous*, because this asunderness is still quite *abstract*, and contains no specific difference within itself.

Remark. A number of different theories have been put forward about the nature of space. I will mention only the Kantian definition that space, like time, is a form of *sensuous intuition*. It has also become usual elsewhere to lay down as a principle that space must be regarded only as something subjective in our ideas. Disregarding what belongs in the Kantian conception to subjective idealism and its determinations, there remains the correct definition that space is a mere form, i.e. an *abstraction*, that of immediate *externality*. It is not permissible to speak of *points of space*, as if they constituted the positive element of space, since space, on account of its lack of difference, is only the possibility and not the actual *positedness* of being-outside-of-one-another and of the negative, and is therefore absolutely continuous; the point, the being-for-self, is consequently rather the *negation* of space, a negation which is posited in space. This also settles the question of the infinitude of space (§100 *Remark*). Space is simply pure Quantity, only no longer as a logical determination, but as existing immediately and externally. Nature, consequently, does not begin with the qualitative but with the quantitative, because its determination is not, like Being in Logic, the abstractly First and immediate, but a Being already essentially *mediated* within itself, an external- and other-being.

§255. Space, as in itself the Notion as such, contains within itself the *differences* of the Notion. (α) In the indifference of space, these are immediately the three *dimensions*, which are merely *diverse* and possess no determination whatever.

Remark. Geometry is not required to deduce that space necessarily has just three dimensions, because it is not a philosophical science, and may presuppose as its subject-matter space with its universal determinations. But apart from this, no thought is given to the necessity of such a deduction. The necessity is based on the nature of the Notion, whose determinations in this first form of asunderness, in *abstract* Quantity, are altogether superficial and a completely empty difference. The reason, therefore, why it cannot be said how *height, length*, and *breadth* differ from each other is that these three dimensions only *ought* to be different, but that they *are* not yet differences. It is not at all fixed whether a direction is called height, length, or breadth. The more precise definition of *height* is to be in the direction of the centre of the earth; but this more concrete determination does not concern the nature of space in itself. Even assuming this definition, it is still immaterial whether this direction is called height or depth; and it also does not serve to determine length and breadth, which is also often called depth.

§256. (β) The difference of space is, however, essentially a determinate, qualitative difference. As such, it is (α), first, the *negation* of space itself, because this is immediate *differenceless* self-externality, the *point*. (β) But the negation is the negation *of space*, i.e. it is itself spatial. The point, as essentially this relation, i.e. as sublating itself, is the *line*, the first other-being, i.e. spatial being, of the point. (γ) The truth of other-being is, however, negation of the negation. The line consequently passes over into the plane, which, on the one hand, is a determinateness opposed to line and point, and so surface, simply as such, but, on the other hand, is the sublated negation of space. It is thus the restoration of the spatial totality which now contains the negative moment within itself, an *enclosing surface* which separates off a *single* whole space.

Remark. That the line does not consist of points, nor the plane of lines, follows from their Notion; for the line is rather the point existing *outside* of itself, i.e. *relating* itself to space and sublating itself, and the plane, similarly, is the sublated line existing outside of itself. Here the point is conceived as the primary and positive element which forms the starting-point. But the converse is also true; inasmuch as space, not point, is in fact the positive element, the plane is the first negation, and the line the second; but as the second negation of space the line is, in its truth, the negation which relates self to self, the point. The necessity of the transition is the same. In the external way of understanding and defining the point, line, etc., no thought is given to the necessity of this transition. It is true that the first kind of transition is envisaged, though only as something contingent, in the form of the definition that when the point *moves*, the line is formed, etc. The other configurations of space considered by geometry are further qualitative limitations of an abstract division of space, of the plane, or of a bounded spatial whole. Here, too, there enters an element of necessity; e.g. that the triangle is the first rectilinear figure, that all other figures can only be determined by reducing them to the triangle or the square, and so on. The principle of these constructions is the identity of the Understanding, which subordinates figures to a *regularity*, and so establishes relationships between them which it is thereby possible to know.

We may note in passing that it was a singular opinion of Kant's that the definition of the *straight line* as the shortest distance between two points is a synthetic proposition, since my *concept* of *straight* involves nothing of quantity, but only a quality. In this sense every definition is a synthetic proposition. What is defined, *the straight line*, is at first only intuition or figurate conception; the definition that it is the shortest distance between two points, first constitutes the *notion* (that is, as it appears in such definitions: §229). That the *notion* is not already given in *intuition*, is the difference between them which makes a definition necessary. However, the definition is obviously analytic, since the straight line can be reduced to simplicity of direction; and simplicity with reference to *manifoldness* yields the determination of the *least* manifold, here of the shortest distance.

2. Time

§257. Negativity, as point, relates itself to space, in which it develops its determinations as line and plane; but in the sphere of self-externality, negativity is equally *for itself* and so are its determinations; but, at the same time, these are posited in the sphere of self-externality, and negativity, in so doing, appears as indifferent to the inert side-by-sideness of space. Negativity, thus posited for itself, is Time.

§258. Time, as the negative unity of self-externality, is similarly an out-and-out abstract, ideal being. It is that being which, inasmuch as it *is*, is *not*, and inasmuch as it is *not*, *is*: it is Becoming directly *intuited*; this means that differences, which admittedly are purely *momentary*, i.e. directly self-sublating, are determined as *external*, i.e. as external to *themselves*.

Remark. Time, like space, is a *pure form* of *sense* or *intuition*, the non-sensuous sensuous; but, as in the case of space, the distinction of objectivity and a subjective consciousness confronting it, does not apply to time. If these determinations were applied to space and time, the former would then be abstract objectivity, the latter abstract subjectivity. Time is the same principle as the I = I of pure self-consciousness, but this principle, or the simple Notion, still in its uttermost externality and abstraction — as intuited mere *Becoming*, pure being-within-self as sheer coming-out-of-self.

Time is *continuous*, too, like space, for it is the negativity abstractly relating self to self, and in this abstraction there is as yet no real difference.

Everything, it is said, *comes to be* and *passes away* in time. If abstraction is made from *everything*, namely from what fills time, and also from what fills space, then what we have left over is empty time and empty space: in other words, these abstractions of externality are posited and represented as if they were for themselves. But it is not *in* time that everything comes to be and passes away, rather time itself is the *becoming*, this coming-to-be and passing away, the *actually existent abstraction*, *Chronos*, from whom everything is born and by whom its offspring is destroyed. The real is certainly distinct from time, but is also essentially identical with it. What is real is limited, and the Other to this negation is *outside* it; therefore the determinateness in it is self-external and is consequently the contradiction of its being; the abstraction of this externality and unrest of its contradiction is time itself. The finite is perishable and *temporal* because, unlike the Notion, it is not in its own self total negativity; true, this negativity is immanent in it as its universal essence, but the finite is not adequate to this essence: it is *one-sided*, and consequently it is related to negativity as to the power that dominates it. The Notion, however, in its freely self-existent identity as I = I, is in and for itself absolute negativity and freedom. Time, therefore, has no power over the Notion, nor is the Notion in time or temporal; on the contrary, *it* is the power over time, which is this negativity only *qua* externality. Only the natural, therefore, is subject to time in so far as it is finite; the True, on the other hand, the Idea, Spirit, is *eternal*. But the notion of eternity must not be grasped negatively as abstraction from time, as existing, as it were, outside of time; nor in a sense which makes eternity come *after* time, for this would turn eternity into futurity, one of the moments of time.

§259. The dimensions of time, *present, future*, and *past*, are the *becoming* of externality as such, and the resolution of it into the differences of being as passing over into nothing, and of nothing as passing over into being. The immediate vanishing of these differences into *singularity* is the present as *Now* which, as singularity, is *exclusive* of the other moments, and at the same time completely *continuous* in them, and is only this vanishing of its being into nothing and of nothing into its being.

Remark. The *finite* present is the *Now* fixed as *being* and distinguished as the concrete unity, and hence as the affirmative, from what is *negative*, from the abstract moments of past and future; but this being is itself only abstract, vanishing into nothing. Furthermore, in Nature where time is a *Now*, being does not reach the *existence* of the difference of these dimensions; they are, of necessity, only in subjective imagination, in *remembrance* and *fear* or *hope*. But the past and future of time as *being* in Nature, are space, for space is negated time; just as sublated space is immediately the point, which developed for itself is time.

There is no *science of time* corresponding to the *science of space*, to *geometry*. The differences of time have not this *indifference* of self-externality which constitutes the immediate determinateness of space, and they are consequently not capable of being expressed, like space, in configurations. The principle of time is only capable of being so expressed when the Understanding has paralysed it and reduced its negativity to the *unit*. This inert One, the uttermost externality of thought, can be used to form external combinations, and these, the numbers of *arithmetic*, can in turn be brought by the Understanding under the categories of equality and inequality, of identity and difference.

One could also conceive the idea of a philosophical mathematics knowing by Notions, what ordinary mathematics deduces from hypotheses according to the method of the Understanding. However, as mathematics is the science of finite determinations of magnitude which are supposed to remain fixed and valid in their finitude and not to pass beyond it, mathematics is essentially a science of the Understanding; and since it is able to be this in a perfect manner, it is better that it should maintain this superiority over other sciences of the kind, and not allow itself to become adulterated either by mixing itself with the Notion, which is of a quite different nature, or by empirical applications. There is nothing in that to hinder the Notion from establishing a more definite consciousness alike of the leading principles of the Understanding and also of order and its necessity in arithmetical operations (§102) as well as in the theorems of geometry.

Furthermore, it would be a superfluous and thankless task to try to express *thoughts* in such a refractory and inadequate medium as spatial figures and numbers, and to do violence to these for this purpose. The simple elementary figures and numbers, on account of their simplicity, can be used for *symbols* without fear of misunderstanding; but even so, these symbols are too heterogeneous and cumbersome to express thought. The first efforts of pure thought had recourse to such aids, and the Pythagorean system of numbers is the famous example of this. But with richer notions these means become completely inadequate, because their *external* juxtaposition and their contingent combination do not accord at all with the nature of the Notion, and it is altogether ambiguous which of the many possible relationships in complex numbers and figures should be stuck to. Besides, the fluid character of the Notion is dissipated in such an external medium, in which each determination is indifferent to and outside the others. This ambiguity could be removed only by an *explanation*; but then the essential expression of the thought is this explanation, so that the representation by symbols becomes a worthless superfluity.

Other mathematical determinations such as the *infinite and its relationships*, the *infinitesimal, factors, powers*, etc., have their true notions in philosophy itself; it is inept to employ these determinations in philosophy, borrowing them from mathematics where they are employed in a notionless, often meaningless way; rather must they await their justification and meaning from philosophy. It is only indolence which, to spare itself the labour of thought and notional determination, takes refuge in formulae which are not even an immediate expression of thought, and in their ready-made schemata.

The truly philosophical science of mathematics as *theory of magnitude*, would be the science of *measures*; but this already presupposes the real particularity of things, which is found only in concrete Nature. On account of the *external* nature of magnitude, this would certainly also be the most difficult of all sciences.

3. Place and Motion

§260. Space is within itself the contradiction of indifferent asunderness and differenceless continuity, the pure negativity of itself, and the *transition, first of all, into time*. Similarly, time is the immediate *collapse* into indifference, into undifferentiated asunderness or *space*, because its opposed moments which are held together in unity, immediately sublate themselves. In this way, the *negative* determination in space, the *exclusive* point, no longer only implicitly conforms to the Notion, but is *posited* and *concrete* within itself, through the total negativity which is time; the point, as thus concrete, is *Place* (§255, 256).

§261. Place, as this *posited* identity of space and time is equally, at first, the posited *contradiction* which space and time are each in themselves. Place is spatial, and therefore indifferent, *singularity*; and it is this only as a *spatial Now*, as time, so that place is immediately indifferent towards itself as *this* place, is external to itself, the negation of itself, and is *another place*. This *vanishing* and *self-regeneration* of space in time and of time in space, a process in which time posits itself spatially as *place*, but in which place, too, as indifferent spatiality, is immediately posited as *temporal*: this is *Motion*. This becoming, however, is itself just as much the collapse within itself of its contradiction, the *immediately identical* and *existent* unity of both, namely, *Matter*.

Remark. The transition from ideality to reality, from abstraction to concrete existence, in this case from space and time to reality, which appears as matter, is incomprehensible to the Understanding; consequently, the transition always presents itself to the Understanding as an external affair, as something already given. The usual conception of space and time takes them to be *empty* and indifferent to what fills them, and yet they are to be considered as always filled, that is, *empty* space and time are *filled* with matter from outside. In this way, material things are, on the one hand, regarded as indifferent to space and time, and yet at the same time as essentially spatial and temporal.

It is said of matter: (α) that it is *composite*; this refers to its abstract asunderness, to space. In so far as abstraction is made from time and all forms generally, it is asserted that matter is eternal and immutable. This, in fact, follows immediately; but such a matter is also only an untrue abstraction. It is said (β) that it is *impenetrable* and *offers resistance*, is tangible, visible, and so on. These predicates signify nothing else than that matter exists, partly for specific forms of perception, in general, for an Other, and partly that it exists just as much *for itself*. Both these determinations belong to matter precisely because it is the *identity* of space and time, of immediate *asunderness* and of *negativity* or *self-subsistent* singularity.

The *transition of ideality into reality* is explicitly demonstrated in the familiar mechanical phenomena, namely, that ideality can take the place of reality, and vice versa; and only the notionless thinking of the imagination and the Understanding are to blame if the identity of both is not inferred from their interchangeability. In connection with the *lever*, for instance, *distance* can take the place of *mass*, and vice versa, and a quantum of ideal moment produces the same effect as the corresponding real amount. Similarly, in connection with the *magnitude of motion, velocity*, which is simply the quantitative relationship of space and time, can take the place of *mass*; and conversely, the real effect is the same if the mass is increased and the velocity proportionately decreased. A brick does not kill a man just because it is a brick, but brings about such a result only by virtue of the velocity it has acquired; that is to say, the man is killed by space and time. It is *Force*, a category of reflection fixed by the Understanding, which presents itself here as ultimate, and prevents the Understanding from inquiring further into the relationship of its categories. But this at least is adumbrated, that the *effect* of force is something real, appealing to sense, also that *force* and its *expression* have the same content and that the *real expression of* this force is achieved through the relation of its ideal moments, space and time.

It is also in keeping with this notionless reflection that the so-called forces are regarded as *implanted* in matter, that is to say, as originally *external* to it, with the result that this very identity of time and space which is vaguely present in the reflective category of Force, and which in truth constitutes the *essence* of matter, is posited as something *alien* to it and *contingent*, something introduced into it from outside.

XI. Philosophy of Mind: Introduction*

377. The knowledge of mind is the highest and hardest, just because it is the most concrete, knowledge. The meaning of that absolute command-ment, *Know thyself*—whether in itself or in the historical circumstances of its first utterance—is not mere self-knowledge in respect of the *particular* capacities, character, propensities, and foibles of the individual. The knowledge it commands means that of man's genuine reality, of what is essentially and ultimately true and real, of mind as the essence itself. Equally little is it the purport of the philosophy of mind to teach what is called *knowledge of men*, whose aim is to detect the *peculiarities*, passions, and foibles of other men, and lay bare what are called the recesses of the human heart. Information of this kind is, for one thing, senseless, unless on‛ the assumption that we know the *universal*—man as man, and thus essen-tially mind. And for another, being only engaged with casual, insignificant and *untrue* existences of mental life, it fails to reach the substantial, the mind itself.

378. Pneumatology, or, as it was also called, rational psychology, has been already alluded to in the Introduction as an *abstract* metaphysic of the understanding. *Empirical* psychology deals with the concrete mind; and, after the revival of the sciences, when observation and experience had become the main foundation of knowledge of the concrete, such psychol-ogy was worked on the same lines as other sciences. Thus the metaphysical element was kept outside the empirical science, and so prevented from getting any concrete determination or content; while at the same time the empirical science clung to the understanding's usual metaphysic, with its forces, various activities, etc., and rejected any speculative treatment.

The books of Aristotle on the soul, along with his discussions on its special aspects and states, are for this reason still by far the most admirable, perhaps even the sole, work of speculative value on this topic. The essen-tial aim of a philosophy of mind can only be to reintroduce the *concept* into the knowledge of mind, and so to redisclose the sense of those Aristotelian books.

*From the third (1830) edition of *The Encyclopaedia of the Philosophical Sciences in Outline*. Translated by William Wallace, with revisions by M. J. Inwood.

379. The feeling of self, of the mind's *living* unity, automatically protests against any attempt to break it up into diverse faculties, forces, or, what comes to the same thing, activities, conceived as independent of each other. But the need for *comprehension* here is still further stimulated, as we soon come across contrasts between the mind's freedom and its determinism, between free *psychic* agency and the corporeity external to it, and again the intimate interconnection of the two. In modern times especially, the phenomena of *animal magnetism* have given, even in experience, an intuitive confirmation of the substantial unity of soul, and of the power of its ideality. Before these facts, the rigid distinctions of the understanding were struck with confusion; and the necessity of a speculative examination with a view to the resolution of the contradictions is more directly displayed.

380. The concrete nature of mind involves for the observer the peculiar difficulty that the particular stages and determinations of the development of its concept do not remain behind as particular existences confronting its deeper structures. It is otherwise in external nature, where matter and movement have their free existence in the solar system; and the determinations of the senses also have a retrospective existence in the properties of *bodies*, and still more freely in the elements. The determinations and stages of the mind, on the contrary, are essential only as moments, states, and determinations in the higher stages of development. Consequently, a lower and more abstract determination betrays the presence in it, empirically, of a higher phase. In sensation, e.g., we may find all the higher mental life as its content or determinacy. And so sensation, which is but an abstract form, may superficially seem to be the essential seat and even the root of that ethical and religious content; and the determinations of that content may seem to call for treatment as particular species of sensation. But at the same time, when lower stages of mental life are under examination, it becomes necessary, if we desire to point to them in their empirical existence, to direct attention to higher stages in which they are present as mere forms. In this way content will be treated of by anticipation which properly belongs to later stages of development (e.g., in dealing with natural awaking from sleep we speak by anticipation of consciousness, or in dealing with mental derangement we must speak of intellect).

CONCEPT OF MIND

381. *For us* mind has for its *presupposition* nature, of which it is the truth, and for that reason its *absolute prius*. In this its truth nature is vanished, and mind has resulted as the Idea entered on its being for itself. Here the subject and object of the Idea are one: the concept. This identity is *absolute negativity*—for whereas in nature the concept has its objectivity perfect but external, this self-externalization has been sublimated and the concept in that externalization has become identical with itself. Thus at the same time it *is* this identity only so far as it is a return out of nature.

382. For this reason the essence of mind is formally liberty, the concept's absolute negativity as self-identity. By this formal determination, it *may* abstract from everything external and from its own externality, its own determinate being; it can thus submit to infinite *pain*, the negation of its individual immediacy; in other words, it can keep itself affirmative in this negativity and possess its own identity. This possibility is its abstract universality within itself, a universality that is for itself.

383. This universality is also its determinate being. As being for itself, the universal is self-particularising, while it still remains self-identical. Hence the determinacy of the mind is *manifestation*. The mind is not some determinacy or content whose utterance or externality is only a form distinct from itself; it does not reveal *something*, but its determinacy and content is this revelation. And thus its possibility is immediately an infinite, absolute, *actuality*.

384. *Revelation*, as the *abstract* Idea, is an unmediated transition to nature that *comes* to be. As mind is free, *its* revelation is to *posit* nature as *its* world; but because it is reflection, it, in thus positing its world, at the same time *presupposes* the world as an independent nature. In the concept to reveal is to create a world as its being — a being in which the mind procures the *affirmation* and *truth* of its freedom.

The absolute is mind — this is the supreme definition of the absolute. To find this definition and to comprehend its sense and content was, we may say, the absolute tendency of all education and philosophy: it was the point to which all religion and science pressed on; from this drive alone can we comprehend the history of the world. The word 'mind,' and the conception of it, was found early on; and the spirituality of God is the content of Christianity. It remains for philosophy in its own element, the concept, to get hold of what was thus given as a conception, and *implicitly* is the essence; and that problem is not genuinely and immanently solved so long as liberty and the concept are not the object and the soul of philosophy.

385. The development of mind is in three stages:

1. In the form of self-relation: within it arises the *ideal* totality of the Idea — i.e., what its concept is becomes for it, and its being is to be self-contained and free. This is *mind subjective.*

2. In the form of *reality* as a *world* produced and to be produced by it; in this world freedom presents itself as necessity. This is *mind objective.*

3. In that *unity* of mind's objectivity and of mind's ideality or its concept, which essentially and actually is and eternally produces itself, mind in its absolute truth. This is *mind absolute.*

386. The two first parts of the doctrine of mind embrace the finite mind. Mind is the infinite Idea; thus finitude here means the disproportion between the concept and the reality with the determination that it is a show within the mind—a show that the mind implicitly posits as a barrier to itself, in order, by its sublimation, *for itself* to have and know freedom as *its* essence, i.e., to be fully *manifested*. The several stages of this activity, on each of which, as the show, it is the destiny of the finite mind to linger, and through which it has to pass, are stages of its liberation. In the full truth of that liberation the following are one and the same: *finding* a world presupposed before it, *generating* a world as posited by it, and gaining freedom from it and in it. To the infinite form of this truth the show purifies itself till it becomes knowledge of it.

A rigid application of the category of finitude by the *understanding* is chiefly seen in dealing with mind and reason: it is held not only a matter of the understanding, but also a moral and religious concern, to adhere to the point of view of finitude, and the wish to go further is reckoned a mark of audacity, if not of insanity, of thought. Whereas in fact such a *modesty* of thought, as treats the finite as something altogether fixed and *absolute*, is the worst of virtues; and to stick to what does not have its ground in itself is the most unsound of cognitions. The category of finitude was much earlier elucidated and explained at its place in the Logic: an elucidation that, as in logic for the further determined though still simple thought-forms of finitude, so in the rest of philosophy for the concrete forms of it, has merely to show that the finite *is not*, i.e., not the truth, but merely a transition and a transcendence of itself. This finite of the previous spheres is the dialectic of having its demise through another and in another; but mind, the concept and the *implicit* eternal, is itself just the consummation within itself of the process by which nullity is nullified and vanity is made vain. The modesty alluded to is a retention of this vanity—the finite—in opposition to the true: It is itself therefore vanity. In the mind's development itself this vanity will appear as *wickedness* at that turning-point at which mind has reached its extreme immersion in its subjectivity and its innermost contradiction.

XII.   Philosophy of Right: Preface*

The immediate inducement to publish this manual is the need for putting into the hands of my audience a text-book for the lectures on the Philosophy of Right which I deliver in the course of my professional duties. This compendium is an enlarged and especially a more systematic exposition of the same fundamental concepts which in relation to this part of philosophy are already contained in a book of mine designed previously for my lectures — the *Encyclopaedia of Philosophical Sciences* (Heidelberg, 1817).

But this manual was to appear in print and therefore it now comes before the general public; and this was my inducement to amplify here a good many of the Remarks which were primarily meant in a brief compass to indicate ideas akin to my argument or at variance with it, further inferences from it, and the like, i.e. material which would receive its requisite elucidation in my lectures. The object of amplifying them here was to clarify occasionally the more abstract parts of the text and to take a more comprehensive glance at current ideas widely disseminated at the present time. Hence the result has been a number of Remarks rather more extensive than is usually consistent with the style and aim of a compendium. Apart from that, however, a compendium proper has as its subject-matter what is taken to be the closed circle of a science; and what is appropriate in it, except perhaps for a small addition here and there, is principally the assembly and arrangement of the essential factors in a content which has long been familiar and accepted, just as the form in which it is arranged has its rules and artifices which have long been settled. *Philosophical* manuals are perhaps not now expected to conform to such a pattern, for it is supposed that what philosophy puts together is a work as ephemeral as Penelope's web, one which must be begun afresh every morning.

I need hardly say that the chief difference between this manual and an ordinary compendium lies in the method which constitutes their guiding principle. But in this book I am presupposing that philosophy's mode of progression from one topic to another and its mode of scientific proof — this

---

*Translated by T. M. Knox. Pages 1–13 (Hegel's Preface) from Hegel's *Philosophy of Right* translated by T. M. Knox (1942). Reprinted by permission of Oxford University Press.

whole speculative way of knowing—is essentially distinct from any other
way of knowing. It is only insight into the necessity of such a difference that
can rescue philosophy from the shameful decay in which it is immersed at
the present time. It is true that the forms and rules of the old logic, of
definition, classification, and syllogism, which include the rules of discur-
sive thinking, have become recognized as inadequate for speculative
science; or rather their inadequacy has not been recognized; it has only
been felt, and then these rules have been thrown off as if they were mere
fetters in order to allow the heart, the imagination, and casual intuition to
say what they pleased. And since reflection and connexions of thought have
after all to come on the scene as well, there is an unconscious relapse into
the despised method of commonplace deduction and argumentation.

Since I have fully expounded the nature of speculative knowing in my
Science of Logic, in this manual I have only added an explanatory note here
and there about procedure and method. In dealing with a topic which is
concrete and intrinsically of so varied a character, I have omitted to bring
out and demonstrate the chain of logical argument in each and every detail.
For one thing, to have done this might have been regarded as superfluous
where acquaintance with philosophical method is presupposed; for another,
it will be obvious from the work itself that the whole, like the formation of
its parts, rests on the logical spirit. It is also from this point of view above all
that I should like my book to be taken and judged. What we have to do
with here is philosophical *science*, and in such science content is essentially
bound up with form.

We may of course hear from those who seem to be taking a profound
view that the form is something external and indifferent to the subject-
matter, that the latter alone is important; further, the task of a writer,
especially a writer on philosophy, may be said to lie in the discovery of
truth, the statement of truth, the dissemination of truth and sound concepts. But if we consider how this task is as a rule actually discharged, what
we find in the first place is that the same old stew is continually warmed up
again and again and served round to everybody—a task that will even be
meritorious in educating and stimulating men's hearts, though it might
preferably be regarded as the superfluous labour of a busybody—'They
have Moses and the Prophets, let them hear them.' In particular, we have
ample opportunity to marvel at the pretentious tone recognizable in these
busybodies when they talk as if the world had wanted for nothing except
their energetic dissemination of truths, or as if their *réchauffé* were productive of new and unheard-of truths and was to be specially taken to heart
before everything else 'to-day' and every day. But in this situation we also
find one party giving out truths of this sort only to have them dislodged and
brushed aside by truths of just the same sort purveyed by other parties. In
this press of truths, there is something neither new nor old but perennial;
yet how else is this to be lifted out of these reflections which oscillate from

this to that without method, how else is it to be separated from them and proved, if not by philosophic science?

After all, the truth about Right, Ethics, and the state is as old as its public recognition and formulation in the law of the land, in the morality of everyday life, and in religion. What more does this truth require — since the thinking mind is not content to possess it in this ready fashion? It requires to be grasped in thought as well; the content which is already rational in principle must win the *form* of rationality and so appear well-founded to untrammelled thinking. Such thinking does not remain stationary at the given, whether the given be upheld by the external positive authority of the state or the *consensus hominum*, or by the authority of inward feeling and emotion and by the 'witness of the spirit' which directly concurs with it. On the contrary, thought which is free starts out from itself and thereupon claims to know itself as united in its innermost being with the truth.

The unsophisticated heart takes the simple line of adhering with trustful conviction to what is publicly accepted as true and then building on this firm foundation its conduct and its set position in life. Against this simple line of conduct there may at once be raised the alleged difficulty of how it is possible, in an infinite variety of opinions, to distinguish and discover what is universally recognized and valid. This perplexity may at first sight be taken for a right and really serious attitude to the thing, but in fact those who boast of this perplexity are in the position of not being able to see the wood for the trees; the only perplexity and difficulty they are in is one of their own making. Indeed, this perplexity and difficulty of theirs is proof rather that they want as the substance of the right and the ethical not what is universally recognized and valid, but something else. If they had been serious with what is universally accepted instead of busying themselves with the vanity and particularity of opinions and things, they would have clung to what is substantively right, namely to the commands of the ethical order and the state, and would have regulated their lives in accordance with these.

A more serious difficulty arises, however, from the fact that man thinks and tries to find in thinking both his freedom and the basis of ethical life. But however lofty, however divine, the right of thought may be, it is perverted into wrong if it is only this [opining] which passes for thinking and if thinking knows itself to be free only when it diverges from what is *universally* recognized and valid and when it has discovered how to invent for itself some *particular* character.

At the present time, the idea that freedom of thought, and of mind generally, evinces itself only in divergence from, indeed in hostility to, what is publicly recognized, might seem to be most firmly rooted in connexion with the state, and it is chiefly for this reason that a philosophy of the state might seem essentially to have the task of discovering and promulgating still another theory, and a special and original one at that. In examining this idea and the activity in conformity with it, we might suppose that no state or constitution had ever existed in the world at all or was even in being at the present time, but that nowadays — and this 'nowadays' lasts for ever — we had to start all over again from the beginning, and that the ethical world had just been waiting for such present-day projects, proofs, and investigations. So far as nature is concerned, people grant that it is nature as it is which philosophy has to bring within its ken, that the philosopher's stone lies concealed somewhere, somewhere within nature itself, that nature is inherently rational, and that what knowledge has to investigate and grasp in concepts is this actual reason present in it; not the formations and accidents evident to the superficial observer, but nature's eternal harmony, its harmony, however, in the sense of the law and essence immanent within it. The ethical world, on the other hand, the state (i.e. reason as it actualizes itself in the element of self-consciousness), is not allowed to enjoy the good fortune which springs from the fact that it is reason which has achieved power and mastery within that element and which maintains itself and has its home there. The universe of mind is supposed rather to be left to the mercy of chance and caprice, to be God-forsaken, and the result is that if the ethical world is Godless, truth lies outside it, and at the same time, since even so reason is supposed to be in it as well, truth becomes nothing but a problem. But it is this also that is to authorize, nay to oblige, every thinker to take his own road, though not in search of the philosopher's stone, for he is saved this search by the philosophizing of our contemporaries, and everyone nowadays is assured that he has this stone in his grasp as his birthright. Now admittedly it is the case that those who live their lives in the state as it actually exists here and now and find satisfaction there for their knowledge and volition (and of these there are many, more in fact than think or know it, because ultimately this is the position of everybody), or those at any rate who *consciously* find their satisfaction in the state, laugh at these operations and affirmations and regard them as an empty game, sometimes rather funny, sometimes rather serious, now amusing, now dangerous. Thus this restless activity of empty reflection, together with its popularity and the welcome it has received, would be a thing on its own, developing in privacy in its own way, were it not that it is philosophy itself which has earned all kinds of scorn and discredit by its indulgence in this occupation. The worst of these kinds of scorn is this, that, as I said just now, everyone is convinced that his mere birthright puts him in a position to pass judgement on philosophy in general and to condemn it. No other art or science is subjected to this last degree of scorn, to the supposition that we are masters of it without ado.

In fact, what we have seen recent philosophical publications proclaiming with the maximum of pretension about the state has really justified anybody who cared to busy himself with the subject in this conviction that he could manufacture a philosophy of this kind himself without ado and so give himself proof of his possession of philosophy. Besides, this self-styled 'philosophy' has expressly stated that 'truth itself cannot be known', that that only is true which each individual allows to rise out of his heart, emotion, and inspiration about ethical institutions, especially about the state, the government, and the constitution. In this connexion what a lot of flattery has been talked, especially to the young! Certainly the young have listened to it willingly enough. 'He giveth to his own in sleep' has been applied to science and hence every sleeper has numbered himself among the elect, but the concepts he has acquired in sleep are themselves of course only the wares of sleep.

A ringleader of these hosts of superficiality, of these self-styled 'philosophers', Herr Fries,* did not blush, on the occasion of a public festival which has become notorious, to express the following ideas in a speech on 'The state and the constitution': 'In the people ruled by a genuine communal spirit, life for the discharge of all public business would come from below, from the people itself; living associations, indissolubly united by the holy chain of friendship, would be dedicated to every single project of popular education and popular service', and so on. This is the quintessence of shallow thinking, to base philosophic science not on the development of thought and the concept but on immediate sense-perception and the play of fancy; to take the rich inward articulation of ethical life, i.e. the state, the architectonic of that life's rationality — which sets determinate limits to the different circles of public life and their rights, uses the strict accuracy of measurement which holds together every pillar, arch, and buttress and thereby produces the strength of the whole out of the harmony of the parts — to take this structure and confound the completed fabric in the broth of 'heart, friendship, and inspiration'. According to a view of this kind, the world of ethics (Epicurus, holding a similar view, would have said the 'world in general') should be given over — as in fact of course it is not — to the subjective accident of opinion and caprice. By the simple family remedy of ascribing to feeling the labour, the more than millenary labour, of reason and its intellect, all the trouble of rational insight and knowledge directed by speculative thinking is of course saved. On this point, Goethe's Mephistopheles, a good authority!, says something like this, a quotation I have used elsewhere already: 'Do but despise intellect and knowledge, the highest of all man's gifts, and thou hast surrendered thyself to the devil and to perdition art doomed.' The next thing is that such sentiments assume even the guise of piety, for this bustling activity has used any and every expedient in its endeavour to give itself authority. With godliness and the Bible, however, it has arrogated to itself the highest

---

*I have borne witness before to the superficiality of his philosophy — see *Science of Logic* (Nuremberg, 1812), Introduction, p. xvii.

of justifications for despising the ethical order and the objectivity of law, since it is piety too which envelops in the simpler intuition of feeling the truth which is articulated in the world into an organic realm. But if it is piety of the right sort, it sheds the form of this emotional region so soon as it leaves the inner life, enters upon the daylight of the Idea's development and revealed riches, and brings with it, out of its inner worship of God, reverence for law and for an absolute truth exalted above the subjective form of feeling.

The particular form of guilty conscience revealed by the type of elo-quence in which such superficiality flaunts itself may be brought to your attention here and above all if you notice that when it is furthest from mind, superficiality speaks most of mind, when its talk is the most tedious dead-and-alive stuff, its favourite words are 'life' and 'vitalize', and when it gives evidence of the pure selfishness of baseless pride, the word most on its lips is 'people'. But the special mark which it carries on its brow is the hatred of law. Right and ethics, and the actual world of justice and ethical life, are understood through thoughts; through thoughts they are invested with a rational form, i.e. with universality and determinacy. This form is law; and this it is which the feeling that stipulates for its own whim, the conscience that places right in subjective conviction, has reason to regard as its chief foe. The formal character of the right as a duty and a law it feels as the letter, cold and dead, as a shackle; for it does not recognize itself in the law and so does not recognize itself as free there, because law is the reason of the thing, and reason refuses to allow feeling to warm itself at its own private hearth. Hence law, as I have remarked somewhere in the course of this text-book, is *par excellence* the shibboleth which marks out these false friends and comrades of what they call the 'people'.

At the present time, the pettifoggery of caprice has usurped the name of philosophy and succeeded in giving a wide public the opinion that such triflings are philosophy. The result of this is that it has now become almost a disgrace to go on speaking in philosophical terms about the nature of the state, and law-abiding men cannot be blamed if they become impatient so soon as they hear mention of a philosophical science of the state. Still less is it a matter for surprise that governments have at last directed their atten-tion to this kind of philosophy, since, apart from anything else, philosophy with us is not, as it was with the Greeks for instance, pursued in private like an art, but has an existence in the open, in contact with the public, and especially, or even only, in the service of the state. Governments have proved their trust in their scholars who have made philosophy their chosen field by leaving entirely to them the construction and contents of philosophy — though here and there, if you like, it may not have been so much confidence that has been shown as indifference to learning itself, and professorial chairs of philosophy have been retained only as a tradition (in France, for instance, to the best of my knowledge, chairs of metaphysics at least have been allowed to lapse). Their confidence, however, has very often been ill repaid, or alternatively, if you preferred to see indifference, you would have to regard the result, the decay of thorough knowledge, as the penalty of this indifference. Prima facie, superficiality seems to be extremely accommodating, one might say, at least in relation to public peace and order, because it fails to touch or even to guess at the substance of the things; no action, or at least no police action, would thus have been taken against it in the first instance, had it not been that there still existed in the state a need for a deeper education and insight, a need which the state required philosophical science to satisfy. On the other hand, superficial thinking about the ethical order, about right and duty in general, starts automatically from the maxims which constitute superficiality in this sphere, i.e. from the principles of the Sophists which are so clearly outlined for our information in Plato. What is right these principles locate in subjective aims and opinions, in subjective feeling and particular conviction, and from them there follows the ruin of the inner ethical life and a good conscience, of love and right dealing between private persons, no less than the ruin of public order and the law of the land. The significance which such phenomena must acquire for governments is not likely to suffer any diminution as a result of the pretentiousness which has used that very grant of confidence and the authority of a professorial chair to support the demand that the state should uphold and give scope to what corrupts the ultimate source of achievement, namely universal principles, and so even to the defiance of the state as if such defiance were what it deserved. 'If God gives a man an office, he also gives him brains' is an old joke which in these days surely no one will take wholly in earnest.

In the fresh importance which circumstances have led governments to attach to the character of philosophical work, there is one element which we cannot fail to notice; this is the protection and support which the study of philosophy now seems to have come to need in several other directions. Think of the numerous publications in the field of the positive sciences, as well as edifying religious works and vague literature of other kinds, which reveal to their readers the contempt for philosophy I have already mentioned, in that, although the thought in them is immature to the last degree and philosophy is entirely alien to them, they treat it as something over and done with. More than this, they expressly rail against it and pronounce its content, namely the speculative knowledge of God, nature, and mind, the knowledge of truth, to be a foolish and even sinful presumptuousness, while reason, and again reason, and reason repeated *ad infinitum* is arraigned, disparaged, and condemned. At the very least such writings reveal to us that to a majority of those engaged in activities supposedly scientific, the claims of the concept are an embarrassment which none the less they cannot escape. I venture to say that anyone with such phenomena before him may very well begin to think that, if they alone are considered,

tradition is now neither worthy of respect nor sufficient to secure for the study of philosophy either tolerance or existence as a public institution.*
The arrogant declamations current in our time against philosophy present the singular spectacle, on the one hand of deriving their justification from the superficiality to which that study has been degraded, and, on the other, of being themselves rooted in this element against which they turn so ungratefully. For by pronouncing the knowledge of truth a wild-goose chase, this self-styled philosophizing has reduced all thoughts and all topics to the same level, just as the despotism of the Roman Empire abolished the distinction between free men and slaves, virtue and vice, honour and dishonour, learning and ignorance. The result of this levelling process is that the concepts of what is true, the laws of ethics, likewise become nothing more than opinions and subjective convictions. The maxims of the worst of criminals, since they too are convictions, are put on the same level of value as those laws; and at the same time any object, however sorry, however accidental, any material however insipid, is put on the same level of value as what constitutes the interest of all thinking men and the bonds of the ethical world.

It is therefore to be taken as a piece of *luck* for philosophic science — though in actual fact, as I have said, it is the *necessity* of the thing — that this philosophizing which like an exercise in scholasticism might have continued to spin its web in seclusion, has now been put into closer touch and so into open variance with actuality, in which the principles of rights and duties are a serious matter, and which lives in the light of its consciousness of these.

It is just this placing of philosophy in the actual world which meets with misunderstandings, and so I revert to what I have said before, namely that, since philosophy is the exploration of the rational, it is for that very reason the apprehension of the present and the actual, not the erection of a beyond, supposed to exist, God knows where, or rather which exists, and we can perfectly well say where, namely in the error of a one-sided, empty, ratiocination. In the course of this book, I have remarked that even Plato's *Republic*, which passes proverbially as an empty ideal, is in essence nothing but an interpretation of the nature of Greek ethical life. Plato was conscious that there was breaking into that life in his own time a deeper principle which could appear in it directly only as a longing still unsatisfied, and so only as something corruptive. To combat it, he needs must have

*I came across a similar view in a letter of Joh. von Müller (*Werke*, Part vii, p. 57). In talking of the state of Rome in 1803 when the city was under French control, he says; 'Asked how the public educational institutions were faring, a professor replied *On les tolère comme les bordels.*' The so-called 'Doctrine of Reason', logic namely, we can indeed still hear recommended, perhaps with the conviction that it is such a dry and profitless science that nobody will busy himself with it, or that if here and there a man does take it up, he will thereby acquire mere empty formulae, unproductive and innocuous, and that therefore in either case the recommendation will do no harm, even if it does no good.

sought aid from that very longing itself. But this aid had to come from on High and all that Plato could do was to seek it in the first place in a particular external form of that same Greek ethical life. By that means he thought to master this corruptive invader, and thereby he did fatal injury to the deeper impulse which underlay it, namely free infinite personality. Still, his genius is proved by the fact that the principle on which the distinctive character of his Idea of the state turns is precisely the pivot on which the impending world revolution turned at that time.

What is rational is actual and what is actual is rational. On this conviction the plain man like the philosopher takes his stand, and from it philosophy starts in its study of the universe of mind as well as the universe of nature. If reflection, feeling, or whatever form subjective consciousness may take, looks upon the present as something vacuous and looks beyond it with the eyes of superior wisdom, it finds itself in a vacuum, and because it is actual only in the present, it is itself mere vacuity. If on the other hand the Idea passes for 'only an Idea', for something represented in an opinion, philosophy rejects such a view and shows that nothing is actual except the Idea. Once that is granted, the great thing is to apprehend in the show of the temporal and transient the substance which is immanent and the eternal which is present. For since rationality (which is synonymous with the Idea) enters upon external existence simultaneously with its actualization, it emerges with an infinite wealth of forms, shapes, and appearances. Around its heart it throws a motley covering with which consciousness is at home to begin with, a covering which the concept has first to penetrate before it can find the inward pulse and feel it still beating in the outward appearances. But the infinite variety of circumstance which is developed in this externa- lity by the light of the essence glinting in it—this endless material and its organization—this is not the subject matter of philosophy. To touch this at all would be to meddle with things to which philosophy is unsuited; on such topics it may save itself the trouble of giving good advice. Plato might have omitted his recommendation to nurses to keep on the move with infants and to rock them continually in their arms. And Fichte too need not have carried what has been called the 'construction' of his passport regulations to such a pitch of perfection as to require suspects not merely to sign their passports but to have their likenesses painted on them. Along such tracks all trace of philosophy is lost, and such super-erudition it can the more readily disclaim since its attitude to this infinite multitude of topics should of course be most liberal. In adopting this attitude, philosophic science shows itself to be poles apart from the hatred with which the folly of superior wisdom regards a vast number of affairs and institutions, a hatred in which pettiness takes the greatest delight because only by venting it does it attain a feeling of its self-hood.

This book, then, containing as it does the science of the state, is to be nothing other than the endeavour to apprehend and portray the state as something inherently rational. As a work of philosophy, it must be poles apart from an attempt to construct a state as it ought to be. The instruction which it may contain cannot consist in teaching the state what it ought to be; it can only show how the state, the ethical universe, is to be understood.

'Ιδοὺ 'Ρόδος ἰδοὺ καὶ τὸ πήδημα.
Hic Rhodus, *hic* saltus.

To comprehend what is, this is the task of philosophy, because what is, is reason. Whatever happens, every individual is a child of his time; so philosophy too is its own time apprehended in thoughts. It is just as absurd to fancy that a philosophy can transcend its contemporary world as it is to fancy that an individual can overleap his own age, jump over Rhodes. If his theory really goes beyond the world as it is and builds an ideal one as it ought to be, that world exists indeed, but only in his opinions, an unsubstantial element where anything you please may, in fancy, be built.

With hardly any alteration, the proverb just quoted would run:

Here is the rose, dance thou here.

What lies between reason as self-conscious mind and reason as an actual world before our eyes, what separates the former from the latter and prevents it from finding satisfaction in the latter, is the fetter of some abstraction or other which has not been liberated [and so transformed] into the concept. To recognize reason as the rose in the cross of the present and thereby to enjoy the present, this is the rational insight which reconciles us to the actual, the reconciliation which philosophy affords to those in whom there has once arisen an inner voice bidding them to comprehend, not only to dwell in what is substantive while still retaining subjective freedom, but also to possess subjective freedom while standing not in anything particular and accidental but in what exists absolutely.

It is this too which constitutes the more concrete meaning of what was described above rather abstractly as the unity of form and content; for form in its most concrete signification is reason as speculative knowing, and content is reason as the substantial essence of actuality, whether ethical or natural. The known identity of these two is the philosophical Idea. It is a sheer obstinacy, the obstinacy which does honour to mankind, to refuse to recognize in conviction anything not ratified by thought. This obstinacy is the characteristic of our epoch, besides being the principle peculiar to Protestantism. What Luther initiated as faith in feeling and in the witness of the spirit, is precisely what spirit, since become more mature, has striven to apprehend in the concept in order to free and so to find itself in the world as it exists to-day. The saying has become famous that 'a half-philosophy leads away from God' — and it is the same half-philosophy that locates knowledge in an 'approximation' to truth — 'while true philosophy leads to God'; and the same is true of philosophy and the state. Just as reason is not content with an approximation which, as something 'neither cold nor hot', it will 'spue out of its mouth', so it is just as little content with the cold despair which submits to the view that in this earthly life things are truly bad or at best only tolerable, though here they cannot be improved and that this is the only reflection which can keep us at peace with the world: There is less chill in the peace with the world which knowledge supplies.

One word more about giving instruction as to what the world ought to be. Philosophy in any case always comes on the scene too late to give it. As the thought of the world, it appears only when actuality is already there cut and dried after its process of formation has been completed. The teaching of the concept, which is also history's inescapable lesson, is that it is only when actuality is mature that the ideal first appears over against the real and that the ideal apprehends this same real world in its substance and builds it up for itself into the shape of an intellectual realm. When philosophy paints its grey in grey, then has a shape of life grown old. By philosophy's grey in grey it cannot be rejuvenated but only understood. The owl of Minerva spreads its wings only with the falling of the dusk.

But it is time to close this preface. After all, as a preface, its only business has been to make some external and subjective remarks about the standpoint of the book it introduces. If a topic is to be discussed philosophically, it spurns any but a scientific and objective treatment, and so too if criticisms of the author take any form other than a scientific discussion of the thing itself, they can count only as a personal epilogue and as capricious assertion, and he must treat them with indifference.

Berlin, June 25th, 1820

XIII. ENCYCLOPAEDIA: OBJECTIVE MIND*

PRACTICAL MIND

469. As will, the mind is aware that it is the author of its own conclusions, the origin of its self-fulfillment. Thus fulfilled, this independency[6] or individuality forms the side of existence or of *reality* for the Idea of mind. As will, the mind steps into actuality; whereas as knowledge it is on the soil of conceptual generality. Supplying its own content, the will is self-possessed, and in the widest sense free: this is its determinate concept. Its finitude lies in the formalism that the spontaneity of its self-fulfillment means no more than a general and abstract ownness, not yet identified with matured reason. It is the function of the essential[5] will to bring liberty to exist in the formal will, and it is therefore the aim of that formal will to fill itself with its concept, i.e. to make liberty its pervading character, content, and aim, as its sphere of existence. This concept, freedom, is, and must always be, thought: Hence the way by which will can make itself objective mind is to rise to be a thinking will, to give itself the content which it can only have as it thinks itself.

True liberty, in the shape of ethical life,[44] consists in the will finding its purpose in a universal content, not in subjective or selfish interests. But such a content is only possible in thought and through thought: it is nothing short of absurd to seek to banish thought from the ethical, religious, and law-abiding life.

470. Practical mind, considered at first as formal or immediate will, contains a double 'ought'—(1) in the contrast which the new mode of being projected outward by the will offers to the immediate positivity of its old existence and condition,—which in consciousness develops at the same time in relation to external objects. (2) That first self-determination, being itself immediate, is not at once elevated into thinking universality: The latter, therefore, virtually constitutes an obligation on the former in point of

*From the third (1830) edition of *The Encyclopaedia of the Philosophical Sciences in Outline.* Translated by William Wallace, with revisions by M. J. Inwood.

form, as it may also constitute it in point of matter — a contrast which at first is only for us.

α. Practical Feeling[24]

471. The autonomy of the practical mind at first is immediate and therefore formal, i.e. it *finds* itself as an *individuality* determined in *its* inward *nature*. It is thus practical feeling. In this phase, as it is at bottom a subjectivity simply identical with reason, it has no doubt a rational content, but a content which as it stands is individual, and for that reason also natural, contingent and subjective, — a content which may be determined quite as much by mere particularity of want and opinion, etc., and by the subjectivity which selfishly sets itself against the universal, as it may be virtually in conformity with reason.

An appeal is sometimes made to the feeling of right and morality, as well as of religion, which man is alleged to possess, to his benevolent dispositions, — and even to his heart generally, — i.e. to the subject so far as the various practical feelings are in it all combined. So far as this appeal implies (1) that these ideas are immanent in his own self, and (2) that when feeling is opposed to the understanding, it, and not the partial abstractions of the latter, *may* be the *totality* — the appeal has a legitimate meaning. But on the other hand feeling too *may* be one-sided, unessential, and bad. The rational, which exists in the shape of rationality when it is apprehended by thought, is the same content as the *good* practical feeling has, but presented in its universality and necessity, in its objectivity and truth.

Thus it is on the one hand *silly* to suppose that in the passage from feeling to law and duty there is any loss of import and excellence; it is this passage which lets feeling first reach its truth. It is equally silly to consider intellect as superfluous or even harmful to feeling, heart, and will; the truth and, what is the same thing, the actual rationality of the heart and will can only be at home in the universality of intellect, and not in the singleness of feeling as feeling. If feelings are of the right sort, it is because of their quality or content, which is right only so far as it is intrinsically universal or has its source in the thinking mind. The difficulty for the logical intellect consists in throwing off the separation it has arbitrarily imposed between the several faculties of feeling and thinking mind, and coming to see that in the human being there is only *one* reason, in feeling, volition, and thought. Another difficulty connected with this is found in the fact that the Ideas which are the special property of the thinking mind, viz. God, law and morality, can also be *felt*. But feeling is only the form of the immediate and peculiar individuality of the subject, in which this content, like any other objective content (which consciousness also sets over against itself), may be placed.

On the other hand, it is *suspicious* or even worse to cling to feeling and heart in place of the intelligent rationality of law, right and duty; because all that the former holds more than the latter is only particular subjectivity with its vanity and caprice.[58] For the same reason it is out of place in a scientific treatment of the feelings to deal with anything beyond their form, and to discuss their content; for the latter, when thought, is precisely what constitutes, in their universality and necessity, the rights and duties which are the true works of mental autonomy. So long as we study practical feelings and dispositions specially, we have only to deal with the selfish, bad, and evil; it is these alone which belong to the individuality which retains its opposition to the universal: their content is the reverse of rights and duties, and precisely in that way do they—but only in antithesis to the latter—retain a speciality of their own.

472. The 'Ought' of practical feeling is the claim of its essential autonomy to control some existing mode of fact—which is assumed to be worth nothing save as adapted to that claim. But as both, in their immediacy, lack objective determination, this relation of the *requirement* to existent fact is the utterly subjective and superficial feeling of pleasant or unpleasant.

Delight, joy, grief, &c., shame, repentance, contentment, &c., are partly only modifications of the formal 'practical feeling' in *general*, but are partly different in the features that give the special tone and character mode to their 'Ought.'

The celebrated question as to the origin of evil in the world, so far at least as evil is understood to mean what is disagreeable and painful merely, arises at this stage of formal practical feeling. Evil is nothing but the incompatibility between what is and what ought to be. 'Ought' is an ambiguous term,—indeed infinitely so, considering that casual aims may also come under the form of Ought. But where the objects sought are thus casual, evil only executes what is rightfully due to the vanity and nullity of their planning: for they themselves were radically evil. The finitude of life and mind is seen in their judgment: the contrary which is separated from them they also have as a negative in them, and thus they are the contradiction called evil. In the dead there is neither evil nor pain: for in inorganic nature the concept does not confront its existence and does not in the difference at the same time remain its permanent subject. Whereas in life, and still more in mind, we have this immanent distinction present: hence arises the Ought: and this negativity, subjectivity, ego, freedom are the principles of evil and pain. Jacob Böhme viewed egoity (selfhood) as pain and torment, and as the source of nature and of spirit.

β. The Impulses and Choice[58]

473. The practical ought is a *real* judgment. Will, which is essentially self-determination, finds in the conformity—as immediate and merely *found* to hand—of the existing mode to its requirement a negation, and something inappropriate to it. If the will is to satisfy itself, if the implicit unity of universality and determinacy is to be realised, the conformity of its inner requirement and of the existent thing ought to be its act and institution. The will, as regards the form of its content, is at first still a natural will, directly identical with its determinacy—natural *impulse* and *inclination*. Should, however, the totality of the practical spirit throw itself into a single one of the many restricted forms of impulse, each being always in conflict to another, it is *passion*.

474. Inclinations and passions embody the same constituent contents as the practical feeling. Thus, while on one hand they are based on the rational nature of the mind; they on the other, as part and parcel of the still subjective and single will, are infected with contingency, and appear as particular to stand to the individual and to each other in an external relation and with a necessity which creates bondage.

The special feature of *passion* is its restriction to one special mode of volition, in which the whole subjectivity of the individual is merged, be the value of that mode what it may. In consequence of this formalism, passion is neither good nor bad; the title only states that a subject has thrown his whole soul,—his interests of spirit, talent, character, enjoyment,—on one aim and object. Nothing great has been and nothing great can be accomplished without passion. It is only a dead, too often, indeed, a hypocritical moralising which inveighs against the form of passion as such.

But with regard to the inclinations, the question is directly raised, Which are good and bad?—Up to what degree the good continue good;—and (as there are many, each with its particular range) In what way have they, being all in one subject and hardly all, as experience shows, admitting of gratification, to suffer at least reciprocal restriction? And, first of all, as regards this mass of impulses and propensities, the case is much the same as with the psychical powers, whose aggregate is to form the mind theoretical,—an aggregate which is now increased by the host of impulses. The formal rationality of impulse and propensity lies merely in their general impulse not to be subjective merely, but to get realised, overcoming the subjectivity by the subject's own agency. Their genuine rationality cannot reveal its secret to a method of outer reflection which pre-supposes a number of *independent* innate tendencies and immediate instincts, and therefore is wanting in a single principle and final purpose for them. But the immanent reflection of mind itself carries it beyond their particularity and their natural immediacy, and gives their contents a rationality and objectivity, in which they exist as necessary ties of relation, as rights and duties. It is this objectification which evinces their real value, their mutual connexions, and their truth. And thus it was a true perception when Plato (especially including as he did the mind's whole nature under its right) showed that the full reality of justice could be exhibited only in the *objective* phase of justice, viz. in the construction of the State as the ethical life.

The answer to the question, therefore, What are the good and rational propensities, and how they are to be co-ordinated with each other? resolves itself into an exposition of the relationships produced by the mind when developing itself as *objective* mind — a development in which the *content* of autonomous action loses its contingency and optionality.[58] The discussion of the true intrinsic worth of the impulses, inclinations, and passions is thus essentially the theory of legal, moral, and ethical *duties*.

475. The subject is the activity of satisfying impulses, an activity of formal rationality, as it translates them from the subjectivity of content (which so far is *purpose*) into objectivity, where the subject is made to close with itself. If the content of the impulse is distinguished as the thing or business[38] from this activity, and we regard the thing which has been brought to pass as involving the element of subjective individuality and its activity, this is what is called the *interest*. Nothing therefore is brought about without interest.

An action is an aim of the subject, and also his activity which executes this aim: unless the subject were in this way in the most disinterested action, i.e. unless he had an interest in it, there would be no action at all. — The impulses and passions are sometimes depreciated by being contrasted with the baseless chimera of a happiness, the free gift of nature, where wants are supposed to find their satisfaction without the agent doing anything to produce a conformity between immediate existence and his own inner requirements. They are sometimes contrasted, quite generally, with the morality of duty for duty's sake. But impulse and passion are the very life-blood of the subject; they are needed if he is really to be in his aim and the execution thereof. The ethical concerns the content of the aim, which as such is the universal, an inactive thing, that finds its actualising in the agent; and finds it only when the aim is immanent in the agent, is his interest and — should it claim to engross his whole efficient subjectivity — his passion.

476. The will, as thinking and implicitly free, distinguishes itself from the particularity of the impulses, and places itself as simple subjectivity of thought above their diversified content. It is thus reflecting will.

477. Such a particularity of impulse has thus ceased to be a mere datum: the reflective will now sees it as its own, because it closes with it and thus gives itself specific individuality and actuality. It is now at the standpoint of *choosing* between inclinations, and is option or *choice*.[58]

478. Will as choice claims to be free, reflected into itself as the negativity of its merely immediate autonomy. However, as the content, in which its formal universality concludes itself to actuality, is nothing but the content of the impulses and appetites, it is actual only as a subjective and contingent will. It realises itself in a particularity, which it regards at the same time as a nullity, and finds a satisfaction in what it has at the same time emerged from. As thus contradictory, it is the process of distracting and suspending[8] one desire or enjoyment by another,—and one satisfaction, which is just as much no satisfaction, by another, without end. But the truth of the particular satisfactions is the universal, which under the name of *happiness* the thinking will makes its aim.

γ Happiness

479. In this idea, which reflective thinking has educed, of a universal satisfaction, the impulses, so far as their particularity goes, are reduced to a mere negative; and it is held that in part they are to be sacrificed to each other for the behoof of that aim, partly sacrificed to that aim directly, either altogether or in part. Their mutual limitation, on one hand, proceeds from a mixture of qualitative and quantitative considerations: on the other hand, as happiness has its sole *affirmative* contents in the impulses, it is on them that the decision turns, and it is subjective feeling and good pleasure which must have the casting vote as to where happiness is to be placed.

480. Happiness is the mere abstract and merely imagined universality of the content—a universality which only ought to be. But the particularity of the satisfaction which just as much *is* as it is abolished, and the abstract singleness, the choice which gives or does not give itself (as it pleases) an aim in happiness, find their truth in the intrinsic *universality* of the will, i.e. its very autonomy or freedom. In this way choice is will only as pure subjectivity, which is pure and concrete at once, by having for its content and aim only that infinite determinacy—freedom itself. In this truth of its autonomy, where concept and object are one, the will is an *actually free will.*

Free Mind

481. Actual free will is the unity of theoretical and practical mind: free will, which realises its own freedom of will, now that the formalism, fortuitousness, and contractedness of the practical content up to this point have been superseded.[8] By superseding the adjustments of means therein contained, the will is the *immediate individuality* self-instituted,—an individuality, however, also purified of all that interferes with its universalism, with freedom itself. This universalism the will has as its object and aim, only so far as it thinks itself, knows this its concept, and is *will* as free *intelligence.*

482. The mind which knows itself as free and wills itself as this its object, which has its true being for characteristic and aim, is in the first instance the rational will in general, or *implicit* Idea, and because implicit only the concept of absolute mind. As *abstract* Idea again, it is existent only in the *immediate* will—it is the *existential* side of reason,—the *single* will as aware of this its universality constituting its contents and aim, and of which it is only the formal activity. If the will, therefore, in which the Idea thus appears is only finite, that will is also the act of developing the Idea, and of investing its self-unfolding content with an existence which, as realising the idea, is *actuality*. It is thus Objective Mind.

No Idea is so generally recognised as indefinite, ambiguous, and open to the greatest misconceptions (to which therefore it actually falls a victim) as the idea of Liberty: none in common currency with so little appreciation of its meaning. Since free mind is *actual* mind, misconceptions about it are of tremendous consequence in practice. When individuals and nations have once got in their heads the abstract concept of full-blown liberty, there is nothing like it in its uncontrollable strength, just because it is the very essence of mind, and that as its very actuality. Whole continents, Africa and the East, have never had this Idea, and are without it still. The Greeks and Romans, Plato and Aristotle, even the Stoics, did not have it. On the contrary, they saw only that it is by birth (as e.g. an Athenian or Spartan citizen), or by strength of character, education, or philosophy (— the sage is free even as a slave and in chains) that the human being is actually free. It was through Christianity that this Idea came into the world. According to Christianity, the individual *as such* has an infinite value as the object and aim of divine love, destined as mind to live in absolute relationship with God himself, and have God's mind dwelling in him: man is implicitly destined to supreme freedom. If, in religion as such, man is aware of this relationship to the absolute mind as his true being, he has also, even when he steps into the sphere of secular existence, the divine mind present with him, as the substance of the state, of the family, &c. These institutions are due to the guidance of that spirit, and are constituted after its measure; whilst by their existence the ethical temper comes to be indwelling in the individual, so that in this sphere of particular existence, of present sensation and volition, he is *actually* free.

If to be aware of the Idea — to be aware, i.e. that men are aware of freedom as their essence, aim, and object — is matter of *speculation*, still this very Idea itself is the actuality of men — not something which they *have*, as men, but which they *are*. Christianity in its adherents has realised an ever-present sense that they are not and cannot be slaves; if they are made slaves, if the decision as regards their property rests with an arbitrary will, not with laws or courts of justice, they would find the very substance of their life outraged. This will to liberty is no longer an *impulse* which demands its satisfaction, but the character — the spiritual consciousness grown into a non-impulsive nature. But this freedom, which has the content and aim of freedom, is itself only a concept — a principle of the mind and heart, intended to develop into an objective phase, into legal, ethical, religious, and not less into scientific actuality.

OBJECTIVE MIND

483. The objective Mind is the absolute Idea, but only existing *in posse*:[5] and as it is thus on the territory of finitude, its actual rationality retains the aspect of external apparency. The free will finds itself immediately confronted by differences which arise from the circumstance that freedom is its *inward* function and aim, and is in relation to an external and already subsisting objectivity, which splits up into different heads: viz. anthropological data (i.e. particular needs), external things of nature which exist for consciousness, and the ties of relation between individual wills which are conscious of their own diversity and particularity. These aspects constitute the external material for the embodiment of the will.

484. But the purposive activity of this will is to realise its concept, Liberty, in these externally-objective aspects, making the latter a world moulded by the former, which in it is thus at home with itself, locked together with it: the concept accordingly perfected to the Idea. Liberty, shaped into the actuality of a world, receives the *form of Necessity*, the substantial nexus of which is the system of the principles of liberty, whilst its phenomenal nexus is power or its recognition, i.e. its authority in consciousness.

485. This unity of the rational will with the single will (this being the peculiar and immediate medium in which the former is actualised) constitutes the simple actuality of liberty. As it (and its content) belongs to thought, and is the virtual *universal*, the content has its true character only in the form of universality. When invested with this character for the intelligent consciousness, or instituted as authoritative power, it is the *Law*.[26] When, on the other hand, the content is freed from the impurity and fortuitousness, attaching to it in the practical feeling and in impulse, and is set and grafted in the individual will, not in the form of impulse, but in its universality, so as to become its habit, temper and character, it exists as custom.[44]

486. This reality, in general, where free will has *existence*, is *Law* (Right),[36] — the term being taken in a comprehensive sense not merely as the limited juristic law, but as the actual body of all the conditions of freedom. These conditions, in relation to the *subjective* will, where they, being universal, ought to have and can only have their existence, are its *Duties*; whereas as its temper and habit they are *Manners*.[44] What is a right is also a duty, and what is a duty, is also a right. For a mode of existence is a right, only as a consequence of the free substantial will: and the same content, when referred to the will distinguished as subjective and individual, is a duty. It is the same content which the subjective consciousness recognises as a duty, and brings into existence in these several wills. The finitude of the objective will thus creates the semblance of a distinction between rights and duties.

In the phenomenal[20] range right and duty are *correlata*, at least in the sense that to a right on my part corresponds a duty in some one else. But, in the light of the concept, my right to a thing is not merely possession, but as possession by a *person* it is *property*, or legal possession, and it is a *duty* to possess things as *property*, i.e. to be as a person. Translated into the phenomenal relationship, viz. relation to another person — this grows into the duty of some one *else* to respect *my* right. The *moral* duty in general is in me — a free subject — at the same time a right of my subjective will or disposition. But in the moral sphere, there arises the division between what is only inward purpose (disposition or intention), which only has its being in me and is merely subjective duty, and the actualisation of that purpose: and with this division a contingency and imperfection which makes the inadequacy of mere morality. In social ethics these two parts have reached their truth, their absolute unity; although even right and duty return to one another and combine by means of certain adjustments[50] and under the guise of necessity. The rights of the father of the family over its members are equally duties towards them; just as the children's duty of obedience is their right to be educated to the liberty of manhood. The penal judicature of a government, its rights of administration, &c., are no less its duties to punish, to administer, &c.; as the services of the members of the State in dues, military services, &c., are duties and yet their right to the protection of their private property and of the general substantial life in which they have their root. All the aims of society and the State are the private aim of the individuals. But the set of adjustments, by which their duties come back to them as the exercise and enjoyment of right, produces an appearance of diversity: and this diversity is increased by the variety of shapes which value assumes in the course of exchange, though it remains intrinsically the same. Still it holds fundamentally good that he who has no rights has no duties and *vice versa.*

Subdivision
487.   The free will is

A. itself at first immediate, and hence as individual — the *person*: the existence which the person gives to its liberty is *property*. *Right as* right is *formal, abstract right.*[36]

B. When the will is reflected into self, so as to have its existence inside it, and to be thus at the same time characterised as *particular*, it is the right of the *subjective* will, — morality.[35]

C. When the free will is the substantial will, made actual in the subject and conformable to its concept and a totality of necessity, — it is ethical life, in family, civil society, and state.

A.   LAW[36]

a.   Property

488.   Mind, in the immediacy of its self-secured liberty, is an individual, but one that knows its individuality as an absolutely free will: it is a *person*, in whom the inward sense of this freedom, as in itself still abstract and empty, has its particularity and fulfillment not yet on its own part, but

in an external *thing*. This thing, as something devoid of will, has no rights against the subjectivity of intelligence and choice, and is by that subjectivity made adjectival to it, the external sphere of its liberty—*possession*.

489. By the judgment of possession, in the outward appropriation, the thing first acquires the predicate of 'mine.' But this predicate, on its own account merely practical, has here the signification that I import my personal will into the thing. As so characterised, possession is *property*, which as possession is a *means*, but as existence of the personality is an *end*.[61]

490. In his property the person is brought into union with itself. But the thing is an abstractly external thing, and the I in it is abstractly external. The concrete return of me into me in the externality is that I, the infinite self-relation, am as a person the repulsion of me from myself, and have the existence of my personality in the *being of other persons*, in my relation to them and in my recognition by them, which is thus mutual.

491. The thing is the *mean* by which the extremes meet in one. These extremes are the persons who, in the knowledge of their identity as free, are at the same time mutually independent. For them my will has its *definite recognisable existence* in the thing by the immediate bodily act of taking possession, or by the formation of the thing or, it may be, by mere designation of it.

492. The casual aspect of property is that I place my will in *this* thing: so far my will is *arbitrary*, I can just as well put it in it as not, —just as well withdraw it as not. But so far as my will lies in a thing, it is only I who can withdraw it: it is only by my will that the thing can pass to another, whose property it similarly becomes only by his will: — *Contract*.

b. Contract

493. The two wills and their agreement in the contract are as an *internal* state of mind different from its realisation in the *performance*. The comparatively ideal utterance (of contract) in the *stipulation* involves the actual surrender of a property by the one, its changing hands, and its acceptance by the other will. The contract is thus thoroughly binding: it does not need the performance of the one or the other to become so — otherwise we should have an infinite regress or infinite division of thing, labour, and time. The utterance in the stipulation is complete and exhaustive. The inwardness of the will which surrenders and the will which accepts the property is in the realm of ideation,[53] and in that realm the word is deed and thing (§ 462) — the full and the complete deed, since here the morality of the will does not come under consideration (whether it is meant in earnest or is a deception), and the will refers only to the external thing.

494. Thus in the stipulation we have the *substantial* being of the contract standing out in distinction from its real utterance in the performance, which is reduced to a sequel. In this way there is put into the thing or performance a distinction between its immediate specific *quality* and its substantial being or *value*, meaning by value the quantitative terms into which that qualitative feature has been translated. One piece of property is thus made comparable with another, and may be made equivalent to a thing which is (in quality) wholly heterogeneous. It is thus treated in general as an abstract, universal thing.

495. The contract, as an agreement which has a voluntary origin and deals with a casual commodity, involves at the same time the giving to this accidental will a positive fixity. This will may just as well not be conformable to law (right), and, in that case, produces a *wrong*: by which however the absolute law (right) is not superseded, but only a relationship originated of right to wrong.

c. Right *versus* Wrong

496. Law (right) considered as the realisation of liberty in externals, breaks up into a multiplicity of relations to this external sphere and to other persons (§§ 491, 493ff.). Thus there are (1) several titles or grounds at law, of which (seeing that property, in respect both of the person and of the thing, is exclusively individual) only one is the right, but which, because they face each other, each and all are invested with a *show*[39] of right, against which the former is defined as the intrinsically right.

497. Now so long as (compared with this show) the one intrinsically right, still in immediate unity with the several titles, is affirmed, willed, and recognised, the only diversity lies in this, that *this* thing is subsumed under the law or right by the *particular* will of *these* persons. This is naive, non-malicious wrong. Such wrong in the several claimants is a simple *negative judgment*, expressing the *civil suit*. To settle it there is required a third judgment, which, as the judgment of the intrinsically right, is disinterested, and a power of giving the right existence as against that semblance.

498. But (2) if the semblance of right is willed as such *against* intrinsic right by the particular will, which thus becomes *wicked*, then the external *recognition* of right is separated from the right's true value; and while the former only is respected, the latter is violated. This gives the wrong of *fraud*—the infinite judgment as identical (§ 173),—where the nominal relation is retained, but the sterling value is let slip.

499. (3) Finally, the particular will sets itself in opposition to the intrinsic right by negating that right itself as well as its recognition or semblance. [Here there is a negatively infinite judgment (§ 173) in which there is denied the genus as a whole, and not merely the particular mode—in this case the apparent recognition.] Thus the will is violently wicked, and commits a *crime*.

500. As an outrage on right, such an action is essentially and actually null. In it the agent, as a volitional and thinking being, sets up a law[26]—a law however which is nominal and recognised by him only—a universal which holds good *for him*, and under which he has at the same time subsumed himself by his action. To display the nullity of such an act, to carry out simultaneously this nominal law and the intrinsic right, in the first instance by means of a subjective individual will, is the work of *Revenge*. But, revenge, starting from the interest of an immediate particular personality, is at the same time only a new outrage; and so on without end. This infinite regress abolishes itself in a third judgment, which is disinterested—*punishment*.

501. The means by which authority is given to intrinsic right are (α) that a particular will, that of the judge, being conformable to the right, has an interest to turn against the crime (which in the first instance, in revenge, is a matter of chance), and (β) that an executive power (also in the first instance casual) negates the negation of right created by the criminal. This negation of right has its existence in the will of the criminal; consequently revenge or punishment is directed against the person or property of the criminal and exercises *coercion* upon him. It is in this legal sphere that coercion in general takes place—compulsion against the thing, in seizing and maintaining it against another's seizure: for in this sphere the will has its existence immediately in externals as such, or in corporeity, and can be seized only in this quarter. But more than *possible* compulsion is not, so long as I can withdraw myself as free from every mode of existence, even from the range of all existence, from life. It is legal only as abolishing a first and original compulsion.

502. A distinction has thus emerged between the law (right) and the subjective will. The reality of right, which the personal will in the first instance gives itself in immediate wise, is seen to be due to the instrumentality of the subjective will,—the factor which gives existence to the essential right, or alternatively cuts itself off from and opposes itself to it. Conversely, the claim of the subjective will to be in this abstraction a power over the law of right is null and empty of itself: the will gets truth and reality essentially only so far as it realises in itself the rational will—*morality*.

The phrase 'Natural Right', which is common in the philosophy of law, involves the ambiguity that it may mean either right as existing ready-formed in nature, or right as governed by the nature of things, by the concept. The former used to be the common meaning, accompanied with the fiction of a *state of nature*, in which the law of nature is supposed to hold sway; whereas the social and political state rather required and implied a restriction of liberty and a sacrifice of natural rights. But in fact the whole law and its every article are based on free personality alone,—on self-determination or autonomy, which is the very contrary of determination by nature. The law of nature is thus the predominance of the strong and the reign of force, and a state of nature a state of violence and wrong, of which nothing truer can be said than that one ought to depart from it. The social state, on the other hand, is the condition in which alone right has its actuality: what is to be restricted and sacrificed is just the wilfulness and violence of the state of nature.

B. MORALITY

503. The free individual, who, in (immediate) right, counts only as a *person*, is now characterised as a *subject*, — a will reflected into itself so that, be its affection what it may, it is distinguished (as existing in it) as *its own* from the existence of freedom in an external thing. Yet because the affection of the will is thus inwardised, the will takes the form of a particular will, and there arise further particularisations of it and relations of these to one another. This affection is partly the essential and implicit will, the reason of the will, the essential basis of law and ethical life: partly it is the existent volition, which is before us and throws itself into actual deeds, and thus comes into relationship with the former. The subjective will is *morally* free, so far as these features are its inward institution, its own, and willed by it. Its utterance in deed with this freedom is *action*, in the externality of which it only admits as its own, and allows to be imputed to it, so much as it has consciously willed.

This subjective or moral freedom is what a European especially calls freedom. In virtue of the right thereto a man must possess a personal knowledge of the distinction between good and evil in general: ethical and religious principles shall not merely lay their claim on him as external laws and precepts of authority to be obeyed, but have their assent, recognition, or even justification in his heart, sentiment, conscience, insight, &c. The subjectivity of the will in itself is an end in itself and absolutely essential.

The 'moral' must be taken in the wider sense in which it does not signify the morally good merely. In French *le moral* is opposed to *le physique*, and means the mental or intellectual in general. But here the moral signifies an affection of the will; so far as it is in the interior of the will in general; it thus includes design and intention, — and also moral wickedness.

a. Design

504. So far as the action comes into immediate touch with *existence, my part* in it is to this extent formal, that external existence is also *independent* of the agent. This externality can pervert his action and bring to light something else than lay in it. Now, though any alteration as such, which is set on foot by the subject's activity, is its *deed*, still the subject does not for that reason recognise it as its *action*, but only admits as its own that existence in the deed which lay in its knowledge and will, which was its design. Only for that does it hold itself *responsible*.

b. Intention and Welfare

505. (1) As regards its empirically concrete *content*, the action has a variety of particular aspects and connexions. In point of *form*, the agent must have known and willed the action in its essential feature, embracing these individual points. This is the right of *intention*. While design regards only the immediate existence, *intention* regards the underlying essence and aim thereof. (2) The agent has no less the right to see that the particularity of content in the action, in point of its matter, is not something external to him, but is a particularity of his own, — that it contains his needs, interests, and aims. These aims, when similarly comprehended in a single aim, as in happiness (§ 479), constitute his *well-being*. This is the right to well-being. Happiness is distinguished from well-being only in this, that happiness implies no more than some sort of immediate existence, whereas well-being regards it as also justified as regards morality.

506. But the essentiality of the intention is in the first instance the abstract form of generality. Reflection can put in this form this or that particular aspect of the empirically-concrete action, thus making it essential to the intention or restricting the intention to it. In this way the supposed essentiality of the intention and the real essentiality of the action may be brought into the greatest contradiction — e.g. a good intention in case of a crime. Similarly well-being is abstract and may be set on this or that: as appertaining to *this* agent, it is always something particular.

c. Good and Evil

507. The truth of these particularities and the concrete unity of their formalism is the content of the universal, essential and actual,[7] will, — the law and substance of every volition, the essential and actual good. It is thus the absolute final aim of the world, and *duty* for the agent who *ought* to have *insight* into the *good*, make it his *intention* and bring it about by his activity.

508. But though the good is the universal of will — a universal determined in itself, and thus including in it particularity, — still so far as this particularity is in the first instance still abstract, there is no principle at hand to determine it. Such determination therefore arises also outside that universal; and as determinance of a will which is free and has rights of its own, there emerges here the deepest contradiction. (α) In consequence of the indeterminate determining of the good, there are always *several sorts* of good and *many kinds of duties*, the variety of which is a dialectic of one against another and brings them into *collision*. At the same time because good is one, they *ought* to stand in harmony; and yet each of them, though it is a particular duty, is as good and as duty absolute. It falls upon the agent to be the dialectic which, superseding this absolute claim of each, concludes such a combination of them as excludes the rest.

509. (β) To the agent, who in his existent sphere of liberty is essentially a *particular*, his *interest and welfare* ought, on account of that existent sphere of liberty, to be an essential aim and therefore a duty. But at the same time in aiming at the good, which is the not-particular but only universal of the will, the particular interest *ought not* to be a factor. On account of this independency of the two principles of action, it is likewise an accident whether they harmonise. But they *ought* to harmonise, because the agent, as individual and universal, is always fundamentally one identity.

(γ) But the agent is not only a mere particular in his existence; it is also a form of his existence to be abstract self-certainty, abstract reflection of freedom into himself. He is thus distinct from reason in the will, and capable of making the universal itself a particular and in that way a semblance. The good is thus reduced to the level of a mere 'may happen' for the agent, who can therefore resolve on something opposite to the good, can be wicked.

510. (δ) The external objectivity, following the distinction which has arisen in the subjective will (§ 503), constitutes a peculiar world of its own, — another extreme which stands in no rapport with the internal will-determination. It is thus a matter of chance, whether it harmonises with the subjective aims, whether the good is realised, and the evil, an aim essentially and actually null, nullified in it: it is no less matter of chance whether the agent finds in it his well-being, and more precisely whether in the world the good agent is happy and the wicked unhappy. But at the same time the world *ought* to allow the good action, the essential thing, to be carried out in it; it *ought* to grant the good agent the satisfaction of his particular interest, and refuse it to the wicked; just as it *ought* also to make the evil itself null and void.

511. The all-round contradiction, expressed by this repeated *ought*, with its absoluteness which yet at the same time is *not* — contains the most abstract analysis of the mind in itself, its deepest descent into itself. The only relation the self-contradictory principles have to one another is in the abstract certainty of self; and for this infinitude of subjectivity the universal will, good, right, and duty, no more exist than not. The subjectivity alone is aware of itself as choosing and deciding. This pure self-certitude, rising to its pitch, appears in the two directly inter-changing forms — *Conscience* and *Wickedness*. The former is the will of goodness; but a goodness which in this pure subjectivity is the *non-objective*, non-universal, the unutterable; and over which the agent is conscious that *he* in his *individuality* has the decision. Wickedness is the same awareness that the single self possesses the decision, so far as the single self does not merely remain in this abstraction, but takes up the content of a subjective interest contrary to the good.

512. This supreme pitch of the *phenomenon* of will, — evaporating into this absolute vanity, into a goodness which has no objectivity, but is only sure of itself, and a self-assurance in the nullity of the universal — collapses by its own force. Wickedness, as the most intimate reflection of subjectivity itself, in opposition to the objective and universal, (which it treats as mere sham,) is the same as the good sentiment of abstract goodness, which reserves to the subjectivity the determination thereof: — the utterly abstract semblance, the bare perversion and annihilation of itself. The result, the truth of this semblance, is, on its negative side, the absolute nullity of this volition which is supposed to hold its own against the good, and of the good, which is supposed to be only abstract. On the affirmative side, in the concept, this semblance thus collapsing is the same simple universality of the will, which is the good. Subjectivity, in this its *identity* with the good, is only the infinite form, which actualises and develops it. In this way the standpoint of bare reciprocity between two independent sides, — the standpoint of the *ought*, is abandoned, and we have passed into the field of ethical life.

C. ETHICAL LIFE

513. Ethical life is the perfection of spirit objective — the truth of the subjective and objective spirit itself. The failure of the latter consists partly in having its freedom *immediately* in reality, in something external therefore, in a thing, — partly in the abstract universality of its goodness. The failure of spirit subjective similarly consists in this, that it is, as against the universal, abstractly self-determinant in its inward individuality. When these two imperfections are superseded subjective *freedom* exists as the covertly and overtly[7] *universal* rational will, which is aware of itself and actively disposed in the consciousness of the individual subject, whilst its practical operation and immediate universal *actuality* at the same time exist as *custom*, — where self-conscious *liberty* has become *nature*.

514. The freely self-aware substance, in which the absolute 'ought' is no less an 'is,' has actuality as the spirit of a nation. The abstract diremption of this spirit singles it out into *persons*, whose independence it however controls and dominates from within. But the person, as an intelligent being, knows that substance to be his own very being — ceases when so minded to be an accident of it — looks upon it as his absolute final aim. In its actuality he sees not less an achieved present, than somewhat he brings about by his activity — yet somewhat which without all question *is*. Thus, without any reflective choice, the person performs his duty as *his own* and as something which *is*; and in this necessity *he* has himself and his actual freedom.

515. Because the substance is the absolute unity of individuality and universality of freedom, it follows that the actuality and activity of each individual to keep and to take care of his own being, while it is conditioned by the presupposed whole in whose complex alone he exists, is also a transition into a universal product. The disposition of the individuals is their knowledge of the substance, and of the identity of all their interests with the whole; and that the other individuals mutually know each other and are actual only in this identity, is confidence — the genuine ethical temper.

516. The relations between individuals in the several situations to which the substance is particularised form their *ethical duties*. The ethical personality, i.e. the subjectivity which is permeated by the substantial life, is *virtue*. In relation to external immediacy, to a fate, virtue is an attitude to being as something not negative, and is thus a quiet repose in itself: in relation to substantial objectivity, to the whole of ethical actuality, it exists as confidence, as deliberate work for the community, and the capacity of sacrificing self thereto; in relation to the contingency of relations with others, it is in the first instance justice and then benevolence. In the latter sphere, and in its attitude to its own being and corporeity, the individuality expresses its particular character, temperament, etc. as *virtues*.

517. The ethical substance is

(a) As immediate or *natural* mind, — the *family*.

(b) The relative totality of the relative relations of the individuals as independent persons to one another in a formal universality — *civil society*.

(c) The self-conscious substance, as the mind developed to an organic actuality — the *political constitution*.

a. The Family

518. The ethical spirit, in its *immediacy*, contains the *natural* factor that the individual has its substantial existence in its natural universal, i.e. in its kind. This is the sexual tie, elevated however to spiritual significance, — the unanimity of love and the temper of trust. In the form of the family, mind appears as feeling.

519. (1) The natural difference of sex thus appears at the same time as a difference of intellectual and ethical type. With their exclusive individualities these personalities combine to form a *single person*: the subjective intimacy, becoming a substantial unity, makes this union an ethical tie — *marriage*. The substantial intimacy makes marriage an indivisible personal bond — monogamic marriage: the bodily conjunction is a sequel to the ethical attachment. A further sequel is community of personal and particular interests.

520. (2) By the community in which the various individuals constituting the family stand in reference to property, that property of the one person (viz. the family) acquires an ethical interest, as do also its income, labour, and care for the future.

521. The ethical principle which is involved in the natural generation of children, and was assumed to have primary importance in first forming the marriage union, is realised in the second or spiritual birth of the children, — in educating them to be independent persons.

522. (3) The children, thus invested with independence, leave the concrete vitality of the family to which they originally belong, acquire an existence of their own, destined however to found anew such an actual family. Marriage is essentially broken up by the *natural* element contained in it, the death of husband and wife: but even their intimacy, as it is a mere substantiality of feeling, contains the germ of liability to chance and decay. In virtue of such fortuitousness, the members of the family take up to each other the status of persons; and it is thus that the family finds introduced into it for the first time the element, originally foreign to it, of *legal* regulation.

b. Civil Society

523. As the substance, being spirit, particularises itself abstractly into many persons (the family is only a single person), into families or individuals, who exist independent and free, as private persons, it at first loses its ethical character: for these persons as such have in their consciousness and as their aim not the absolute unity, but their own particularity and selfhood. Thus arises the system of atomism: by which the substance is reduced to a general system of adjustments to connect self-subsisting extremes and their particular interests. The developed totality of this connective system is the state as civil society, or *state external*.

a. The System of Needs

524. (1) The particularity of persons includes in the first instance their needs. The possibility of satisfying these needs is here laid on the social system, the general stock from which all derive their satisfaction. In the condition in which this method of indirect adjustment is realised, immediate seizure (§ 488) of external objects as means thereto exists barely or not at all: the objects are property. To acquire them is only possible by the intervention, on one hand, of the possessors' will, which as particular has in view the satisfaction of their variously defined needs; while on the other hand it is conditioned by the ever-continued production of fresh means of exchange by the exchangers' *own labour*. This process, by which the labour of all facilitates satisfaction, constitutes the general stock.

525. (2) The first glimmer of universality in this particularity of needs is found in the way intellect creates differences in them, and thus causes an indefinite multiplication both of needs and of means for satisfying them. Both are thus rendered more and more abstract. This *morcellement* of their content by abstraction gives rise to the *division of labour*. The habit of this abstraction in enjoyment, information, knowledge and demeanour, constitutes training in this sphere or formal culture in general.

526. The labour which thus becomes more abstract tends on one hand by its uniformity to make labour easier and to increase production, — on the other, to limit each person to a single skill, and thus produce more unconditional dependence on the social system. The skill itself becomes in this way mechanical, and gets the capability of letting the machine take the place of human labour.

527.   (3) But the concrete division of the general stock—which is also a general, communal business—into particular masses determined by the factors of the concept—each mass possessing its own basis of subsistence, and corresponding modes of labour, of needs, and of means for satisfying them, of aims and interests, as well as of mental culture and habit—constitutes the difference of estates (orders or ranks). Individuals apportion themselves to these according to natural talent, skill, choice and chance. Belonging to such a definite and stable sphere, they have their actual existence, which as existence is essentially particular; and in it they have their ethic as *integrity*, their recognition and their *honour*.

Where civil society, and with it the state, exists, there arise the several estates in their difference: for the universal substance *exists* vitally only so far as it organically *particularises* itself. The history of constitutions is the history of the growth of these estates, of the legal relationships of individuals to them, and of these estates to one another and to their centre.

528.   To the substantial, natural estate the fruitful soil and ground supply a natural and stable capital; its activity gets direction and content through natural features, and its ethical life is founded on faith and trust. The second, the reflected estate has as its allotment the social capital, the medium created by the action of middlemen, of agents, and an ensemble of contingencies, where the individual has to depend on his subjective skill, talent, intelligence and industry. The third, thinking estate has for its business the general interests; like the second it has a subsistence procured by means of its own skill, and like the first a certain subsistence, certain however because guaranteed through the whole society.

b. Administration of Justice

529.   When matured through the operation of natural need and free choice into a system of universal relationships and a course of external necessity, the principle of contingent particularity gets the explicitly stable determination of liberty first of all in *formal right*. (1) The actualisation which right gets in this sphere of intellectual[52] consciousness is that it be brought to consciousness as the stable universal, that it be known and stated in its specificity with the voice of authority—the *law*.[26]

The *positive* element in laws concerns only their form of *publicity* and *authority*—which makes it possible for them to be known by all in a customary and external way. Their content *per se* may be reasonable—or it may be unreasonable and so wrong. But when right, involved in determinate existence, is developed in detail, and its content analyses itself to gain definiteness, this analysis, because of the finitude of its materials, falls into a falsely infinite progression: the *final* definiteness, which is absolutely essential and breaks off this progression of unreality, can in this sphere of finitude be attained only in a way that savours of contingency and arbitrariness. Thus whether three years, ten thalers, or only $2\frac{1}{2}$, $2\frac{3}{4}$, $2\frac{4}{5}$ years, and so on *ad infinitum*, be the right thing, can by no means be decided conceptually—and yet it should be decided. Hence, though of course only at the final points of specification, on the side of external existence, the positive principle automatically enters into right as contingency and arbitrariness. This happens and has always happened in all legislations: it is just necessary to be clearly aware of it, and not be misled by the supposed goal and by suggestions that the law can and should be, at *every* point, determined through reason or legal intellect, on purely rational and intellectual grounds. It is a futile perfectionism to have such expectations and requirements in the sphere of the finite.

There are some who look upon laws as an evil and a profanity, and who regard governing and being governed from natural love, hereditary divinity or nobility, by faith and trust, as the genuine order; while the reign of law is held an order of corruption and injustice. These people forget that the stars—and cattle too—are governed and well governed too by laws;—laws however which are only internally in these objects, not *for them*, not as laws *set to* them:—whereas it is man's privilege to *know* his law. They forget that he can thus truly obey only such known law,—even as his law can only be a just law, if it is a *known* law, while otherwise it must be, even in its essential content, contingency and caprice, or at least mixed and polluted with them.

The same empty requirement of perfection is employed for an opposite thesis—viz. to support the opinion that a code is impossible or impracticable. In this case there comes in the additional absurdity of putting essential and universal provisions in one class with the particular detail. The finite material is determinable on and on to false infinity: but this advance is not, as in our conception of space, a generation of spatial intervals of the same quality as the preceding ones, but an advance into greater and ever greater speciality by the acumen of the analytic intellect, which discovers new distinctions, which again make new decisions necessary. To provisions of this sort one may give the name of *new* decisions or *new* laws; but in proportion to the advance in specialisation the interest and value of these provisions declines. They fall within the already subsisting substantial, general laws, like improvements on a floor or a door, within the house—which though something *new*, are not a new *house*. But there is a contrary case. If the legislation of a rude age began with single provisos, which go on by their nature always increasing their number, there arises, with the advance in multitude, the need of a simpler code, of embracing that mass of singulars in their general features. To find and be able to express these principles befits an intelligent and civilised nation. Such a gathering up of single rules into general forms, first really deserving the name of laws, has lately been begun in some directions by the English Minister Peel, who has by so doing gained the gratitude, even the admiration, of his countrymen.

530. (2) The positive form of laws—to be *promulgated and made known* as laws—is a condition of the *external obligation* to obey them; inasmuch as, being laws of strict right, they touch only the abstract will— itself at bottom external—not the moral or ethical will. The subjectivity to which the will has in this direction a right is here only publicity. This subjective existence is as existence of the essential and developed truth in this sphere, Right, at the same time an externally objective existence, as universal authority and necessity.

The legality of property and of private transactions concerned therewith —in consideration of the principle that all law must be promulgated, recognised, and thus authoritative—gets its universal guarantee through *formalities*.

531. (3) Legal forms get the necessity, to which objective existence determines itself, in the *judicial system*. Intrinsic right has to exhibit itself to the *court*—to individualised right—*as proven*:—a process in which there may be a difference between what is intrinsically right and what is provably right. The court judges and acts in the interest of right as such, strips the existence of right of its contingency, and in particular transforms this existence—in the form of revenge—into *punishment* (§ 500).

The comparison of the two species, or rather two elements, of judicial reasoning, bearing on the actual facts of the case in relation to the accused, —according as that reasoning is (1) based on mere circumstances and other people's witness alone, or (2) in addition requires the confession of the accused, constitutes the main point in the question of the so-called jury-courts. It is an essential point that the two ingredients of a judicial verdict, the judgment as to the facts, and the judgment as application of the law to them, should, as at bottom different sides, be exercised as *different functions*. By the said institution they are allotted even to bodies differently qualified,—from the one of which members of the official judiciary are expressly excluded. To carry this separation of functions as far as this separation in the courts rests rather on extra-essential considerations: the main point remains only the separate performance of these essentially different functions.—It is a more important point whether the confession of the accused is or is not to be made a condition of penal judgment. The institution of the jury-court loses sight of this condition. The point is that in this area certainty is completely inseparable from truth: but confession is to be regarded as the very acme of assurance, which in its nature is subjective. The final decision therefore lies with the confession. To this therefore the accused has an absolute right, if the proof is to be final and the judges convinced. This factor is incomplete, because it is only one factor; but still more incomplete is the other when no less abstractly taken,—mere cir-cumstantial evidence. The jurors are essentially judges and pronounce a judgment. In so far, then, as all they have to go on are such objective proofs, whilst at the same time incomplete certainty (incomplete in so far as it is only *in them*) is admitted, the jury-court shows traces of its barbaric origin in a confusion and admixture of objective proof with subjective or so-called 'moral' conviction. It is easy to call *extraordinary* punishments an absurdity; but the fault lies rather with the shallowness which takes offence at a mere name. Materially the principle involves the difference of objective proof according as it goes with or without the factor of absolute assurance which lies in confession.

532. The function of judicial administration is only to actuate to necessity the abstract side of personal liberty in civil society. But this actuation rests at first on the particular subjectivity of the judge, since here as yet there is not found the necessary unity of it with intrinsic right. Conversely, the blind necessity of the system of needs is not lifted up into consciousness of the universal, and actuated from that direction.

c. *Police and Corporation*

533. Judicial administration automatically has no concern with such part of actions and interests as belongs only to particularity, and leaves to chance not only the occurrence of crimes but also care for welfare. In civil society the end is to satisfy needs — and that, because it is man's need — in a stable general way, so as to *secure* this satisfaction. But the machinery of social necessity leaves in many ways a contingency about this satisfaction. This is due to the variability of needs themselves, in which opinion and subjective caprice play a great part. It results also from circumstances of locality, from the connexions between nation and nation, from errors and deceptions which can be foisted on individual parts of the whole mechanism and are capable of creating disorder in it, — as also and especially from the limited capacity of individuals to take advantage of that general stock. The onward march of this necessity also sacrifices the particularities by which it is brought about, and does not itself contain the affirmative aim of securing the satisfaction of individuals. So far as concerns them, it *may* be far from beneficial: yet here the individuals are the morally justifiable end.

534. To keep in view this essential end, to ascertain the way in which the powers and variable ingredients composing that necessity operate, and to maintain that end in them and against them, is the work of an institution which assumes on *one* hand, to the concrete of civil society, the position of an external universality. Such an order acts with the power of an external state, which, insofar as it is rooted in the higher or substantial state, appears as state-police. On the *other* hand, in this sphere of particularity the aim of substantial universality and the carrying of it out is restricted to the business of particular branches and interests. Thus we have the *corporation*, in which the particular citizen in his private capacity finds the securing of his stock, whilst at the same time he in it emerges from his individual private interest, and has a conscious activity for a comparatively universal end just as in his legal and professional duties he has his ethical life.

c. The State

535. The state is the *self-conscious* ethical substance, the unification of the family principle with that of civil society. The same unity, which is in the family a feeling of love, is its essence, receiving however at the same time through the second principle of conscious and spontaneously active volition the *form* of conscious universality. This universality, with all its evolution in detail, is the absolute aim and content of the knowing subject, which thus identifies itself in its volition with the system of rationality.

536. The state is (α) its inward structure as a self-relating development—constitutional (inner-state) law: (β) a particular individual, and therefore in relations with other particular individuals,—international (outer-state) law; (γ) but these particular minds are only stages in the universal Idea of mind in its actuality: universal history.

α. CONSTITUTIONAL LAW[36]

537. The essence of the state is the universal, self-originated and self-developed,—the rationality of will; but, as self-knowing and self-actuating, sheer subjectivity, and as an actuality, it is one individual. Its *work* generally—in relation to the extreme of individuality as the multitude of individuals—consists in a double function. First it maintains them as persons, thus making right a necessary actuality, then it promotes their welfare, which each originally takes care of for himself, but which has a thoroughly general side; it protects the family and guides civil society. Secondly, it brings back both, and the whole disposition and activity of the individual—whose tendency is to become a centre of his own—into the life of the universal substance; and, in this sense, as a free power it interferes with those subordinate spheres and keeps them in substantial immanence.

538. The laws express the special provisions for objective freedom. First, to the immediate agent, his independent self-will and particular interest, they are restrictions. But, secondly, they are an absolute final end and the universal work: hence they are a product of the functions of the various classes which become more specialised in the general particularisation, and of all the activity and private concerns of individuals. Thirdly, they are the substance of the volition of individuals—which volition is thereby free—and of their disposition: they are thus exhibited as authoritative custom.

539. As a living mind, the state can only be an organised whole, differentiated into particular agencies, which, proceeding from the one concept (though not known as concept) of the rational will, continually produce it as their result. The *constitution* is the articulation of state-power. It provides for the rational will,—insofar as it is in the individuals only *implicitly* the universal will, — coming to a consciousness and an understanding of itself and being *found*; also for that will being brought to actuality, through the action of the government and its several branches, and maintained in it, and also protected against the contingent subjectivity both of the government and of individuals. The constitution is existent *justice*, — the actuality of liberty in the development of all its rational provisions.

Liberty and equality are the simple categories into which is frequently concentrated what should form the fundamental principle, the final aim and result of the constitution. However true this is, the defect of these terms is their utter abstractness: if stuck to in this abstract form, they are principles which either prevent the rise of concreteness of the state, i.e. its articulation into a constitution and a government in general, or destroy them. With the state there arises inequality, the difference of governing powers and of governed, magistracies, authorities, directories, etc. The principle of equality, applied consistently, rejects all differences, and thus allows no sort of political condition to exist. Liberty and equality are indeed the foundation of the state, but also the most abstract and the most superficial of principles, and for that very reason naturally the most familiar. It is of interest therefore to study them closer.

As regards, first, equality, the familiar proposition, 'All men are by nature equal,' blunders by confusing the natural with the concept. It ought to read: '*By nature* men are only unequal.' But the concept of liberty, as it exists as such, without further specification and development, is abstract subjectivity, a person capable of property (§ 488). This single abstract feature of personality constitutes the actual *equality* of human beings. But that this freedom should exist, that it should be *man* (and not as in Greece, Rome, etc. *some* men) that is recognised and legally regarded as a person, is so little *by nature*, that it is rather only a result and product of the consciousness of the deepest principle of mind, and of the universality and expansion of this consciousness. That the citizens are equal before the law contains a great truth, but so expressed it is a tautology: it only states that the legal condition in general exists, that the laws rule. But, as regards the concrete, the citizens, apart from their personality, are equal before the law only in respects in which they are already equal *outside the law*. Only that equality which (in whatever way it be) they, as it happens, otherwise have in property, age, physical strength, talent, skill, etc. — or even in crime, can and ought to justify equal treatment before the law: only it can make them — as regards taxation, military service, eligibility to office, etc. — punishment, etc. — equal in the concrete. The laws themselves, except insofar as they concern that narrow sphere of personality, presuppose unequal conditions, and provide for the unequal legal duties and entitlements resulting therefrom.

As for liberty, it is initially taken partly in a negative sense against the

self-will of others and lawless treatment, partly in the affirmative sense of
subjective freedom; but this freedom is allowed great latitude both as
regards the agent's self-will and activity for his particular ends, and as
regards his claim to have a personal insight and activity and a personal share
in general affairs. Formerly the legally defined rights, private as well as
public rights of a nation, town, etc. were called its 'liberties.' Really, every
genuine law is a liberty: it contains a rational principle of objective mind;
thus it embodies a liberty. Nothing has become, on the contrary, more
familiar than the idea that each must *restrict* his liberty in relation to the
liberty of others: that the state consists in such reciprocal restriction, and
that the laws are restrictions. In such ideas liberty is viewed as only casual
self-will and caprice. Hence it has also been said that modern nations are
only susceptible of equality, or of equality more than liberty: and that for
no other reason than that, with an assumed definition of liberty (chiefly the
participation of all in political affairs and actions), it was impossible to
make ends meet in actuality—which is at once more rational and more
powerful than abstract presuppositions. On the contrary, it should be said
that it is just the great development and maturity of modern states which
produces the supreme concrete inequality of individuals in actuality: while,
through the deeper rationality of laws and the greater stability of the legal
state, it gives rise to greater and more stable liberty, which it can without
incompatibility allow. Even the superficial distinction of the words 'liberty'
and 'equality' points to the fact that the former tends to inequality:
whereas, on the contrary, the current concepts of liberty only carry us back
to equality. But the more we fortify liberty,—as security of property, as
possibility for each to develop and make the best of his talents and good
qualities, the more it gets taken for granted: and then the consciousness
and appreciation of liberty especially turns to its *subjective* sense. By this is
meant the liberty to attempt action on every side, and to throw oneself at
pleasure into activity for particular and for general spiritual interests, the
independence of individual particularity, as well as the inward liberty in
which the subject has principles, has an insight and conviction of his own,
and thus gains moral independence. But this liberty itself on one hand
implies that supreme differentiation in which men are unequal and make
themselves more unequal by education; and on the other it only grows up
under conditions of that objective liberty, and has, and could have, grown to
such height only in modern states. If, with this development of particularity, there be an endless increase in the number of needs, and of the
difficulty of satisfying them, of the lust of argument and the fancy of
detecting faults, with its insatiate vanity, it is all but part of that indiscri-
minating relaxation of particularity in this sphere which generates all
possible complications, and must deal with them as it can. This sphere is of
course also the field of restrictions, because liberty is there involved with
natural self-will and caprice, and has therefore to restrict itself: and that,

not merely with regard to the naturalness, self-will and self-conceit of others, but especially and essentially with regard to rational liberty.

The term 'political liberty,' however, is often used to mean formal participation in the public affairs of state by the will and action even of those individuals who otherwise find their chief function in the particular aims and business of civil society. And it has in part become usual to give the title 'constitution' only to the side of the state which concerns such participation of these individuals in general affairs, and to regard a state, in which this is not formally done, as a state without a constitution. On this use of the term, the only thing to remark is that by 'constitution' must be understood the determination of rights, i.e. of liberties in general, and the organisation of the actualisation of them; and that political freedom can in any case only constitute a part of it. Of it the following paragraphs will speak.

540. The guarantee of a constitution (i.e. the necessity that the laws be rational, and their actualisation secured) lies in the spirit of the whole nation, — especially in the specific way in which it is itself conscious of its reason. (Religion is that consciousness in its absolute substantiality.) But the guarantee lies also in an actual organisation or development of that principle conformable to the spirit. The constitution presupposes that consciousness of the spirit, and conversely that spirit presupposes the constitution: for the actual spirit only has a definite consciousness of its principles, insofar as it has them actually existent before it.

The question: To whom (to what authority and how organised) belongs the power to make a constitution? is the same as the question, Who has to make the spirit of a nation? Separate our idea of a constitution from that of the spirit, as if the latter exists or has existed without a constitution conforming to it, and your fancy only proves how superficially you have apprehended the nexus between the spirit, its self-consciousness and its actuality. What is thus called 'making' a constitution, has — just because of this inseparability — never happened in history, just as little as the making of a code of laws. A constitution only develops from the spirit identically with that spirit's own development, and runs through at the same time with it the grades of formation and the alterations necessitated by the concept. It is the indwelling spirit and the history of the nation (and, be it added, the history is only that spirit's history) by which constitutions have been and are made.

541. The living totality, that which preserves, i.e. continually produces the state in general and its constitution, is the *government*. The organisation which natural necessity gives is seen in the rise of the family and of the estates of civil society. The government is the *universal* part of the constitution, i.e. the part which intentionally aims at preserving those parts, but at the same time gets hold of and carries out those general aims of the whole which rise above the function of the family and of civil society.

The organisation of the government is likewise its differentiation into powers, as their peculiarities have a basis in the concept; yet without the difference losing touch with the *actual unity* they have in the subjectivity of the concept.

As the most obvious categories of the concept are those of *universality* and *individuality*, and their relationship that of *subsumption* of individual under universal, it has come about that in the state the legislative and executive power have been so distinguished as to make the former *exist* apart as the absolute superior, and to subdivide the latter again into administrative (government) power and judicial power, according as the laws are applied to public or private affairs. The *division* of these powers has been treated as *the* condition of political equilibrium, meaning by 'division' their *independence* one of another in existence, — subject always however to the above-mentioned subsumption of the powers of the individual under the power of the general. The theory of such division unmistakably implies the elements of the concept, but so combined by understanding as to result in an absurd collocation, instead of the self-redintegration of the living spirit. The one essential canon to make liberty deep and real is to give every business belonging to the general interests of the state a separate organisation wherever they are essentially distinct. Such real division must be: for liberty is only deep when it is differentiated in all its fullness and these differences manifested in existence. But to make the business of legislation an independent power — to make it the first power, with the further proviso that all citizens shall have part therein, and the government be merely executive and dependent, presupposes ignorance that the true Idea,[32] and therefore the living and spiritual actuality, is the self-redintegrating concept, and thus the subjectivity which contains in it universality as only one of its moments. (A mistake still greater, if it goes with the idea that the constitution and the fundamental laws were still one day to make, — in a state of society, which includes an already existing development of differences.) Individuality is the first and supreme principle which permeates the state's organisation. Only through the government, and by its embracing in itself the particular businesses (including the abstract legislative business, which in itself is particular), is the state *one*. These, as always, are the terms on which the different elements essentially and alone truly stand towards each other in the logic of reason, as opposed to the external footing they stand on in understanding, which never gets beyond subsuming the individual and particular under the universal. What disorganises the unity of logical reason, equally disorganises actuality.

542.   In the government — as organic totality — the sovereign power (principate) is (a) *subjectivity* as the *infinite* self-unity of the concept in its development; — the all-sustaining, all-decreeing will of the state, its highest peak and all-pervasive unity. In the perfect form of the state, in which every element of the concept has reached free existence, this subjectivity is

not a so-called 'moral person,' or a decree issuing from a majority (forms in which the unity of the decreeing will has not an *actual* existence), but an actual individual, — the will of a decreeing individual, — *monarchy*. The monarchical constitution is therefore the constitution of developed reason: all other constitutions belong to lower grades of the development and realisation of reason.

The unification of all concrete state powers into one existence, as in the patriarchal society, — or, as in a democratic constitution, the participation of all in all affairs — impugns the principle of the division of powers, i.e. the developed liberty of the constituent factors of the Idea. But equally the division (the working out of these factors each to a free totality) must be reduced to ideal unity, i.e. to *subjectivity*. The mature differentiation or realisation of the Idea means, essentially, that this subjectivity should grow to be a *real* moment, an *actual* existence; and this actuality can only be the individuality of the monarch — the subjectivity of abstract and final decision existent in *one* person. All those forms of collective decreeing and willing, a common will which shall be the sum and the resultant (on aristocratic or democratic principles) of the atomism of single wills, have on them the mark of the unreality of an abstraction. Two points only are important, the necessity of a conceptual factor, and the form in which it is actualised. It is only the nature of the speculative concept which can really give light on the matter. That subjectivity — being the moment of abstract deciding in general — partly leads on to the proviso that the name of the monarch appear as the bond and sanction under which everything is done in the government; partly, being simple self-relation, it has attached to it the characteristic of *immediacy*, and thus of *nature*—whereby the destination of individuals for the dignity of the princely power is fixed by inheritance.

543.(b) In the *particular* government-power there emerges, first, the division of state-business into its branches (previously defined), legislative power, administration of justice or judicial power, administration and police, and its consequent distribution between particular boards or offices, which having their business appointed by law, to that end and for that reason possess independence of action, without thereby ceasing to stand under higher supervision. Second, there arises the participation of *several* in state-business, who together constitute the universal class (§ 528) in so far as they take on themselves the charge of universal ends as the essential function of their particular life; — the further condition for being able to take individually part in this business being a certain training, aptitude, and skill for such ends.

544. The estates-collegium or provincial council is an institution by which all who belong to civil society in general, and are to that degree private persons, participate in the governmental power, especially in legislation — viz. in matters of general interest which do not, like peace and

war, involve the emergence and action of the state as an individual, and therefore do not belong specially to the province of the princely power. By virtue of this participation subjective liberty and conceit, with their public opinion, can show themselves palpably efficacious and enjoy the satisfaction of counting for something.

The division of constitutions into democracy, aristocracy and monarchy is still the most definite statement of their difference in relation to sovereignty. They must at the same time be regarded as necessary structures[27] in the development, thus in the history, of the state. Hence it is superficial and absurd to represent them as an object of *choice*. The pure forms — necessary to the process of evolution — are, insofar as they are finite and in course of change, conjoined both with forms of their degeneration, such as ochlocracy, etc., and with earlier transition-forms. These two forms are not to be confused with those genuine structures. Thus, it may be — if we look only at the fact that the will of one individual stands at the head of the state — oriental despotism is included under the vague name 'monarchy,' — as also feudal monarchy, to which indeed even the favourite name of 'constitutional monarchy' cannot be refused. The true difference of these forms from genuine monarchy depends on the substance of those principles of right which are in force and have their actuality and guarantee in the state-power. These principles are those expounded earlier, liberty of property, and also personal liberty, civil society, with its industry and its communities, and the regulated activity of the particular bureaus in subordination to the laws.

The question which is most discussed is in what sense we are to understand the participation of private persons in state affairs. For it is as private persons that the members of bodies of estates are primarily to be taken, be they treated as mere individuals, or as representatives of a number of people or of the nation. The aggregate of private persons is often spoken of as the *nation*: but as such an aggregate it is *vulgus*, not *populus*: and in this connection, it is the sole aim of the state that a nation should *not* come to existence, to power and action, *as such an aggregate*. Such a condition of a nation is a condition of lawlessness, demoralisation, irrationality: in it the nation would only be a shapeless, wild, blind force, like that of the stormy, elemental sea, which however is not self-destructive, as the nation — a spiritual element — would be. Yet such a condition may be often heard described as that of true freedom. If there is to be any sense in embarking on the question of the participation of private persons in public affairs, it is not a brutish mass, but an already organised nation — one in which a governmental power exists — which must be presupposed. The desirability of such participation however does not lie in the superiority of particular intelligence, which private persons are supposed to have over state officials — the contrary is necessarily the case — nor in the superiority of their good will for the general interest. The members of civil society as such are rather people who find their nearest duty in their private interest and (especially in feudal society) in the interest of their privileged corporation. Take the case of *England* which, because private persons have a predominant share in public affairs, has been regarded as having the freest of all constitutions. Experience shows that that country — as compared with the other civilised states of Europe — is the most backward in civil and criminal legislation, in the law and liberty of property, in arrangements for art and science, and that objective freedom or rational right is rather *sacrificed* to formal right and particular private interest; and that this happens even in the institutions and possessions supposed to be dedicated to religion. The desirability of private persons taking part in public affairs lies partly in their concrete, and therefore more urgent, sense of general needs, but essentially in the right of the collective spirit to appear as an *externally universal* will, acting with orderly and express efficacy for public concerns. By this satisfaction of this right it gets its own life quickened, and at the same time breathes fresh life in the administrative officials; who thus have it brought home to them that not merely have they to enforce duties but also to have regard to rights. Private citizens are in the state the incomparably greater number, and form the multitude of such as are recognised as persons. Hence volitional reason exhibits its existence in them as a plurality of freemen, or in its reflectional universality, which has its actuality vouchsafed it as a participation in the sovereignty. But it has already been noted as a moment of civil society (§§ 527, 534) that the individuals rise from external into substantial universality, and form a *particular* kind — the estates: and it is not in the inorganic form of individuals as such (after the *democratic* fashion of election), but as organic factors, as estates, that they enter upon that participation. In the state a power or agency must never appear and act as a formless, inorganic shape, i.e. basing itself on the principle of plurality and mere numbers.

Assemblies of estates have been wrongly designated as the *legislative power*, so far as they form only one branch of that power, a branch in which the special government-officials have an essential share, while the sovereign power has the privilege of final decision. In a civilised state moreover legislation can only be a further modification of existing laws, and so-called new laws can only deal with minutiae of detail and particularities (cf. § 529), the main drift of which has been already prepared or preliminarily settled by the practice of the law-courts. The so-called *financial law*, in so far as it requires the assent of the estates, is essentially a government affair: it is only improperly called a law, in the general sense of embracing a wide, indeed the whole, range of the external means of government. The finances deal with what in their nature are only particular needs, ever newly recurring, even if they touch on the sum total of such needs. If the main part of the requirement were — as it very likely is — regarded as permanent, the provision for it would have more the nature of a law: but to be a law, it would have to be made once for all, and not be made yearly, or every few years, afresh. The part which varies according to time and circumstances concerns in reality the smallest part of the amount, and the provisions with regard to it have even less the character of a law: and yet it is and may be only this slight variable part which is in dispute, and can be subjected to a varying yearly estimate. It is this last then which falsely bears the high-sounding name of the 'Grant' of the Budget, i.e. of the whole of the finances. A law for one year and made each year has even to the plain man something palpably absurd: for he distinguishes the essential and developed universal, as content of a true law, from the reflectional universality which only externally embraces what in its nature is many. To give the name of a law to the annual fixing of financial requirements only serves — with the presupposed separation of legislative from executive — to keep up the illusion of that separation having real existence, and to conceal the fact that the legislative power, when it makes a decree about finance, is really engaged with strict executive business. But the importance attached to the power of from time to time granting supply, on the ground that the assembly of estates possesses in it a *check* on the government, and thus a guarantee against injustice and violence, — this importance is in one way rather illusory than real. The financial measures necessary for the state's subsistence cannot be made conditional on any other circumstances, nor can the state's subsistence be put yearly in doubt. It would be a parallel absurdity if the government were e.g. to grant and arrange the judicial institutions always for a limited time merely; and thus, by the threat of suspending the activity of such an institution and the fear of a consequent state of brigandage, reserve for itself a means of coercing private individuals. Then again, the ideas of a condition of affairs, in which it might be useful and necessary to have in hand means of compulsion, are partly based on the false conceptions of a contract between rulers and ruled, and partly presuppose the possibility of such a divergence in spirit between these two parties as would make constitution and government quite out of the question. If we suppose the empty possibility of getting *help* by such compulsive means brought into existence, such help would rather be the derangement and dissolution of the state, in which there would be no longer a government, but only parties, and the violence and oppression of one party would only be redressed by the other. To fit together the several parts of the state into a constitution after the fashion of mere understanding — to adjust within it the machinery of a balance of powers external to each other — is to contravene the fundamental idea of what a state is.

545.   The final aspect of the state is to appear in immediate actuality as a single nation naturally determined. As a single individual it is exclusive against other like individuals. In their mutual relations, waywardness and chance have a place; for each person in the totality is autonomous; the universal of right ought to obtain between them, but actually does not. This

independence reduces disputes between them to terms of mutual violence, a *state of war*, to meet which the universal estate in the community assumes the particular function of maintaining the state's independence against other states, and becomes the estate of bravery.

546. This state of war shows the substance of the state in its individuality—an individuality that goes even to abstract negativity. The state then appears as the power by which the particular independence of individuals and their absorption in the external existence of possession and in natural life feels its own nullity,—as the power which procures the maintenance of the general substance by the patriotic sacrifice on the part of these individuals of this natural and particular existence,—so making nugatory the nugatoriness that confronts it.

β. EXTERNAL PUBLIC LAW

547. In the state of war the independence of states is at stake. In one case the result may be the mutual recognition of free national individualities (§ 430): and by peace-conventions supposed to be for ever, both this general recognition, and the special claims of nations on one another, are settled and fixed. External state-right rests partly on these positive treaties, but to that extent contains only rights falling short of true actuality (§ 545): partly on so-called *international* law, the general principle of which is its presupposed recognition by the several states. It thus restricts their otherwise unchecked action against one another in such a way that the possibility of peace is left; and distinguishes individuals as private persons (nonbelligerents) from the state. In general, international law rests on customs.

γ. UNIVERSAL HISTORY

548. As the spirit of a definite nation is actual and its liberty is under natural conditions, it admits on this nature-side the influence of geography and climate. It is in time; and as regards its range and scope, has essentially a *particular* principle on the lines of which it must run through a development of its consciousness and its actuality. It has a history of its own. But as a restricted mind its independence is something secondary; it passes into universal world-history, the events of which exhibit the dialectic of the particular national spirits—the judgment of the world.

549. This movement is the path of liberation for the spiritual substance, the deed by which the absolute final aim of the world is realised in it, and the merely implicit mind achieves consciousness and self-consciousness. It is thus the revelation and actuality of its essential and completed[7] essence, whereby it becomes an externally universal spirit—a world-mind. As this development is in time and in real existence, as it is history, its several stages and steps are the national minds, each of which, as single and endued by nature with a specific character, is appointed to occupy only one grade, and accomplish one task in the whole deed.

The presupposition that history has an essential and actual end, from which certain characteristics develop conceptually, is called an *a priori* view of it, and philosophy is reproached with *a priori* history-writing. On this point, and on history-writing in general, we must go into further detail. That history, and essentially world-history, is founded on an essential and actual aim, which actually is and will be realised in it—the plan of providence; that, in short, there is reason in history, must be decided on strictly philosophical ground, and thus shown to be essentially and in fact necessary. To presuppose such aim is blameworthy only when the assumed conceptions or thoughts are arbitrarily adopted, and when a determined attempt is made to force events and actions into conformity with such conceptions. For such *a priori* methods at the present day, however, those are chiefly to blame who profess to be purely historical, and who at the same time take opportunity expressly to raise their voice against the habit of philosophising, first in general, and then in history. Philosophy is to them a troublesome neighbour: for it is an enemy of arbitrariness and brain-waves. Such *a priori* history-writing has sometimes won ground in quarters where one would least have expected it, especially on the philological side, and in Germany more than in France and England, where the art of historical writing has gone through a process of purification to a firmer and maturer character. Fictions, like that of a primitive age and its primitive people, possessed from the first of the true knowledge of God and all the sciences,—of sacerdotal races,—and, when we come to minutiae, of a Roman epic, supposed to be the source of the reports which pass current for the history of ancient Rome etc., have taken the place of the pragmatising which detected psychological motives and associations. There is a wide circle of persons who seem to consider it incumbent on a *learned* and *ingenious* historian drawing from the original sources to concoct such baseless fancies, and form bold combinations of them from a learned rubbish-heap of out-of-the-way and trivial facts, in defiance of the best-accredited history.

Setting aside this subjective treatment of history, we find what is properly the opposite view forbidding us to import into history an *objective purpose*. This is after all synonymous with what *seems* to be the still more legitimate demand that the historian should proceed with *impartiality*. This is a requirement often and especially made on the *history of philosophy*: where it is insisted there should be no prepossession in favour of an idea or opinion, just as a judge should have no special sympathy for one of the contending parties. In the case of the judge it is at the same time assumed that he would administer his office ill and foolishly, if he had not an interest, and an exclusive interest, in justice, if he had not that for his aim and one sole aim, or if he declined to judge at all. This requirement on the judge may be called *partiality* for justice; and there is no difficulty here in distinguishing it from *subjective* partiality. But in speaking of the impartiality required of the historian, this self-satisfied insipid chatter lets the distinction disappear, and rejects both kinds of interest. It demands that the historian bring with him no definite aim and view by which he may sort out, state and assess events, but narrate them exactly in the casual mode he finds them, in their unconnected and uninterpreted particularity. Now it is at least admitted that a history must have an object, e.g. Rome and its fortunes, or the decline of the grandeur of the Roman empire. But little reflection is needed to discover that this is the presupposed purpose which lies at the basis of the events themselves, as of the assessment of their comparative importance, i.e. their closer or remoter relation to it. A history without such aim and such assessment would be only an imbecile mental divagation, not even a fairy tale, for even children expect a *motif* in their stories, a purpose at least dimly surmiseable with which events and actions are put in relation.

In the existence of a *nation* the substantial aim is to be a state and preserve itself as such. A nation with no state formation, (*a mere nation*), has strictly speaking no history, like the nations which existed before the rise of states and others which still exist in a condition of savagery. What happens to a nation, and takes place within it, has its essential significance in relation to the state: the mere particularities of individuals are at the greatest distance from the true object of history. It is true that the general spirit of an age leaves its imprint in the character of its celebrated individuals, and even their particularities are but the very distant and the dim media in which it still plays in fainter colours. Even such singularities as a petty occurrence, a word, express not a subjective particularity, but an age, a nation, a civilisation, with striking vividness and brevity; and to select such trifles shows the hand of a historian of genius. But, on the other hand, the main mass of singularities is a superfluous mass, by the painstaking accumulation of which the objects of real historical value are overwhelmed and obscured. The essential characteristic of the spirit and its age is always contained in the great events. It was a correct instinct which sought to banish such depictions of the particular and the gleaning of insignificant traits, into the *novel* (as in the celebrated novels of Walter Scott, etc.). Where the picture presents an unessential aspect of life it is certainly in good taste to conjoin it with unessential material, such as the novel takes from private events and subjective passions. But to take the individual trivia of an age and of the persons in it, and, in the interest of so-called truth, weave them into the representation of general interests, is not only against taste and judgment, but violates the concept of objective truth. The only truth for mind is the substantial and underlying essence, and not the trivialities of external existence and contingency. It is therefore completely indifferent whether such insignificancies are duly vouched for by documents, or, as in the novel, invented to suit the character and ascribed to this or that name and circumstances.

The point of interest of *biography* — to say a word on that here — appears to run directly counter to any universal aim. But biography too has for its background the historical world, with which the individual is involved: even purely personal originality, humour, etc. hints at that central reality and its interest is thus enhanced. But mere homely detail has no place or interest in history.

The requirement of impartiality on the history of philosophy (and also, we may add, on the history of religion, first in general, and secondly, on church history) generally implies an even more decided bar against presupposition of any objective aim. As the state was already called the point to which in political history judgment had to refer all events, so here the *truth* must be the object to which the several deeds and events of the spirit would have to be referred. What is actually done is rather to make the contrary presupposition. Histories of religion or philosophy are understood to have only subjective aims for their theme, i.e. only opinions and ideas, not an essential and realised object like the truth. And that on the simple ground that there is no truth. On this assumption the sympathy with truth appears as only a partiality in the usual sense, a partiality for opinions and ideas, which all alike have no substance to them, and are all treated as indifferent. In that way historical truth means but correctness — an accurate report of externals, without judgment save as regards this correctness — admitting, in this case, only qualitative and quantitative judgments, no judgments of necessity or of the concept (§§ 172, 175). But, really, if Rome or the German empire etc. are an actual and genuine object of history, and the aim to which the phenomena are to be related and by which they are to be judged; then in universal history the universal spirit, the consciousness of it and of its essence, is even in a higher degree a true and actual object and theme, and an aim to which all other phenomena are essentially and actually subservient. Thus through their relationship to it, i.e. through the judgment in which they are subsumed under it, while it inheres in them, they have their value and even their existence. It is the spirit which not merely broods over history as over the waters, but lives in it and is alone its principle of movement: and in the voyage of that spirit, liberty, i.e. a development determined by the concept of spirit, is the guiding principle and only its concept its final aim, i.e. truth. For spirit is consciousness. Such a doctrine — or in other words that reason is in history — will be partly at least a plausible faith, partly it is a cognition of philosophy.

550. This liberation of mind, in which it proceeds to come to itself and to realise its truth, and the business of so doing, is the supreme and absolute right. The self-consciousness of a particular nation is the vehicle for the current stage of development of the universal spirit in its actual existence: it is the objective actuality in which that spirit invests its will. Against this absolute will the other particular national minds have no rights: *that* nation dominates the world: yet the universal will steps onward over its property for the time being, as over a particular stage, and then delivers it over to its chance and doom.

551. Since this business of actuality appears as an action, and therefore as the work of *individuals*, these individuals, as regards the substantial content of their labour, are *instruments*, and their subjectivity, which is what is peculiar to them, is the empty form of activity. What they personally have gained therefore through the individual share they took in the substantial business (prepared and appointed independently of them) is a formal universality or subjective conception — *fame*, which is their reward.

552. The national spirit contains nature-necessity, and stands in external existence (§ 483): the ethical substance, internally infinite, is actually a particular and limited substance (§§ 549, 550); on its subjective side it labours under contingency, in the shape of unreflective custom, and its content is presented to it as something *existing* in time and confronting an external nature and external world. The spirit, however, which *thinks* in this ethical organism, supersedes within itself the finitude attaching to it as national spirit in its state and the state's temporal interests, in the system of laws and customs. It rises to apprehend[60] itself in its essentiality. Such apprehension, however, still has the immanent limitedness of the national spirit. But the spirit which thinks in universal history, stripping off at the same time those limitations of the particular national minds and its own worldliness, lays hold of its concrete universality, and rises to apprehend the absolute mind, as the eternally actual truth in which apprehending reason enjoys freedom, while the necessity of nature and the necessity of history are only ministrant to its revelation and the vessels of its honour.

The formal aspects of the mind's elevation to God have been spoken of in the Introduction to the Logic (cf. especially § 51). As regards the starting-point of that elevation, Kant has on the whole adopted the most correct, when he treats belief in God as proceeding from practical reason. For the starting-point contains implicitly the material or content which constitutes the content of the concept of God. But the true concrete material is neither being (as in the cosmological) nor mere purposive activity (as in the physico-theological proof) but the mind, the absolute characteristic of which is effective reason, i.e. the self-determining and self-realising concept itself, liberty. That the elevation of subjective mind to God which these considerations give is by Kant again deposed to a *postulate* — a mere 'ought' — is the peculiar perversity, formerly noticed, of simply reinstating as true and valid that very antithesis — finitude —, the supersession[8] of which into truth is the essence of that elevation.

As regards the mediation which, as has been already shown (§ 192, cf. § 204), that elevation to God involves, the point specially calling for note is the moment of negation through which the essential content of the start-ing-point is purged of its finitude so as to come forth free. This factor, abstract in the formal treatment of logic, now gets its most concrete interpretation. The finite, from which the start is now made, is the real ethical self-consciousness. The negation through which that consciousness raises its spirit to its truth, is the purification, *actually* accomplished in the ethical world, whereby its knowledge is purged of subjective opinion and its will freed from the selfishness of desire. Genuine religion and genuine religiosity only issue from the ethical life; religion is that life rising to think, becoming aware of the free universality of its concrete essence. Only from ethical life and by ethical life is the Idea of God seen to be free spirit: outside the ethical spirit therefore it is vain to seek for true religion and religiosity.   `

But — as is the case with all speculative process — this development of one thing out of another means that what appears as sequel and derivative is rather the absolute *prius* of what it appears to be mediated by, and is here in mind also known as its truth.

Here then is the place to go more deeply into the relations between the state and religion, and in doing so to elucidate the categories customary on the topic. It is apparent from what has preceded that ethical life is the state retracted into its inner heart and substance, while the state is the organisa-tion and actualisation of ethical life; and that religion is the very substance of ethical life itself and of the state. Correspondingly, the state rests on the ethical sentiment, and that on the religious. If religion is the consciousness of *absolute truth*, then whatever is to rank as right and justice, as law and duty, i.e. as *true* in the world of free will, can do so only as it participates in that truth, as it is subsumed under it and is its sequel. But if the truly ethical is to be a sequel of religion, then perforce religion must have the *genuine* content; the idea of God it knows must be the true and real. The ethical life is the divine spirit as indwelling in self-consciousness, as it is actually present in a nation and its individual members. This self-con-sciousness retiring into itself out of its empirical actuality and bringing its truth to consciousness, has in its *faith* and in its *conscience* only what it has in its certainty of itself, in its spiritual actuality. The two are inseparable: there cannot be two kinds of conscience, one religious and another ethical, differing from the former in substance and content. But in point of form, i.e. for thought and knowledge — (and religion and ethical life belong to intelligence and are a thinking and knowing) — the content of religion, as the pure self-subsisting and therefore supreme truth, exercises a sanction over the ethical life which lies in empirical actuality. Thus for self-con-sciousness religion is the basis of ethical life and of the state. It has been the monstrous blunder of our times to try to look upon these inseparables as separable from one another, and even as mutually indifferent. The view taken of the relationship of religion and the state has been that, whereas the state had an independent existence of its own, springing from some force and power, religion was a later addition, something desirable perhaps for strengthening the political bulwarks, but purely subjective in individuals: — or it may be, religion is treated as something without effect on the ethical life of the state, i.e. its rational law and constitution which are based on a ground of their own.

As the inseparability of the two sides has been indicated, it may be worth while to note the separation as it appears on the side of religion. It is primarily a point of form: the relation which self-consciousness has to the content of truth. So long as this content is the very substance or indwelling spirit of self-consciousness in its actuality, then self-consciousness in this content has the certainty of itself and is free. But there may arise, in point of form, a condition of spiritual slavery, even though the *implicit* content of religion is absolute spirit. This great difference (to cite a specific case) comes out within the Christian religion itself, even though here it is not the nature-element in which the idea of God is embodied, and though nothing of the sort even enters as a factor into its central dogma and sole theme of a God who is known in spirit and in truth. And yet in Catholicism this spirit is in actuality set in rigid opposition to the self-conscious spirit. First of all, God is the 'host' presented to religious adoration as an *external thing*. (In the Lutheran Church, on the contrary, the host *as such* is not consecrated, but only in the act of enjoyment, i.e. in the annihilation of its externality, and in faith, i.e. in the free self-certain spirit: only then is it consecrated and exalted to be present God.) From that first and supreme relation of externality flows every other external relation — of bondage, non-spiritual-ity, and superstition. It leads to a laity, receiving its knowledge of divine truth, as well as the direction of its will and conscience, from without and from another order — which order itself does not get possession of that knowledge in a spiritual way only, but to that end essentially requires an external consecration. It leads to the non-spiritual style of praying — partly as mere moving of the lips, partly in the way that the subject foregoes his right of directly addressing God, and prays others to pray — addressing his devotion to miracle-working images, even to bones, and expecting miracles from them. It leads, generally, to justification by external works, a merit which is supposed to be gained by acts, and even to be capable of being transferred to others. All this binds the spirit under an externalism by which the very concept of spirit is perverted and misconceived at its source, and law and justice, ethics and conscience, responsibility and duty are corrupted at their root.

Along with this principle of spiritual bondage, and this development of it in the religious life, there can only go in the legislative and constitutional system a legal and ethical bondage, and a state of injustice and immorality in the actual state. Catholicism has been loudly praised and is still often praised — consistently enough — as the one religion which secures the stability of governments. But in reality this applies only to governments which are bound up with institutions founded on the bondage of the spirit (of that spirit which should have legal and ethical liberty), i.e. with institutions that embody injustice and with an ethically corrupt and barbaric state of society. But these governments are not aware that in fanaticism they have a terrible power, which does not rise in hostility against them, only so long as and only on condition that they remain sunk in the thraldom of injustice and immorality. But in the mind there is yet another power available; against that externalism and dismemberment, consciousness collects itself into its inward free actuality. Philosophy awakes in the spirit of governments and nations, the wisdom to discern what is essentially and actually right and rational in the real world. It was well to call the products of thought, and more precisely philosophy, the 'wisdom of the world'; for thought makes the spirit's truth an actual present, leads it into the world, and thus liberates it in its actuality and in its own self.

Thus set free, the content of religion assumes quite another shape. So long as the form, i.e. our knowledge and subjectivity, lacked liberty, it followed that self-consciousness was conceived as not immanent in that content, and the content as so remote from it as to seem to have true being only as negative to actual self-consciousness. In this unreality ethical content gets the name of *holiness*. But once the divine spirit introduces itself into actuality, and actuality emancipates itself to spirit, then what in the world was a postulate of holiness is supplanted by ethical life. Instead of the vow of chastity, *marriage* now ranks as the ethical relation; and, therefore, as the highest on this side of humanity stands the family. Instead of the vow of poverty (muddled up into a contradiction of assigning merit to whoever gives away goods to the poor, i.e. whoever enriches them) is the precept of activity to acquire goods through intelligence and industry, of honesty in commercial dealing, and in the use of property, in short, ethical life in civil society. Instead of the vow of obedience, true religion sanctions obedience to the law and the legal arrangements of the state — an obedience which is itself the true freedom, because the state is one's own, self-actualising reason — in short, ethical life in the state. Thus, and thus only, can law and morality exist. The precept of religion, 'Give to Caesar what is Caesar's and to God what is God's' is not enough: the question is to settle what is Caesar's, what belongs to the secular authority: and it is familiar enough that the secular no less than the spiritual authority has arbitrarily claimed almost everything as its own. The divine spirit must interpenetrate the entire secular life: whereby wisdom is concrete within it, and it carries the terms of its own justification. But that concrete indwelling is only the aforesaid ethical formations. It is the ethics of marriage as against the sanctity of a celibate order; the ethics of economic and industrial activity against the sanctity of poverty and its indolence; the ethics of an obedience dedicated to the law of the state as against the sanctity of an obedience from which law and duty are absent and where conscience is enslaved. With the need of law and ethics and of insight into the spirit's essential liberty, there sets in a conflict of spirit with the religion of unfreedom. It is no use to organise laws and the political system on principles of right and reason, so long as in religion the principle of unfreedom is not abandoned. A free state and a slavish religion are incompatible. It is silly to suppose that we may try to allot them separate spheres, under the impression that their diverse natures will maintain tranquility one to another and not break out in contradiction and conflict. Principles of legal freedom can be but abstract and superficial, and political institutions derived from them must be, if taken alone, untenable, so long as those principles in their wisdom mistake religion so much as not to know that the principles of reason in actuality have their ultimate and supreme sanction in the religious conscience, in subsumption under the consciousness of absolute truth. Let us suppose that, no matter how, a code of law should arise, so to speak *a priori*, founded on principles of reason, but in contradiction with an established religion based on principles of spiritual unfreedom; still, as the duty of carrying out the laws lies in the hands of *individual* members of the government, and of the various classes of the administrative *personnel*, it is vain to delude ourselves with the abstract and empty idea that individuals will act only according to the letter or meaning of the law, and not in the spirit of their religion where their inmost conscience and supreme obligation lies. Opposed to what religion pronounces holy, the laws appear something made by human hands: even though backed by penalties and externally introduced, they could offer no lasting resistance to the contradiction and attacks of the religious spirit. Such laws, however sound their provisions may be, thus founder on the conscience, whose spirit is different from the spirit of the laws and refuses to sanction them. It is nothing but a modern folly to try to alter a corrupt ethical system, its political constitution and code of laws without changing the religion, — to make a revolution without having made a reformation, to suppose that a political constitution opposed to the old religion could live in peace and harmony with it and its sanctities, and that stability could be procured for the laws by external guarantees, e.g. so-called 'chambers,' and the power given them to fix the budget, etc. (cf. § 544). At best it is only a temporary expedient — when it is obviously too great a task to descend into the depths of the religious spirit and to raise that spirit to its truth — to seek to separate law and justice from religion. Those guarantees are but rotten bulwarks against the consciences of the subjects charged with administering the laws — among which laws these guarantees are included. It is indeed the height and profanity of contradiction to seek to bind and subject to the secular code the religious conscience to which that code is a thing profane.

The perception had dawned upon Plato with great clearness of the gulf which in his day had begun to divide the established religion and the political constitution, on one hand, from those deeper requirements which, on the other, were made on religion and politics by liberty which was now becoming conscious of its inner life. Plato has the thought that a genuine constitution and political life have their deeper foundation in the Idea, — in the essentially and actually universal and genuine principles of eternal justice. Now to see and ascertain what these are is certainly the function and the business of *philosophy*. It is from this point of view that Plato breaks out into the celebrated or notorious passage where he makes Socrates emphatically state that philosophy and political power must coincide, that the Idea must be regent, if the distress of nations is to come to an end. What Plato here definitely had in mind was that the Idea — which implicitly of course is the free self-determining thought — could not come to consciousness except in the form of thought; that the substance of the thought could only be true when set forth as a universal, and as such brought to consciousness in its most abstract form.

For a fully exact comparison of the Platonic position with the point of view from which the relationship of state and religion is here regarded, the conceptual distinctions on which everything turns must be recalled. The first of these is that in natural things their substance or genus is different from their existence in which that substance is the subject: further that this subjective existence of the genus is distinct from that which the genus, or in general the universal, gets when it is specially set in relief *as such*, in the conceiving, thinking subject. This additional individuality — the terrain on which the universal substance *freely* exists, — is the spiritual and thinking *self*. In the case of *natural* things their content does not get the form of universality and essentiality through themselves and their individuality is not itself the form: the form is only found in subjective thinking, which in philosophy gives that universal content an existence of its own. In man's case it is otherwise: his content is the free mind itself, and it comes to existence in his self-consciousness. This absolute content — mind intrinsically concrete — is just this — to have the form (thinking) itself for a content. To the height of the thinking consciousness of this principle Aristotle ascended in his concept of the entelechy of thought, which is νόησις τῆς νοήσεως, thus rising above the Platonic Idea (the genus, or essential being). But thought in general — and that on account of this very feature — contains the immediate being-for-self of subjectivity no less than it contains universality; to the genuine Idea of the intrinsically concrete mind the one of its features (subjective consciousness) is just as essential as the other, universality; and in the one as in the other it is the same substantial content. To the subjective form, however, belong feeling, intuition, conception;[53] and it is in fact necessary that in point of time the consciousness of the absolute Idea should be first acquired in this form; it must exist in its immediate reality as religion, earlier than it does as philosophy. Philosophy is a later development from this basis, just as Greek philosophy itself is later than Greek religion and in fact reached its completion by catching and comprehending in all its definite essentiality that principle of spirit which first manifests itself in religion. But Greek philosophy could set itself up only in opposition to Greek religion: the unity of thought and the substantiality of the Idea could take up none but a hostile attitude to an imaginative polytheism, and to the gladsome and frivolous humours of its poetic creations. The *form* in its infinite truth, the *subjectivity* of mind, broke forth at first only as subjective free *thinking*, which was not yet identical with the *substantiality* itself, — and thus this substantiality was not yet apprehended as *absolute mind*. Thus religion could appear as first purified only through philosophy, — through pure self-existent thought: but the form pervading this substantial element — the form which philosophy attacked — was that creative imagination.

The state, which develops similarly, but earlier than philosophy, from religion, exhibits the onesidedness, which in the actual world may infect its *implicitly* true Idea, as corruption. Plato, in common with all his thinking contemporaries, perceived this corruption of democracy and the defectiveness even of its principle; he set in relief accordingly the underlying principle of the state, but could not work into his idea of it the infinite form of subjectivity, which still eluded his spirit. His state is therefore, on its own showing, wanting in subjective liberty (§ 503, § 513, etc.). The truth which should be immanent in the state, should knit it together and control it, he, for these reasons, got hold of only in the form of thought-out truth, of philosophy; and hence he makes that utterance that 'so long as philosophers do not rule in states, or those who are now called kings and rulers do not soundly and comprehensively philosophise, then neither the state nor the race of men can be liberated from evils, — then the Idea of the political constitution will fall short of possibility and not see the light of the sun.' It was not vouchsafed to Plato to go on to say that so long as true religion does not spring up in the world and hold sway in states, then the genuine principle of the state has not come into actuality. But then too this principle could not emerge even in thought, nor could thought grasp the genuine idea of the state, — the idea of the substantial ethical life, with which is identical the liberty of an independent self-consciousness. Only in the principle of the mind which is aware of its own essence, is implicitly absolutely free, and has its actuality in the activity of self-liberation, does the absolute possibility and necessity exist for state power, religion, and the principles of philosophy to coincide, and for accomplishing the reconciliation of actuality in general with the mind, of the state with the religious conscience as well as with philosophical knowledge. Self-realising subjectivity is in this case absolutely identical with substantial universality. Hence religion as such, and the state as such, — both as forms in which the principle exists — each contain the absolute truth: so that the truth, in its philosophic phase, is after all only in one of its forms. But even religion, as it develops, lets the distinct aspects of the Idea develop also (§ 566 ff.). As it is left therefore behind, in its first immediate, and so also one-sided phase, religion may, or rather *must* appear in its existence degraded to sensuous externality, and thus in future come to oppress liberty of spirit and to deprave political life. Still the principle has in it the infinite elasticity of the absolute form, so as to overcome this depraving of the form-determinations and that of the content by means of them and to bring about the reconciliation of the spirit in itself. Thus ultimately, in the Protestant conscience, the principles of the religious and of the ethical conscience come to be one and the same: the free spirit knowing itself in its rationality and truth. In the Protestant state, the constitution and the code, as well as their applications, embody the principle and the development of ethical life, which proceeds and can only proceed from the truth of religion, when reinstated in its original principle and in that way first become actual as such. The ethical life of the state and the religious spirituality of the state are thus firm guarantees of each other.

XIV. PHILOSOPHY OF HISTORY: INTRODUCTION*

Second Draft (1830)
The Philosophical History of the World

[begun] 8. xi. 1830

Gentlemen,
The subject of these lectures is the philosophy of world history.

As to what is meant by history or world history, I need say nothing; the common conception of it is adequate, and we are more or less agreed on what it is. But what may strike you about the title of these lectures and call for a word of elucidation, or rather of justification, is that we are here concerned with a philosophy *of world history, and are about* to consider history from a philosophical point of view.

But the philosophy of history is nothing more than the application of thought to history; and thinking is something we cannot stop doing. For man is a thinking *being, and it is this which distinguishes him from the animals. All that is truly* human, *as distinct from animal — feeling, knowledge, and cognition — contains an element of thought, and this applies to all historical studies. But to appeal in this way to the participation of thought in all human activities may seem inadequate, for it could be argued that thought is subordinate to being, to the data of reality, and is based upon and determined by the latter. Philosophy, on the other hand, is credited with* independent *thoughts produced by pure speculation, without reference to actuality; speculation, it might further be contended, approaches history as something to be manipulated, and does not leave it as it is, but* forces it to conform *to its preconceived notions and* constructs a history a priori.

History, however, is concerned with what actually happened. Its methods would therefore seem completely at variance with the essentially self-determining activity of conceptual thought. It is, of course, possible to present events in such a way that we can imagine they are taking place directly before our eyes. Even then, however, the links between the events must be taken into account; in other words, our procedure must be **pragmatic**, for we have to discover the causes and reasons behind the events. But as one can imagine, this will require the assistance of concepts, which

From G. W. F. Hegel's *Lectures on the Philosophy of World History*, translated by H. B. Nisbet, published by Cambridge University Press. Reprinted by permission. Hegel's own text is printed in italics; passages added from students' notes are in Roman type.

does not, however, imply that the conceptual thought involved will be at odds with its own nature. Nevertheless, in a procedure of this kind, the events will always remain basic, and the activity of the concept will be limited to the formal and general aspects of the factual material, i.e. to rules, fundamentals, and principles. It is generally accepted that logical thinking is required for all such deductions from history; their justification, however, must come from the world of experience. But what philosophy understands by conceptual thinking is something quite different; in this case, comprehension is the activity of the concept itself, and not a conflict between a **material** and a **form** of separate origin. An alliance of disparates such as is found in pragmatic history is not sufficient for the purposes of conceptual thinking as practised in philosophy; for the latter derives its content and material essentially from within itself. In this respect, therefore, despite the alleged links between the two, the original dichotomy remains: the historical event stands opposed to the independent concept.

But [even if we disregard philosophy,] the same relationship emerges in the study of history itself as soon as we look at it from a higher vantage point. For on the one hand, we have in history ingredients and higher determinants which are remote from the conceptual world — i.e. all kinds of human arbitrariness and external necessity. On the other hand, we set up against this the idea of a higher necessity, an eternal justice and love, the absolute and ultimate end which is truth in and for itself. In contrast to natural being, this second, opposite pole is based on abstract elements, on the freedom and necessity of the concept. This opposition contains many interesting features; it comes to our notice once again in the Idea of world history. Our present aim is to show how it is resolved in and for itself in the world-historical process.

The sole end of history is to comprehend clearly what is and what has been, the events and deeds of the past. It gains in veracity the more strictly it confines itself to what is given, and — although this is not so immediately evident, but in fact requires many kinds of investigations in which thought also plays a part — the more exclusively it seeks to discover what actually happened. This aim seems to contradict the function of philosophy; and it is this contradiction, and the accusation that philosophy imports its own ideas into history and manipulates it accordingly, that I wish to discuss in the **Introduction** *to these lectures. In other words, we must first obtain a* **general definition of the philosophy of world history** *and then consider its immediate implications. As a result, the relationship between thought and the events should automatically appear in the correct light. For this reason, and since I do not wish the introduction to become too long-winded (for the material of world history itself is so abundant), there is no need for me to spend time refuting and correcting the endless individual misconceptions and mistaken reflections — some of which are current now, others of which are periodically resuscitated — regarding perspectives, principles, and opinions on the aim and interests of historical studies, and in particular on the* *relationship of conceptual thought and philosophy to historical fact. I can omit all this entirely, or merely touch on it in passing.*

A. [ITS GENERAL CONCEPT]

The first thing I wish to say concerning our provisional concept of world history is this. As already remarked, the main objection levelled at philosophy is that it imports its own thoughts into history and considers the latter in the light of the former. But the only thought which philosophy brings with it is the simple idea of **reason** — *the idea that reason governs the world, and that world history is therefore a rational process. From the point of view of history as such, this conviction and insight is a* **presupposition.** *Within philosophy itself, however, it is not a presupposition; for it is* **proved** *in philosophy by speculative cognition that reason — and we can adopt this expression for the moment without a detailed discussion of its relationship to God — is* substance *and* **infinite power**; *it is itself the* **infinite material** *of all natural and spiritual life, and the* **infinite form** *which activates this material content. It is* substance, *i.e. that through which and in which all reality has its being and subsistence; it is infinite* **power**, *for reason is sufficiently powerful to be able to create something more than just an ideal, an obligation which supposedly exists in some unknown region beyond reality (or, as is more likely, only as a particular idea in the heads of a few individuals); and it is the infinite* **content**, *the essence and truth of everything, itself constituting the material on which it operates through its own activity. Unlike finite actions, it does not require an external material as a condition of its operation, or outside resources from which to derive its sustenance and the objects of its activity; it is self-supporting, and is itself the material of its own operations. On the one hand, it is its own sole precondition, and its end is the absolute and ultimate end of everything; and on the other, it is itself the agent which implements and realises this end, translating it from potentiality into actuality both in the natural universe and in the spiritual world — that is, in world history. That this Idea is true, eternal, and omnipotent, that it reveals itself in the world, and that nothing is revealed except the Idea in all its honour and majesty — this, as I have said, is what philosophy has proved, and we can therefore* **posit** *it as demonstrated for our present purposes.*

The sole aim of philosophical enquiry is **to eliminate the contingent. Contingency is the same as external necessity, that is, a necessity which originates in causes which are themselves no more than external circumstances.** In history, we must look for a general design, the ultimate end of the world, and not a particular end of the subjective spirit or mind; and we must comprehend it by means of reason, which cannot concern itself with particular and finite ends, but only with the absolute. This absolute end is a content which speaks for itself and in which everything of interest to man has its foundation. The rational is that which has being in and for itself, and from which everything else derives its value. It assumes varying shapes; but in none of them is it more obviously an end than in that whereby the spirit explicates and manifests itself in the endlessly varying forms which we call nations. We must bring to history the belief and conviction that the realm of the will is not at the mercy of contingency. That world history is governed by an ultimate design, that it is a rational process — whose rationality is not that of a particular subject, but a divine and absolute reason — this is a proposition whose truth we must assume; its proof lies in the study of world history itself, which is the image and enactment of reason. The real proof, however, comes from a knowledge of reason itself; for reason appears in world history only in a mediate form. World history is merely a manifestation of this one original reason; it is one of the particular forms in which reason reveals itself, a reflection of the archetype in a particular element, in the life of nations.

Reason is self-sufficient and contains its end within itself; it brings itself into existence and carries itself into effect. Thought must become conscious of this end of reason. The philosophical method may at first strike us as odd; bad habits of thinking may even lead us to imagine that it is itself contingent or no more than an arbitrary whim. But anyone who does not accept that thought is the sole truth and the highest factor in existence is not in a position to pass any judgment whatsoever on the philosophical method.

Some of you gentlemen, may not yet be acquainted with philosophy. I could easily appeal to all such persons to approach these lectures on world history with a faith in reason and a thirst for knowledge of it; — and we must surely assume that a desire for rational insight, for knowledge, and not just for a collection of assorted information, is the subjective motive which inspires those who seek to study the learned disciplines. But I need not, in fact, make any such claims upon your faith. These provisional remarks and the observations I shall subsequently add to them are not, even within our own discipline, to be regarded simply as prior assumptions, but as a preliminary survey of the whole, as the result of the ensuing enquiry; for the result is already known to me, as I have covered the whole field in advance. It has already been shown and will again emerge in the course of this enquiry that the history of the world is a rational process, the rational and necessary evolution of the world spirit. This spirit [is] the substance of history; its nature is always one and the same; and it discloses this nature in the existence of the world. (The world spirit is the absolute spirit.) This, as I have said, must be the result of our study of history. But we must be sure to take history as it is; in other words, we must proceed historically and empirically. For example, we must not allow ourselves to be misled by the professional historians; for certain of them, at least in Germany (and they even include some leading authorities who pride themselves on what they call their study of the sources), are guilty of precisely what they accuse the philosophers of doing — of introducing a priori fictions into history. Thus it is a widely accepted fiction (to quote one example) that there was an original primeval people, directly instructed by God, living in perfect under-

standing and wisdom, and possessing a thorough knowledge of all natural laws and spiritual truth; or again, that various nations of priests at one time existed; or (to take a more specific example) that the Roman historians based their accounts of ancient history on a lost Roman epic, etc. Let us leave such a priori inventions to those ingenious professional historians, among whom (at any rate in Germany) they are not uncommon.

We can therefore lay it down as our first condition that history must be apprehended accurately. *But general expressions such as* apprehend *and* accurately *are not without ambiguity. Even the ordinary, run-of-the-mill historian who believes and professes that his attitude is entirely receptive, that he is dedicated to the facts, is by no means passive in his thinking; he brings his categories with him, and they influence his vision of the data he has before him. The truth is not to be found on the superficial plane of the senses; for, especially in subjects which claim a scientific status, reason must always remain alert, and conscious deliberation is indispensable. Whoever looks at the world rationally will find that it in turn assumes a rational aspect; the two exist in a reciprocal relationship.*

It is perfectly correct to say that the design of the world should be distinguishable by observation. But to recognise the universal and the rational, it is necessary to use reason too. The objects are stimuli to thought; otherwise, we find that the world takes on an aspect corresponding to the way in which we look at it. Anyone who views the world purely subjectively will see it in terms of his own nature; he will know everything better than everyone else, and see how things ought to have been done and what course events ought to have taken. But the overall content of world history is rational, and indeed has to be rational; a divine will rules supreme and is strong enough to determine the overall content. Our aim must be to discern this substance, and to do so, we must bring with us a rational consciousness. Physical perception and a finite understanding are not enough; we must see with the eye of the concept, the eye of reason, which penetrates the surface and finds its way through the complex and confusing turmoil of events. Yet people say that this approach to history is an a priori procedure, and intrinsically wrong. Whether they do so or not is a matter of indifference to philosophy. In order to perceive the substance, we must apply our own reason to it. This does not mean, however, that one-sided reflections are admissible; for they distort history and arise out of mistaken subjective opinions. But philosophy is not concerned with these. Sure in the knowledge that reason governs history, philosophy is convinced that the events will match the concept; it does not pervert the truth after the fashion which is now prevalent — especially among the philologists, who employ their so-called acumen to introduce wholly a priori ideas into history. Admittedly, philosophy does follow an a priori method in so far as it presupposes the Idea. But the Idea is undoubtedly there, and reason is fully convinced of its presence.

The perspective adopted by the philosophical history of the world is accordingly not just one among many general perspectives, an isolated abstraction singled out at the expense of the rest. Its spiritual principle is the sum total of all possible perspectives. It concentrates its attention on the concrete spiritual principle in the life of nations, and deals not with individual situations but with a universal thought which runs throughout the whole. This universal element is not to be found in the world of contingent phenomena; it is the unity behind the multitude of particulars. The object of history is the most concrete of all, for it comprehends every aspect of existence; the world spirit is its individuality. What philosophy is therefore concerned with in its treatment of history is the concrete object in its concrete form, and it traces the necessary development of this object. Thus the destinies, passions, and energies of nations are not its prime consideration, with the events following on in second place. On the contrary, its chief concern is the spirit of the events themselves, the moving spirit within them, for this is the true Mercury, the leader of nations. We must therefore not imagine that the universal object of the philosophical history of the world is only one aspect of history (no matter how important this aspect might be), with other alternative determinants existing independently of it. On the contrary, the universal object is infinitely concrete, all-comprehending and omnipresent, for the spirit is eternally present to itself; it has no past, and remains for ever the same in all its vigour and strength.

The understanding must always be brought to bear on history in order that we may comprehend the causes and effects at work in it. In this way, we try to discover what is essential in world history and to disregard what is inessential. The understanding brings out everything that is important and inherently significant. Its criteria of the essential and the inessential will vary according to the end it is pursuing in its examination of history, and the ends it sets itself can also vary enormously. Whenever a particular aim is chosen, further considerations at once present themselves, and we are compelled to distinguish between principal and secondary aims. Accordingly, when we are comparing the facts of history with the ends of the spirit, we will ignore everything which might otherwise be of interest and stick to essentials. Thus the historical content which presents itself to reason is not simply equivalent to the entire events of the past. Some ends are of essential interest to the intellect, and others to the emotions, so that we can be moved to sorrow, admiration, or joy when we read about them.

But it is not our business to discuss the various types of reflection, attitudes, and judgements, not even the ways of distinguishing the important from the unimportant (and these are the most obvious categories), or [of deciding what to emphasize most] in the unlimited material at our disposal.

[Nevertheless, we ought to give a brief account of the categories under which the historical process generally presents itself to thought.] The first category comes from our observation of the changing individuals, nations, and states which flourish for a while, capture our interest, and then disappear. This is the category of **change**.

We witness a vast spectacle of events and actions, of infinitely varied constellations of nations, states, and individuals, in restless succession. Everything that can occupy and interest the human mind, every sensation of the good, the beautiful and the great, comes into play; everywhere we see others pursuing aims which we ourselves affirm and whose fulfilment we desire, and we share their hopes and fears. In all these events and contingencies, our first concern is with the deeds and sufferings of men; we see elements of ourselves in everything, so that our sympathies constantly oscillate from one side to the other. Sometimes we are captivated by beauty, freedom, and riches, sometimes we are impressed by human energy, which can invest even vice with greatness. Sometimes we see the accumulated weight of a popular cause lose its impetus and finally disintegrate, to be sacrificed to an infinite complex of minor exigencies. Sometimes we see how a huge expenditure of effort can produce only a trifling result, or conversely, how an apparently insignificant thing can have momentous consequences. Everywhere we see a motley confusion which draws us into its interests, and when one thing disappears, another at once takes its place.

The negative aspect of the idea of change moves us to sadness. It oppresses us to think that the richest forms and the finest manifestations of life must perish in history, and that we walk amidst the ruins of excellence. History cuts us off from the finest and noblest of our interests: the passions have destroyed them, for they are transient. It seems that all must perish and that nothing endures. Every traveller has experienced this melancholy. Who has stood among the ruins of Carthage, Palmyra, Persepolis or Rome without being moved to reflect on the transience of empires and men, to mourn the loss of the rich and vigorous life of bygone ages? It is not a sorrow like that which we experience at the graves of those dear to us, when we lament our personal losses and the transience of our own aspirations; it is rather a disinterested sorrow at the downfall of the brilliant cultures of the past.

But the category of change has another, positive side to it. For out of death, new life arises. The Orientals have understood this idea; it is perhaps the greatest idea they have ever produced, and it is certainly the most sublime of their metaphysical doctrines. It is implicit, but with individual reference, in their notion of metempsychosis: but an even more celebrated example is the image of the Phoenix, of natural life, which for ever constructs its own funeral pyre and is for ever consumed upon it, only to rise again from the ashes as fresh and rejuvenated life. This, however, is only an image of the East; it applies to the body, but not to the spirit. Its Western counterpart is the realisation that the spirit too rises up again, not only rejuvenated but also enhanced and transfigured. Admittedly, it becomes divided against itself and destroys the form it earlier occupied, but in so doing, it rises up to a new stage of development. But when it abandons the shell of its former existence, it does not merely migrate into a new shell; it emerges as a purified spirit from the ashes of its earlier form. This is the second category of the spirit, the category of **rejuvenation**. The rejuvenation of the spirit is not just a return to an earlier shape; it is a purification or further elaboration of itself. The solution of its problem creates new problems for it to solve, so that it multiplies the materials on which it operates. Thus we see how the spirit in history issues forth in innumerable directions, indulging and satisfying itself in them all. But the only result of its labour is that its activity is once more increased, and it is again consumed. Each of the creations in which it found temporary satisfaction presents itself in turn as a new material, challenging the spirit to develop it further still. The forms it produced become the material on which it labours to raise itself up to new forms. It manifests all its powers in every possible way. We learn what powers it possesses from the very wealth of forms it produces. In this sheer delight in activity, it is entirely absorbed in itself. Nature admittedly imposes internal and external limitations on it, and these not only resist it and place obstacles in its path but can even cause it to fail completely in its endeavours. But even when it is frustrated, it remains true to its character as a spiritual being, a being whose end is not the finished product but the activity of production, so that it still affords the spectacle of having exhibited its active nature.

But the immediate result of these intriguing speculations is that we grow weary of particulars and ask ourselves to what end they all contribute. We cannot accept that their significance is exhausted in their own particular ends; everything must be part of a **single** enterprise. Surely some ultimate end must be promoted by this enormous expenditure of spiritual resources. We are compelled to ask whether, beneath the superficial din and clamour of history, there is not perhaps a silent and mysterious inner process at work, whereby the energy of all phenomena is conserved. What may well perplex us, however, is the great variety and even inconsistency of the content of history. We see complete opposites venerated as equally sacred, capturing the attention of different ages and nations. We feel the need to find a justification in the realm of ideas for all this destruction. This reflection leads us to the third category, to the question of whether there is such a thing as an ultimate end in and for itself. This is the category of **reason** proper; it is present in our consciousness as a belief that the world is governed by reason. Its proof is to be found in the study of world history itself, which is the image and enactment of reason.

I only wish to mention two points concerning the general conviction that reason has ruled and continues to rule the world and hence also world history; for these should give us an opportunity to examine more closely the main difficulty which confronts us, and to touch provisionally on matters which will have to be discussed later.

The first point is as follows. As history tells us, the Greek **Anaxagoras** *was the first to declare that the world is governed by a 'nous', i.e. by reason or understanding in general. This does not signify an intelligence in the sense of a self-conscious reason or a spirit as such, and the two must not be confused. The movement of the solar system is governed by unalterable laws; these laws are its inherent reason. But neither the sun nor the planets which revolve around it in accordance with these laws are conscious of them. It is man who abstracts the laws from empirical reality and acquires knowledge of them. An idea of this kind, that there is reason in nature or that it is governed by unalterable general laws, does not strike us as in any way strange, and Anaxagoras had as yet applied it only to nature. We are accustomed to such ideas, and do not find them at all extraordinary. One of the reasons why I mentioned this historical fact at all was to show how we can learn from history that what may now seem trivial was once unknown to the world, and that such ideas were in fact of epoch-making significance in the history of the human spirit. Aristotle says of Anaxagoras, as the originator of this idea, that he stood out like a sober man in a company of drunkards.*

This idea was taken over from Anaxagoras by **Socrates**, *and it then became the ruling principle in philosophy — except in the case of* **Epicurus**, *who attributed everything to* **chance**. *We shall see in due course what other religions and nations came to accept it.* **Plato** *(Phaedo, 97–8) makes Socrates say of this discovery that thought (not conscious thought but thought of a nature as yet undefined, equivalent to neither conscious nor unconscious reason) governs the world: 'I was delighted with it and hoped I had at last discovered a teacher who would explain nature to me rationally, who would reveal the particular end of each particular phenomenon and also the ultimate end, the good, in nature as a whole. It was a hope which I was not at all eager to relinquish. But how very disappointed I was', Socrates continues, 'when I turned, full of anticipation, to the writings of Anaxagoras himself! I discovered that, instead of reason, he dealt only with external causes such as air, ether, water, and the like.' It is evident from this that what Socrates took exception to was not Anaxagoras' principle as such, but his failure to apply it adequately to concrete nature, and to interpret nature in the light of the principle; for this principle was never anything more than an abstraction, or more precisely, nature was not presented as a development of the principle, as an organisation produced by it, with reason as its cause.*

I wish, from the outset, to emphasise this distinction between a definition, principle, or truth which remains abstract, and one whose specific determination and concrete development are also explained. This distinction is to be found throughout our subject, and one of the principal occasions on which we shall encounter it will be at the end of our survey of world history when we come to examine the political situation in recent times.

Another of the main reasons why I have cited this earliest instance of the idea that reason rules the world and discussed its inadequacy is because it has also been applied more fully to another subject with which we are all familiar and of whose truth we are **personally** *convinced — I refer, of course, to the religious truth that the world is not a prey to chance and external, contingent causes, but is* *governed by* **providence**. *I declared earlier that I did not wish to make any demands on your* **faith** *in the above-mentioned principle. I might, however, have appealed to your faith in it in this religious form, if it were not that the peculiar nature of philosophy forbids us to attach authority to prior assumptions; or, to put it differently, I cannot do so, because the discipline we are studying must itself furnish the proof of the principle's* **correctness** *(if not of its actual* **truth***), and display its concrete reality. The* **truth***, then, that the world's events are controlled by a providence, indeed by divine providence, is consistent with the principle in question. For divine providence is wisdom, coupled with infinite power, which realises its ends, i.e. the absolute and rational design of the world; and reason is freely self-determining* **thought***, or what the Greeks called 'nous'.*

But there is also a difference, indeed a contradiction, between this faith in providence and our original principle, a difference akin to that between the principle of Anaxagoras and the expectations with which Socrates approached it. For this general **faith in providence** *is likewise indeterminate, and lacks a determinate application to the whole, to the entire course of world events. [Instead of giving it this] application [men are content] to explain history [by natural causes. They confine themselves to] human passions, the relative strengths of armies, the abilities and genius of this or that individual, or the lack of such an individual in a given state — in short, to so-called natural causes of a purely contingent nature, such as Socrates [criticised in the work of Anaxagoras. They conceive of providence as an] abstraction [and] make do with a general idea of it [without discussing its determinate application]. The determinate aspects of providence, the specific actions it performs, constitute the providential* **plan** *(i.e. the end and means of its destiny and aims). But this plan is supposed to be hidden from our view, and we are told that it is presumptuous to try to comprehend it. The ignorance of Anaxagoras as to how understanding manifests itself in reality was unfeigned; the development of thought, and man's awareness of its develop-ment, had not progressed beyond this point either in him or in Greece as a whole. He was as yet unable to apply his general principle to concrete reality, or to interpret reality in terms of the principle. It was Socrates who took the first step towards finding a means of combining the concrete with the universal, if only in a subjective and one-sided way; thus his polemics were not directed against concrete applications of the principle. But those who believe in providence are hostile to all attempts to apply the idea on a large scale, i.e. to any attempts to comprehend the providential plan. No-one objects to it being applied in isolated cases, and pious souls discern in numerous particular occurrences, where others see only the agency of chance, not just dispensations of God himself, but of divine providence — i.e. the ends which providence pursues by means of such dispensations. But this usually happens only in isolated instances; and when, for example, an individual in great perplexity and distress receives unexpected help, we must not hold it against him if his gratitude at once leads him to see the hand of God at work. But* *the design of providence in such cases is of a limited nature; its content is merely the particular end of the individual in question. In world history, however, the individuals we are concerned with are nations, totalities, states. We cannot, therefore, be content with this (if the word be permitted) trivial faith in providence, nor indeed with a merely abstract and indeterminate faith which conceives in general terms of a ruling providence but refuses to apply it to determinate reality; on the contrary, we must tackle the problem seriously. The concrete events are the* **ways** *of providence, the means it uses, the phenomena in which it manifests itself in history; they are open to our inspection, and we only have to relate them to the general principle referred to above.*

But in mentioning the possibility of comprehending the plan of divine providence, I have touched on a question which is of central importance today: I mean the question of whether it is possible to obtain knowledge of God — or rather, since it has ceased to be a question — the doctrine, now hardened into a prejudice, that it is impossible to know God, notwithstanding the teaching of the Scriptures that it is our highest duty not only to love God but also to know him. This prejudice goes against the Scriptural saying that the spirit leads into truth, searches all things, and penetrates even into the deep things of God.

Simple faith can well dispense with a fuller understanding of history and make do with the general notion of a divine world order; and we ought not to condemn those who take this course, so long as their faith does not become a polemical one. But it is also possible to defend such views in a spirit of prejudice, and the general proposition, by virtue of its very generality, can also be given a specifically negative application, so as to suggest that the divine being is remote from all human things and transcends human knowledge. Those who adopt this attitude reserve the right to dismiss the claims of truth and rationality, with the added advantage of being able to indulge their own fancies at will. Seen from this point of view, all ideas of God are reduced to empty talk. If God is placed beyond the reach of our rational consciousness, we are no longer obliged to trouble ourselves about his nature, or indeed to look for reason in world history; the way is then open for any arbitrary hypotheses. Pious humility knows very well what it stands to gain from its sacrifices.

I could have refrained from mentioning that our principle (i.e. that reason governs the world and always has done so) has a religious equivalent in the doctrine of a ruling providence; this would have allowed me to avoid the question of whether it is possible to obtain knowledge of God. But I did not wish to do so, partly in order to bring out some further implications of these questions, and partly also to allay any suspicions that philosophy has or should have any cause to fear discussing religious truths, or that it circumvents them because it does not, so to speak, have an easy conscience about them. On the contrary, we have recently reached the point where philosophy has had to defend the content of religion against certain kinds of theology.

As I have said, we are often told that it is presumptuous to try to fathom the plan of providence. This is a direct consequence of the idea (which has now become an almost universally accepted axiom) that it is impossible to obtain knowledge of God. And when theology itself is in so desperate a position, we must take refuge in philosophy if we wish to learn anything about God. Certainly, reason is often accused of arrogance in presuming to attain such knowledge. But it would be more accurate to say that true humility consists precisely in recognising and revering God in everything, especially in the theatre of world history. Furthermore, the traditional view that God's wisdom is manifest in nature has not yet been altogether abandoned. It was indeed fashionable at one time to admire the wisdom of God as manifested in animals and plants. But to marvel at human destinies or products of nature is already an indication that we have some knowledge of God. If we admit that providence reveals itself in such objects and materials, why should we not do the same in world history? Is it because history seems too vast a subject? It is certainly customary to conceive of providence as taking a hand only in minor matters, to picture it as a wealthy benefactor who distributes alms among men and furthers their ends. But it is a mistake to think that the material of world history is too vast for providence to cope with; for the divine wisdom is one and the same in great things and in small. It is the same in plants and insects as in the destinies of entire nations and empires, and we must not imagine that God is not powerful enough to apply his wisdom to things of great moment. To believe that God's wisdom is not active in everything is to show humility towards the material rather than towards the divine wisdom itself. Besides, nature is a theatre of secondary importance compared with that of world history. Nature is a field in which the divine Idea operates in a non-conceptual medium; the spiritual sphere is its proper province, and it is here above all that it ought to be visible. Armed with the concept of reason, we need not fear coming to grips with any subject whatsoever.

The contention that we should not attempt to know God in fact requires closer examination than is possible within the scope of these lectures. But since this matter has so close a bearing upon our present aim, it is essential that we should consider at least the general perspectives involved. Thus if knowledge of God is impossible, the only thing left for the mind to occupy itself with is the non-divine, the limited, the finite. Of course it is necessary for man to occupy himself with finite things; but there is also a higher necessity which requires that there should be a sabbath in his existence, a time when he can rise above his daily labours to occupy his mind consciously with truth.

If the name of God is to be more than an empty word, we must consider God as benevolent, or at least as in some way communicative. In the earlier phases of Greek thought, God was seen as subject to envy, and there was much talk of the envy of the gods; it was said that the divinity is hostile to greatness, and that it is the mission of the gods to humble the great.

Aristotle says, however, that poets are much given to lying, for envy cannot be an attribute of God. And if we were to maintain in turn that God does not reveal himself at all, this would amount to an allegation that he is envious. But God cannot lose anything by communication any more than a light can be diminished when a second one is lit from it.

It is often said that God does reveal himself, but only in nature on the one hand, and in the heart, in the feelings of men, on the other. We are usually told nowadays that this is the point at which we must draw a halt, for God is present only to our immediate consciousness or intuition. Intuition and emotion, however, are both unreflecting forms of consciousness, and we must insist in reply to such arguments that man is a thinking being, for it is thought which distinguishes him from the animals. He behaves as a thinking being even when he is himself unaware of it. When God reveals himself to man, he reveals himself essentially through man's rational faculties; if he revealed himself essentially through the emotions, this would imply that he regarded man as no better than the animals, who do not possess the power of reflection—yet we do not attribute religion to the animals. In fact, man only possesses religion because he is not an animal but a thinking being. It is a trivial commonplace that man is distinguished from the animals by his ability to think, yet this is something which is often forgotten.

God is the eternal being in and for himself; and the universal in and for itself is an object of thought, not of feeling. It is true that all spiritual things, all data of the consciousness, all products and objects of thought—and above all religion and morality—must also come to us through the medium of feeling, and indeed primarily through this medium. Feeling, however, is not the source from which they are derived, but only the form which they assume in man; and it is the basest form they can assume, a form which man shares in common with the animals. All substantial things must be able to assume the form of emotion, yet they can also assume a higher and worthier form. But to insist on translating all morality and truth and every spiritual substance into feeling, and to endeavour to preserve them in this form is tantamount to saying that their proper form is the animal one—although the latter is in fact incapable of comprehending their spiritual content. Feeling is the lowest form which any such content can assume, for its presence in feeling can only be minimal. So long as it retains this form, it remains inchoate and completely indeterminate. The content of our feelings remains entirely subjective, and is only subjectively present to us. To say 'I feel such and such' is to shut oneself up within oneself. Everyone else is equally entitled to say 'But I feel differently,' and then all common ground is lost. In purely particular matters, feelings are perfectly justified. But to maintain that a given content is present in the feelings of everyone is to contradict the emotional point of view one has adopted, the point of view of personal subjectivity. As soon as the emotions have a content, everyone is placed in a position of subjectivity. And if one person should choose to say unpleasant things about another who has acted only on his feelings, the second is entitled to say the same of the first, and both would be equally justified — from their own point of view — in taking offence. If one man says that he has religious emotions, and another says that he cannot feel God, they are both right. If the divine content — i.e. the revelation of God, the relationship between man and God, and the being of God for mankind — is reduced in this way to mere emotion, it is thereby confined to the level of individual subjectivity, of arbitrariness, of random inclinations. In fact, this has been a convenient way of getting round the problem of the truth which exists in and for itself. If I rely only on my emotions, which are indeterminate, and have no knowledge of God and his nature, I have nothing to guide me except random inclinations; the finite alone has validity and is the dominant power. And if I know nothing whatsoever of God, there can be no serious talk about the limits of such knowledge either.

The truth is inherently universal, essential, and substantial; and as such, it exists solely in thought and for thought. But that spiritual principle which we call God is none other than the truly substantial, inherently and essentially individual and subjective truth. It is the source of all thought, and its thought is inherently creative; we encounter it as such in world history. Whatever else we describe as true is merely a particular form of this eternal truth, which is its sole foundation; it is but a single ray of the universal light. If we know nothing of this truth, we must remain ignorant of all truth, rightness, and morality.

But what, we may ask, is the plan of providence in world history? Has the time come for us to understand it? *[I shall confine myself for the present to] the following general remarks.*

God has revealed himself through the Christian religion; that is, he has granted mankind the possibility of recognising his nature, so that he is no longer an impenetrable mystery. The fact that knowledge of God is possible also makes it our duty to know him, and that development of the thinking spirit which the Christian revelation of God initiated must eventually produce a situation where all that was at first present only to the emotional and representational faculties can also be comprehended by thought. Whether the time has yet come for such knowledge will depend on whether the ultimate end of the world has yet been realised in a universally valid and conscious manner.

Now the distinctive feature of Christianity is that, with its advent, this time has indeed come. Its significance for the history of the world is therefore absolutely epoch-making, for the nature of God has at last been made manifest. If we say that we know nothing of God, Christianity becomes something superfluous, a belated arrival, or even a symptom of decay. But this is not the case, for Christianity does give us knowledge of God. Its content, admittedly, appeals to our emotions too. But since the feeling it evokes is a spiritual one, it at least brings into play the faculty of representation — and not just sensory representation either, but also representational thought, the true medium through which man perceives God. Christianity is the religion which has revealed the nature and being of God to man. Thus we know as Christians what God is; God is no longer an unknown quantity: and if we continue to say that he is, we are not Christians. Christianity demands that humility to which we have already referred, a humility which makes us seek to know God not through our own unaided efforts but with the help of divine knowledge and wisdom. Christians, then, are initiated into the mysteries of God, and this also supplies us with the key to world history. For we have here a definite knowledge of providence and its plan. It is one of the central doctrines of Christianity that providence has ruled and continues to rule the world, and that everything which happens in the world is determined by and commensurate with the divine government. This doctrine is opposed both to the idea of chance and to that of limited ends (such as the preservation of the Jewish people). Its end is the ultimate and absolutely universal end which exists in and for itself. Religion does not go beyond this general representation; it remains on the level of generality. But we must proceed from this general faith firstly to philosophy and then to the philosophy of world history — from the faith that world history is a product of eternal reason, and that it is reason which has determined all its great revolutions.

We can therefore conclude that, even in the absolute sense, the time has come in which this conviction and inner certainty need no longer remain a mere representation, but can also be thought, developed, and recognised as a definite piece of knowledge. The original faith makes no attempt to elaborate its content further or to gain any insight into historical necessity — for only knowledge can do that. The fact that the spirit never stands still guarantees that such a time must eventually come; the culminating phase of the spirit — thought or the concept — insists on its rights, and it alone, in its most general and essential being, constitutes the true nature of the spirit.

A distinction is often made between faith and knowledge, and the two have come to be commonly accepted as opposites. It is taken for granted that they are different, and that we therefore have no knowledge of God. People are affronted if we tell them that we seek to know and understand God, and to impart such knowledge to others. But if it is defined correctly, the distinction between faith and knowledge is in fact an empty one. For if I have faith in something, I also know it and am convinced of it. In religion, we have faith in God and in the doctrines which explain his nature more fully; but this is something we know and of which we are certain. To know means to have something as an object of one's consciousness and to be certain of it; and it is exactly the same with faith. Cognition, however,

perceives that the content of knowledge — and indeed of faith — is necessary, and discerns the reasons behind it; it does so without reference to the
authority of the Church or of feeling, which is something immediate, and
goes on to analyse this content into its various determinate elements.
These determinate elements must first become objects of thought before
we can obtain a true cognition of them and perceive them in their concrete
unity within the concept. And if there is any further suggestion that it is
presumptuous to seek such cognition, we might then reply that all this fuss
is unnecessary, since cognition merely takes note of necessity and watches
the inner development of the content unfold before its eyes. As a further
reason why such cognition cannot be branded as presumptuous, one might
also maintain that it differs from faith only in its greater knowledge of
particulars. But this argument would be misplaced, and indeed inherently
false. For the spiritual is not by nature abstract, but a living thing, a
universal individual, a subjective, self-determining, decision-making being.
We cannot therefore truly know the nature of God unless we recognise its
determinate elements. Christianity too speaks of God in this way, for it
recognises him as a spirit, and this spirit is not an abstraction, but the
process in itself; and this in turn presupposes the existence of absolute
distinctions — in fact, the very distinctions which Christianity has made
known to mankind.

God does not wish to have narrow-minded and empty-headed children.
On the contrary, he demands that we should know him; he wishes his
children to be poor in spirit but rich in knowledge of him, and to set the
highest value on acquiring knowledge of God. History is the unfolding of
God's nature in a particular, determinate element, so that only a determinate form of knowledge is possible and appropriate to it.

*The time has now surely come for us to comprehend even so rich a product of
creative reason as world history. The aim of human cognition is to understand
that the intentions of eternal wisdom are accomplished not only in the natural
world, but also in the realm of the [spirit] which is actively present in the world.
From this point of view, our investigation can be seen as a theodicy, a justification
of the ways of God (such as Leibniz attempted in his own metaphysical manner,
but using categories which were as yet abstract and indeterminate). It should
enable us to comprehend all the ills of the world, including the existence of evil, so
that the thinking spirit may be reconciled with the negative aspects of existence;
and it is in world history that we encounter the sum total of concrete evil.
(Indeed, there is no department of knowledge in which such a reconciliation is
more urgently required than in world history, and we shall accordingly pause for
a moment to consider this question further.)*

*A reconciliation of the kind just described can only be achieved through a
knowledge of the affirmative side of history, in which the negative is reduced to a
subordinate position and transcended altogether. In other words, we must first of
all know what the ultimate design of the world really is, and secondly, we must see*

that this design has been realised and that evil has not been able to maintain a position of equality beside it.

In order to justify the course of history, we must try to understand the role of evil in the light of the absolute sovereignty of reason. We are dealing here with the category of the negative, as already mentioned, and we cannot fail to notice how all that is finest and noblest in the history of the world is immolated upon its altar. Reason cannot stop to consider the injuries sustained by single individuals, for particular ends are submerged in the universal end. In the rise and fall of all things it discerns an enterprise at which the entire human race has laboured, an enterprise which has a real existence in the world to which we belong. Phenomena have become real independently of our efforts, and all that we need to understand them is consciousness, or more precisely, a thinking consciousness. For the affirmative element is not to be found merely in emotional enjoyment or in the imagination, but is something which belongs to reality and to us, or to which we ourselves belong.

Reason, it has been said, rules the world. But 'reason' is just as indefinite a word as 'providence'. People continually speak of reason, without being able to define it correctly, to specify its content, or to supply a criterion by which we might judge whether something is rational or irrational. Reason in its **determinate** *form is the true* **substance***; and the rest—if we confine ourselves to reason in general—is mere words. With this task before us, we may proceed to the second point which, as earlier remarked, has to be considered in this introduction. . . .*

C. THE COURSE OF WORLD HISTORY

a. [The principle of development]

Historical change in the abstract sense has long been interpreted in general terms as embodying some kind of progress towards a better and more perfect condition. Changes in the natural world, no matter how great their variety, exhibit only an eternally recurring cycle; for in nature there is nothing new under the sun, and in this respect its manifold play of forms produces an effect of boredom. Only in those changes which take place in the spiritual sphere does anything new emerge. This peculiarity of spiritual phenomena has given rise to the idea that the destiny of man is quite different from that of merely natural objects. For in the latter we always encounter one and the same determination and a constantly stable character to which all change can be reduced, and from which all change follows as a secondary consequence; whereas man displays a real capacity for change, and, as already remarked, for progress towards a better and more perfect condition—in short, he possesses an impulse of **perfectibility***. This principle, which reduces change itself to a law-governed process, has met with disfavour both from religions—for example Catholicism—and from states, which claim a genuine right to a fixed (or at least stable) position. Although it is* *generally conceded that worldly things, including the state, are subject to change, an exception is made in the case of religion — as the religion of truth — on the one hand; and on the other, it is always possible to ascribe changes, revolutions, and the destruction of legitimate institutions to accidents or errors of judgement, but above all to the levity, depravity, and evil passions of man. In fact, perfectibility is almost as indeterminate a concept as that of change in general; it is without aim or purpose, and the better and more perfect condition to which it supposedly tends is of a completely indefinite nature.*

It is important that we should recognise that the development of the spirit is a form of progress, for although this idea is widespread enough, it is just as frequently attacked (as we have already noticed). For it may well appear incompatible with the idea of peaceful stability and of a permanent constitution and legislation. Stability is a value which must certainly be accorded the highest respect, and all activity ought to contribute to its preservation. The idea of progress is unsatisfactory simply because it is usually formulated in such a way as to suggest that man is perfectible, i.e. that it is possible and even necessary for him to become increasingly perfect. From this point of view, stability does not appear as the highest value; on the contrary, the highest value is that of change itself. For the sole consideration here is that of ever increasing perfection, which is so indefinite that we are left only with the idea of change in general; we are offered no criterion whereby change can be measured, nor any means of assessing how far the present state of affairs is in keeping with right and with the universal substance. We have no principle which can help us to exclude irrelevant factors, and no goal or definite end is in sight; and the only definite property which remains is that of change in general. **Lessing's** idea of the education of the human race is an ingenious one, but it is only remotely connected with what we are discussing here. For such doctrines invariably present progress in quantitative terms — as a constant growth of knowledge, as increasing refinement of culture, and other such comparatives; one can go on in this manner at great length without ever reaching any definite conclusions or making any qualitative pronouncements. The object in hand, the qualitative element, is given from the start, but no indication is given of the goal which is supposed to be ultimately reached; the goal itself remains completely indefinite. If, however, we wish to discuss progress in definite terms, we must realise that the idea of quantitative change is devoid of intellectual content. We must know the goal which is supposed to be ultimately attained, because the activity of the spirit is such that its productions and changes must be presented and recognised as variations in quality.

But the principle of **development** *has further implications, for it contains an inner determination, a* **potentially** *present condition which has still to be realised. This formal determination is an essential one; the spirit, whose theatre, province, and sphere of realisation is the history of the world, is not something* *which drifts aimlessly amidst the superficial play of contingent happenings, but is in itself the absolute determining factor; in its own peculiar destiny, it is completely proof against contingencies, which it utilises and controls for its own purposes. But organic entities in the natural world are also capable of development. Their existence is not just an immediate one which can be altered only by external influences; on the contrary, it has its source within itself, in an unchanging inner principle, a simple essence whose own existence as a germ is at first equally simple, but which subsequently develops distinct parts. These then enter into relations with other objects and consequently undergo a continuous process of change — although this process itself leads to the very opposite of change, in that it takes on the new function of conserving the organic principle and the forms it creates. Thus the individual organism produces itself: it makes itself actually what it already was potentially; and the spirit too is only what it makes itself, for it likewise makes itself actually what it already was potentially. But the development of natural organisms takes place in an immediate, unopposed, and unhindered fashion, for nothing can intrude between the concept and its realisation, between the inherently determined nature of the germ and the actual existence which corresponds to it. But it is otherwise in the world of the spirit. The process whereby its inner determination is translated into reality is mediated by consciousness and will. The latter are themselves immersed at first in their immediate natural life; their primary object and aim is to follow their natural determination as such, which, since it is the spirit which animates it, is nevertheless endowed with infinite claims, power, and richness. Thus, the spirit is divided against itself; it has to overcome itself as a truly hostile obstacle to the realisation of its end. That development which, in the natural world, is a peaceful process of growth — for it retains its identity and remains self-contained in its expression — is in the spiritual world at once a hard and unending conflict with itself. The will of the spirit is to fulfil its own concept; but at the same time, it obscures its own vision of the concept, and is proud and full of satisfaction in this state of self-alienation.*

Development, therefore, is not just a harmless and peaceful process of growth like that of organic life, but a hard and obstinate struggle with itself. Besides, it contains not just the purely formal aspect of development itself, but involves the realisation of an end whose content is determinate. And we have made it clear from the outset what this end is: it is the spirit in its essential nature, i.e. as the concept of freedom. This is the fundamental object, so that the guiding principle of development endows the development itself with meaning and significance; thus, in Roman history, Rome is the object which guides our consideration of the events, and, conversely, the events have their source in this object alone, so that their entire significance and import are derived from it. In the history of the world, there have been several great periods of development which have come to an end without any apparent continuation; whereupon, in fact, the whole enormous gains of past culture have been destroyed, with the unfortunate result that everything had to start again from the beginning, in the hope of regaining — perhaps with some help from fragments salvaged from the lost treasures of the past and with an incalculable new expenditure of time and energy, crimes and sufferings — one of the provinces of past culture which had originally been conquered long ago. But there have also been unbroken processes of development, structures and systems of culture existing in their own peculiar elements, rich in quality and radiating in every direction. The formal principle of development in general can neither assign to one product superiority over another, nor help us to comprehend the purpose which underlies the destruction of earlier periods of development; instead, it must regard such happenings — or more precisely, the retrogressions they embody — as external contingencies, and it can only evaluate the gains by indeterminate criteria (which, since development is the ultimate factor, are relative rather than absolute ends).

The concept of the spirit is such that historical development must take place in the temporal world. But time entails the property of negativity. A given entity or event has a positive existence for us, but its opposite is equally possible, and this relation to non-existence is a function of time; it is a relation which exists not only for thought, but also for our immediate perception. Time, then, is the completely abstract dimension of the sensory world. If non-existence does not encroach upon something, we describe it as permanent. If we compare spiritual changes with those of nature, we observe that, in the natural world, individual things are subject to change, whereas the species themselves are enduring. Thus a planet, for example, leaves each particular position it occupies, although its orbit as a whole is constant. And the same is true of animal species. For change is a cyclic process, a repetition of identical phases. Thus, everything moves in cycles, and it is only within these, in the world of particular things, that change takes place. In nature, the life which arises from death is itself only another instance of particular life; and if the species is taken as the substantial element behind this change, the destruction of particular things will appear as a relapse on the part of the species into particularity. Consequently, the survival of the species consists purely in a uniform repetition of one and the same mode of existence. But with spiritual forms, it is otherwise; for in this case, change occurs not just on the surface but within the concept, and it is the concept itself which is modified. In the natural world, the species does not progress, but in the world of the spirit, each change is a form of progress. Admittedly, the hierarchy of natural forms also constitutes a gradual sequence, extending from light at the one extreme to man at the other, so that each successive step is a modification of the preceding one, a higher principle which arises out of the dissolution[8] and destruction of its predecessor. But in nature, this sequence is fragmented, and all its individual elements coexist simultaneously; the transitions between them are only apparent to the thinking mind, which comprehends their overall relationship. Nature cannot comprehend itself, so that the negation of the forms it creates does not exist for it. But in the case of spiritual phenomena, higher forms are produced through the transformation of earlier and less advanced ones. The latter accordingly cease to exist; and the fact that each new form is the transfiguration of its predecessor explains why spiritual phenomena occur within the medium of time. Thus, world history as a whole is the expression of the spirit in time, just as nature is the expression of the Idea in space.

But in one respect, the nations of history, which are spiritual forms, are also natural entities. Accordingly, the various patterns they assume appear to coexist indifferently in space, i.e. to exist perennially. For if we cast our eyes around the world, we can discern three main principles in the older continents: the Far Eastern (i.e. Mongolian, Chinese, or Indian) principle, which is also the first to appear in history; the Mohammedan world, in which the principle of the abstract spirit, of monotheism, is already present, although it is coupled with unrestrained arbitrariness; and the Christian, Western European world, in which the highest principle of all, the spirit's recognition of itself and its own profundity, is realised. This universal series has been described here as existing perennially; but in world history we encounter it as a sequence of successive stages. For although these great spiritual principles coexist perennially, this does not mean that all the forms which have come and gone with the passage of time should also endure permanently. We might expect, for example, to find a Greek nation with its noble paganism etc. still existing in the present, or a Roman one of the same kind. But these nations belong to the past. Similarly, we encounter in every nation forms which have disappeared while the nation itself continued to exist. Why they disappear and do not likewise endure permanently in space can only be explained by their own peculiar nature, which only allows them to exist within the medium of world history itself. And it will at the same time emerge that only the most general forms endure, and that the more specific ones must inevitably disappear as soon as they have expressed themselves in restless activity.

All progress takes the form of following the successive stages in the evolution of consciousness. Man begins life as a child, and is only dimly conscious of the world and of himself; we know that he has to progress through several stages of empirical consciousness before he attains a knowledge of what he is in and for himself. The child starts out with sensory emotions; man next proceeds to the stage of general representations, and then to that of comprehension, until he finally succeeds in recognising the soul of things, i.e. their true nature. In spiritual matters, the child lives at first by relying on its parents and its environment, and is aware of their efforts to guide it in the ways of rectitude, which appear to it to have been laid down arbitrarily. A further stage is that of youth; its distinctive feature is that the human being now looks for independence within himself, that he becomes self-sufficient, and that he recognises that what is right and ethically proper, what is essential for him to perform and accomplish, is present in his own consciousness. And the consciousness of the adult contains even more principles regarding what is essential. Since progress consists in a development of the consciousness, it is not just a quantitative process but a sequence of changing relationships towards the underlying essence.

The history of the world accordingly represents the **successive stages** *in the development of that principle whose substantial content is the consciousness of freedom. This development is* **gradual***, not only because the spirit appears in it in a mediate rather than an immediate form — in that the spirit mediates itself with itself; but also because it is internally differentiated, for it involves a division or differentiation of the spirit within itself. The more specific determination of these various stages in their universal form belongs to the province of logic, but in its concrete aspect it is part of the philosophy of spirit. As regards its abstract qualities, it need only be mentioned here that, during the first and immediate stage in the process, the spirit, as already pointed out, is still immersed in nature, in which it exists in a state of unfree particularity (only One is free). But during the second stage it emerges into an awareness of its own freedom. The first departure from nature is, however, imperfect and partial — only Some are free — for it is derived indirectly from a state of nature, and is therefore related to it and still encumbered with it as one of its essential moments. The third stage witnesses the ascent of the spirit out of this as yet* **specific** *form of freedom into its purely universal form — man as such is free — in which the spiritual essence becomes conscious of itself and aware of its own nature.*

Thus, the first stage we shall consider in the spirit's development can be compared with the spirit of childhood. In it, that so-called unity of the spirit with nature which we encounter in the **Oriental World** still prevails. This natural spirit is still immersed in nature and is not yet self-sufficient; it is therefore not yet free, and has not undergone the process by which freedom comes into being. Even at this initial stage in the spirit's evolution, we find states, arts, and the rudiments of learning already in existence; but they are still rooted in the soil of nature. In this early patriarchal world, spirituality is still an underlying substance to which the individual is related only as an accidental property. In relation to the will of the One, all the others are in the position of children or subordinates.

The second phase of the spirit is that of separation, in which the spirit is reflected within itself and in which it emerges from a position of mere obedience and trust. This phase is made up of two distinct parts. The first is the youthful age of the spirit, in which it possesses freedom for itself, but a freedom which is still bound up with the underlying substance. Freedom has not yet been reborn from within the depths of the spirit. This youthful age is that of the **Greek World**. The second part of the phase is that of the spirit's manhood, in which the individual has his own ends for himself, but can only attain them in the service of a universal, of the state. This is the **Roman World**. In it, the personality of the individual and service towards the universal stand in opposition.

Then fourthly, there follows the Germanic age, the **Christian World**. If it were possible to compare the spirit's development to that of the individual in this case too, this age would have to be called the old age of the spirit. But it is a peculiarity of old age that it lives only in memories, in the past rather than in the present, so that the comparison is no longer applicable. In his negative aspects, the individual human being belongs to the elemental world and must therefore pass away. The spirit, however, returns to its concepts. In the Christian age, the divine spirit has come into the world and taken up its abode in the individual, who is now completely free and endowed with substantial freedom. This is the reconciliation of the subjective with the objective spirit. The spirit is reconciled and united with its concept, in which it had developed from a state of nature, by a process of internal division, to be reborn as subjectivity. All this is the a priori structure of history to which empirical reality must correspond.

These stages are the basic principles which underlie the universal process; but to show in detail how each of them contains within itself a further process whereby it achieves specific form, and what constitutes the dialectic of transitions between them, must be left to the later part of this investigation.

We must merely note for the present that the spirit begins *in a state of infinite potentiality—but no more than potentiality—which contains its absolute substance as something as yet* implicit, *as the object and goal which it only attains as the end result in which it at last achieves its realisation. In actual existence, progress thus appears as an advance from the imperfect to the more perfect, although the former should not be understood in an abstract sense as merely imperfect, but as something which at the same time contains its own opposite, i.e. what is commonly called perfection, as a germ or impulse: just as potentiality—at least in terms of reflection—points forward to something which will eventually attain reality, or—to take a more specific example—just as the Aristotelian* dynamis *is also* potentia, *i.e. power and strength. Thus the imperfect, in so far as it contains its own opposite within itself, is a contradiction; and although it certainly exists, it must just as surely be overcome[8] and resolved. It is the drive and inherent impulse of spiritual life to break through the shell of natural and sensory existence, of all that is alien to it, and to arrive at the light of consciousness, i.e. as its own true nature.*

b. [The beginning of history]

In connection with the idea of a state of nature in which freedom and justice are—or were—supposedly present in perfect form, we have already remarked in general terms on how the commencement of the history of spirit should be interpreted in relation to the concept which underlies it. But the idea of a state of nature was merely an assumption *as far as historical existence is concerned, an assumption made in the twilit regions of hypothetical reflection. But a claim of an altogether different kind—i.e. one put forward not as an assumption based on thought but as a historical fact guaranteed by a higher authority—is made by another idea which is now frequently advanced in certain quarters. It takes up the old doctrine of the primitive paradisiac condition of man, which the theologians originally elaborated after their own fashion (for example, in the theory that God conversed with Adam in Hebrew), but adapts it to suit other requirements.* For it has been argued (by **Schelling**, for example; cf. also **Schlegel's** *On the Language and Wisdom of the Indians*) that a primitive nation once existed, and that all our knowledge and art has simply been handed down to us from it. This original nation, it is contended, existed before mankind proper had come into being, and is immortalised in ancient legends under the image of the gods; distorted fragments of its highly developed culture are allegedly also to be found in the myths of the earliest nations. And the condition of the earliest nations, as described in history, is represented as a gradual decline from the high level of culture which preceded it. All this is put forward with the claim that philosophy requires that it should be so, and that it is also supported by historical evidence. *The high authority to which appeal is made in the first instance is that of the biblical narrative. But on the one hand, this narrative portrays the primitive condition only in its few well known characteristics, and on the other, it describes it and its various changes either in relation to mankind at large—i.e. as part of human nature in general—or, in so far as Adam is to be taken as a single individual or at most as two people, as present and complete only in this one individual or in a single human couple. The biblical account does not justify us in imagining that a nation and its historical condition actually existed in that primitive form, let alone in inferring that it had developed a perfect knowledge of God and of nature. Nature, so the fiction runs, originally lay open and transparent like a bright mirror of God's creation before the clear eye of man, and the divine truth was equally transparent to him. It is also hinted—albeit in an indefinite and obscure manner—that in this primeval condition, man was in possession of a definite and already extensive knowledge of religious truths, revealed to him directly by God. Furthermore, all religions had their historical origin in this primitive condition, although they subsequently adulterated and obscured the original truth with figments of error and depravity. But in all the mythologies which error has created, traces of that original state and of the early doctrines of religious truth are present and can still be recognised. It is accordingly claimed that the study of the history of ancient peoples gains its essential interest from the fact that it is possible to follow it back to the point where such fragments of the earliest revealed knowledge can still be encountered in a purer form.*

We certainly owe very much that is valuable to the interest which has fired such historical research, but this same research can also be indicted on its own direct testimony. For it sets out to prove by historical methods that whose historical existence it has already presupposed. Besides, it begins with a highly concentrated amalgam of historical data, and even these are eventually lost sight of altogether. Neither that advanced state of theological knowledge, or of other scientific (e.g.

astronomical) knowledge (such as astronomers themselves, including **Bailly,**
have fancifully attributed to the Indians), nor the assumption that such a state of
affairs prevailed at the beginning of history or that the religions of the various
nations were traditionally derived from it and subsequently developed by a
process of degeneration and deterioration (as is claimed by the crudely conceived
so-called 'system of emanation')—none of these assumptions has any historical
foundation, nor—if we may contrast their arbitrary and purely subjective origin
with the true concept of history—can they ever hope to attain one.

This notion of a perfect primeval condition does, however, contain a
philosophical element—namely the realisation that man cannot have originally existed in a state of animal insensibility. This is perfectly correct; man
cannot have developed from a state of animal insensibility, although he may
well have developed from a state of human insensibility. Animal humanity
is altogether different from animality proper. The spirit is present from the
beginning; but the spirit at first exists only in itself, as natural spirit, on
which the character of humanity is nevertheless already imprinted. The
child has no rationality, but it does have the real capability of becoming
rational. The animal, on the other hand, is incapable of attaining self-consciousness. Even the simple movements of the child have a human quality
about them; its first movement of all, its crying, is of a completely non-ani-
mal nature. For man is from the start an intelligent being; but those who
persist in believing that man, in his original condition, lived in pure consciousness of God and of nature—surrounded, as it were, by everything
which we have to acquire through laborious efforts, and in the centre of all
arts and sciences—have failed to appreciate what intelligence and thought
are. They cannot have understood that spirit is that infinite movement,
ἐνέργεια, ἐντελέχεια (energy, activity) which never rests, that it abandons
its original condition and is drawn on to a new one which it works upon in
turn, discovering itself through the work it performs: for it is through this
work alone that the spirit externalises its universal concept and attains a
real existence. This, accordingly, is not the first but the last stage in its
development. The customs, laws, institutions, and symbols of ancient
nations are indeed the vessels of speculative ideas, for they are products of
the spirit. But this inner reality of the Idea and its recognition of itself in
the form of the Idea are two quite different things. The speculative Idea as
an object of knowledge cannot have come first; on the contrary, it is the
fruit of the spirit's highest and most abstract endeavours.

The only appropriate and worthy method of philosophical investigation is to
take up history at that point where rationality begins to manifest itself in worldly
existence—i.e. not where it is still a mere potentiality **in itself** *but where it is in*
a position to express itself in consciousness, volition, and action. The inorganic
existence of the spirit or of freedom—i.e. unconscious indifference (whether
savage or mild in temper) towards good and evil, and hence towards laws in
general, or, if we prefer to call it so, the perfection of innocence—is not itself an

*object of history. The natural (and at the same time religious) form of ethical life
is family piety. In a society where this prevails, ethical life consists in the members
behaving towards each other not as individuals or distinct persons with a will of
their own; and for this very reason, the family in itself lies outside that development from which history takes its source. But if this spiritual unit steps beyond the
sphere of emotion and natural love and attains a consciousness of personality, we
have before us that dark and impenetrable intermediate zone in which neither
nature nor spirit is open and transparent, and for which nature and spirit can
become open and transparent only through a further process whereby the will,
which has now become conscious of itself, develops over a protracted period of
time. The quality of openness pertains solely to consciousness, and it is to consciousness alone that God—and indeed all other things too—can be revealed; in
their true and universal form, which exists in and for itself, they can only be
revealed to a consciousness which has become capable of reflective thought.
Freedom is nothing more than a knowledge and affirmation of such universal and
substantial objects as law and justice, and the production of a reality which
corresponds to them—i.e. the state.*

*Nations may have had a long history before they finally reach their destination
—i.e. that of forming themselves into states—and may even have developed
considerably in some respects before they attain this goal. But, as already indicated, this* **pre-historical period** *lies outside the scope of our present investigation, irrespective of whether a real history followed it or whether the nations in
question never finally succeeded in forming themselves into states. A great historical discovery, like the discovery of a new world, has been made in the last twenty
[years] or upwards in connection with the Sanskrit language and its affinities
with the languages of Europe. In particular, it has given us an insight into the
historical links between the Germanic nations and those of India, an insight which
carries as much certainty with it as can ever be achieved in such matters. Even at
the present time, we know of peoples which scarcely form a society, let alone a
state, but which have long been known to exist; and with others again, although it
is primarily their advanced condition which interests us, their traditions extend
beyond the history of their first constitution, and they underwent numerous
changes before this epoch began. In the above-mentioned connection between the
languages of nations so widely separated in space and so very different in religion,
constitutions, ethics, and in every variety of spiritual and even physical culture
(differences which have existed not only in the present, but also in the already
remote ages in which they first became known to us), we have before us a result
which proves as an irrefutable fact that these nations spread outwards from a
centre in Asia and developed in disparate ways from an original family relationship; and this is not a fact established by the favourite method of combining and
reasoning from circumstances of greater and lesser import—a method which has
enriched history with so many fabrications given out as facts, and which, since
alternative combinations of the same circumstances (either among themselves or
with others) are equally possible, will continue to enrich it in the same fashion.*

But all these events, whose range appears so extensive, lie outside history proper: they in fact preceded it.

In our language, the word 'history' *combines both objective and subjective meanings, for it denotes the* historia rerum gestarum *as well as the* res gestae *themselves, the historical narrative and the actual happenings, deeds, and events—which, in the stricter sense, are quite distinct from one another. But this conjunction of the two meanings should be recognised as belonging to a higher order than that of mere external contingency: we must in fact suppose that the writing of history and the actual deeds and events of history make their appearance simultaneously, and that they emerge together from a common source. Family memorials and patriarchal traditions have an interest only within the family or tribe itself. The uniform course of their existence is not an object worthy of commemoration, although distinct deeds or turns of fate may well inspire Mnemosyne to retain their images, just as love and religious emotion impel the imagination to confer shape upon impulses which are initially lacking in form. But it is the state which first supplies a content which not only lends itself to the prose of history but actually helps to produce it. Instead of the merely subjective dictates of authority—which may suffice for the needs of the moment—a commonwealth in the process of coalescing and raising itself up to the position of a state requires formal commandments and laws, i.e. general and universally valid directives. It thereby creates a record of its own development, and an interest in intelligible, determinate, and—in their results—enduring deeds and events, on which Mnemosyne, for the benefit of the perennial aim which underlies the present form and constitution of the state, is impelled to confer a lasting memory. All deeper emotions such as love, as well as religious contemplation and the forms it creates, are wholly immediate and satisfying in themselves; but the external existence of the state, despite the rational laws and principles it contains, is an incomplete present which cannot understand itself and develop an integrated consciousness without reference to the past.*

Those periods—whether we estimate them in centuries or millennia—which elapsed in the life of nations before history came to be written, and which may well have been filled with revolutions, migrations, and the most violent changes, have no objective history precisely because they have no subjective history, i.e. no historical narratives. It is not that the records of such periods have simply perished by chance; on the contrary, the reason why we have no records of them is that no such records were possible. It is only within a state which is conscious of its laws that clearly defined actions can take place, accompanied by that clear awareness of them which makes it possible and necessary to commit them to posterity. It is obvious to anyone with even a rudimentary knowledge of the treasures of Indian literature that this country, so rich in spiritual achievements of a truly profound quality, nevertheless has no history. In this respect, it at once stands out in stark contrast to China, an empire which possesses a highly distinguished and detailed historical record going back to the earliest times. India not only has ancient religious books and splendid works of poetry, but also ancient books of law—and the latter have already been mentioned as a prerequisite for the growth of history proper; nevertheless, it still does not have a history. But in this particular case, the incipient organisation which first created social distinctions immediately became petrified into natural determinations—i.e. the caste system—so that, although the laws are concerned with civil rights, they make these very rights dependent on distinctions of natural origin; their principal aim is to define the duties (in terms of wrongs rather than rights) of these classes towards one another, i.e. the privileges of the higher over the lower. The ethical element is thereby excluded from the splendour of Indian life and from every one of its provinces. Given this state of bondage in an order based firmly and permanently on nature, all social relations are wild and arbitrary, an ephemeral activity—or rather madness—with no ultimate end in the shape of progress and development; thus, no intelligent recollection, no object worthy of Mnemosyne presents itself, and a profound but extravagant fantasy drifts at random over a region which ought to have had a fixed purpose—a purpose rooted at least in substantial (i.e. implicitly rational, if [not] yet also subjective) freedom and reality—and thereby rendered itself worthy of history.

Since such conditions must be fulfilled before history is possible, it has happened that so rich and immeasurable an enterprise as the growth of families into tribes and of tribes into nations, which have then spread out in space as a result of their increase in size (a process which, as one can imagine, has led to innumerable complications, revolutions, and catastrophes) has taken place without giving rise to history; and what is more, that the concomitant expansion and development of the realm of spoken sounds has itself remained dumb, and has taken place in a silent and surreptitious manner. It is a fact attested by the monuments of literature that languages spoken by uncivilised nations have attained a high degree of development, and that the human understanding, by an intelligible process, has fully acquainted itself with this theoretical region. A full and consistent grammar is the product of thought, and the categories of thought are apparent within it. It is also a fact that, as society and the state become progressively more civilised, this systematic completeness of the understanding is gradually eroded, and, in this respect, language becomes correspondingly poorer and less refined—for it is a peculiar phenomenon that progress towards greater spirituality, although it promotes and cultivates rationality, allows the elaborate and precise constructions of the understanding to fall into neglect, seeing them as an obstruction and finally dispensing with them altogether. Language is the **activity** *of the theoretical* **intelligence** *in the proper sense, for it is through language that it receives its external expression. The activities of memory and of the imagination, if not expressed in language, are no more than internal utterances. But this whole theoretical activity, together with its further development and the more concrete process which accompanies it—i.e. the dissemination of peoples, their separation from one another, their interminglings and their migrations—remains buried in the obscurity of a voiceless past; these are not acts of a will becoming conscious of itself, of freedom giving itself an external embodiment and a proper reality. Since* *they do not partake of this true substance, all such changes — regardless of the linguistic advances which accompany them — have not attained the status of history. The precocious development of language and the progress and diffusion of nations have acquired their significance and interest for concrete reason partly in so far as the nations in question have had contact with the other states, and partly as they have begun to form political constitutions of their own.*

c. The course of development

After these remarks concerning the **beginning** *of world history and that pre-historical period which lies outside it, we must now define more precisely* **the nature** *of its* **course** *— but for the present only in its formal aspects; the further definition of its concrete content is a problem of detailed classification.*

World history, as already pointed out, represents the development of the spirit's consciousness of its own freedom and of the consequent realisation of this freedom. This development is by nature a **gradual progression,** *a series of successive determinations of freedom which proceed from the concept of the material in question, i.e. the nature of freedom in its development towards self-consciousness. The logical — and even more so the dialectical — nature of the concept in general, i.e. the fact that it determines itself, assumes successive determinations which it progressively overcomes,[8] thereby attaining a positive, richer, and more concrete determination — this necessity, and the necessary series of pure abstract determinations of the concept, are comprehended by means of philosophy. All that need be noted here is that each step in the process, since it is different from all the others, has its own peculiar determinate principle. In history, such principles constitute the determinate characteristics of the spirit of a nation. Each historical principle, in its concrete form, expresses every aspect of the nation's consciousness and will, and indeed of its entire reality; it is the common denominator of its religion, its political constitution, its ethical life, its system of justice, its customs, its learning, art, and technical skill, and the whole direction of its industry. These special peculiarities should be interpreted in the light of the general peculiarity, the particular principle of the nation in question, just as this general peculiarity can be detected in the factual details with which history presents us. The question of whether this or that particular characteristic actually constitutes the distinctive principle of a nation is one which can only be approached empirically and demonstrated by historical means. To accomplish this, a trained capacity for abstraction and a thorough familiarity with ideas are necessary; one must have, so to speak, an a priori knowledge of the entire sphere to which the principles in question belong, just as* **Kepler** *— to name the greatest exponent of this mode of cognition — had to have an a priori knowledge of ellipses, cubes, and squares and of the ideas concerning their relations before he could discover his immortal laws from the empirical data at his disposal; and the laws themselves consist of definitions borrowed from the above-mentioned class of conceptions. Anyone who approaches such matters without a knowledge of these elementary general princi-*

ples, however long he may contemplate the heavens and the movements of the celestial bodies, can no more understand these laws than he could hope to formulate them himself. This ignorance of ideas concerning the gradual develop-ment of freedom is responsible for some of the objections commonly levelled against the philosophical approach to a subject which usually confines itself to empirical matters — objections to its so-called a priori method and to its alleged attempts to foist ideas on to the data of history. In the eyes of the objectors, these determina-tions of thought appear as something alien and extraneous to the object in hand. To a subjectively conditioned mind which is unfamiliar with ideas and unaccus-tomed to using them, they will indeed appear alien, and they have no place in the conceptions and theories which so limited an intellect forms of its object. It is this which has given rise to the saying that philosophy **does not understand** *such subjects. Philosophy must indeed admit that it does not have the kind of under-standing which prevails in other disciplines, i.e. that it does not proceed according to the categories of the understanding, but according to the categories of reason — although it is fully acquainted with the understanding and with its value and position. In the process of scientific understanding — just as in philosophy itself — the* **essential** *must be separated from the so-called inessential and clearly distinguished from it. But this is impossible unless we* **know** *what is essential, and in relation to world history in general, the essential is precisely that conscious-ness of freedom and those determinate phases in its development which we have already mentioned. The relationship of all particular things to these categories is their relationship to the truly essential.*

Among the more direct kinds of objection levelled against the interpretation of any determinate object in a universal sense, some instances can usually be traced back to an inability to grasp and understand Ideas. If, in natural history, some monstrous and abnormal specimen or hybrid is cited as an instance against clearly defined species and genera, we can rightly reply with that saying which is so often used in an imprecise sense: namely that the exception proves the rule, i.e. that the exception reveals either the particular conditions under which the rule applies, or the deficiency and hybridism which occur in deviations from the norm. Nature is not strong enough to preserve its general classes and species from the influence of other elemental factors and agencies. But although the organisation of man, for example, is defined by the concrete form it assumes, and the brain, the heart, etc., are specified as essential ingredients of it, it is quite possible to adduce some wretched abortion or freak which possesses a generally human form (or at least parts of it) and which has been conceived in a human body, lived in it, been born from it, and drawn the breath of life, but which lacks either a brain or a heart. If such a specimen is quoted against the defining properties of an authentic human constitution, we can proceed no further than the abstract name of man and its superficial definition, from which the idea of a real, concrete human being is of course altogether different: for the latter must have a brain in its head and a heart in its breast.

A similar situation arises when it is maintained — quite correctly — that genius, talent, moral virtues, moral sentiments, and piety can be encountered in every region, under all constitutions, and in all political circumstances; and there is no lack of examples to prove this assertion. But if this is meant to imply that those distinctions which arise out of the degree of self-consciousness which freedom has attained are unimportant or inessential in relation to the above-mentioned qualities, reflection remains tied to abstract categories and lacks any determinate content, for which no principles are provided by the categories in question. The intellectual attitude which adopts such formal points of view certainly affords unlimited scope for ingenious questions, scholarly opinions, striking comparisons, and seemingly profound reflections and declamations; their brilliance may in fact seem to increase in proportion to their capacity for indefiniteness, and they may be the more readily refurbished and modified the less their attempts to achieve great results lead to anything of rational substance. From this point of view, one might well compare the familiar Indian epics, as they are called, with those of Homer, and argue that, since imaginative greatness is the true test of poetic genius, they are superior to the latter; in the same way, similarities between certain imaginary traits or attributes of the deities have led some to feel justified in identifying figures of Greek mythology with those of India. Similarly, the philosophy of China, in so far as it takes the **One** *as its basis, has been equated with what later appeared as the Eleatic philosophy or the system of Spinoza; and since it also expresses itself in abstract numbers and lines, some have claimed to detect Pythagorean philosophy or even Christian dogma in it. Examples of bravery, indefatigable courage, qualities of magnanimity, self-denial and self-sacrifice, etc., which are encountered in the most savage and the most faint-hearted of nations, are deemed sufficient evidence for the view that there is as much — or even more — virtue and morality in such nations as in the most civilised Christian states, and so on. With such examples in mind, some have seen fit to doubt whether men have become better with the progress of history and of culture in general, and whether their morality has increased — the assumption being that morality depends upon the agent's subjective intentions and insights, on what he considers as justice or injustice, good or evil, and not on what is considered to be just and good or unjust and evil in and for itself or within a particular religion which is generally recognised as true.*

We can spare ourselves the task of analysing the formalism and error of such attitudes here, and of establishing the true principles of morality — or rather of ethical life — in opposition to false morality. For world history moves on a higher plane than that to which morality properly belongs, for the sphere of morality is that of private convictions, the conscience of individuals, and their own particular will and mode of action; and the latter have their value, imputation, and reward or punishment within themselves. Whatever is required and accomplished by the ultimate end of the spirit, which exists in and for itself, and whatever providence does, transcends the obligations, liability, and responsibility which attach to individuality by virtue of its ethical existence. Those who, on ethical grounds (and hence with a noble intention), have resisted what the progress of the

Idea of the spirit required, stand higher in moral worth than those whose crimes have been transformed by a higher order into the instruments of realising its will. But in revolutions of this kind, both parties alike stand within the same circle of corruptible existence, so that it is merely a formal kind of justice, abandoned by the living spirit and by God, which those who have the existing law on their side defend. The deeds of the great men who are the individuals of world history thus appear justified not only in their inner significance (of which the individuals in question are unconscious), but also in a secular sense. But from this latter point of view, no representations should be made against world-historical deeds and those who perform them by moral circles to which such individuals do not belong. The litany of private virtues — modesty, humility, charity, liberality, etc. — must not be raised against them. World history might well disregard completely the sphere to which morality and the much discussed and misunderstood dichotomy between morality and politics belong — and not merely by refraining from judgements (for the principles of world history and the necessary relationship of men's actions to these principles themselves constitute the judgement), but by ignoring individuals altogether and leaving them unmentioned; for what it has to record is the activity of the spirit of nations, and the individual forms which the spirit has assumed in the sphere of external reality could well be left to the attention of ordinary historians.

The same kind of formalism as that practised in morality also makes use of the indefinite notions which surround genius, poetry, and even philosophy, and likewise manages to discover them in everything. These notions are products of reflective thought, and the ability to manipulate such generalities — which do signalise and designate essential distinctions, but without bringing out the true depth of their significance — is what we call **culture;** *it is a purely formal property, in that its sole aim, irrespective of the content it has before it, is to analyse the latter into its component parts and to comprehend these in forms and definitions of thought. Culture as such does not contain that free universality which would enable it to make itself the object of its own consciousness. Such a consciousness of thought itself and of the forms of thought taken in isolation from any particular material, is philosophy, for whose existence culture is admittedly a prerequisite; but the function of culture consists merely in clothing whatever content it has before it in the form of universality, so that the two are inseparably united within it — so inseparably that it regards its content (which, through the analysis of one conception into a multitude of subordinate conceptions, can be enlarged to an immeasurable degree of richness) as a purely empirical element in which thought plays no part whatsoever. It is nevertheless just as much an act of thought — or, more specifically, of the understanding — to reduce to a simple conception (such as earth, man, etc., or Alexander or Caesar) an object which itself encompasses a rich and concrete content and to designate it by a single word, as it is to analyse it into its separate parts, to isolate the determinations which such a conception contains, and to bestow particular names on each of them. All this [had to be said] to avoid the risk of making indefinite and empty pronounce-*

ments on culture. But to return to the view which originally provoked the above remarks, it is at least clear that, just as reflection produces the universal notions of genius, talent, art, science, etc., and equally general observations concerning their nature, formal culture, at every stage of spiritual evolution, not only can *but also* must *make its appearance, grow, and blossom out to the full; for each stage in the process must develop itself into a state, and advance from this basis of civilisation to reflective understanding and to forms of generalisation, both in laws and in all other things. Political life as such inevitably gives rise to formal culture, and hence also to learning and to a fully developed poetry and art in general. Besides, what we call the plastic arts, even in their technical aspects, presuppose a civilised community of men. Poetry, which has less need of external means and accessories and whose medium is the voice, the instrument of the spirit's immediate self-expression, emerges in all its boldness and with highly developed powers of expression even in nations which have not yet reached the stage of uniting to form a law-governed community; for as already remarked, language attains a high level of reflective development in its own right even before civilisation has emerged.*

Philosophy, too, must make its appearance as soon as political life is established. For that which confers the property of culture upon any given content is, as already mentioned, the form proper to thought itself; whereas philosophy is merely the consciousness of this form, the thinking of thinking, so that the material which it requires for its own peculiar edifice is already prepared for it through the general progress of culture. And in the development of the state itself, periods must occur in which the spirit of nobler natures is forced to flee from the present into ideal regions, and to find in them that reconciliation with itself which it can no longer enjoy in an internally divided reality; for the reflective understanding attacks all those sacred and profound elements which were artlessly introduced into the religion, laws, and customs of nations, and debases and dilutes them into abstract and godless generalities. Thought is then impelled to become thinking reason, and to pursue and accomplish in its own element the undoing of that destruction which had previously overtaken it.

Thus, in all world-historical nations, we do indeed encounter poetry, plastic art, science, and even philosophy. But these differ not only in their tone, style, and general tendency, but even more so in their basic import; and this import involves the most important difference of all, i.e. that of rationality. It is pointless for a presumptuous aesthetic criticism to insist that their subject-matter, i.e. the substantial part of their content, should not be determined by the pleasure we derive from it, and to argue that beauty of form as such, imaginative greatness, and the like, are the aims of fine art and the only factors which should be registered and appreciated by a liberal disposition and cultivated mind. If the substance itself is insignificant, or wild and fantastic or absurd, a healthy common sense cannot bring itself to abstract from it in such a way as to derive enjoyment from the work in question. For even if one ranks the Indian epics as highly as Homer's on account of numerous formal qualities of this kind—greatness of invention and imagination, vividness of imagery and sentiments, beauty of diction, etc.—they neverthe-

less remain infinitely different in their import and hence in their very substance; and the latter involves the interest of reason, which is directly concerned with the consciousness of the concept of freedom and the way in which it expresses itself in individuals. There is not only a classical form, but also a **classical** *content; and besides, form and content are so intimately connected in works of art that the former can only be classical in so far as the latter is also classical. If the content is fantastic and not self-contained — and it is reason alone which supplies both measure and goal — the form becomes unbalanced and amorphous, or awkward and trivial.*

In the same way, it is equally possible to draw parallels between Chinese and Indian philosophy, and between Eleatic, Pythagorean, and Spinozistic metaphysics — or even modern metaphysics in general — for all of them do indeed base themselves on the One or on unity, the wholly abstract universal; but to compare or even to identify them in this way is a highly superficial procedure. For it overlooks the one essential factor, i.e. the determinate characteristics of the unity in question; and this involves an essential distinction, for the unity may be understood either in an abstract or in a concrete sense (concrete to the point of being a unity in itself, which is the same thing as spirit). Those who treat them as identical merely prove that they have recognised only the abstract kind of unity; and although they pass judgements on philosophy, they are ignorant of the very factor from which philosophy derives its interest.

On the other hand, there are also areas which remain the same despite all differences in the substantial content of the cultures in question. These differences concern the thinking reason; and freedom, whose self-consciousness consists in this reason, has **one and the same** *root as thought. Since man alone — as distinct from the animals — is a thinking being, he alone possesses freedom, and he possesses it solely by virtue of his ability to think. Consciousness of freedom consists in the fact that the individual comprehends himself as a person, i.e. that he sees himself in his distinct existence as inherently universal, as capable of abstraction from and renunciation of everything particular, and therefore as inherently infinite. Consequently, the areas which lie outside this variety of comprehension are a common denominator amidst the substantial differences referred to above. Even morality, which is so closely connected with the consciousness of freedom, can attain a high degree of purity before any such consciousness is present; for it may simply enunciate universal duties and rights as objective commandments, or even remain purely negative in character, prescribing a formal elevation of the mind and a renunciation of the sensual and of all sensual motives.* **Chinese** *morality, since the Europeans have become acquainted with it and with the writings of* **Confucius,** *has received the highest praise and the most flattering tributes to its merits even from those who are familiar with Christian morality; in the same way, men have acknowledged the sublimity with which the religion and poetry of* **India** *(or at least the higher kinds of these), and in particular the Indian philosophy, express and enjoin the removal and sacrifice of all sensual things. Yet these two nations are lacking — indeed completely lacking — in the essential self-*

consciousness of the concept of freedom. The Chinese look on their moral rules as if they were laws of nature, positive external commandments, coercive rights and duties, or rules of mutual courtesy. Freedom, through which the substantial determinations of reason can alone be translated into ethical attitudes, is absent; morality is a political matter which is administered by government officials and courts of law. Their writings on the subject are not, however, collections of legal statutes, but are addressed to the subjective will and disposition of the reader. Like the moral writings of the Stoics, they read like a series of commands which purport to be necessary for the attainment of happiness, so that it is left to the individual to adopt and follow such commands or not; in the same way, the idea of an abstract subject, *the wise man, is the culmination of such doctrines with both the Chinese and the Stoic moralists. And in the* Indian *doctrine of the renunciation of sensuality, desires, and all earthly interests, positive ethical freedom is not the goal and end, but rather the extinction of consciousness and the suspension of spiritual and even physical life.*

A nation is only world-historical in so far as its fundamental element and basic aim have embodied a universal principle; only then is its spirit capable of producing an ethical and political organisation. If nations are impelled merely by desires, their deeds are lost without trace (as with all fanaticism), and no enduring achievement remains. Or the only traces they leave are ruin and destruction. In this way, the Greeks speak of the rule of Chronos or Time, who devours his own children (i.e. the deeds he has himself produced); this was the Golden Age, which produced no ethical works. Only Zeus, the political god from whose head Pallas Athene sprang and to whose circle Apollo and the Muses belong, was able to check the power of time; he did so by creating a conscious ethical institution, i.e. by producing the state.

An achievement is only objective in so far as it is an object of knowledge. It contains the determination of universality or thought in its very element; without thought, it has no objectivity, for thought is its basis. The nation must know the universal on which its ethical life is based and before which the particular vanishes away, and it must therefore know the determinations which underlie its justice and religion. The spirit cannot rest content with the mere existence of an order or cult; its will is rather to attain this knowledge of its own determinations. Only in this way can it succeed in uniting its subjectivity with the universal of its objectivity. Admittedly, its world is also composed of distinct elements to which it responds through the medium of external intuition, etc., but the unity of its innermost nature with this external world must also be present to it. This is its supreme liberation, since thought is its innermost nature. The highest point in the development of the nation is reached when it has understood its life and condition by means of thought, and acquired a systematic knowledge of its laws, justice, and ethical life; for in this achievement lies the closest

possible unity which the spirit can attain with itself. The aim of its endeavours is for it to have itself as its own object; but it cannot have itself as its
object in its true essentiality unless it thinks itself. At this point, then, the
spirit knows its own principles, the universal aspect of its real world. Thus,
if we wish to know what Greece really was, we find the answer in Sophocles
and Aristophanes, Thucydides and Plato; in them, we find the historical
expression of what Greek life actually was. For in these individuals, the
Greek spirit comprehended itself through representation and thought.

This spiritual self-consciousness is the nation's supreme achievement;
but we must remember in the first place that it is also only ideal. In this
achievement of thought lies the profounder kind of satisfaction which the
nation can attain; but since it is of a universal nature, it is also ideal, and
accordingly different in form from the real activity, the real work and life
which made such an achievement possible. The nation now has both a real
and an ideal existence. At such a time, we shall therefore find that the
nation derives satisfaction from the idea of virtue and from discussion of
it—discussion which may either coexist with virtue itself or become a
substitute for it. All this is the work of the spirit, which knows how to bring
the unreflected—i.e. the merely factual—to the point of reflecting upon
itself. It thereby becomes conscious to some degree of the limitation of
such determinate things as belief, trust, and custom, so that the consciousness now has reasons for renouncing the latter and the laws which they
impose. This is indeed the inevitable result of any search for reasons; and
when no such reasons—i.e. no completely abstract universal principles—
can be found as the basis of the laws in question, men's ideas of virtue
begin to waver, and the absolute is no longer regarded as valid in its own
right, but only in so far as it has reasons to justify it. At the same time,
individuals gradually became isolated from one another and from the
whole, selfishness and vanity intervene, and men seek to obtain their own
advantage and satisfaction at the expense of the whole. For the consciousness is subjective in nature, and subjectivity carries with it the need to
particularise itself. Vanity and selfishness accordingly make their appearance, and passions and personal interests emerge unchecked and in a
destructive form. This is not, however, the natural death of the national
spirit, but merely a state of internal division.

And thus Zeus, who set limits to the depredations of time and suspended
its constant flux, had no sooner established something inherently enduring
than he was himself devoured along with his whole empire. He was devoured by the principle of thought itself, the progenitor of knowledge, of
reasoning, of insight based on rational grounds, and of the search for such
grounds. Time is the negative element in the world of the senses; thought
is equally negative, but it is at the same time that innermost and infinite
form into which all existence—and in the first place finite being or
determinate form—is dissolved. Time, then, is indeed the corrosive aspect

of negativity; but spirit likewise has the property of dissolving every determinate content it encounters. For it is the universal, unlimited, innermost and infinite form itself, and it overcomes all that is limited. Even if the objective element does not appear finite and limited in content, it does at least appear as something given, immediate, and authoritative in nature, so that it is not in a position to impose restrictions on thought or to set itself up as a permanent obstacle to the thinking subject and infinite internal reflection.

This dissolving activity of thought also inevitably gives rise to a new principle. Thought, in so far as it is universal in character, has the effect of dissolving every determinate content; but in this very dissolution, the preceding principle is in fact preserved, with the sole difference that it no longer possesses its original determination. The universal essence is preserved, but its universality as such has been brought out into relief. The preceding principle has been transfigured by universality; its present mode must be considered as different from the preceding one, for in the latter, the present mode existed only implicitly and had an external existence only through a complex series of manifold relationships. What formerly existed only in concrete particulars now has the form of universality conferred upon it; but a new element, another further determination, is also present. The spirit, in its new inward determination, has new interests and ends beyond those which it formerly possessed. This change in the principle's form also brings with it new and additional determinations of content. Everyone knows that a cultured man has quite different expectations from those of his uncultured fellow-countryman, although the latter lives within the same religion and ethical community and his substantial condition is precisely the same. Culture would at first seem to be purely formal in character, but it does also give rise to differences in content. The cultured and the uncultured Christian appear completely identical in one respect, but their needs are nevertheless completely different. And it is precisely the same with property relations. Even the serf has property, but it is coupled with obligations which render another person the joint owner of it. If, however, we define property in terms of **thought**, it of course follows that only one man can be the owner. For thought brings out the universal aspect, thereby creating a different interest and different needs.

The determinate nature of the transition which takes place in all such changes is therefore as follows: what at present exists becomes an object of thought, and it is thereby elevated into universality. The nature of the spirit is to comprehend the universal, i.e. that which is essential. Universality, in its truest sense, is the substance, the essence, that which truly exists. In the case of the slave, for example, the appropriate universal is that of the human being; for it is at this point that particularity passes over into universality. If, therefore, particularity is transcended in a given nation — for example, in that of Athens — by means of thought, and if thought develops to the point where the particular principle of the nation in question is no longer essential, that nation cannot continue to exist; for another principle has meanwhile emerged. World history then passes over to another nation. Such principles are present in world history in the shape of national spirits; but the latter also have a natural existence. The particular stage which the spirit has reached is present as the **natural principle** of the people in question or as the **nation**. According to the different ways in which it manifests itself in this determinate natural element, the spirit appears in various forms. Thus, although its new and higher determination within a particular national spirit does appear as the negation or destruction of the preceding one, its positive side also emerges in the shape of a new nation. A nation cannot pass through several successive stages in world history or make its mark in it more than once. If it were possible for genuinely new interests to arise within a nation, the national spirit would have to be in a position to will something new — but where could this new element come from? It could only take the shape of a higher and more universal conception of itself, a progression beyond its own principle, or a quest for a more universal principle — but this would mean that a further determinate principle, i.e. a new spirit, was already present. In world history, a nation can be dominant only once, because it can only have one task to perform within the spiritual process.

This advance or progression appears to be a process of infinite duration, in keeping with the notion of perfectibility — a constant progress which must always remain distant from its goal. But even if, in the advance towards a new principle, the content of the preceding one is comprehended in a more universal sense than before, it is at least certain that the new form which emerges will again be a determinate one. Furthermore, history has to do with reality, in which the universal must in any case assume a determinate form. And no limited form can establish itself permanently in face of thought or the concept. If there were something which the concept could not digest or resolve, it would certainly represent the highest degree of fragmentation and unhappiness. But if something of the kind did exist, it could be nothing other than thought itself in its function of self-comprehension. For thought alone is inherently unlimited, and all reality is determined within it. In consequence, the fragmentation would cease to exist, and thought would be satisfied within itself. This, then, would be the ultimate purpose of the world. Reason recognises that which is truthful, that which exists in and for itself, and which is not subject to any limitations. The concept of the spirit involves a return upon itself, whereby it makes itself its own object; progress, therefore, is not an indeterminate advance ad infinitum, for it has a definite aim — namely that of returning upon itself. Thus, it also involves a kind of cyclic movement as the spirit attempts to discover itself.

It is sometimes said that goodness is the ultimate end. But in the first place, this is an indefinite kind of expression. One might well be reminded — and should be reminded — of the equivalent form in religion. For in philosophy, we must on no account adopt the attitude of ignoring other venerable insights out of a misplaced sense of awe. From the point of view of religion, the ultimate aim is that man should attain a state of holiness. This, in religious terms, is indeed the proper aim so far as individuals are concerned. The subject gains itself as such and fulfils its end within the institution of religion. But seen in this light, the end already presupposes a content of a universal kind, i.e. a state in which souls may find their salvation. One might well object that this conception of salvation is no concern of ours, since salvation is a future end whose fulfilment lies in another world. But then we would still be left with existence in this world as a preparation for that future state. This whole distinction, however, is only subjectively valid; it would leave individuals with no choice but to regard whatever leads them to salvation as nothing more than a means. But this is not at all the case, for the latter must undoubtedly be understood in an absolute sense. From the point of view of religion, the aim of both natural existence and spiritual activity is the **glorification of God**. Indeed, this is the worthiest end of the spirit and of history. The nature of the spirit is to make itself its own object and to comprehend itself. Only then is it really present as the product and result of its own activity. 'To comprehend itself' means, of course, to comprehend itself by means of thought. But this implies not merely a knowledge of arbitrary, casual, and ephemeral determinations, but a comprehension of the absolute itself. The aim of the spirit is therefore to make itself conscious of the absolute, and in such a way that this consciousness is given to it as the sole and exclusive truth, so that everything must be — and actually is — brought into conformity with it, and world history is ruled by it in reality as it was all along. To become actively aware of this means to do honour to God or to glorify the truth. This is the absolute and ultimate end, and truth is itself the power which produces its own glorification. In honouring God, the individual spirit is itself honoured — not, however, in a particular sense, but through the knowledge that the activity it performs in honour of God is of an absolute nature. Here, the individual spirit exists in truth, and participates in the absolute; it is therefore self-sufficient. Here also, the dichotomy which besets the limited spirit (which knows its own being only as a restriction, and raises itself above it by means of thought) is removed. And here again, not even natural death can intervene.

In our understanding of world history, we are concerned with history primarily as a record of the past. But we are just as fully concerned with the present. Whatever is true exists eternally in and for itself — not yesterday or tomorrow, but entirely in the present, 'now', in the sense of an absolute present. Within the Idea, even that which appears to be past is never lost. The Idea is of the present, and the spirit is immortal; there is no past or future time at which it did not exist or would not exist; it is not over and done with, nor does it not yet exist—on the contrary, it exists absolutely now. This in fact means that the present world and the present form and self-consciousness of the spirit contain within them all the stages which appear to have occurred earlier in history. These did admittedly take shape independently and in succession; but what the spirit is now, it has always been implicitly, and the difference is merely in the degree to which this implicit character has been developed. The spirit of the present world is the concept which the spirit forms of its own nature. It is this which sustains and rules the world, and it is the result of 6000 years of effort; it is all that the spirit has created for itself through the labours of world history, and all that was destined to emerge from these labours. This, then, is how we should understand world history, which presents us with the work of the spirit in its progressive recognition of its own nature and in its application of this knowledge to all the various spheres which are affected by it.

In this connection, it should be remembered that every individual, in his cultural development, must pass through various spheres which together form the basis of his concept of the spirit and each of which has taken shape and developed independently at some time in the past. But what the spirit is now, it has always been; the only difference is that it now possesses a richer consciousness and a more fully elaborated concept of its own nature. The spirit has all the stages of the past still adhering to it, and the life of the spirit in history consists of a cycle of different stages, of which some belong to the present and others have appeared in forms of the past. Since we are concerned with the Idea of the spirit and look upon everything in world history merely as a manifestation of it, we are invariably occupied with the present whenever we review the past, no matter how considerable that past may be. For philosophy is concerned with what is present and real. Those moments which the spirit appears to have outgrown still belong to it in the depths of its present. Just as it has passed through all its moments in history, so also must it pass through them again in the present—in the concept it has formed of itself.

XV.   Philosophy of Art: Introduction*

Before it is possible for us to turn . . . to our subject proper, it is our business to devote a brief introductory discussion to the objections and doubts which have been raised. In the first place, as regards the *worthiness* of art to be scientifically considered, it is no doubt the case that art can be employed as a fleeting pastime, to serve the ends of pleasure and entertainment, to decorate our surroundings, to impart pleasantness to the external conditions of our life, and to emphasize other objects by means of ornament. In this mode of employment art is indeed not independent, not free, but servile. But what *we* mean to consider, is the art which is *free* in its end as in its means.

That art is in the abstract capable of serving other aims, and of being a mere pastime, is moreover a relation which it shares with thought. For, on the one hand, science, in the shape of the subservient understanding, submits to be used for finite purposes, and as an accidental means, and in that case is not self-determined, but determined by alien objects and relations; but, on the other hand, science liberates itself from this service to rise in free independence to the attainment of truth, in which medium, free from all interference, it fulfils itself in conformity with its proper aims.

Fine art is not real art till it is in this sense free, and only achieves its highest task when it has taken its place in the same sphere with religion and philosophy, and has become simply a mode of revealing to consciousness and bringing to utterance the Divine Nature, the deepest interests of humanity, and the most comprehensive truths of the mind. It is in works of art that nations have deposited the profoundest intuitions and ideas of their hearts; and fine art is frequently the key—with many nations there is no other—to the understanding of their wisdom and of their religion.

This is an attribute which art shares with religion and philosophy, only in this peculiar mode, that it represents even the highest ideas *in sensuous forms*, thereby bringing them nearer to the character of natural phenomena, to the senses, and to feeling. The world, into whose depths *thought* penetrates, is a supra-sensuous world, which is thus, to begin with, erected as a

* From *The Introduction to Hegel's Philosophy of Fine Art*, translated by B. Bosanquet (1886).

beyond over against immediate consciousness and present sensation; the power which thus rescues itself from the *here*, that consists in the actuality and finiteness of sense, is the freedom of thought in cognition. But the mind is able to heal this schism which its advance creates; it generates out of itself the works of fine art as the first middle term of reconciliation between pure thought and what is external, sensuous, and transitory, between nature with its finite actuality and the infinite freedom of the reason that comprehends.

δ. The *element* of art was said to be in its general nature an *unworthy* element, as consisting in appearance and deception. The censure would be not devoid of justice, if it were possible to class appearance as something that ought not to exist. An appearance or show, however, is essential to existence. Truth could not be, did it not appear[20] and reveal itself,[39] were it not truth *for* some one or something, *for* itself as also *for* Mind. Therefore there can be no objection against appearance in general, but, if at all, against the particular mode of appearance in which art gives actuality to what is in itself real and true. If, in this aspect, the *appearance* with which art gives its conceptions life as determinate existences is to be termed a *deception*, this is a criticism which primarily receives its meaning by comparison with the external world of phenomena and its immediate contact with us as *matter*, and in like manner by the standard of our own world of feeling, that is, the inner world of *sense*. These are the two worlds to which, in the life of daily experience, in our own phenomenal life, we are accustomed to attribute the value and the title of actuality, reality, and truth, in contrast to art, which we set down as lacking such reality and truth. Now, this whole sphere of the empirical inner and outer world is just what is not the world of genuine reality, but is to be entitled a mere appearance more strictly than is true of art, and a crueller deception. Genuine reality is only to be found beyond the immediacy of feeling and of external objects. Nothing is genuinely real but that which is actual in its own right,[7] that which is the substance of nature and of mind, fixing itself indeed in present and definite existence, but in this existence still retaining its essential and self-centred being, and thus and no otherwise attaining genuine reality. The dominion of these universal powers is exactly what art accentuates and reveals. The common outer and inner world also no doubt present to us this essence of reality, but in the shape of a chaos of accidental matters, encumbered by the immediateness of sensuous presentation, and by arbitrary states, events, characters, etc. Art liberates the real import of appearances from the semblance and deception of this bad and fleeting world, and imparts to phenomenal semblances a higher reality, born of mind. The appearances of art, therefore, far from being mere semblances, have the higher reality and the more genuine existence in comparison with the realities of common life.

Just as little can the representations of art be called a deceptive semblance in comparison with the representations of historical narrative, as if that had the more genuine truth. For history has not even immediate existence, but only the intellectual presentation of it, for the element of its portrayals, and its content remains burdened with the whole mass of contingent matter formed by common reality with its occurrences, complications, and individualities. But the work of art brings before us the eternal powers that hold dominion in history, without any such superfluity in the way of immediate sensuous presentation and its unstable semblances.

Again, the mode of appearance of the shapes produced by art may be called a deception in comparison with philosophic thought, with religious or moral principles. Beyond a doubt the mode of revelation which a content attains in the realm of thought is the truest reality; but in comparison with the show or semblance of immediate sensuous existence or of historical narrative, the artistic semblance has the advantage that in itself it points beyond itself, and refers us away from itself to something spiritual which it is meant to bring before the mind's eye. Whereas immediate appearance does not give itself out to be deceptive, but rather to be real and true, though all the time its truth is contaminated and infected by the immediate sensuous element. The hard rind of nature and the common world give the mind more trouble in breaking through to the idea than do the products of art.

But if, on the one side, we assign this high position to art, we must no less bear in mind, on the other hand, that art is not, either in content or in form, the supreme and absolute mode of bringing the mind's genuine interests into consciousness. The form of art is enough to limit it to a restricted content. Only a certain circle and grade of truth is capable of being represented in the medium of art. Such truth must have in its own nature the capacity to go forth into sensuous form and be adequate to itself therein, if it is to be a genuinely artistic content, as is the case with the gods of Greece. There is, however, a deeper form of truth, in which it is no longer so closely akin and so friendly to sense as to be adequately embraced and expressed by that medium. Of such a kind is the Christian conception of truth; and more especially the spirit of our modern world, or, to come closer, of our religion and our intellectual culture, reveals itself as beyond the stage at which art is the highest mode assumed by man's consciousness of the absolute. The peculiar mode to which artistic production and works of art belong no longer satisfies our supreme need. We are above the level at which works of art can be venerated as divine, and actually worshipped; the impression which they make is of a more considerate kind, and the feelings which they stir within us require a higher test and a further confirmation. Thought and reflection have taken their flight above fine art. Those who delight in grumbling and censure may set down this phenomenon for a corruption, and ascribe it to the predominance of passion and selfish interests, which scare away at once the seriousness and the cheerfulness of art. Or we may accuse the troubles of the present time and the complicated condition of civil and political life as hindering the feelings, entangled in minute preoccupations, from freeing themselves, and rising to the higher aims of art, the intelligence itself being subordinate to petty needs and interests, in sciences which only subserve such purposes and are seduced into making this barren region their home.

However all this may be, it certainly is the case, that art no longer affords that satisfaction of spiritual wants which earlier epochs and peoples have sought therein, and have found therein only; a satisfaction which, at all events on the religious side, was most intimately and profoundly connected with art. The beautiful days of Greek art, and the golden time of the later middle ages are gone by. The reflective culture of our life of to-day, makes it a necessity for us, in respect of our will no less than of our judgment, to adhere to general points of view, and to regulate particular matters according to them, so that general forms, laws, duties, rights, maxims are what have validity as grounds of determination and are the chief regulative force. But what is required for artistic interest as for artistic production is, speaking generally, a living creation, in which the universal is not present as law and maxim, but acts as if one with the mood and the feelings, just as, in the imagination, the universal and rational is contained only as brought into unity with a concrete sensuous phenomenon. Therefore, our present in its universal condition is not favourable to art. As regards the artist himself, it is not merely that the reflection which finds utterance all round him, and the universal habit of having an opinion and passing judgment about art infect him, and mislead him into putting more abstract thought into his works themselves; but also the whole spiritual culture of the age is of such a kind that he himself stands within this reflective world and its conditions, and it is impossible for him to abstract from it by will and resolve, or to contrive for himself and bring to pass, by means of peculiar education or removal from the relations of life, a peculiar solitude that would replace all that is lost.

In all these respects art is, and remains for us, on the side of its highest destiny, a thing of the past. Herein it has further lost for us its genuine truth and life, and rather is transferred into our *ideas* than asserts its former necessity, or assumes its former place, in reality. What is now aroused in us by works of art is over and above our immediate enjoyment, and together with it, our judgment; inasmuch as we subject the content and the means of representation of the work of art and the suitability or unsuitability of the two to our intellectual consideration. Therefore, the *science* of art is a much more pressing need in our day, than in times in which art, simply as art, was enough to furnish a full satisfaction. Art invites us to consideration of it by means of thought, not to the end of stimulating art production, but in order to ascertain scientifically what art is.

ε. As soon as we propose to accept this invitation we are met by the difficulty which has already been touched upon in the suggestion that, though art is a suitable subject for philosophical reflection in the general sense, yet it is not so for systematic and scientific discussion. In this objection there lies the false idea that a philosophical consideration may, nevertheless, be unscientific. On this point it can only be remarked here with brevity, that, whatever ideas others may have of philosophy and philosophizing, I regard the pursuit of philosophy as utterly incapable of existing apart from a scientific procedure. Philosophy has to consider its object in its necessity, not, indeed, in its subjective necessity or external arrangement, classification, etc., but it has to unfold and demonstrate the object out of the necessity of its own inner nature. Until this evolution is brought to pass the scientific element is lacking to the treatment. In as far, however, as the objective necessity of an object lies essentially in its logical and metaphysical nature, the isolated treatment of art must be conducted with a certain relaxation of scientific stringency. For art involves the most complex presuppositions, partly in reference to its content, partly in respect of its medium and element, in which art is constantly on the borders of the arbitrary or accidental. Thus it is only as regards the essential innermost progress of its content and of its media of expression that we must call to mind the outline prescribed by its necessity.

The objection that works of fine art elude the treatment of scientific thought because they originate out of the unregulated fancy and out of the feelings, are of a number and variety that defy the attempt to gain a conspectus, and therefore take effect only on feeling and imagination, raises a problem which appears still to have importance. For the beauty of art does in fact appear in a form which is expressly contrasted with abstract thought, and which the latter is forced to destroy in exerting the activity which is its nature. This idea coheres with the opinion that reality as such, the life of nature and of mind, is disfigured and slain by comprehension; that, so far from being brought close to us by the thought which comprehends, it is by it that such life is absolutely dissociated from us, so that, by the use of thought as the *means* of grasping what has life, man rather cuts himself off from this his purpose. We cannot speak fully on this subject in the present passage, but only indicate the point of view from which the removal of this difficulty, or impossibility depending on maladaptation, might be effected.

It will be admitted, to begin with, that the mind is capable of contemplating itself, and of possessing a consciousness, and that a *thinking* consciousness, of itself and all that is generated by itself. Thought — to think — is precisely that in which the mind has its innermost and essential nature. In gaining this thinking consciousness concerning itself and its products, the mind is behaving according to its essential nature, however much freedom and caprice those products may display, supposing only that in real truth they have mind in them. Now art and its works as generated and created by the mind (spirit), are themselves of a spiritual nature, even if their mode of representation admits into itself the semblance of sensuous being, and pervades what is sensuous with mind. In this respect art is, to begin with, nearer to mind and its thinking activity than is mere external unintelligent nature; in works of art, mind has to do but with its own. And even if artistic works are not abstract thought and notion, but are an evolution of the notion *out of* itself, an alienation from itself towards the sensuous, still the power of the thinking spirit (mind) lies herein, *not merely* to grasp *itself only* in its peculiar form of the self-conscious spirit (mind), but just as much to recognize itself in its alienation in the shape of feeling and the sensuous, in its other form, by transmuting the metamorphosed thought back into definite thoughts, and so restoring it to itself. And in this preoccupation with the other of itself the thinking spirit is not to be held untrue to itself as if forgetting or surrendering itself therein, nor is it so weak as to lack strength to comprehend what is different from itself, but it comprehends both itself and its opposite. For the notion is the universal, which preserves itself in its particularizations, dominates alike itself and its "other," and so becomes the power and activity that consists in undoing the alienation which it had evolved. And thus the work of art in which thought alienates itself belongs, like thought itself, to the realm of comprehending thought, and the mind, in subjecting it to scientific consideration, is thereby but satisfying the want of its own inmost nature. For because thought is its essence and notion, it can in the last resort only be satisfied when it has succeeded in imbuing all the products of its activity with thought, and has thus for the first time made them genuinely its own. But as we shall see more definitely below, art is far from being the highest form of mind, and receives its true ratification only from science.

Just as little does art elude philosophical consideration by unbridled caprice. As has already been indicated, it is its true task to bring to consciousness the highest interests of the mind. Hence it follows at once with respect to the *content* that fine art cannot rove in the wildness of unfettered fancy, for these spiritual interests determine definite bases for its content, how manifold and inexhaustible soever its forms and shapes may be. The same holds true for the forms themselves. They, again, are not at the mercy of mere chance. Not every plastic shape is capable of being the expression and representation of those spiritual interests, of absorbing and of reproducing them; every definite content determines a form suitable to it.

In this aspect too, then, we are in a position to find our bearings according to the needs of thought in the apparently unmanageable mass of works and types of art. . . .

THE CONCEPTION OF ARTISTIC BEAUTY

Part I.   The Work of Art as Made and as Sensuous

After the above prefatory remarks, we approach closer to our subject, the philosophy of artistic beauty. Inasmuch as we are undertaking to treat it scientifically we must begin with its *Conception*.[9] Not till we have established this conception can we map out the division, and with it the plan of the entirety of the science; for a division, if it is not, as is the case with unphilosophical inquiries, taken in hand in a purely external manner, must find its principle in the conception of the object itself.

In presence of such a demand we are at once met by the question, "Whence do we get this conception?" If we begin with the given conception of artistic beauty itself, that is enough to make it a *pre-supposition* and mere assumption; now, mere assumptions are not admitted by the philosophical method, but whatever it allows to pass must have its truth demonstrated, *i.e.* displayed as necessary.

We will devote a few words to coming to an understanding upon this difficulty, which concerns the introduction to every philosophical branch of study when taken in hand by itself.

The object of every science presents *prima facie* two aspects: in the first place, that such an object *is*; in the second place, *what* it is.

In ordinary science little difficulty attaches to the first of these points. It might even, at first sight, look ridiculous, if the requirement were presented that in astronomy and physics it should be demonstrated that there was a sun, heavenly bodies, magnetic phenomena, etc. In these sciences, which have to do with what is given to sense, the objects are taken from external experience, and instead of demonstrating them it is thought sufficient to show them. Yet even within the non-philosophical sciences, doubts may arise about the existence of their objects, as *e.g.* in psychology, the science of mind, it may be doubted if there *is* a soul, a mind, *i.e.* something subjective, separate, and independent, distinct from what is material; or in theology, whether a God *is*. If, moreover, the objects are of subjective kind, *i.e.* are given only in the mind, and not as external sensuous objects, we are confronted by our conviction that there is nothing in the mind but what its own activity has produced. This brings up the accidental question whether men have produced this inner idea or perception in their minds or not, and even if the former is actually the case, whether they have not made the idea in question vanish again, or at any rate degraded it to a merely *subjective idea*, whose content has no natural and independent being. So, for instance, the beautiful has often been regarded as not naturally and independently necessary in our ideas, but as a mere subjective pleasure or accidental sense. Our external intuitions, observations, and perceptions are often deceptive and erroneous, but still more is this the case with the inner ideas, even if they have in themselves the greatest vividness, and are forcible enough to transport us irresistibly into passion.

This doubt whether an object of inward ideas and inward perception as such is or is not, as also the accidental question whether the subjective consciousness has produced it in itself, and whether the act or mode in which it brought it before itself was in its turn adequate to the object in its essential and independent nature—all this is just what aroused in men the higher scientific need, which demands that, even if we have an idea that an object is, or that there is such an object, the object must yet be displayed or demonstrated in terms of its necessity.

This proof, if it is developed in a really scientific way, must also satisfy the further question *What* an object is. But to expound this relation would carry us too far in this place, and we can only make the following remarks on the point.

If we are to display the necessity of our object, the beautiful in art, we should have to prove that art or beauty was a result of antecedents such as, when considered in their true conception, to lead us on with scientific necessity to the idea of fine art. But in as far as we begin with *art*, and propose to treat of the essence of *its* idea and of the realization of that idea, not of antecedents which go before it *as demanded by* its idea, so far art, as a peculiar scientific object, has, for us, a pre-supposition which lies beyond our consideration, and which, being a different content, belongs in scientific treatment to a different branch of philosophical study. For it is nothing short of the whole of philosophy that is the knowledge of the universe as in itself *one single* organic totality which develops itself out of its own conception, and which, returning into itself so as to form a whole in virtue of the necessity in which it is placed towards itself, binds itself together with itself into *one single* world of truth. In the coronal of this scientific necessity, each individual part is just as much a circle that returns into itself, as it has, at the same time, a necessary connection with other parts. This connection is a backward out of which it derives itself, as well as a forward, to which in its own nature it impels itself on and on, in as far as it is fertile by creating fresh matter out of itself, and issuing it into the further range of scientific knowledge. Therefore, it is not our present aim to demonstrate the idea of beauty from which we set out, that is, to derive it according to its necessity from the pre-suppositions which are its antecedents in science. This task belongs to an encyclopaedic development of philosophy as a whole and of its particular branches. For us, the idea of beauty and of art is a pre-supposition given in the system of philosophy. But as we cannot in this place discuss this system, and the connection of art with it, we have not yet the idea of the beautiful before us *in a scientific form*; what we have at command are merely the elements and aspects of it, as they are or have at former periods been presented, in the diverse ideas of the beautiful and of art in the mere common consciousness. Having started from this point, we shall subsequently pass to the more profound consideration of the views in question, in order thereby to gain the advantage of, in the first place, obtaining a general idea of our object, and further, by a brief criticism effecting a preliminary acquaintance with its higher principles, with which we shall have to do in the sequel. By this mode of treatment our final introduction will act, so to speak, as the overture to the account of the subject itself, and will serve the purpose of a general collection and direction of our thoughts towards the proper object-matter of our discussion.

What we know, to begin with, as a current idea of the work of art, comes under the three following general predicates: —

1. We suppose the work of art to be no natural product, but brought to pass by means of human activity.
2. To be essentially made *for* man, and, indeed, to be more or less borrowed from the sensuous and addressed to man's sense.
3. To contain an *end*.

1. As regards the first point, that a work of art is taken to be a product of human activity, this view has given rise (*a*) to the view that this activity, being the *conscious* production of an external object, can also be *known*, and *expounded*, and learnt, and prosecuted by others. For, what one can do, it might seem, another can do, or imitate, as soon as he is acquainted with the mode of procedure; so that, supposing universal familiarity with the rules of artistic production, it would only be a matter of any one's will and pleasure to carry out the process in a uniform way; and so to produce works of art. It is thus that the above-mentioned rule-providing theories and their precepts, calculated for practical observance, have arisen. But that which can be executed according to such instruction, can only be something formally regular and mechanical. For only what is mechanical is of such an external kind that no more than a purely empty exercise of will and dexterity is required to receive it among our ideas and put it in act; such an exercise not needing to be supplemented by anything concrete, or anything that goes beyond the precepts conveyed in general rules. This is most vividly displayed when precepts of the kind in question do not limit themselves to what is purely external and mechanical, but extend to the meaning-laden spiritual activity of true art. In this region the rules contain nothing but indefinite generalities; *e.g.* "The theme ought to be interesting, and each individual ought to be made to speak according to his rank, age, sex, and position." But if rules are meant to be adequate on this subject, their precepts ought to have been drawn up with such determinateness that they could be carried out just as they are expressed, without further and original activity of mind. Being abstract, however, in their content, such rules reveal themselves, in respect of their pretension of being adequate to fill the consciousness of the artist, as wholly inadequate, inasmuch as artistic production is not formal activity in accordance with given determinations. For it is bound as spiritual activity to work by drawing on its own resources, and to bring before the mind's eye a quite other and richer content and ampler individual creations than any abstract formulae can dictate. Such rules may furnish guidance in case of need, if they contain anything really definite, and therefore of practical utility; but their directions can only apply to purely external circumstances.

(*b*) The tendency which we have just indicated has therefore been abandoned, and, in place of it, the opposite principle has been pursued to no less lengths. For the work of art came to be regarded no longer as the product of an *activity general* in mankind, but as the work of a mind endowed with wholly peculiar gifts. This mind, it is thought, has then nothing to do but *simply* to give free play to its particular gift, as though it were a specific force of nature, and is to be entirely released from attention to laws of universal validity, as also from the interference of reflection in its instinctively creative operation. And, indeed, it is to be guarded therefrom, inasmuch as its productions could only be infected and tainted by such a consciousness. In this aspect the work of art was pronounced to be the product of *talent* and *genius*, and stress was laid on the natural element which talent and genius contain. The view was partly right. Talent is specific, and genius universal capability, with which a man has not the power to endow himself simply by his own self-conscious activity. We shall treat this point more fully in the sequel.

In this place we have only to mention the aspect of falsity in the view before us, in that all consciousness respecting the man's own activity was held, in the case of artistic production, not merely superfluous, but even injurious. Production on the part of talent and genius then appears, in general terms, as a *state*, and, in particular, as a state of *inspiration*. To such a state, it is said, genius is in part excited by a given object, and in part it has the power of its own free will to place itself therein, in which process, moreover, the good service of the champagne bottle is not forgotten. This notion became prominent in Germany in the so-called *epoch of genius*, which was introduced by the early poetical productions of Goethe, and subsequently sustained by those of Schiller. In their earliest works these poets began everything anew, in scorn of all the rules which had then been fabricated, transgressed these rules of set purpose, and, while doing so, distanced all rivals by a long interval. I will not enter more closely into the confusions which have prevailed respecting the conception of inspiration and genius, and which prevail even at the present day respecting the omnipotence of inspiration as such. We need only lay down as essential the view that, though the artist's talent and genius contains a natural element, yet it is essentially in need of cultivation by thought, and of reflection on the mode in which it produces, as well as of practice and skill in producing. A main feature of such production is unquestionably external workmanship, inasmuch as the work of art has a purely technical side, which extends into the region of handicraft; most especially in architecture and sculpture, less so in painting and music, least of all in poetry. Skill in this comes not by inspiration, but solely by reflection, industry, and practice; and such skill is indispensable to the artist, in order that he may master his external material, and not be thwarted by its stubbornness.

Moreover, the higher an artist ranks, the more profoundly ought he to represent the depths of heart and mind; and these are not known without learning them, but are only to be fathomed by the direction of a man's own mind to the inner and outer world. So here, too, *study* is the means whereby the artist brings this content into his consciousness, and wins the matter and burden of his conceptions.

In this respect one art may need the consciousness and cognition of such matter more than others. Music, for instance, which concerns itself only with the undefined movement of the inward spiritual nature, and deals with musical sounds as, so to speak, feeling without thought, needs little or no spiritual content to be present in consciousness. It is for this reason that musical talent generally announces itself in very early youth, while the head is still empty and the heart has been but little moved, and is capable of attaining to a very considerable height in early years, before mind and life have experience of themselves. And again, as a matter of fact we often enough see very great expertness in musical composition, as also in execution, subsist along with remarkable barrenness of mind and character. The reverse is the case with poetry. In poetry all depends on the representation, — which must be full of matter and thought — of man, of his profounder interests, and of the powers that move him; and therefore mind and heart themselves must be richly and profoundly educated by life, experience, and reflection, before genius can bring to pass anything mature, substantial, and self-complete. Goethe's and Schiller's first productions are of an immaturity, and even of a rudeness and barbarism, that are absolutely terrifying. This phenomenon, that the greater part of those attempts display a predominant mass of thoroughly prosaic and in part of frigid and common-place elements, furnishes the chief objection to the common opinion, that inspiration is inseparable from youth and youthful fire. Those two men of genius, it may be said, were the first to give our nation works of true poetry, and yet it was only their mature manhood that presented us with creations profound, substantial, and the outcome of genuine inspiration, while no less thoroughly perfect in form. Thus, too, it was not till his old age that Homer devised and uttered his immortal songs.

(*c*) A third view, which concerns the idea of the work of art as a product of human activity, refers to the position of such a work towards the external appearances of nature. It was an obvious opinion for the common consciousness to adopt on this head, that the work of art made by man ranked *below* the product of nature. The work of art has no feeling in itself, and is not through and through a living thing, but, regarded as an external object, is dead. But we are wont to prize the living more than the dead. We must admit, of course, that the work of art has not in itself movement and life. An animated being in nature is within and without an organization appropriately elaborated down to all its minutest parts, while the work of art attains the semblance of animation on its surface only, but within is common stone, or wood and canvas, or, as in the case of poetry, is idea, uttering itself in speech and letters. But this aspect, viz. its external

existence, is not what makes a work into a production of fine art; it is a
work of art only in as far as, being the offspring of mind, it continues to
belong to the realm of mind, has received the baptism of the spiritual, and
only represents that which has been moulded in harmony with mind. A
human interest, the spiritual value which attaches to an incident, to an
individual character, to an action in its plot and in its *dénoûment*, is apprehended in the work of art, and exhibited more purely and transparently
than is possible on the soil of common unartistic reality. This gives the
work of art a higher rank than anything produced by nature, which has not
sustained this passage through the mind. So, for instance, by reason of the
feeling and insight of which a landscape as depicted by an artist is a
manifestation, such a work of mind assumes a higher rank than the mere
natural landscape. For everything spiritual is better than anything natural.
At any rate, no existence in nature is able, like art, to represent divine
ideals.

Upon that which, in works of art, the mind borrows from its own inner
life it is able, even on the side of external existence, to confer *permanence*;
whereas the individual living thing of nature is transient, vanishing, and
mutable in its aspect, while the work of art persists. Though, indeed, it is
not mere permanence, but the accentuation of the character which animation by mind confers, that constitutes its genuine preeminence as compared with natural reality.

Nevertheless, this higher rank assigned to the work of art is in turn
disputed by another idea of the common consciousness. It is said that
nature and its products are a work of God, created by his goodness and
wisdom, whereas the work of art is *merely* a human production, made after
man's devising by man's hands. In this antithesis between natural production as a divine creation and human activity as a merely finite creation, we
at once come upon the misconception, that God does *not* work in man and
through man, but limits the range of his activity to nature alone. This false
opinion is to be entirely abandoned if we mean to penetrate the true
conception of art. Indeed, in opposition to such an idea, we must adhere to
the very reverse, believing that God is more honoured by what mind does
or makes than by the productions or formations of nature. For not only is
there a divinity in man, but in him it is operative under a form that is
appropriate to the essence of God, in a mode quite other and higher than in
nature. God is a Spirit, and it is only in man that the medium through
which the divine element passes has the form of conscious spirit, that
actively realizes itself. In nature the corresponding medium is the unconscious, sensible, and external, which is far below consciousness in value. In
the products of art God is operative neither more nor less than in the
phenomena of nature; but the divine element, as it makes itself known in
the work of art, has attained, as being generated out of the mind, an
adequate thoroughfare for its existence; while existence in the unconscious

sensuousness of nature is not a mode of appearance adequate to the Divine Being.

(*d*) Granting, then, that the work of art is made by man as a creation of mind, we come to the last question, which will enable us to draw a deeper result from what has been said. What is man's need to produce works of art? On the one hand the production may be regarded as a mere toy of chance and of man's fancies, that might just as well be let alone as pursued. For, it may be said, there are other and better means for effecting that which is the aim of art, and man bears in him interests that are yet higher and of more import than art has power to satisfy. But, on the other hand, art appears to arise from the higher impulse and to satisfy the higher needs, at times, indeed, even the highest, the absolute need of man, being wedded to the religious interests of whole epochs and peoples, and to their most universal intuitions respecting the world. This inquiry concerning the not contingent but absolute need of art we cannot as yet answer completely, seeing that it is more concrete than any shape which could here be given to the answer. We must, therefore, content ourselves for the present with merely establishing the following points.

The universal and absolute need out of which art, on its formal side, arises has its source in the fact that man is a *thinking* consciousness, *i.e.* that he draws out of himself, and makes explicit *for himself*, that which he is, and, generally, whatever is. The things of nature are only *immediate and single*, but man as mind *reduplicates* himself, inasmuch as *prima facie* he *is* like the things of nature, but in the second place just as really is *for* himself, perceives himself, has ideas of himself, thinks himself, and only thus is active self-realizedness.[6] This consciousness of himself man obtains in a twofold way: *in the first place theoretically*, in as far as he has inwardly to bring himself into his own consciousness, with all that moves in the human breast, all that stirs and works therein, and, generally, to observe and form an idea of himself, to fix before himself what thought ascertains to be his real being, and, in what is summoned out of his inner self as in what is received from without, to recognize only himself. Secondly, man is realized for himself by *practical* activity, inasmuch as he has the impulse, in the medium which is directly given to him, and externally presented before him, to produce himself, and therein at the same time to recognize himself. This purpose he achieves by the modification of external things upon which he impresses the seal of his inner being, and then finds repeated in them his own characteristics. Man does this in order as a free subject to strip the outer world of its stubborn foreignness, and to enjoy in the shape and fashion of things a mere external reality of himself. Even the child's first impulse involves this practical modification of external things. A boy throws stones into the river, and then stands admiring the circles that trace themselves on the water, as an effect in which he attains the sight of something that is his own doing. This need traverses the most manifold phenomena, up to the mode of self-production in the medium of external things as it is known to us in the work of art. And it is not only external things that man treats in this way, but himself no less, *i.e.* his own natural form, which he does not leave as he finds it, but alters of set purpose. This is the cause of all ornament and decoration, though it may be as barbarous, as tasteless, as utterly disfiguring or even destructive as crushing Chinese ladies' feet, or as slitting the ears and lips. It is only among cultivated men that change of the figure, of behaviour, and of every kind and mode of self-utterance emanates from spiritual education.

The universal need for expression in art lies, therefore, in man's rational impulse to exalt the inner and outer world into a spiritual consciousness for himself, as an object in which he recognizes his own self. He satisfies the need of this spiritual freedom when he makes all that exists explicit for himself *within*, and in a corresponding way realizes this his explicit self *without*, evoking thereby, in this reduplication of himself, what is in him into vision and into knowledge for his own mind and for that of others. This is the free rationality of man, in which, as all action and knowledge, so also art has its ground and necessary origin. The specific need of art, however, in contradistinction to other action, political or moral, to religious imagination and to scientific cognition, we shall consider later.

2.   We have so far been considering that aspect of the work of art in which it is made by man. We have now to pass on to its second characteristic, that it is made for man's *sense*, and for this reason is more or less borrowed from the sensuous.

(*a*) This reflection has furnished occasion for the consideration to be advanced that fine art is intended to arouse feeling, and indeed more particularly the feeling which we find suits us — that, is pleasant feeling. Looking at the question thus, men have treated the investigation of fine art as an investigation of the feelings, and asked what feelings it must be held that art ought to evoke, — fear, for example, and compassion; and then, how these could be pleasant — how, for example, the contemplation of misfortune could produce satisfaction. This tendency of reflection is traceable particularly to Moses Mendelssohn's times, and many such discussions are to be found in his writings. Yet such an investigation did not lead men far, for feeling is the indefinite dull region of the mind; what is felt remains wrapped in the form of the most abstract individual subjectivity, and therefore the distinctions of feeling are also quite abstract, and are not distinctions of the actual object-matter itself. For instance, fear, anxiety, alarm, terror, are no doubt of one and the same sort of feeling variously modified, but in part are mere quantitative heightenings, in part are forms which in themselves have nothing to do with their content itself, but are indifferent to it. In the case of fear, for instance, an existence is given in which the subject (*i.e.* a person) has an interest, but at the same time sees approaching the negative that threatens to annihilate this existence, and so finds immediately in himself, as a contradictory affection of his subjectivity, the two at once, this interest and that negative. Now, such fear considered in itself is not enough to condition any content, but is capable of receiving into itself the most diverse and opposite matters. Feeling, as such, is a thoroughly empty form of subjective affection. No doubt this form may in some cases be manifold in itself, as is hope, grief, joy, or pleasure; and, again, may in such diversity comprehend varied contents, as there is a feeling of justice, moral feeling, sublime religious feeling, and so forth. But the fact that such content is forthcoming in different forms of feeling is not enough to bring to light its essential and definite nature; they remain purely subjective affections of myself, in which the concrete matter vanishes, as though narrowed into a circle of the utmost abstraction. Therefore, the inquiry into the feelings which art arouses, or ought to arouse, comes utterly to a standstill in the indefinite, and is a mode of study which precisely abstracts from the content proper and from its concrete essence and notion. For reflection upon feeling contents itself with the observation of the subjective affection in its isolation, instead of diving into and fathoming the matter in question itself, the work of art, and, while engaged with it, simply letting go the mere subjectivity and its states. In feeling it is just this vacant subjectivity that is — not merely retained, but — given the first place, and that is why men are so fond of having emotions. And for the same reason such a study becomes tedious from its indefiniteness and vacancy, and repulsive from its attentiveness to little subjective peculiarities.

(*b*) Now, as a work of art is not merely to do in general something of the nature of arousing emotion — for this is a purpose which it would have in common, without specific difference, with eloquence, historical composition, religious edification, and so forth — but is to do so only in as far as it is beautiful, reflection hit upon the idea, seeing that beauty was the object, of searching out a *peculiar feeling of beauty* to correspond to it, and of discovering a particular *sense of beauty*. In this search it soon appeared that such a sense is no blind instinct made rigidly definite by nature, and capable from the beginning in its own independent essence of discerning beauty. Hence it followed that education came to be demanded for this sense, and the educated sense of beauty came to be called *taste*, which, although an educated appreciation and apprehension of the beautiful, was yet supposed to retain the nature of immediate feeling. We have already mentioned how abstract theories undertook to educate such a sense of taste, and how external and one-sided that sense remained. The criticism of the time when those views prevailed, was not only defective in *universal* principles, but also, in its particular references to individual works of art, was less directed to justifying a *definite* judgment — the power to make one not having at that time been acquired — than to advancing the general education of taste. For this reason such education in its turn came to a standstill in the indefinite, and merely endeavoured so to equip feeling as sense of beauty by help of reflection, that there might thenceforth be capacity to find out beauty whenever and wherever it should exist. Yet the depths of the matter remained a sealed book to mere taste, for these depths demand not only sensibility and abstract reflection, but the undivided reason and the mind in its solid vigour; while taste was only directed to the external surface about which the feelings play, and on which one-sided maxims may pass for valid. But, for this very reason, what is called good taste takes fright at all more profound effects of art, and is silent where the reality comes in question, and where externalities and trivialities vanish. For when great passions and the movements of a profound soul are unveiled, we are no longer concerned with the finer distinctions of taste and its pettifogging particularities. It feels that genius strides contemptuously over such ground as this, and, shrinking before its power, becomes uneasy, and knows not which way to turn.

(c) And thus, as we should expect, men have abandoned the tendency to consider works of art solely with an eye to the education of taste, and with the purpose of merely displaying taste. The *connoisseur*, or scholar of art, has replaced the art-judge, or man of taste. The positive side of art-scholarship, so far as it concerns a thorough acquaintance with the entire circumference of the individual character in a given work of art, we have already pronounced to be essential to the study of art. For a work of art, owing to its nature as at once material and individual, is essentially originated by particular conditions of the most various kinds, to which belong especially the time and place of its production, then the peculiar individuality of the artist, and in particular the grade of technical development attained by his art. Attention to all these aspects is indispensable to distinct and thorough insight and cognition, and even to the enjoyment of a work of art; it is with them that connoisseurship, or art-scholarship, is chiefly occupied; and all that it can do for us in its own way is to be accepted with gratitude. Yet, though such scholarship is entitled to rank as something essential, still it ought not to be taken for the sole or supreme element in the relation which the mind adopts towards a work of art, and towards art in general. For art-scholarship (and this is its defective side) is capable of resting in an acquaintance with purely external aspects, such as technical or historical details, etc., and of guessing but little, or even knowing absolutely nothing, of the true and real nature of a work of art. It may even form a disparaging estimate of the value of more profound considerations in comparison with purely positive, technical, and historical information. Still, even so, art-scholarship, if only it is of a genuine kind, at least strives after definite grounds and information, and an intelligent judgment, with which is closely conjoined the more precise distinction of the different, even if partly external, aspects in a work of art, and the estimation of their importance.

(d) After these remarks upon the modes of study which have arisen out of that aspect of a work of art in which, being a sensuous object, it is invested with a relation to man as a sensuous being, we will now consider this aspect in its more essential relation to art as such, and so (α) partly as regards the work of art as object, (β) partly with respect to the subjectivity of the artist, his genius, talent, and so on; but without entering into matter relative to these points that can only proceed from the knowledge of art in its universal idea. For we are not yet on genuinely scientific ground, but have only reached the province of external reflection.

(α) The work of art then, of course, presents itself to sensuous apprehension. It is addressed to sensuous feeling, outer or inner, to sensuous perception and imagination, just as is the nature that surrounds us without, or our own sensitive nature within. Even a speech, for instance, may be addressed to sensuous imagination and feeling. Notwithstanding, the work of art is not only for the *sensuous* apprehension as sensuous object, but its position is of such a kind that as sensuous it is at the same time essentially addressed to the *mind*, that the mind is meant to be affected by it, and to find some sort of satisfaction in it.

This intention of the work of art explains how it is in no way meant to be a natural product and to possess natural life, whether a natural product is to be ranked higher or lower than a *mere* work of art, as it is often called in a depreciatory sense.

For the sensuous aspect of the work of art has a right to existence only in as far as it exists for man's mind, but not in as far as *qua* sensuous thing it has separate existence by itself. If we examine more closely in what way the sensuous is presented to man, we find that what is sensuous may bear various relations to the mind.

(αα) The lowest mode of apprehension, and that least appropriate to the mind, is purely sensuous apprehension. It consists naturally in mere looking, listening, feeling, just as in seasons of mental fatigue it may often be entertaining to go about without thought, and just to hear and look around us. The mind, however, does not rest in the mere apprehension of external things by sight and hearing, it makes them objects for its own inner nature, which then is itself impelled in a correspondingly sensuous form to realize itself in the things, and relates itself to them as *desire*. In the appetitive relation to the outer world, the man stands as a sensuous particular over against the things as likewise particulars; he does not open his mind to them with general ideas as a thinking being, but has relations dictated by particular impulses and interests to the objects as themselves particulars, and preserves himself in them, inasmuch as he uses them, consumes them, and puts in act his self-satisfaction by sacrificing them to it. In this negative relation desire requires for itself not merely the superficial appearance of external things, but themselves in their concrete sensuous existence. Mere pictures of the wood that it wants to use, or of the animals that it wants to eat, would be of no service to desire. Just as little is it possible for desire to let the object subsist in its freedom. For its impulse urges it just precisely to destroy this independence and freedom of external things, and to show that they are only there to be destroyed and consumed. But, at the same time, the subject himself, as entangled in the particular limited and valueless interests of his desires, is neither free in himself, for he does not determine himself out of the essential universality and rationality of his will, nor free in relation to the outer world, for his desire remains essentially determined by things, and related to them. This relation of desire is not that in which man stands to the work of art. He allows it to subsist as an object, free and independent, and enters into relation with it apart from desire, as with an object which only appeals to the theoretic side of the mind. For this reason the work of art, although it has sensuous existence, yet, in this point of view, does not require concrete sensuous existence and natural life; indeed, it even *ought* not to remain on such a level, seeing that it has to satisfy only the interests of mind, and is bound to exclude from itself all desire. Hence it is, indeed, that practical desire rates individual things in nature, organic and inorganic, which are serviceable to it, higher than works of art, which reveal themselves to be useless for its purpose, and enjoyable only for other modes of mind.

(*ββ*) A second mode in which the externally present may be related to the mind is, in contrast with singular sensuous perception and desire, the purely theoretical relation to the *Intelligence*. The theoretic contemplation of things has no interest in consuming them as particulars, in satisfying itself sensuously, and in preserving itself by their means, but rather in becoming acquainted with them in their universality, in finding their inner being and law, and in conceiving them in terms of their notion. Therefore the theoretical interest lets the single things be, and holds aloof from them as sensuous particulars, because this sensuous particularity is not what the contemplation exercised by the intelligence looks for. For the rational intelligence does not belong, as do the desires, to the individual subject as such, but only to the individual as at the same time in his nature universal. In as far as man has relation to things in respect of this universality, it is his universal reason which attempts to find himself in nature, and thereby to reproduce the inner essence of things, which sensuous existence, though having its ground therein, cannot immediately display. But again, this theoretic interest, the satisfaction of which is the work of science, is in the scientific form no more shared by art, than the latter makes common cause with the impulse of the purely practical desires. Science may, no doubt, start from the sensuous thing in its individuality, and may possess a sensuous idea of the way in which such an individual presents itself in its individual colour, shape, size, etc. Still, this isolated sensuous thing, as such, has no further relation to the mind, inasmuch as the intelligence aims at the universal, the law, the thought and notion of the object. Not only, therefore, does it abandon all intercourse with the thing as a given individual, but transforms it within the mind, making a concrete object of sense into an abstract matter of thought, and so into something quite other than the same object *qua* sensuous phenomenon. The artistic interest, as distinguished from science, does not act thus. Artistic contemplation accepts the work of art just as it displays itself *qua* external object, in immediate determinateness and sensuous individuality clothed in colour, figure, and sound, or as a single isolated perception, etc., and does not go so far beyond the immediate appearance of objectivity which is presented before it, as to aim, like science, at apprehending the notion of such an objective appearance as a universal notion.

Thus, the interest of art distinguishes itself from the practical interest of *desire* by the fact that it permits its object to subsist freely and in independence, while desire utilizes it in its own service by its destruction. On the other hand, artistic contemplation differs from theoretical consideration by the scientific intelligence, in cherishing interest for the object as an individual existence, and not setting to work to transmute it into its universal thought and notion.

(γγ) It follows, then, from the above, that though the sensuous must be present in a work of art, yet it must only appear as surface and *semblance* of the sensuous. For, in the sensuous aspect of a work of art, the mind seeks neither the concrete framework of matter, that empirically thorough completeness and development of the organism which desire demands, nor the universal and merely ideal thought. What it requires is sensuous presence, which, while not ceasing to be sensuous, is to be liberated from the apparatus of its merely material nature. And thus the sensuous in works of art is exalted to the rank of a mere *semblance* in comparison with the immediate existence of things in nature, and the work of art occupies the mean between what is immediately sensuous and ideal thought. This semblance of the sensuous presents itself to the mind externally as the shape, the visible look, and the sonorous vibration of things — supposing that the mind leaves the objects uninterfered with (physically), but yet does not descend into their inner essence (by abstract thought), for if it did so, it would entirely destroy their external existence as separate individuals *for it*. For this reason the sensuous aspect of art only refers to the two *theoretical* senses of *sight* and *hearing*, while smell, taste, and feeling remain excluded from being sources of artistic enjoyment. For smell, taste, and feeling have to do with matter as such, and with its immediate sensuous qualities; smell with material volatilization in air, taste with the material dissolution of substance, and feeling with warmth, coldness, smoothness, etc. On this account these senses cannot have to do with the objects of art, which are destined to maintain themselves in their actual independent existence, and admit of no purely sensuous relation. The pleasant for these latter senses is not the beautiful in art. Thus art on its sensuous side purposely produces no more than a shadow-world of shapes, sounds, and imaginable ideas;[4] and it is absolutely out of the question to maintain that it is owing to simple powerlessness and to the limitations on his actions that man, when evoking worlds of art into existence, fails to present more than the mere surface of the sensuous, than mere *schemata*. In art, these sensuous shapes and sounds present themselves, not simply for their own sake and for that of their immediate structure,[27] but with the purpose of affording in that shape satisfaction to higher spiritual interests, seeing that they are powerful to call forth a response and echo in the mind from all the depths of consciousness. It is thus that, in art, the sensuous is *spiritualized*, *i.e.* the *spiritual* appears in sensuous shape.

(β) But for this very reason we have a product of art only in so far as it has found a passage through the mind, and has been generated by spiritually productive activity. This leads us to the other question which we have to answer — how, that is, the sensuous side, which is indispensable to art, is operative in the artist as a productive state of the subject or person. This, the method and fashion of production, contains in itself as a subjective activity just the same properties which we found objectively present in the work of art; it must be a spiritual activity which, nevertheless, at the same time has in itself the element of sensuousness and immediateness. It is neither, on the one hand, purely mechanical work, as mere unconscious skill in sensuous sleight of hand, or a formal activity according to fixed rules learnt by rote; nor is it, on the other hand, a scientific productive process, which passes from sense to abstract ideas and thoughts, or exercises itself exclusively in the element of pure thinking; rather the spiritual and the sensuous side must in artistic production be as one. For instance, it would be possible in poetical creation to try and proceed by first apprehending the theme to be treated as a prosaic thought, and by then putting it into pictorial ideas, and into rhyme, and so forth; so that the pictorial element would simply be hung upon the abstract reflections as an ornament or decoration. Such a process could only produce bad poetry, for in it there would be operative as two *separate activities* that which in artistic production has its right place only as undivided unity. This genuine mode of production constitutes the activity of artistic *fancy*. It is the rational element which, *qua* spirit, only exists in as far as it actively extrudes itself into consciousness, but yet does not array before it what it bears within itself till it does so in sensuous form. This activity has, therefore, a spiritual import, which, however, it embodies in sensuous shape. Such a process may be compared with the habit even of a man with great experience of the world, or, again, with that of a man of *esprit* or wit, who, although he has complete knowledge of the main stakes of life, of the substantive interests that hold men together, of what moves them, and of what is the power that they recognize, yet neither has himself apprehended this content in the form of general rules, nor is able to explain it to others in general reflections, but makes plain to himself and to others what occupies his consciousness always in particular cases, whether real or invented, in adequate instances, and the like. For in his ideas, everything shapes itself into concrete images, determinate in time and place, to which, therefore, names and other external circumstances of all kinds must not be wanting. Yet such a kind of imagination rather rests on the recollection of states that he has gone through, and of experiences that have befallen him, than is creative in its own strength. His recollection preserves and reproduces the individuality and external fashion of occurrences that had such and such results with all their external circumstances, and prevents the universal from emerging in its own shape. But the productive fancy of the *artist* is the fancy of a great mind and heart, the apprehension and creation of ideas and of shapes, and, indeed, the exhibition of the profoundest and most universal human interests in the definite sensuous mould of pictorial representation. From this it follows at once, that in one aspect Fancy unquestionably rests on natural gifts — speaking generally, on talent — because its mode of production requires a sensuous medium. It is true that we speak in the same way of scientific "talent," but the sciences only presuppose the universal capacity of thought, which has not, like Fancy, a natural mode (as well as an intellectual one), but abstracts just precisely from all that is natural (or native) in an activity; and thus it would be more correct to say that there is no specifically scientific talent in the sense of a *mere* natural endowment. Now, Fancy *has* in it a mode of instinct-like productiveness, inasmuch as the essential plasticity and sensuousness of the work of art must be subjectively present in the artist as natural disposition and natural impulse, and, considering that it is unconscious operation, must belong to the natural element in man, as well as to the rational. Of course, natural capacity leaves room for other elements in talent and genius, for artistic production is just as much of a spiritual and self-conscious nature; we can but say that its spirituality must, somehow, have an element of natural, plastic, and formative tendency. For this reason, though nearly every one can reach a certain point in an art, yet, in order to go beyond this point, with which the art in the strict sense begins, it is impossible to dispense with native artistic talent of the highest order.

Considered as a natural endowment, moreover, such talent reveals itself for the most part in early youth, and is manifested in the impelling restlessness that busies itself, with vivacity and industry, in creating shapes in some particular sensuous medium, and in seizing on this species of utterance and communication as the only one, or as the chief and the most suitable one. And thus, too, a precocious technical facility, that up to a certain grade of attainment is without effort, is a sign of natural talent. A sculptor finds everything transmute itself into shapes, and he soon begins to take up the clay and model it. And, speaking generally, whatever men of such talents have in their imagination, whatever rouses and moves their inner nature, turns at once into shape, drawing, melody, or poem.

(γ) Thirdly, and to conclude: the *content* of art is also in some respects borrowed from the sensuous, from nature; or, in any case, even if the content is of a spiritual kind, it can only be seized and fixed by representing the spiritual fact, such as human relations, in the shape of phenomena with external reality.

Part II.   The End[61] of Art

3.   The question then arises, what the interest or the *End* is which man proposes to himself when he reproduces such a content in the form of works of art. This was the third point of view which we set before us with reference to the work of art, and the closer discussion of which will finally make the transition to the actual and true conception of art.

If in this aspect we glance at the common consciousness, a current idea which may occur to us is —

(*a*) The principle of the *imitation of nature*. According to this view the essential purpose of art consists in imitation, in the sense of a facility in copying natural forms as they exist in a way that corresponds precisely to them; and the success of such a representation, exactly corresponding to nature, is supposed to be what affords complete satisfaction.

(*α*) This definition contains, *prima facie*, nothing beyond the purely formal aim that whatever already exists in the external world, just *as* it is therein, is now to be made a second time by man as a copy of the former, as well as he can do it with the means at his command. But we may at once regard this repetition as —

(*αα*) A *superfluous* labour, seeing that the things which pictures, theatrical representations, etc., imitate and represent — animals, natural scenes, incidents in human life — are before us in other cases already, in our own gardens or our own houses, or in cases within our closer or more remote circle of acquaintance. And, looking more closely, we may regard this superfluous labour as a presumptuous sport which —

(*ββ*) Comes far short of nature. For art is restricted in its means of representation; and can produce only *one-sided* deceptions, *i.e.* for instance, a semblance of reality addressed to one sense only; and, in fact, it invariably gives rise, if it rests in the formal purpose of *mere imitation*, to a mere parody of life, instead of a genuine vitality. Just so the Turks, being Mohammedans, tolerate, as is well known, no pictures copied from men or the like; and when James Bruce, on his journey to Abyssinia, showed paintings of fish to a Turk, the man was amazed at first, but soon enough made answer: "If this fish shall rise up against you on the last day, and say, 'You have created for me a body, but no living soul,' how will you defend yourself against such an accusation?" The prophet, moreover, it is recorded in the Sunna, said to the two women, Ommi Habiba and Ommi Selma, who told him of pictures in Ethiopian churches — "These pictures will accuse their authors on the day of judgment!"

There are, no doubt, as well, examples of completely deceptive imitation. Zeuxis' painted grapes have from antiquity downward been taken to be the triumph of this principle of the imitation of nature, because the story is that living doves pecked at them. We might add to this ancient example the modern one of Büttner's monkey, which bit in pieces a painted cockchafer in Rösel's "Diversions of the Insect World," and was pardoned by his master, in spite of his having thereby spoilt a beautiful copy of this valuable work, because of this proof of the excellence of the pictures. But when we reflect on these and similar instances, it must at once occur to us that, in place of commending works of art because they have *actually* deceived *even* pigeons and monkeys, we ought simply to censure the people who mean to exalt a work of art by predicating, as its highest and ultimate quality, so poor an effect as this. In general, we may sum up by saying that, as a matter of mere imitation, art cannot maintain a rivalry with nature, and, if it tries, must look like a worm trying to crawl after an elephant.

(γγ) Considering the unvarying failure — comparative failure, at least — of imitation when contrasted with the original in nature, there remains as end nothing beyond our pleasure in the sleight of hand which can produce something so like nature. And it is doubtless open to man to be pleased at producing over again what is already present in its own right, by his labour, skill, and industry. But enjoyment and admiration, even of this kind, naturally grow frigid or chilled precisely in proportion to the resemblance of the copy to the natural type, or are even converted into tedium and repugnance. There are portraits which, as has been wittily said, are sickeningly like; and Kant adduces another instance relative to this pleasure in imitation as such, viz. that we soon grow tired of a man — and there are such men — who is able to mimic the nightingale's strain quite perfectly; and as soon as it is discovered that a man is producing the notes, we are at once weary of the song. We then recognize in it nothing but a conjuring trick, neither the free production of nature, nor a work of art; for we expect from the free productive capacity of human beings something quite other than such music as this, which only interests us when, as is the case with the nightingale's note, it gushes forth from the creature's own vitality without special purpose, and yet recalls the utterance of human feeling. In general, such delight at our skill in mimicking can be but limited, and it becomes man better to take delight in what he produces out of himself. In this sense the invention of any unimportant and technical product has the higher value, and man may be prouder of having invented the hammer, the nail, and so forth, than of achieving feats of mimicry. For this fervour of abstract copying is to be evened with the feat of the man who had taught himself to throw lentils through a small opening without missing. He displayed this skill of his before Alexander, and Alexander presented him with a bushel of lentils as a reward for his frivolous and meaningless art.

(β) Moreover, seeing that the principle of imitation is purely formal, to make it the end has the result that *objective beauty* itself disappears. For the question is in that case no longer *of what nature* that is which is to be copied, but only whether it is *correctly* copied. The object and content of the beautiful comes then to be regarded as matter of entire indifference. That is to say, if we go outside the principle and speak of a difference of beauty and ugliness in considering beasts, men, landscapes, actions, or characters, this must nevertheless, in presence of the maxim in question, be set down as a distinction that does not belong particularly to art, for which nothing is left but abstract imitation. In this case the above-mentioned lack of criterion in dealing with the endless forms of nature reduces us, as regards the selection of objects and their distinction in beauty and ugliness, to subjective *taste* as an ultimate fact, which accepts no rule and admits of no discussion. And, in fact, if in selecting objects for representation we start from what *men* think beautiful or ugly, and therefore deserving artistic imitation — that is, from their taste, — then all circles of natural objects open to us, and not one of them will be likely to fail of a patron. Among men, for instance, it is the case that at any rate every bridegroom thinks his bride beautiful, and indeed, perhaps, he alone; though not, it may be, every husband his wife; and that subjective taste for such beauty has no fixed rule one may hold to be the good fortune of both parties. If we, moreover, look quite beyond individuals and their accidental taste, to the taste of nations, this again is full of extreme diversity and contrast. How often we hear it said that a European beauty would not please a Chinese or even a Hottentot, in as far as the Chinaman has quite a different conception of beauty from the negro, and the negro in turn from the European, and so forth. Indeed, if we look at the works of art of those extra-European peoples — their images of the gods, for instance — which their fancy has originated as venerable and sublime, they may appear to us as the most gruesome idols, and their music may sound to our ears as the most horrible noise; while they, on their side, will regard our sculptures, paintings, and musical productions as trivial or ugly.

(γ) But even if we abstract from an objective principle of art, and if beauty is to be based on subjective and individual taste, we shall still soon find on the side of art itself that the imitation of nature, which certainly appeared to be a universal principle and one guaranteed by high authority, is at any rate not to be accepted in this universal and merely abstract form. For if we look at the different arts it will at once be admitted that even if painting and sculpture represent objects which appear like those of nature, or the type of which is essentially borrowed from nature, yet works of architecture on the other hand — and architecture belongs to the fine arts — and the productions of poetry, in as far as they do not confine themselves to mere description, are by no means to be called imitations of nature. At least, if we desired to maintain the principle as valid in the case of these latter arts, we should have to make a long circuit by conditioning the proposition in various ways, and reducing the so-called truth at any rate to probability. But if we admitted probability we should again be met by a great difficulty in determining what is probable and what is not; and still, moreover, one would neither consent nor find it possible to exclude from poetry all wholly arbitrary and completely original imaginations.

The end of art must, therefore, lie in something different from the purely formal imitation of what we find given, which in any case can bring to the birth only *tricks* and not *works* of art. It is, indeed, an element essential to the work of art to have natural shapes for its foundation; seeing that its representation is in the medium of external and therefore of natural phenomena. In painting, for instance, it is an important study to know how to copy with precision the colours in their relations to one another, the effects of light, reflections, etc., and, no less, the forms and figures of objects down to their subtlest characteristics. It is in this respect chiefly that the principle of naturalism in general and of copying nature has recovered its influence in modern times. Its aim is to recall an art which has grown feeble and indistinct to the vigour and crispness of nature; or, again, to invoke against the purely arbitrary and artificial conventionalism, as unnatural as. it was inartistic, into which art had strayed, the uniform, direct, and solidly coherent sequences of nature. But however true it is that there is something right in this endeavour from one point of view, yet still the naturalism at which it aims is not as such the substantive and primary concern that underlies fine art. And, therefore, although external appearance in the shape of natural reality constitutes an essential condition of art, yet, nevertheless, neither is the given natural world its *rule*, nor is the mere imitation of external appearance *as* external its *end*.

(*b*) The further question then arises — What *is* the true content of art, and with what aim is this content to be presented. On this subject our consciousness supplies us with the common opinion that it is the task and aim of art to bring in contact with our sense, our feeling, our inspiration, *all* that finds a place in the mind of man. Art, it is thought, should realize in us that familiar saying, "Homo sum: humani nihil a me alienum puto." Its aim is therefore placed in arousing and animating the slumbering emotions, inclinations, and passions; in filling the *heart*, in forcing the human being, whether cultured or uncultured, to feel the whole range of what man's soul in its inmost and secret corners has power to experience and to create, and all that is able to move and to stir the human breast in its depths and in its manifold aspects and possibilities; to present as a delight to emotion and to perception all that the mind possesses of real and lofty in its thought and in the Idea — all the splendour of the noble, the eternal, and the true; and no less to make intelligible misfortune and misery, wickedness and crime; to make men realize the inmost nature of all that is shocking and horrible, as also of all pleasure and delight; and, finally, to set imagination roving in idle toyings of fancy, and luxuriating in the seductive spells of sense-stimulating visions. This endlessly varied content, it is held, art is bound to embrace, partly in order to complete the natural experience in which our external existence consists, and partly with the general aim of provoking the passions of our nature, both in order that the experiences of life may not leave us unmoved, and because we desire to attain to a receptivity that welcomes all phenomena. Now, such a stimulus is not given in this sphere by actual experience itself, but can only come by the semblance thereof, by art, that is, deceptively substituting its creations for reality. The possibility of this deception by means of artistic semblance rests on the fact that all reality must, for man, traverse the medium of perception and ideas, and cannot otherwise penetrate the feelings and the will. In this process it is quite indifferent whether his attention is claimed by immediate external reality, or whether this effect is produced by another means—that is, by images, symbols, and ideas, containing or representing *the content* of reality. Man can frame to himself ideas of things that are not actual as though they were actual. Hence it is all the same to our feelings whether external reality or only the semblance of it is the means of bringing in contact with us a situation, a relation, or the import of a life. Either mode suffices to awaken our response to its burden, in grief and in rejoicing, in pathos and in horror, and in traversing the emotions and the passions of wrath, hatred, compassion, of anxiety, fear, love, reverence, and admiration, or of the desire of honour and of fame.

This awakening of all feelings in us, the dragging of the heart through the whole significance of life, the realization of all such inner movements by means of a presented exterior consisting merely in deception—all this was what, from the point of view which we have been considering, constituted the peculiar and pre-eminent power of art.

Now, as this mode of treatment credits art with the vocation of impressing on the heart and on the imagination good and bad alike, and of strengthening man to the noblest, as of enervating him to the most sensuous and selfish emotions, it follows that the task set before art is still purely formal, and so it would have no certain purpose, but would merely furnish the empty form for every possible kind of significance and content.

(c) It is a fact that art does include this formal side, in that it has power to present every possible subject-matter in artistic dress, before perception and feeling, just exactly as argumentative reflection has the power of manipulating all possible objects and modes of action, and of furnishing them with reasons and justifications. But when we admit so great a variety of content we are at once met by the remark that the manifold feelings and ideas, which art aims at provoking or reinforcing, intersect and contradict, and by mutual interference cancel one another. Indeed, in this aspect, in so far as art inspires men to directly opposite emotions, it only magnifies the contradiction of our feelings and passions, and either sets them staggering like Bacchantes, or passes into sophistry and scepticism, in the same way as argumentation. This diversity of the material of art itself compels us, therefore, not to be content with so formal an aim for it, seeing that rationality forces its way into this wild diversity, and demands to see the emergence of a higher and more universal purpose from these elements in spite of their self-contradiction, and to be assured of its being attained. Just in the same way the State and the social life of men are, of course, credited with the purpose that in them *all* human capacities and *all* individual powers are to be developed and to find utterance in *all* directions and with *all* tendencies. But in opposition to so formal a view there at once arises the question in what *unity* these manifold formations must be comprehended, and what *single end* they must have for their fundamental idea and ultimate purpose.

As such an end, reflection soon suggests the notion that art has the capacity and the function of mitigating the fierceness of the desires.

(α) In respect to this first idea, we have only to ascertain in what feature peculiar to art it is that the capacity lies of eliminating brutality and taming and educating the impulses, desires, and passions. Brutality in general has its reason in a direct selfishness of the impulses, which go to work right away, and exclusively for the satisfaction of their concupiscence. Now, desire is most savage and imperious in proportion as, being isolated and narrow, it occupies the *whole man*, so that he does not retain the power of separating himself as a universal being from this determinateness, and becoming aware of himself as universal. Even if the man in such a case says, "The passion is stronger than I," it is true that the abstract I is then separated for consciousness from the particular passion; but still only in a formal way, inasmuch as this separation is only made in order to pronounce that, against the power of the passion, the I as such is of no account whatever. The savageness of passion consists, therefore, in the oneness of the I as universal with the limited content of its desires, so that the man has no will outside this particular passion. Now, such brutality and untamed violence of passion is softened through art, to begin with, by the mere fact that it brings before the man as an idea what in such a state he feels and does. And even if art restricts itself to merely setting up pictures of the passions before the mind's eye, or even if it were actually to flatter them, still this is by itself enough to have a softening power, inasmuch as the man is thereby at least *made aware*, of what, apart from such presentation, he simply *is*. For then the man observes his impulses and inclinations, and whereas before they bore him on without power of reflection, he now sees them outside himself, and begins already to be free from them, in so far as they form an object which he contrasts with himself. Hence it may frequently be the case with the artist that when attacked by grief he softens and weakens the intensity of his own feelings in its effect on his own mind by representing it in art. Tears, even, are enough to bring comfort; the man, who to begin with is utterly sunk and concentrated in grief, is able thus, at any rate, to utter in a direct fashion this his inner state. Still more of a relief, however, is the utterance of what is within in words, images, pictures, sounds, and shapes. For this reason it was a good old custom at deaths and funerals to appoint wailing women, in order to bring the grief before the mind in its utterance. Manifestations of sympathy, too, hold up the content of a man's misfortune to his view; when it is much talked about he is forced to reflect upon it, and is thereby relieved. And so it has always been held that to weep or to speak one's fill is a means to obtain freedom from the oppressive weight of care, or at least to find momentary relief for the heart. Hence the mitigation of the violence of passion has for its universal reason that man is released from his immediate sunkenness in a feeling, and becomes conscious of it as of something external to him, towards which he must now enter into an *ideal* relation. Art, by means of its representations, while remaining within the sensuous sphere, delivers man at the same time from the power of sensuousness. Of course we may often hear those favourite phrases about man's duty being to remain in immediate oneness with nature, but such oneness in its abstraction is simply and solely coarseness and savagery; and art, in the very process of dissolving this oneness for man, is raising him with gentle hand above and away from mere sunkenness in nature. Man's mode of occupying himself with works of art is always purely contemplative, and educates thereby, in the first place, no doubt, merely attention to the representations themselves, but then, going beyond this, it cultivates attention to their significance, the power of comparison with other contents, and receptivity for the general consideration of them, and for the points of view which it involves.

(β) To the above there attaches itself in natural connection the second characteristic which has been ascribed to art as its essential purpose, viz. the *purification* of the passions, instruction and *moral* perfecting. For the characteristic that art was to bridle savageness and educate the passions remained quite abstract and general, so that a question must again arise about a *determinate* kind and an essential *end* of this education.

(αα) The doctrine of the purification of passion suffers indeed under the same defect as the above doctrine of the mitigation of the desires; yet, when more closely looked at, it at any rate arrives at the point of accentuating the fact that the representations of art may be held to lack a standard by which their worth or unworthiness could be measured. This standard simply means their effectiveness in separating pure from impure in the passions. It therefore requires a content that has capacity to exercise this purifying power, and, in as far as the production of such an effect is taken to constitute the substantive end of art, it must follow that the purifying content must be brought before consciousness in its *universality* and *essentiality*.

(ββ) In this latter aspect the end of art has been pronounced to be that it should *teach*. Thus, on the one side, the peculiar character of art would consist in the movement of the emotions and in the satisfaction which lies in this movement, even in fear, compassion, in painful pathos and shock — that is to say, in the satisfying engagement of the emotions and passions, and to that extent in a complacency, entertainment, and delight in the objects of art, in their representation and effect; but, on the other side, this purpose (of art) is held to find its higher standard only in its instructiveness, in the *fabula docet*, and thus in the useful influence which the work of art succeeds in exerting on the subject. In this respect the Horatian saw, "Et prodesse volunt et delectare poetae," ("Poets aim at utility and entertainment alike") contains, concentrated in a few words, all that has subsequently been elaborated in infinite degrees, and diluted into the uttermost extreme of insipidity as a doctrine of art. As regards such instruction we have, then, to ask, whether it is meant to be directly or indirectly, explicitly or implicitly contained in the work of art.

If, speaking generally, we are concerned about a purpose which is universal and not contingent, it follows that this purpose, considering the essentially spiritual nature of art, cannot but be itself spiritual, and indeed, moreover, one which is not contingent, but actual in its nature and for its own sake. Such a purpose in relation to teaching could only consist in bringing before consciousness, by help of the work of art, a really and explicitly significant spiritual content. From this point of view it is to be asserted that the higher art ranks itself, the more it is bound to admit into itself such a content as this, and that only in the essence of such a content can it find the standard which determines whether what is expressed is appropriate or inappropriate. Art was, in façt, the first *instructress* of peoples.

But the purpose of instruction may be treated as *purpose*, to such a degree that the universal nature of the represented content is doomed to be exhibited and expounded directly and obviously as abstract proposition, prosaic reflection, or general theorem, and not merely in an indirect way in the concrete form of a work of art. By such a severance the sensuous plastic form, which is just what makes the work of art a work of *art*, becomes a mere otiose accessory, a husk which is expressly pronounced to be mere husk, a semblance expressly pronounced to be mere semblance. But thereby the very nature of the work of art is distorted. For the work of art ought to bring a content before the mind's eye, not in its generality as such, but with this generality made absolutely individual, and sensuously particularized. If the work of art does not proceed from this principle, but sets in relief its generalized aspect with the purpose of abstract instruction, then the imaginative and sensuous aspect is only an external and superfluous adornment, and the work of art is a thing divided against itself, in which form and content no longer appear as grown into one. In that case the sensuously individual and the spiritually general are become external to one another.

And further, if the purpose of art is limited to this *didactic* utility, then its other aspect, that of pleasure, entertainment, and delight, is pronounced to be in itself *unessential*, and ought to have its substance merely in the utility of the teaching on which it is attendant. But this amounts to pronouncing that art does not bear its vocation and purpose in itself, but that its conception is rooted in something else, to which it is a *means*. Art is, in this case, only one among the several means which prove useful and are applied for the purpose of instruction. This brings us to the boundary at which art is made no longer to be an end on its own merits, seeing that it is degraded into a mere toy of entertainment or a mere means of instruction.

(γγ) This boundary becomes most sharply marked when a question is raised, in its turn, about a supreme end and aim for the sake of which the passions are to be purified and men are to be instructed. This aim has often, in modern times, been declared to be *moral* improvement, and the aim of art has been placed in the function of preparing the inclinations and impulses for moral perfection, and of leading them to this goal. This idea combines purification with instruction, inasmuch as art is, by communicating an insight into genuine moral goodness — that is, by instruction, — at the same time to incite to purification, and in this way alone to bring about the improvement of mankind as its useful purpose and supreme goal.

Regarding art in reference to moral improvement, the same has *prima facie* to be said as about the didactic purpose. We may readily grant that art must not as a principle take for its aim the immoral and its furtherance. But it is one thing to take immorality for the express aim of representation, and another to abstain from taking morality. Every genuine work of art may have a good moral drawn from it, but, of course, in doing so much depends on interpretation and on him who draws the moral. Thus one may hear the most immoral representations defended by saying that we must know evil, or sin, in order to act morally; and, conversely, it has been said that the portrayal of Mary Magdalene, the beautiful sinner who afterwards repented, has seduced many into sin, because art makes it look so beautiful to repent, and you must sin before you can repent. But the doctrine of moral improvement, if consistently carried out, goes in general yet further. It would not be satisfied with the possibility of extracting a moral from a work of art by interpretation, but it would, on the contrary, display the moral instruction as the substantive purpose of the work of art, and, indeed, would actually admit to portrayal none but moral subjects, moral characters, actions, and incidents. For art has the choice among its subjects, in contradistinction to history or the sciences which have their matter fixed for them.

In order that we may be able to form a thoroughly adequate estimate of the idea that the aim of art is moral from this point of view, we must inquire first of all for the definite standpoint of the morality on which this doctrine is based. If we look closely at the standpoint of morality as we have to understand it in the best sense at the present day, we soon find that its conception does not immediately coincide with what apart from it we are in the habit of calling in a general way virtue, respectability,[44] uprightness, etc. To be respectable and virtuous is not enough to make a man moral.[35] Morality involves *reflection* and the definite consciousness of that which duty prescribes, and acting out of such a prior consciousness. Duty itself is the law of the will, which man nevertheless lays down freely out of his own self, and then is supposed to determine himself to this duty for duty's and its fulfilment's sake, by doing good solely from the conviction which he has attained that it is the good. Now this law, the duty which is chosen for duty's sake to be the guide of action, out of free conviction and the inner conscience, and is then acted upon, is, taken by itself,[6] the abstract universal of the will, and is the direct antithesis of nature, the sensuous impulses, the self-seeking interests, the passions, and of all that is comprehensively entitled the feelings and the heart. In this antagonism the one side is regarded as *negativing* the other; and, seeing that both are present as antagonists within the subject (person), he has, as determining himself out of himself, the choice of following the one or the other. But, according to the view under discussion, a *moral* aspect is acquired by such a decision, and by the act performed in accordance with it, only through the free conviction of duty on the one hand, and, on the other hand, through the conquest, not only of the particular or separate will, of the natural motives, inclinations, passions, etc., but also through that of the nobler emotions and the higher impulses. For the modern moralistic view starts from the fixed antithesis of the will in its spiritual universality to its sensuous natural particularity, and consists not in the completed reconciliation of these contrasted sides, but in their conflict with one another, which involves the requirement that the impulses which conflict with duty ought to yield to it.

This antithesis does not merely display itself for our consciousness, in the limited region of moral action; but also emerges as a fundamental distinction and antagonism between that which is real essentially and in its own right,[7] and that which is external reality and existence. Formulated in the abstract, it is the contrast of the universal and particular, when the former is explicitly fixed over against the latter, just as the latter is over against the former; more concretely, it appears in nature as the opposition of the abstract law against the abundance of individual phenomena, each having its own character; in the mind, as the sensuous and spiritual in man, as the battle of the spirit against the flesh, of duty for duty's sake, the cold command, with the individual interest, the warm feelings, the sensuous inclinations and impulses, the individual disposition as such; as the hard conflict of inward freedom and of natural necessity; further, as the contradiction of the dead conception—empty in itself—compared with full concrete vitality, or of theory and subjective thought contrasted with objective existence and experience.

These are antitheses which have not been invented, either by the subtlety of reflection or by the pedantry of philosophy, but which have from all time and in manifold forms preoccupied and disquieted the human consciousness, although it was modern culture that elaborated them most distinctly, and forced them up to the point of most unbending contradiction. Intellectual culture and the modern play of understanding create in man this contrast, which makes him an amphibious animal, inasmuch as it sets him to live in two contradictory worlds at once; so that even consciousness wanders back and forward in this contradiction, and, shuttle-cocked from side to side, is unable to satisfy itself *as* itself on the one side as on the other. For, on the one side, we see man a prisoner in common reality and earthly temporality, oppressed by want and poverty, hard driven by nature, entangled in matter, in sensuous aims and their enjoyments; on the other side, he exalts himself to eternal ideas, to a realm of thought and freedom, imposes on himself as a *will* universal laws and attributions, strips the world of its living and flourishing reality and dissolves it into abstractions, inasmuch as the mind is put upon vindicating its rights and its dignity simply by denying the rights of nature and maltreating it, thereby retaliating the oppression and violence which itself has experienced from nature. Such a discrepancy in life and consciousness involves for modern culture and its understanding the demand that the contradiction should be resolved. Yet the understanding cannot release itself from the fixity of these antitheses. The solution, therefore, remains for consciousness a mere *ought*, and the present and reality only stir themselves in the unrest of a perpetual to and fro, which seeks a reconciliation without finding it. Then the question arises, whether such a many-sided and fundamental opposition which never gets beyond a mere ought and a postulated solution, can be the genuine and complete[7] truth, and, in general, the supreme purpose. If the culture of the world[2] has fallen into such a contradiction, it becomes the task of philosophy to undo or cancel it, *i.e.* to show that neither the one alternative in its abstraction nor the other in similar one-sidedness possesses truth, but that they are essentially self-dissolving; that truth only lies in the conciliation and mediation of the two, and that this mediation is no mere postulate, but is in its nature and in reality accomplished and always self-accomplishing. This intuition agrees directly with the natural faith and will, which always has present to the mind's eye precisely this resolved antithesis, and in action makes it its purpose and achieves it. All that philosophy does is to furnish a reflective insight into the essence of the antithesis in as far as it shows that what constitutes truth is merely the resolution of this antithesis, and that not in the sense that the conflict and its aspects in any way *are not*, but in the sense that they *are, in reconciliation.*

(*d*) Now, as an ultimate aim implied a higher standpoint in the case of moral improvement, we shall have to vindicate this higher standpoint for art no less than for morals. Thereby we at once lay aside the false position, which has already been remarked upon, that art has to serve as a means for moral ends, and to conduce to the moral end of the world, as such, by instruction and moral improvement, and thereby has its substantive aim, not in itself, but in something else. If, therefore, we now continue to speak of an aim or purpose, we must, in the first instance, get rid of the perverse idea, which, in asking "What is the aim?" retains the accessory meaning of the question, "What is the *use*?". The perverseness of this lies in the point that the work of art would then be regarded as aspiring to something else which is set before consciousness as the essential and as what ought to be; so that then the work of art would only have value as a useful instrument in the realization of an end having substantive importance *outside* the sphere of art. Against this it is necessary to maintain that art has the vocation of revealing *the truth* in the form of sensuous artistic shape, of representing the reconciled antithesis just described, and, therefore, has its purpose in itself, in this representation and revelation. For other objects, such as instruction, purification, improvement, pecuniary gain, endeavour after fame and honour, have nothing to do with the work of art as such, and do not determine its conception.

It is from this point of view, into which *reflective* consideration of the matter resolves itself, that we have to apprehend the idea of art in its inner necessity, as indeed it was from this point of view, historically speaking, that the true appreciation and understanding of art took its origin. For that antithesis, of which we spoke, made itself felt, not only within general reflective culture, but no less in philosophy as such, and it was not till philosophy discovered how to overcome this antithesis absolutely, that it grasped its own conception and, just in as far as it did so, the conception of nature and of art.

Hence this point of view, as it is the re-awakening of philosophy in general, so also is the re-awakening of the science of art; and, indeed, it is this re-awakening to which alone aesthetic as a science owes its true origin, and art its higher estimation. . . .

DIVISION OF THE SUBJECT

1. After the above introductory remarks, it is now time to pass to the study of our object-matter. But we are still in the introduction, and an introduction cannot do more than lay down, for the sake of explanation, the general sketch of the entire course which will be followed by our subsequent scientific considerations. As, however, we have spoken of art as proceeding from the absolute Idea, and have even assigned as its end the sensuous representation of the absolute itself, we shall have to conduct this review in a way to show, at least in general, how the particular divisions of the subject spring from the conception of artistic beauty as the representation of the absolute. Therefore we must attempt to awaken a very general idea of this conception itself.

It has already been said that the content of art is the Idea, and that its form lies in the plastic use of images accessible to sense. These two sides art has to reconcile into a full and united totality. The *first* attribution which this involves is the requirement that the content, which is to be offered to artistic representation, shall show itself to be in its nature worthy of such representation. Otherwise we only obtain a bad combination, whereby a content that will not submit to plasticity and to external presentation, is forced into that form, and a matter which is in its nature prosaic is expected to find an appropriate mode of manifestation in the form antagonistic to its nature.

The *second* requirement, which is derivable from this first, demands of the content of art that it should not be anything abstract in itself. This does not mean that it must be concrete as the sensuous is concrete in contrast to everything spiritual and intellectual, these being taken as in themselves simple and abstract. For everything that has genuine truth in the mind as well as in nature is concrete in itself, and has, in spite of its universality, nevertheless, both subjectivity and particularity within it. If we say, *e.g.*, of God that he is simply *One*, the supreme Being as such, we have only enunciated a lifeless abstraction of the irrational understanding. Such a God, as he himself is not apprehended in his concrete truth, can afford no material for art, least of all for plastic art. Hence the Jews and the Turks have not been able to represent their God, who does not even amount to such an abstraction of the understanding, in the positive way in which Christians have done so. For God in Christianity is conceived in His truth, and therefore, as in Himself thoroughly concrete, as a person, as a subject, and more closely determined, as mind or spirit. What He is as spirit unfolds itself to the religious apprehension as the Trinity of Persons, which at the same time in relation with itself is *One*. Here is essentiality, universality, and particularity, together with their reconciled unity; and it is only such unity that constitutes the concrete. Now, as a content in order to possess truth at all must be of this concrete nature, art demands the same concreteness, because a mere abstract universal has not in itself the vocation to advance to particularity and phenomenal manifestation and to unity with itself therein.

If a true and therefore concrete content is to have corresponding to it a sensuous form and modelling, this sensuous form must, in the third place, be no less emphatically something individual, wholly concrete in itself, and one. The character of concreteness as belonging to both elements of art, to the content as to the representation, is precisely the point in which both may coincide and correspond to one another; as, for instance, the natural shape of the human body is such a sensuous concrete as is capable of representing spirit, which is concrete in itself, and of displaying itself in conformity therewith. Therefore we ought to abandon the idea that it is a mere matter of accident that an actual phenomenon of the external world is chosen to furnish a shape thus conformable to truth. Art does not appropriate this form either because it simply finds it existing or because there is no other. The concrete content itself involves the element of external and actual, we may say indeed of sensible manifestation. But in compensation this sensuous concrete, in which a content essentially belonging to mind expresses itself, is in its own nature addressed to the inward being; its external element of shape, whereby the content is made perceptible and imaginable, has the aim of existing purely for the heart and mind. This is the only reason for which content and artistic shape are fashioned in conformity with each other. The *mere* sensuous concrete, external nature as such, has not this purpose for its exclusive ground of origin. The birds' variegated plumage shines unseen, and their song dies away unheard, the *Cereus* which blossoms only for a night withers without having been admired in the wilds of southern forests, and these forests, jungles of the most beautiful and luxuriant vegetation, with the most odorous and aromatic perfumes, perish and decay no less unenjoyed. The work of art has not such a naive self-centred being, but is essentially a question, an address to the responsive heart, an appeal to affections and to minds.

Although the artistic bestowal of sensuous form is in this respect not accidental, yet on the other hand it is not the highest mode of apprehending the spiritually concrete. Thought is a higher mode than representation by means of the sensuous concrete. Although in a relative sense abstract, yet it must not be one-sided but concrete thinking, in order to be true and rational. Whether a given content has sensuous artistic representation for its adequate form, or in virtue of its nature essentially demands a higher and more spiritual embodiment, is a distinction that displays itself at once, if, for instance, we compare the Greek gods with God as conceived according to Christian ideas. The Greek god is not abstract but individual, and is closely akin to the natural human shape; the Christian God is equally a concrete personality, but in the mode of pure spiritual existence, and is to be known as *mind* and in mind. His medium of existence is therefore essentially inward knowledge and not external natural form, by means of which He can only be represented imperfectly, and not in the whole depth of His idea.

But inasmuch as the task of art is to represent the idea to direct perception in sensuous shape, and not in the form of thought or of pure spirituality as such, and seeing that this work of representation has its value and dignity in the correspondence and the unity of the two sides, *i.e.* of the Idea and its plastic embodiment, it follows that the level and excellency of art in attaining a realization adequate to its idea, must depend upon the grade of inwardness and unity with which Idea and Shape display themselves as fused into one.

Thus the higher truth is spiritual being that has attained a shape adequate to the conception of spirit. This is what furnishes the principle of division for the science of art. For before the mind can attain the true notion of its absolute essence, it has to traverse a course of stages whose ground is in this idea itself; and to this evolution of the content with which it supplies itself, there corresponds an evolution, immediately connected therewith, of the plastic forms of art, under the shape of which the mind as artist presents to itself the consciousness of itself.

This evolution within the art-spirit has again in its own nature two sides. In the *first* place the development itself is a spiritual and universal one, in so far as the graduated series of definite *conceptions of the world* as the definite but comprehensive consciousness of nature, man and God, gives itself artistic shape; and, in the *second* place, this *universal* development of art is obliged to provide itself with external existence and sensuous form, and the definite modes of the sensuous art-existence are themselves a totality of necessary distinctions in the realm of art—which are *the several arts*. It is true, indeed, that the necessary kinds of artistic representation are on the one hand *qua* spiritual of a very general nature, and not restricted to any one material; while sensuous existence contains manifold varieties of matter. But as this latter, like the mind, has the Idea potentially for its inner soul, it follows from this that particular sensuous materials have a close affinity and secret accord with the spiritual distinctions and types of art presentation.

In its completeness, however, our science divides itself into three principal portions.

First, we obtain a *general part*. It has for its content and object the universal Idea of artistic beauty—this beauty being conceived as the Ideal—together with the nearer relation of the latter both to nature and to subjective artistic production.

Secondly, there develops itself out of the idea of artistic beauty a *particular* part, in as far as the essential differences which this idea contains in itself evolve themselves into a scale of *particular* plastic forms.

In the *third* place there results a *final* part, which has for its subject the individualization of artistic beauty, that consists in the advance of art to the sensuous realization of its shapes and its self-completion as a system of the several arts and their genera and species.

2.   With respect to the first part, we must begin by recalling to mind, in order to make the sequel intelligible, that the Idea *qua* the beautiful in art is not the Idea as such, in the mode in which a metaphysical logic apprehends it as the absolute, but the Idea as developed into concrete form fit for reality, and as having entered into immediate and adequate unity with this reality. For the *Idea as such*, although it is the essentially and actually true, is yet the truth only in its generality which has not yet taken objective shape; but the *Idea* as the *beautiful in art* is at once the Idea when specially determined as in its essence individual reality, and also an individual shape of reality essentially destined to embody and reveal the Idea. This amounts

to enunciating the requirement that the Idea, and its plastic mould as concrete reality, are to be made completely adequate to one another. When reduced to such form the Idea, as a reality moulded in conformity with the conception of the Idea, is the *Ideal*. The problem of this conformity might, to begin with, be understood in the sense that any Idea would serve, so long as the actual shape, it did not matter what shape, represented this particular Idea and no other. But if so, the required truth of the Ideal is confounded with mere correctness, which consists in the expression of any meaning whatever in appropriate fashion so that its import may be readily recognized in the shape created. The Ideal is not to be thus understood. Any content whatever may attain to being represented quite adequately, judged by the standard of its own nature, but it does not therefore gain the right to claim the artistic beauty of the Ideal. Compared indeed with ideal beauty, even the presentation will in such a case appear defective. From this point of view we must remark to begin with, what cannot be proved till later, that the defects of a work of art are not to be regarded simply as always due, for instance, to individual unskilfulness. *Defectiveness of form* arises from *defectiveness of content*. So, for example, the Chinese, Indians, and Egyptians in their artistic shapes, their forms of deities, and their idols, never got beyond a formless phase, or one of a vicious and false definiteness of form, and were unable to attain genuine beauty; because their mythological ideas, the content and thought of their works of art, were as yet indeterminate in themselves, or of a vicious determinateness, and did not consist in the content that is absolute in itself. The more that works of art excel in true beauty of presentation, the more profound is the inner truth of their content and thought. And in dealing with this point, we have not to think merely perhaps of the greater or lesser skill with which the natural forms as given in external reality are apprehended and imitated. For in certain stages of art-consciousness and of representation, the distortion and disfigurement of natural structures is not unintentional technical inexpertness and want of skill, but intentional alteration, which emanates from the content that is in consciousness, and is required thereby. Thus, from this point of view, there is such a thing as imperfect art, which may be quite perfect, both technically and in other respects, *in its determinate* sphere, yet reveals itself to be defective when compared with the conception of art as such, and with the Ideal. Only in the highest art are the Idea and the representation genuinely adequate to one another, in the sense that the outward shape given to the Idea is in itself essentially and actually the true shape, because the content of the Idea, which that shape expresses, is itself the true and real content. It is a corollary from this, as we indicated above, that the Idea must be defined in and through itself as concrete totality, and thereby possess in itself the principle and standard of its particularization and determination in external appearance. For example, the Christian imagination will be able to represent God only in human form and with man's intellectual expression, because it is herein that God Himself is completely known in Himself as mind. Determinateness is, as it were, the bridge to phenomenal existence. Where this determinateness is not totality derived from the Idea itself, where the Idea is not conceived as self-determining and self-particularizing, the Idea remains abstract and has its determinateness, and therefore the principle that dictates its particular and exclusively appropriate mode of presentation, not in itself but external to it. Therefore, the Idea when still abstract has even its shape external, and not dictated by itself. The Idea, however, which is concrete in itself bears the principle of its mode of manifestation within itself, and is by that means the free process of giving shape to itself. Thus it is only the truly concrete Idea that can generate the true shape, and this correspondence of the two is the Ideal.

3. Now because the Idea is in this fashion concrete unity, it follows that this unity can enter into the art-consciousness only by the expansion and re-conciliation of the particularities of the Idea, and it is through this evolution that artistic beauty comes to possess a *totality of particular stages and forms.* Therefore, after we have studied the beauty of art in itself and on its own merits, we must see how beauty as a whole breaks up into its particular determinations. This gives, as our *second part, the doctrine of the types of art.* These forms find their genesis in the different modes of grasping the Idea as artistic content, whereby is conditioned a difference of the form in which it manifests itself. Hence the types of art are nothing but the different relations of content and shape, relations which emanate from the Idea itself, and furnish thereby the true basis of division for this sphere. For the principle of division must always be contained in *that* conception whose particularization and division is in question.

We have here to consider *three* relations of the Idea to its outward shaping.[27]

α. First, the Idea gives rise to the beginning of Art when, being itself still in its indistinctness and obscurity, or in vicious untrue determinateness, it is made the import of artistic creations. As indeterminate it does not yet possess in itself that individuality which the Ideal demands; its abstractness and one-sidedness leave its shape to be outwardly bizarre and defective. The first form of art is therefore rather a mere search after plastic portrayal than a capacity of genuine representation. The Idea has not yet found the true form even within itself, and therefore continues to be merely the struggle and aspiration thereafter. In general terms we may call this form the *Symbolic* form of art. In it the abstract Idea has its outward shape external to itself in natural sensuous matter, with which the process of shaping begins, and from which, *qua* outward expression, it is inseparable.

Natural objects are thus primarily left unaltered, and yet at the same time invested with the substantial Idea as their significance, so that they receive the vocation of expressing it, and claim to be interpreted as though the Idea itself were present in them. At the root of this is the fact that natural objects have in them an aspect in which they are capable of representing a universal meaning. But as an adequate correspondence is not yet possible, this reference can only concern *an abstract attribute*, as when a lion is used to mean strength.

On the other hand, this abstractness of the relation brings to consciousness no less strongly the foreignness of the Idea to natural phenomena; and the Idea, having no other reality to express it, expatiates in all these shapes, seeks itself in them in all their unrest and disproportion, but nevertheless does not find them adequate to itself. Then it proceeds to exaggerate the natural shapes and the phenomena of reality into indefiniteness and disproportion, to intoxicate itself in them, to seethe and ferment in them, to do violence to them, to distort and explode them into unnatural shapes, and strives by the variety, hugeness, and splendour of the forms employed to exalt the phenomenon to the level of the Idea. For the Idea is here still more or less indeterminate and non-plastic, but the natural objects are in their shape thoroughly determinate.

Hence, in view of the unsuitability of the two elements to each other, the relation of the Idea to objective reality becomes a *negative* one, for the former, as in its nature inward, is unsatisfied with such an externality, and as being its inner universal substance persists in exaltation or *Sublimity* beyond and above all this inadequate abundance of shapes. In virtue of this sublimity the natural phenomena and the human shapes and incidents are accepted, and left as they were, though at the same time understood to be inadequate to their significance, which is exalted far above every earthly content.

These aspects may be pronounced in general terms to constitute the character of the primitive artistic pantheism of the East, which either charges even the meanest objects with the absolute import, or again coerces nature with violence into the expression of its view. By this means it becomes bizarre, grotesque, and tasteless, or turns the infinite but abstract freedom of the substantive Idea disdainfully against all phenomenal being as null and evanescent. By such means the import cannot be completely embodied in the expression, and in spite of all aspiration and endeavour the reciprocal inadequacy of shape and Idea remains insuperable. This may be taken as the first form of art, — Symbolic art with its aspiration, its disquiet, its mystery and its sublimity.

(*β*) In the second form of art, which we propose to call "*Classical*," the double defect of symbolic art is cancelled. The plastic shape of symbolic art is imperfect, because, in the first place, the Idea in it only enters into consciousness in *abstract* determinateness or indeterminateness, and, in the second place, this must always make the conformity of shape to import defective, and in its turn merely abstract. The classical form of art is the solution of this double difficulty; it is the free and adequate embodiment of the Idea in the shape that, according to its conception, is peculiarly appropriate to the Idea itself. With it, therefore, the Idea is capable of entering into free and complete accord. Hence, the classical type of art is the first to afford the production and intuition of the completed Ideal, and to establish it as a realized fact.

The conformity, however, of notion and reality in classical art must not be taken in the purely *formal* sense of the agreement of a content with the external shape given to it, any more than this could be the case with the Ideal itself. Otherwise every copy from nature, and every type of countenance, every landscape, flower, or scene, etc., which forms the purport of any representation, would be at once made classical by the agreement which it displays between form and content. On the contrary, in classical art the peculiarity of the content consists in being itself concrete idea, and, as such, the concrete spiritual; for only the spiritual is the truly inner self. To suit such a content, then, we must search out that in Nature which on its own merits belongs to the essence and actuality of the mind. It must be the absolute notion[9] that *invented* the shape appropriate to concrete mind, so that the *subjective* notion — in this case the spirit of art — has merely *found* it, and brought it, as an existence possessing natural shape, into accord with free individual spirituality. This shape, with which the Idea as spiritual — as individually determinate spirituality — invests itself when manifested as a temporal phenomenon, is *the human form*. Personification and anthropomorphism have often been decried as a degradation of the spiritual; but art, in as far as its end is to bring before perception the spiritual in sensuous form, must advance to such anthropomorphism, as it is only in its proper body that mind is adequately revealed to sense. The migration of souls is in this respect a false abstraction, and physiology ought to have made it one of its axioms that life had necessarily in its evolution to attain to the human shape, as the sole sensuous phenomenon that is appropriate to mind. The human form is employed in the classical type of art not as mere sensuous existence, but exclusively as the existence and physical form corresponding to mind, and is therefore exempt from all the deficiencies of what is merely sensuous, and from the contingent finiteness of phenomenal existence. The outer shape must be thus purified in order to express in itself a content adequate to itself; and again, if the conformity of import and content is to be complete, the spiritual meaning which is the content must be of a particular kind. It must, that is to say, be qualified to express itself completely in the physical form of man, without projecting into another world beyond the scope of such an expression in sensuous and bodily terms. This condition has the effect that Mind is by it at once specified as a particular case of mind, as human mind, and not as simply absolute and eternal, inasmuch as mind in this latter sense is incapable of proclaiming and expressing itself otherwise than as intellectual being.[25]

Out of this latter point arises, in its turn, the defect which brings about the dissolution of classical art, and demands a transition into a third and higher form, viz. into the *romantic* form of art.

(γ) The romantic form of art destroys the completed union of the Idea and its reality, and recurs, though in a higher phase, to that difference and antagonism of two aspects which was left unvanquished by symbolic art. The classical type attained the highest excellence, of which the sensuous embodiment of art is capable; and if it is in any way defective, the defect is in art as a whole, *i.e.* in the limitation of its sphere. This limitation consists in the fact that art as such takes for its object Mind—the conception of which is *infinite* concrete universality—in the shape of *sensuous* concreteness, and in the classical phase sets up the perfect amalgamation of spiritual and sensuous existence as a Conformity of the two. Now, as a matter of fact, in such an amalgamation Mind cannot be represented according to its true notion. For mind is the infinite subjectivity of the Idea, which, as absolute inwardness, is not capable of finding free expansion in its true nature on condition of remaining transposed into a bodily medium as the existence appropriate to it.

As *an escape from such a condition* the romantic form of art in its turn dissolves the inseparable unity of the classical phase, because it has won a significance which goes beyond the classical form of art and its mode of expression. This significance—if we may recall familiar ideas—coincides with what Christianity declares to be true of God as Spirit, in contradistinction to the Greek faith in gods which forms the essential and appropriate content for classical art. In Greek art the concrete import is potentially, but not explicitly, the unity of the human and divine nature; a unity which, just because it is purely *immediate* and *not explicit*, is capable of adequate manifestation in an immediate and sensuous mode. The Greek god is the object of naive intuition and sensuous imagination. His shape is, therefore, the bodily shape of man. The circle of his power and of his being is individual and individually limited. In relation with the subject, he is, therefore, an essence and a power with which the subject's inner being is merely in latent unity, not itself possessing this unity as inward subjective knowledge. Now the higher stage is the *knowledge* of this *latent* unity, which as latent is the import of the classical form of art, and capable of perfect representation in bodily shape. The elevation of the latent or potential into self-conscious knowledge produces an enormous difference. It is the infinite difference which, *e.g.*, separates man as such from the animals. Man is animal, but even in his animal functions he is not confined within the latent and potential as the animal is, but becomes conscious of them, learns to know them, and raises them—as, for instance, the process of digestion—into self-conscious science. By this means Man breaks the boundary of merely potential and immediate consciousness, so that just for the reason that he knows himself to be animal, he ceases to be animal, and, as *mind*, attains to self-knowledge.

If in the above fashion the unity of the human and divine nature, which in the former phase was potential, is raised from an *immediate* to a *conscious* unity, it follows that the true medium for the reality of this content is no longer the sensuous immediate existence of the spiritual, the human bodily shape, but *self-conscious inward intelligence.* Now, Christianity brings God before our intelligence *as spirit*, or mind — not as particularized individual spirit, but as absolute, in *spirit* and in truth. And for this reason Christianity retires from the sensuousness of imagination into intellectual inwardness, and makes this, not bodily shape, the medium and actual existence of its significance. So, too, the unity of the human and divine nature is a conscious unity, only to be realized by *spiritual* knowledge and in *spirit*. Thus the new content, won by this unity, is not inseparable from sensuous representation, as if that were adequate to it, but is freed from this immediate existence, which has to be posited as negative, absorbed, and reflected into the spiritual unity. In this way, romantic art must be considered as art transcending itself, while remaining within the artistic sphere and in artistic form.

Therefore, in short, we may abide by the statement that in this third stage the object (of art) is *free*, concrete intellectual being, which has the function of revealing itself as spiritual existence for the inward world of spirit. In conformity with such an object-matter, art cannot work for sensuous perception. It must address itself to the inward mind, which coalesces with its object simply and as though this were itself, to the subjective inwardness, to the heart, the feeling, which, being spiritual, aspires to freedom within itself, and seeks and finds its reconciliation only in the spirit within. It is this *inner* world that forms the content of the romantic, and must therefore find its representation as such inward feeling, and in the show or presentation of such feeling. The world of inwardness celebrates its triumph over the outer world, and actually in the sphere of the outer and in its medium manifests this its victory, owing to which the sensuous appearance sinks into worthlessness.

But, on the other hand, this type of Art, like every other, needs an external vehicle of expression. Now the spiritual has withdrawn into itself out of the external and its immediate oneness therewith. For this reason, the sensuous externality of concrete form is accepted and represented, as in Symbolic art, as something transient and fugitive. And the same measure is dealt to the subjective finite mind and will, even including the peculiarity or caprice of the individual, of character, action, etc., or of incident and plot. The aspect of external existence is committed to contingency, and left at the mercy of freaks of imagination, whose caprice is no more likely to mirror what is given *as* it is given, than to throw the shapes of the outer world into chance medley, or distort them into grotesqueness. For this external element no longer has its notion and significance, as in classical art, in its own sphere, and in its own medium. It has come to find them in the feelings, the display of which is *in themselves* instead of being in the external and *its* form of reality, and which have the power to preserve or to regain their state of reconciliation with themselves, in every accident, in every unessential circumstance that takes independent shape, in all misfortune and grief, and even in crime.

Owing to this, the characteristics of symbolic art, in difference, discrepancy, and severance of Idea and plastic shape, are here reproduced, but with an essential difference. In the sphere of the romantic, the Idea, whose defectiveness in the case of the symbol produced the defect of external shape, has to reveal itself in the medium of spirit and feelings as perfected in itself. And it is because of this higher perfection that it withdraws itself from any adequate union with the external element, inasmuch as it can seek and achieve its true reality and revelation nowhere but in itself.

This we may take as in the abstract the character of the symbolic, classical, and romantic forms of art, which represent the three relations of the Idea to its embodiment in the sphere of art. They consist in the aspiration after, and the attainment and transcendence of the Ideal as the true Idea of beauty.

4. The third part of our subject, in contradistinction to the two just described, presupposes the conception of the Ideal, and the general types of art, inasmuch as it simply consists of their realization in particular sensuous media. Hence we have no longer to do with the inner development of artistic beauty in conformity with its general fundamental principles. What we have to study is how these principles pass into actual existence, how they distinguish themselves in their external aspect, and how they give actuality to every element contained in the idea of beauty, separately and by itself *as a work of art*, and not merely as a general type. Now, what art transfers into external existence are the differences proper to the idea of beauty and immanent therein. Therefore, the general types of art must reveal themselves in this third part, as before, in the character of the fundamental principle that determines the arrangement and definition of the *several arts*; in other words, the species of art contain in themselves the same essential modifications as those with which we become acquainted as the general types of art. External objectivity, however, to which these forms are introduced through the medium of a sensuous and therefore *particular* material, affects these types in the way of making them *separate* into independent and so particular forms embodying their realization. For each type finds its definite character in some one definite external material, and its adequate actuality in the mode of portrayal which that prescribes. But, moreover, these types of art, being for all their determinateness, its *universal* forms, break the bounds of *particular* realization by a determinate form of art, and achieve existence in other arts as well, although in subordinate fashion. Therefore, the particular arts belong each of them specifically to *one* of the general types of art, and constitute *its adequate* external actuality; and also they represent, each of them after its own mode of external plasticity, the totality of the types of art.

Then, speaking generally, we are dealing in this third principal division with the beautiful of art, as it unfolds itself in the several arts and in their creations into a *world* of actualized beauty. The content of this world is the beautiful, and the true beautiful, as we saw, is spiritual being in concrete shape, the Ideal; or, more closely looked at, the absolute mind, and the truth itself. This region, that of divine truth artistically represented to perception and to feeling, forms the centre of the whole world of art. It is the independent, free, and divine plasticity, which has thoroughly mastered the external elements of form and of medium, and wears them simply as a means to manifestation of itself. Still, as the beautiful unfolds itself in this region in the character of *objective* reality, and in so doing distinguishes within itself its individual aspects and elements, permitting them independent particularity, it follows that this centre erects its extremes, realized in their peculiar actuality, into its own antitheses. Thus one of these extremes comes to consist in an objectivity as yet devoid of mind, in the merely natural vesture of God. At this point the external element takes plastic shape as something that has its spiritual aim and content, not in itself, but in another.

The other extreme is the divine as inward, as something known, as the variously particularized *subjective* existence of the Deity; it is the truth as operative and vital in sense, heart, and mind of individual subjects, not persisting in the mould of its external shapes, but as having returned into subjective, individual inwardness. In such a mode, the Divine is at the same time distinguished from its first manifestation as Deity, and passes thereby into the diversity of particulars which belongs to all subjective knowledge —emotion, perception, and feeling. In the analogous province of religion, with which art at its highest stage is immediately connected, we conceive this same difference as follows. *First*, we think of the earthly natural life in its finiteness as standing on one side; but, then, *secondly*, consciousness makes God its object, in which the distinction of objectivity and subjectivity is done away. And at last, *thirdly*, we advance from God as such to the devotion of the community, that is, to God as living and present in the subjective consciousness. Just so these three chief modifications present themselves in the world of art in independent development.

(α) The *first* of the particular arts with which, according to their fundamental principle, we have to begin, is architecture considered as a fine art. Its task lies in so manipulating external inorganic nature that it becomes cognate to mind, as an artistic outer world. The material of architecture is matter itself in its immediate externality as a heavy mass subject to mechanical laws, and its forms do not depart from the forms of inorganic nature, but are merely set in order in conformity with relations of the abstract understanding, *i.e.* with relations of symmetry. In this material and in such forms, the ideal as concrete spirituality does not admit of being realized. Hence the reality which is represented in them remains contrasted with the Idea, as something external which it has not penetrated, or has penetrated only to establish an abstract relation. For these reasons, the fundamental type of the fine art of building is the *symbolical* form of art. It is architecture that pioneers the way for the adequate realization of the God, and in this its service bestows hard toil upon existing nature, in order to disentangle it from the jungle of finitude and the abortiveness of chance. By this means it levels a space for the God, gives form to his external surroundings, and builds him his temple as a fit place for concentration of spirit, and for its direction to the mind's absolute objects. It raises an enclosure round the assembly of those gathered together, as a defense against the threatening of the storm, against rain, the hurricane, and wild beasts, and reveals the will to assemble, although externally, yet in conformity with principles of art. With such import as this it has power to inspire its material and its forms more or less effectively, as the determinate character of the content on behalf of which it sets to work is more or less significant, more concrete or more abstract, more profound in sounding its own depths, or more dim and more superficial. So much, indeed, may architecture attempt in this respect as even to create an adequate artistic existence for such an import in its shapes and in its material. But in such a case it has already overstepped its own boundary, and is leaning to sculpture, the phase above it. For the limit of architecture lies precisely in this point, that it retains the spiritual as an inward existence over against the external forms of the art, and consequently must refer to what has soul only as to something other than its own creations.

(β) Architecture, however, as we have seen, has purified the external world, and endowed it with symmetrical order and with affinity to mind; and the temple of the God, the house of his community, stands ready. Into this temple, then, in the *second* place, the God enters in the lightning-flash of individuality, which strikes and permeates the inert mass, while the infinite and no longer merely symmetrical form belonging to mind itself concentrates and gives shape to the corresponding bodily existence. This is the task of *Sculpture*. In as far as in this art the spiritual inward being which architecture can but indicate makes itself at home in the sensuous shape and its external matter, and in as far as these two sides are so adapted to one another that neither is predominant, sculpture must be assigned the *classical form of art* as its fundamental type. For this reason the sensuous element itself has here no expression which could not be that of the spiritual element, just as, conversely, sculpture can represent no spiritual content which does not admit throughout of being adequately presented to perception in bodily form. Sculpture should place the spirit before us in its bodily form and in immediate unity therewith at rest and in peace; and the form should be animated by the content of spiritual individuality. And so the external sensuous matter is here no longer manipulated, either in conformity with its mechanical quality alone, as a mass possessing weight, nor in shapes belonging to the inorganic world, nor as indifferent to colour, etc.; but it is wrought in ideal forms of the human figure, and, it must be remarked, in all three spatial dimensions.

In this last respect we must claim for sculpture, that it is in it that the inward and spiritual are first revealed in their eternal repose and essential self-completeness. To such repose and unity with itself there can correspond only that external shape which itself maintains its unity and repose. And this is fulfilled by shape in its abstract spatiality. The spirit which sculpture represents is that which is solid in itself, not broken up in the play of trivialities and of passions; and hence its external form too is not abandoned to any manifold phases of appearance, but appears under this one aspect only, as the abstraction of space in the whole of its dimensions.

(γ) Now, after architecture has erected the temple, and the hand of sculpture has supplied it with the statue of the God, then, in the third place, this god present to sense is confronted in the spacious halls of his house by the *community*. The community is the spiritual reflection into itself of such sensuous existence, and is the animating subjectivity and inner life which brings about the result that the determining principle for the content of art, as well as for the medium which represents it in outward form, comes to be particularization [dispersion into various shapes, attributes, incidents, etc.], individualization, and the subjectivity which they require. The solid unity which the God has in sculpture breaks up into the multitudinous inner lives of individuals, whose unity is not sensuous, but purely ideal.

It is only in this stage that God Himself comes to be really and truly spirit—the spirit in His community; for He here begins to be a to-and-fro, an alternation between His unity within himself and his realization in the individual's knowledge and in its separate being, as also in the common nature and union of the multitude. In the community, God is released from the abstractness of unexpanded self-identity, as well as from the simple absorption in a bodily medium, by which sculpture represents Him. And He is thus exalted into spiritual existence and into knowledge, into the reflected appearance which essentially displays itself as inward and as subjectivity. Therefore the higher content is now the spiritual nature, and that in its absolute shape. But the dispersion of which we have spoken reveals this at the same time as particular spiritual being, and as individual character. Now, what manifests itself in this phase as the main thing is not the serene quiescence of the God in Himself, but appearance as such, being which is *for* another, self-manifestation. And hence, in the phase we have reached, all the most manifold subjectivity in its living movement and operation—as human passion, action, and incident, and, in general, the wide realm of human feeling, will, and its negation,—is for its own sake the object of artistic representation. In conformity with this content, the sensuous element of art has at once to show itself as made particular in itself and as adapted to subjective inwardness. Media that fulfil this requirement we have in colour, in musical sound, and finally in sound as the mere indication of inward perceptions and ideas; and as modes of realizing the import in question by help of these media we obtain painting, music, and poetry. In this region the sensuous medium displays itself as subdivided in its own being and universally set down as ideal. Thus it has the highest degree of conformity with the content of art, which, as such, is spiritual, and the connection of intelligible import and sensuous medium develops into closer intimacy than was possible in the case of architecture and sculpture. The unity attained, however, is a more inward unity, the weight of which is thrown wholly on the subjective side, and which, in as far as form and content are compelled to particularize themselves and give themselves merely ideal existence, can only come to pass at the expense of the objective universality of the content and also of its amalgamation with the immediately sensuous element.

The arts, then, of which form and content exalt themselves to ideality, abandon the character of symbolic architecture and the classical ideal of sculpture, and therefore borrow their type from the romantic form of art, whose mode of plasticity they are most adequately adapted to express. And they constitute a *totality* of arts, because the romantic type is the most concrete in itself.

i. The articulation of this *third sphere* of the individual arts may be determined as follows. The *first* art in it, which comes next to sculpture, is painting. It employs as a medium for its content and for the plastic embodiment of that content visibility as such in as far as it is specialized in its own nature, *i.e.* as developed into colour. It is true that the material employed in architecture and sculpture is also visible and coloured; but it is not, as in painting, visibility as such, not the simple light which, differentiating itself in virtue of its contrast with darkness, and in combination with the latter, gives rise to colour. This quality of visibility, made subjective in itself and treated as ideal, needs neither, like architecture, the abstractly mechanical attribute of mass as operative in the properties of heavy matter, nor, like sculpture, the complete sensuous attributes of space, even though concentrated into organic shapes. The visibility and the rendering visible which belong to painting have their differences in a more ideal form, in the several kinds of colour, and they liberate art from the sensuous completeness in space which attaches to material things, by restricting themselves to a plane surface.

On the other hand, the content also attains the most comprehensive specification. Whatever can find room in the human heart, as feeling, idea, and purpose; whatever it is capable of shaping into act — all this diversity of material is capable of entering into the varied content of painting. The whole realm of particular existence, from the highest embodiment of mind down to the most isolated object of nature, finds a place here. For it is possible even for finite nature, in its particular scenes and phenomena, to make its appearance in the realm of art, if only some allusion to an element of mind endows it with affinity to thought and feeling.

ii. The *second* art in which the romantic type realizes itself is contrasted with painting, and is music. Its medium, though still sensuous, yet develops into still more thorough subjectivity and particularization. Music, too, treats the sensuous as ideal, and does so by negating,[8] and idealizing into the individual isolation of a single point, the indifferent externality of space, whose complete semblance is accepted and imitated by painting. The single point, *qua* such a negativity (excluding space) is in itself a concrete and active process of positive negation[8] within the attributes of matter, in the shape of a motion and tremor of the material body within itself and in its relation to itself. Such an inchoate ideality of matter, which appears no longer as under the form of space, but as temporal ideality, is sound, the sensuous set down as negated, with its abstract visibility converted into audibility, inasmuch as sound, so to speak, liberates the ideal content from its immersion in matter. This earliest inwardness of matter and inspiration of soul into it furnishes the medium for the mental inwardness — itself as yet indefinite, — and for the soul into which mind concentrates itself; and finds utterance in its tones for the heart with its whole gamut of feelings and passions. Thus music forms the centre of the romantic arts, just as sculpture represents the central point between architecture and the arts of romantic subjectivity. Thus, too, it forms the point of transition between abstract spatial sensuousness, such as painting employs, and the abstract spirituality of poetry. Music has within itself, like architecture, a relation of quantity conformable to the understanding, as the antithesis to emotion and inwardness; and has also as its basis a solid conformity to law on the part of the tones, of their conjunction, and of their succession.

iii. As regards the *third* and most spiritual mode of representation of the romantic art-type, we must look for it in *poetry*. Its characteristic peculiarity lies in the power with which it subjects to the mind and to its ideas the sensuous element from which music and painting in their degree began to liberate art. For sound, the only external matter which poetry retains, is in it no longer the feeling of the sonorous itself, but is a *sign*, which by itself is void of import. And it is a sign of the idea which has become concrete in itself, and not merely of indefinite feeling and of its *nuances* and grades. This is how sound develops into the *Word*, as voice articulate in itself, whose import it is to indicate ideas and notions. The merely negative point up to which music had developed now makes its appearance as the completely concrete point, the point which is mind, the self-conscious individual, which, producing out of itself the infinite space of its ideas, unites it with the temporal character of sound. Yet this sensuous element, which in music was still immediately one with inward feeling, is in poetry separated from the content of consciousness. In poetry the mind determines this content for its own sake, and apart from all else, into the shape of ideas, and though it employs sound to express them, yet treats it solely as a symbol without value or import. Thus considered, sound may just as well be reduced to a mere letter, for the audible, like the visible, is thus depressed into a mere indication of mind. For this reason the proper medium of poetical representation is the poetical imagination and intellectual portrayal itself. And as this element is common to all types of art, it follows that poetry runs through them all and develops itself independently in each. Poetry is the universal art of the mind which has become free in its own nature, and which is not tied to find its realization in external sensuous matter, but expatiates exclusively in the inner space and inner time of the ideas and feelings. Yet just in this its highest phase art ends by transcending itself, inasmuch as it abandons the medium of a harmonious embodiment of mind in sensuous form, and passes from the poetry of imagination into the prose of thought.

5. Such we may take to be the articulated totality of the particular arts, viz. the external art of architecture, the objective art of sculpture, and the subjective art of painting, music and poetry. Many other classifications have been attempted, for a work of art presents so many aspects, that, as has often been the case, first one and then another is made the basis of classification. For instance, one might take the sensuous medium. Thus architecture is treated as crystallization; sculpture, as the organic modelling of the material in its sensuous and spatial totality; painting, as the coloured surface and line; while in music, space, as such, passes into the point of time possessed of content within itself, until finally the external medium is in poetry depressed into complete insignificance. Or, again, these differences have been considered with reference to their purely abstract attributes of space and time. Such abstract peculiarities of works of art may, like their material medium, be consistently explored in their characteristic traits; but they cannot be worked out as the ultimate and fundamental law, because any such aspect itself derives its origin from a higher principle, and must therefore be subordinate thereto.

This higher principle we have found in the types of art—symbolic, classical, and romantic—which are the universal stages or elements[34] of the Idea of beauty itself. For *symbolic art* attains its most adequate reality and most complete application in *architecture*, in which it holds sway in the full import of its notion, and is not yet degraded to be, as it were, the inorganic nature dealt with by another art. The *classical* type of art, on the other hand, finds adequate realization in sculpture, while it treats architecture only as furnishing an enclosure in which it is to operate, and has not acquired the power of developing painting and music as absolute forms for its content. The *romantic* type of art, finally, takes possession of painting and music, and in like manner of poetic representation, as substantive and unconditionally adequate modes of utterance. Poetry, however, is conformable to all types of the beautiful, and extends over them all, because the artistic imagination is its proper medium, and imagination is essential to every product that belongs to the beautiful, whatever its type may be.

And, therefore, what the particular arts realize in individual works of art, are according to their abstract conception simply the universal types which constitute the self-unfolding Idea of beauty. It is as the external realization of this Idea that the wide Pantheon of art is being erected, whose architect and builder is the spirit of beauty as it awakens to self-knowledge, and to complete which the history of the world will need its evolution of ages.

XVI.   Encyclopaedia: Absolute Mind*

553.   The concept of mind has its *reality* in the mind. If this reality in identity with that concept is to exist as the knowledge of the absolute Idea, then the necessary aspect is that the *implicitly* free intelligence be in its actuality liberated to its concept, if that actuality is to be a vehicle worthy of it. The subjective and the objective spirit are to be looked on as the road on which this aspect of *reality* or existence rises to maturity.

554.   The absolute mind, while it is self-centred *identity*, is eternally also identity returning and ever returned into itself: if it is the one and universal *substance* it is so as a spirit, discerning[49] itself into a self and a knowledge, for which it is as substance. *Religion*, as this supreme sphere may be in general designated, if it has on one hand to be studied as issuing from the subject and having its home in the subject, must no less be regarded as objectively issuing from the absolute spirit which as spirit is in its community.

That here, as always, belief or faith is not opposite to knowledge,[60] but to a sort of knowledge, and that belief is only a particular form of the latter, has been remarked already (§63). If nowadays there is so little consciousness of God, and his objective essence is so little dwelt upon, while people speak so much more of the subjective side of religion, of God's indwelling in us, and if that and not the truth as such is called for, — in this there is at least the correct principle that God must be apprehended as spirit in his community.

555.   The subjective consciousness of the absolute spirit is essentially and intrinsically a process, the immediate and substantial unity of which is *belief* on the testimony of the spirit as the *certainty* of objective truth. Belief, at once this immediate unity and containing it as a reciprocal dependence of these different terms, has in *devotion* — the implicit or more explicit act of worship (*cultus*) — passed over into the process of elevating[8] the antithesis to spiritual liberation, the process of authenticating that first certainty by this mediation, and of gaining its concrete determination, viz. the reconciliation, the actuality of the spirit.

*From the third (1830) edition of *The Encyclopaedia of the Philosophical Sciences in Outline*. Translated by William Wallace, with revisions by M. J. Inwood.

A. ART

556. In its first, immediate form, this knowledge is the phase of finitude in art. On one hand, it breaks up into a work of external common existence, into the subject who produces that work, and the subject who intuits and worships it. But, on the other hand, it is the concrete intuition and conception of implicitly absolute spirit as the *ideal*. In this ideal, the concrete shape born of the subjective spirit, its natural immediacy, which is only a *sign* of the Idea, is so transfigured by the informing spirit in order to express the Idea, that the shape shows it and it alone: — the shape or form of *beauty*.

557. The sensuous externality attaching to the beautiful, — the *form of immediacy* as such, — at the same time *qualifies* what it *embodies*: and the God (of art) has with his spirituality at the same time the stamp upon him of a natural element or existence — He contains the so-called *unity* of nature and spirit — i.e. the immediate unity in intuitional form — hence not the spiritual unity, in which the natural would be put only as 'ideal,' as superseded in spirit, and the spiritual content would be self-contained. It is not the absolute spirit which enters this consciousness. On the subjective side the community has of course ethical life, aware, as it is, of the spirituality of its essence; and its self-consciousness and actuality are in it elevated to substantial liberty. But with the stigma of immediacy upon it, the subject's liberty is only a custom, without the infinite self-reflection and the subjective inwardness of *conscience*. These considerations govern in their further developments devotion and worship in the religion of fine art.

558. For the objects of intuition it has to produce, art requires not only external given material (which also includes subjective images and ideas), but also — for the expression of spiritual content — the given forms of nature with a significance which art must divine and master (cf.§411). Of all such forms the human is the highest and the true, because only in it can the spirit have its corporeity and thus its visible expression.

This disposes of the principle of the *imitation of nature* in art: an issue which cannot be settled while a contrast is left thus abstract, — in other words, so long as the natural is only taken in its externality, not as the characteristic, meaningful nature-form which is significant of spirit.

559. In such single shapes the absolute mind cannot be made explicit: in fine art therefore the spirit is a limited national spirit whose implicit universality, when steps are taken to specify its fullness in detail, breaks up into an indeterminate polytheism. With the essential restrictedness of its content, beauty in general goes no further than a penetration of the intuition or image by the spiritual — a mere formality — so that the thought embodied, or the idea, can, like the material which it uses to work in, be of the most diverse and unessential kind, and still the work be something beautiful and a work of art.

560. The one-sidedness of *immediacy* on the part of the ideal involves the opposite one-sidedness (§556) that it is something *made* by the artist. The subject or agent is the mere technical activity: and the work of art is only an expression of the God, when there is no sign of subjective particularity in it, and the content of the indwelling spirit is conceived and born into the world, without admixture and unspotted by its contingency. But as liberty only goes as far as there is thought, the activity engrossed by this indwelling content, the artist's inspiration, is like the alien force of an unfree passion; the artist's *production* has on its part the form of natural immediacy, it belongs to the *genius* of *this* particular subject — and is at the same time a labour concerned with technical understanding and mechanical externalities. The work of art therefore is just as much a work due to free self-will, and the artist is the master of the God.

561. In such inspiration the reconciliation appears at the outset: it is immediately accomplished in the subjective self-consciousness, which is thus confident and of good cheer, without the depth and without the consciousness of its antithesis to the absolute essence. It is in classical art that beauty achieves its perfection in such reconciliation. Beyond it lies the art of sublimity, *symbolic art*, in which the figuration[27] suitable to the Idea is not yet found, and the thought as going forth and wrestling with the figure[27] is exhibited as a negative attitude to it, and yet all the while toiling to work itself into it. The meaning or content thus shows it has not yet reached the infinite form, is not yet known, not yet conscious of itself, as free spirit. The content only is as the abstract God of pure thought, or a striving towards him, — a restless and unappeased effort which throws itself into shape after shape as it vainly tries to find its goal.

562. In another way the Idea and the sensuous figure it appears in are ill-suited; and that is where the infinite form, subjectivity, is not, as in the first extreme, a mere superficial personality, but its inmost depth, and God is known not as only seeking his form or satisfying himself in an external form, but as only finding himself in himself, and thus giving himself his adequate figure in the spiritual alone. *Romantic art* gives up the task of showing him as such in external form and by means of beauty: it presents him as only condescending to appearance, and the divine as the heart of hearts in an externality from which it always disengages itself. Thus the external can here appear as contingent towards its significance.

The philosophy of religion has to cognise the logical necessity in the progress by which the essence, known as the absolute, assumes fuller and firmer features; it has to note to what particular feature the kind of cultus corresponds, — and then to see how the secular self-consciousness, the consciousness of what is the supreme vocation of man, — in short how the nature of a nation's ethical life, the principle of its law, of its actual liberty, and of its constitution, as well as of its art and science, corresponds to the principle which constitutes the substance of a religion. That all these elements of a nation's actuality constitute one systematic totality, that one spirit creates and informs them, is an insight on which follows the further insight that the history of religions coincides with world-history.

As regards the close connexion of art with the various religions it may be specially noted that *beautiful* art can only belong to those religions in which the spiritual principle, though concrete and intrinsically free, is not yet absolute. In religions where the Idea has not yet been revealed and known in its free determinacy, though the need for art is felt to bring in imaginative intuition to consciousness the idea of the *essence*, and though art is the sole organ in which the abstract and radically indistinct content, — a mixture from natural and spiritual sources, — can try to bring itself to consciousness; — still this art is defective; its form is defective because its content is so, for the defect in content comes from the form not being immanent in it. The representations of this symbolic art keep a certain tastelessness and spiritlessness — for the principle it embodies is itself spiritless, and hence has not the power freely to transmute the external to significance and shape. Beautiful art, on the contrary, has for its condition the self-consciousness of the free spirit, — the consciousness that compared with it the natural and sensuous has no standing of its own: it makes the natural wholly into the mere expression of spirit, which is thus the inner form that manifests itself alone.

But this connects with a further and deeper point: the advent of art, in a religion still in bonds of sensuous externality, shows that such religion is on the decline. At the very time it seems to give religion the supreme glorification, expression and brilliancy, it has lifted the religion over its limitation. In the sublime divinity to which the work of art succeeds in giving expression the artistic genius and the spectators find themselves at home, with their personal sense and feeling, satisfied and liberated: to them the intuition and the consciousness of free spirit has been vouchsafed and attained. Beautiful art, from its side, has thus performed the same service as philosophy: it has purified the spirit of its thraldom. The religion in which the need of fine art, and just for that reason, is first generated, looks up in its principle to an other-world which is sensuous and devoid of thought; the images adored by its devotees are hideous idols regarded as wonder-working talismans, which point to the unspiritual objectivity of that other world, — and bones perform a similar or even a better service than such images. But fine art is only a stage of liberation, not the supreme liberation itself. Genuine objectivity, which is only in the medium of thought, — the medium in which alone the pure spirit is for the spirit, and where liberation is accompanied by reverence, — is also absent in the sensuous beauty of the work of art, still more in that external, unbeautiful sensuousness.

563.   Beautiful art, like the religion peculiar to it, has its future in true religion. The restricted content of the Idea passes utterly and naturally into the universality identical with the infinite form; — the intuition in which knowledge depends on the senses passes into a self-mediating knowledge,

into an existence which is itself knowledge, into *revelation*. Thus the content of the Idea has as its principle the feature of free intelligence, and as absolute *spirit it is for the spirit.*

B. REVEALED RELIGION

564. It lies essentially in the concept of genuine religion, the religion whose content is absolute mind, that it be *revealed*, and, what is more, revealed *by God*. Knowledge (the principle by which the substance is mind) is a self-determining principle, as infinite self-realising form; thus it is manifestation simply. The spirit is only spirit in so far as it is for the spirit, and in the absolute religion it is the absolute spirit which manifests no longer abstract elements of its being but itself.

The old conception—due to the as yet abstract understanding—of Nemesis, which made the divinity and its action in the world only a levelling power, dashing to pieces the high and great,—was confronted by Plato and Aristotle with the doctrine that God is not *envious*. The same answer may be given to the modern assertions that man cannot know[19] God. These assertions (and more than assertions they are not) are the more illogical, when made within a religion which is expressly called 'revealed'; for according to them it would rather be the religion in which nothing of God was revealed, in which he had not revealed himself, and those belonging to it would be the heathen 'who know not God.' If the world 'God' is taken in earnest in religion at all, it is from Him, the content and principle of religion, that the definition of it may and must begin: and if self-revelation is refused Him, then the only thing left to constitute His content would be to ascribe envy to him. But clearly if the word 'mind' is to have a meaning, it implies the revelation of itself.

If we recall how difficult is knowledge[19] of God as spirit, since it ought not to be content with the homely ideas of faith but proceed to thought,—at first only rationalising[52] reflection, but afterwards conceptual thought,—it need hardly surprise us that so many, and especially theologians whose vocation it is to deal with these Ideas, have tried to get off their task by gladly accepting anything offered them for this purpose. And nothing serves better than to adopt the conclusion that man knows[60] nothing of God. To know what God as spirit is—to apprehend this accurately and distinctly in thoughts—requires thorough speculation. It includes, first of all, the propositions: God is God only so far as he knows himself: his self-knowledge is, further, a self-consciousness in man and man's knowledge *of* God, which proceeds to man's self-knowledge *in* God.—See the profound elucidation of these propositions in the work from which they are taken: *Aphorisms on Knowing and Not-knowing, etc.*, by C. F. G[öschel]: Berlin 1829.

565. When the immediacy and sensuousness of shape and knowledge

is superseded, the absolute spirit is, in content, the essential and actual
spirit of nature and spirit, while in form it is, first of all, presented to
knowledge as a *conception*. This conception gives independence to the
elements of his content, on one hand, making them presuppositions
towards each other, and phenomena which succeed each other; their relationship it makes a series of events according to finite reflective categories.
But, on the other hand, such a form of finite mode of conception is also
overcome[8] in the faith in the one spirit, and in the devotion of worship.

566. In this separating, the form parts from the content: and in the
form the different elements of the concept part into special spheres or
media, in each of which the absolute content exhibits itself; (α) as eternal
content, abiding self-centred in its manifestation; (β) as distinction of the
eternal essence from its manifestation, which by this difference becomes
the phenomenal world into which the content enters; (γ) as infinite return,
and reconciliation with the eternal essence, of the world it gave away—the
withdrawal of the eternal from the phenomenal into the unity of its
fullness.

567. (α) In the moment of *universality*,—the sphere of pure thought
or the abstract medium of essence,—it is therefore the absolute spirit,
which is at first the presupposed principle, not however staying aloof and
inert, but (as substantial power in the reflective category of causality)
creator of heaven and earth: but yet in this eternal sphere rather only
begetting himself as his *son*, with whom, though different, he still remains
in original identity,—just as, again, this differentiation of him from the
universal essence eternally supersedes itself and through this mediating of
a self-superseding mediation, the first substance is essentially as *concrete
individuality* and subjectivity,—is the *Spirit*.

568. (β) In the moment of *particularity*, or of judgment, it is this
concrete eternal essence which is presupposed: its movement is the creation of the phenomenal world. The eternal moment of mediation—of the
only Son—divides itself to become the antithesis of two independent
worlds. On one hand is heaven and earth, the elemental and the concrete
nature,—on the other hand, standing in relation with such nature, the
spirit, which therefore is finite spirit. That spirit, as the extreme of inherent
negativity, completes its independence till it becomes wickedness, and is
that extreme through its connexion with a confronting nature and through
its own naturalness thereby entailed. Yet, amid that naturalness, it is, since
it thinks, directed towards the Eternal, though, for that reason, only standing to it in an external connexion.

569. (γ) In the moment of *individuality* as such,—of subjectivity and
the concept itself, in which the contrast of universal and particular has sunk
to its identical ground, (1) the place of presupposition is taken by the
universal substance, as actualised out of its abstraction into *individual*
self-consciousness. This individual, who is directly identical with the

essence, — (in the eternal sphere he is called the Son) — is transplanted into the world of time, and in him wickedness is implicitly overcome. Further, this immediate, and thus sensuous, existence of the absolutely concrete puts itself in judgement and expires in the pain of *negativity*, in which, as infinite subjectivity, it remains self-identical, and thus, as absolute return from that negativity and as universal unity of universal and individual essentiality, has realised its being as the Idea of the spirit, eternal, but alive and present in the world.

570. (2) This objective totality is the implicit presupposition for the *finite* immediacy of the individual subject. For such subject therefore it is at first an other, an object of intuition, but the intuition of implicit truth, through which witness of the spirit in him, he, on account of his immediate nature, at first characterises himself as nought and wicked. But, secondly, after the example of his truth, by means of the faith in the unity (in that example implicitly accomplished) of universal and individual essence, he is also the movement to throw off his immediacy, his natural aspect and his own will, to close himself in unity with that example and his implicit essence in the pain of negativity, and thus to know himself made one with the essential being. Thus this being (3) through this mediation brings about its own indwelling in self-consciousness, and is the actual presence of the essential and self-subsisting spirit as the universal spirit.

571. These three syllogisms, constituting the one syllogism of the absolute self-mediation of spirit, are the revelation of that spirit whose life is set out as a cycle of concrete shapes in conception. From this separation into parts, with a temporal and external sequence, the unfolding of the mediation contracts itself in the result, — where the spirit closes in unity with itself, — not merely to the simplicity of faith and devotional feeling, but even to thought. In the immanent simplicity of thought the unfolding still has its expansion, yet is all the while known as an indivisible coherence of the universal, simple, and eternal spirit in itself. In this form of truth, truth is the object of *philosophy*.

If the result — the realised[6] spirit in which all mediation has superseded itself — is taken in a merely formal, contentless sense, so that the spirit is not also at the same time known as *implicitly*[5] existent and objectively self-unfolding, then that infinite subjectivity is the merely formal self-consciousness, knowing itself in itself as absolute, — irony. Irony, which can make every objective reality nought and vain, is itself the emptiness and vanity, which from itself, and therefore by chance and its own caprice, gives itself direction and content, remains master over it, is not bound by it, — and, with the assertion that it stands on the very summit of religion and philosophy, falls rather back into the vanity of wilfulness. It is only when the pure infinite form, the self-centred manifestation, throws off the one-sidedness of subjectivity in which it is the vanity of thought, that it is the free thought which has its infinite power at the same time as essential and actual content, and has that content as an object in which it is also free. Thinking to that extent is only the formal aspect of the absolute content.

C. PHILOSOPHY

572.   This science is the unity of art and religion. Whereas art's mode of intuition, external in form, is but subjective production and shivers the substantial content into many independent shapes, and whereas religion, with its separation into parts, opens its totality out in conception, and mediates what is thus opened out; philosophy not merely keeps it together to make a whole, but even unifies it into the simple spiritual intuition and then in that raises it to self-conscious thought. Such knowledge is thus the concept (cognised by thought) of art and religion, in which the diverse elements in the content are cognised as necessary, and this necessity as free.

573.   Philosophy thus characterises itself as a cognition of the necessity in the content of the absolute conception, as also of the necessity in the two forms — on one hand, immediate intuition and its poetry, and the objective and external revelation presupposed by conception, — on the other hand, first the subjective retreat inwards, then the subjective movement of faith and its identification with the presupposed object. This cognition is thus the *recognition* of this content and its form; it is the liberation from the one-sidedness of the forms, elevation of them into the absolute form, which determines itself to content, remains identical with it, and is thus the cognition of that essential and actual necessity. This movement, which philosophy is, finds itself already accomplished, when at the close[40] it grasps its own concept — i.e. just *looks back* on its knowledge.

This might seem the place to treat in a definite exposition of the relation of philosophy to religion. The whole question turns entirely on the difference of the forms of speculative thought from the forms of conception and reflecting intellect. But the whole cycle of philosophy, and of logic in particular, has not merely made known this difference, but also assessed it, or rather has let its nature develop and judge itself by these very categories. It is only by this cognition of the forms that the genuine conviction can be gained, that the content of religion and philosophy is the same, — leaving aside the further details of external nature and finite mind which fall outside the range of religion. But religion is the truth *for all men*: faith rests on the witness of the spirit, which as witnessing is the spirit in man. This witness — in itself substantial — first resorts, when driven to expound itself, to the cultural forms which already clothe secular consciousness and intellect. In this way the truth becomes liable to the categories and relations of finitude in general. This does not prevent the spirit, even in employing sensuous ideas and finite categories of thought, from retaining its content (which as religion is essentially speculative) with a tenacity which does violence to them, and acts *inconsistently* towards them. By this inconsistency it corrects their defects. Nothing easier therefore for the intellect than to point out contradictions in the exposition of the faith, and so prepare triumphs for its principle of formal identity. If the spirit yields to this finite reflection, which has usurped the title of reason and philosophy ('Rationalism') it strips religious truth of its infinity and makes it in reality nought. Religion in that case is completely in the right in guarding itself against such reason and philosophy and treating them as enemies. But it is another thing when religion sets itself against conceptual reason, and against philosophy in general, and specially against a philosophy of which the content is speculative, and so religious. Such opposition proceeds from failure to appreciate the difference indicated and the value of spiritual forms in general, and particularly of the logical forms; or, to be more precise, from failure to note the difference of the content—which may be in both the same—from these forms. It is on the ground of form that philosophy has been reproached and accused by the religious party; just as conversely its speculative content has brought the same charges upon it from a self-styled philosophy—and from a pithless piety. It had too little of God in it for the former; too much for the latter.

The charge of *atheism*, which used often to be brought against philosophy (that it has *too little* of God), has grown rare: the more wide-spread grows the charge of pantheism, that it has *too much* of him: so much so, that it is treated not so much as an imputation, but as a proved fact, or a sheer fact which needs no proof. Piety, in particular, which with its pious airs of superiority fancies itself free to dispense with proof, goes hand in hand with empty rationalism—(which means to be so much opposed to it, though both rest really on the same habit of mind)—in the assertion, almost as if it merely mentioned a familiar fact, that philosophy is the All-one doctrine, or pantheism. It must be said that it was more to the credit of piety and theology when they accused a philosophical system (e.g. Spinozism) of atheism than of pantheism, though the former imputation at first glance looks more cruel and invidious (cf.§71). The imputation of atheism pre-supposes a definite idea of a full and real God, and arises because conception does not detect in the philosophical concepts the peculiar form to which it is attached. Philosophy indeed can recognise its own forms in the categories of religious representation, and thus its own content in the content of religion—which therefore it does not disparage. But the converse is not true: the religious mode of conception does not apply the criticism of thought to itself, does not comprehend itself, and is therefore, in its immediacy, exclusive. To impute pantheism instead of atheism to philosophy is part of the modern habit of mind—of the new piety and new theology. For them philosophy has too much God:—so much so, that, if we believe them, it asserts that God is everything and everything God. This new theology, which makes religion only a subjective feeling and denies knowledge of the divine nature, thus retains nothing more than a God in general without objective characteristics. Without interest of its own in the concrete, fulfilled concept of God, it treats it only as an interest which *others* once had, and hence treats what belongs to the doctrine of God's concrete nature as something merely historical. The indeterminate God is to be found in all religions; every kind of piety (§72) — that of the Hindu to asses, cows, — or to dalai-lamas — that of the Egyptians to the ox — is always adoration of an object which, with all its absurdities, also contains the generic abstract, God in general. If this view needs no more than such a God, so as to find God in everything called religion, it must at least find such a God recognised even in philosophy, and can no longer accuse it of atheism. The mitigation of the reproach of atheism into that of pantheism has its ground therefore in the superficial idea to which this mildness has attenuated and emptied God. As that idea clings to its abstract universality, from which all definiteness is excluded, all such definiteness is only the non-divine, the secular existence of things, thus left standing in fixed undisturbed substantiality. On such a presupposition, even after philosophy has maintained God's absolute universality, and the consequent untruth of the being of external things, they still cling as much as before to the belief that secular things still keep their being, and form all that is definite in the divine universality. They thus change that universality into what they call 'pantheistic' universality: *Everything is*— (empirical things, without distinction, whether higher or lower in the scale, *are*) — all possess substantiality; and this being of secular things is God. It is only their own thoughtlessness and a consequent falsification of concepts which generate the idea and allegation of pantheism.

But if those who allege that a certain philosophy is pantheism, are unable and unwilling to see this — for it is just insight into concepts that they reject — they should before everything have verified the alleged fact that *any philosopher, or any man*, had really ascribed substantial or objective and inherent reality to *all* things and regarded them as God; that such an idea had ever come into anyone's head but their own. This allegation I will further elucidate in this exoteric discussion: and the only way to do so is to set down the facts. If we want to take so-called pantheism in its most poetical, most sublime, or, if you will, its grossest form, we must, as is well known, consult the oriental poets; and the most copious delineations of it are found in Hindu literature. Among the abundant sources on this topic, I select — as the most authentic statement accessible — the Bhagavad-Gita, and among its effusions, prolix and reiterative *ad nauseam*, some of the most telling passages. In the 10th lesson Krishna says of himself: 'I am the self, seated in the hearts of all beings. I am the beginning and the middle and the end also of all beings. . . . I am the beaming sun amongst the shining ones, and the moon among the lunar mansions. . . . Amongst the Vedas I am the Sâma-Veda: I am mind amongst the senses: I am consciousness in living beings. And I am Sankara (Siva) among the Rudras, . . . Meru among the high-topped mountains, . . . the Himalaya among the firmly-fixed (mountains). . . . Among beasts I am the lord of beasts. . . . Among letters I am the letter A. . . . I am the spring among the seasons. . . . I am also that which is the seed of all things: there is nothing moveable or immoveable which can exist without me.'

Even in these totally sensuous delineations, Krishna (and we must not suppose there is, apart from Krishna, God, or a God, besides; as he said before that he was Siva, also Indra, so it is afterwards said that Brahma too is in him) claims to be not everything, but only the most excellent of all. Everywhere there is a distinction drawn between external, unessential existences, and one essential among them, which He is. Even when, at the beginning of the passage, he is said to be the beginning, middle, and end of living things, this totality is distinguished from the living things themselves as individual existences. Even such a picture which extends deity far and wide in its existence cannot be called pantheism: we must rather say that the infinitely multiple empirical world, the All, is reduced to a limited number of essential existences, to a polytheism. But even what has been quoted shows that even these substantialities of the externally-existent do not retain the independence entitling them to be named Gods; even Siva, Indra, etc. melt into the one Krishna.

This reduction is more expressly made in the following scene (7th lesson). Krishna says: 'I am the origin and the dissolution of the whole world. There is nothing else higher than myself; all this is woven upon me, like numbers of pearls upon a thread. I am the taste in water; . . . I am the light of the sun and the moon; I am "Om" in all the Vedas. . . . I am life in all beings. . . . I am the discernment of the discerning ones. . . . I am also the strength of the strong.' Then he adds: 'The whole universe deluded by these three states of mind developed from the qualities [sc. goodness, passion, darkness] does not know me who am beyond them and inexhaustible: for this delusion of mine' [even Maya is *his*, nothing independent], 'developed from the qualities is divine and difficult to transcend. Those cross beyond this delusion who resort to me alone.' Then the conception gathers itself up in a simple expression: 'At the end of many lives, the man possessed of knowledge approaches me, (believing) that Vasudeva is everything. Such a high-souled mind is very hard to find. Those who are deprived of knowledge by various desires approach other divinities. . . . Whichever form of deity one worships with faith, from it he obtains the beneficial things he desires really given by me. But the fruit thus obtained by those of little judgment is perishable. . . . The undiscerning ones, not knowing my transcendent and inexhaustible essence, than which there is nothing higher, think me who am unperceived to have become perceptible.'

This 'All,' which Krishna calls himself, is not, any more than the Eleatic One or Spinoza's Substance, the Every-thing. This every-thing, rather, the infinitely-multiple sensuous manifold of the finite is in all these conceptions defined as the accidental, without essential being of its own, but having its truth in the substance, the One which, as different from that accidental, is alone the divine and God. Hinduism advances besides, to the conception of Brahma, the pure unity of thought in itself, where the empirical everything of the world, as also those proximate substantialities, called Gods, vanish.

Colebroke and many others have described Hindu religion as essentially monotheism. That this description is not incorrect is clear from these short citations. But so little concrete is this divine unity — spiritual as its idea of God is — so powerless, so to speak, that Hinduism, with a monstrous confusion, is also the maddest of polytheisms. But the idolatry of the wretched Hindu, when he adores the ape, or whatever, is still a long way from that wretched idea of pantheism, that everything is God, and God everything. Hindu monotheism moreover is itself an example how little comes of mere monotheism, if the Idea of God is not deeply determinate in itself. For that unity, if it be intrinsically abstract and thus empty, tends of itself to let the concrete — whether a collection of Gods or of secular, empirical individuals — keep its independence outside it. That pantheism indeed — on the shallow conception of it — might with consistency as well be called a monotheism: for if God is identical with the world, then as there is only one world there would be in that pantheism only one God. Perhaps empty numerical unity must be predicated of the world; but this abstract predicate has no further special interest; on the contrary, this numerical unity just means that its *content* is an infinite plurality and variety of finitudes. But it is that delusion of empty unity, which alone makes possible and induces the bad idea of pantheism. It was only the idea — floating in the indefinite blue — of the world as *one thing, the all*, that could ever be considered compatible with God: only on that assumption could philosophy be supposed to teach that God is the world: for if the world were taken as it is, as everything, as the endless mass of empirical existences, then it would hardly have been even held possible for there to be a pantheism which asserted of such content that it is God.

But to go back again to the question of fact. If we want to see the consciousness of the One not, as with Hindus, split between the featureless unity of abstract thought and the long-winded weary story of its particular detail, but in its finest purity and sublimity, we must turn to the Mohammedans. If e.g. in the excellent Jelaleddin-Rumi in particular, we find the unity of the soul with the One set forth, and this unity described as love, this spiritual unity is an elevation above the finite and common, a transfiguration of the natural and the spiritual, in which the externality and transitoriness of immediate nature, and of empirical secular spirit, is discarded and absorbed. . . .

I refrain from accumulating further examples of the religious and poetic conceptions customarily called pantheistic. Of the philosophies to which that name is given, the Eleatic, or Spinozist, it has been remarked earlier (§50) that so far are they from identifying God with the world and making him finite, that in these systems this 'everything' has no truth, and that we should rather call them monotheistic, or, in relation to the idea of the world, acosmist. They are most accurately called systems which apprehend the absolute only as substance. Of the oriental, especially the Mohammedan, modes of conception, we may rather say that they represent the absolute as the utterly universal genus which dwells in the species or existences, but in such a way that these existences have no actual reality. The fault of all these modes of conception and systems is that they stop short of defining substance as subject and as mind.

These systems and modes of conception originate from the one need common to all philosophies and all religions of getting an idea of God, and, secondly, of the relationship of God and the world. (In philosophy we find the more precise cognition that the determination of God's nature determines his relations with the world.) The reflective understanding begins by rejecting all systems and modes of conception, which, whether they spring from heart, imagination or speculation, express the interconnexion of God and the world: and in order to have God pure in faith or consciousness, he is as essence separated from appearance, as infinite from the finite. But, after this separation, the conviction arises also that the appearance has a relation to the essence, the finite to the infinite, and so on: and thus arises the reflective question as to the nature of this relation. It is in the form of reflection on this relation that the whole difficulty of the matter lies. It is this relation that is called the 'incomprehensible' by those who want to know nothing of God's nature. The close of philosophy is not the place, even in a general exoteric discussion, to waste a word on what 'comprehension' means. But as the view taken of this relation is closely connected with the view taken of science generally and with all imputations against it, we may still add the remark that philosophy certainly has to do with unity in general, not however abstract unity, mere identity, and the empty absolute, but concrete unity (the concept), and that in its whole course it has to do with nothing else; — that each step in its advance is a peculiar determination of this concrete unity, and that the deepest and final determination of unity is that of absolute mind. Would-be judges and critics of philosophy might be recommended to go into these determinations of unity and take the trouble to get acquainted with them, at least to know this much: that of these determinations there are a great many, and that among them there is great variety. But they show so little acquaintance with them — and still less take trouble about it — that, when they hear of unity — and relation *ipso facto* implies unity — they rather stick to quite abstract indeterminate unity, and lose sight of the sole point of interest — the way in which the unity is qualified. Hence all they can say about philosophy is that dry identity is its principle and result, and that it is the system of identity. Sticking to this unconceptual thought of identity, they have laid hands on, not the concrete unity, the concept and content of philosophy, but rather its reverse. In this field they proceed, as in the physical field the physicist; who also is well aware that he has before him a variety of sensuous properties and stuffs—or usually stuffs alone, (for properties get similarly transformed into stuffs for the physicist)—and that these stuffs also stand in *relation* to one another. But the question is, In what kind of relation? Every peculiarity and the whole difference of natural things, inorganic and living, depend solely on the different modes of this unity. But instead of ascertaining these different modes, the ordinary physicist (chemist included) takes up only one, the most external and the worst, viz. *composition*, applies only it in the whole range of natural structures, which he thus renders for ever inexplicable.

The aforesaid shallow pantheism is an immediate consequence of this shallow identity. All that those who employ this invention of their own to accuse philosophy learn from the study of God's *relation* to the world is that one (but only one) factor of this category of relation—and that the factor of indeterminateness—is identity. Then they stick fast in this half-perception, and assert—falsely as a fact—that philosophy asserts the identity of God and the world. And as, for them, each of the two,—the world as much as God—has solid substantiality, they infer that in the philosophic Idea God is *composed* of God and the world. This is then the idea they form of pantheism, and which they ascribe to philosophy. Unaccustomed in their own thinking and apprehending of thoughts to go beyond such categories, they import them into philosophy, where they are quite absent; they thus make it itch so that they can scratch it. If any difficulty emerges in comprehending God's relation to the world, they at once and very easily avoid it by admitting that this relation contains for them an inexplicable contradiction; and that hence, they must stop at the indeterminate conception of such relation, and also of its specific modes, e.g. omnipresence, providence, etc. Faith, in this sense, means no more than a refusal to define the conception, or to go more closely into the content. That men and classes of untrained intellect are satisfied with indeterminate ideas, is what one expects; but when a trained intellect and an interest in reflective study is satisfied, in matters admitted to be of superior, if not even of supreme interest, with indefinite ideas, it is hard to decide whether the mind is really in earnest with the content. But if those who cling to this bare rationalism were in earnest, e.g. in affirming God's omnipresence, so far as to realise their faith in it in a definite idea, in what difficulties would they be involved by their belief in the true reality of the things of sense! They would hardly like, as Epicurus does, to let God dwell in the interspaces of things, in the pores of the physicists,— pores being the negative, something supposed to exist *beside* the material reality. This very 'Beside' would give their pantheism its spatiality,—their everything, conceived as the mutual exclusion of parts in space. But in ascribing to God, in his relation to the world, an action on and in the space thus filled, on the world and in it, they would endlessly split up the divine actuality into infinite materiality. They would have thus the misconception they call pantheism or all-one-doctrine, just as the necessary consequence, in fact, of their misconceptions of God and the world. But to put that sort of thing, this stale gossip of oneness or identity, on the shoulders of philosophy, shows such recklessness about justice and truth that it can only be explained by the difficulty of getting into the head thoughts and concepts, not abstract unity, but the multiform modes of determinacy. If statements as to facts are put forward, and the facts are thoughts and concepts, it is indispensable to grasp them. But even the fulfilment of this requirement has been rendered superfluous, now that it has long been a foregone conclusion that philosophy is pantheism, a system of identity, an All-one doctrine, so that the person who is unaware of this fact is treated either as merely unaware of a matter of common notoriety, or as prevaricating for a purpose. On account of this chorus of assertions, then, I have believed myself obliged to speak at more length and exoterically on the outward and inward truth of this alleged fact: for exoteric discussion is the only way of dealing with the external apprehension of concepts as mere facts,—by which concepts are perverted into their opposite. The esoteric study of God and identity, as of cognition and concepts, is philosophy itself.

574. This concept of philosophy is the self-thinking Idea, the truth aware of itself (§236),—the logical system, but with the signification that it is universality proved in concrete content as in its actuality. In this way science has gone back to its beginning: its result is the logical system but as a spiritual principle: out of the presupposing judgment, in which the concept was only implicit and the beginning an immediate—and thus out of the *appearance* which it had there—it has risen into its pure principle and thus also into its proper medium.

575. It is this appearing which motivates the further development. The first appearance is constituted by the syllogism based on the logical system as a starting-point, with nature for the middle term which couples the mind with logic. The logical principle becomes nature and nature mind. Nature, standing between the mind and its essence, sunders them not indeed to extremes of finite abstraction, nor itself to something away from them and independent,—which, as other than they, only serves as a link between them; for the syllogism is *in the Idea* and nature is essentially defined as a transition-point and negative factor, and as implicitly the Idea; but the mediation of the concept has the external form of *transition*, and science has the form of the course of necessity, so that it is only in the one extreme that the liberty of the concept is explicit as a coupling with itself.

576. In the second syllogism this appearance is so far superseded, that

this syllogism is the standpoint of the mind itself, which — as the mediating agent in the process — presupposes nature and couples it with the logical. It is the syllogism of spiritual reflection in the Idea: philosophy appears as a subjective cognition, of which liberty is the aim, and which is itself the way to produce it.

577. The third syllogism is the Idea of philosophy, which has self-knowing reason, the absolutely-universal, for its middle term: a middle, which divides itself into mind and nature, making the former its presupposition, as process of the Idea's subjective activity, and the latter its universal extreme, as process of the objectively and implicitly existing Idea. The self-judging of the Idea into its two appearances (§§575, 576) determines both as its (self-knowing reason's) manifestations: and in it there is a unification of the two aspects: it is the nature of the subject-matter, the concept, which causes the movement and development, yet this same movement is equally the activity of cognition. The eternal Idea, in full fruition of its essence, eternally sets itself to work, engenders and enjoys itself as absolute mind.

Thought in itself deals with that which is best in itself, and that which is thought in the fullest sense with that which is best in the fullest sense. And intellect thinks itself because it shares the nature of the object of thought; for it becomes an object of thought in coming into contact with and thinking its objects, so that intellect and object of thought are the same. For that which is *capable* of receiving the object of thought, i.e. the essence, is intellect. And it is *active* when it *possesses* this object. Therefore the latter (possession) rather than the former (receptivity) is the divine element which intellect seems to contain, and contemplation is what is most pleasant and best. If, then, God is always in that good state in which we sometimes are, this compels our wonder; and if in a better this compels it yet more. And God *is* in a better state. And life also belongs to God; for the actuality of intellect is life, and God is that actuality; and God's essential actuality is life most good and eternal. We say therefore that God is a living being, eternal, most good, so that life and duration continuous and eternal belong to God; for this *is* God. (Aristotle, *Metaphysics, XII, 7)**

---

*I have substituted Sir David Ross's translation (1908), slightly amended, for Hegel's Greek quotation.

XVII. History of Philosophy: The Final Result*

The present standpoint of philosophy is that the Idea is known in its necessity; the sides of its diremption, nature and spirit, are each recognized as representing the totality of the Idea, and not only as being in themselves identical, but as producing this one identity from themselves; and thus the identity is recognized as necessary. Nature, and the spiritual world, history, are the two actualities; what exists as actual nature is an image of divine reason; the forms of self-conscious reason are also forms of nature. The ultimate aim and concern of philosophy is to reconcile thought or the concept with actuality. It is easy to adopt subordinate standpoints, to find satisfaction in modes of intuition and of feeling. But the deeper the spirit goes within itself, the stronger the opposition, the more abundant the wealth without; depth is to be measured by the greatness of the need with which spirit seeks to find itself in what lies outside of itself. We saw the thought which apprehends itself emerge; it strove to make itself concrete within itself. Its first activity is formal; Aristotle was the first to say that νοῦς is the thinking of thinking. The result is the thought which is at home with itself, and at the same time embraces the universe, and transforms it into an intelligent world. In conceptualisation the spiritual and the natural universe interpenetrate as one harmonious universe, which flees from itself into itself, and in its aspects develops the absolute into a totality, to become thereby conscious of itself in its unity, in thought. Philosophy is thus the true theodicy, as contrasted with art and religion and the feelings which these call up—a reconciliation of spirit, of the spirit which has apprehended itself in its freedom and in the riches of its actuality.

To this point the world-spirit has come, and each stage has its own form in the true system of philosophy; nothing is lost, all principles are preserved, since philosophy in its final aspect is the totality of forms. This concrete Idea is the result of the strivings of spirit during almost twenty-five centuries of earnest work to become objective to itself, to know itself:

*From the second (1840) edition of the *Lectures on the History of Philosophy*. Translated by E. S. Haldane and F. H. Simson (1892–1896), with revisions by M. J. Inwood.

Tantae molis erat, se ipsam cognoscere mentem.

All this time was required to produce the philosophy of our day; so tardily and slowly did the world-spirit work to reach this goal. What we pass in rapid review when we recall it, stretched itself out in actuality to this great length of time. For in this period, the concept of spirit, invested with its entire concrete development, external subsistence, wealth, strives to bring spirit to perfection, to make progress itself and to emerge from spirit. It goes ever on and on, because spirit is progress alone. Spirit often seems to have forgotten and lost itself, but inwardly opposed to itself, it is inwardly working ever forward (as Hamlet says of the ghost of his father, "Well said, old mole! canst work i' the ground so fast?"), until grown strong in itself it bursts asunder the crust of earth which divided it from the sun, its concept, so that the earth crumbles away. At such a time, when the encircling crust, like a soulless decaying tenement, crumbles away, and spirit displays itself arrayed in new youth, the seven league boots are put on. This work of the spirit to know itself, this activity to find itself, is the life of the spirit and the spirit itself. Its result is the concept which it takes up of itself; the history of philosophy is a revelation of what has been the aim of spirit in its history; it is therefore the world's history in its innermost signification. This work of the human spirit in inner thinking is parallel with all the stages of actuality. No philosophy oversteps its own time. The importance of the determinations of thought is another matter, which does not belong to the history of philosophy. These concepts are the simplest revelation of the world spirit: in their more concrete form they are history.

We must, therefore, firstly, not esteem lightly what spirit has won, and won now. Older philosophy is to be reverenced as necessary, and as a link in this sacred chain, but all the same only a link. The present is the highest stage. Secondly, all the various philosophies are no mere fashions or the like; they are neither chance products nor the blaze of a fire of straw, nor casual eruptions here and there, but a spiritual, rational, forward advance; they are of necessity one philosophy in its development, the revelation of God, as He knows Himself to be. Where several philosophies appear at the same time, they are different sides which make up one totality forming their basis; and on account of their one-sidedness we see the refutation of the one by the other. Thirdly, we do not find here feeble little efforts to establish or to criticize this or that particular point; each philosophy sets up a *principle* of its own, and this must be recognized.

If we glance at the main epochs in the whole history of philosophy, and grasp the necessary succession of stages in the leading moments, each of which expresses a determinate Idea, we find that after the Oriental whirl of subjectivity, which attains to no understanding and therefore to no subsistence, the light of thought dawned among the Greeks.

1. The philosophy of the ancients had the absolute Idea as its thought;

and the realization or reality of it consisted in comprehending the existing present world, and regarding it as it is in and for itself. This philosophy did not start from the Idea itself, but from the objective as something given, and transformed it into the Idea: the being of Parmenides.

2. Abstract thought, νὸυς, became known to itself as universal essence, not as subjective thinking: the universal of Plato.

3. In Aristotle the concept emerges, free and unconstrained, as conceptual thinking, permeating and spiritualizing all the formations of the universe.

4. The concept as subject, its becoming for itself, its inwardness, abstract separation, is represented by the Stoics, Epicureans and Sceptics: not the free concrete form, but universality abstract and in itself formal.

5. The thought of totality, the intelligible world, is the concrete Idea as we have seen it in the Neo-Platonists. This principle is ideality in general in all reality, the Idea as totality, but not the Idea which knows itself: this is not reached until the principle of subjectivity, individuality, found a place in it, and God as spirit became actual to Himself in self-consciousness.

6. But it is the work of modern times to grasp this Idea as spirit, as the Idea that knows itself. In order to proceed from the knowing Idea to the self-knowing, we must have the infinite opposition, the Idea must have come to the consciousness of its bifurcation. As spirit had the thought of objective essence, philosophy thus perfected the intellectuality of the world, and produced this spiritual world as an object existing beyond present actuality, like a nature—the first creation of spirit. The work of the spirit now consisted in bringing this Beyond back to actuality and into self-consciousness. This is accomplished by self-consciousness thinking itself, and recognizing the absolute essence to be the self-consciousness that thinks itself. With Descartes pure thought directed itself on that bifurcation. Self-consciousness, first, thinks of itself as consciousness; therein is contained all objective actuality and the positive, intuitive connexion of its actuality with the other. With Spinoza thought and being are opposed and yet identical; he has the intuition of substance, but the knowledge of substance in his case is external. We have here the principle of reconciliation taking its rise from thought as such, in order to sublimate the subjectivity of thought: this is the case in Leibniz's monad, which possesses the power of representation.

7. Secondly, self-consciousness thinks of itself as being self-consciousness; in being self-conscious it is for itself, but still for itself it has a negative connexion with another. This is infinite subjectivity, which appears at one time as the critique of thought in Kant, and at another time, in Fichte, as the impulse towards the concrete. Absolutely pure, infinite form is expressed as self-consciousness, the ego.

8. This is a light that breaks forth on spiritual substance, and shows absolute content and absolute form to be identical; substance is in itself

identical with knowledge. Self-consciousness thus, thirdly, recognizes its positive connexion as its negative, and its negative as its positive, — or it recognizes these opposite activities as the same, i.e. it recognizes pure thought or being as self-equality, and this again as bifurcation. This is intellectual intuition; but it is requisite in order that it be in truth intellectual, that it should not be that merely immediate intuition of the eternal and the divine which we hear of, but absolute knowledge. This intuition which does not cognize itself is taken as starting-point as if it were absolutely presupposed; it has in itself intuition only as immediate knowledge, not as self-knowledge: or it knows nothing, and what it intuits it does not really know, — for, at its best, it consists of beautiful thoughts, but not knowledge.

But intellectual intuition is known, since firstly, in spite of the separation of each of the opposed sides from the other, all external reality is known as internal. If it is known according to its essence, as it is, it shows itself as not existing of itself, but as essentially consisting in the movement of transition. This Heraclitean or sceptical principle, that nothing is at rest, must be demonstrated of each individual thing; and thus in this consciousness — that the essence of each thing lies in determinacy, in the opposite of itself — there appears the comprehended unity with its opposite. Similarly this unity is, secondly, to be cognized even in its essence; its essence as this identity is likewise to pass over into its opposite, or to realize itself, to become something different; and thus the opposition in it is brought about by itself. Again, it may be said of the opposition, thirdly, that it is not in the absolute; this absolute is the essence, the eternal, etc. This is however itself an abstraction in which the absolute is apprehended in a one-sided manner only and the opposition is only ideal; but in fact it is form, as the essential moment of the movement of the absolute. This absolute is not at rest, and that opposition is not the unresting concept; for the Idea, unresting though it is, is yet at rest and satisfied in itself. Pure thought has advanced to the opposition of the subjective and objective; the true reconciliation of the opposition is the perception that this opposition, when pushed to its absolute extreme, resolves itself; as Schelling says, the opposites are in themselves identical — and not only in themselves, but eternal life consists in the very process of eternally producing the opposition and eternally reconciling it. To know opposition in unity, and unity in opposition — this is absolute knowledge; and science is the knowledge of this unity in its whole development by means of itself.

This is now the need of the time in general and of philosophy. A new epoch has arisen in the world. It would appear as if the world-spirit had at last succeeded in stripping off from itself all alien objective being, and apprehending itself at last as absolute spirit, in developing from itself what for it is objective, and keeping it in its power, yet remaining at rest. The strife of the finite self-consciousness with the absolute self-consciousness, which seemed to the former to lie outside itself, now ceases. Finite self-consciousness has ceased to be finite; and in this way absolute self-consciousness has, on the other hand, acquired the actuality which it lacked before. This is the whole history of the world in general up to the present, and the history of philosophy in particular, which only depicts this strife. Now it seems to have reached its goal, when this absolute self-consciousness, which it had the work of representing, has ceased to be alien, and when spirit is thus actualized as spirit. For it becomes such only by knowing itself to be absolute spirit, and this it knows in science. Spirit produces itself as nature, as the state; nature is its unconscious work, in which it appears to itself something different, not spirit; but in the deeds and life of history, as also of art, it brings itself to pass with consciousness; it knows very various modes of its actuality, yet they are only modes. In science alone it knows itself as absolute spirit; and this knowledge, or spirit, is its only true existence. This then is the standpoint of the present day, and the series of spiritual forms is with it for now concluded.

At this point I bring this history of philosophy to a close. It has been my desire that you should learn from it that the history of philosophy is not a blind collection of brain-waves, nor a fortuitous progression. I have rather sought to show the necessary development of the successive philosophies from one another, so that the one of necessity presupposes the preceding. The general result of the history of philosophy is this: (1) at all times there has been only one philosophy, the contemporary differences of which constitute the necessary aspects of the one principle; (2) the succession of philosophic systems is not due to chance, but the necessary succession of stages in the development of this science; (3) the final philosophy of a period is the result of this development, and is truth in the highest form which the self-consciousness of spirit affords of itself. The latest philosophy contains therefore those which went before; it embraces in itself all the stages; it is the product and result of those that preceded it. We can now be Platonists no longer. We must rise above the pettinesses of individual opinions, thoughts, objections, and difficulties; and also above our own vanity, as if our own thoughts were of particular value. For to apprehend the inward substantial spirit is the standpoint of the individual; within the whole, individuals are like blind men, driven forward by the inner spirit. Our standpoint now is accordingly the knowledge of this Idea as spirit, as absolute spirit, which in this way opposes another spirit, the finite, the principle of which is to know absolute spirit, so that absolute spirit is for it. I have tried to develop and bring before your thoughts this series of spiritual forms of philosophy in its progress, and to indicate the connection between them. This series is the true kingdom of spirits, the only kingdom of spirits that there is — it is a series which is not a multiplicity, nor does it even remain a series or succession, but in the very process of coming to knowledge of itself it is transformed into the moments of the one spirit, of the one self-present spirit. This long procession of spirits is formed by the individual pulses which beat in its life; they are the organism of our substance, an absolutely necessary progression, which expresses nothing less than the nature of spirit itself, and which lives in us all. We have to give ear to its urgency — when the mole within forces its way on — and we have to give it actuality. It is my desire that this history of philosophy should contain for you a summons to grasp the spirit of the time, which is in us by nature, and — each in his own place — consciously to bring it from its natural condition, from its lifeless seclusion, into the light of day.

I have to express my thanks to you for the attention with which you have listened to me while I have been making this attempt; it is also due to you that my efforts have met with so great a measure of success. And it has been a source of pleasure to myself to have been associated with you in this spiritual community; I ought not to speak of it as if it were a thing of the past, for I hope that a spiritual bond has been knit between us which will prove permanent. I bid you a most hearty farewell.

Bibliographical Essay

This bibliography is inevitably selective. More information may be found in the *Hegel Bibliography* by K. Steinhauer and G. Hausen (1980), which lists 12,032 items up to 1975. A survey of recent work in English up to 1970 will be found in "Recent Work on Hegel," by F. G. Weiss and H. Kainz, in the *American Philosophical Quarterly*, Vol. 8, no. 3 (July, 1971). Several journals are devoted to articles about Hegel and to reviews of work on Hegel, most notably *The Owl of Minerva*, *The Bulletin of the Hegel Society of Great Britain*, and *Hegel-Studien*. The long defunct *Journal of Speculative Philosophy*, edited by W. T. Harris, contains many pieces about and translations from Hegel, as well as other German idealists.

1. **Translations of Works by Hegel.** Most of Hegel's writings have been translated, or retranslated, in recent years. In particular, translations are beginning to appear of critical German editions of Hegel's lectures — editions, that is, that separate material delivered in different years, and that distinguish Hegel's own notes from those of his pupils. I list the main translations of Hegel's works, roughly in the order in which he composed and/or published them:

   (a) *Early Theological Writings* (1793–1800), translated by T. M. Knox, with an introduction by R. Kroner.

   (b) *Three Essays, 1783–1795*, translated by P. Fuss and J. Dobbins, with an introduction and notes(1984), contains the "Tübingen Essay," the "Berne Fragments," and the "Life of Jesus."

   (c) *Difference between the Systems of Fichte and Schelling* (1801), translated by H. S. Harris and W. Cerf (1977) and also by J. P. Surber, under the title *The Difference between the Fichtean and Schellingian Systems of Philosophy* (1978). Both translations have an introduction and notes.

   (d) *Faith and Knowledge* (1802), translated by W. Cerf and H. S. Harris (1977). This and the following item were first published in the *Critical Journal of Philosophy*, edited jointly by Hegel and Schelling in 1802/3. Several of Hegel's shorter pieces from the journal are translated in *Between Kant and Hegel: Texts in the Development of Post-Kantian Idealism* (1985) by G. di Giovanni and H. S. Harris, including the "Relationship of Scepticism to Philosophy."

   (e) *Natural Law* (1802/3), translated by T. M. Knox, with an introduction by H. B. Acton.

(f) *System of Ethical Life* (1802/3) and *First Philosophy of Spirit* (1803/4), translated by H. S. Harris and T. M. Knox (1979).

(g) *The Jena System (1804–5): Logic and Metaphysics*, translated by J. Burbidge and G. di Giovanni, with an introduction and notes by H. S. Harris (1986).

(h) *Hegel and the Human Spirit: A Translation of the Jena Lectures on the Philosophy of Spirit* (1805/6), with a commentary, by L. Rauch (1983).

(i) *Political Writings* (1798–1832), translated by T. M. Knox, with an introduction by Z. A. Pelczynski (1964).

(j) *Phenomenology of Mind* (or *Spirit*) (1807), Hegel's first major published work, translated in full by J. B. Baillie (1937) and by A. V. Miller (1977), with an introduction and analysis by J. N. Findlay.

(k) *The Philosophical Propaedeutic* (1986), edited by M. George and A. Vincent, and translated by A. V. Miller, contains Hegel's notes for his lectures, from 1808 to 1811, at the Nuremberg Gymnasium, where he was Rector. The notes provide a brief and accessible, if somewhat bald, introduction to Hegel's main concepts and their interrelationships.

(l) *Science of Logic* (1812/16). The first book, the "Doctrine of Being," was extensively revised by Hegel before his death in 1831, and republished in 1832. Only the revised version is translated. The third book, the "Subjective Logic," was translated by H. S. Macran in two volumes, *Hegel's Doctrine of Formal Logic* (1912), and *Hegel's Logic of World and Idea* (1929), each with a substantial introduction. The work is translated in full by W. H. Johnston and L. G. Struthers (1929) and by A. V. Miller (1969).

(m) The *Philosophy of Right* (1821) is translated, together with the "Additions" — material collected from the lecture notes of Hegel and his pupils for the posthumous edition of 1833 — adequately by S. W. Dyde (1896) and superbly by T. M. Knox (1942).

(n) *Encyclopaedia of the Philosophical Sciences* (published by Hegel, with successive revisions and additions, in 1817, 1827, and 1830. The posthumous edition of 1840/5 contains "Additions" assembled from lecture notes). The Introduction and Part I, the *Logic*, were translated by W. Wallace in 1874 and, with revisions, in 1892; Wallace's second edition was re-issued in 1975 with an introduction by J. N. Findlay. Part II, the *Philosophy of Nature*, is translated by A. V. Miller (1970), with an introduction by J. N. Findlay, and also by M. J. Petry (1970), who also supplies an extensive and valuable introduction and commentary. Part III, the *Philosophy of Mind*, was translated by W. Wallace in 1894, omitting the posthumous Additions; these were added, in A. V. Miller's translation, to a reissue of Wallace's translation in 1971, together with an introduction by J. N. Findlay. The first section of Part III, the *Philosophy of Subjective Spirit*, was translated, together with some of Hegel's lecture notes, by M. J. Petry (1978), again with an extensive introduction and commentary. Petry has published his translation of the commentary on the second subsection of "Subjective Spirit," the "Phenomenology of Spirit" — together with a new introduction — as a separate volume, entitled *The Berlin Phenomenology* (1981). (In my selections from the Encyclopaedia, I have omitted the posthumous Additions, for the reason that, in view of the appearance of critical editions of Hegel's lectures, their republication can no longer be justified.)

(o) The *Lectures on the Philosophy of History* (delivered biennially from 1822/3 to 1830/1) were translated in full by J. Sibree (1857, with many reprintings). The Introduction to the lectures is translated by R. S. Hartman as *Reason in History* (1953) and by H. B. Nisbet as *Lectures on the Philosophy of World History: Introduction* (1975), with an introduction by D. Forbes.

(p) The *Lectures on Aesthetics* (delivered in 1823, 1826, and 1828/9) are translated in full by T. M. Knox as *Hegel's Aesthetics: Lectures on Fine Art* (1975). The Introduction to the lectures is published separately, with an introduction by C. Karelis, as *Hegel's Introduction to Aesthetics* (1979). A translation, by M. Donougho, of the transcription of the lectures made by H. Hotho in 1823 is in preparation.

(q) The *Lectures on the Philosophy of Religion* (delivered in 1821, 1824, 1827, and 1831) were translated by E. B. Speirs and J. B. Sanderson (1895), together with the *Lectures on the Proofs of the Existence of God*, which Hegel himself prepared for publication. The critical edition of the lectures is translated by R. F. Brown, P. C. Hodgson and J. M. Stewart (1984/7).

(r) The *Lectures on the History of Philosophy* (delivered on nine occasions from 1805/6 to 1831) are translated in full by E. S. Haldane and F. H. Simson (1892/6). The Introduction to the lectures is translated separately by Q. Lauer, together with a commentary, in *Hegel's Idea of Philosophy* (1971) and also by T. M. Knox and A. V. Miller as *Introduction to the Lectures on the History of Philosophy* (1985). A translation of the 1825/6 version of the lectures, by R. F. Brown and J. M. Stewart, is in preparation.

(s) A translation, by Z. A. Pelczynski and J. M. Stewart, of a transcription of the *Lectures on Natural Law and Political Science* delivered in 1817/8 is in preparation.

(t) A translation, by T. Geraets and H. S. Harris, of a transcription of Hegel's *Lectures on Logic* (1831) is in preparation.

(u) Hegel's voluminous correspondence is translated by C. Butler and C. Seiler as *Hegel: The Letters* (1984).

2. General Works on Hegel.

(a) *Hegel* (1883), by E. Caird, is still valuable. It pays more attention to Hegel's life than do most books on Hegel, but it also gives a fair summary of Hegel's main works in a brief span.

(b) *The Philosophy of Hegel* (1924), by W. T. Stace, expounds and assesses the argument of the first and third parts of Hegel's Encyclopaedia; only a few pages are allotted to the philosophy of nature. Stace also provides summaries of Hegel's predecessors, from the Greeks onward, and assesses their influence on him. The work is still valuable for its clarity and acumen.

(c) H. Marcuse, *Reason and Revolution* (2nd ed.,1955) is an insightful study from a Marxist viewpoint. Marcuse's early work, *Ontology and the Theory of Historicity*, provides a Heideggerian reading of Hegel. It is translated with an introduction by S. Benhabib (1987).

(d) J. N. Findlay, *Hegel: A Re-examination* (1958) is a classic work by an "analytical" philosopher. It covers the whole range of Hegel's system from the Phenomenology on, but neglects the early writings.

(e) F. Copleston, *Fichte to Hegel* (1965), Vol. VII, Part I of his *A History of Philosophy*, provides a clear and sober introduction to Hegel. Copleston is unusual among Hegel scholars in being as familiar with the works of Fichte and Schelling as with those of Hegel himself.

(f) G. R. G. Mure, *The Philosophy of Hegel* (1965) is an interesting work by a devoted Hegelian.

(g) W. Kaufmann, *Hegel: Reinterpretation, Texts, and Commentary* (1965) is perhaps the most readable book about Hegel in English. It supplies a wealth of biographical and bibliographical information and it finally put to rest some of the more obvious misunderstandings of Hegel.

(h) A. Kojève, *Introduction to the Reading of Hegel* (1969) — a translation and abridgement of the French edition (1947) — presents Hegel as an atheistic humanist who anticipated Heidegger by giving death the central place in his system. [I have expressed doubts about Kojève's thesis in my "Hegel on Death," in the *International Journal of Moral and Social Studies*, Vol. 1, no. 2 (Summer 1986).]

(i) I. Soll, *An Introduction to Hegel's Metaphysics* (1969) is probably the best short book on this aspect of Hegel in English. It considers Hegel in relation to Kant, and is a model of clarity and precision.

(j) S. Rosen, *G. W. F. Hegel: An Introduction to the Science of Wisdom* (1974) is a difficult but interesting book.

(k) C. Taylor, *Hegel* (1975) is a rich yet lucid presentation of Hegel's whole system. It provides illuminating commentary on Hegel's main works, notably the Logic.

(l) D. Lamb, *Hegel: From Foundation to System* (1980) considers Hegel from a Wittgensteinian standpoint.

(m) M. Rosen, *Hegel's Dialectic and its Criticism* (1983) interprets Hegel as an emanationist in the tradition of neo-Platonism. Though rigorously critical of Hegel, it is one of the most stimulating books of recent years.

(n) M. J. Inwood, *Hegel* (1983) sets out to provide an analytical examination of Hegel's main arguments, while preserving a sense of his thought as a system and of the interconnection of its parts.

(o) P. Singer, *Hegel* is an excellent brief account of Hegel's thought.

(p) S. Houlgate, *Hegel, Nietzsche and the Criticism of Metaphysics* (1986) considers Hegel in relation to Nietzsche's criticisms of him and finds in Hegel's favour.

(q) Chapter 4 ("One Way to Read Hegel") of E. Craig's *The Mind of God and the Works of Man* (1987) is an excellent critical assessment of some of Hegel's central arguments.

(r) E. Tugendhat, *Self-consciousness and Self-determination* (1986) gives a critical account of these two concepts in Hegel and other philosophers. It is an important contribution to philosophy as well as to scholarship.

3. **Reference Works on Hegel.** J. Royce's article "Hegel's Terminology" in J. M. Baldwin, ed. *Dictionary of Philosophy and Psychology* (1901), Vol. I, pp. 454–464, gives a good, brief account of some of Hegel's vocabulary. Apart from this, the most useful works are in German. J. Hoffmeister's *Wörterbuch der philosophischen Begriffe* (2nd ed. 1955), though not exclusively concerned with Hegel, is the work of a distinguished Hegel scholar. Two German editions of Hegel's works are accompanied by a complete index—H. Glockner's *Jubiläumsausgabe* (1927/30) has a *Hegel-Lexicon* as volumes 23–26, and the *Werke* edited by E. Moldenhauer and K. M. Michel (1970/1) has a *Register* compiled by H. Reinicke (1979). However, neither of these editions include all the works listed in section 1 above. Only a little knowledge of German is needed to make some use of these works.

4. **General Collections of Articles.** Much interesting work on Hegel appears in articles rather than books. The following collections may be recommended:
    (a) D. C. Travis, ed., *A Hegel Symposium* (1962).
    (b) W. E. Steinkraus, ed., *New Studies in Hegel's Philosophy* (1971).
    (c) A. C. MacIntyre, ed., *Hegel: A Collection of Critical Essays* (1972).
    (d) J. O'Malley et al., eds., *The Legacy of Hegel* (1973).
    (e) F. G. Weiss, ed., *Beyond Epistemology: New Studies in the Philosophy of Hegel* (1974).
    (f) R. Schacht, *Hegel and After* (1975).
    (g) H.-G. Gadamer, *Hegel's Dialectic: Five Hermeneutical Studies* (1976).
    (h) M. J. Inwood, ed., *Hegel* (1985).
    (i) J. M. E. MacTaggart's *Studies in Hegelian Cosmology* (2nd ed. 1918) deserves special mention. The essays range over Hegel's political philosophy and philosophy of religion. Though his interpretations of Hegel are often questionable, MacTaggart is perhaps the only indisputably great philosopher to have written at length on Hegel in English, and his works on Hegel are a rare blend of competent exegesis and first-rate philosophy. He should not be missed.
    (j) W. Desmond, ed., *Hegel and his Critics* (1988).

5. **The Early Hegel.** By far the best work in English (and possibly in any language) on Hegel's early life and thought is H. S. Harris' two-volume work *Hegel's Development: Toward the Sunlight* (1972) and *Night Thoughts (Jena 1801–1806)* (1983). These cover, with as much scholarship as one could possibly require, Hegel's career before the publication of the Phenomenology, and provide translations of many writings of this period. G. Lukacs's *The Young Hegel: Studies in the Relations between Dialectics and Economics* (1975) is also useful and stimulating. L. Dickey's *Hegel: Religion, Economics and the Politics of Spirit, 1770–1807* (1987) provides a masterly account of Hegel's early studies in theology, economics, and ethics, against the background of the political and religious culture of his native Württemberg.

6. Hegel and his Predecessors.

(i) Ancient Philosophy. Despite Hegel's interest in and indebtedness to
Greek philosophy (when, for example, Hegel speaks of "skepticism,"
he is more likely to have Sextus Empiricus in mind than Hume),
relatively little has appeared in English on his connections with the
Greeks:

(a) J. G. Gray's *Hegel's Hellenic Ideal* (1941), reprinted as *Hegel and
Greek Thought* (1968), gives a useful account of Hegel's relationship to Greece in general.

(b) G. R. G. Mure's *An Introduction to Hegel* (1940) considers Hegel
in relation to Aristotle.

(c) F. G. Weiss' *Hegel's Critique of Aristotle's Philosophy of Mind* (1969)
is useful, but, like Mure's book, it lacks the depth and refinement
characteristic of much recent work on ancient philosophy.

(ii) Modern Philosophy. More work has been done on Hegel's relationships to other modern philosophers, especially Kant:

(a) F. Copleston's "Pantheism in Spinoza and the German Idealists"
in *Philosophy* (1946) is a useful account of the revival of Spinoza
towards the end of the eighteenth century and its effects on the
German idealists.

(b) F. H. Burkhardt has translated one of the products of this revival,
J. G. Herder's *God: Some Conversations* (1940) and, in a long
introduction, surveys the seminal "Spinoza Controversy" between
F. H. Jacobi and M. Mendelssohn.

(c) In his "Hegel, Pantheism, and Spinoza," in the *Journal of the
History of Ideas* (1977), G. H. R. Parkinson assesses Hegel's interpretation and criticisms of Spinoza.

(d) W. H. Walsh, *Reason and Experience* (1947) is one of the few
works on Kant that take seriously Hegel's objections to Kant.

(e) Hegel's relationship to Kant has been thoroughly explored in
Hegel's Critique of Kant (1987), ed. S. Priest. The essays consider
and assess — not always to Hegel's advantage — Hegel's criticisms
of Kant over the whole range of his thought.

(f) An excellent survey of German philosophy between Kant and
Fichte is provided by F. C. Beiser in *The Fate of Reason: German
Philosophy from Kant to Fichte* (1987).

(g) G. di Giovanni and H. S. Harris translate excerpts from some of
the philosophers dealt with by Beiser — Reinhold, Schulze,
Fichte, Maimon, and Beck — as well as some early pieces by
Hegel and Schelling, in their *Between Kant and Hegel* (1985).

(h) E. L. Schaub, "Hegel's Criticisms of Fichte's Subjectivism" in the
Philosophical Review (1912,1913) is still useful.

(i) J. Royce, in his *The Spirit of Modern Philosophy* (1892) and his
briefer *Lectures on Modern Idealism* (1919) provides valuable guidance on the route from Kant to Hegel, as does

(j) R. C. Solomon, in his entertaining *Introducing the German Idealists*
(1980).

(k) J. O'Malley et al., eds., *Hegel and the History of Philosophy* (1974)
contains pieces on Hegel's relations with other philosophers from

Plato onwards, as well as an exhaustive bibliography.

(l) W. H. Walsh, "Hegel on the History of Philosophy" in *History and Theory*, Beiheft 5 (1965) provides a balanced assessment of Hegel's view of the history of philosophy.

7. The *Phenomenology of Mind*.

(a) J. Loewenberg, *Hegel's Phenomenology: Dialogues on the Life of Mind* (1965) is an interesting exploration of the Phenomenology, in the form of a dialogue.

(b) M. Heidegger, *Hegel's Concept of Experience* (1970) is concerned with the introduction to the Phenomenology only. Like most of Heidegger's writings on other philosophers, it tells us more about Heidegger than about his subject, but is no less interesting for that. Heidegger's lectures on the Phenomenology—which get as far as the chapter on "self-consciousness"—are not yet translated, but his *Identity and Difference*, translated by J. Stambaugh (1969), contains an interesting discussion of the Logic.

(c) J. Hyppolite, *Genesis and Structure of Hegel's "Phenomenology of Spirit"* (1974) is a massive and learned commentary. It is less perverse, but perhaps less interesting, than Kojève's work.

(d) R. Norman, *Hegel's Phenomenology: a Philosophical Introduction* (1976) is probably the best short introduction to the Phenomenology in English. It covers the whole work in a clear and critical, though occasionally somewhat brisk, manner.

(e) H. P. Kainz, *Hegel's Phenomenology Part I: Analysis and Commentary* (1976) is a difficult but interesting book.

(f) J. Shklar, *Freedom and Independence: A Study of the Political Ideas of Hegel's "Phenomenology of Mind"* (1976) is useful for, among other things, its attempt to trace the Greek influences on Hegel's thought.

(g) Q. Lauer, *A Reading of Hegel's Phenomenology of Spirit* (1976) is a learned, thorough commentary. Unusually among recent studies, it endorses Hegel's claim to theological orthodoxy.

(h) J. Robinson, *Duty and Hypocrisy in Hegel's "Phenomenology of Mind"* (1977) is a detailed examination of some of the ethical ideas in the Phenomenology.

(i) M. Westphal, *History and Truth in Hegel's Phenomenology* (1982) attempts to find a single coherent argument in the Phenomenology, namely that "transcendental subjectivity has a social history and that absolute knowledge is both an historically conditioned and essentially collective or social event."

(j) R. C. Solomon, *In the Spirit of Hegel* (1983) is a lively, readable commentary. It provides a survey of Hegel's earlier writings and of the cultural and philosophical background. Its interpretation is distinctly left-Hegelian, arguing that Hegel was neither a theist nor a Christian. (I have reviewed this book, together with Lauer's, in *The Bulletin of the Hegel Society of Great Britain*, No. 9, Spring/Summer 1984.)

(k) D. P. Verene, *Hegel's Recollection: A Study of Images in the "Phenomenology of Spirit"* (1985) focuses on Hegel's concept of *Erinnerung* ("recollection," with, for Hegel, the additional connotation of "internalization").

8. **Logic.**
   (a) J. M. E. MacTaggart, *Studies in the Hegelian Dialectic* (1896) examines Hegel's notion of dialectic, primarily in the context of logic.
   (b) J. M. E. MacTaggart, *A Commentary on Hegel's Logic* (1910) deals primarily with the *Science of Logic*. Both these books, despite their philosophical excellence, fail to keep pace with Hegel's interest in history, mathematics, and the natural sciences.
   (c) G. R. G. Mure, *A Study of Hegel's Logic* (1950) is primarily a commentary on the Encyclopaedia Logic. Mure lacked MacTaggart's lucidity and acumen, but is probably a more reliable interpreter.
   (d) M. Clark, *Logic and System: A Study of the Transition from "Vorstellung" to Thought in the Philosophy of Hegel* (1971) explores the relationship of the Logic to the rest of Hegel's system.
   (e) W. E. Steinkraus and K. L. Schmitz, eds., *Art and Logic in Hegel's Philosophy* (1980) contains some interesting papers and a useful bibliography.
   (f) E. E. Harris, *An Interpretation of the Logic of Hegel* (1983) is primarily an account of the Encyclopaedia Logic.
9. **Philosophy of Nature.** After years of neglect, Hegel's philosophy of nature is now receiving a great deal of attention. Apart from M. J. Petry's commentary, *Hegel and the Sciences*, eds. R. S. Cohen and M. W. Wartofsky (1983), is invaluable. Another recent collection, though published in Germany, contains some articles in English: *Hegels Philosophie der Natur*, eds. R.-P. Horstmann and M. J. Petry (1986). *Hegel und die Naturwissenschaften*, ed. M. J. Petry (1987), contains many valuable pieces, all of them in German.
10. **Philosophy of Mind and Action.**
    (a) G. Von Wright, *Explanation and Understanding* (1971) examines Hegel's account of teleology in the *Science of Logic* in relation to the theory of action and of practical reasoning.
    (b) R. J. Bernstein, *Praxis and Action* (1972) considers Hegel's account of action in relation to other more recent accounts.
    (c) M. Greene, *Hegel on the Soul: A Speculative Anthropology* (1973) is the only book in English on this subject.
    (d) C. Elder, *Appropriating Hegel* (1980) sees Hegel's Logic as providing a solution to the mind-body problem. Both the solution itself and its attribution to Hegel are questionable, but the book is nevertheless clear, ingenious, and stimulating. (I have reviewed this book in *The Bulletin of the Hegel Society of Great Britain*, No. 6, Autumn/Winter, 1982.)
    (e) *Hegel's Philosophy of Action* (1983), eds. L. S. Stepelevich and D. Lamb, contains some valuable papers ranging over the whole of Hegel's ethical and social thought.
    (f) The essays in *Hegel's Philosophy of Spirit* (1987), ed. P. G. Stillman, focus on various aspects of Hegel's notion of *Geist* as it occurs in Part III of the Encyclopaedia.
11. **Ethics and Politics.**
    (a) H. A. Reyburn, *The Ethical Theory of Hegel: A Study of the Philosophy of*

Right (1921) is useful introduction to the subject and, indeed, to Hegel's system as a whole.

(b) G. A. Kelly, *Idealism, Politics and History: Sources of Hegelian Thought* (1969) is an excellent account of the Enlightenment and Romantic background of Hegel's thought.

(c) *The Political Thought of the German Romantics: 1793–1815* (1955), edited and introduced by H. S. Reiss, provides a useful selection of the political writings of Fichte, Novalis, Adam Müller, Schleiermacher, and Savigny.

(d) W. H. Walsh, *Hegelian Ethics* (1969) considers Hegel's ethical views in relation to Kant's. It is the clearest and probably the best brief introduction to Hegel's ethics, though it tends to neglect the systematic aspect of Hegel's thought.

(e) M. B. Foster, *The Political Philosophies of Plato and Hegel* (1935) is an eccentric but stimulating work.

(f) In Volume II of his *Man and Society*, J. Plamenatz provides a clear and careful analysis and assessment of Hegel's thoughts on politics and history.

There are several recent monographs on Hegel's political and social thought. The following may be recommended:

(g) S. Avineri, *Hegel's Theory of the Modern State* (1972).

(h) B. Cullen, *Hegel's Social and Political Thought* (1979).

(i) C. Taylor, *Hegel and Modern Society* (1979).

(j) R. Plant, *Hegel: An Introduction* (2nd ed. 1983) relates Hegel's political thought to the rest of his system.

(k) M. Riedel, *Between Tradition and Revolution: The Hegelian Transformation of Political Philosophy* (1984) is a work by a distinguished German Hegel scholar.

There are also several collections of essays:

(l) *Hegel's Political Philosophy* (1970), ed. W. Kaufmann, is a lively collection concerned with the extent to which Hegel was a nationalist, a "totalitarian," and/or a reactionary.

(m) At a higher level, Z. A. Pelczynski has edited two collections that are indispensable to any serious student of Hegel's political thought: *Hegel's Political Philosophy* (1971), the essays in which range widely over the whole of Hegel's ethical, political, and historical thought, and *The State and Civil Society* (1984), which focuses on Hegel's seminal notion of "civil society."

(n) *Hegel's Social and Political Thought: the Philosophy of Objective Spirit* (1980), ed. D. P. Verene, is also a useful collection.

We still lack a detailed commentary on Hegel's *Philosophy of Right*, but the following go some way toward meeting this need:

(o) A. T. Peperzak, *Philosophy and Politics: A Commentary on the Preface to Hegel's Philosophy of Right* (1987).

(p) K. Marx's *Critique of Hegel's "Philosophy of Right,"* translated by A. Jolin and J. O'Malley (1970), is a penetrating assessment of the later parts of the *Philosophy of Right*.

12. Philosophy of History. Many of the works mentioned in section 11 above also deal with Hegel's philosophy of history. In addition, however, the following works may be recommended:

(a) Chapter VII of W. H. Walsh's *An Introduction to Philosophy of History* (3rd ed. 1967) is probably the best short introduction to the subject. Like all of Walsh's work, it is a model of clarity and precision.

(b) B. T. Wilkins's *Hegel's Philosophy of History* (1974) is also clear and brief. It provides illuminating accounts of parts of Hegel's Logic and uses them to elucidate the philosophy of history.

(c) A somewhat longer work, though still of manageable compass, is G. D. O'Brien's *Hegel on Reason and History* (1975). It takes issue with the sharp distinction between "critical" and "speculative" philosophy of history—as drawn, for example, by Walsh—and argues that Hegel wants to write a "history of historical consciousness." The work is controversial, accessible, and stimulating.

(d) *History and System: Hegel's Philosophy of History* (1984), ed. R. L. Perkins, is a useful collection of essays on the subject.

(e) Hegel's account of history and historical writing can be usefully compared with Nietzsche's. The best starting point is Nietzsche's "On the Uses and Disadvantages of History for Life," the second of his *Untimely Meditations*, translated by R. J. Hollingdale (1983).

13. Philosophy of Art. Apart from the translations referred to in section 1, two useful collections of translations from Hegel have appeared, both with introductions:

(a) H. Paolucci, ed., *Hegel: On the Arts* (1979).

(b) A. and H. Paolucci, eds., *Hegel on Tragedy* (1960).

(c) Also useful is *German Aesthetic and Literary Criticism: Kant, Fichte, Schelling, Schopenhauer, Hegel* (1984), ed. D. Simpson. This contains excerpts from Kant, etc., together with an introduction and notes.

(d) I. Knox's *The Aesthetic Theories of Kant, Hegel, and Schopenhauer* (1936) sets Hegel's views against their background.

(e) K. E. Gilbert and H. Kuhn, *A History of Esthetics* (2nd ed. 1956) is also helpful on the background, as well as on Hegel's own views.

(f) J. Kaminsky, *Hegel on Art* (1962), though scornful of Hegel's metaphysics, gives a competent survey of his account of art.

(g) S. Bungay, *Beauty and Truth: A Study of Hegel's Aesthetics* (1984) does justice both to Hegel's aesthetic theories and to their relationship to the rest of his system. It is by far the best book in English on Hegel's aesthetics.

(h) Some interesting essays, as well as an exhaustive bibliography, will be found in *Art and Logic in Hegel's Philosophy* (1980), eds. W. E. Steinkraus and K. L. Schmitz.

14. Philosophy of Religion.

(a) B. M. G. Reardon, *Hegel's Philosophy of Religion* (1977) is a competent survey of Hegel's lectures on the subject.

(b) E. L. Fackenheim, *The Religious Dimension in Hegel's Thought* (1967) is a stimulating, if occasionally eccentric, attempt to steer a central course between the extremes of Left and Right Hegelianism—which maintain respectively that Hegel was an atheist and that he was an orthodox Lutheran.

(c) Reasons for doubting that Hegel was an orthodox Christian are succinctly presented by H. Meynell in his *Sense, Nonsense and Christianity* (1964). This book also contains brief summaries of the religious views of Kant and Schleiermacher.

(d) Hegel and Schleiermacher, though colleagues at the university of Berlin, had little regard for one another. But their views may be usefully compared, and R. B. Brandt's *Philosophy of Schleiermacher* (1941) contains some useful remarks on this.

(e) *Hegel and the Philosophy of Religion* (1970), ed. D. E. Christensen contains some valuable essays.

(f) Q. Lauer, *Hegel's Concept of God* (1982) is a difficult but rewarding exploration of the subject in relation to Hegel's Logic.

(g) Hegel's view on the relationship between philosophy and religion is illuminated by Max Scheler's discussion of the topic in his *On the Eternal in Man*, trans. B. Noble (1960), pp. 107–160. Scheler, though he did not write about Hegel at any length, shares with MacTaggart the distinction of a first-rate philosophical mind.

Whether or not Hegel was, as he supposed, an orthodox Lutheran, he was at least steeped in religion, and references to it pervade his works. Hence virtually all the items in this bibliography are relevant to his views on it.

15. **Conclusion.** In the face of the vast accumulation of secondary literature on Hegel the reader should perhaps bear in mind the following points:

(i) When Hegel scholars differ in style or content this is often as much Hegel's responsibility as theirs: Hegel's work approaches a complete civilization in its richness, complexity, and ambiguity. No single commentary, and perhaps no single mind, could do justice to all its aspects. What Leibniz said (with Hegel's approval) of philosophical sects is applicable to Hegel scholars: "I have found that most sects are right in a good part of what they assert, but not so much in what they deny." [This dictum, from a letter to Rémont de Montmort, is quoted by Jacobi in his *On the Doctrine of Spinoza* (2nd ed. 1789) and by Hegel in his "Relationship of Scepticism to Philosophy" (1802).]

(ii) Nevertheless, the reader should not persevere with a commentary that fails to meet acceptable standards of clarity and of philosophical competence. If a commentary is obscure, it fails to serve its purpose of explaining to the reader what Hegel is saying; and if it is philosophically incompetent, it defeats the main object of studying Hegel — namely, to extract good philosophy from him.

(iii) Hegel is often his own best commentator: Passages illuminate other passages. In particular his lectures often illuminate his published texts.

(iv) As often as not, more is to be gained from reading the philosophers who influenced Hegel — Plato, Aristotle, Proclus, Spinoza, Kant, and so on — than from modern commentaries on him. Hegel should not be read in isolation; his readers should turn to his great predecessors. That, after all, is what Hegel himself did.